Based on

NIELIT 'O' Level Revised Syllabus of year 2020 for M4–R5

'O' LEVEL *made simple* MODULE - 4

INTERNET OF THINGS AND ITS APPLICATIONS

by

Satish Jain

B.Sc., B.E.(IISc), M.E.(IISc), M.Tech.(IIT Kanpur),
Ex-Professor of Information Technology,
Institute of Information Technology & Management
GGS Indraprastha University, Delhi.

Shashi Singh

MCA, M.Phil

REPRINTED 2026

Second Revised & Updated Edition 2023

First Edition 2020

ISBN: 978-93-8984-576-1

Distributors:

BPB PUBLICATIONS
20, Ansari Road, Darya Ganj
New Delhi-110002
Ph: 23254990/23254991

DECCAN AGENCIES
4-3-329, Bank Street,
Hyderabad-500195
Ph: 24756967/24756400

MICRO MEDIA
Shop No. 5, Mahendra Chambers,
150 DN Rd. Next to Capital Cinema,
V.T. (C.S.T.) Station, MUMBAI-400 001
Ph: 22078296/22078297

NIELIT is in no way connected with this book. This book is written solely for the benefit and guidance of students appearing of NIELIT Examination

Published by Manish Jain for BPB Publications, 20 Ansari Road, Darya Ganj, New Delhi-110002 and Printed at Akash Press, Delhi

www.bpbonline.com

Dedicated to

Sri Raja Rajeshwari, Mata Sharda Devi and Sri Sai Baba

Whose blessings will overcome all the hurdles in life

PREFACE

This book is an up-to-date edition based on NIELIT '*O*' *Level* Module-4 (M4–R5) syllabus for **Internet of Things and Its Applications**. This is a text book that explains this highly technical subject in very simple language. The complicated concepts for solving problems using the 'C' language in Arduino IDE are brought out in an easy-to-understand manner through various examples and diagrams. It is felt that most of the books available in the market do not cover the entire syllabus of the course.

The 'O' Level Module-4 (M4–R5) course revised by NIELIT is very comprehensive and needs very thorough study of the applied knowledge of both the IoT based applications and data flows between things. We have made great efforts to cover the entire syllabus so that students would get hands on experience in the writing C program in Arduino IDE.

There are rapid changes in the field of programming and many new concepts are introduced from time to time. Accordingly, there is a major change in the syllabus for 'O' Level Module-4 (M4–R5). Hence, the scope for the questions set in the examination will cover many more new terms. This has prompted us to bring out this book by inserting prescribed topics and latest concepts. It focuses on understanding how connected devices work together to update other applications. A separate chapter is included to acquire knowledge to interface sensors and actuators with microcontroller based on Arduino platform. Security is one of the major challenges in IoT so, a separate chapter is included discussing security aspect of IoT devices. In addition chapter on Personality development is covered to enhance skills set towards better personality development and maintain a positive outlook in life. The book contains ample concise and practical example programs. Also many solved and unsolved examples are provided at the end of each chapter. An effort is made to explain all topics in layman's language with a large number of illustrations and examples. The book elucidates both basic and advanced topics in "IoT".

A special feature throughout this book is that the salient and crucial information has been encapsulated within parallel and horizontal lines with a (☞) mark to draw the attention of the reader .

We shall feel obliged if you could send us your critical opinion regarding the presentation, readability and coverage in this book and request you to mail your suggestions, if any, to improve the same.

16th April, 2020 Authors

M4-R5 : Internet of Things and Its Applications

Outline of Course

S.No.	TOPIC	Written Marks (Max.)
1.	Introduction to IoT – Applications/Devices, Protocols and Communication Model	10
2.	Things and Connections	10
3.	Sensors, Actuators and Microcontrollers	15
4.	Building IoT Applications	40
5.	Security and Future of IoT Ecosystem	5
6.	Soft skills-Personality Development	20
	Total Marks	**100**

Detailed Syllabus

1. Introduction to Internet of Things – Applications/Devices, Protocols and Communication Model

Introduction - Overview of Internet of Things(IoT), the characteristics of devices and applications in IoT ecosystem, building blocks of IoT, Various technologies making up IoT ecosystem, IoT levels, IoT design methodology, The Physical Design/Logical Design of IoT, Functional blocks of IoT and Communication Models.

2. Things and Connections

Working of Controlled Systems, Real-time systems with feedback loop e.g. thermostat in refrigerator, AC, etc. Connectivity models – TCP/IP versus OSI model, different type of modes using wired and wireless methodology, The process flow of an IoT application.

3. Sensors, Actuators and Microcontrollers

Sensor – Measuring physical quantities in digital world e.g. light sensor, moisture sensor, temperature sensor, etc.

Actuator – moving or controlling system e.g. DC motor, different type of actuators.

Controller – Role of microcontroller as gateway to interfacing sensors and actuators, microcontroller vs microprocessor, different type of microcontrollers in embedded ecosystem.

4. Building IoT applications

Introduction to Arduino IDE – writing code in sketch, compiling-debugging, uploading the file to Arduino board, role of serial monitor.

Embedded 'C' Language basics – Variables and Identifiers, Built-in Data Types, Arithmetic operators and Expressions, Constants and Literals, assignment.

Conditional Statements and Loops – Decision making using Relational Operators, Logical Connectives – conditions, if-else statement, Loops: while loop, do while, for loop, Nested loops, Infinite loops, Switch statement.

Arrays – Declaring and manipulating single dimension arrays.

Functions – Standard Library of C functions in Arduino IDE, Prototype of a function: Formal parameter list, Return Type, Function call.

Interfacing sensors – The working of digital versus analog pins in Arduino platform, interfacing LED, Button, Sensors-DHT, LDR, MQ135. Display the data on Liquid Crystal Display(LCD), interfacing keypad.

Serial communication – interfacing HC-05(Bluetooth module).
Control/handle 220v AC supply – interfacing relay module.

5. Security and Future of IoT Ecosystem

Need of security in IoT – Why Security? Privacy for IoT enabled devices- IoT security for consumer devices- Security levels, protecting IoT devices

Future IoT eco system – Need of power full core for building secure algorithms, Examples for new trends - AI, ML penetration to IoT

6. Soft skills-Personality Development

Personality Development – Determinants of Personality– self-awareness, motivation, self-discipline, etc., building a positive personality, gestures.

Self-esteem, self-efficacy, self-motivation, time management, stress management, Etiquettes & manners.

Communication and writing skills – objective, attributes and categories of communication, Writing Skills – Resume, Letters, Report, Presentation, etc. Interview skills and body language.

USEFUL TIPS FOR THE EXAMINEE

Dear Reader,

Every examination has its peculiarity and the best results are often obtained by identifying that particular feature and working with the help of right strategies, which in turn can be adopted by correctly analyzing the question paper.

The 'O' Level Examination being no exception to this rule, the authors present an effective aid to guide you to analyze the question paper and thus help to chalk out your own effective plan of action.

The instructions given on the first page of the question paper should always be read *very* carefully. As the answer sheets of Part ONE will be evaluated with the help of a computer, you have to be extra cautious.

The answer sheet contains separate boxes for writing answers to each question in this part. You should read the following paragraphs to avoid mistakes and clear the first part without any difficulty.

How to avoid mistakes?

If you are not sure about a particular answer - *do not fill* the box in the first try itself, but make an attempt later. After having given an initial reading to all the questions, first attempt only those questions about which you are very ***sure*** regarding the correct answer. It is while taking a second go at the questions, that you answer the remaining ones, always making sure that you spend only a *limited* amount of time on each one of them. Finally, go through all the answers once decided and fill the boxes with black ink as per the instructions given in the question paper.

How to answer the questions of Part TWO?

Once you have done well in Part ONE, rest assured, passing Part TWO will not pose much of a problem, if you have effectively followed the instructions given below. While answering Part TWO, the time limit should be strictly kept in mind and every effort must be made to complete all the questions, by keeping the answers brief and to the point. Remember you can also resort to making a sketch/diagram in your answer wherever possible, instead of describing it in words, because "a thousand words of description can be effectively expressed by a small diagram." As the number of questions are normally more for an average student, this precious time saved, enables you to have a wider coverage of the paper.

While attempting the descriptive type of questions, keep a check on the length of your answers and keep in mind the time frame available for answering the remaining questions.

The last stage, being the revision stage, you should save at least 5 to 10 minutes to revise all your answers. Try to find the gross errors, like units of measurement, or wrong question number you might have put for a specific answer, etc. This does happen because of the inherent tension of the examination.

This book has covered the complete syllabus in an easy to understand manner. It is advised, however, that in addition to this book, you should also refer to a few books on 'Internet of Things'. This will enable you to broaden the horizon of your knowledge.

Make your own notes, by reading each topic from this book and other standard books. Once you are quite sure about the comprehension of the topic, try to answer the Exercises given at the end of each chapter of this book.

In the second reading, go through the sample papers given at the end of the book. Solve these papers without consulting any book. After you have answered them, compare your response with the relevant matter available in the text of this book. Where you find your answers differ, re-study that part again.

WISH YOU A GRAND SUCCESS in the 'O' Level Examination, and a very bright future in the field of computer science.

Authors

Contents

Internet of Things and its Applications

Chapter 2. Things and Connections 55

Chapter 3. Sensors, Actuators and Microcontrollers 90

CHAPTER 1

Introduction to Internet of Things

1.1 INTRODUCTION

Internet of Things (IoT) means when things or objects are more connected to the Internet rather than people. The things in IoT is defined as objects that can be the person or machine with a built-in sensor having IP addresses with the ability to collect and transfer the data over the Internet. It is a platform where everyday devices become smarter, everyday processing becomes intelligent, and everyday communication becomes informative. It has controlled connection between digital and physical world.

Before the invention of IoT, there were only two types of communication either human-human or human-devices, but the invention of IoT made it possible to establish communication among Machines-to-Machines (M2M) without any human interference or interaction. It helps in connecting to the cloud and able to manage and collect the data.

IoT is being widely used in organizations of different industries. It helps them to work with more efficiency, deliver the enhanced service to a customer, improving decision making and increasing the value of the business.

M2H, M2M and IoT

Machine-to-Human (M2H) refers to a set of technologies that enable machines to interact with human beings. Some common examples of M2H interfaces include wearables, home automation devices, and autonomous vehicles. Based on the data collected and algorithmic calculations, machines have the potential to convey suggestive actions to individuals who then exercise their discretion to take or not to take the recommended action.

Machine-to Machine (M2M) refers to a set of technologies that enable machines to communicate with other machines and drive action. It is a networking of machines (or devices) for the purpose of remote monitoring and control and data exchange. M2M communication aims to enable seamless integration of physical and virtual objects into larger and geographically distributed enterprises by eliminating the need for human intervention. M2M is defined as the technologies that allow machines, typically (small) computing sensors that perform specific tasks (intelligence) to communicate or relay information as needed. In IoT, things communicate themselves to its owner indicating its location and conditions. To make the IoT and M2M communication possible there is a need for fast, high-capacity networks.

M2M

- M2M is about direct communication between machines.
- It supports point-to-point communication and uses non-IP protocols.
- Devices do not necessarily rely on an Internet connection.
- Data can be stored locally.
- M2M is mostly hardware-based technology.
- Machines normally communicate with a single machine at a time.
- A device can be connected through mobile or other network.

IoT

The IoT is a broader concept that includes Machine-to-Machine (M2M) and Machine-to-Human (M2H) interfaces, as well as support systems that facilitate the management of information in a way that creates value.

- The IoT is about sensors automation and Internet platform.

- It supports cloud communication and uses IP networks & protocols as the communication is multi-point.
- Device rely on an Internet connection.
- Data can be stored locally and also in cloud.
- The IoT is both hardware and software technology.
- Many users can access at one time over the Internet.
- Data delivery depends on the Internet Protocol(IP) network.

Internet and Web

The Internet is the physical layer or network made up of switches, routers, and other equipment. Its primary function is to transport information from one point to another quickly, reliably, and securely. The web, on the other hand, is an application layer that operates on top of the Internet. Its primary role is to provide an interface that makes the information flowing across the Internet usable.

IoT and Internet

The basic idea of the IoT is that virtually every physical thing in this world can also become a computer that is connected to the Internet. In fact, the IoT is all about sensing the physical world. It provides the infrastructure that for the first time enables us to measure the world.

Web of Things (WoT)

Web of Things (WoT) is a computing concept that describes a future where everyday objects are fully integrated with the Web. The requirement for WoT is for the 'things' to have embedded computer systems that enable communication with the Web. Such smart devices would then be able to communicate with each other using existing Web standards. Similarly to what the Web (Application Layer) is to the Internet (Network Layer), the Web of Things provides an Application Layer that simplifies the creation of Internet of Things applications. Rather than re-inventing completely new standards, the Web of Things reuses existing and well-known Web standards.

Industrial Internet of Things (IIoT)

The Industrial Internet of Things (IIoT) is the use of Internet of Things (IoT) technologies in manufacturing. Also known as the Industrial Internet, IIoT incorporates machine learning and big data technology, control the sensor data, Machine-to-Machine (M2M) communication and automation technologies that have existed in industrial settings for years.

Internet of Everything (IoE)

IoE brings together people (humans), process (manages the way people, data, and things work together), data (rich information), and things (still objects and devices) to make networked connections more relevant and valuable than ever before-turning information into actions that create new capabilities, richer experiences, and new economic opportunity for businesses, individuals, and countries.

1.2 OVERVIEW OF INTERNET OF THINGS(IoT)

IoT stands for Internet of Things which means accessing and controlling daily usable equipment and devices using Internet. The term "Things" in the Internet of Things refers to anything and everything in day to day life which is accessed or connected through the Internet (See Figure 1.1). The Internet of Things potential has a lot to offer for the daily life of every human. It makes everything so efficient, productive, and advance.

☞ *Internet of Things (IoT) is a system of interconnected objects, usually called smart devices, through the Internet.*

The vision of IoT is to use smart technologies to connect things anytime, anyplace for anything. The term Internet of Things was first developed in year *1999* by *Kevin Ashton,* one of the founders of the Auto-ID Center at MIT. It is concept that refers to connections between physical devices like vehicles, home appliances, and other items embedded in electronics such as sensors, software which enables these things to connect, collect and exchange data (See Figure 1.2). The

Internet of Things idea is to connect any device to an Internet switch. These devices may include everything from coffee makers, cell phones, lamps, washing machines, wearable devices or anything one can think of.

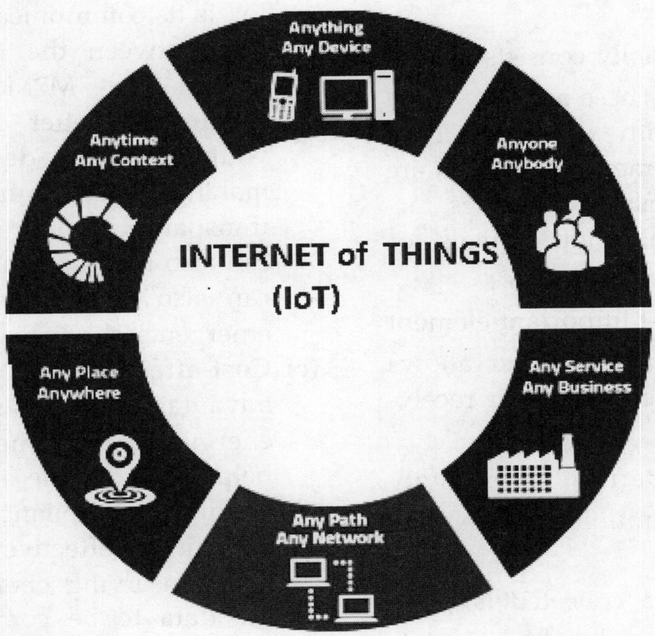

Figure 1.1 Everything and anything connected to IoT

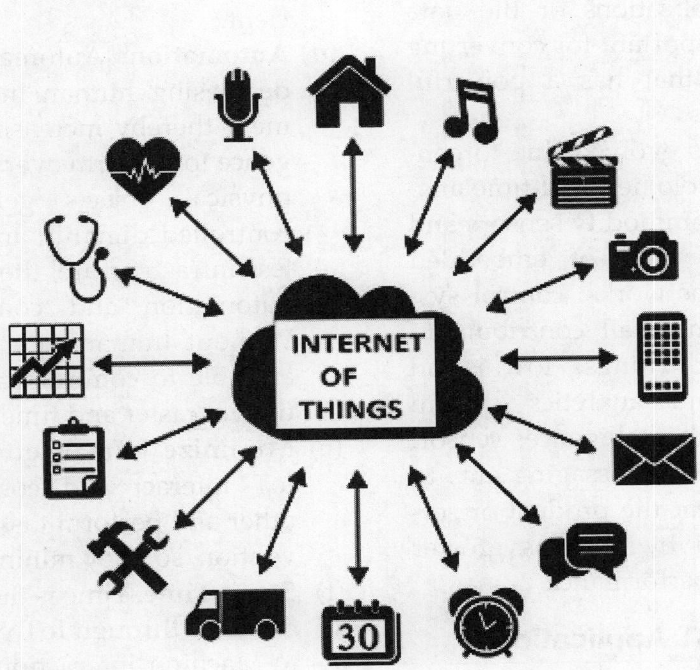

Figure 1.2 Internet of Things

The minimum things required for an IoT application to function are the hardware device, the software, device unique identifier or IP (Internet Protocol) address, Internet connectivity and a cloud platform.

- The device hardware usually consists of sensors or embedded chips. These are very small inexpensive devices with varying CPUs, operating systems and memory. These are placed in various locations like buildings, factories and cities or even inside animals for data collection purposes.
- The IP address is the most important element of the device. This unique identifier allows you to identify the device sending or receiving the information.
- Communications or Internet connectivity allows the device to communicate with each other.
- Since the volume of data collected is more than 100 exabytes per month, a cloud platform that offers low-cost storage is essential. Finally, the cloud applications or the data analytics software is important for converting this data into action that has a powerful impact on your business.

The Internet of Things has evolved due to convergence of multiple technologies, real-time analytics, machine learning, commodity sensors and embedded systems. The field of embedded systems, wireless sensor networks, control systems, automation and others all contribute to enabling the Internet of Things. IoT is an advanced automation and analytics system which deals with artificial intelligence, sensor, networking, electronic, cloud messaging etc., to deliver complete systems for the product or services. The system created by IoT has greater transparency, control and performance.

1.2.1 Advantages of IoT Applications

(a) **Access information:** You can easily access any information sitting from any part of the globe, in real time. This makes it very convenient for people to go about their work, even if they are not physically present.

(b) **Communication:** The biggest advantage of IoT is its communication, as it can communicate between the devices which are also known as M2M communication. IoT encourages better communication between your connected devices and the Internet, making the communication of devices more transparent, which reduces inefficiencies. It can also maintain the quality of service. You can also take necessary action in case of emergencies.

(c) **Cost-effective and efficient:** The biggest advantage of IoT is saving money, time and energy. IoT fundamentally proves to be very helpful to people in their daily tasks by making the appliances communicate to each other in an effective manner thereby saving and conserving energy and cost. Allowing the data to be communicated and shared between deviçes and then translating it into the required way, it makes our systems efficient.

(d) **Automation:** Automation is the process of decreasing human intervention or involvement thereby increasing the machine intelligence to perform every tasks by itself. Due to physical objects getting connected and controlled digitally and centrally with wireless infrastructure, there is a large amount of automation and control in its working. Without human intervention, the machines are able to communicate with each other to deliver faster and timely output.

(e) **Minimize human effort:** As the devices of IoT interact and communicate with each other and perform task without human intervention, so, they minimize the human effort.

(f) **Saves Time:** Time is the primary factor which can save through IoT platform. The Machine-to-Machine interaction provides better efficiency, improved response time, thus reducing the time taken to do any job and accurate results can be obtained fast. This results in saving valuable time.

(g) **Useful in monitoring:** One of the most apparent advantages of IoT is monitoring. It provides the benefit of knowing things in advance. The computers keep a track both on the quality and the viability of things at home. Knowing the expiry date of products before one consumes them improves safety and quality of life. Also, you will never run out of anything when you need it at the last moment. It also takes necessary action in case of disasters and emergencies.

1.2.2 Disadvantages of IoT Applications

(a) **Security:** IoT security is the technology area concerned with safeguarding connected devices and networks in the Internet of Things (IoT). You can monitor your home through your mobile phones, with the ability to control it. They can provide personal safety. As the IoT systems are interconnected and communicate over networks. The system offers little control which lead the various kinds of network attacks like hackers could break into the network and steal the information. So, data encryption is very much necessary for maintaining the privacy of the data shared over the Internet.

(b) **Complexity:** A diverse network that connects various devices is what you call IoT. A single loop-hole can affect the entire system. Also the designing, developing, and maintaining and enabling the large technology to IoT system is quite complicated.

(c) **Unemployment:** With every task being automated will lead to a lower need for manpower and eventually loss of jobs. This will have a direct impact on employment.

(d) **Dependability:** There is no doubt that technology is dominating our lifestyle, reflecting a human's dependability on technology. In case of a bug in the system, there are high chances of every related device getting corrupted.

(e) **Becoming Lazy:** People are more habituated to have a click based work making them lazy to any sort of physical activity.

☞ *Automation means to manage everyday tasks without human intervention.*

1.3 CHARACTERISTICS OF IoT

The fundamental characteristics of the IoT are as follows:

1.3.1 Connectivity

Connectivity refers to establish a proper connection between all the things of IoT to IoT platform, it may be server or cloud. Connectivity enables network accessibility and compatibility. Accessibility is getting on a network while compatibility provides the common ability to consume and produce data.

1.3.2 Interconnectivity

Interconnectivity in IoT means anything can be interconnected with the global information and communication infrastructure. After connecting the IoT devices, it needs a high speed messaging between the devices and cloud to enable reliable, secure and bi-directional communication.

1.3.3 Things-related services

The IoT is capable of providing thing-related services within the restriction of things, such as privacy protection and semantic consistency between physical things and their associated virtual things.

1.3.4 Heterogeneity

The devices in the IoT are heterogeneous which supports different hardware platforms and networks. They can interact with other devices or service platforms through different networks.

1.3.5 Interoperability

Interoperability is the ability of two or more systems or components to exchange data and use information. Technical Interoperability is usually associated with hardware/software components, systems and platforms that enable Machine-to-Machine communication to take place. This kind of interoperability is often centered on (communication) protocols and the infrastructure needed for those protocols to operate. Syntactical Interoperability is usually associated with data formats. As for the IoT, future networks will continue to be heterogeneous, multi-vendors, multi-services and largely distributed. Consequently, the risk of non-interoperability will increase.

1.3.6 Dynamic changes

IoT devices and systems should change dynamically based on the context and changing conditions and take actions based on their operating conditions, user's context, or sensed environment. For example, in surveillance system, cameras can adapt their modes (normal or infra-red night modes) based on whether it is day or night.

1.3.7 Enormous scale

The number of devices that need to be managed and that communicate with each other will be at least an order of magnitude larger than the devices connected to the current Internet.

1.3.8 Safety

The number of devices that need to be managed and that communicate with each other will be at least an order of magnitude larger than the devices connected to the current Internet.

1.4 IoT APPLICATIONS

There are many applications of the Internet of Things in various sectors like consumer IoT, enterprise IoT & manufacturing, and industrial IoT (See Figure 1.3). These applications can be telecom, energy, automotive, etc. Smart homes, smart appliances, connected heating, lighting can be controlled with the help of computers and mobile devices. The devices having sensor helps to collect and analyze the user data, and sending the information to other technologies for making the life of users easy. The other examples are smart health, smart city, smart farming, smart TV, wearable's, smart car, etc. Smart buildings help in reducing energy cost and helps the temperature to adjust automatically. The smart farming system can help in monitoring the instance, light, temperature, humidity and soil moisture of crops. IoT helps the smart city like street lights, smart meters, and sanitation, etc.

Smart means automation the process of decreasing human intervention or involvement thereby increasing the machine intelligence to perform every tasks by itself, which could be done by IoT. IoT has great importance in the future market as everything today is based on the Internet and smart devices. The Internet helps in connecting the devices to collect and send information over the network, so it will be a very big thing in the near future. Some uses of IoT applications are discussed below:

1.4.1 Home Automation

In smart homes, various sensors are deployed, which provide intelligent and automated services to the user. They help in automating daily tasks and help in maintaining a routine for individuals. They help in energy conservation by turning off lights and electronic gadgets automatically. For example, an application can automatically turn on the AC when the humidity rises. Or, when there is a gas leak, it can turn all the lights off. Smart home applications are really beneficial for ill people. Their health is monitored and relatives are informed immediately in case of emergencies.

1.4.2 Smart Water Systems

It is very important to manage our water resources efficiently. As a result most cities are opting for smart solutions that place a lot of meters on water supply lines and storm drains. These meters can be used to measure the degree of water inflow and outflow to identify possible leaks. IoT embed smart water tap automatically open when you approach towards it as per your requirements water will flow. Smart water metering systems are also help us predict flooding.

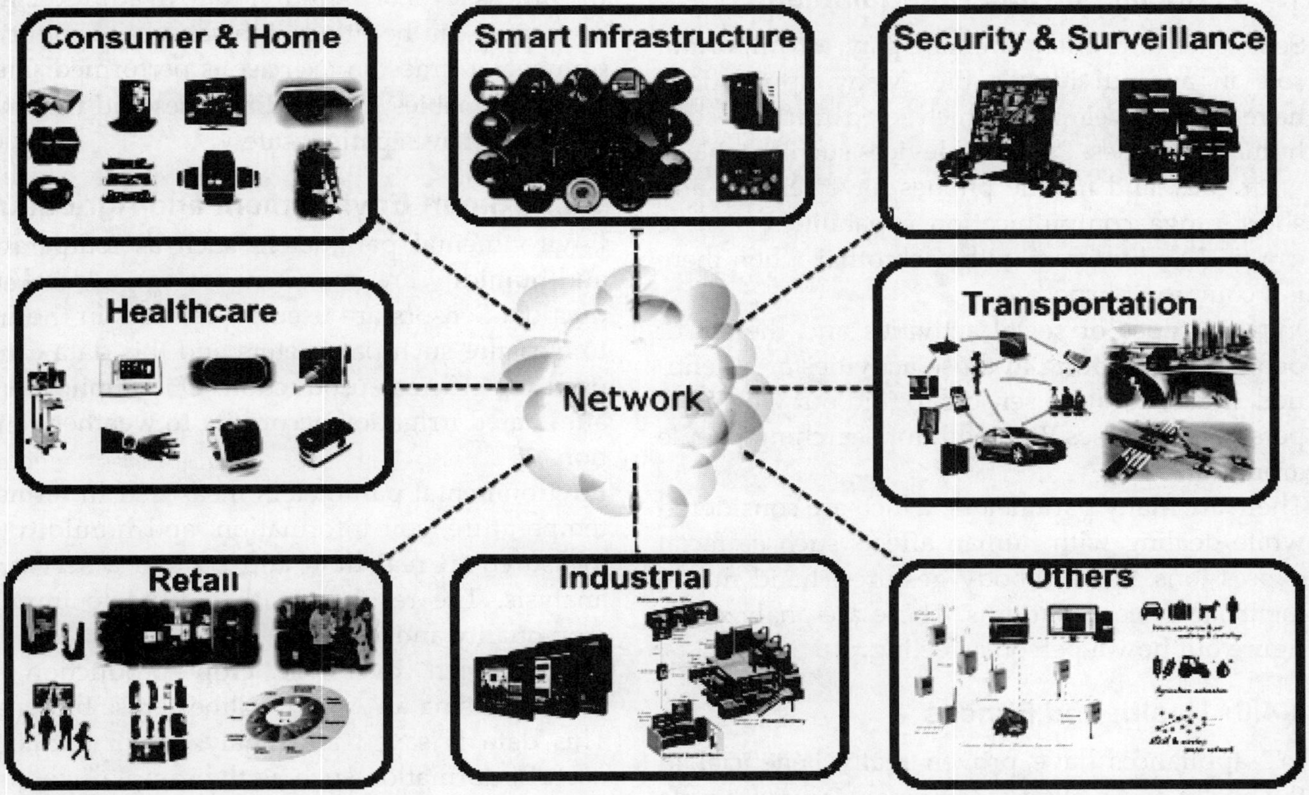

Figure 1.3 IoT Applications

1.4.3 Smart Transport

Smart transport applications can manage daily traffic in cities using sensors and intelligent information processing systems. The main aim of intelligent transport systems is to minimize traffic congestion, ensure easy and hassle-free parking, and avoid accidents by properly routing traffic and spotting drunk drivers. The transportation system will highly beneficial by navigation on any route within the city, such congestion will avoid by guiding drivers to follow the alternative route, the whole traffic with real time monitored and drivers will instantly get the information regarding traffic congestion on the particular track. Also at public bus stoppage it displays the expected time of arrival of all buses on that route. As a result there will less traffic jam and hassle free journey and passenger can save the precious time. The sensor technologies governing these types of applications are GPS sensors for location, accelerometers for speed, gyroscopes for direction, RFIDs (Radio Frequency Identification) for vehicle identification, infrared sensors for counting passengers and vehicles, and cameras for recording vehicle movement and traffic.

1.4.4 Smart Cities

Smart city is the city with thousands of sensors for smart traffic, smart water management applications, and smart parking system etc. Smart transportation is implemented using a network of sensors, centralized analysis, and smart traffic lights. In smart parking, it is possible to easily locate parking spots nearby. Parking lots have sensors, which let a server know about their usage. Once a driver queries the server with his/her GPS location, he/she is guided to the nearest parking lot with free slots. It helps to locate parking slot faster, lesser CO_2 emission from the car, and ultimately lesser traffic problems.

1.4.5 Social Life and Entertainment

Social life and entertainment play an important role in an individual's life. Many applications have been developed, which keep track of such human activities. Personal devices such as tablets, wearables, and mobile phones have sensing and short range communication capabilities. People can find and interact with each other when there is a common purpose.

Various types of social activities and the set of people participating in those activities are identified. It uses location sensors to find out where the person is and uses Bluetooth for searching people around it.

There are many parameters, which are considered while dealing with human affects such as facial expressions, speech, body gestures, hand movements, and sleep patterns. These are analyzed to figure out how a person is feeling.

1.4.6 Health and Fitness

IoT appliances have proven really beneficial in the health and wellness domains. Many wearable devices are being developed, which monitor a person's health condition. Health applications make independent living possible for the elderly and patients with serious health conditions. Currently, IoT sensors are being used to continuously monitor and record their health conditions and transmit warnings in case any abnormal indicators are found. If there is a minor problem, the IoT application itself may suggest a prescription to the patient.

IoT applications can be used in creating an Electronic Health Record (EHR), which is a record of all the medical details of a person. It is maintained by the health system. An EHR can be used to record allergies, surges in blood sugar and blood pressure.

Smartphone accelerometer data can be used for activity detection by applying complex algorithms. For example, you can measure the number of steps taken and the amount of exercise done by using fitness trackers. Fitness trackers are available in the market as wearables to monitor the fitness level of an individual. In addition, gym apparatus can be fitted with sensors to count the number of times an exercise is performed. These IoT data enables precise diagnoses and treatment plans, improves patient safety.

1.4.7 Smart Environment and Agriculture

Environmental parameters such as temperature and humidity are important for agricultural production. Sensors are used by farmers in the field to measure such parameters and this data can be used for efficient production. One application is automated irrigation according to weather conditions.

Environmental parameters measured in terms of temperature, soil information, and humidity are measured in real time and sent to a server for analysis. The results are then used to improve crop quality and yield.

Pesticide left overs in crop production are detected using an Acetylcholinesterase biosensor. This data is saved and analyzed for extracting useful information such as the sample size, time, location, and amount of left overs. You can thus maintain the quality of the crop.

Air pollution is an important concern today because it is changing the climate of the earth and degrading air quality. Vehicles cause a lot of air pollution on the roads. It also tracks vehicles that cause an undue amount of pollution. Electrochemical toxic gas sensors can also be used to measure air pollution.

Agricultural drones are a very good example of IoT applications in Agriculture. Agriculture industries today, have become one of the major industries where drones can incorporate. Two types of drones, that is, ground-based and aerial-based drones are being incorporated in agriculture in many ways such as, for crop health assessment, irrigation, planting, and soil & field analysis. From the data collected by the drone, useful insights can be drawn on various factors such as plant counting and yield prediction, plant health indices, plant height measurement, canopy cover mapping, nitrogen content in wheat, drainage mapping, and so on.

1.4.8 Livestock Monitoring

IoT applications help farmers to collect data regarding the location, well-being, and health of their cattle. This information helps them in identifying the condition of their livestock. Such as, finding animals that are sick so that they can separate from the herd, preventing the spread of the disease to the entire cattle.

1.4.9 Smart Greenhouses

Greenhouse farming is a technique that enhances the yield of crops, vegetables, fruits etc. Since manual intervention has disadvantages such as production loss, energy loss, and labor cost, these methods are less effective. A smart greenhouse through IoT embedded systems not only monitors intelligently but also controls the climate. Thereby eliminating any need for human intervention. The sensors in the IoT system in the greenhouse provide information on temperature, pressure, humidity, light levels. The greenhouse state and water consumption can supervise with these sensors through sending SMS alerts to the farmer with an on-line portal.

1.4.10 Supply Chain and Logistics

IoT tries to simplify real world processes in business and information systems. IoT connects all phases of the Industrial Internet of Things (IIoT) process from supply chain to delivery for a cohesive view of production, process and product data. The goods in the supply chain can be tracked easily from the place of manufacture to the final places of distribution using sensor technologies such as RFID and NFC (Near Field Communication). Real time information is recorded and analyzed for tracking. Information about the quality and usability of the product can also be saved in RFID tags attached with the shipments. Thus, IoT enhances safety and reduce costs by managing, tracking and monitoring connected vehicles, and other mobile assets in real time. The IoT system can also process workflow and change equipment settings to optimize performance.

1.4.11 Energy Conservation

IoT offers sophisticated ways to analyze and optimize use of energy not only throughout the entire system of the house but also at a particular device level. This can range from very basic functions such as dimming of lights, or be switching them off or modifying multiple home settings or changing device settings to optimize energy use.

The smart grid is information and communication technology enabled modern electricity generation, transmission, distribution, and consumption system, to make electric power generation, transmission, and distribution smart, the concept of smart grids adds intelligence at each step and also allows the two-way flow of power (back from the consumer to the supplier). This can save a lot of energy and help consumers better understand the flow of power and dynamic pricing. In a smart grid, power generation is distributed. There are sensors deployed throughout the system to monitor everything. It is actually a distributed network of microgrids. Microgrids generate power to meet demands of local sites and transmit back the surplus energy to the central grid. Microgrids can also demand energy from the central grid in case of a shortfall. Two-way flow of power also benefits consumers, who are also using their own generated energy occasionally (say, solar, or wind power); the surplus power can be transmitted back so that it is not wasted. The user will also get paid for that power.

Some of the IoT applications in a smart grid are on-line monitoring of transmission lines for disaster prevention and efficient use of power in smart homes by having a smart meter for monitoring energy consumption.

Smart meters read and analyze consumption patterns of power at regular and peak load times. This information is then sent to the server and also made available to the user. The generation is then set according to the consumption patterns. In addition, the user can adjust her/his use so as to reduce costs. Smart power appliances can control this information and operate when the prices are low.

1.5 WORKING AND IMPLEMENTATION OF IoT

The IoT basically consists of web-enabled devices that can read or collect, send and respond to the data they acquired from the environment by the use of highly functioning sensors, hardware that can communicate, network connection and processors. These devices that are connected to the IoT hub or gateway, share the data they collected and analyze it locally. These devices may connect with other devices as well and act on the information they get from another device like smartphones, smartwatches, electronic appliances like TV, Washing machine which helps you to communicate with the IOT platform. (See Figure 1.4). These devices mainly work without any human interaction or intervention. The main aim of IoT is to transform the real world objects into an intelligent virtual object in order to make human's lives much safer and easier.

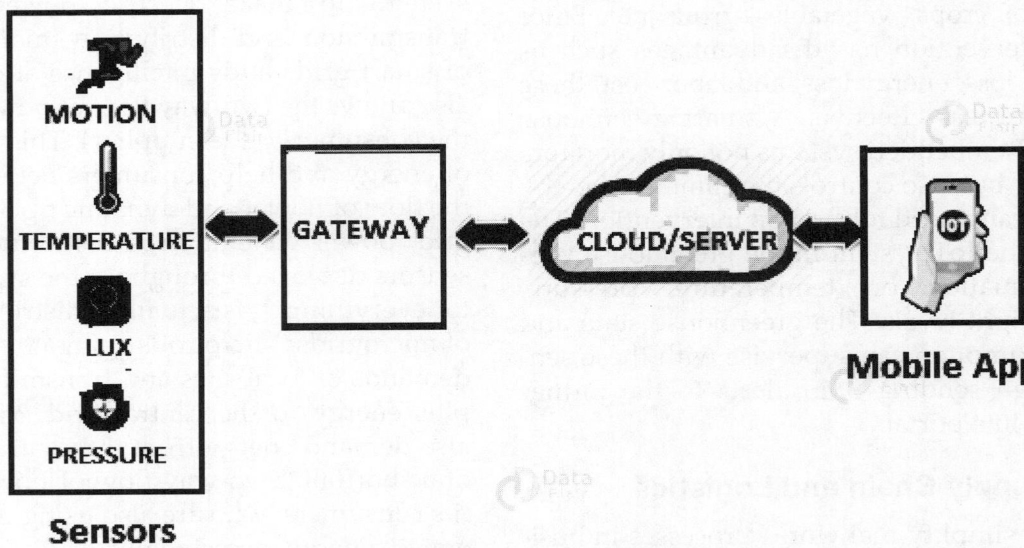

Figure 1.4 Working of IoT

Let us discuss real life example depicting working of IoT say, you have an AC in your room, now the temperature sensor installed in it in the room will be integrated with a gateway. The gateway connects the temperature sensor (inside the AC) to the Internet by making use of a cloud infrastructure. A Cloud/Server infrastructure has detailed records about each and every device connected to it such as device id, a status of the device, what time was the device last accessed, number of times the device has been accessed etc. A connection with the cloud then implement by making use of web services. Human in this system, act as end-users and through the mobile app interact with cloud (and in turn devices installed in our homes). A request will send to the cloud infrastructure with the authentication of the device and device information. It requires authentication of the device to ensure cyber security. Once the cloud has authenticated the device, it sends a request to the appropriate sensor network using gateways. After receiving the request, the temperature sensor inside the AC will read the current temperature in the room and will send the response back to the cloud. Cloud infrastructure will then identify the particular user who has requested the data and will then push the requested data to the app. So, a user will get the current information about the temperature in the room, pick up through AC's temperature sensors directly on his screen.

You know that IoT refers to a network of devices that can communicate with each other through the Internet. These devices also have the ability to send and receive data. When connected with a computer or smart phone, they have the ability to automate processes and form a network of integrated applications. Some of the examples of these 'things' are smart meters, smart TVs, fitness trackers, home appliances, medical devices and even shoes or clothes using sensors. Any object embedded with a computer chip can form a system in the IoT.

1.6 COMPONENTS OF AN IoT SYSTEM

IoT component includes hardware such as the sensors, communication hardware etc. Middleware such as data analytical tools and storage and presentation for delivery of the information to the end users. Here we are discussing about four fundamental components of an IoT system:

1.6.1 Sensors/Devices

Sensors or devices are a key component that helps you to collect live data from the surrounding environment. A device may have various types of sensors such as temperature sensor, motion sensor, air quality sensor, moisture sensor, and light sensor, etc., which performs multiple tasks apart from sensing. These sensors are automatically connected and collect or receive information from different environments or devices that help in making the correct decisions. For example, when sensors show that the soil is dry, watering systems get an automatic command to water plants.

☞ *Sensing is the method of capturing information from the environment by some highly functioning hardware and respond to it.*

1.6.2 Connectivity

Connectivity element plays a very significant task in IoT. The communication enables messaging for the devices. All the collected data is sent to a cloud infrastructure where devices connect to the cloud to perform different operations. The sensors can be connected to the cloud through various mediums of communication and transports such as cellular networks, satellite networks, Wi-Fi, Bluetooth, Wide Area Networks (WAN), Low Power Wide Area Network etc. And the information that is sensed at the machine level is further transmitted to the cloud-based service for sequential processing.

1.6.3 Data Processing

Once that data is collected, and it gets to the cloud, the software performs processing on the gathered data. This process can be checking the temperature, reading on devices like AC or heaters etc.

1.6.4 Delivery of information

Delivery of information is the last element of IoT where the data after being processed are delivered to the end-users in some way which can be achieved by triggering alarms on their phones or sending them notification through email or text message. The data delivery may be a person or it may be to another device in M2M (Machine-to-Machine) workflow. The user sometimes might need an interface which actively checks their IoT system, for example, the user has a camera installed in his home, he wants to access video recording and all the feeds with the help of a web server.

1.7 IoT ARCHITECTURE AND LEVELS

IoT architecture shows the building blocks of an IoT system and how they are connected to collect, store and process data. IoT architecture also contains device and user management components to provide stable and secure functioning of things and control user access issues. Developing an IoT architecture of a particular solution, it is also important to focus on consistency (giving enough attention to every element of IoT architecture and making them work together), flexibility (opportunity to add new functions and new logic) and integration with enterprise systems and delivery management systems and more.

There is not such a unique or standard consensus on the Internet of Things (IoT) architecture which is universally defined. The IoT architecture differs from their functional area and their solutions. However, the IoT architecture technology mainly consists of four major components:

- Sensors/Devices
- Gateways and Networks
- Cloud/Management Service Layer
- Application Layer

1.7.1 Three and Five-Layer Architectures

There are several layers of IoT built upon the capability and performance of IoT elements that provides the optimal solution to the business enterprises and end-users. The most basic architecture is a three-layer architecture as shown in Figure 1.5. It was introduced in the early stages of research in this area. It has three layers, namely, the Perception, Network, and Application layers. The three-layer architecture defines the main idea of the Internet of Things, but it is not sufficient for research on IoT because research often focuses on finer aspects of the Internet of Things. That is why, you have many more layered architectures proposed such as five-layered architecture, which additionally includes the *Processing* and *Business layers* as shown in Figure 1.6. The layers of IoT are as follows:

(a) **Perception (recognition) Layer:** This layer is the physical layer, which has sensors for sensing and gathering information about the environment. It senses some physical parameters or identifies other smart objects in the environment. One of the important functions of this layer is that it linked and converts the information gathered by the sensors into digital signals which are further transferred to the Network layer. The most generic sensor available today is the smartphone. The smartphone itself has many types of sensors embedded in it such as the location sensor (GPS), movement sensors (accelerometer, gyroscope), camera, light sensor, microphone, proximity sensor, and magnetometer. These are being heavily used in different IoT applications.

(b) **Network Layer:** The Network layer is responsible for connecting to other smart things, network devices, and servers. The functions of this layer are to receive and transmit the digital data to the Processing (Middleware) layer that are received from the Perception layer for processing. Those data are transmitted onto the middleware layer over some transmission medium such as Wi-Fi, 4G, and GSM etc along with protocols like IPv4, DDS etc.

(c) **Processing Layer:** The data that are received from the Network layer is processed in this layer. This layer uses the technologies like cloud computing, big data processing etc. The Processing layer is also known as the *Middleware layer*. The middleware creates an abstraction for the programmer such that the details of the hardware can be hidden. This enhances interoperability of smart things and makes it easy to offer different kinds of services.

(d) **Application Layer:** This layer is responsible for delivering application specific services to the user. It defines various applications in which the Internet of Things can be deployed, based on the processed data, the IoT's result is finally released to the end-user for example, smart homes, smart cities, and smart health.

(e) **Business Layer:** This layer acts as the manager for the application and services of the IoT.

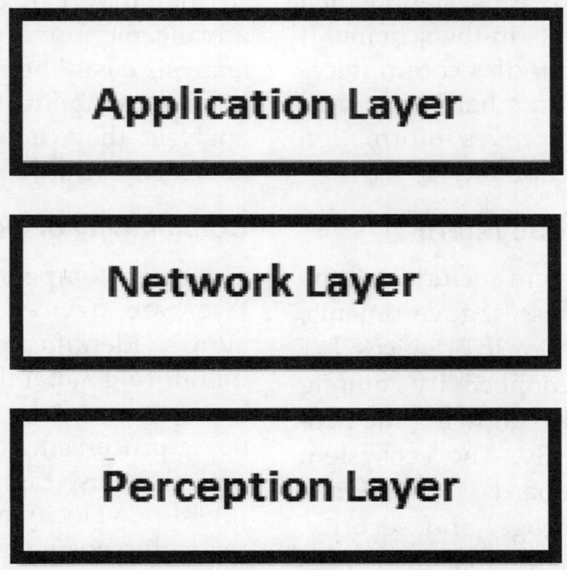

Figure 1.5 Three-layer-IoT Architecture

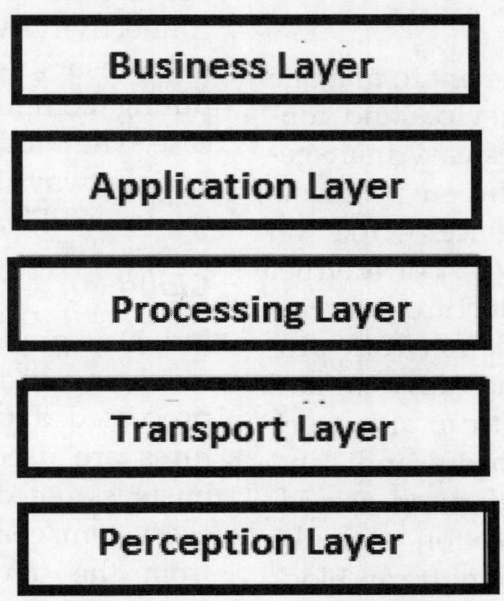

Figure 1.6 Five-layer-IoT Architecture

1.8 IoT ECOSYSTEM

The IoT ecosystem is a connection of various kind of devices that sense and analyze the data and communicates with each other over the networks. In the IoT ecosystem, the user uses smart devices such as smartphones, tablet, sensors, etc., to send the command or request to devices over the networks. The device response and execute the command to send information back to the user after it is analyzed. The IoT ecosystem uses different technologies, software and application to communicate and connect with smart devices and environment.

An IoT Ecosystem is a combination of various IoT layers beginning from the user layer to the connectivity layer. This new chain of development is the best way to connect companies together. Even in future, the companies will be offering the IoT ecosystem similar to risk management and cyber security. Also, IoT ecosystem is used to make the protocols easily accessible, reasonably priced, efficient and secure.

IoT is a key part of a large IoT ecosystem, which promotes and links all elements in the scheme. It allows device management, handles communication protocols on software and hardware, collects/analyses information, improves information flow and intelligent apps functionality.

1.8.1 Components IoT Ecosystem

The Internet of Things ecosystem includes all the components that enable businesses, governments, and consumers to connect to their IoT devices. IoT is not just transforming connectivity among devices and objects but it is also allowing the people to get remote access easily. The ecosystem includes remotes, dashboards, networks, gateways, analytics, data storage, and security. The main ecosystem components that IoT works on are discussed below:

Gateway

Gateways are an important component to manage the Internet traffic between IoT devices and connected networks. Gateway enables easy management of data traffic flowing between protocols and networks. Different IoT device works on different kinds of network protocols. For Internet applications TCP/IP, based architecture is generally followed. It also translates the network protocols and makes sure that the devices and sensors are connected properly. It can also work to preprocess the data from sensors and send them off to next level if it is configured accordingly. It also gives proper encryption with the network flow and data transmission. It can block the particular IP addresses, protocols, even application layers components.

Analytics

Analytics software analyzes the data generated by IoT devices and stores the results in the cloud database. Analysis can be used for a variety of use-cases, most common would be predictive maintenance.

The most important function of IoT technology is that it supports real-time analysis that easily observes the irregularities and prevents any loss or scam. The big companies collect the data in bulk and analyze it to see the future opportunity so that they can easily develop more business advancement and gain something out of it. This analysis easily helps in setting future trends that have a capability to rule the market. From this analysis, they can be one step ahead of the time and easily achieve success.

Connectivity of Devices

The main component that complete connectivity layer are devices and sensors. An IoT device allows identification, remote sensing, remote monitoring capabilities. Sensors collect the information and send it off to the next layer where it is being processed. For example, for automotive use cases, you use Light detection sensors along with pressure, velocity and imagery sensors. Choosing the right sensing components is a key step for a successful use case.

An important aspect of the IoT environment is connectivity. Without joint connectivity between IoT sensors, end devices, and analytics or computing components, you cannot execute a use case. The modern smart sensors and devices use various ways to be connected. The wireless networks, Wi-Fi, and Bluetooth etc.

Cloud

Industry grade IoT solutions require acquiring, managing and manipulating large scale raw and processed data. Generally, cloud-based architectures are used to serve the purpose based on business needs. With the help of IoT Cloud ecosystem, companies are able to collect bulk data from the devices and applications. It is also responsible for managing the connected devices and networks, manage device to device communications and implement IOT applications by operating and synchronizing different IOT devices and communication between them. Also, there are various tools that are used for the purpose of data collection that can collect, process, handle and store the data efficiently in real time.

It is a huge high-performance network that connects servers together to optimize the performance of data process that is being processed by many devices at once. It also helps in controlling traffic and delivering accurate data analytics results. With advanced analytics, users of IoT

solutions can interrogate high volumes of data to optimise the systems being monitored, predict trends, and perform simulations.
With cloud-based IoT applications, business users can quickly enhance existing processes for supply chains, customer service, human resources, and financial services. There's no need to recreate entire business processes.

User Interface

It provides a visible and physical part that can be easily accessed by the user. It is important for the developer to create a user-friendly interface that could be accessed without putting any extra efforts in it and that can help in easy interaction.

Dashboard

Dashboard displays information about the IoT ecosystem to users and enables them to control their IoT ecosystem. It is generally housed on a remote. Remotes enable entities that utilize IoT devices to connect and control them using a dashboard, such as a mobile application. Examples of remotes would be smartphones, tablets, PCs, smartwatches, connected TVs, and non-traditional remotes.

Standards And Protocols

The webpages are now using the HTML format with the cascading style sheet. They are the most used standard protocols making it not just user friendly but easily acceptable. However, IoT doesn't have that standard. So, it is important to choose a platform for IoT that can help in determining the way your platform will interact with the system. Thus, you will be able to have an interaction with devices and networks with the same standard as yours. It is important for having the same protocol to have a successful interaction. IoT applications can be based on both the internet and intranets. For internet applications TCP/IP, based architecture is generally followed. For Intranet IoT use cases, devices are connected using LAN, RF, Wi-Fi, and Li-Fi, etc.

Database

It is essential to have a proper database system that can store and manage the data that is being gathered from various device and end-users. Generally, cloud-based architectures are used to serve the purpose based on business needs.

Automation

The database system is using the automotive features that help in managing data and accumulating it.
It is now used for a much more advanced version that allows the automatic adjustment of the wireless things. For example, you can easily control light with a click of the remote. The air conditioner is now connected to your smartphone and you can switch them on and off whenever you want. Even it is possible to adjust the temperature.

Development

Internet of Things is the latest advancement in technology. The need for the development is growing and increasing with time.

1.9 VALUE CHAIN AND GLOBAL VALUE CHAIN

The value chain describes the full range of activities that firms and workers do to bring a product/good or service from its conception to its end use and beyond. This includes activities such as design, production, marketing, distribution and support to the final consumer. A value chain can be contained within a single geographic location or even a single firm. From a technological perspective, the value chain of any IoT product includes connected assets, the network used to enable communication between devices, IoT platforms, IoT applications, and IoT solutions.
Following components make up the IoT value chain:
IoT platform: If the IoT is the wired or wireless networks of sensors and actuators, embedded in physical objects, and the communication and data-sharing activities that they carry out via the internet, then an IoT platform, or enablement platform, is widely understood as the underlying software that allows devices to share large quantities of data, and ensures that this data can be analyzed and put to use.

IoT application: An IoT application is a software programme that can be added on top of an IoT platform, and uses the latter, along with data it aggregates from the connected assets and network, to produce actionable insights for specific pain-point areas.

IoT solution: An IoT solution is an end-to-end service which integrates all of the above elements of the IoT value chain from the connected assets to the communication network, the IoT platform and the specific business applications. IoT solutions are therefore made up of a number of parts, which can often be separated and sold on their own (for example as applications), but that together comprise a comprehensive, outcome-based IoT service that is usually adapted to individual organizations needs.

A global value chain is divided among multiple firms and geographic spaces. For example, a computer uses labor and materials from multiple suppliers in different countries, is assembled in another country, and was designed and will ultimately be sold in other places. The global value chain initiative is particularly interested in understanding value chains that are divided among multiple firms and spread across several locations.

1.10 TYPES OF NETWORKS

Networking has been developed on all levels, from local to international, in diverse sectors of society. Before we get to the specifics of IoT connectivity protocols, let's review a few of the basic network types, as organized by the range of communication they offer. There are many types of computer networks that are described as follows:

- **Body Area Network (BAN):** The term BAN (Body Area Networks) have been invented to refer to the wireless network technology used in combination with wearables. The main purpose of these networks is to transmit data produced by wearable devices outside to a WLAN or the Internet. Number of intelligent physiological sensor can be combined into a wearable WBAN (Wireless Body Area Network), which can be used to detect medical conditions.
- **Personal Area Network (PAN):** Starting with the smallest network type, a PAN often relies on Bluetooth or WiFi connectivity to link up a number of personal devices such as a laptop, printer, media system and so on. The radius of a PAN network may be as small as the size of a room or part of a house. The wireless variety is known as Wireless Personal Area Network (WPAN) and is based on technologies such as Bluetooth, Wireless USB, Insteon, IrDA, ZigBee, and Z-Wave.
- **Home Area Network (HAN):** It is a network contained within a user's home that connects a person's digital devices.
- **Neighborhood Area Network (NAN):** NAN is an offshoot of Wi-Fi hotspots and Wireless Local Area Networks (WLAN), which enable users to connect to the Internet quickly and at very little expense. A NAN is generally installed by an individual to serve a family or a number of neighbors.
- **Local Area Network (LAN):** As the name suggests, LAN is a computer network that spans a relatively small area. Most LANs are confined to a single building or group of buildings. However, one LAN can be connected to other LANs over any distance via use of cable or wireless technology such as WiFi. If a local network is implemented via radio, it is referred to as a Wireless Local Area Network (WLAN). The WLAN standard's technical basis is defined by the IEEE 802.11 family of standards.
- **Metropolitan Area Network (MAN):** A Metropolitan Area Network (MAN) is a network that interconnects users with computer resources in a geographical area or region larger than that covered by even a large local area network but smaller than the area covered by a Wide Area Network. It is data network designed for a town or city. MANs are usually characterized by very high-speed connections using fibre optical cable or microwave transmission which is facilitated by dedicated microwave antennae. A standard for larger regional radio networks, known as Wireless Metropolitan Area Networks

(WMAN), was developed with IEEE 802.16. This technology known as WiMAX (Worldwide Interoperability for Microwave Access) makes it possible to set up WiFi hotspots. These are several WiFi access points working together in different locations.

- **Wide Area Network (WAN):** The term Wide Area Network (WAN) usually refers to a network which covers a large geographical area. Some WANs are very extensive, spanning the globe using satellite communications.
- **Virtual Private Network (VPN):** A Virtual Private Network (VPN) is a virtual communication network that uses the infrastructure of a physical network to logically connect computer systems. It allows restrict access to your network while allowing authorized users the ability to access the network from remote locations by encrypting the connection process.
- **Campus Area Network (CAN):** The computers are within a limited geographic area, such as a campus or military base.
- **Global Area Networks (GAN):** A Global Area Network (GAN) refers to a network composed of different interconnected networks that cover an unlimited geographical area. It is a network used for supporting mobile across an arbitrary number of wireless LANs, satellite coverage areas, etc.

1.11 IoT TECHNOLOGIES AND PROTOCOLS

The primary idea behind the Internet of Technology is to exchange information between real-world objects around us, with the help of leading technologies. In IoT, no one technology is involved but it consists of multiple technologies. An IoT device may consist of several interfaces for connections to other devices, both wired (such as coaxial cables, copper wires, fiber optic cables) and wireless. With respect to sending and receiving data, wired and wireless communication technologies have also improved such that nearly every type of electronic equipment can provide data connectivity.

Networking technologies, such as fixed, mobile, wired and wireless networks, allowing the highly available bi-directional communication on different levels. The communication between IoT devices is mainly wireless because they are generally installed at geographically dispersed locations. The typical wireless technologies used widely are Zigbee, Zwave, RFID, NFC etc. The most common communication technologies for short range low power communication protocols are RFID (Radio Frequency Identification) and NFC (Near Field Communication). For the medium range, they are Bluetooth, Zigbee, and WiFi. These technologies support the specific networking functionality needed in an IoT system in contrast to a standard uniform network of common systems.

Like we human communicate with each other, same way IoT devices can communicate with each other through protocols which are known as IoT protocols. The protocol is defined as a set of rules and regulation guidelines having how to react for commands from another device. There are several IoT communication protocols available, and they have different capabilities, data rates, communication range, power, and memory. Communication protocols selected depends on the number of devices to be connected to this network.

IoT has power to make the complete system automatic. There are various IOT communication protocols which are used in communication between devices in the IoT network. The wireless communication protocol is a standard set of rules with reference to which various electronic devices communicate with each other wirelessly. In Communication protocols, we will discuss popular wireless Protocols.

1.12 TECHNOLOGIES USED IN IoT

The protocols for allowing IoT sensors to relay data include wireless technologies such as RFID, NFC, Wi-Fi, Bluetooth, Bluetooth Low Energy(BLE), XBee, ZigBee, Wireless MBus and NuelNET, as well as satellite connections and mobile networks using GSM, GPRS, 3G, LTE, or WiMAX

(See Figure 1.7). Wired protocols, usable by stationary smart objects, include Ethernet, HomePlug, HomePNA and LonWorks as well as conventional telephone lines.

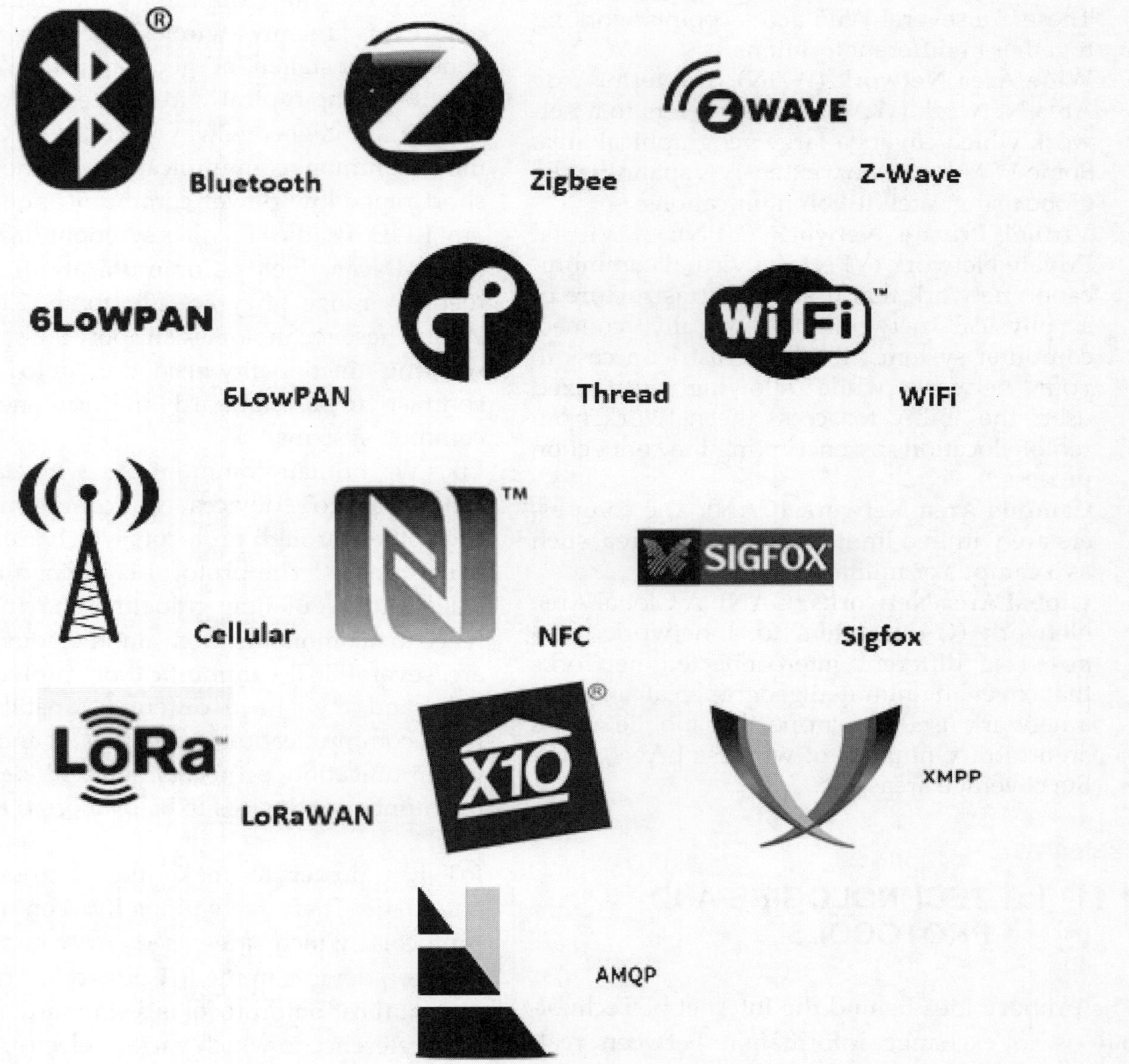

Figure 1.7 Technologies used in IoT

Some of the most common technologies used in IoT implementation are discussed below:

1.12.1 Bluetooth

Bluetooth is a Wireless Personal Area Network (WPAN) protocol designed by the Bluetooth Special Interest Group (SIG). It is an open standard for short-range transmission of digital voice and data. Some bluetooth applications have been used in cellphones, providing a wireless connection to a headset and to an automobile's audio system for hands-free operation (See Figure 1.8). It operates in the frequency band of 2.45 GHz. Data transfer rate of bluetooth is 2.1 Mbps. Some of the features of bluetooth are:

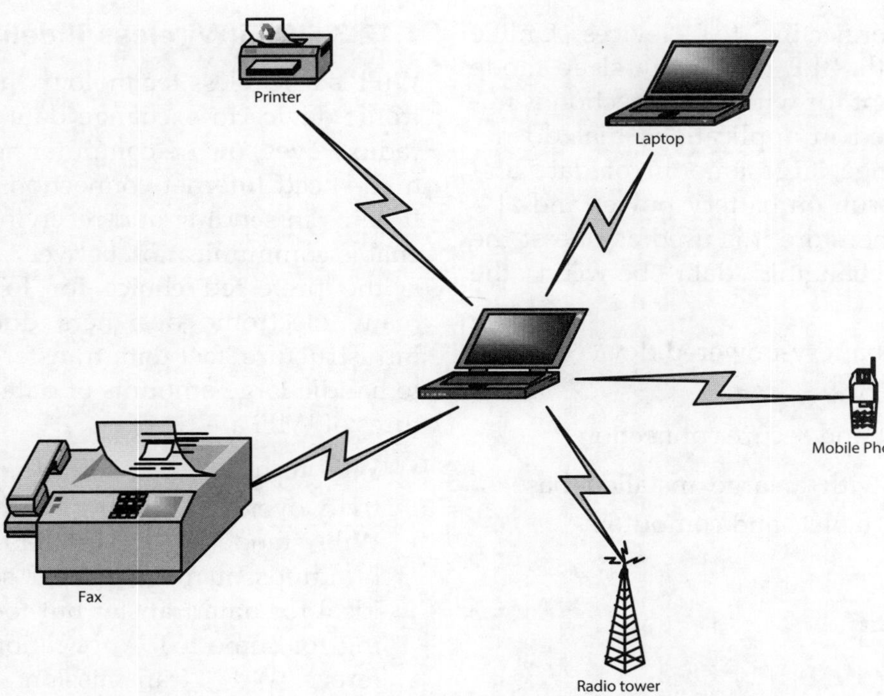

Figure 1.8 Bluetooth

- Bluetooth is one of the most widely used protocols for short-range communication.
- It supports point-to-point and multi-point applications.
- Replaces cables connecting many types of devices. It is a standard IoT protocol for wireless data transmission.
- This communication protocol is secure and perfect for short-range, low-power, low-cost, and wireless transmission between electronic devices.

Advantages of Bluetooth

- It has low power consumption.
- It has range better than Infrared communication.
- It creates adhoc connection immediately without any wires.
- Bluetooth devices are available at very cheap cost.

Disadvantages of Bluetooth

- The bandwidth is lower compare to WiFi.
- Battery usage is more compare to the condition when bluetooth is powered OFF.

1.12.2 Bluetooth Low Energy (BLE)

The Bluetooth Low Energy is commonly known as BLE or Bluetooth 4.0 and marketed as Bluetooth Smart. It is a wireless standard and is intended to exchange data over short distances and build Personal Area Networks (PANs). Due to improved energy consumption, it is suited for sensors and other devices that require low power. Internet-enabled nodes often use BLE to act with local nodes and send collected data to the backend for more actions. The devices usually transmit a small amount of data as bursts at 1 Mbps speed. However, it is not suitable for sending data in real-time. It is used in applications such as smart building, smart transportation, smartphones, fitness trackers and wearables. Some of the features of BLE are:

- Bluetooth Low Energy provides reduced power consumption, cost and plays an important role in connecting IoT devices. Unlike classic Bluetooth, BLE remains in sleep mode constantly except for when a connection is initiated. It is used in applications that do not need to exchange large amount of data and can, therefore, run on battery power and at a cheaper cost, therefore it is used as one of the means of exchanging data between the devices.

- BLE is used in battery-powered devices developed for industries.
- Low cost, faster and secure connection.
- Compatibility with a large installed base of mobile phones, tablets and computers.

Advantages of BLE

- It offers very low power consumption, thus battery life is very long.
- BLE are inexpensive
- It offers reliability and enables digital life.
- Devices from different manufacturers are compatible with the others.

Disadvantages of BLE

- It can not be used for higher data rates as offered by WiFi and cellular technologies. It supports 1 Mbps and 2 Mbps data rates.
- It can not be used for long distance wireless communications unlike cellular and WiFi devices.
- It is open to interception and attack due to wireless transmission/reception.

☞ *Bluetooth is today commonly referred to as Classic Bluetooth, to distinguish it from Bluetooth low energy. BLE is an intelligent and low-power version of the classic Bluetooth wireless technology.*

1.12.3 WiFi(Wireless Fidelity)

WiFi is a wireless technology that allows an electronic device to exchange data wirelessly (using radio waves) over a computer network, including high-speed Internet connections (See Figure 1.9). It helps in sending and receiving data packets to enable communication between IoT devices. WiFi is the preferred choice for IoT integration for many electronic designers due to its existing infrastructure, fast data transfer rates, and ability to handle large amounts of data. Some of the features of WiFi are:

- WiFi technology enables IoT wireless connectivity over a LAN using IEEE 802.11 standards. WiFi standard 802.11 offers transfer rates of hundreds of megabits per second, making it ideal for data transfer but too power consuming for some IoT Applications. There are different WiFi transmission standards, IEEE 802.11a, b and g. Currently, the most common WiFi standard used in homes and many businesses is 802.11n, which offers serious throughput in the range of hundreds of megabit per second, which is fine for file transfers, but may be too power-consuming for many IoT applications.
- In car radios and TV sets, broadcasts are on different channels to avoid interference. 802.11 b and g have only 3 non-overlapping channels. To avoid interference, the radio power, and therefore transmission distances are short. Much longer links can be achieved with specialized antennae and amplifiers. Note that the distance is lower for higher frequency transmission. The frequency ranges are referred to as 2.4ghz and 5ghz. IEEE 802.11n has been agreed upon and standard products are expected. Speeds will be around 300 Mbps (100 effective) and distances increased.

☞ *WiFi is based on the IEEE 802.11 family of standards and is primarily a local area networking (LAN) technology designed to provide in-building broadband coverage.*

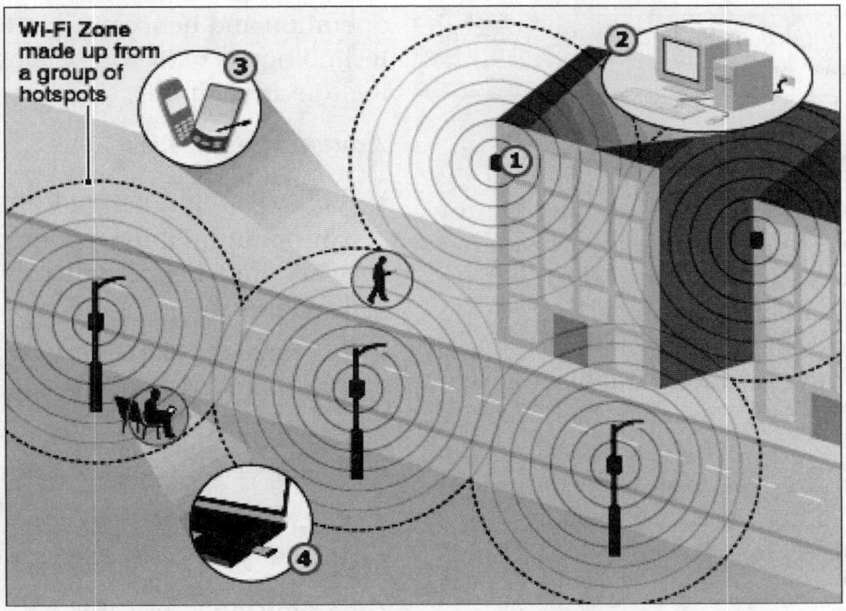

Figure 1.9 WiFi connection

Advantages of WiFi

- The main advantages of using WiFi technology is the lack of wires. This is a wireless connection that can merge multiple devices together.
- Wi-Fi allows managing or communicating network. It can reduce the cost of cables and laying charges.
- It is easy to setup WiFi and also you can add any number of WiFi clients.
- You can send and receive any amount of data in the air; its completely safe and it will not interfere with any network.
- WiFi networks are widely used to connect a variety of devices, not only between themselves but also to the Internet. And almost all modern laptops, tablets, and some mobile phones have this feature. It is very convenient and allows you to connect to the Internet almost anywhere, not just where the cables are laid.

Disadvantages of WiFi

- WiFi has a limited radius of action and it is suitable for home networking, which is more dependent on the environment. For example, a typical home router with WiFi in the room has a range of up to 45 meters and up to 450 meters outside.
- At high density WiFi-points operating in the same or adjacent channels, they can interfere with each other. This affects the quality of the connection. This problem is common in apartment buildings, where many residents are using this technology.
- WiFi technology is not perfect and has many flaws that limit its use.
- WiFi network implementation is more costly than wired network. There are some limit to transfer the data rate, it can't send the huge data compared to wired technology.
- WiFi will generates some radiation which effects on human health. Switch off the WiFi devices or equipment when it is not in use to reduce the radiation.
- Although WiFi is a highly suited protocol for communication between IoT devices, it consumes high power for its operations. However, it is the most powerful protocol for file transfer among most of the IoT devices at present.

☞ *WiFi has been modified to Low-power WiFi to suite the IoT power requirement.*

1.12.4 Low Power WiFi (WiFi-HaLow)

The original WiFi standards are not suitable for IoT applications due to their frame overhead and high power consumption. Hence, IEEE 802.11 working group initiated 802.11ah task group to develop a standard that supports low overhead, power friendly communication suitable for sensors and motes. The WiFi alliance has recently developed 'WiFi HaLow' which is based on the IEEE 802.11ah standard. 802.11ah is far more IoT-centric than many other WiFi counterparts. This protocol is suitable for Internet of Things applications.

Advantages of Low Power WiFi

- It consumes lower power than a traditional WiFi device
- The range of WiFi HaLow is nearly twice that of traditional WiFi.
- Designed specifically for low data rate, long-range sensors and controllers.

Disadvantages of Low Power WiFi

- Because of the relatively lower frequency, the range is longer since higher frequency waves suffer from higher attenuation.

1.12.5 LiFi(Light Fidelity)

It is a new wireless technology that offers high speed data transmission based on Visible Light Communication (VLC) principle. It uses two main components LiFi controller or coordinator and LiFi dongles. The technology uses LED lamps on source side and photo detector based LiFi dongles on destination side. Li-Fi can also utilize energy efficient Light-Emitting Diode (LED) lights to reduce energy costs. However, the Li-Fi scheme is limited to the line of sight and is subject to interference or failure due to objects blocking the light signals. The LiFi devices consume low power for operation and hence used in IoT applications. LiFi technology is used for various applications which include street lights, sign boards, Internet etc.

Advantages of LiFi

- LiFi uses light as medium for data communication. In LiFi, light does not pass through the walls and hence will provide a much secure data transfer.
- It transfers data very rapidly and securely through LOS (Line of Sight) operation of optical signals.
- The speed of data provided by these LEDs is 100 times faster than the WiFi speed.
- It is very efficient in terms of cost and energy.

Disadvantages of LiFi

- Internet cannot be used without a light source.
- A new infrastructure for Li-Fi is required to be constructed.

1.12.6 Cellular Networks

A cellular network is a radio network distributed over land through cells where each includes a fixed location transceiver known as *base station*. Cellular technology is the basis of mobile phone networks. These networks exists in various generations such as 3G and 4G of cellular network standards that are often employed in smartphones but are also suitable for IoT due to their high mobility and speed. Any IoT application that requires operation over longer distances can take advantage of GSM/3G/4G/5G cellular communication capabilities. However, Narrowband-IoT (NB-IoT) along with LTE-M are newer standards that were developed especially for running IoT systems using existing cellular networks. LTE-M is an abbreviation for LTE (Long Term Evolution) Cat-M1. This technology is for Internet of Things devices that need to connect directly to a 4G mobile network. It is a subset of the LTE cellular technology that is optimized for low data rate devices running from small batteries.

Advantages of Cellular Networks

- It is used in areas where cables can not be laid out due to its wireless nature.
- It provides voice/data services even while roaming.
- It connects both fixed and wireless telephone users.

Disadvantages of Cellular Networks

- The technology is able to transfer high quantities of data, but the power consumption and the expenses are high.
- The wireless communication is influenced by physical obstructions, climatic conditions and interference from other wireless devices.
- It offers less data rate compare to wired networks such as fiber optics, DSL etc. The data rate varies based on wireless standards such as GSM, CDMA, LTE etc.
- It requires higher cost in order to setup cellular network infrastructure.

1.12.7 Z-Wave

Z-Wave is a wireless network standard that consumes very low power and it is widely used for connecting smart devices in the Internet of Things (IoT) like home automation, lighting controls, security systems, Energy saving etc. Z-Wave devices can be attached to home appliances, which enable them to be controlled over the Internet. Z-Wave is a complete communications solution, which consists of everything from the Physical layer to the Applications layer.

Advantages of Z-Wave

- Easy to install the system.
- Easy to add or remove devices.
- Interoperable with other devices.
- Uses low-energy radio waves to communicate.
- Uses a simpler protocol than some others, which can enable faster and simpler development.

Disadvantages of Z-Wave

- Cannot be deployed over a wide area as the range is less.
- Applicable for less data speed and small data size applications.

1.12.8 RFID(Radio Frequency Identification)

RFID stands for Radio Frequency Identification. The acronym refers to small electronic devices that consist of a small chip and an antenna. RFID tags store identifiers and data. It uses electromagnetic signals to detect chips containing electronically stored information placed within objects. RFID systems consist of a reading device called a reader, and one or more tags. The reader is a powerful device with ample memory and computational resources. The RFID tag is attached to the object to be tracked and the reader detects and records its presence when the object passes by it. In this manner, object movement can be tracked and RFID can serve as a search engine for smart things. The typical range of RFID is less than a meter. RFID used to track consumer product worldwide. RFID is an intelligent barcode that can be operated using the networked system to track the product, vehicles or any object. But unlike a traditional bar code, it does not require line of sight communication between the tag and the reader and can identify itself from a distance even without a human operator. RFID is used in indoor moving navigation, smart parking, supply chain management, and battery-less remote control devices applications. RFID tags can be of following types:

- **Active:** An active tag has an on-board battery i.e., power source and periodically transmits its ID signal.
- **Passive:** Passive tags do not have any power source. Passive tags derive power from the electromagnetic waves emitted by the reader and are thus cheap and have a long lifetime. These tags are ideal for devices without batteries, as the ID is passively read by the reader.

- **Assisted passive:** Assisted passive tags become active when RFID reader is present.

Advantages of RFID

- They work on radio frequencies and do not require a direct line of site between tag and reader.
- Some RFID devices will only use battery power in the presence of an RFID reader which makes it ideal for lower power consumption applications.
- RFID is similar to a barcode reader based technology but the performance is more efficient
- RFID is inexpensive and uses very little power.
- Established and widely used technology.

Disadvantages of RFID

- Highly insecure.
- Tags need to be present as identifier and be handed over before.
- Not compatible with smartphones.

1.12.9 X-10

X-10 is a protocol for communication among IoT devices, mainly in the home automation sector. It is called as the *father of modern home automation*. The existing household wiring, which powers the house, acts as the physical layer to transmit and receive data. X-10 devices are connected to the plugs in the wall, like a normal electrical appliance. A remote interface could be provided so that lights and other appliances can be turned *on* and *off*. Depending on your budget, there are some very hi-tech approaches that can be adopted. For example, touch-screens to control X10 devices within the house.

☞ *X10 has become very popular with consumers who wish to use home automation to make life easier.*

Advantages of X-10

- The infrastructure for the medium of communication exists and thus needs less effort to set-up. And the equipment is also inexpensive.
- No new or specialised wiring is required.
- It is simple to install - no need for qualified engineers or professionals.

Disadvantages of X-10

- The data rate of signal transmission is very less, in the order of 20 bits/s. Thus, this technology facilitates for turning on and off devices only.
- Other electrical devices in the house can create interference on the power lines, which may prevent X10 signals being received by modules.
- It is not suitable as a safety device.
- There is a time delay in sending signals - up to one second.

1.12.10 Sigfox

Sigfox is a cellular style system that enables remote devices to connect using ultra-narrow band, to provide low power low data rate, and low cost communications for remote connected devices.

It a subscription based service that offers connectivity solutions over dedicated LPWAN networks. Sigfox uses a technology called Ultra Narrow Band (UNB) and is only designed to handle low data-transfer speeds of 10 to 1,000 bits per second. The concept behind Sigfox is to provide an effective connectivity solution for low-power M2M applications requiring low levels of data transfer for which the WiFi range is too short, and cellular range is too expensive. Sigfox is ideal for IoT applications that need to send infrequent and small bursts of data, such as alarm systems, smart meters, smart street lighting, patient monitors etc.

Advantages of Sigfox

- Sigfox offers significant cost and battery-life.

- The Sigfox network provides very long-range wireless connectivity for the Internet of Things.
- It is lightweight protocol which handles smaller messages efficiently.
- Due to less overhead, more space will be available for the user data to be transported.

Disadvantages of Sigfox

- Sigfox supports one way communication without acknowledgement. This necessitates multiple transmissions if server does not receive data without errors. Due to this, power consumption will increase which depends on number of re-transmissions.
- Due to low data rate support, it cannot be used for high data rate applications.
- Sigfox system works well in fixed location. There are issues such as interference and frequency inaccuracies in the mobility environments.

1.12.11 Zigbee

Zigbee is a low powered, low cost standard on a wireless mesh network designed for battery-powered devices and cheaper alternative to Bluetooth. It is based on the IEEE 802.15.4 communication protocol standard and is used for personal area networks or PANs. The range of Zigbee device communication is very small (10-100 meters). For example, if you just need to communicate inside a small building, you can use Zigbee. ZigBee devices often transmit data over longer distances by passing data through intermediate devices to reach remote ones, creating a mesh network. They can used in applications that require a low data rate, long battery life, and secure networking. Street lighting and electric meters which provides low power consumption, use the ZigBee communication protocol. It is also used with security systems, smart homes, remote controls, road map products-tracking and health-care systems.

Advantages of ZigBee

- Low-power consumption, powerful and direct communication.
- It support a large number of nodes and these nodes are capable of multi-year battery lives.
- Zigbee has a flexible network structure.
- It is less complex than bluetooth.

Disadvantages of ZigBee

- Working on small distance with low speed.
- Its high maintenance cost.
- Low transmission, as well as low network stability.
- Zigbee is not secure like WiFi based secured system.

1.12.12 Low Range Wide Area Network(LoRaWAN)

LoRaWAN is a newly developed Long-Range Wide-Area Network Wireless technology designed for IoT applications with power saving, low cost, mobility, security, and bi-directional communication requirements. LoRaWAN defines the communication protocol and system architecture for the network in the Medium Access Control (MAC) layer protocol. It is ideal for smart cities and industrial applications.

Advantages of LoRaWAN

- Low-cost, mobile, and secure bi-directional communication.
- Low power consumption and supports large networks with millions of nodes.
- Battery life for the attached node is normally very long.
- It is easy to deploy due to its simple architecture.

Disadvantages of LoRaWAN

- It is not ideal to be used for real time applications.

- It can be used for applications requiring low data rate i.e., upto about 27 Kbps.

1.12.13 6LoWpan

6LoWPAN is an acronym of IPv6 over Low Power Wireless Personal Area Networks. It is a protocol that is primarily intended for long-range wireless battery-operated IoT devices in regional, national, or global networks. It is specifically known for its ability to communicate in long-range with the least power consumption and detects the signals below the noise level. This protocol is mainly used in smart cities, where there is a large network with millions and millions of devices connected to each other that function with less power, memory, low-cost mobile secure communication in IoT devices, and a wide range of industrial applications.

The 6LoWPAN group has defined encapsulation and header compression mechanisms that allow IPv6 packets to be sent to and received from over IEEE 802.15.4 based networks.

Advantages of 6LoWpan

- The 6LoWPAN standard enables any low-power radio to communicate to the internet, including 804.15.4, Bluetooth Low Energy and Z-Wave for home automation applications.
- 6LoWPAN uses reduced transmission time (typically short time pulses) and thus saves energy.
- 6LowPAN is a mesh network that is robust, scalable and self-healing.
- It offers one-to-many and many-to-one routing.

Disadvantages of 6LoWpan

- 6LoWPAN offers a secure and non-secure mode but the overall security in 6LoWPAN is still in progress. In comparison, Zigbee has more robust and tested security protocol.
- The greatest challenge to 6LoWPAN is the lack of application that utilizes 6LoWPAN because it require extensive training as it is complicated to work with and require extensive knowledge of IPv6 protocol.

1.12.14 5G

It is the fifth generation of wireless, popularly known as 5G. The "G" stands for a *generation of mobile technology*, installed in phones and on cellular networks. 5G is a medium range communication that offers many improvement over 4G(called LTE-Advanced), such as increased speed and better coverage. It enable a larger number of nodes to be connected with extra mobility.

Advantages of 5G

- Provides high data transfer rates.
- More effective and efficient.
- Easily manageable with the previous generations.
- Possible to provide uniform, uninterrupted, and consistent connectivity across the world.

Disadvantages of 5G

- Technology is still under process and research on its viability is going on.
- Developing infrastructure needs high cost.
- Many of the old devices would not be competent to 5G, hence, all of them need to be replaced with new one

1.12.15 Low Power Wide Area Networks (LPWAN)

It is a type of wireless network used for low power IoT and M2M applications. It defines Low Power Wide Area Networks (LPWAN) standard to enable IoT and can transmit data over long distances while having low power consumption. Mainly its aim is to guarantee interoperability between various operators in one open global standard.

Advantages of LPWAN

- The LPWAN network offers longer range from 5 Km to 30 Km.
- The LPWAN devices will consume low power and hence they offer longer life time.
- It offers simple network installation and easy network management due to smart architecture.
- It offers secured data communication between nodes and gateways due to use of encryption algorithms.

Disadvantages of LPWAN

- LPWAN supports low data rate, hence LPWAN can not be used for high data rate applications.
- It offers high latency between end to end nodes. Hence, LPWAN is not ideal for low latency applications.

1.12.16 Thread

A very new IP-based IPv6 networking protocol aimed at the home automation environment is Thread. Thread uses IPv6 for the Internet Protocol addressing and each of the devices is IP-addressable. Thread enables device-to-device and device-to-cloud communications and reliably connects hundreds (or thousands) of products and includes mandatory security features. Thread wireless connectivity has been developed specifically to support the Internet of Things, IoT, and as a result, it incorporates many features that have not been available in previous standards.
Thread is based on the broadly supported IEEE 802.15.4 radio standard, which is designed from the ground up for extremely low power consumption and low latency.

Advantages of Thread

- Thread guarantees to be a 'no single point of failure system'.
- Uses good security features such as proper authentication in order to join a network.
- IP-addressable devices.
- Simple Management i.e., creating a thread, switching between threads and synchronization between threads can all be done without the intervention of the kernel.

Disadvantages of Thread

- There is a lack of coordination between threads and operating system kernel.
- User-level threads require non-blocking systems call i.e., a multi-threaded kernel.

1.12.17 Near Field Communication (NFC)

NFC is a set of the communication-based protocol used for communication between two devices in the range of approximately 10 cm. All types of data can be transferred between two NFC enabled devices in seconds by bringing them close to each other. In this two-way, short-range communication, one of the devices must be portable for the purpose of finding a suitable location. NFC make it possible to use our phone as readers. You can extract information from certain objects just by tapping it or bringing our device close to it. The most used applications are smartphones, contactless payment systems, parking meters, E-ticket booking etc.

Advantages of NFC

- Offers a low-speed connection with extremely simple setup.
- NFC has a short range and supports encryption.
- Very easy to used.

Disadvantages of NFC

- Only works in short ranges. Short range might not be feasible in many situations.
- Low data transfer rate.
- NFC is an expensive technology.

1.12.18 GSM (Global System for Mobile communications)

GSM stand for Global System for Mobile communications. It is digital cellular phone technology based on TDMA that is the predominant system in Europe. Developed in the 1980s, GSM was first deployed in seven European countries in 1992. Text Messaging GSM provides a *Short Messaging Service (SMS)* that enables text messages up to 160 characters in length to be sent to and from a GSM phone. It also supports data transfer to packet networks, ISDN and POTS users. GSM is a fast-growing communications technology.

The SIM Card GSM phones use a *Subscriber Identity Module (SIM)* smart card that contains user account information. Any GSM phone becomes immediately programmed after plugging in the SIM card, thus allowing GSM phones to be easily rented or borrowed. SIM cards can be programmed to display custom menus for personalized services.

☞ *GSM is an open, digital cellular technology used for transmitting mobile voice and data services.*

Advantages of GSM

- It provides very cost effective products and solutions.
- The GSM based networks (i.e. base stations) are deployed across the world and hence same mobile phone works across the globe.
- Advanced versions of GSM with higher number of antennas will provide high speed download and upload of data.
- It is easy to maintain GSM networks due to availability of large number of network engineers at affordable cost.
- The phone works based on SIM card and hence it is easy to change the different varieties of phones by users.

Disadvantages of GSM

- GSM provides limited data rate capability, for higher data rate GSM advanced version devices are used.
- GSM uses pulse based burst transmission technology and hence it interferes with certain electronics.

1.12.19 GPRS

GPRS stands for *General Packet Radio Service*. It is the first high-speed digital data service provided by cellular carriers that used the GSM technology. GPRS works on GPRS cellphones as well as laptops and portable devices that have GPRS modems. Users have typically experienced downstream data rates up to 80 Kbps.

Advantages of GPRS

- As GPRS is available in all the mobile devices, it provides wireless internet access.
- It allows simultaneous use of both voice and data services. Hence, user can have both voice call and data call together.

Disadvantage of GPRS

- Network can be affected, when more number of GPRS users in the same area utilize the GPRS services at the same time. This leads to congestion which results into slower data connection.

1.12.20 LTE-A

LTE-A, or LTE Advanced, delivers an important upgrade to LTE technology by increasing not only its coverage, but also reducing its latency and raising its throughput.
Long-term Evolution Advanced (LTE-A) is a collection of cellular networking standards that is designed to meet M2M and IoT requirements in such networks. It is one of the most scalable and cost effective standards compared to other cellular protocols.

Advantages of LTE

- LTE network uses all IP network architecture. Due to this fact, it is dedicated for packet switched operations. It supports data as well voice. The voice can be transported using voice over LTE protocols (i.e. VOIP) and fall-back to legacy networks (i.e. 2G/3G).
- As LTE supports MIMO, higher data rate can be achieved.
- LTE downloads the files faster.

Disadvantages of LTE

- The existing mobile phones can not be used to access LTE network features. The user need to have mobile phone which supports LTE functionality. This will incur cost to the user to avail the LTE service.
- LTE network is completely new network which requires installation of equipments and antennas to make it operational.
- LTE system is complex and hence requires skilled engineers to maintain and manage the system. They need to be paid higher salaries in order to retain them.

1.12.21 WSN (Wireless Sensor Network)

A Wireless Sensor Network (WSN) is the networks that are wireless in nature which comprises of distributed devices with sensors which are used to sense or monitor the environmental and physical conditions like temperature, gyroscope, pressure, etc., and make the embedded processing using these devices. They collect data about the environment and communicate it to gateway devices that relay the information to the cloud over the Internet. These devices are connected through different devices such as GPS, WiFi, RFID, etc. over the networks. For example Weather monitoring system, Soil moisture monitoring system, Surveillance system, Healthcare monitoring, Indoor air quality monitoring system etc.

Advantages of WSN

- WSN is the flexible network and it can adapt to the changes.
- WSN are used in very hard and poor environments where wired cannot be deployed.
- WSN save a lot of wiring cost.

Disadvantages of WSN

- It is not fully secure.
- In WSN communication speed is very poor, on the other hand, wired networks have good speed of communication.
- It is distracted by other wireless devices like bluetooth.

1.13 COMMUNICATION PROTOCOLS

Communication protocols form the backbone of IoT systems and enable network connectivity. Communication protocols allow devices to exchange data over the network.

By the term protocol, we mean the set of rules or standards designed to enable computers to connect with one another and to exchange information. Protocol can describe low-level details of machine-to-machine interfaces (e.g. the order in which bits and bytes are sent across a wire) or high-level exchange between allocation programs (e.g. the way in which two programs transfer a file across the Internet).

An example will be able to make the idea clear. Suppose, there are two people one speaks Hindi and the other French. Since they have no common language, they each engage a translator whose common language is English.

Protocols can include rules concerning any or all of the following functions:

- Data transmission mechanisms.
- Communication session initialization and termination.
- Addressing and routing.
- Authentication and verification.
- Encryption and compression.
- Error correction.

Protocols are usually classified according to the layer they correspond to in the *Open Systems Interconnection (OSI)* reference model for networking. Types of protocols include the following:

(a) Data-link protocols
(b) Communication or Network protocols
(c) Transport protocols
(d) Application layer protocols

Here, we discuss communication protocols in detail.

1.13.1 Application Layer Protocols

CoAP(Constrained Application Protocol)

CoAP is an internet-utility protocol created specifically for connecting devices with limited (constrained) resources such as a small memory or short battery life. This protocol is primarily used for Machine-to-Machine (M2M) communication and is particularly designed for IoT systems that are based on HTTP protocols. Using this protocol, the client can send a request to the server and the server can send back the response to the client in HTTP. It makes use of UDP *(User Datagram Protocol)* and reduces space usage. CoAP is an application layer protocol for IoT and uses request-response model, uses client/server architecture, and supports methods such as GET, POST, PUT and DELETE. CoAP protocol is used mainly in automation, mobiles, and microcontrollers.

Advantages of CoAP

- It has reduced power requirements as it operates over UDP.
- Has smaller packet size, leading to faster communication.
- It has lower latency and consumes less power compare to HTTP.

Disadvantages of CoAP

- CoAP is unreliable protocol due to use of UDP.
- It acknowledges each receipt of the message and hence increases processing time.
- It does not verify whether the received message has been decoded properly or not.

MQTT(Message Queue Telemetry Transport)

Message Queue Telemetry Transport (MQTT) is an open light-weight easy-to-implement messaging protocol for M2M communications. It is based on publish-subscribe model where the system consists of three main components: Publishers, Subscribers, and a Broker. The publisher collects data and sends it to subscribers. The broker tests publishers and subscribers, checking their authorization and ensuring security.

It is well suited for constrained environments where devices have limited processing, low memory and low bandwidth requirement particularly for sensors and mobile devices on unreliable networks. MQTT collects data from various electronic devices and supports remote device monitoring. MQTT is ISO-approved and offers low power consumption and efficient data distribution via its minimized packet system. This makes it a great option for industrial IoT and mobile applications. MQTT is mainly used in devices which are economical and requires less power and memory. For instance, fire detectors, car sensors, smart watches, and apps for text-based messaging.

☞ *MQTT-S/MQTT-SN is an extension of MQTT, which is designed for low power and low cost devices.*

Advantages of MQTT

- MQTT is bandwidth efficient, lightweigth and is best used when your internet connection is unreliable.
- MQTT is extremely simple, offering few control options and easy-to-implement.
- Low power consumption and efficient data distribution.
- MQTT is best used when your node sends data at irregular intervals of time.
- MQTT is an asynchronous messaging protocol. This is best used for real time systems.

Disadvantages of MQTT

- MQTT is a very light messaging protocol and cannot support heavy payloads.
- MQTT is best used to send your sensor data. You cannot send photos or video clips or audio using MQTT.

XMPP(Extensible Messaging and Presence Protocol)

The Extensible Messaging and Presence Protocol (XMPP) is an open technology for real-time communication originally designed for chats and messages exchange applications. It is used for applications such as instant messaging, presence, multi-party chat, voice and video calls etc. Other than the instant messaging apps such as Google Talk and WhatsApp, XMPP is also used in on-line gaming, news websites, and Voice over Internet Protocol (VoIP).

Advantages of XMPP

- XMPP offers an easy way to address a device.
- Like MQTT, XMPP also makes use of the publish/subscribe mechanism of data sharing.

Disadvantages of XMPP

- XMPP does not have a Quality of Service (QoS), like that of MQTT.
- Further, the text-based communication increases the overhead when compared to its binary based equivalent.

DDS(Data Distribution Service)

DDS (Data Distribution Service) is an IoT standard for real-time, scalable and high-performance machine-to-machine communication. It was developed by the *Object Management Group (OMG)*. It uses a publish/subscribe architecture where publishers create topics to which subscribers can use. In real-time distributed applications, publish/subscribe is the most efficient communication design pattern to use. It enables delivery of data to multiple destinations without having to add a lot of code to your applications to track all of these destinations.

DDS first gained widespread acceptance in aerospace and defense. DDS has now emerged as a standout technology for the Industrial Internet of Things (IIoT). DDS is a core connectivity standard for the rapidly growing Industrial Internet of Things (IIoT). IIoT has completely changed the industrial automation, healthcare, transportation, energy, smart cities etc. It is used in applications like financial trading, air-traffic control, smart grid management, and other big data applications.

Advantages of DDS

- DDS is a feature-rich standard that transparently handles much of an IoT system's data connectivity complexity, therefore, easing developer efforts.
- DDS provides low-latency, high-throughput, scalable, real-time and reliable communication.
- DDS can be used in small devices which occupies less area and as well as in the cloud.
- DDS implementations provide high-performance data communications, suitable for real-time.

Disadvantages of DDS

- DDS is too heavyweight to be used in embedded systems.
- DDS does not interface with web services.
- DDS always consumes approximately twice the bandwidth when compared against MQTT.

AMQP(Advanced Message Queuing Protocol)

Advanced Message Queuing Protocol (AMQP) is an open source published standard for asynchronous messaging by wire. AMQP enables encrypted and interoperable messaging between organizations and applications. The protocol is used in client/server messaging and in IoT device management. Advanced Messaging Queuing Protocol used for business messaging. AMQP doesn't require the systems to be simultaneously available and works reliably over a distance or over poor networks. Like MQTT, AMQP also supports the publish/subscribe protocol of communication. It also has the Quality of Service (QoS) implemented, ensuring the safe passage of important data.

Advantages of AMQP

- Like MQTT, AMQP also makes use of the publish/subscribe mechanism of data sharing.
- AMQP is a wire-level protocol (data send as stream of bytes), ensuring interoperability.
- Simple peer-to-peer and communication with intermediaries possible.

Disadvantage of AMQP

- Backward compatibility with older versions is not supported.

WebSocket

WebSocket is a protocol that provides bi-directional, full-duplex communications channels, over a single Transmission Control Protocol (TCP) socket. It is designed to be implemented in web browsers and web servers, but it can be used by any client or server application. It is part of the HTML 5 specification.

Advantages of WebSocket

- Supports Duplex communication.
- With WebSockets, you can send and receive your data immediately.
- Faster than HTTP.

Disadvantages of WebSocket

- Browser must be fully HTML5 compliant.
- Takes over the communications protocol between the client and the server for a particular connection.

HTTP (HyperText Transfer Protocol)

HyperText Transfer Protocol is the best example of IoT network protocol. HTTP is the foundation of the client-server model used for data communication over the web. It is the most common protocol that is used for IoT devices when there is a lot of data to be published. HTTP is common application layer protocol in the TCP/IP stack to transfer web content over the internet. HTTP works as a request-response protocol between a client and server. It defines what actions browsers and servers should take in response to certain commands or messages. A web browser may be the client, and an application on a computer that hosts a web site may be the server. For example, when you enter a URL in your browser, this actually sends an HTTP command to the web server directing it to fetch and transmit the requested web page.

☞ *HTTPS is the more secure version of HTTP, where S stands for secure.*

Advantages of HTTP

- HTTP is a TCP/IP based communication protocol, that is used to deliver data (HTML files, image files, query results, etc.) on the World Wide Web.
- HTTP is a generic and stateless protocol which can be used for other purposes as well using extensions of its request methods, error codes, and headers.

Disadvantages of HTTP

- HTTP protocol is not preferred because of its cost, battery-life, energy saving, and more constraints.
- HTTP does not encrypt the data while transferring data between client and server. The data transferred over HTTPS gets encrypted.
- HTTP saves cookies/data on the client system.

1.13.2 Transport Layer Protocol

Transmission Control Protocol (TCP)

TCP is a standard that defines how to establish and maintain a network conversation via which application programs can exchange data. TCP works with the Internet Protocol (IP), which defines how computers send packets of data to each other. TCP is based on a client-server communication model by which a user (client) receives a service such as a loaded web page from a server in the same network. TCP is not suited for IoT applications as IoT devices offer a varying traffic pattern due to their limitations.

Advantages of TCP

- Ensures reliable transmission and ensures that data which arrives out of sequence should put back into order.
- Provides Error Detection.
- Capability to ensure no duplicacy of packets and retransmit lost packets.
- It helps you to establish/set up a connection between different types of computers. It operates also independently of the operating system.

Disadvantages of TCP

- The speed for TCP is slower.
- You can't use for broadcast or multicast transmission.

- It doesn't offer clear separation from its services, interfaces, and protocols.

User Datagram Protocol (UDP)

UDP (User Datagram Protocol) is an alternative communications protocol to Transmission Control Protocol (TCP) used primarily for establishing low-latency and loss tolerating connections between applications on the Internet. With UDP, computer applications can send messages, in this case referred to as datagrams, to other hosts on an Internet Protocol (IP) network without prior communications to set up special transmission channels or data paths. UDP is also better suited for real-time data applications such as voice and video.

UDP is a connectionless protocol that works at the transport layer. UDP transports datagrams but does not acknowledge their receipt. UDP also uses a port address to achieve datagram delivery, but this port address is simply a pointer to a process, not a connection identifier, as it is with TCP. The lack of overhead makes UDP faster than TCP. Hence, a sender wishing to send a small message and does not care much about reliability can use UDP.

If UDP detects some error while transmitting a datagram, it simply drops the datagram and does not inform the sender about the same.

☞ *UDP provides no flow control or acknowledgements for received packets.*

Advantages of UDP

- UDP method is largely used by time-sensitive applications as well as by servers that answer small queries from a larger client base.
- Broadcast and multicast transmission are also available with UDP.
- UDP is ideal to use with multimedia like VoIP.

Disadvantages of UDP

- In UDP protocol, a packet may not be delivered or delivered twice. It may be delivered out of order, so you get no indication.
- UDP has no congestion control, and flow control.
- UDP mostly like to suffer from worse packet loss

How does UDP Work?

UDP gives a connectionless service. Each user datagram sent by UDP is an independent datagram. There is no relationship between the various user datagrams even when they are coming from the same source process and going to the same destination program. The user datagrams are not numbered. Moreover, each user datagram can travel a different path.

☞ *Each request must be small enough to fit into one user datagram. Only those processor sending short messages need to use UDP because it cannot cut messages into small segments.*

Difference between TCP and UDP

- TCP is a connection-oriented protocol, whereas UDP is a connectionless protocol.
- The speed for TCP is slower while the speed of UDP is faster
- TCP does error checking and also makes error recovery. On the other hand, UDP performs error checking, but it discards erroneous packets.
- TCP has acknowledgment segments, but UDP does not have any acknowledgment segment.
- TCP is heavy-weight, and UDP is lightweight.

1.13.3 Network Layer Protocol

IPv4 (Internet Protocol version 4)

IP (Internet Protocol) is the main networking protocol. There are two version of IP (IPv4 and IPV6). IPv4 is limited to 32-bit addresses, which only provide around 4.3 billion addresses in total, which is less than the current number of IoT devices that are connected

Advantages of IPv4

- IPv4 allows data to be secured with encryption.
- IPv4 is still widely used and the world is slow to convert to IPv6.

Disadvantages of IPv4

- The most significant drawback related to IPv4 is that it is difficult to configure it.
- The lack of address space - the number of different devices connected to the Internet grows exponentially, and the size of the address space is quickly exhausted.
- Weak protocol extensibility - the insufficient size of the IPv4 header, which does not accommodate the required number of additional parameters.
- The problem of security of communications - no means are provided to limit access to information hosted on the network. IPv4 has never been designed for security.

IPv6 (Internet Protocol version 6)

IPv6 is the latest revision of the Internet Protocol (IP), the communications protocol that provides an identification and location system for computers on networks and routes traffic across the Internet. Every device on the Internet must be assigned an IP address in order to communicate with other devices. IPv6 uses a 128-bit address. Some of the features of the IPv6 are as following:

(a) Options are specified in an extension to the header that is examined only at the destination. Thus, network performance are speeded up.

(b) The introduction of an "any cast" address provides the possible gateway hosts. With this idea, any one of them can manage the forwarding of the packet to others. Anycast messages can be used to update routing tables along the line.

(c) Packets can be identified as belonging to a particular "flow". Thus, packets that are part of a multimedia presentation, which needs to arrive in "real-time" can provide higher quality-of-service relative to other customers.

(d) The IPv6 header now includes extensions that allow a packet to specify a mechanism for authenticating its origin. This helps for ensuring data integrity, and privacy.

Advantages of IPv6

- IPv6 addressing scheme is much more efficient than IPv4 and has more Unique Addresses.
- Auto-configuration.
- No more private address collisions.
- Built-in authentication and privacy support

Disadvantage of IPv6

- The process of making the switch to IPv6 from IPv4 is slow and tedious.

Differences between IPv6 and IPv4

IPv6	IPv4
Doesn't provide broadcast messaging.	Provides broadcast messaging.
Addresses are the 128-bit length.	Addresses are 32 bit long.
No checksum field available in the header.	Checksum field available.
Binary represented in hexadecimal.	Binary represented in decimals.
Placket flow identification is there.	Packet flow identification isn't there.

6LoWpan (IPv6 Low power Wireless Personal Area Networks)

6LoWPAN, an acronym for IPv6 over Low power Wireless Personal Area Networks, is a very popular standard for wireless communication. It is really the first wireless connectivity standard that was created for the IoT. 6LoWPAN has also an advantage over other Personal Area Networks, because peer-to-peer communication is simpler to implement when each device has a global address. The 6LoWPAN group has defined encapsulation and header compression mechanisms that allow IPv6 packets to be sent to and received from over IEEE 802.15.4 wireless based networks. 6LoWPAN gives IoT connectivity to very small, low-power devices to directly communicate with any other IP-based (Ethernet or Wi-Fi) server or device on the internet. The main aim of the protocol is to enable the smallest devices to use the internet protocol. This takes into consideration the low-power working condition and the low bandwidth of the devices. And thus, developing a protocol which acts as a bridge between the bigger and smaller devices was very hard.

Advantage of 6LoWPAN

- 6LowPAN is a mesh network that is robust and scalable.

Disadvantages of 6LoWPAN

- The greatest challenge to 6LoWPAN is the lack of application that utilizes 6LoWPAN because it require extensive training as it is complicated to work with and requires extensive knowledge of IPv6 protocol.
- Another challenge with 6LoWPAN is that end users could not deploy this protocol easily as it requires extensive knowledge of stack and the workability.

1.13.4 Link Layer Protocols

802.3 - Ethernet

Ethernet is based upon the IEEE 802.3 standard and is widely used to build LANs. IoT networks do not necessarily have to be wireless and by using Ethernet, an IoT system can be built upon existing electrical cable networks. For example, sensor units installed within a building automation system can use wired networking technologies like Ethernet.

802.11 - WiFi

IEEE 802.11 is a collection of Wireless Local Area Network (WLAN) communication standards defines the WLAN specification, which is the baseline of the Wi-Fi standard. WiFi provides communication range in the order of 20 m (indoor) to 100 m (outdoor).

802.16 - WiMAX

IEEE 802.16 is a collection of wireless broadband standards. WiMAX (Worldwide Interoperability for Microwave Access) standards provide data rates from 1.5 Mb/s to 1 Gb/s.

802.15.4 - LR-WPAN

IEEE 802.15.4 is a collection of Low-Rate Wireless Personal Area Networks (LR-WPAN) standards. These standards form the basis of specifications for high level communications protocols such as Zigbee, 6LoWPAN and Wireless Highway Addressable Transducer Protocol (HART).

2G/3G/4G/5G - Mobile communication

There are different generations of mobile communication standards including second generation (2G including GSM and CDMA), third generation (3G-including UMTS ad CDMA2000) and fourth generation (4G-including LTE). IoT devices based on these standards can communicate over cellular networks.

1.14 IoT ENABLING TECHNOLOGIES

IoT enabling technologies includes Sensors, Cloud computing, Big data analytics, Communication protocols, Embedded system. These technologies are discussed below:

1.14.1 Sensors

A sensor is a device that is used to sense a physical condition or event. A sensor works by converting a non-electrical input into an electrical signal that can be sent to an electronic circuit. A sensor does not function by itself, it is a part of a larger system that comprises microprocessors, modem chips, power sources, and other related devices. The sensors, actuators, chipsets, MEMS, etc. that are embedded into 'smart' physical assets and devices. There has been a rapid growth in the use of smaller sensors that can be embedded in smartphones and wearables. Micro-electro-mechanical Systems (MEMS) Sensors.

A sensor converts a non-electrical input into an electrical signal that can be sent to an electronic circuit. An electronic device that produces electrical, optical, or digital data derived from a physical condition or event. Data produced from sensors is then electronically transformed, by another device, into information (output) that is useful in decision making done by 'intelligent' devices or individuals (people).

1.14.2 Cloud Computing

Cloud computing or on-demand computing is an Internet-based computing service which involves the use of the network of remote servers rather than local server or personal computer, which host on the Internet for storing, managing, and processing the data (See Figure 1.10).

Cloud computing is a transformative computing paradigm that involves delivering applications and services over the Internet. For example a cloud based application is used for visualizing the moisture level over a period of time, which can help in making decisions about irrigation schedule.

Cloud computing involves provisioning of computing, networking and storage resources on demand and providing these resources as metered services to the users in a 'pay as you go model'.

In cloud computing, Cloud is a large group of interconnected computers, which may be personal or public.

Consider an example: If you have a Gmail or Yahoo account, then you are already using Cloud Computing. As you do not know where exactly your e-mail and contacts are stored, and you can access your account via Internet.

Figure 1.10 Cloud Computing

Cloud computing allows:

- Companies to focus on only projects which differentiate their businesses instead of on infrastructure and to avoid upfront infrastructure costs.
- Enterprises to get their applications up and run faster, with less maintenance.
- To rapidly adjust the resources, to meet fluctuating and unpredictable business demand.

Cloud computing is highly demanded service or utility because of its:

- High computing power and performance.
- Cheap cost of services.
- Scalability, accessibility and availability.

Properties

The key properties of Cloud computing are:

- **User-centric:** Once the user gets connected to cloud, any data which is present there, such as images, videos, applications, becomes his/her property.
- **Task Centric:** In this, documents are given more priority than applications from which they are created.
- **Powerful:** Due to its computing power and mass data storage capability.
- **Self-Healing:** Backups of every document is created automatically in the cloud.
- **Multi-tenancy & Intelligence:** Multi-tenancy means sharing of data among a large number of users, by using data mining and analysis for accessing information in an intelligent manner.
- **Programmable:** Programming is associated with cloud computing, as processes such as backing up of data is done automatically, which requires programming.
- **Flexible:** It matches with the needs of user.

Characteristics

Key characteristics of cloud computing are:

- **Agility:** It improves with users' ability to re-provision technological infrastructure resources.
- **Cost reductions claimed by cloud providers:** The capital investment in the data centre is assumed by the cloud provider and operation costs are passed onto the cloud data centre user.
- **Device and location independence:** It enables the users to access systems through web browser irrespective of their location or the device they are using.
- **Maintenance:** Cloud computing applications maintenance is easier, as it does not need to be installed on each user's computer and can be accessed from many places, provided that there must be an internet connection.
- **Multitenancy:** It enables the sharing of resources and costs across a large number of users.
- **Productivity:** It is increased as multiple users work on the same data simultaneously than waiting for it to be saved and e-mailed.

- **Time:** Time is saved as information does not need to be re-entered again and again when fields are matched, nor the users need to install an application software upgrades to their computer.
- **Reliability:** It enables the use of multiple redundant sites, which makes well-designed cloud computing suitable for business continuity.
- **Security:** It is improved due to centralization of data, security-focused resources, etc.

Service Model

Service-oriented architecture advocates "everything as a service", whereas, on the other hand, cloud-computing providers offer their "services" according to different models. The three generally accepted modes of type of service offered are:

IaaS - Infrastructure as a Service (Servers and storage)

It provides physical hardware and software required by companies on the Internet. In other terms, IaaS refers to an on-line service which abstract the user from the detail of infrastructure (Infrastructure includes physical computing resources, location, data partitioning, scaling, security, backup etc.)

In this basic requirement for the consumer is to send a provisioning request for the number of server with data storage requirement. The server is provisioned and the access to the server is granted by the service provider.

IaaS provides a cloud-based platform for servers, storage, memory, bandwidth and computing power on demand. User needs a platform substantial customization of IaaS services. Vendors such as Rack space and Amazon's EC2 provides server and storage on demand. What applications to be use and how to configure the data storage are left to the client. Sub-class of IaaS is "Communications as service".

PaaS - Platform as a Service (Development)

It provides a development environment or a real-time in cloud environment. The provider mainly develops toolkit and standards for the development and channels for distribution and payment. Generally, developer use PaaS (who develop and run their software solutions on a cloud platform without the cost and complexity of buying and managing the underlying hardware and software layers) and consumer user SaaS.

In this, cloud providers deliver a computing platform (which includes operating system, programming-language execution environment, database, and web server), on which an application developer can develop and run their software solutions without spending much cost.

Example, web-hosting platform or a collaboration program which provides access to document sharing or video archival and retrieval.

SaaS- Software as a Service (Application)

It provides software applications over the Internet, Cloud based software services such as customer resource management or enterprise resource management and user gain access to application software and database.

Example: Microsoft Live, which duplicates the Microsoft office suite for free on the Internet.

SaaS is sometimes referred to as "on-demand software" as in this cloud providers manage the platform and infrastructure, on which the applications are run. It is priced on a pay-per-use basis or using a subscription fee.

1.14.3 Big Data Analytics

The data transfer or receive through smart devices and environments are communicated through cloud computing or others servers and stored as big data. Big data is a collections of data sets whose volume, velocity or variety is so large that it is difficult to store, manage, process and analyze the data using traditional databases and data processing tools. Examples of big data generated by IoT systems are Weather Monitoring Stations, Machine sensor data from industrial systems, Health and fitness data, Location and tracking systems etc.

Characteristics of Big Data

Volume: A particular data can actually be considered as a Big Data or not, is dependent upon the volume of data. Hence, 'volume' is one characteristic which needs to be considered while dealing with Big Data.

Variety: It refers to heterogeneous sources and the nature of data, both structured and unstructured. Data in the form of email, photos, videos, monitoring devices, PDFs, audio etc. are also being considered in the analysis applications.

Velocity: It refers to the speed of generation of data i.e., how fast the data is generated and processed to meet the demands.

Variability: It refers to the disparity which can be shown by the data at times, thus restrict the process of being able to handle and manage the data effectively.

Big data analytics refers to the method of analyzing huge volumes of big data. It is the process of collecting, organizing and analyzing a large amount of data to uncover hidden patterns, correlations, market trends and other meaningful information. It helps an organization understand the information contained in their data and use it to provide new opportunities to improve their business, which in turn leads to more efficient operations and higher profits.

☞ *Big Data Analytics refers to the process of collecting, organizing, analyzing large data sets to discover different patterns and other useful information.*

1.14.4 Communication Protocols

Communication protocol are format descriptions of digital message formats and rules. They are required to exchange messages in or between computing systems. Many wireless technologies are available today that are being used to interconnect IoT devices and the internet, consisting of various ranges WPAN and WLAN such as Wi-Fi, Infrared, Bluetooth etc.

1.14.5 Embedded Systems

An Embedded system is a system that has computer hardware and software embedded to perform specific tasks. They include a processing unit, usually a general-purpose microcontroller(i.e. CPUs with integrated memory or peripheral interfaces), along with on-board peripheral components such as I/O ports, memory (program memory, RAM and EEPROM), A/D converter, oscillators, and more. An embedded system may be connected to sensors that collect information about the environment and actuators that are used to trigger functions within the system. Embedded system range from low-cost miniaturized devices such as Digital watch, Digital cameras, Vending machines appliances etc. Embedded systems are used in a range of industrial, commercial, and residential applications that range from controlling manufacturing systems to enabling vehicle safety features to powering home security systems and smart appliances.

Characteristics of Embedded Systems

- All Embedded Systems are task specific. They do the same task repeatedly /continuously over their lifetime.
- Embedded systems are created to perform the task within a certain time frame. It must therefore perform fast enough.
- Built to function with little or no human intervention. A fully automatic washing machine works on its own after the programme is set and stops once the task is over.
- Some embedded systems are designed to react to external stimuli and react accordingly. For example, a GPS tracking device.
- The hardware of an embedded-system is used for security and performance.

☞ *Embedded systems are small computers that are implemented as part of a larger system or product and designed to execute a specific function or application.*

Advantages of Embedded system

- These systems are highly stable and reliable.
- Embedded systems are made for specific tasks.
- The embedded systems are very small in size, hence can be carried and loaded anywhere.
- These systems are fast. They also use less power.
- The embedded systems optimize the use or resources available.
- The embedded system is highly reliable.

Disadvantages of Embedded system

- Once configured, these systems cannot be changed.
- Troubleshooting is difficult for embedded systems.
- It has hard to take backup of embedded files.

1.14.6 Fog Computing

Fog computing also known as *Edge Computing* is a term created by Cisco and it extends the concept of cloud computing to the network edge, making it ideal for Internet of Things (IoT) and other applications that require real-time interactions. It refers to a decentralized computing structure, where resources, including the data and applications, get placed in logical locations between the data source and the cloud. The fog computing platform lies between the cloud servers and the users. In a fog-enabled environment, the devices at the fog layer usually perform operations related to networking such as routers, gateways, bridges, and hubs.

☞ *Fog computing is a type of network architecture that links cloud computing to the Internet of Things (IoT). It is a medium weighted extension of cloud computing in IoT domain.*

1.14.7 Fog Computing Applications

Fog computing has many real-world applications. Popular fog computing applications include smart grid, smart city, smart buildings, vehicle networks and software-defined networks.

Smart traffic management

Traffic management systems can use edge and fog computing for real-time data analysis to alter traffic lights and intelligent road signs the moment an accident or road blockage occurs. Also, better connectivity can reduce accidents and promote safe driving.

Smart cities and grids

For utilities and systems to run smoothly and effectively in smart cities, real-time, accurate data is essential. Also to run efficiently, a smart grid relies heavily on real time data of electrical production and consumption. Real-time data processing allows fog data being collected across a city to be processed faster.

Industrial IoT (IIoT)

Fog computing has also been applied in manufacturing in the IIoT (Industrial Internet of Things). This allows connected manufacturing devices with sensors and cameras to gather and process data locally, rather than send all of this data to the cloud. This achieves higher data accuracy while decreasing the amount of data packets (i.e., units of data) that need to be transported back and forth.

1.14.8 How Fog Computing Works?

A fog computing framework can have a variety of components and functions depending on its application. It could include computing gateways that accept data from data sources or diverse collection endpoints such as routers and switches connecting assets within a network. Data parsing and analysis occurs in a smart hub, gateway, or router, thus limiting the amount of information that needs to be sent to the cloud for processing. Data that needs to be processed at once are analyzed at the gateway (i.e., within the network), while the rest are filtered then sent directly to the cloud.

Fog Computing vs Edge Computing

The terms fog computing and edge computing are used interchangeably, as both involve bringing intelligence and processing closer to where the data is created. However, the key difference between the two is where the intelligence and compute power is placed.

In a fog environment, intelligence is at the local area network. Data is transmitted from endpoints to a gateway where it is then transmitted to sources for processing and return transmission. In edge computing, intelligence and power of the edge gateway or appliance are in devices such as programmable automation controllers.

Advantages of Fog Computing

- Since fog computing is connected to various nodes and the system is very complex so it maintains high security. Fog computing has all applicable security controls and processes in place which solves the problems of security risks.
- With fog computing, manufacturers and service providers offer their services at affordable rates.
- Fog computing is the physical location of the devices, which are much closer to the users than the cloud servers. Such placement of the devices reduces latency (Latency is the delay between the transfer from one point to another) requirements and hence quick decisions can be made. This helps in avoiding accidents.
- It offers better security. Fog nodes can be protected using same procedures followed in IT environment.
- It processes selected data locally instead of sending them to the cloud for processing. So, it offers better privacy to the users data as they are analyzed locally. By keeping the process local, the IT team can keep track and control the devices that collect, analyze and store data.
- Power efficiency of fog computing is one of the important advantage. Many likes to use fog computing due to its quality of being efficient, faster performance and processes.
- The fog node, which is located in a smart router or gateway device, allows fog data to be processed on this smart device, so that only the necessary data gets further transmitted to the cloud, and decreases the bandwidth used. This leads to lower operational costs.

Disadvantages of Fog Computing

- To achieve high data consistency in the fog computing is challenging and requires more efforts.
- Fog computing will realize global storage concept with infinite size and speed of local storage but data management is a challenge.
- Scheduling is complex as tasks can be moved between client devices, fog nodes and back end cloud servers.
- Power consumption is high in fog nodes compare to centralized cloud architecture. Also, cloud is more scalable than fog computing.
- Using fog computing, a large volume of data is stored on the devices themselves. These devices are often located outside the office's physical location, and many companies or business managers feel that this configuration increases the risk of a data leak or hack.
- Enhanced edge devices and fog nodes may be located in less secure environments than a central cloud platform in a secure data centre can provide.
- Fog computing is very expensive because the organization needs to buy devices like hubs, routers, gateways.

1.15 BUILDING BLOCKS OF IoT

Four things form basic building blocks of IoT system -sensors, processors, gateways, applications. The sensors at access layer connected to switches called processors then gateways called routers then data stored in cloud. Each of these nodes has to have their own characteristics in order to form an useful IoT system.

1.15.1 Sensors & Actuators

These form the front end of the IoT devices. Sensors are active in nature which means that real-time information is to be collected and processed. For example, sensors help monitor the state of industrial equipment, and in case of a pre-failure situation, an IoT system generates and sends automatic notifications to field engineers.

You have different sensors for different applications - temperature sensor for collecting temperature data, water quality for examining water quality, moisture sensor for measuring moisture content of the atmosphere or soil etc. The main purpose of sensor is to collect static or dynamic data from the physical world and give out data to its surrounding (actuators) to act upon. An actuator is a device, which can effect a change in the environment by converting electrical energy into some form of useful energy. As an example, you can consider a smart home system, which consists of many sensors and actuators. The actuators are used to lock/unlock the doors, switch on/off the lights or other electrical appliances, alert users of any threats through alarms or notifications, and control the temperature of a home etc.

☞ *Sensors are devices which converts physical parameters like temperature, motion etc. into the electrical signals.*

☞ *Actuators are devices which is a contrast to sensors. It transforms electrical signals into physical movements.*

1.15.2 Processors

Processors are the brain of the IoT system. Their main function is to process the data captured by the sensors and to extract the valuable data from the enormous amount of raw data collected.

Processors mostly work on real-time basis and can be easily controlled by applications. These are also responsible for securing the data - that is performing encryption and decryption of data.

1.15.3 Gateways

Gateways are responsible for routing the processed data and send it to proper locations for its (data) proper utilization. It provides network connectivity to the data. Network connectivity is essential for any IoT system to communicate. LAN, WAN, PAN etc., are examples of network gateways.

1.15.4 Applications

Applications form another end of an IoT system. Applications are essential for proper utilization of all the data collected.

These cloud based applications which are responsible for rendering effective meaning to the data collected. Applications are controlled by users and are delivery point of particular services. Examples of applications are: home automation apps, security systems, industrial control hub etc.

1.16 THE LOGICAL AND PHYSICAL DESIGN OF IoT

Logical design of an IoT system refers to an abstract representation of the entities and processes without going into the low-level detail of the implementation. The logical design is more conceptual and abstract than the physical design. In the logical design, you look at the logical relationships among the objects. In the physical design, you look at the most effective way of storing and retrieving the objects. Here, physical design means more than creating connected products, but forming an overall intelligent system. Your design should be oriented toward the needs of the end users.

Comparison of logical and physical design is given below:

Logical Design	Physical Design
It is a high-level design without any detail.	It is very detailed.
Here focus is on satisfying the design factors such as requirements, risks, assumptions, and constraints.	Here focus is on specific solutions i.e., how they are assembled and configured.
It can be graphical, textual, or both.	It is more graphical than textual, but can be both.

1.17 FUNCTIONAL BLOCKS OF IoT

An IoT system comprises of a number of functional blocks that provide the system the capabilities for identification, sensing, actuation, communication, and management. These functional blocks are as follows:

1.17.1 Device

An IoT devices provide sensing, actuation, monitoring and control functions.

1.17.2 Communication

It handles communication for the IoT system.

1.17.3 Security

It secures the IoT system by providing authentication, authorization, message and content integrity, and data security.

1.17.4 Application

It provides an interface that the user's can use to control and monitor various aspects of IoT system.

1.17.5 Services

An IoT system uses various types of IoT services such as services for device monitoring, device control services, data publishing services and services for device discovery.

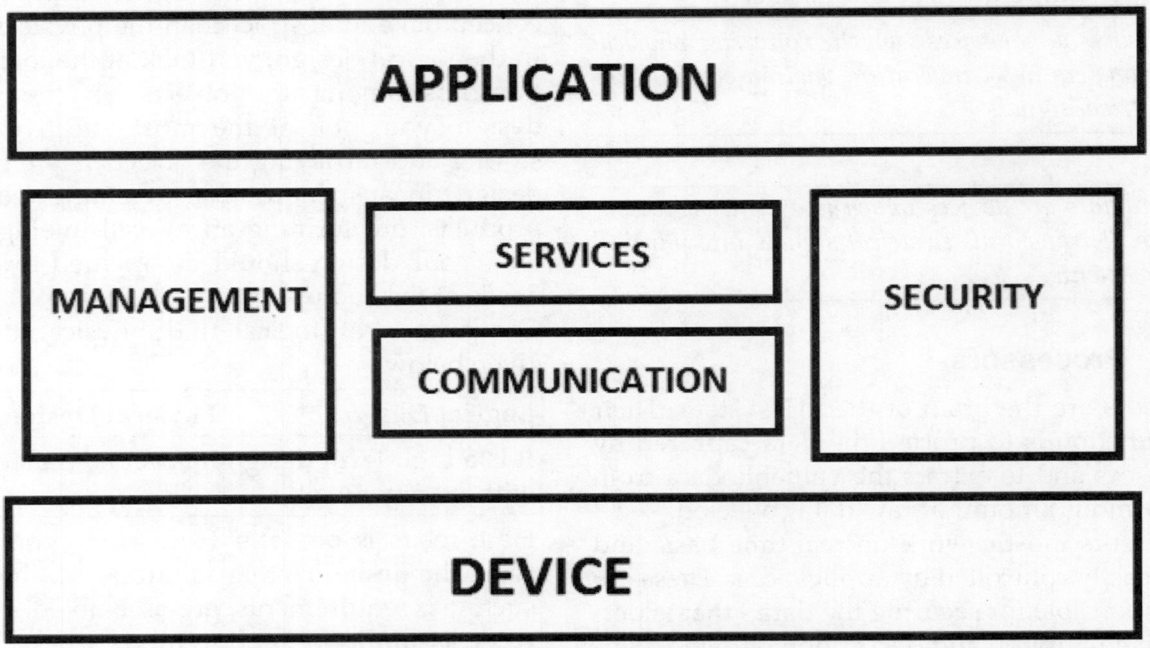

Figure 1.11 Functional blocks of IoT

1.18 IoT DESIGN METHODOLOGY

Design methodology refers to the development of a system or method for a unique situation. Designing for the Internet of Things (IoT) is the designing of connected products. IoT systems combine physical and digital components that collect data from physical devices and deliver actionable, operational insights. These components include: physical devices, sensors, data extraction and secured communication, gateways, cloud servers, analytics, and dashboards. (See Figure 1.12).

Purpose & requirements specification

The first step in IoT design methodology is to define the purpose and requirements of the system. In this step, the system purpose, behavior and requirements such as data collection requirements, data analysis requirement, system management requirements, data privacy and security requirements, user interface requirements are captured.

Process specification

The second step in the IoT design methodology is to define the process specification. In this step, the use cases of the IoT system are formally described based on the derived from the purpose and requirement specification.

Domain Model Specification

The third step in the IoT design methodology is to define the Domain Model. This model describes the main concepts, entities and objects in the domain of IoT system to be designed. It also defines the attributes of the objects and relationships between objects. The domain model provides an abstract representation of the concepts, objects and entities in the IoT domain, independent of any specific technology or platform.

Information Model Specification

The fourth step in the IoT design methodology is to define the Information Model. Information Model defines the structure of all the information in the IoT system, say, attributes of virtual entities, relations, etc. Information model does not describe the specifics of how the information is represented or stored.

Services Specifications

The fifth step in the IoT design methodology is to define the service specifications. Service specifications define the services in the IoT system, service types, service input/output, service endpoints, service schedules, service preconditions and service effects.

IoT Level Specification

The sixth step in the IoT design methodology is to define the IoT level for the system.

Functional View Specification

The seventh step in the IoT design methodology is to define the Functional view. The functional view defines the functions of the IoT systems grouped into various Functional groups. Each functional group either provides functionalities for interacting with instances of concepts defined in the Domain Model or provides information related to these concepts.

Operational View Specification

The eighth step in the IoT design methodology is to define the Operational view specifications. In this step, various options pertaining to the IoT system deployment and operation are defined, such as, service hosting options, storage options, device options, application hoisting options, etc.

Device and Component Integration

The ninth step in the IoT design methodology is the integration of the devices and components.

Application Development

The final step in the IoT design methodology is to develop the IoT application. The application has controls for the mode (auto on or auto off) and the light (on or off).

1.19 COMMUNICATION MODELS

1.19.1 Request-Response Communication Model

Request-Response is a communication model in which the client sends requests to the server and the server responds to the requests. When the server receives a request, it decides how to respond, fetches the data, retrieves resource representations, prepares the response and then sends the response to the client. Request-response is a stateless communication model and each request-response pair is independent of others. In stateless each request from client to server must contain all the information necessary to understand the request, and cannot take advantage of any stored context on the server. HTTP works as a request-response protocol between a client and server. (See Figure 1.13).

Module 4: M4–R5

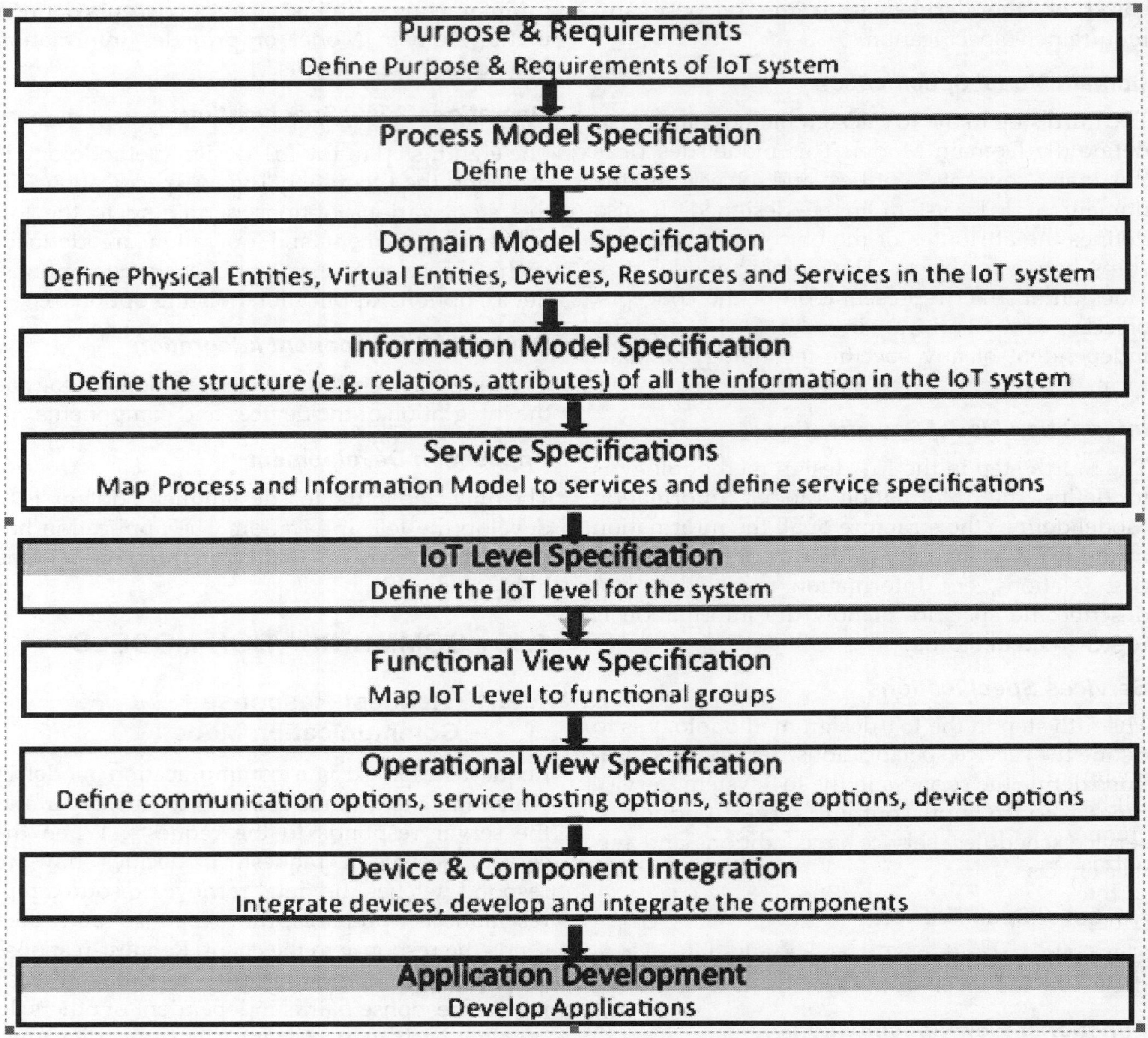

Figure 1.12 IoT Design Methodology

Figure 1.13 Request-Response Communication Model

1.19.2 Publish-Subscribe Communication Model

Publish-Subscribe is a communication model that involves publishers, brokers and consumers. Publishers are the source of data. Publishers send the data to the topics which are managed by the broker. Publishers are not aware of the consumers. Consumers subscribe to the topics which are managed by the broker. When the broker receives data for a topic from the publisher, it sends the data to all the subscribed consumers. (See Figure 1.14).

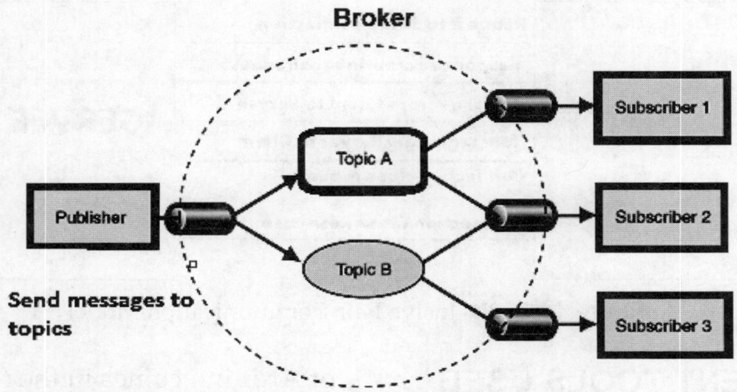

Figure 1.14 Publish-Subscribe Communication Model

1.19.3 Push-Pull Communication Model

Push-Pull is a communication model in which the data producers push the data to queues and the consumers pull the data from the queues. In a pull-based communication model, the user issues a request for any specific information object. In contrast, in a push-based model interested parties get the information if they have previously subscribed it, and information gets distributed when it is available. Therefore, producers push information periodically or based on events to consumers.

Producers do not need to be aware of the consumers. Queues help in decoupling the messaging between the producers and consumers. Queues also act as a buffer which helps in situations when there is a mismatch between the rate at which the producers push data and the rate at which the consumers pull data. (See Figure 1.15).

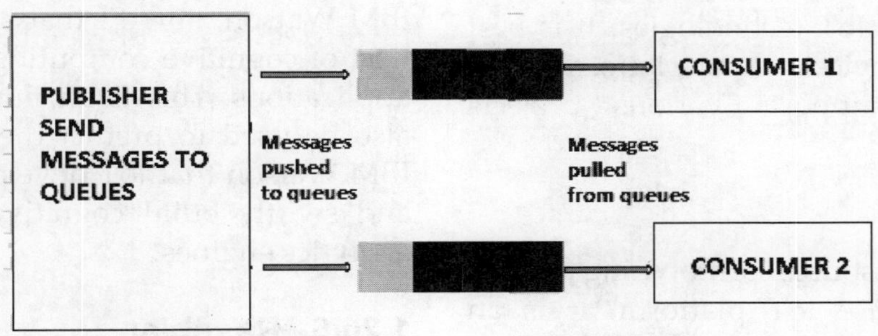

Figure 1.15 Push-Pull Communication Model

1.19.4 Exclusive Pair Communication Model

Exclusive Pair is a bi-directional, fully duplex communication model that uses a persistent connection between the client and the server. Once the connection is set up it, remains open until the client sends a request to close the connection. Client and server can send messages to each other after connection setup. Exclusive pair is stateful communication model and the server is aware of all the open connections. (See Figure 1.16).

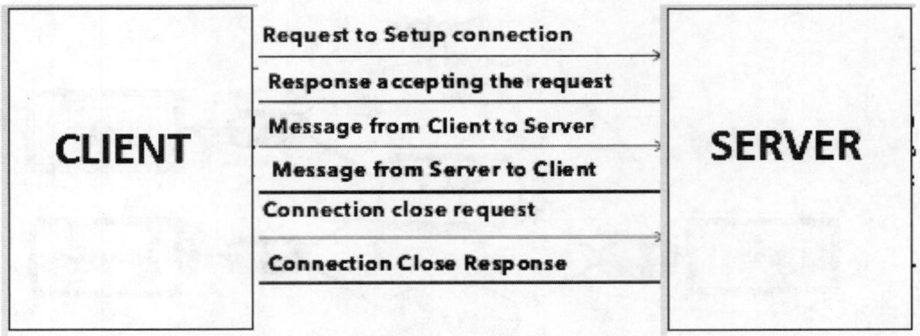

Figure 1.16 Exclusive Pair Communication Model

1.20 DEVELOPMENT TOOLS USED IN IoT

These tools help the developers to explore and create innovative IoT applications and devices.

1.20.1 Tessel 2

It is used to build basic IoT prototypes and applications. Tessel 2 is a board which can hold up to a dozen modules including the RFID, camera, GPS and the accelerometer. Using Tessel 2 board, a developer can avail Ethernet connectivity, Wi-Fi connectivity, two USB ports, a micro USB port etc.

1.20.2 Eclipse IoT

This tool allows the user to develop, adopt and promote open source IoT technologies. It is best suited to build IoT devices, cloud platforms, and gateways. Eclipse supports various projects related to IoT.

1.20.3 Arduino

Arduino is an open-source prototyping and is easy and simple-to-use IoT platform. It is an open-source prototyping platform that offers both IoT hardware and software. Arduino operates through a set of hardware specifications that can be applied to interactive electronics. The software of Arduino comes in the form of the Arduino programming language and Integrated Development Environment (IDE). It is the most preferable IDEs in all IoT development tools.

1.20.4 PlatformIO

It is a cross-platform IoT development environment. This platform comes with a build system, supported by a library manager and IDE. It comes with the integrated debugger and is compatible with more than 200 boards. It is the best for mobile app development and developers can use a friendly IoT environment for development.

1.20.5 IBM Watson

IBM Watson, an API that allows you to attach a host of cognitive computing features to your IoT applications. This is an innovative tool that can also be used to predict the future. It is through IBM Watson that IoT developers can successfully and swiftly build cognitive search and content analytics engines.

1.20.6 Raspbian

This IoT IDE is created for Raspberry Pi board. It is regarded as the best tool for Raspberry Pi for IoT app development. Another best part about this tool is that it is under constant development and has widened the reach for computing so that users can gain maximum benefits.

1.20.7 Kaax

It provides end to end support for IoT devices connected across the cloud. Due to its multi-purpose middleware, it allows users to build connected applications. It helps developers to distribute firmware updates remotely, and to enable cross-platform interoperability.

1.20.8 Home Assistant

It is an open source tool mostly used for functions based on the Python coding system and home automation. Desktop and mobile browsers help to control their IoT system.

1.21 SDN AND NFV FOR IoT

Software Defined Networking (SDN) is a new networking paradigm to make the current wireless and mobile networks more intelligent, efficient, secure, and scalable in order to handle the large amount of data produced in the IoT. SDN has been applied to IoT to facilitate networking applications such as heterogeneity, mobility management, QoS management and security.

A complementary approach to SDN is Network Function Virtualization (NFV). NFV separates the physical network equipment's (i.e., network address translator, firewall) from the functions that run on them. This way, numerous service providers can create several isolated virtual networks which could then share the physical network equipment's provided by the network infrastructure providers.

REVIEW QUESTIONS WITH ANSWERS

1. Multiple Choice Questions

1. The ________ is the "Central Nervous System" that takes care of global services in the IoTs.
   a. Perception layer
   b. Network layer
   c. Application layer
   d. None of the above
2. Remotes enable entities that utilize IoT devices to connect and control them using a dashboard:
   a. Smartphones
   b. Tablets & PCs
   c. Smartwatches
   d. All of the above
3. WiFi-ah (HaLow) designed specifically for:
   a. Low data rate
   b. Long-range sensors
   c. Controllers
   d. All of the above
4. The RFID is a useful IoT architecture layer of the perception layer for:
   a. Object identifying
   b. Tracking
   c. Exchanging useful information
   d. All of the above
5. What is the full form of HTTP?
   a. Hyphenation Text Test Program
   b. Hypertext Transfer Protocol
   c. Hypertext Transfer Package
   d. None of the above
6. An entity in IoT:
   a. Businesses b. Governments
   c. Consumers d. All of the above
7. Which of there following wireless technology provide mesh network architecture in easiest way?
   a. Bluetooth b. ZigBee
   c. Wi-Fi d. None of the above
8. ZigBee is based on which of the following standard:
   a. IEEE 802.15.4 b. IEEE 802.5
   c. IEEE 802.4.13 d. Both a and b
9. Mostly used protocols in IoT:
   a. MQTT b. Zigbee
   c. XMPP d. All of the above
10. Which of the following is Light weight protocol used in IoT Applications?
   a. MQTT b. WebSocket
   c. HTTP d. All of the above
11. Advantage of MQTT over HTTP is:
   a. More secure b. Lightweight

c. Polling is not required
d. Both (a) and (b)

12. MQTT suits are:
a. Small & cheap devices
b. Low-memory devices
c. Low-power devices
d. All of the above

13. Which protocol provide Full-Duplex communication?
a. WebSocket
b. HTTP
c. MQTT
d. CoAP

14. IPv4 is ______ bit address.
a. 24
b. 32
c. 64
d. 128

15. Acroname of 6LoWPAN is:
a. IPv6 over Low Power Wireless Personal Area Network
b. IPv4 over Low Power Wireless Private Area Network
c. IPv6 over Low Energy Wire Personal Area Network
d. IPv4 over LongRange Wireless Private Area Network

16. The different wireless standards used in cellular networks:
a. GSM
b. CDMA
c. LTE
d. All of the above

17. The full form of LoRa is:
a. Level Range Radio
b. Long Radio Range
c. Long Range Radio
d. None of these

18. The RFID technology consists of:
a. Antenna
b. Transponder
c. Transceiver
d. All of these

19. Which protocol provide Full-Duplex communication?
a. WebSocket
b. HTTP
c. MQTT
d. CoAP

20. Connected car is:
a. BAN
b. LAN
c. WAN
d. None of these

2. State True or False for the following:

1. An IoT ecosystem is a network of organizations that drives the creation and delivery of IoT products and services.
2. BLE is a low-power version of the popular Bluetooth 2.4 GHz wireless communication protocol.
3. Bluetooth low energy is also called Bluetooth smart.
4. CoAP can be thought of as an alternative to HTTP.
5. MQTT is a lightweight protocol, which makes it suitable for IoT applications.
6. The Sigfox network provides very long-range Wireless connectivity for the Internet of Things.
7. RFID is inexpensive and uses very little power.
8. The phrase 'Internet of Things' was coined by Kevin Ashton an expert on digital innovation in 1999.
9. IoE stands for Internet of Environment.
10. 6LoWPAN is an acronym of IPv6 over Low power Wireless Personal Area Networks.
11. Zigbee supports low data exchange rates, low power operation, security, and reliability.
12. Smart farming through the use of IoT technologies will help farmers to reduce generated wastes and enhance productivity.

3. Match the following:

1. Middleware	a. Data from IoT devices is stored
2. Data storage	b. Data analytical tools and storage
3. BLE	c. A small chip with an antenna
4. RFID tag	d. Connectionless Internet protocol
5. ZigBee	e. Fitness trackers
6. Nodes	f. IoT protocol
7. MQTT	g. Miniature devices
8. XMPP	h. Connection oriented protocol
9. TCP	i. A good example of an existing Web technology

10. UDP	j.	Useful for remote communication
11. LoRaWAN	k.	People, process, data, and things
12. IoE components	l.	Wireless network
13. Processors	m.	Track and measure activity
14. Sensors	n.	Brain of the IoT system

4. Fill in the blanks:

1. Delivery of the information to the end user is known as ________.
2. ________ is the method of capturing information by some highly functioning hardware.
3. ________ transmits the data collected by the physical layer to different devices.
4. ________ protocols and interfaces that devices use to identify and communicate with each other.
5. ________ software systems analyze the data generated by IoT devices.
6. ________ has been modified to Bluetooth Low Energy (BLE).
7. ________ is a publish/subscribe protocol that runs over TCP.
8. ________ uses a technology called Ultra Narrow Band (UNB).
9. ZigBee is based on the ______ standard.
10. ________ used to track consumer product worldwide.
11. ________ layer is responsible for delivery of various applications to different users in IoT.
12. The full form of LoRa is ________.

Answers

1. 1. b 2. d 3. d 4. d 5. b 6. d 7. b 8. a 9. d 10. a 11 d 12 d 13. a 14. b 15. a 16. d 17. c 18. d 19. a 20. c

2. 1. T 2. T 3. T 4. T 5. T 6. T 7. T 8. T 9. F 10. T 11. T 12. T

3. 1. b 2. a 3. e 4. c 5. f 6. g 7. j 8. i 9. h 10. d 11. l 12. k 13. n 14. m

4. 1. Presentation 2. Sensing 3. Network layer 4. Application layer 5. Analytics 6. Bluetooth 7. MQTT 8. Sigfox 9. IEEE 802.15.4 10. RFID 11. Application 12. Long Range Radio

Short Answers Questions

1. What is Things in IoT?

Ans Things - IoT device that individuals can use to combine sensors such as accelerometers, gyroscopes, and magnetometers with other sensors that measure temperature, humidity, pressure, and light in order to collect personally interesting data. For example, a home security system that comes with a combination of temperature, motion, light, and humidity sensors.

2. What do you mean by IoT?

Ans IoT stands for Internet of Things. It is concept that refers to connections between physical devices like vehicles, home appliances, and other items embedded in electronics such as sensors, software which enables these things to connect, collect and exchange data. So, Internet of Things refers to everything in day to day life which is accessed or connected through the Internet.

3. Explain any two features of IoT.

Ans The two features of IoT are:

Connectivity: It refers to establish a proper connection between all the things of IoT platform it may be server or cloud.

Analyzing: It comes to real-time analyzing the data collected and use them to build effective business intelligence.

4. What do you mean by Wearable devices?

Ans Wearable devices are the small electronic devices that can be worn on arms, neck, head, feet etc. These devices are not only the part of IoT system, but they enable access for improved productivity.

5. Differentiate between Data and Big Data.

Ans *Data* refers to the quantities, characters, or symbols on which operations are performed by a computer, which may be stored and transmitted in the form of electrical signals and recorded on magnetic, optical or mechanical recording media.

Big Data is also data but with large size. It is a term used to describe a collection of data that is large in size and yet growing with time. Examples of Big Data are BSE stock exchange data, Social media data such as photo and video uploads, message exchanges, putting comments etc.

6. What are the important components of an Internet of Things?

Ans The important components that exist in the Internet of Things are as follows:

Hardware: This will make physical items responsive and give them functionality to store records and respond to instructions.

Software: It allows the facts collection such as storing, processing, manipulating and instructing.

Infrastructure: Infrastructure which consists of protocols and technologies which allow two bodily gadgets to exchange information.

7. What does Big Data Analytics mean?

Ans The term *Big data analytics* refers to the strategy of analyzing large volumes of data, or big data. The large amount of data which grouped a wide variety of sources, including social network, videos, digital images, sensors and sales transactions record is called Big Data. The main purpose in analyzing all this data is to uncover patterns and connections that might otherwise be invisible, and that might provide valuable insights about the users who created it.

8. Why is big data analytics is important?

Ans The most important advantages of Big Data analysis is, it helps organizations harness their data and use it to identify new opportunities. With the help of this, companies lead to smarter business, more efficient operations, higher profits and happier customers.

9. What is Cloud?

Ans A cloud is an amalgamation of hardware, network, services, storage and interfaces that aid in delivering computing as a service. It has three users:

(a) **End users**: The end users is the one who uses the services provided by the cloud.

(b) **Business management users**: The business management user in the cloud takes the responsibility of the data and the services provided by the cloud.

(c) **Cloud service provider**: The cloud service provider is the one who takes car or is responsible for the maintenance of the IT assets of the cloud. It acts as a common center for its users to fulfill their computing needs.

10. What are the basic characteristic of cloud computing?

Ans The four basic characteristic of cloud computing are given as follows:

(a) Elasticity and scalability.

(b) Self-Service provisioning and automatic de-provisioning.

(c) Standardized interfaces.

(d) Billing self-service based usage model.

11. Write short note on Bluetooth.

Ans Bluetooth is also a short-range communication technology useful for communication between two devices up to almost 100 m in range. It works similarly to the master-slave based architecture. It is designed for low consumption of power. The most common used applications are home automation, communication with peripherals etc.

12. What are the advantages of Bluetooth?

Ans Advantages of bluetooth are:

(a) It is cheap and Easy to install.

(b) It is wireless and makes connecting to different devices convenient.

13. What are the disadvantages of Bluetooth?

Ans Disadvantages of bluetooth are:

(a) It only allows short range communication between devices.

(b) It can only connect two devices at once.

14. Write Pros and Cons of WiFi.

Ans Pros of WiFi are:

(a) Universal smartphone compatibility.

(b) Affordable, Well protected and controlled.

Cons of WiFi are:

(a) Relatively high power usage

15. Write application area of RFID tag.

Ans RFID (Radio Frequency Identification) devices are wireless microchips used for tagging objects for automated identification. RFID was designed specifically so devices without batteries could send a signal. In most systems, one side of an RFID system is powered, creating a magnetic field, which induces an electric current in the chip. This creates a system with enough power to send data wirelessly over and over again. Because of this, RFID tags are used for shipping and tracking purposes.

16. Compare BLE and NFC.

Ans BLE and NFC are both short-range communication technologies that are integrated into mobile phones.

(a) Speed: BLE is faster.

(b) Transfer: BLE has higher transfer rate.

(c) Power: NFC consumes less power.

(d) Pairing: NFC does not require pairing.

(e) Time: NFC takes less time to set up.

(f) Connection: Automatically established for NFC.

17. What is the abbreviation of MQTT and what is its purpose?

Ans MQTT stands for Message Queue Telemetry Transport. It provides the connectivity between applications and users at one end, network and communications at the other end.

18. Differentiate between LiFi and WiFi technologies.

Ans Basic difference between LiFi and WiFi technologies are:

(a) LiFi stands for Light Fidelity and WiFi stands for Wireless Fidelity.

(b) LiFi uses light as medium for data communication with the help of LED bulbs where as WiFi uses Electro-magnetic waves at various radio frequencies for data communication with the help of WiFi router.

(c) LiFi is an optical communication technology where as WiFi is a radio communication technology.

(d) LiFi do not have any intereference issues similar to radio frequency waves where as WiFi will have intereference issues from nearby access points(routers).

(e) In LiFi, light does not pass through the walls and hence will provide a much secure data transfer.
In WiFi, RF signal passess through the walls and hence there is a need to employ techniques to achieve secure data transfer.

19. What is LoRaWAN?

Ans LoRaWAN (Long Range Wide Area Network), a protocol for wide area networks, it's designed to support huge networks, such as smart cities, with millions of low-power devices.

20. What is the purpose of NFC?

Ans NFC, short for Near Field Communication, is a short range wireless RFID technology that makes use of interacting electromagnetic radio fields instead of the typical direct radio transmissions used by technologies such as Bluetooth. NFC is a short-range, low-power wireless way to transfer small amounts of data between devices.

21. Write pros and cons of NFC.

Ans Pros of NFC are:

(a) Offers a low-speed connection with extremely simple setup.

(b) NFC has a short range and supports encryption.

Cons of NFC are:

(a) Short range might not be feasible in many situations.

(b) NFC is an expensive technology.

22. Differentiate between MQTT and DDS protocols.

Ans MQTT is optimized for centralized data collection and analysis - connecting sensors and mobile devices to applications running in a data center. All communication routes through this centralized broker.

DDS is optimized for distributed processing - directly connecting sensors, devices and applications to each other without any dependence on centralized IT infrastructure. DDS is decentralized.

23. Explain smart parking IoT application.

Ans In smart parking, it is possible to easily locate parking spots nearby. Parking lots have sensors, which let a server know about their usage. Once a driver queries the server with his/her GPS location, he/she is guided to the nearest parking lot with free slots.

24. Discuss in detail Smart City application of IoT.

Ans Smart city is the city with thousands of sensors for smart traffic, smart water management applications, and smart parking system etc. Smart transportation is implemented using a network of sensors, centralized analysis, and smart traffic lights. The reason why it is so popular is that it tries to remove the discomfort and problems of people who live in cities. IoT solutions offered in the smart city area solve various city-related problems comprising of traffic, reduce air and noise pollution and help make cities safer.

25. Explain with the examples how IoT conserves energy and saves money?

Ans. (a) IoT-based real-time monitoring systems brings optimum use of energy and saves money. For example, thermostats enable people to remotely monitor and control the temperature of their heating and cooling systems. The advantage of using a smart thermostat, is that we can override the scheduled programming to raise and lower the temperature remotely.

(b) Similar to thermostats, smart water heaters enable us to raise and lower the water temperature in our tank from anywhere we have an internet connection. For example, suppose we take a shower every night at 9:00 p.m. We can program our hot water heater to start heating the tank at 8:00 p.m. so that by the time we need it, the water is nice and hot. The rest of the day, the hot water heater is turned off.

(c) Sensors integrate with the lighting system in order to turn lights on or off depending on the presence of people in the room. A smart lighting system will notify us via text messaging if a light was left on. The energy savings of a smart lighting system can be very significant.

(d) A smart grid basically promises to extract information on the behaviors of consumers and electricity suppliers in an automated fashion in order to improve the efficiency, economics, and reliability of electricity distribution.

26. What is an IoT ecosystem?

Ans IoT ecosystem is like a community that consists of data and monetary flows that helps in connecting enterprises and vendors together. This new chain of development is the best way to connect companies together. Even in future, the companies will be offering the IoT ecosystem similar to risk management and cyber security.

The IoT ecosystem includes all those technologies that enable consumers, businesses, and governments to connect, control and derive value from their connected objects in diverse environments, including manufacturing, agriculture, transportation, smart cities, construction, oil, and gas.

27. Write short note on cloud computing.

Ans Cloud computing is an infrastructure of shared resources (such as servers, networks, and software applications and services) that allow users to scale up their data management and processing abilities while keeping the costs low. A cloud vendor invests in and maintains the cloud infrastructure; a user pays for only the resources and applications he wishes to use.

28. What is Big data?

Ans Big data is a term popularly used to describe large data sets that cannot be handled efficiently by traditional data management systems. In addition to the large volume, the concept of big data also refers to the variety of data sets i.e., structured and unstructured as well as the velocity or the rate at which the data are incoming.

29. What is Internet Protocol (IP)?

Ans Internet Protocol (IP) is an open network protocol that provides unique addresses to various devices connected to the Internet. There are two versions of IP: IP version 4 (IPv4) and IPv6.

IP version 4 (IPv4) is an older version of the Internet Protocol (IP) whereas IPv6 is a most recent version.

30. What is the Internet of Everything? What are its elements?

Ans The Internet of Everything is the intelligent connection of people, process, data, and things.

The elements of the Internet of Everything are Human beings, Procedure, Things and Information.

31. Name a few IoT protocols.

Ans A few IoT protocols are:

XMPP: Extensible Messaging and Presence Protocol.

AMQP: Advanced Message Queuing Protocol.

CoAP: Constrained Application Protocol.

MQTT: Message Queue Telemetry Transport.

DDS: Data Distribution Service.

32. Explain service models of cloud computing.

Ans Service models of cloud computing are:

(a) **Infrastructure-as-a-Service (IaaS)**: It is supply an on-demand environment for developing, testing, delivering and managing software applications.

(b) **Platform-as-a-Service (PaaS)**: This type of solution allows you to rent cloud infrastructure and an IoT platform all from a single technology provider. Also, there might be ready-to-use IoT solutions (IoT cloud services) offered by the provider, built and hosted on its infrastructure.

(c) **Software-as-a-Service (SaaS)**: This method is used for delivering software applications over the Internet, on demand and typically on a subscription basis. IoT applications are pre-built software-as-a-service (SaaS) applications that can analyze and present captured IoT sensor data to business users via dashboards.

33. What is fog computing? Who has coined it?

Ans Fog computing is a type of network architecture (i.e., how the systems are connected within a network and to the Internet) that links cloud computing (storage of data and programs over the Internet) to the Internet of Things (IoT). The term fog computing (or fogging) was coined by Cisco in 2014.

34. What is fog node?

Ans The device with network connection, storage and computing feature is known as fog node. Examples include switches, controllers, routers, servers, cameras and so on.

35. How fog computing decreases the bandwidth used?

Ans The fog node is located in a smart router or gateway device, allows fog data to be processed on this smart device, so that only the necessary data gets further transmitted to the cloud, and decreases the bandwidth used.

36. Write Pros of Fog computing.

Ans The pros of fog computing are:

(a) Fog is geographically closer to users and is able to provide instant responses.

(b) Loss of connection is impossible due to multiple interconnected channels.

37. Write the key differences between Fog Computing and Cloud Computing.

Ans Key difference between cloud and fog computing are:

(a) Cloud architecture is centralized and consists of large data centers that can be located around the globe, a thousand miles away from client devices. Fog architecture is distributed and consists of millions of small nodes located as close to client devices as possible.

(b) In cloud computing, data processing takes place in remote data centers. Fog processing and storage are done on the edge of the network close to the source of information.

(c) The cloud consists of a few large server nodes. Fog includes millions of small nodes.

(d) Fog performs short-term edge analysis due to instant responsiveness, while the cloud aims for long-term deep analysis due to slower responsiveness.

(e) Fog provides low latency, where as cloud provide high latency.

(f) Fog is a more secure system than the cloud due to its distributed architecture.

(g) Fog is the layer between the cloud and the devices like computer, laptop, mobile etc. As Fog acts as a mediator, it is less time consuming to transfer the data. When there is no layer then cloud needs to communicate directly to the end devices which take more time than using Fog computing.

EXERCISE

1. Write short note on the following:
(a) MQTT
(b) IoT Ecosystem
(c) Big Data Analytics
(d) Arduino
(e) PaaS

2. What are the key features of IoT?

3. What is the role of things and internet in IoT?

4. What is an IOT device?

5. What is difference between IPv4 and IPv6 address?

6. Discuss various application areas of IoT.

7. Define M2M. Explain reasons of shifting from M2M to IoT.

8. Explain layered IoT architecture.

9. What is a cloud? What is the role of cloud platforms in IoT?

10. What is middleware?

11. What are Big Data and Big Data Analytics?

12. What are the governance issues of Internet of Things.

13. Differentiate M2M and IoT.

14. Discuss the advantages and disadvantages of IoT.

15. Define IoT. Explain different characteristics of IoT.

16. Explain different components of IoT System.

17. Explain different development tools used in IoT.

18. Explain working of different communication models.

19. Differentiate between logical and physical design of IoT.

20. What is Wireless Sensor Network? Explain its advantages and disadvantages.

21. What is RFID? Where is it used?

22. Explain different steps of IoT design methodology.

23. Explain any two Link Layer Protocols.

24. Explain Request-Response Communication Model.

25. What role does the network play in the Internet of Everything?

26. What are advantages and disadvantage of Cloud computing?

27. What are the benefits of IoT?

28. What is fog computing?

29. Explain working of fog computing.

30. What are the advantages and disadvantage of fog computing?

31. What are the drawbacks of edge computing in IoT?

32. Where fog computing is applied?

CHAPTER 2

Things and Connections

2.1 INTRODUCTION TO CONTROL SYSTEMS

Control system is a way of arranging and combining components in such a way that the desired output is obtained. In other words, a system is said to be 'controlled', if it is working in a stable mode without getting unstable in any span of time. (See Figure 2.1).

2.2 WORKING OF CONTROLLED SYSTEMS

A control system as a system responds to input signals from the plant (a system to be controlled) and/or an operator and causes the plant or equipment to operate in the desired manner. Control systems usually involve one or more input devices, a controller, one or more output devices, power supplies, and any associated information connections.

☞ *In the context of control systems, a plant is a system to be controlled.*

A control system is a set of mechanical or electronic devices that regulates other devices or systems by way of control loops. Typically, control systems are computerized. Control systems are an important and pervasive part of modern industry. They range from simple devices, for example, a temperature sensor operating a switch that controls a heating element, to complex computer-controlled systems with many inputs and outputs.

Control systems today have various uses. In industry these systems are used to control the production or working of other machines. Different types of control systems work for different purposes. Control systems manage the behavior and working of a machine. The usefulness of control systems is in the precision and reliability of functions and equipment they can deliver. The field of control systems has its roots in industry and home appliances as well.

Control systems are used to enhance production, efficiency and safety in many areas, including Agriculture, Chemical plants, Pulp and paper mills, Quality control, Boiler controls and power plant, Nuclear power plants, Environmental control, Water treatment plants, Sewage treatment plants, Food processing, Metal and mines, Pharmaceutical manufacturing, Sugar refining plants etc.

Programmable Logic Controllers (PLCs), Programmable Automation Controllers (PACs), Remote Terminal Units (RTUs), Control Servers, Intelligent Electronic Devices (IEDs) and sensors are some of the elements of control loops that are in turn a part of control systems. The control loops that make up control systems are generally made themselves of a sensor, a controller and a final control element. The sensor reads the process variable or a related measurement. The controller receives the signal from the sensor and then forwards it to instrumentation, to remote terminal units and to final control elements where the process variable is adjusted, to be kept constant at what is known as a *set point*.

There are various types of control systems, but all of them are created to control outputs. The system used for controlling the position, velocity, acceleration, temperature, pressure, voltage and current etc., are examples of control systems. Systems measure, monitor and control manufacturing processes and activities. They identify and correct any abnormalities or variations from specified values, either manually or automatically. The aim is to make sure that production is consistent and that as little energy is wasted as possible.

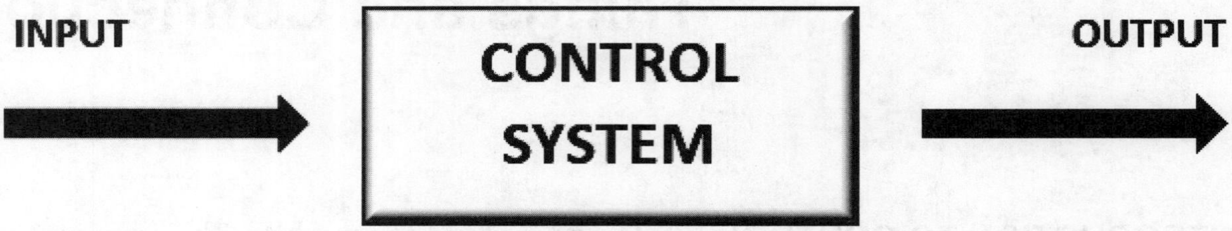

Figure 2.1 A Control System

2.2.1 Manual Control System

Let us take an example of the simple temperature controller of the room, to clear the concept. Suppose there is a simple heating element, which is heated up as long as the electric power supply is switched *on*. The temperature of the room rises and after achieving the desired temperature of the room, the power supply is switched *off*. Again due to ambient temperature, the room temperature falls and then manually the heater element is switched *on* to achieve the desired room temperature again. In this way, one can manually control the room temperature at the desired level. This is an example of manual control system.

2.2.2 Automatic Control System

An automatic control system is defined as one in which the value of a controlled condition is compared with a desired value and corrective action is taken dependent on the deviation, without the inclusion of a human element. From above example temperature controller system can further be improved by using timer switching arrangement of the power supply where the supply to the heating element is switched *on* and *off* in a pre-determined interval to achieve desired temperature level of the room.

There is another improved way of controlling the temperature of the room. Here, one sensor measures the difference between actual temperature and desired temperature. If there is difference between them, the heating element functions to reduce the difference and when the difference becomes lower than a pre-determined level, the heating elements stop functioning. Both forms of the system are automatic control system. Thus, an automatic control system includes the plant, the detecting or sensing element, the measuring or indicating element, the controller.

2.2.3 Features of a Control System

Accuracy

Accuracy is the measurement tolerance of the instrument and defines the limits of the errors made when the instrument is used in normal operating conditions. Detecting faults early means throughput, yield and quality are maintained. Accuracy can be improved by using feedback elements. To increase the accuracy of any control system, error detector should be present in the control system.

Sensitivity

The parameters of a control system are always changing with the change in surrounding conditions, internal disturbance or any other parameters. This change can be expressed in terms of sensitivity. Any control system should be insensitive to such parameters but sensitive to input signals only.

Energy savings

Energy wastage is reduced when your plant and machinery are efficiently operated.

Improved safety

Control systems automatically warn you of any abnormalities which minimizes the risk of accidents.

Figure 2.2 An open Loop System

Noise

An undesired input signal is known as *noise*. A good control system should be able to reduce the noise effect for better performance.

Stability

It is an important characteristic of the control system. For the bounded input signal, the output must be bounded and if the input is zero then output must be zero then such a control system is said to be a *stable system*.

Bandwidth

An operating frequency range decides the bandwidth of the control system. Bandwidth should be as large as possible for the frequency response of good control system.

Speed

It is the time taken by the control system to achieve its stable output. A good control system possesses high speed. The transient period for such system is very small.

Oscillation

A small numbers of oscillation or constant oscillation of output tend to indicate the system to be stable.

2.2.4 Types of Control Systems

There are three basic types of control systems that are feed forward control systems, open loop control systems and the third type is feedback or closed loop control systems. All the three types of control systems are discussed in the following sections:

Feed Forward Control System

Feed forward is a type of system which counters the changes in its surroundings. It is used to maintain the wanted status of the system. The biggest advantage of this system is that it does not permit the huge disturbance in the output. The objective of feed forward control, also known as *predictive control*, is to measure or predict any potential open-loop disturbances and compensate for them manually before the controlled variable deviates too far from the original set point.

Open Loop Control System

A control system in which the control action is totally independent of output of the system then it is called open loop control system as shown in Figure 2.2. A manual control system is also an open loop control system. An open-loop control system is also referred as a *non-feedback control system*. These systems may not require a mathematical model of the physical system. It takes input under the consideration and does not react on the feedback to determine the state of output. It does not encounter any disturbance within the system or recompense them.

An open-loop system is defined by the fact that the output signal or condition is neither measured nor fed back for comparison with the input signal or system set point. Therefore open-loop systems are commonly referred to as *Non-feedback systems*. Also, as an open-loop system does not use feedback to determine if its required output was achieved, it assumes that the desired goal of the input was successful because it cannot correct any errors it could make, and so cannot compensate for any external disturbances to the system.

Automatic washing machine is a good example of Open loop control system. Open-loop control systems are often used with processes that require the sequencing of events with the aid of "ON-OFF" signals. For example a washing machines which requires the water to be switched

'ON' and then when full is switched 'OFF' followed by the heater element being switched 'ON' to heat the water and then at a suitable temperature is switched 'OFF', and so on.

This type of 'ON-OFF' open-loop control is suitable for systems where the changes in load occur slowly and the process is very slow acting, necessitating infrequent changes to the control action by an operator.

Some other examples of open loop control system are:

- **Electric Hand Drier:** Hot air (output) comes out as long as you keep your hand under the machine, irrespective of how much your hand is dried.
- **Automatic Tea/Coffee Maker:** These machines also function for pre-adjusted time only.
- **Bread Toaster:** This machine runs as per adjusted time irrespective of toasting is completed or not.
- **Traffic lights control system:** A sequence of input signal is applied to this control system and the output is one of the three lights that will be *on* for some duration of time. During this time, the other two lights will be *off*. Based on the traffic study at a particular junction, the *on* and *off* times of the lights can be determined. Accordingly, the input signal controls the output. So, the traffic lights control system operates on time basis.
- **Electric clothes dryer:** In an electric clothes dryer, depending upon the amount of clothes or how wet they are, a user or operator would set a timer (controller) say 30 minutes and at the end of the 30 minutes the drier will automatically stop and turn-off even if the clothes where still wet or moist. In this case, the control action is the manual operator assessing the wetness of the clothes and setting the process (the drier) accordingly.

Advantages of Open Loop Control System

- Simple in construction and design.
- Economical.
- Easy to maintain.
- Generally stable.
- Convenient to use as output is difficult to measure.

Disadvantages of Open Loop Control System

- They are inaccurate.
- They are unreliable.
- Any change in output cannot be corrected automatically.

☞ *Open-loop control system is a control system where its control action only depends on input signal and does not depend on its output response.*

Closed Loop or Feedback Control System

Control system in which the output has an effect on the input quantity in such a manner that the input quantity will adjust itself based on the output generated is called *Closed loop control system* as shown in Figure 2.3. A feedback control system is also known as closed loop control system. Open loop control system can be converted in to closed loop control system by providing a feedback. This feedback automatically makes the suitable changes in the output due to external disturbance. In this way closed loop control system is called *Automatic control system*.

Some examples of Closed loop control system are:

- **Automatic Electric Iron:** Heating elements are controlled by output temperature of the iron.
- **Water Level Controller:** Input water is controlled by water level of the reservoir.
- **An Air Conditioner:** An air conditioner functions depending upon the temperature of the room.
- **Missile Launched and Auto Tracked by Radar:** The direction of missile is controlled by comparing the target and position of the missile.

☞ *Closed-loop control system is a control system where its control action depends on both of its input signal and output response.*

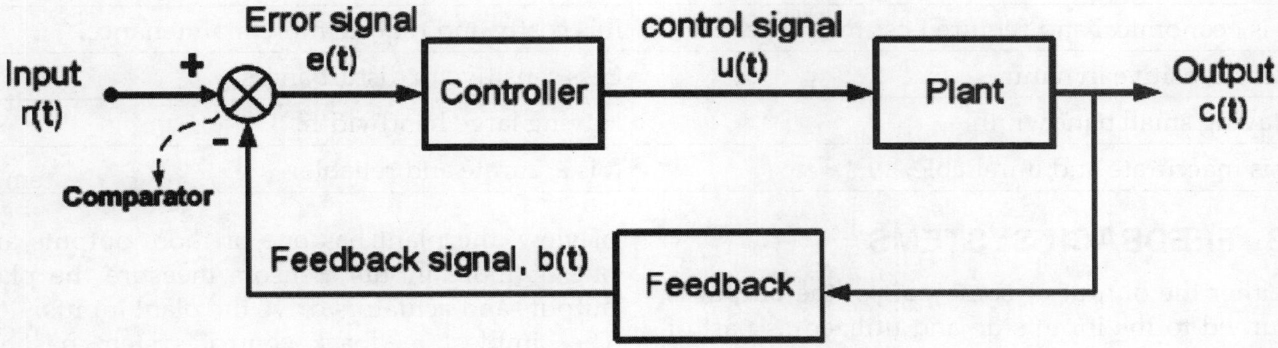

Figure 2.3 A Closed loop Control System

Characteristics of Closed-loop Control System

- To reduce errors by automatically adjusting the systems input.
- To improve stability of an unstable system.
- To increase or reduce the systems sensitivity.
- To enhance robustness against external disturbances to the process.
- To produce a reliable and repeatable performance.

Advantages of Closed Loop Control System

- Closed loop control systems are more accurate even in the presence of non-linearity.
- Highly accurate as any error arising is corrected due to presence of feedback signal.
- Bandwidth range is large.
- Facilitates automation.
- This system is less affected by noise.

Disadvantages of Closed Loop Control System

- They are costlier.
- They are complicated to design.
- Required more maintenance.
- Feedback leads to oscillatory response.
- Overall gain is reduced due to presence of feedback.
- Stability is the major problem and more care is needed to design a stable closed loop system.

Comparison of Open Loop and Closed Loop Control Systems

Comparison of Open Loop and Closed Loop Control Systems are discussed in Table 2.1.

Table 2.1 Comparison of Open Loop and Closed Loop Control Systems

Open Loop Control System	Closed Loop Control System
No feedback is given to the control system, i.e., the feedback element is absent.	A feedback is given to the control system, i.e., the feedback element is always present.
The output will not very for a constant input, provided the system parameters remain unaltered.	In the system the output may vary for a constant input, depending upon the feedback.
Cannot be intelligent.	Intelligent controlling action.
An error detector is not present.	An error detector is always present.
More stable.	Less stable or prone to instability.

(Conti..)

Easy to construct, i.e., simple design.	Complicated construction, i.e., complex design.
It is economical and require Less maintenance.	It is costly and require more maintenance.
Very sensitive in nature.	Less sensitive to disturbances.
Having small bandwidth.	Having large bandwidth.
It is inaccurate and unreliable.	It is accurate and reliable.

2.3 FEEDBACK SYSTEMS

If either the output or some part of the output is returned to the input side and utilized as part of the system input, then it is known as *feedback*. Feedback plays an important role in order to improve the performance of the control systems. A feedback system is one in which the output signal is sampled and then fed back to the input to form an error signal that drives the system. Feedback systems are very useful and widely used in amplifier circuits, oscillators, process control systems as well as other types of electronic systems. But for feedback to be an effective tool it must be controlled as an uncontrolled system with either oscillate or fail to function. This basic feedback loop of sensing, controlling and actuation is the main concept behind a feedback control system.

2.3.1 Feedback Loop of Control System

A feedback is a common and powerful tool when designing a control system. Feedback loop is the tool which take the system output into consideration and enables the system to adjust its performance to meet a desired result of system.

In any control system, the output is affected due to change in environmental condition or any kind of disturbance. So one signal is taken from the output and is fed back to the input. This signal is compared with a reference input and the error signal is generated. This error signal is applied to controller and output is corrected. Such a system is called *Feedback system*.

The controller inputs are the reference input (also called a set point) and the plant output signal (measured by the sensor), which is used as feedback. The controller output is the actuator signal that drives the plant. From the controller's point of view, the plant has one or more outputs and one or more inputs. Sensors measure the plant outputs and actuators drive the plant inputs.

The simplest feedback control system has one input and one output, and is called a Single-Input-Single-Output (SISO) system. In a SISO system, a sensor measures one signal and the controller produces one signal to drive an actuator.

Control systems with more than one input or output are called *MIMO systems*, meaning Multiple-Input-Multiple-Output systems. Because of the added complexity, fewer MIMO system design procedures are available.

☞ *The open loops operates with human input, and closed loops are fully autonomous. Some loops can be switched between closed and open modes. When open, a switchable loop is manually controlled and when closed it is fully automated.*

2.3.2 Classification of Feedback Systems

The main types of feedback control systems are *Positive Feedback* and *Negative Feedback*. These are discussed in the following sections:

Positive Feedback Systems

When the feedback signal is positive then system called positive feedback system. For positive feedback system, the error signal is the addition of reference input signal and a feedback signal. The effect of positive (or regenerative) feedback is to 'increase' the systems gain, i.e, the overall gain with positive feedback applied will be greater than the gain without feedback. For example, if someone praises you or gives you positive feedback about something, you feel happy and more positive.

However, in electronic and control systems to much praise and positive feedback can increase the systems gain far too much which would give rise to oscillatory circuit responses as it increases the magnitude of the effective input signal. An example of a positive feedback systems could be an electronic amplifier.

Negative Feedback Systems

When the feedback signal is negative then the system is called negative feedback system. For negative feedback system, the error signal is given by the difference of reference input signal and the feedback signal. In a negative feedback control system, the set point and output values are subtracted from each other as the feedback is 'out-of-phase' with the original input. The effect of negative (or degenerative) feedback is to 'reduce' the gain. For example, if someone criticizes you or gives you negative feedback about something, you feel unhappy and less positive.

Because negative feedback produces stable circuit responses, improves stability and increases the operating bandwidth of a given system, the majority of all control and feedback systems is degenerative reducing the effects of the gain.

Thermostat

Thermostat is a revolutionary concept which gives you many benefits. Its breakthrough technology and Internet of Things based concepts make it highly efficient electric appliance. Usually thermostats incur almost half of the energy bills. In the aspect of energy conservation, household appliances can suggest optimal setting based on the user's energy consumption like turning the ideal temperature just before the owner arrives home as well as turning on and off the lights whenever the owner is out on vacation just to create the impression that somebody is still left inside the house to prevent burglars from attempting to enter. Imagine that you can control the temperature of your home from anywhere, with just a simple touch on your smart phone or tablet, and you get the desired temperature before getting home so that you don't need to wait. Thermostat not only controlled from anywhere but also it learns by itself by following your daily routing and change the temperature of your home without bothering you, Like if you have set low temperature at night continuously for 7 days, then this device learns that and automatically lowers the temperature at night. This is very helpful device for saving the energy.

2.4 CONNECTIVITY MODELS

The architecture for the Internet of Things (IoT) has evolved over a period of time. The existing systems of communication over the internet have had its share of influence. Moreover, it was essential to build a system compatible with the existing system and structure. So, in order to understand the existing IoT architectures, let us take a look at its predecessors, the conceptual and existing models of architecture.

It would be useful to have a set of protocols and rules for data transmission for the variety of network types to ensure that the information can be shared. For this reason, OSI and TCP/IP models were created. These models describe network systems as being made up of a number of layers, each with its own set of protocols and functionality.

The OSI Model is a logical and conceptual model that defines network communication used by systems open to interconnection and communication with other systems. The Open System Interconnection (OSI Model) also defines a logical network and effectively describes computer packet transfer by using various layers of protocols. It does not take into account the underlying technology. This model is considered as a concept, over which designing of practical models took place.

TCP/IP stands for *Transmission Control Protocol/Internet Protocol*. It is specifically designed as a model to offer highly reliable and end-to-end byte stream over an unreliable internetwork.

TCP/IP helps you to determine how a specific computer should be connected to the Internet and how you can transmit data between them. It helps you to create a virtual network when multiple computer networks are connected together.

All the layers of the OSI model are not present in the TCP/IP model but most of the functionalities are distributed among the four layers. Thus, the functionality of each layer remains the same as that of OSI model.

2.5 OSI MODEL

The Open Systems Interconnection (OSI) model is the foundation of Internet communications, including for devices connected to the Internet of Things (IoT).

The OSI model was developed to standardize the procedures for exchange of information between processing systems. The OSI is a communications reference model that has been defined by the *International Standards Organization* (ISO). It is a seven-layer communications protocol intended as a standard for the development of communications systems worldwide.

Characteristics of the OSI Model

- In the OSI model, each layer relies on the next lower layer to perform primitive functions.
- A layer should only be created where the definite levels of abstraction are needed.
- The function of each layer should be selected as per the internationally standardized protocols.
- Changes made in one layer should not need changes in other layers.

Advantages of the OSI Model

- OSI model distinguishes well between the services, interfaces and protocols.
- It helps you to standardize router, switch, motherboard, and other hardware.
- Reduces complexity and standardizes interfaces.
- It offers flexibility to adapt to various types of protocols.
- Supports connectionless and connection-oriented services.

Disadvantages of the OSI Model

- Fitting of protocols is a tedious task.
- You can only use it as a reference model.
- Layers can't work in parallel as each layer need to wait to obtain data from the previous layer.

2.5.1 Protocol Stacks

This model conceptually organizes the process of communications between computers in terms of seven layers called Protocol Stacks. The seven layers of the OSI model provide a way for you to understand how communications across various protocols take place.

A protocol stack is a group of rules or procedures called protocols arranged on top of each other as part of a communication process. Each layer of the OSI model has different protocols associated with it. When more than one protocol is needed to complete a communication process, the protocols are grouped together in a stack. A popular protocol stack is TCP/IP, which is widely used for UNIX and the Internet. Each layer in the protocol stack receives services from the layer below it and provides services to the layer above it. That means, layer N uses the services of the layer below it (layer N-1) and provides services to the layer above it (layer N+1). For two computers to communicate, the same protocol stacks must be running on each computer.

☞ *Each layer of the protocol stack on one computer communicates with its equivalent, or peer, on the other computer. The entities comprising the corresponding layers on different machines are called peers.*

The computers can have different operating systems and still be able to communicate if they are running the same protocol stacks.

2.5.2 Layers and their Functions

When a message is sent from one machine to another, it travels down the layers on one machine and then up the layers on the other machine. This route is illustrated in Figure 2.4 and 2.5 of OSI model. As the message travels down the first stack, each layer it passes through (except the physical layer and application layer) adds a header. These headers contain pieces of control information that are read and processed by the corresponding layer on the receiving stack.

As the message travels up the stack of the other machine, each layer strips the header added by its peer layer.

☞ *The OSI model divides communication tasks into smaller pieces called subtasks. Protocol implementations are computer processes that relate to these subtasks. Specific protocols fulfill subtasks at specific layers of the OSI model. When these protocols are grouped together to complete a whole task, you get a protocol stack.*

☞ *In reality, no data is directly transferred from layer n on one machine to layer **n** on another machine. Instead, each layer transfers data and control information to the layer immediately below it, until the lowest layer is reached. Below layer 1 is the physical medium through which actual communication occurs.*

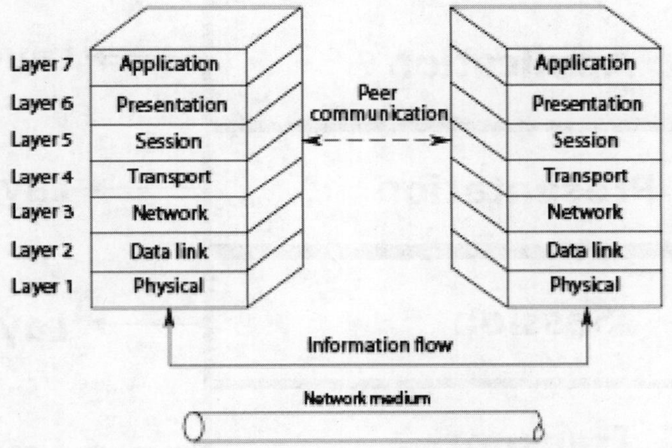

Figure 2.4 Peer-to-peer communication between two computers

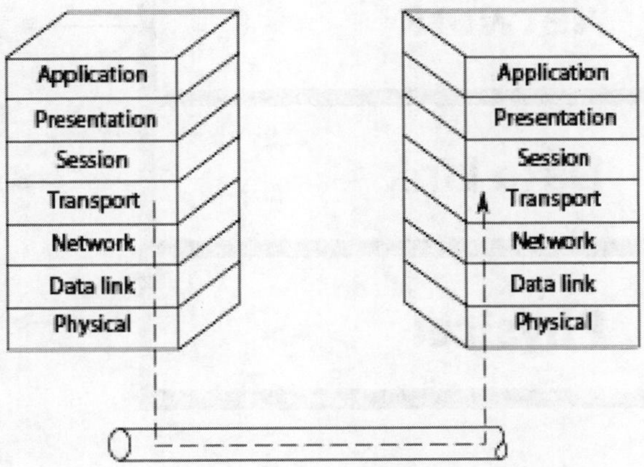

Figure 2.5 A message sent from one peer layer to another peer layer

From top to bottom, the layers of the OSI model are shown in Figure 2.6. These layers are further described in the following section.

Layer 1 — Physical Layer

Physical layer is the lowest layer of the OSI reference model. The physical layer deals with the description of the characteristics of the interface between the devices and the transmission media, representation of bits, synchronization of the bits, data rate, physical topology, line configuration, transmission mode.

- It activates, maintains and deactivates the physical connection.
- It converts the digital/analog bits into electrical signal or optical signals.
- Data encoding is also done in this layer.
- It is responsible for sending bits from one computer to another. The physical layer defines the actual set of wires, plugs and electrical signals that connect the sending and receiving devices to the network.

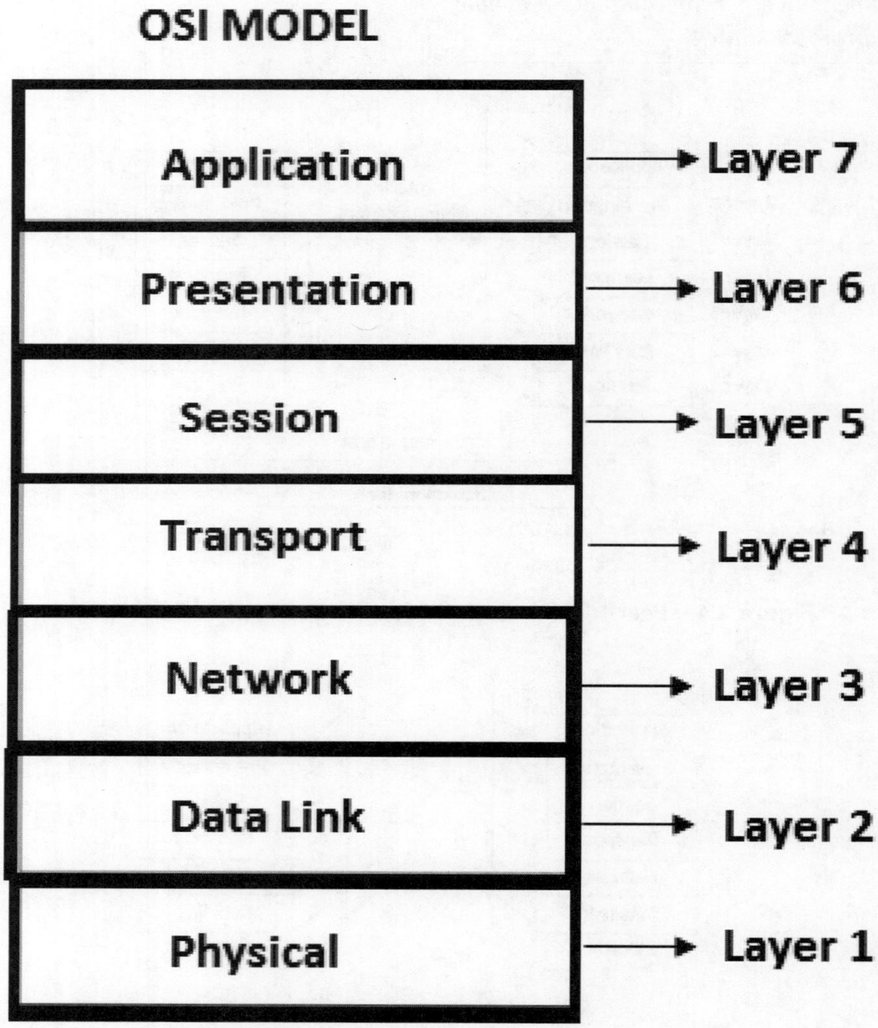

Figure 2.6 The OSI seven layer model

☞ *A physical layer makes a physical circuit with electrical, optical or radio signals. Passive hubs, simple active hubs, terminators, couplers, cables, connectors, repeaters, multiplexers, transmitters, receivers, and trans-receivers are devices associated with the physical layer.*

Layer 2 — Data Link Layer

The data link layer is responsible for gaining access to the network and transmitting the physical block of data from one device to another. It includes the *error checking* necessary to ensure an accurate transmission. This layer uses the communications protocol that is most commonly referenced and often implies the specifications for Layer 1 as well. The data-link layer is the OSI layer where data transfer between two directly connected nodes in a network takes place.

- Data link layer synchronizes the information which is to be transmitted over the physical layer.
- The main function of this layer is to make sure data transfer is error free from one node to another, over the physical layer.
- In this layer, the input data is split into frames. Also, transmitting and receiving data frames sequentially is managed by this layer.
- This layer establishes a logical layer between two nodes and also manages the Frame traffic control over the network.

Layer 3 — Network Layer

The network layer makes *routing decisions* and forwards packets for devices that are farther away than a single link. A link connects two network devices and is implemented by the data link layer. Two devices connected by a link communicate directly with each other and not through a third device. In larger networks, there may be intermediate systems between any two end systems, and the network layer makes it possible for the transport layer and layers above it to send packets without being concerned about whether the end system is immediately adjacent or several hops away.

The network layer translates *logical network addresses* into physical machine addresses. This layer also determines the quality of service (namely, priority of the message) and the route a message will take if there are several ways a message can get to its destination.

The network layer may also break large packets into smaller chunks if the packet is larger than the largest data frame the data link layer will accept. The network reassembles the chunks into packets at the receiving end.

The network layer performs several important functions that enable data to arrive at its destination. The protocols at this layer may choose a specific route through an internetwork to avoid the excess traffic caused by sending data over networks and segments that do not need access to it.

- Logical addressing and routing are the major operations performed by the network layer.
- Network Layer routes the signal through different channels from one node to other.
- It acts as a network controller and also decides which route data should take. To avoid congestion it enable the automatic updation of the routes.
- It divides the outgoing messages into packets and assembles the incoming packets into messages for higher levels.

☞ *Routers and gateways operate in the network layer.*

Layer 4 — Transport Layer

Layer 4 is the transport layer which breaks large messages from the session layer into packets to be sent to the destination computer and reassembles packets into messages to be presented to the session layer. The transport layer typically sends an acknowledgment to the originator for messages received. The *Transmission Control Protocol* (TCP) and *User Datagram Protocol* (UDP) are popular transport layer protocols for devices that connect to the Internet.

- Transport layer breaks the message (data) into small units so that they are handled more efficiently by the network layer.
- It receives messages from the Session layer above it, convert the message into smaller units and passes it on to the Network layer in proper order.
- Transport layer decides if data transmission should be on parallel path or single path.
- Functions such as Multiplexing, Segmenting or Splitting on the data are done by this layer.

Layer 5 — Session Layer

Layer 5 establishes and terminates the session, queues of the incoming messages and is responsible for recovering from an abnormally terminated session. This layer allows applications on separate computers to share a connection called a *session*. This layer provides services, such as name lookup and security to allow two programs to find each other and establish the communication link. The session layer also provides for data synchronization and check points so that in the event of a network failure, only the data sent after the point of failure need be re-sent.

The session layer also controls the dialog between two processes determining whom they can transmit and from whom can they receive at what point during the communication. The session layer can provide for full-duplex, half-duplex, or simplex communications.

- This is the layer used to open and close the communication between the two machines. The period between the opening and closing of the correspondence is known as the session.
- Session Layer manages and synchronize the conversation between two different applications and maintain the interaction between them.
- The services provided by the session layer are dialog control, token management and synchronization.

☞ *The session layer provides for dialog between application programs.*

Layer 6 — Presentation Layer

The presentation layer translates data between the formats the network requires and the formats the computer expects. The presentation layer does protocol conversion, data translation, compression and encryption, character set conversion, and the interpretation of graphics commands. A network redirector is what makes the files on a file server visible to the client computer.

The network redirector also makes remote printers act as though they are attached to the local computer. The network redirector operates at presentation layer.

☞ *The presentation layer adapts information to the local environment.*

- Presentation layer takes care that the data is sent in such a way that the receiver will understand the information (data) and will be able to use the data.
- Presentation layer focuses on the syntax and semantics of the transmitting information.
- It performs tasks such as Data compression, Data encryption, Data conversion etc., where the actual information existing in the form of character strings, numbers, symbols is encoded into bit streams, converted into another form and compressed.

Layer 7 — Application Layer

The application layer is the topmost layer of the OSI model. It provides services that directly support user applications, such as database access, e-mail, and file transfers. It also allows applications to communicate with applications on other computers as though they were on the same computer. When a programmer writes an application program that uses network services, this is the layer the application program will access.

- Transferring of files disturbing the results to the user is also done in this layer. Mail services, directory services, network resource etc., are services provided by application layer.

- This layer mainly holds application programs to act upon the received and to be sent data.
- With this layer, the users can access the network by using interfaces and services like electronic mail, shared database management, file access/transfer and the other services.

☞ *The Application layer provides for the connection of application programs on separate machines.*

A summary of functions performed by different layers in the OSI model is given in Table 2.2.

Table 2.2 Function performed by different layers in the OSI model

Layer Number	Layer Name	Description
7	Application layer	Interfaces user applications with network functionality, controls how applications access the network, and generates error messages. Protocols at this level include HTTP, FTP (File Transfer Protocol), SMTP (Simple Mail Transfer Protocol), and NFS (Network File System).
6	Presentation layer	Translates data to be transmitted by applications into a format suitable for transport over the network. Redirector software is located at this level. Network shells are also defined at this layer.
5	Session layer	Defines how connections can be established, maintained, and terminated. Also performs name resolution functions.
4	Transport layer	Sequences packets so that they can be reassembled at the destination in the proper order. Generates acknowledgments and retransmits packets. Assembles packets after they are received.
3	Network layer	Defines logical host addresses such as IP (*Internet Protocol*) addresses, creates packet headers, and routes packets across an internetwork using routers and Layer 3 switches. Strips the headers from the packets at the receiving end.
2	Data link layer	Specifies how data bits are grouped into frames, and specifies frame formats. Responsible for error correction, flow control, hardware addressing (such as MAC addresses), and how devices such as hubs, bridges, repeaters, and Layer 2 switches operate.
1	Physical layer	Defines network transmission media, signaling methods, bit synchronization, architecture (such as Ethernet or Token Ring), and cabling topologies. Defines how network interface cards (NICs) interact with the media (cabling). You can think of each layer as being logically connected to the same layer on a different computer on the network. For example, the application layer on one machine communicates with the application layer on another machine. But this communication is logical only; physical communication occurs when packets of data are sent down from the application layer of the transmitting computer, encapsulated with header information by each lower layer, and then put on the wire at the physical layer of the transmitting computer. After traveling along the wire, the packets are picked up by the physical layer of the receiving computer, passed up the seven layers while each layer strips off its associated header information and then passes to the application layer of the receiving computer, where the receiving application can process the data.

2.6 TCP/IP MODEL

TCP/IP (*Transmission Control Protocol/Internet Protocol*) is based on a client-server communication model by which a user (client) receives a service such as a loaded web page from a server in the same network. It is the network model used in the current Internet architecture as well.

Protocols are set of rules which govern every possible communication over a network. These protocols describe the movement of data between the source and destination or the Internet. They also offer simple naming and addressing schemes.

TCP/IP is an industry-standard protocol suite for *Wide Area Networks* (WANs) developed in the 1970s and 1980s by the U.S. *Department of Defense* (DoD). TCP/IP is a routable protocol that is suitable for connecting dissimilar systems in heterogeneous networks. It is the protocol of the worldwide network known as the Internet. The Internet began as a project funded by the United States Department of Defence in the 1970s to interconnect educational institutions and government installations. At that time it was called ARPAnet (*Advanced Research Projects Agency Network*). Over time it has evolved into the huge, worldwide network known as the Internet. The protocols that make up the Internet protocol suite, the best known being TCP and IP, have become de-facto standards because of the success of the Internet. The entire protocol suite is referred to as TCP/IP.

Characteristics of TCP/IP model

- Support for a flexible architecture.
- Adding more systems to a network is easy.
- In TCP/IP, the network remains intact until the source and destination machines were functioning properly.
- TCP is a connection-oriented protocol.
- TCP offers reliability and ensures that data which arrives out of sequence should put back into order.

Advantages of the TCP/IP model

- It helps you to establish/set up a connection between different types of computers.
- It operates independently of the operating system.
- It has a highly scalable client-server architecture.
- It can be used to establish a connection between two computers.
- Supports a number of routing protocols.

Disadvantages of the TCP/IP model

- TCP/IP is a complicated model to set up and manage.
- It has no clear separation from its services, interfaces, and protocols.
- Replacing protocol is not easy.

The TCP/IP is divided into 4 layers as per functionality, with each layer having its own set of protocols. (See Figure 2.7).

Layer 1 — Network Interface Layer

This layer acts as an interface between hosts and transmission links and used for transmitting datagrams. It also specifies what operation must be performed by links like serial link and classic ethernet to fulfil the requirements of the connectionless Internet layer.

- Lowest layer of the all.
- Protocol is used to connect to the host, so that the packets can be sent over it.
- The Internetwork layer in the TCP/IP model handles software, or logical, addressing.

Layer 2 — Internet Layer

Selection of a packet switching network which is based on a connectionless internetwork layer is called a *Internet layer*. It manages the use of addresses for routing message packets over the network. For IoT device connectivity, IPv6 is the protocol most commonly used on this layer. The Internet layer transports network packets from a host device to a target device specified by its IP address. It supports processes and functions for

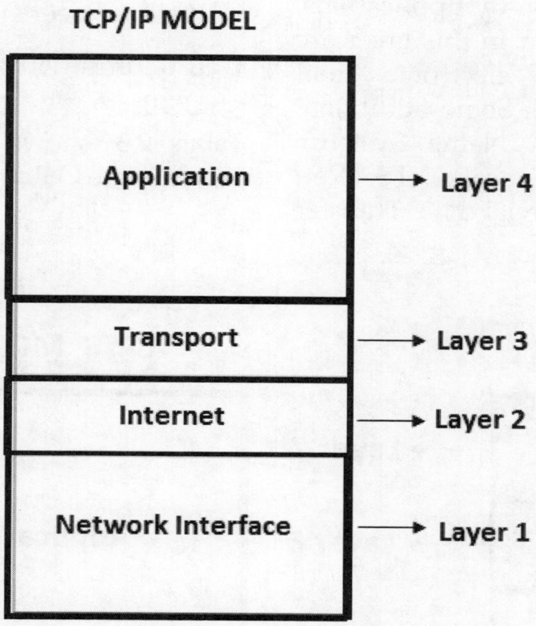

Figure 2.7 TCP/IP four layer model

sending and receiving packets, as well as detecting and diagnosing errors. All the machines, Web servers, nodes that are attached to the TCP/IP network are assigned in this layer.

- It is the layer which holds the whole architecture together.
- It helps the packet to travel independently to the destination.
- Order in which packets are received is different from the way they are sent.
- The various functions performed by the Internet Layer are delivering IP packets, performing routing, and avoiding congestion.

Layer 3 — Transport Layer

It provides end-to-end communications of the data between the source and destination hosts in the form of datagrams and also monitors reliability, message order and prevents congestion across the network. The transport layer of the TCP/IP protocol stack implements either the Transmission Control Protocol (TCP) or the User Datagram Protocol (UDP). TCP provides reliable, connection-oriented communications between two hosts. UDP provides connectionless, datagram services between two hosts. TCP requires more network overhead than UDP because data is acknowledged as it is received. UDP is faster, but less reliable, because the recipient does not acknowledge data as it is received.

- The applications can read and write to the transport layer.
- Transport layer breaks the message (data) into small units so that they are handled more efficiently by the network layer.
- Transport layer also arrange the packets to be sent, in sequence.
- It decides if data transmission should be on parallel path or single path.
- Functions such as multiplexing, segmenting or splitting on the data is done by transport layer.

Layer 4 — Application Layer

The application layer of the TCP/IP protocol stack combines functions that are represented in the application layer, presentation layer, and session layers of the OSI model. It facilitates standardized data exchange for use by applications. The various protocols described in this layer are virtual terminal (TELNET), electronic mail (SMTP) and file transfer (FTP). Some additional protocols like DNS (Domain Name System), HTTP (Hypertext Transfer Protocol), NFS (Network File System), TFTP (Trivial File Transfer Protocol).

- It allows peer entities to carry conversation.
- It defines two end-to-end protocols: TCP and UDP.

Table 2.3 shows some important differences between the OSI and TCP/IP models.

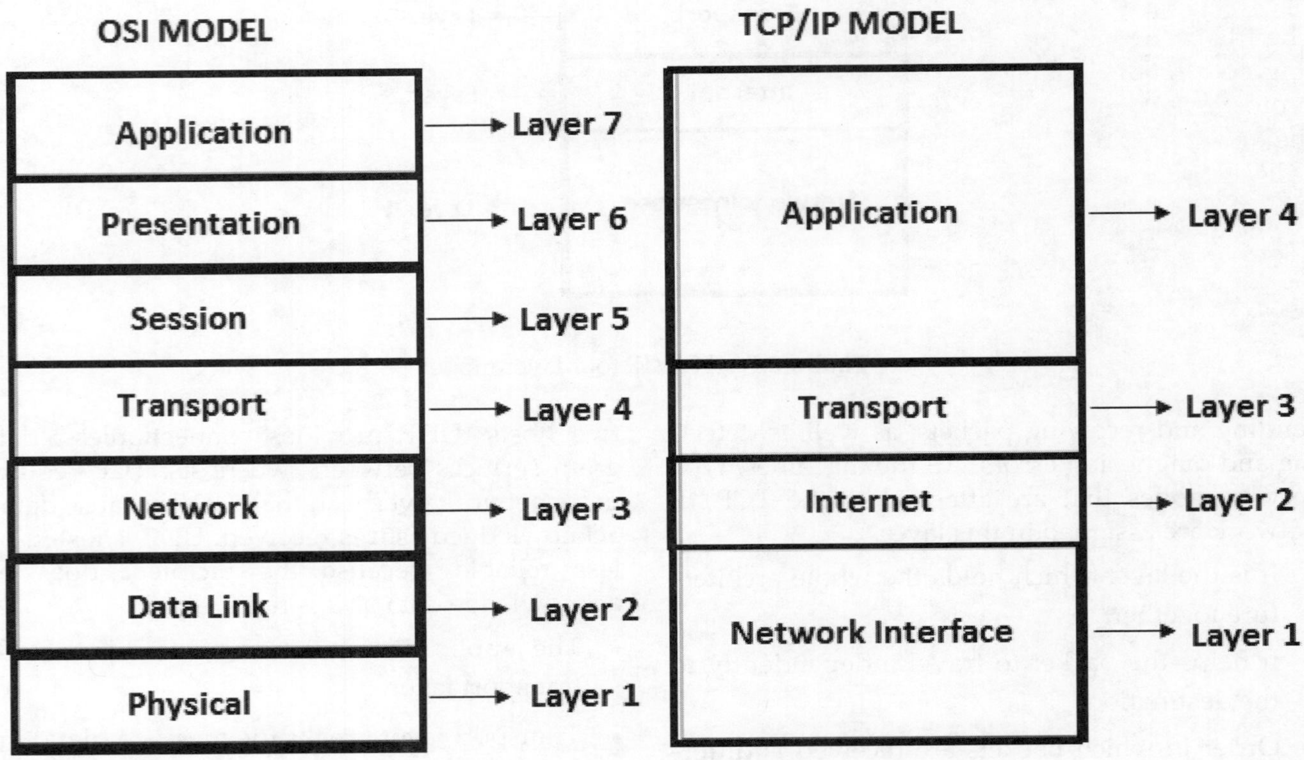

Figure 2.8 OSI and TCP/IP Model

Table 2.3 Function performed by different layers in the OSI model

OSI Model	TCP/IP Model
It is developed by ISO (International Standard Organization).	It is developed by ARPANET (Advanced Research Project Agency Network).
OSI model provides a clear distinction between interfaces, services, and protocols.	TCP/IP doesn't have any clear distinguishing points between services, interfaces, and protocols.
OSI refers to Open Systems Interconnection.	TCP refers to Transmission Control Protocol.
OSI uses the network layer to define routing standards and protocols.	TCP/IP uses only the Internet layer.
OSI follows a vertical approach.	TCP/IP follows a horizontal approach.

(conti...)

OSI layers have seven layers.	TCP/IP has four layers.
In the OSI model, the transport layer is only connection-oriented.	A layer of the TCP/IP model is both connection-oriented and connectionless.
In the OSI model, the data link layer and physical are separate layers.	In TCP, physical and data link are both combined as a single host-to-network layer.
Session and presentation layers are a part of the OSI model.	There is no session and presentation layer in the TCP model.
It is defined after the advent of the Internet.	It is defined before the advent of the internet.

The Internet of Things (IoT) will utilize the existing networking infrastructure, technologies and protocols currently used. The IoT will run over the existing TCP/IP network. The existing TCP/IP networking model uses a four layer model with protocols defined at each level. The Figure 2.9 shows side by side comparison of the Internet protocols currently in use and those that are used for the IoT.

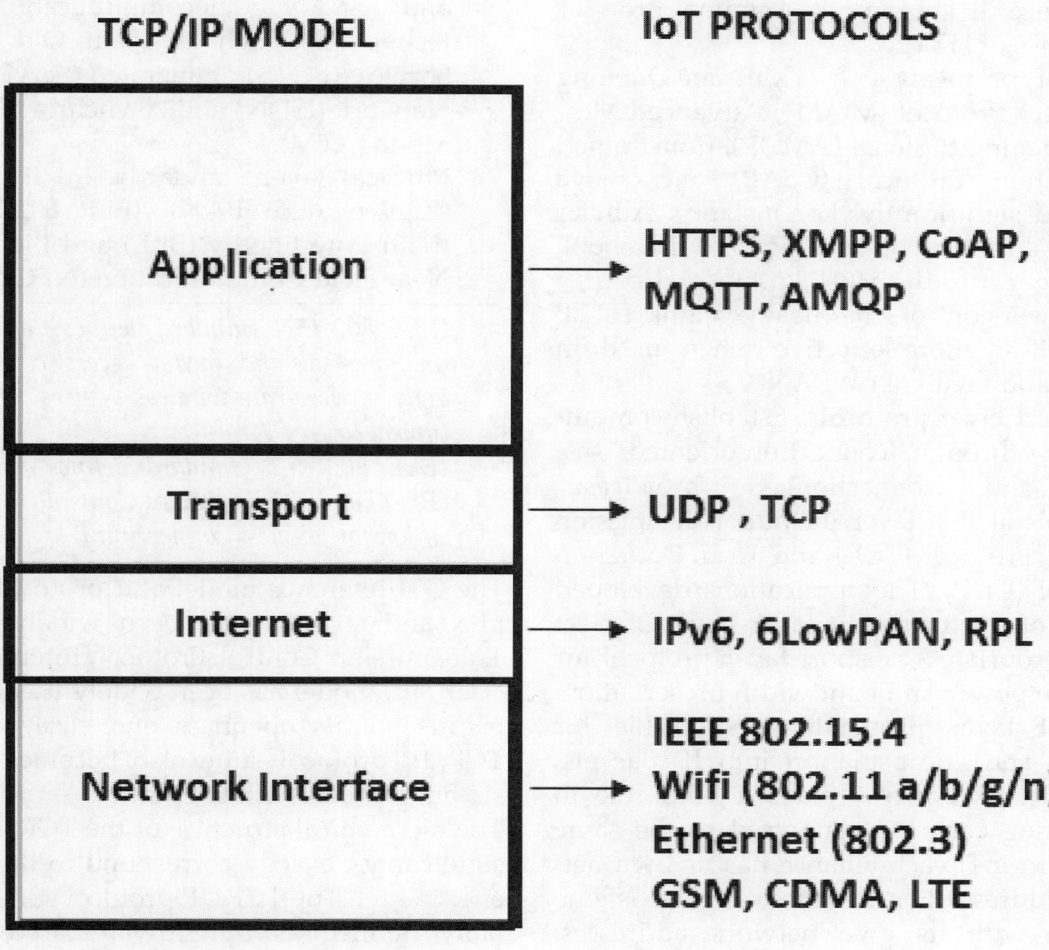

Figure 2.9 IoT protocols mapped with TCP/IP model

Each layer of the TCP/IP protocol suite has its associated component protocols, the most important of which are as given below.

(a) **Application layer protocols:** The application layer serves as the interface between the user and the desired sensor application. Application layer protocol are responsible for application-level access to TCP/IP networking services. These include Dynamic Host Configuration Protocol (DHCP), Domain Name System (DNS), Hypertext Transfer Protocol (HTTP), File Transfer Protocol (FTP), Telnet, Simple Mail Transfer Protocol (SMTP), and Simple Network Management Protocol (SNMP). Protocols such as HTTP/HTTPS have been in existence ever since IP began. A common browser makes use of HTTP.

With IoT, protocols such as Message Queuing Telemetry Protocol (MQTT), Advanced Message Queuing Protocol (AMQP), Constrained Application Protocol (CoAP), etc., have emerged significantly. For instance, Adhaar card makes use of AMQP, and Facebook Messenger uses the MQTT protocol. CoAP, a lighter version of the heavyweight HTTP protocol, is more effective when used in combination with 6LoWPAN.

(b) **Transport layer protocols:** Establish communication through connection-oriented sessions and connectionless broadcasts. Protocols at this layer include Transmission Control Protocol (TCP) and User Datagram Protocol (UDP). The applications developed on top of the Transport layer have to select the appropriate Transport layer protocol for effective power and bandwidth preservation.

(c) **Internet layer protocols:** Responsible for routing and encapsulation into IP packets. The network address plays a vital role in identifying each PC connected to the same router. In IoT, each alliance has its own network address. For instance, ZigBee is one alliance with its own network addresses. Similarly, BLE and Z-Wave have their own network addresses respective to their environments.

Wi-Fi devices come with IP stack in their chip, enabling IP-based connectivity. The IP layer aids the respective devices to effectively communicate within their operating range.

6LoWPAN devices also operate in IEEE 802.15.4, but they have the network stack with IP connectivity (IPv6). Protocols at this layer include Internet Protocol (IP), Address Resolution Protocol (ARP), Internet Control Message Protocol (ICMP), and Internet Group Management Protocol (IGMP), Routing Protocol for Low-Power and Lossy Networks (RPL).

(d) **Network Interface layer protocols:** It places frames on the network. The protocols include the various local area network (LAN) architectures (such as Ethernet and Token Ring) and WAN telecommunication service technologies-such as Plain Old Telephone Service (POTS), Integrated Services Digital Network (ISDN) and Asynchronous Transfer Mode (ATM).

Physical layer standards are IEEE 802.15.4 (ZigBee, 6LoWPAN), IEEE 802.15.1 (Bluetooth Low Energy (BLE) and Bluetooth 4.0), Near Field Communication (NFC), X-10 etc.

☞ *IEEE 802.15.4 standard defines the operation of the physical and media access control (MAC) layer for low-rate wireless devices, which are the typical IoTs.*

IEEE 802.15.1 standard defines physical layer (PHY) and Media Access Control (MAC) specification for wireless connectivity.

The OSI reference model and protocols are complex and so have not been widely used. The Transmission Control Protocol/Internet Protocol (TCP/IP) model has been widely used in practice because of its openness and ease of use. The TCP/IP protocol suite also becomes the mainstream protocols of the Internet.

The hierarchical structure of the TCP/IP protocol suite cannot exactly correspond to the OSI reference model. The TCP/IP protocol suite was originally defined as a hardware-based four-layer architecture: including the Application layer, Transport layer, Internet layer, and Network interface layer (also called link layer). The IoT protocol stack can be visualized as an extension of

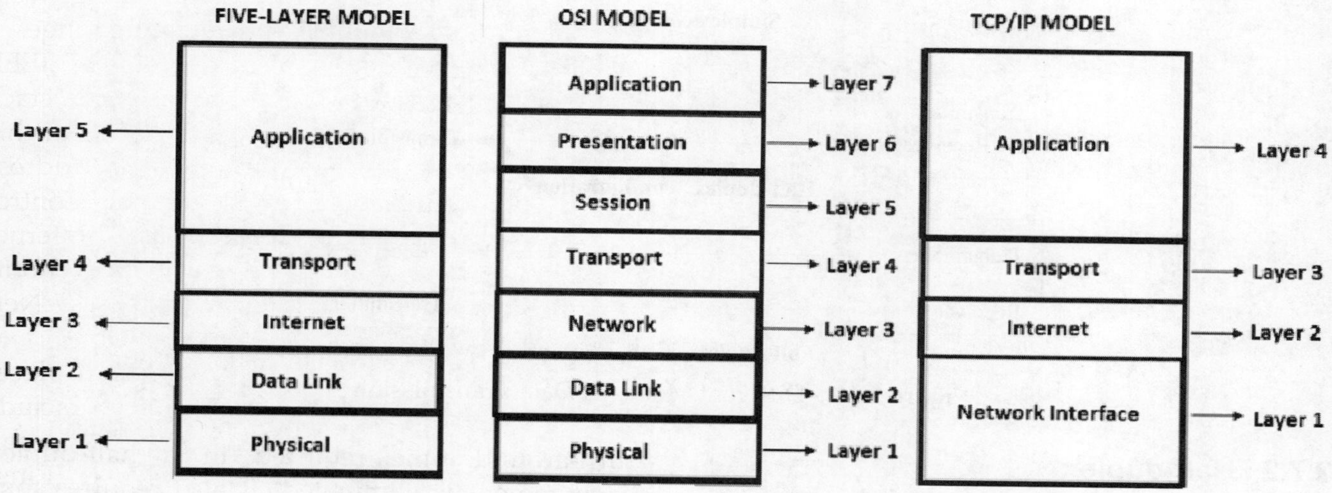

Figure 2.10 Five-layer protocol model mapped with OSI and TCP/IP model

the TCP/IP layered protocol model and is comprised of the following five layers: Physical layer, Data Link layer, Network layer, Transport layer, and Application layer. This five-layer protocol model is adopted to combine the characteristics of the OSI and TCP/IP, as shown in Figure 2.10.

Internet-specific IoT protocols have been developed to meet the requirements of devices with small amounts of memory, and networks with low bandwidth and high latency. IoT protocols are optimized for constrained devices and networks, and produce a much smaller data overhead of tens of bytes.

2.7 TYPES OF MODES

There are three modes of data transmission that correspond to the three types of circuits available. (See Figure 2.11). These modes are:

(i) Simplex
(ii) Half-duplex
(iii) Full-duplex

2.7.1 Simplex

Simplex communications imply a simple method of communication. In simplex communications mode, there is a one-way communication transmission. Television transmission is a very good example of simplex communication. The main transmitter sends out a signal (broadcast), but it does not expect a reply as the receiving units cannot issue a reply back to the transmitter. Examples include a data collection terminal on a factory floor (send only) or a line printer (receive only). Another example of simplex communication is a keyboard attached to a computer because the keyboard can only send data to the computer.

At first thought, it might appear adequate for many types of applications in which flow of information is unidirectional. However, in almost all data processing applications, communication in both directions is required. Even for a "one-way" flow of information from a terminal to a computer, the system will be designed to allow the computer to signal the terminal that data has been received. Without this capability, the remote user might enter data and never know that it was not received by the other terminal.

☞ *Simplex circuits are seldom used because a return path is generally needed to send acknowledgement, control or error signals.*

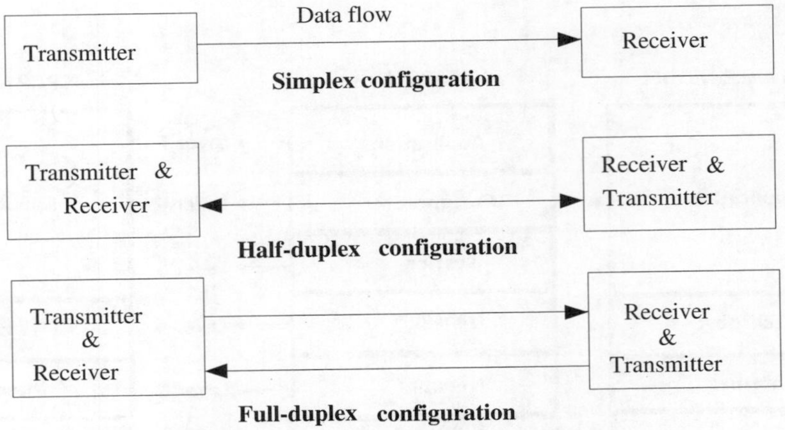

Figure 2.11 Different Modes of Data Transmission

2.7.2 Half-duplex

In half-duplex mode, both units communicate over the same medium, but only one unit can send at a time. While one is in send mode, the other unit is in receive mode. It is like two polite people talking to each other—one talks, the other listens, but both of them could not talk at the same time. Thus, a half duplex line can alternately send and receive data. It requires two wires. This is the most common type of transmission for voice communications because only one person is supposed to speak at a time. It is also used to connect a terminal with a computer. The terminal might transmit data and then the computer responds with an acknowledgement. The transmission of data to and from a hard disk is also done in half duplex mode.

2.7.3 Full-duplex

In a half-duplex system, the line must be *"turned around"* each time the direction is reversed. This involves a special switching circuit and requires a small amount of time (approximately 150 milliseconds). With high speed capabilities of the computer, this turn-around time is unacceptable in many instances. Also, some applications require simultaneous transmission in both directions. In such cases, a full-duplex system is used that allows information to flow simultaneously in both directions on the transmission path. Use of a full-duplex line improves efficiency as the line turn-around time required in a half-duplex arrangement is eliminated. It also requires four wires for full-duplex system.

2.8 WIRED AND WIRELESS METHODOLOGY

Communications or Internet connectivity allows the device to communicate with each other. The Internet connection can be wired, through Ethernet cables, or wireless, such as a Wi-Fi or cellular network.

IoT technology is deployed in many ways so no single network solution is right. It depends on the situation and where the devices are located. Some of the factors affecting the selection of the type of network are network range, network bandwidth, power usage, interoperability, intermittent connectivity and security.

As you know "wired" is the term refers to any physical medium consisting of cables. Wired connections provide a very reliable communications medium as connectivity expands between machines on factory floors to devices and corporate offices to provide secure, reliable, high-speed communication. Physically connected equipment is less likely to experience interference or interruption. More data can often be transferred for a lower cost, as companies reduce the risk of running up high cellular charges. A wired network uses Ethernet cable to connect to the network. The cables can be copper wire, twisted pair or fiber optic. Wired network is used to carry different forms of electrical signals from one end to the other.

Even in the case of wireless network, those networks are usually connected to a wired network at some point; hence the most commonly used network is a hybrid of both wired and wireless network connectivity.

"Wireless" is the term refers to medium made of electromagnetic waves (i.e. EM Waves) or infrared waves. All the wireless devices will have antenna or sensors. Typical wireless devices include cellular mobile, wireless sensors, TV remote, satellite disc receiver, laptops with WLAN card etc. Wireless network does not use wires for data or voice communication; it uses radio frequency waves as mentioned above. With the evolution of network technologies, you see a wide range of wireless technologies like RFID, Bluetooth, BLE, WiFi, ZigBee, Z-Wave, 6LoWPAN, GSM, CDMA, WiMAX, LTE, Satellite etc. Table 2.4 Compares Wired and Wireless networks.

Table 2.4 Comparison of Wired and Wireless network

Specification	Wired network	Wireless network
Speed	Higher	Lower compare to wired networks
Bandwidth	High	Low
Cost	Less as cables are not expensive	More as wireless subscriber stations, wireless routers, wireless access points and adapters are expensive
Installation	Not easy	Easy
Time	Requires more time	Requires less time as newer wireless technologies use plug and play including auto-discovery that helps with reduced installation times.
Mobility	Limited, as it operates in the area covered by connected systems with the wired network	Not limited, as it operates in the entire wireless network coverage
Transmission medium	Copper wires, optical fiber cables, ethernet	EM waves or radiowaves or infrared
Channel Interference and signal power loss	Interference is less as one wired network will not affect the other	Interference is higher due to obstacles between wireless transmitter and receiver for example, weather conditions, reflection from walls, etc.

☞ *Wire or fiber-optic media are referred to as bounded media. Wireless media are sometimes referred to as unbounded media.*

2.9 TRANSMISSION MEDIA

Media is the general term used to describe the data path that forms the physical channel between sender and the receiver. Media can be twisted-pair wire such as that used for telephone installations. It can be coaxial cable of various sizes and electrical characteristics. It can also be fiber-optic cables and wireless supporting either light waves or radio waves.

There are several types of physical channels (communication media) through which data can be transmitted from one point to another. The media of transmission of energy can be either guided or unguided. Some of the most common data transmission media are briefly described in the following sections.

2.10 GUIDED MEDIA

Guided media refers to the method of transmission of data over which signal can travel in a network. Examples of guided media include the following:

(a) Twisted-pair wire
(b) Coaxial cabling
(c) Fiber-optic cabling

2.10.1 Twisted-pair wire

A twisted pair of wires consists of two insulated copper wires, typically about 1 mm thickness (See Figure 2.12). The wires are twisted together in a helical shape. The purpose of twisting the wires is to reduce electrical interference from similar pairs that are close by. Twisted pair cabling, are of two types such as unshielded twisted pair (UTP) and shielded twisted pair (STP) cabling.

Twisted pair wires are commonly used in local telephone communication and for digital data transmission over short distances up to 1 km. When many twisted pairs run in parallel for a substantial distance, such as all the wires coming from a multistory apartment building to the telephone exchange, they are bundled together and placed in a protective sheath.

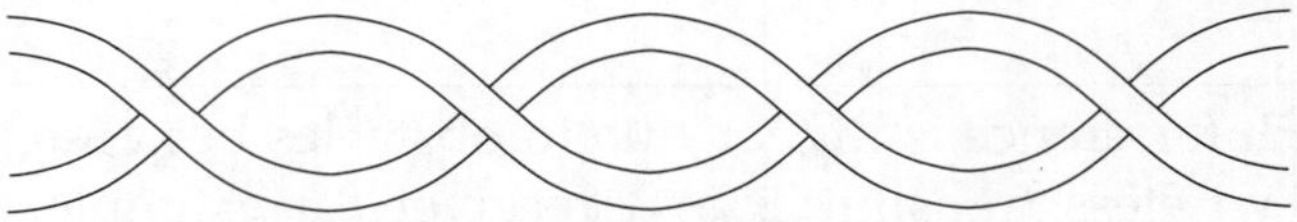

Figure 2.12 A twisted-pair of wires

Wire pairs are normally used to connect terminals to the main computer up to short distances from the main computer. Data transmission speeds up to 9600 bits per second can be achieved if the distance is not more than 100 meters.

Advantages

(a) Being the oldest method of data transmission, trained manpower to repair and service this media of communications are easily available.
(b) In a telephone system, signals can travel several kilometres without amplification when twisted pair wires are used.
(c) This media can be used for both analog and digital data transmission. The bandwidth depends on the thickness of the wire and the distance traveled, but several megabits per second can be achieved for a few kilometres in many cases.
(d) It is the least expensive media of transmission for short distances.
(e) If portion of a twisted-pair cable is damaged, the entire network is not shut down as it may be the case with coaxial cable.

Disadvantages

(a) Easily picks up noise signals which results in higher error rates when the line length exceeds 100 metres.
(b) Being thin in size, it is likely to break easily.
(c) It can support 19,200 bps up to 50 feet on RS-232 port. On a 10BaseT, which supports 10 Mbps, twisted-pair wires can be used up to 100 metres.

Unshielded Twisted Pair (UTP) Cable

Unshielded Twisted Pair (UTP) is a very flexible, low cost media, and can be used for either voice or data communications (Figure 2.13). Its greatest disadvantage is the limited bandwidth, which restricts long distance transmission with low error rates.

UTP cabling is commonly used in Ethernet or Fast Ethernet environments while STP is used for token ring networks and sometimes for gigabit Ethernet installations. Copper cabling (such as thinnet or thicknet) are used mainly in industrial environments.

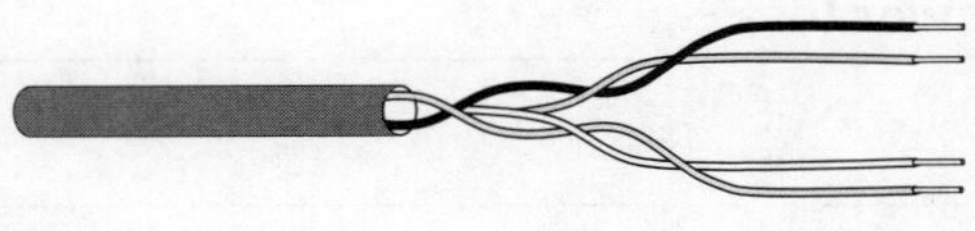

Figure 2.13 Unshielded twisted-pair (UTP) cable

Shielded Twisted Pair (STP) Cable

Shielded Twisted Pair (STP) is heavier and more difficult to manufacture, but it can greatly improve the signaling rate in a given transmission scheme (See Figure 2.14). Although UTP cable is the least expensive cable, it may be susceptible to radio and electrical frequency interference (it should not be too close to electric motors, fluorescent lights, etc.). Shielded cables can also help to extend the maximum distance of the cables. The pairs in STP cable have an individual shield, and the individual shielded cables are wrapped in an overall shield. The primary advantages of STP cable are that it has less attenuation at higher frequencies and is less susceptible to electromagnetic interference. Shielded twisted pair cable is available in three different configurations.

Shielded wire is used in an electrically noisy environment to limit the effects of noise absorption. Twisted-pair wiring is more commonly used for LAN media. The twisted pair version of Ethernet is designated as 10BASE-T, in which 10 refers to the Ethernet rate of 10 Mbps.

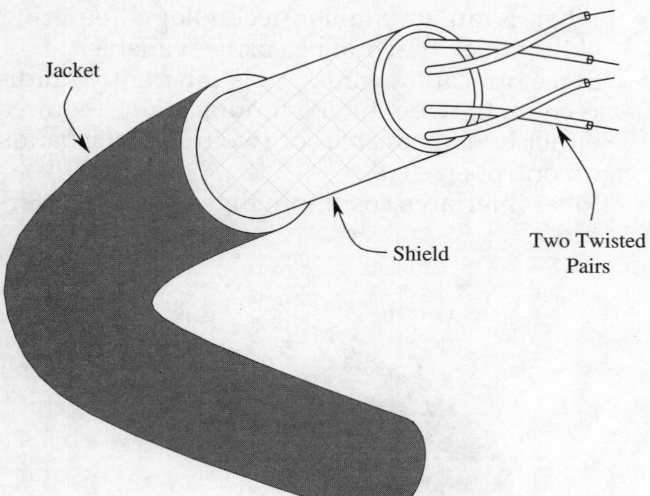

Figure 2.14 Shielded two pair cable

☞ *Unshielded twisted pair, commonly referred to as UTP is by far the more common of the two configurations.*

2.10.2 Coaxial Cable

Coaxial cables are the guided media that carry the signal of higher frequency range compared to twisted pair cable. Coaxial cables are also called coax. (short form). Two types of coaxial cables are widely used: 50 ohm cable and 75 ohm cable. 50 ohm cable is used for digital transmission and 75 ohm cable is used for analog transmission. Due to the shield provided, this cable has excellent noise immunity. It has a large bandwidth and low losses. Co-axial cables are easy to install.

Coaxial cable consists of a stiff copper wire as the core, surrounded by an insulating material. The insulator is encased by a cylindrical conductor, often as a closely woven braided mesh. The outer conductor is covered in a protective plastic sheath. A cutaway view of a coaxial cable is shown in Figure 2.15. The signal is transmitted by the inner copper wire and it is electrically shielded by the outer metal sleeve.

There are two types of coaxial cables: Baseband & Broadband Coaxial Cable. A baseband coaxial cable transmits a single signal at a time at very high speed. A broadband coaxial cable can transmit many simultaneous signals using different frequencies. A baseband cable is mainly used for LANs. Baseband coaxial cable supports frequency range of a-4kHz and are used for digital signaling. Broadband coaxial cable supports the frequency range above 4kHz and are used for analog signals. So it must be used with a modem.

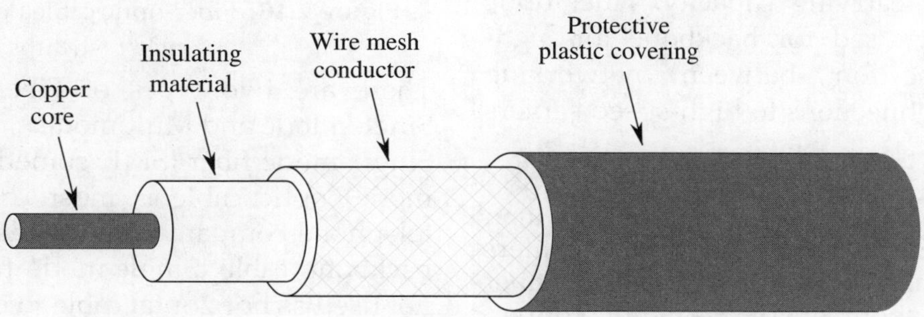

Figure 2.15 Coaxial cable

Coaxial cables are used in Analog telephone networks, Digital telephone network, Cable TV, Traditional Ethernet LANs, Digital transmission, Thick Ethernet etc.

Advantages of Coaxial Cables

- It can be used for both analog and digital transmission.
- It offers higher bandwidth as compared to twisted pair cable and can span longer distances.
- Because of better shielding in coaxial cable, loss of signal or attenuation is less.
- Better shielding also offers good noise immunity.
- It is relatively inexpensive as compared to optical fibers.
- It has lower error rates as compared to twisted pair.
- It is not as easy to tap as twisted pair because copper wire is contained in plastic jacket.

Disadvantages of Coaxial Cables

- It is usually more expensive than twisted pair.
- The thick the cable, the more difficult to work with.
- Installation charges are more as compared to twisted pair.
- Coaxial cable lose signal in long distance but they are suitable for home use.

2.10.3 Fiber Optic Cable

Fiber optic cable is made of glass strands that transmit signals as light waves or pulses. Each fiber is surrounded by a plastic sheath (See Figure 2.16). It can be either single mode, which is used for the longest cable run, or multimode, which has much higher carrying capacity. Fiber optic cable is generally used for backbone for high-speed interconnection between networking devices and for connections to high-speed servers and workstations.

Advantages

- It can handle much higher bandwidth than copper. Due to the low attenuation, repeaters are needed only about every 30 Km on fiber lines, versus about every 5 km for copper. Transmission distances can be much greater than with copper cable.
- Fiber is not affected by power surges, electromagnetic interference, or power failures. Nor is it affected by corrosive chemicals in the air, making it ideal for factory environments where electrical interference is very high.
- Fiber is lighter than copper. One thousand twisted pairs copper cables of 1 km long weigh 800 kg. But fibers have only 100 kg.
- Fibers do not leak light and are quite difficult to tap. This gives them excellent security against potential wire-tappers.
- Fiber-optic cable can easily handle data at speeds above 1Gbps; in fact, it has been demonstrated to handle data rates exceeding 200Gbps.

☞ *Fiber optic is not susceptible to outside EMI or crosstalk interference, nor does it generate EMI or crosstalk.*

Disadvantages

- Fiber is an unfamiliar technology requiring skills which may not be easily available.
- Since optical transmission is inherently unidirectional, two-way communication requires either two fiber cables or two frequency bands on one fiber.
- Fiber interfaces cost more than electrical interfaces.

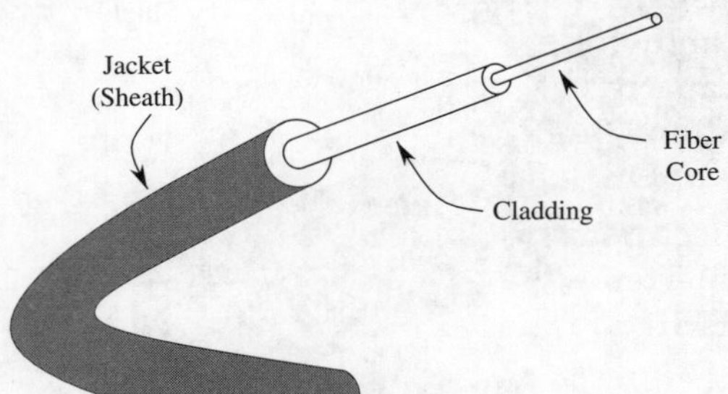

Figure 2.16 Fiber-optic cables with cladding and jacket (sheaths)

There are two types of Fiber-optic cables are Single-mode and Multimode:

Single-mode fiber (SMF, sometimes called mono-mode) optic cable is most commonly used by telephone companies and in data installations as backbone cable. Single-mode fiber optic cable is not used as horizontal cable to connect computers to hubs. The light in a single-mode cable travels straight down the fiber and does not bounce off the surrounding cladding as it travels. Typical single-mode wavelengths are 1,310 and 1,550 nanometers. Before you install single-mode fiber optic cable, make sure the equipment you are using supports it. The equipment that uses single-mode fiber typically uses lasers to transmit light through the cable because a laser is the only light source capable of inserting light into the very small (8- to 10-micron) core of a single-mode fiber.

Multimode fiber (MMF) optic cable is usually the fiber optic cable used with networking applications such as FDDI, ATM, and others that require fiber optics for both horizontal and backbone cable. Multimode cable allows more than one mode of light to propagate through the cable. Typical wavelengths of light used in multimode cable are 850 and 1,300 nanometers. There are two types of multimode fiber optic cable:

- Step Index
- Graded Index

Step-index multimode fiber optic cable indicates that the refractive index between the core and the cladding is very distinctive. The graded-index fiber optic cable is the most common type of multimode fiber. The core of a graded-index fiber contains many layers of glass; each has a lower index of refraction going outward from the core of the fiber. Both types of multimode fiber permit multiple modes of light to travel through the fiber simultaneously. Graded-index fiber is preferred because less light is lost as the signal travels around bends in the cable.

Following factors give the comparison among twisted pair, coaxial cable and fiber optic wiring as transmission media. A brief comparison is given in Table 2.5.

Table 2.5 Characteristics of different types of Cable Media (Bounded Media)

Factor	Unshielded Twisted-pair cable (UTP)	Shielded Twisted-pair cable (STP)	Coaxial Cable	Fiber optic
Cost	Lowest	Moderate	Moderate	Highest
Installation	Easy	Fairly easy	Fairly easy	Difficult
Bandwidth Capacity	1 to 155 Mbps (typically 10 Mbps)	1 to 155 Mbps (typically 100 Mbps)	typically 100 Mbps	2 Gbps (typically 100 Mbps)
Attenuation	High (Range of a few hundred metres)	High (Range of a few hundred metres)	Lower (range of a few kilometres)	Lowest (range of tens of kilometres)
Electromagnetic Interference (EMI)	Most vulnerable to EMI and eavesdropping	Less vulnerable than UTP but still vulnerable to EMI and eavesdropping	Less vulnerable than UTP but still vulnerable to EMI and eavesdropping	Not affected by EMI or eavesdropping

2.11 UNGUIDED MEDIA

Media in which the signals are not guided through a solid medium are known as unguided media. Air is the media through which electromagnetic energy can flow easily. Therefore, there are several methods which are in use to send electromagnetic energy through air. These methods are:

(a) Radio waves
(b) Micro waves
(c) Infrared Waves

2.11.1 Radio waves

Electromagnetic waves ranging in frequencies between 10 kilohertz (kHz) and 1 gigahertz (GHz). Radio waves can be broadcasted omnidirectionally or unidirectionally. Various kinds of antennae can be used to broadcast radio signals. The power of the Radio Frequency (RF) signal is determined by the antenna and trans-receiver (a device that TRANSmits and reCEIVEs a signal over a medium such as copper, radio waves or fiber optic cables).

Characteristics of Radio waves

(a) Radio waves are easy to generate.

(b) They can travel long distances.
(c) They can penetrate buildings easily, thus they are widely used for communications both indoors and outdoors.
(d) Radio waves are omnidirectional, meaning that they travel in all directions from the source, so that the transmitter and receiver do not have to be carefully aligned physically.

In Very Low Frequency (VLF), Low Frequency (LF) and Medium Frequency (MF) bands, radio waves follow the ground. Amplitude modulated radio broadcasting uses the MF band. This band of frequencies cannot be used for data transfer because they offer relatively *low bandwidth.* The omnidirectional characteristics of radio waves make them useful for multicasting in which there is one sender but many receivers. FM radio, television, cordless phones, and paging are examples of multicasting.

VHF (Very High Frequency) is the radio frequency band extending from 30 MHz to 300 MHz. The wavelengths corresponding to these limit frequencies are 10 meters and 1 meter, respectively. Unlike the High Frequencies (HF) band, the ionosphere does not usually reflect VHF radio and thus transmissions are restricted to the local area. Thus, one transmission on VHF does not interfere with transmissions thousands of kilometres away.

VHF is also less affected by atmospheric noise and interference from electrical equipment than lower frequencies.

Common uses for VHF are FM radio broadcast, television broadcast, land mobile stations (emergency, business, and military), long range data communication with radio modems, marine communications, air traffic control communications and air navigation systems. A great deal of satellite communication and broadcasting is done at VHF.

2.11.2 Microwave

Above 100 MHz, the waves travel in straight lines and can therefore be narrowly focused. Concentrating all the energy into a small beam using a parabolic antenna (like the satellite TV dish) gives a much higher signal to noise ratio, but the transmitting and receiving antennas must be accurately aligned with each other. Before the advent of fiber optics, these microwaves formed the heart of the long distance telephone transmission system. In order to overcome the problems of line-of-sight and power amplification of weak signals, microwave systems use repeaters at intervals of about 25 to 30 km in between the transmitting and receiving stations (Figure 2.17).

Microwave transmission is weather and frequency dependent. The frequency band of 10 GHz is in the routine use. Microwave communication is widely used for long-distance telephone communication, cellular telephones, television distribution and other uses so that a severe shortage of spectrum has developed. Microwave systems permit data transmission rates of about 16 Giga bits per second (1 giga = 10^9). At such high frequencies, microwave systems can carry 250,000 voice channels at the same time. They are mostly used to link big metropolitan cities which have heavy telephone traffic between them.

Microwaves, due to their unidirectional properties, are very useful when unicast(one-to-one) communication is needed between the sender and the receiver. They are used in cellular phones, satellite networks and wireless LANs.

Characteristics of Microwave

(a) Microwave is inexpensive as compared to fiber optics system.
(b) Very high-frequency microwaves cannot penetrate walls. This characteristic can be a disadvantage if receivers are inside the buildings.
(c) Micro waves are unidirectional. When an antenna transmits microwaves, they can be narrowly focused. This means that the sending and receiving antennas need to be aligned.

Types of Microwave Communication Systems

There are two types of microwave data communication systems. These are:

(a) Terrestrial
(b) Satellite

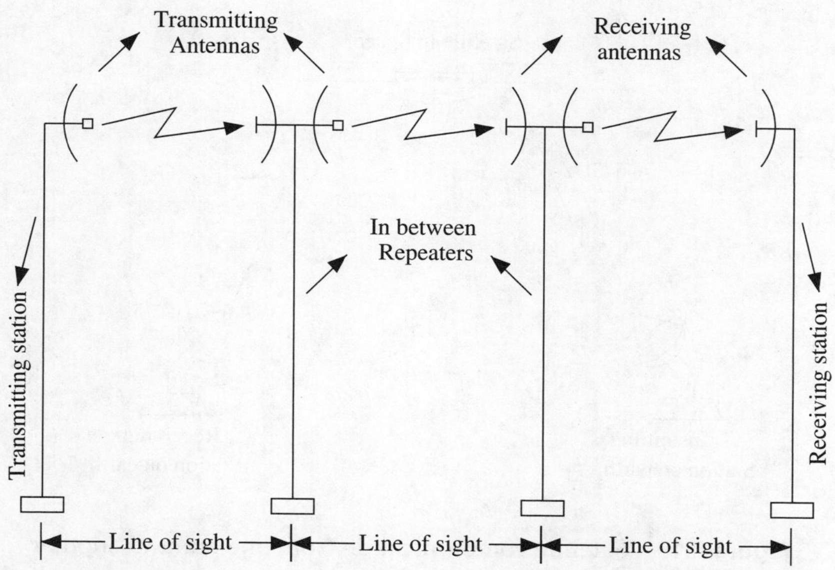

Figure 2.17 Illustration of microwave communication from one point to another

Terrestrial Microwave Systems

Terrestrial Microwave systems typically use directional parabolic antennas to send and receive signals in the lower giga hertz range. The signals are highly focussed and the physical path must be line-of-sight. Relay towers and repeaters are used to extend signals. Terrestrial microwave systems are used whenever cabling is cost-prohibitive such as in hilly areas or crossing rivers, etc.

Because terrestrial microwave system does not use cables, microwave links often connect separate buildings where cabling would be too expensive, difficult to install or prohibited. For example, if two buildings are separated by a public road, you may not be able to get permission to install cable over or under the road. Microwave links would be a good choice in this type of situation.

Satellite Microwave Systems

Satellite Microwave systems transmit signals between directional parabolic antennas (See Figure 2.18). Like terrestrial microwave systems, they use low giga hertz frequencies and must be in line-of-sight. The main difference with satellite systems is that one antenna is on the satellite in geo-synchronous orbit about 36,000 kilometers (22,300 miles) above the equator. As the satellite is positioned in a geo-synchronous orbit, it is stationery relative to earth and always stays over the same point on the ground. This is usually done to allow ground stations to aim antenna at a fixed point in the sky. Because of this, satellite microwave systems can reach the most remote places on earth and communicate with mobile devices.

2.11.3 Infrared Waves

Unguided infrared and millimetre waves are widely used for short-range communication. The remote controls used on television, VCRs, and stereos use infrared communication. They are relatively directional, cheap and easy to build but do not pass through solid objects. An infrared system in one room of a building will not interfere with a similar system in adjacent rooms. Further, security of infrared systems against eves dropping is better than that of radio systems precisely for this reason. No government licence is needed to operate an infrared system in contrast to radio systems which must be licensed.

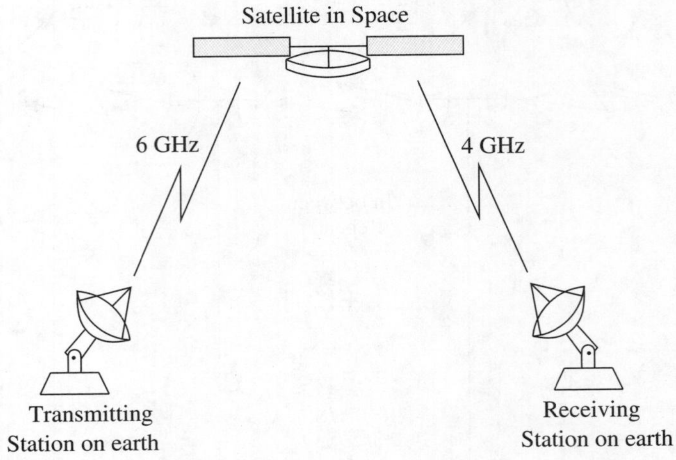

Figure 2.18 Satellite communication from one point to another

Infrared communication is used for indoor wireless LANs. For example, the computers and offices in a building can be equipped with relatively unfocussed infrared transmitters and receivers. In this way, portable computers with infrared capability can be on the local LAN without having to physically connect to it. When several people show up for a meeting with their laptop computers, they can just sit down in the conference room and be fully connected without having to plug in.

2.12 THE PROCESS FLOW OF IoT

Internet of Things is a concept or a technology which aims to connect all the devices to the internet and help them communicate with each other using the internet as a medium.

First of all, sensors or devices collect data from the surrounding environment. The collected data could be as simple as a geographical location or as complex as health essentials of a patient. Once the data is collected, it is sent to a cloud infrastructure of an IoT platform with the help of a medium such as satellite networks, Bluetooth, Wi-Fi, Cellular Networks, LPWAN, Ethernet, etc. This medium is chosen by its specifications between power consumption, bandwidth, and range. Once the data gets to the cloud infrastructure, it is stored, analyzed, and processed securely using a Big Data Analytics Engine for better decision making. The last step involves notifying the end user about the action through an email, text, notification, or alert sound triggered on their IoT application.

REVIEW QUESTIONS WITH ANSWERS

1. Multiple Choice Questions

1. This output signal is feedback so that it subtracts from the input signal:
   a. Negative feedback
   b. Positive feedback
   c. Both (a) and (b)
   d. None of the above
2. A system that utilizes a device to control the process without using feedback:
   a. Open-loop control system
   b. Closed-loop feedback control system
   c. Regulator
   d. All of the above
3. A system that uses a measurement of the output and compares it with the desired output:
   a. Open-loop control system
   b. Closed-loop feedback control system

c. Both (a) and (b)
d. None of the above

4. Natural control system:
 a. Solar system
 b. Digestive system
 c. Both (a) and (b)
 d. None of the above
5. It is a control system that has only one input and one output:
 a. SISO
 b. MIMO
 c. Both (a) and (b)
 d. None of the above
6. Which of the following is not a guided medium?
 a. Twisted-pair cable b. Fiber optic cable
 c. Coaxial cable d. Atmosphere
7. The inner core of an optical fiber is ________ in composition.
 a. Glass or plastic b. Bimetallic
 c. Copper d. Liquid
8. The OSI layer that arranges signals into logical units of information called frames:
 a. Transport b. Physical
 c. Data-link d. Application
9. The Internet Protocol generally corresponds to which OSI layer?
 a. Network Layer b. Transport Layer
 c. Data Link Layer d. Session Layer
10. Transmission media are usually categorized as:
 a. Fixed or unfixed b. Guided or unguided
 c. Determinate or indeterminate d. None of the above
11. Which of the following is not a guided medium?
 a. Twisted-pair cable b. Fiber-optic cable
 c. Coaxial cable d. Atmosphere
12. Which type of cable has glass center core?
 a. UTP b. Fiber-Optic
 c. STP d. Coaxial
13. A wireless network uses ________ waves to transmit signals.
 a. Radio b. Microwave
 c. Sound d. Mechanical
14. Which layer of the OSI model does data compression?
 a. Network b. Data Link
 c. Physical d. Presentation
15. End-to-end connection is established by ________ protocol of the TCP/IP suite.
 a. IP b. UDP
 c. TCP d. All of these
16. Bits from physical layer are converted into frames by the:
 a. Data link layer b. Network layer
 c. Transport layer d. None of these
17. The main function of transport layer is:
 a. Node-to-node delivery
 b. Process-to-process delivery
 c. Synchronization
 d. Updating and maintenance of routing tables
18. Which protocol is a Network layer protocol?
 a. IP b. Telnet
 c. FTP d. None of the above

2. State True or False for the following:

1. The control system where the outputs are mechanical quantities like acceleration, velocity or position is called Servo system.
2. Coaxial cable can be used for data rates over 10 Mbps and frequencies up to 400 MHz.
3. Single mode used in fiber optics does not have any dispersion problem.
4. UTP category 3 can be used in Fast Ethernet networks.
5. In a single-mode optic fibres, the core is 8 to 10 microns and a micron is one millionth of an inch.
6. Coaxial cable can support data rates of up to several tens of Mbps at distance up to several thousand feet.
7. Twisted-wire pair is affected by the electromagnetic interference.
8. UTP category 3 can be used in Fast Ethernet networks.

9. Coaxial cable can support data rates of up to several tens of Mbps at distance up to several thousand feet.
10. The OSI model divides network activity into nine layers.
11. Hyper Text Transfer Protocol (HTTP) works at the Application layer of the OSI model.
12. The receiving computer passes the reassembled data to the Session layer in a usable form.

3. Match the following:

1.	Automation	a.	Closed-loop control system.
2.	Man-made control system	b.	The control of a process by automatic means
3.	Feedback control system	c.	Data Link Layer
4.	Fiber optic network	d.	Power plants
5.	Above 100 MHz electromagnetic waves	e.	SONET
6.	Cat7 cable	f.	Straight line
7.	TCP	g.	Data encryption
8.	Error Control	h.	10 Gigabit
9.	Transmission Mode	i.	Connection-oriented protocol
10.	Presentation Layer	j.	Simplex

4. Fill in the blanks:

1. ________ is the signal or excitation supplied to a control system.
2. ________ is the actual response obtained from the control system.
3. ________ is the part or component of a system that controls the plant.
4. The signal that has adverse effect on the performance of a control system is called __________.
5. A system that can command, direct or regulate itself or another system to achieve a certain goal is called ________.
6. ________ is the device that causes the process to provide the output.
7. STP and ________ can be used for both analog and digital data transmission.
8. Intermodal dispersion is absent in ________ fibers.
9. ________ fiber suffers from high signal dispersion.
10. ________ is one of the most common network media.
11. In fibre optics, ________ prevents light from escaping out.
12. In __________, the bandwidth is highest.
13. The advantage of optical fiber is __________.
14. ________ medium transport electromagnetic waves without using a physical conductor.
15. ________ waves are omnidirectional.
16. Satellite manufacturing cost is very ________.

Answers

1.	1. a	2. a	3. b	4. c	5. a	6. d
	7. a	8. c	9. a	10. b	11 d	12 b
	13. a	14. c	15. c	16. a	17. a	18. a
2.	1. T	2. T	3. T	4. F	5. F	6. T
	7. T	8. F	9. T	10. F	11 T	12 F
3.	1. b	2. d	3. a	4. e	5. f	6. h
	7. i	8. c	9. j	10. g		

4.	1. Input	2. Output
	3. Controller	4. Disturbances
	5. Control system	6. Actuator
	7. UTP	8. Single-mode
	9. Multi-mode	10. Co-axial
	11. Cladding	12. Fiber-optic cable
	13. High bandwidth	14. Unguided
	15. Radio	16. High

Short Answers Questions

1. Write short notes on the following:

(a) STP

(b) Coaxial cable
(c) Twisted-pair wire

Ans They are available in different varieties.

a. Category 3 twisted pairs consist of two insulated wires gently twisted together. Four such pairs are typically grouped together in a plastic sheath for protection and to keep the eight wires together. Effect of noise due to (Electromagnetic Interference (EMI) is comparatively low because of shielding. Being thin in size, the wires are likely to break.

b. Coaxial cable consists of a stiff copper wire as the core surrounded by insulating material. The signal is transmitted by the inner copper wire and it is electrically shielded by the outer sleeve. Effect of noise due to (Electromagnetic Interference (EMI) is very low. Can support up to tens of Mbps at a distance of several thousand feet. Emits very low radiation and causes less interference with the communication equipment.

c. Two insulated copper wires twisted together in a helical shape. The copper conductors are typically about 1 mm thick. Transmission of electromagnetic energy along the wires. Least expensive than coaxial cable. Attenuation is high because of the electromagnetic radiation of energy. Being the oldest method of data communication, ample trained manpower is available to maintain the twisted pair cables.

2. Why do you connect the wire mesh conductor of a coaxial cable to the ground?

Ans In order to avoid the interference caused by the electromagnetic noise. The voltage induced by electromagnetic interference (EMI) is sent to earth by grounding the outer conductor of a coaxial cable.

3. What are the advantages of Optical fiber?

Ans The advantages of Optical fiber are:

- It can handle much higher bandwidth than copper. Due to the low attenuation, repeaters are needed only about every 30 km on fiber lines versus about every 5 km for copper.
- Fiber is not affected by power surges, electromagnetic interference or power failures. It is not even affected by corrosive chemicals in the air, making it ideal for factory environments where electrical interference is very high.
- Fiber cable is lighter than copper cable. One thousand twisted pair copper cables of 1 km long weigh 8000 kg. But fibers have more capacity and weigh only 100 kg, which greatly reduces the need for expensive mechanical support systems that must be maintained.
- Fibers do not leak light and are quite difficult to tap. This gives them excellent security against potential wire-tappers.

4. Write one advantage and disadvantage of Microwave Transmission.

Ans Advantage of Microwave Transmission is:

- Carries 1000's of voice channels at the same time.

Disadvantage of Microwave Transmission is:

- It is very costly.

5. Write one advantage and disadvantage of Satellite Microwave

Ans Advantages of Satellite Microwave

- A single microwave relay station which is visible from any point.

Disadvantages of Satellite Microwave.

- Cost of launching satellite is very expensive.

6. Write one application of Infrared Waves.

Ans Infrared waves has established standards for using these signals for communication between devices such as keyboards, mouse, PCs and printers.

7. Write advantage of Unshielded Twisted Pair Cable.

Ans Advantages of Unshielded Twisted Pair Cable are:

- Installation is easy.
- Higher grades of UTP are used in LAN technologies like Ethernet.
- Flexible and Cheap.

8. Write disadvantages of Unshielded Twisted Pair Cable.

Ans Disadvantages of Unshielded Twisted Pair Cable are:

- Bandwidth is low when compared with Coaxial Cable.
- Provides less protection from interference.

9. Write advantages and disadvantages of Shielded Twisted Pair Cable.

Ans Advantages of Shielded Twisted Pair Cable are:

- Easy to install and can be used for Analog or Digital transmission.
- Higher capacity than unshielded twisted pair.
- Eliminates crosstalk.

Disadvantages of Shielded Twisted Pair Cable are:

- Difficult to manufacture
- Heavy

10. Write short note on Application layer of OSI stack.

Ans The data to be transmitted is obtained from this layer with the help of various applications such as web, ftp, telnet etc. These applications will have data in different formats such as binary, ASCII, EBCDIC etc.

11. What is the usage of Transport layer?

Ans It does flow control, fragmentation, reassembly of the data to be transmitted or received.

12. Write short note on TCP.

Ans TCP is a connection-oriented transport protocol. TCP provides end-to-end reliable services. Each TCP connection has only two endpoints. The data transmitted over a TCP connection is error-free, not lost, not duplicated, and arrives in order. TCP provides functions such as timeout and retransmission management, window management, traffic control, and congestion control to ensure that TCP provides reliable services.

13. What is Internet Protocol (IP)?

Ans The Internet Protocol (IP) is the method or protocol by which data is sent from one computer to another on the Internet. Each computer has a unique identifiable address on the Internet which is used to distinguish between each other.

14. Write important characteristics for IOT Pr tocols.

Ans The important characteristics for IOT Pro cols are:

- Speed: Amount of data that can be transf red/second.
- Latency: amount of time a message takes be transferred.
- Power consumption.
- Security
- Availability of software stacks.

15. Why MQTT is considered better than HT in IoT?

Ans HTTP is the best known protocol that po ers the Web (WWW). However because the high protocol overhead HTTP is r likely to be a major IOT protocol. MQ (Message Queuing Telemetry Transport) h emerged as the main IOT messaging pro col because it is lightweight and easy to us

16. Write disadvantage of Coaxial Cable.

Ans Disadvantage of Coaxial Cable are:

- It tends to be more ridged and more diffic to bend around tight corners.
- It has a tendency to pick up signals arounc unless shielded .
- Imperfect shielded can cause a ground loop.
- For the most part 10 base 2 is about as fast you will ever get on a coaxial cable withc special circumstances.
- It is ancient and being phased out phas out except for special use by cable compan and some telecoms.

17. Write advantages of Coaxial cable.

Ans Advantages of Coaxial Cables are:

- It can be used for both analog and digi transmission.
- It offers higher bandwidth as compared twisted pair cable and can span longer d tances.
- Because of better shielding in coaxial cab loss of signal or attenuation is less.
- Better shielding also offers good no immunity.
- It is relatively inexpensive as compared optical fibers.
- It has lower error rates as compared twisted pair.

It is not as easy to tap as twisted pair because copper wire is contained in plastic jacket.

. Explain types of control loops.

ns Types of control loops are:

There are two main types of control loops: Open loops, which operate with human input, and closed loops, which are fully autonomous. Some loops can be switched between closed and open modes. When open, a switchable loop is manually controlled and when closed it is fully automated.

Open-loop and closed-loop control

In an open-loop control system, the control action from the controller is independent of the process variable. An example of this is a central heating boiler controlled only by a timer. The control action is the switching *on* or *off* of the boiler. The process variable is the building temperature. This controller operates the heating system for a constant time regardless of the temperature of the building.

In a closed-loop control system, the control action from the controller is dependent on the desired and actual process variable. In the case of the boiler analogy, this would utilize a thermostat to monitor the building temperature, and feed back a signal to ensure the controller output maintains the building temperature close to that set on the thermostat. A closed loop controller has a feedback loop which ensures the controller exerts a control action to control a process variable at the same value as the setpoint. For this reason, closed-loop controllers are also called feedback controllers.

. What are advantages of wired network?

ns Reliability: Ethernet connections have been in existence much longer than Wi-Fi technology, which makes it much more reliable. They are less prone to dropped connections and are more reliable.

) Speed: Wired connections are less affected by local factors like walls, floors, cabinets, length of the room, interference from other electronic devices etc. This enables wired connectivity to be much faster than wireless.

20. Draw a neat diagram of TCP/IP model.

Ans

LAYER 4 (APPLICATION LAYER)
LAYER 3 (TRANSPORT LAYER)
LAYER 2 (INTERNET LAYER)
LAYER 1 (NETWORK INTERFACE LAYER)

Figure 1 Diagram of TCP/IP Model

21. Write one advantage and disadvantage of wireless network.

Ans Advantage

Scalable: Wireless networks do not require any hardware installations. They typically involve configurations and can be up and running in a short time. They can also be extended very easily.

Disadvantage

Slower speed: When dealing with real-time data, it is imperative that data is transmitted and available as fast as possible. Wireless networks are susceptible to increased latency and signal interference that impacts the speed and consistency of the data.

22. Why do you connect the wire mesh conductor of a coaxial cable to the ground?

Ans In order to avoid the interference caused by the electromagnetic noise. The voltage induced by electromagnetic interference (EMI) is sent to earth by grounding the outer conductor of a coaxial cable.

23. Mention the various components of signal loss in a typical fiber optic link.

Ans Losses are due to the following reasons:

(a) Absorption and attenuation of the cable because the cladding is not completely opaque. So, some of the light energy is absorbed into the cladding.

(b) Large losses result from the physical connections that bring light sources and detectors into alignment with the fiber cable.

(c) Losses also occur between the splices which are the connectors that attach two cables together.

(d) Misalignment of the light source to cable causes loss of light energy. The misalignments are reduced by precise fittings coupling and splices and by carefully following the connecting processes given by the manufacturer.

(e) Loss of light also occurs because of bends in laying the cable.

24. Describe how losses occur due to the bends in fiber optic cables.

Ans Bends in the fiber cause reflected and refracted rays to change directions. This can increase the absorption loss and distort the light pattern at the receiving end.

25. What is the resulting effect on the light signal due to scattering?

Ans The effect of scattering is to attenuate the light energy as the ray travels through the core.

26. Write short note on Terrestrial microwave link

Ans Terrestrial microwave link

(a) Construction: Consists of directional parabolic antennas. Both antennas are on the ground.

(b) Range of operation: With in line of sight. Repeaters are needed for higher range of communication. Relay towers are used to extend the range

(c) Frequency range: 4 to 6 GHz and 21 to 23 GHz.

(d) Cost: Compared to satellite communication, the cost is low.

(e) Bandwidth and capacity: Data rates are from 1 to 10 Mbps.

27. Compare Twisted-pair wire and optical fiber cable.

Comparison of Twisted-pair wire and Optical fiber:

Characteristics	Twisted-Pair wire	Optical Fiber
Construction	Two insulated copper wires twisted together in a helical shape. The copper conductors are typically about 1 mm thick.	Made up of tiny threads of glass or plastic. The core is about the size of hair, i.e. 8-10 microns in single mode fiber and 50 microns diameter in multimode fibers.
Principle of transmission	Transmission of electromagnetic energy along the wires.	Transmission of optical/light energy along the fiber.
Cost	Least expensive.	Very expensive.
Bandwidth	Low. Depends on the thickness of the wire and the length of the cable. Several mega bits/sec can be sent for a few km.	Very high. A common multimode installation can support 100 Mbps over several km length.
Attenuation	Attenuation is high because of the electromagnetic radiation of energy.	Attenuation is very low because there is light beam travelling in the fiber.
Transmission mode	Full-duplex	Half-duplex
Effect of the damage in the cable	Only a part of the network will be affected.	The whole system containing many channels will suffer total damage.
Availability of trained manpower	Being the oldest method of data communication, ample trained manpower is available to maintain the twisted pair cables.	It is a new technology, therefore only a few trained mechanics are available.
Uses	Can be used for both analog and digital data.	Used mainly for digital data.

EXERCISE

1. Write short notes on the following:
   (a) Control system
   (b) TCP/IP Model
   (c) IoT Protocols
   (d) Transport Layer
   (e) Wireless Network
   (f) Feedback systems
   (g) Negative Feedback Systems
2. Differentiate between Wired network and Wireless network.
3. What are the merits and demerits of TCP/IP model?
4. Draw the layered structure of OSI and TCP/IP model.
5. List two ways in which the OSI reference model and the TCP/IP reference model the same. Now, list the two ways in which they are different.
6. Explain the layered architecture of TCP/IP suite. Mention the different protocols working in each layer.
7. Explain the main services provided by the transport layer of a network.
8. Why Presentation layer is important?
9. Differentiate between Positive Feedback and Negative Feedback Systems.
10. Write characteristics of the OSI Model.
11. Write characteristics TCP/IP Model.
12. Differentiate between OSI Model and TCP/IP Model.
13. What are the major benefits of using the OSI model?
14. What are drawbacks of using the OSI model?
15. What is UDP?
16. What are benefits of TCP/IP model?
17. What is the usage of Internet layer of TCP/IP model?
18. Differentiate between TCP and UDP.
19. What is the primary goal of Presentation Layer of OSI Model?
20. Differentiate between Infrared waves and Micro waves.
21. What do you mean by unguided media?
22. How UTP is different from STP?
23. What are the different communication modes available to connect things in an IoT domain?
24. What factors to be considered while selecting a Transmission Medium?
25. What is Automatic Control System? Explain with an example.
26. Write few features of a Control System.
27. Explain working of controlled system.
28. Explain different types of Control Systems.

CHAPTER 3

Sensors, Actuators and Microcontrollers

3.1 INTRODUCTION

Measurement is an important subsystem in any major system, whether it may be a mechanical system or an electronic system. A measurement system consists of *sensors, actuators, transducers* and *signal processing devices*. The use of these elements and devices is not limited to measuring systems. These are also used in the systems which perform specific tasks, to communicate with the real world. The communication can be anything like reading the status of a signal from a switch or to trigger a particular output to light up an LED.

Sensors and actuators are two critical components of every closed loop control system. Such a system is also called a *mechatronics system*. A typical mechatronics system consists of a sensing unit, a controller, and an actuating unit. A sensing unit can be as simple as a single sensor or can consist of additional components such as filters, amplifiers, modulators, and other signal conditioners. The controller accepts the information from the sensing unit, makes decisions based on the control algorithm, and outputs commands to the actuating unit. The actuating unit consists of an actuator and optionally a power supply and a coupling mechanism. (See Figure 3.1).

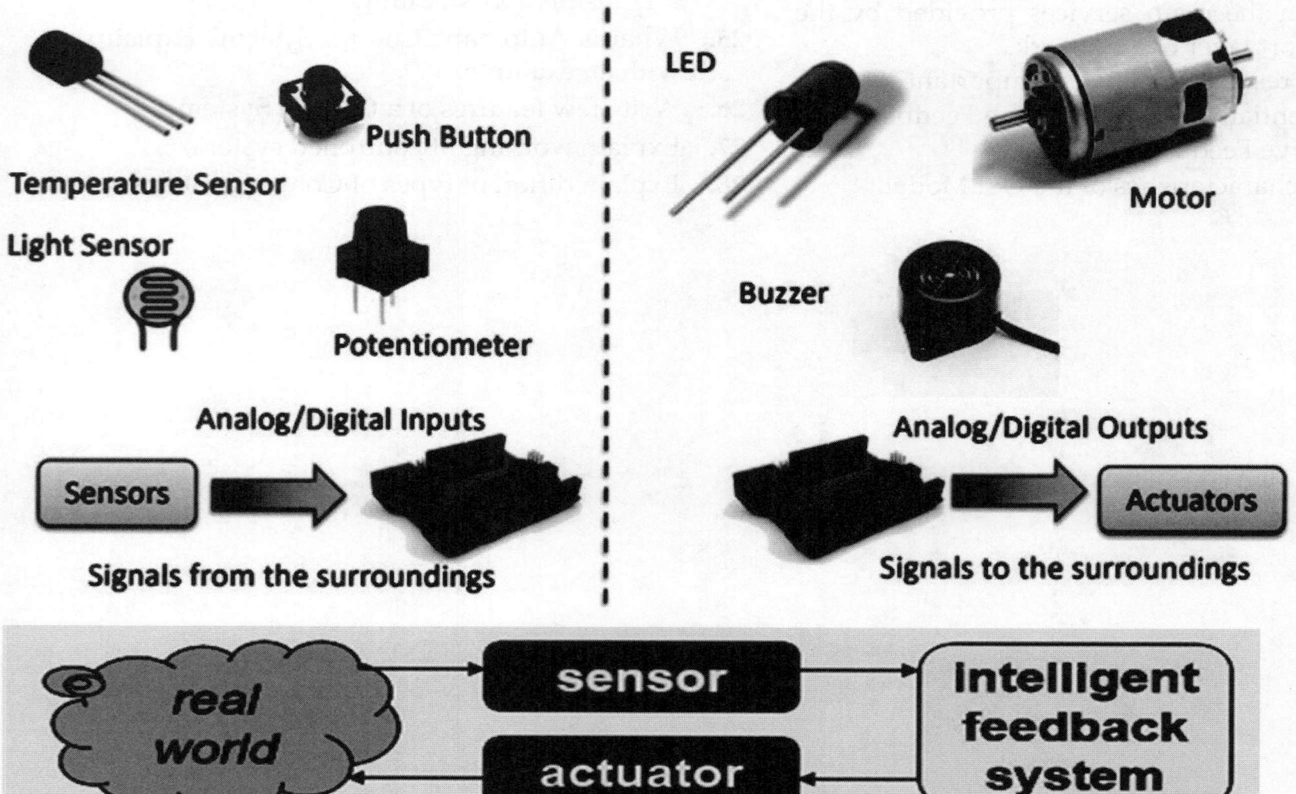

Figure 3.1 Sensor and Actuators

☞ *Linear and rotational position sensors are two of the most fundamental of all measurements used in a typical mechatronics system.*

Any device which has a sensor attached to it and has the capability to transfer data from one device to another through the Internet is known as an *IoT device*. IoT devices consist of softwares, wireless sensors, actuators and computer devices. They are connected to a particular device that operates with the help of Internet, enabling the data to transfer among the devices or people. For instance, IoT systems in your car detect the heavy flow of traffic and send a message automatically to the person waiting for you.

3.2 SENSOR

Sensors are devices that perform input function in a system as they sense the changes in a quantity. The best example of a sensor is mercury thermometer. Here, the quantity that is being measured is heat or temperature. The measured temperature is converted to a readable value on the calibrated glass tube, based on the expansion and contraction of liquid mercury. So, Sensor when exposed to a physical phenomenon (temperature, displacement, force, etc.) produces a proportional output signal (electrical, mechanical, magnetic, etc.). Sensor measures, evaluates and gathers data. The Internet of Things really comes together with the connection of sensors and machines. Due to physical objects getting connected and controlled digitally and centrally with wireless infrastructure, there is a large amount of automation and control in the workings. Without human intervention, the machines are able to communicate with each other leading to faster and timely output. Thus, provide better, more cost effective service through real-time higher solution visibility/capture and analysis of real-time product performance information. This is useful for efficient decision making. For example, doctors supervising patients can monitor their medicine intake as well as measure blood pressure, sugar levels and alert them when something goes wrong to their patients online.

In the aspect of energy conservation, household appliances can suggest optimal setting based on the user's energy consumption like turning the ideal temperature just before the owner arrives home as well as turning on and off the lights whenever the owner is out on vacation just to create the impression that somebody is still left inside the house to prevent burglars from attempting to enter. Smart refrigerators, on the other hand, can suggest food supplies that are low on inventory and needs immediate supply.

☞ *A sensor is a device which can quantitatively measure a certain physical quantity and converts a physical quantity into an electrical signal.*

The term *transducer* is often used synonymously with sensors. However, ideally, a sensor is a device that responds to a change in the physical phenomenon. On the other hand, a transducer is a device that converts one form of energy into another form of energy i.e., it converts a signal from one physical form to a corresponding signal having a different physical form. Therefore, it is an energy converter. Sensors are transducers when they sense one form of energy input and output in a different form of energy. For example, a thermocouple responds to a temperature change (thermal energy) and outputs a proportional change in electromotive force (electrical energy). Therefore, a thermocouple can be called a sensor and or transducer.

Transducers are classified as Active Transducers and Passive Transducers based on the source of energy.

In *Active Transducers*, the energy from the input is used as a control signal in the process of transferring energy from power supply to proportional output. For example, a strain gauge is an active transducer, in which the strain is converted into resistance.

In *Passive Transducers*, the energy from the input is directly converted into the output. For example, a thermocouple is a passive transducer, where the heat energy, which is absorbed from input, is converted into electrical signals (voltage).

☞ *A transducer is a device which converts one physical quantity to another from of physical quantity.*

3.3 CLASSIFICATION OF SENSORS

All the sensors can be classified into two types based on the power or signal requirement. They are active sensors and passive sensors.

Active sensors are the type of sensors that produces output signal with help of external excitation supply. In order to operate active sensors, require power signal from an external source. This signal is called an excitation signal, and based on this excitation signal the sensor produces output. Strain gauge is an example of active sensor.

☞ *Active sensors is also called as Self Generating Sensors.*

Passive sensors are the type of sensors that produces output signal without the help of external excitation supply. They do not need any extra stimulus or voltage. All the power required by a passive sensor is obtained from the measurand. A thermocouple is a passive sensor which generates a voltage value corresponding to the heat, applied. It does not require any external power supply.

Furthermore, sensors are classified as analog or digital based on the type of output signal. *Analog sensors* produce an analog output i.e. a continuous output signal with respect to the quantity being measured and typically require analog-to-digital conversion before feeding to the digital controller. The quantity that is being measured like speed, temperature, pressure, displacement, strain, etc. are all continuous in nature and hence they are analog quantities. For example, accelerometers, speed sensors, pressure sensors, light sensors, temperature sensors etc.

☞ *The sensor that produces continuous signal with respect to time with analog output is called as Analog sensors.*

Digital sensors on the other hand work with discrete or digital data that can be directly interfaced with the digital controller. The output of a digital sensor has only two states, namely 'ON' and 'OFF'. ON is logic 1 and OFF is logic 0. A push button switch is the best example of a digital sensor. In general, the accuracy of a digital sensor is high when compared to an analog sensor.

☞ *Digital sensors produce digital outputs that can be directly interfaced with the digital controller.*

Often, the digital outputs are produced by adding an analog-to-digital converter to the sensing unit. If many sensors are required, it is more economical to choose simple analog sensors and interface them to the digital controller equipped with a multi-channel analog-to-digital converter.

There are some sensors which are capable of sensing a physical quantity to convert it to other form and also sense the output signal form to get back the quantity in original form known as *Inverse sensors*. For example a piezoelectric crystal when subjected to vibration generates voltage. At the same time when a piezo crystal is subjected to varying voltage they begin to vibrate. This property make them suitable to use in microphone and speakers.

The other type of classification is based on the means of detection used in the sensor. Some of the means of detection are Electric, Biological, Chemical, Radioactive etc.

There are different types of sensors used to measure the physical properties like heartbeat & pules, Speed, Heat transfer, temperature etc. Some of the most commonly used sensors and transducers for different stimuli (the quantity to be measured) are:

a. For sensing presence of an object, are proximity sensor implemented using different techniques like Optical (like Infrared or Laser), Ultrasonic, Hall Effect, Capacitive, etc. Proximity Sensors are used in Mobile Phones, Cars (Parking Sensors), industries (object alignment), Ground Proximity in Aircrafts, etc.
b. For sensing light, the input devices or sensors are photo diode, photo transistor, light dependent resistor and solar cells. The output devices or actuators are LEDs, displays, lamps and fiber optics. Infrared Sensor are light based sensor that are used in various applications like Proximity and Object Detection. IR Sensors are used as proximity sensors in almost all mobile phones, Robots, Industrial assembly, automobiles etc. IR Sensors are used to turn on street lights.

c. For sensing temperature, the sensors are thermistor, thermocouple, resistance temperature detectors (RTDs) and thermostat. Based on the requirement, different types of sensors are used for measuring temperature in different applications. The actuators are heaters. A temperature sensor, senses the temperature i.e., it measures the changes in the temperature. Temperature sensors are used everywhere like computers, mobile phones, automobiles, air conditioning systems, industries etc.
d. For sensing position, the input devices are potentiometer, proximity sensor, and differential transformer. The output devices are motor and panel meter. Accelerometer is a type of sensor that is used to detect changes in position, velocity, and vibration by sensing motion. It can be either analog or digital type. Gyroscope sensor to sense and determine the orientation with the help of Earth's gravity i.e. it measures the angular velocity.
e. For sensing pressure, the sensors are strain gauge and load cell. The actuators are lifts and jacks and electromagnetic vibrations. Pressure sensor works on the application of input voltage and pressure value. It produces an analog output voltage.
f. For sensing sound, the input devices are microphones and output devices are loudspeakers and buzzers.
g. For sensing speed, the sensors used are tachogenerator and Doppler Effect sensors. The actuators are motors and brakes. An Ultrasonic Sensor can be used to measure distance as well as velocity of an object. An Ultrasonic Sensor works based on the properties of the sound waves with frequency greater than that of the human audible range.

3.4 TYPES OF SENSORS

3.4.1 Position

A position sensor measures the position of an object; the position measurement can be either in absolute terms (absolute position sensor) or in relative terms (displacement sensor). Position sensors can be linear, angular, or multi-axis. (See Figure 3.2).

Figure 3.2 Position and Speed Sensor

3.4.2 Occupancy and motion

Occupancy sensors detect the presence of people and animals in a surveillance area, while motion sensors detect movement of people and objects. The difference between the two is that occupancy sensors will generate a signal even when a person is stationary, while a motion sensor will not. For example, Electric eye, Radar.

3.4.3 Velocity and Acceleration

Velocity (speed of motion) sensors may be linear or angular, indicating how fast an object moves along a straight line or how fast it rotates.

3.4.4 Force

Force sensors detect whether a physical force is applied and whether the magnitude of force is beyond a threshold. For example, force gauge, viscometer, tactile sensor (touch sensor).

3.4.5 Pressure

Pressure sensors are related to force sensors and measure the force applied by liquids or gases. Pressure is measured in terms of force per unit area. These sensors make it possible to create IoT systems that monitor systems and devices that are pressure propelled. With any deviation from standard pressure range, the device notifies the system administrator about any problems that should be fixed. (See Figure 3.3). For example, Barometer, Bourdon gauge, Piezometer.

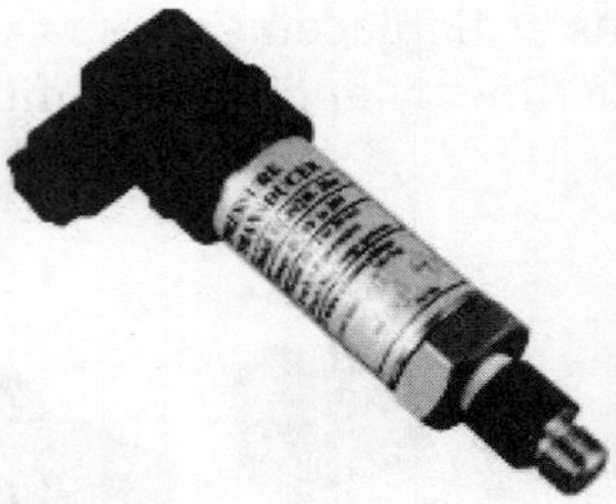

Figure 3.3 Pressure Sensor

3.4.6 Flow

Flow sensors detect the rate of fluid flow. They measure the volume (mass flow) or rate (flow velocity) of fluid that has passed through a system in a given period of time. For example, Anemometer, Mass flow sensor, Water meter etc.

3.4.7 Acoustic

Acoustic sensors measure sound levels and convert that information into digital or analog data signals. (See Figure 3.4). For example, Microphone, Geophone, Hydrophone.

Figure 3.4 Microphone and Sound Sensor

3.4.8 Humidity

Humidity is defined as the amount of water present in the surrounding air. Humidity sensors detect humidity (amount of water vapor) in the air or a mass. (See Figure 3.5). Humidity Sensor is one of the most important devices that has been widely in consumer, industrial, biomedical, and environmental applications for measuring and monitoring Humidity. For example, Hygrometer, Humistor, Soil moisture sensor. (See Figure 3.6).

Figure 3.5 Humidity Sensor

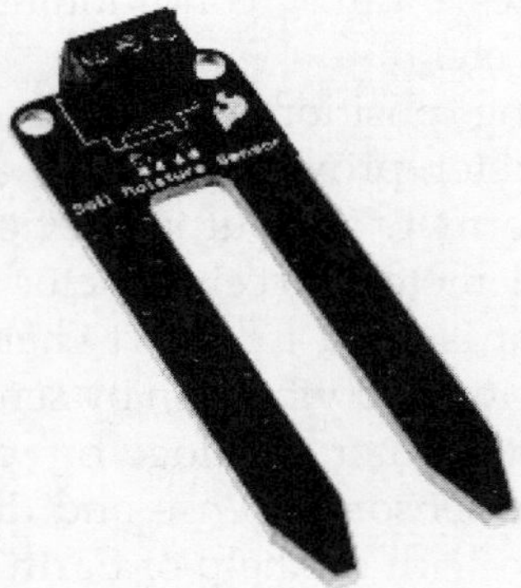

Figure 3.6 Soil and Moisture Sensor

3.4.9 Light

Light sensors detect the presence of light (visible or invisible). For example, Infrared sensor, Photodetector, Flame detector.

3.4.10 Radiation

Radiation sensors detect radiations in the environment. Radiation can be sensed by scintillating or ionization detection. For example, Scintillator, Neutron detector.

3.4.11 Temperature

Temperature sensors measure the amount of heat or cold that is present in a system. They can be broadly of two types: *contact* and *non-contact*. Contact temperature sensors need to be in physical contact with the object being sensed. Non-contact sensors do not need physical contact, as they measure temperature through convection and radiation. For example, Thermometer, Calorimeter, Temperature gauge.

3.4.12 Chemical

Chemical sensors measure the concentration of chemicals in a system. Chemical sensors are applied in a number of different industries. Their goal is to indicate changes in liquid or to find out air chemical changes. They play an important role in bigger cities, where it is necessary to track changes and protect the population. For example, Breathalyser, Smoke detector etc.

3.4.13 Image

Image sensors are instruments which are used to convert optical images into electronic signals for displaying or storing files electronically. The major use of image sensor is found in digital camera & modules, medical imaging and night vision equipment, thermal imaging devices, radar, sonar, media house, biometric etc.

3.4.14 Optical

Optical sensors measures the physical quantity of light rays and convert it into electrical signal which can be easily readable by user or an electronic instrument/device is called optical sensor. For example, Photodetector, Fiber Optics, Pyrometer etc.

3.4.15 Gas

Gas sensor plays a major role in detecting the gas leakage. These gas sensors are classified into various types based on the type of gas that to be detected. They are used in numerous industries such as manufacturing, agriculture and health and used for air quality monitoring, detection of toxic or combustible gas, hazardous gas monitoring in coal mines, oil & gas industries, chemical laboratory research.

3.4.16 Ultrasonic

Ultrasonic means the range of the frequencies. Its range is greater than audible range (>20 kHz) so even it is switched on, you can't sense these sound signals. Only specific speakers and receivers can sense those ultrasonic waves. It is used to detect the presence or to measure the distance of targets similar to radar or sonar.

3.4.17 Hall

Hall Sensor is the sensor which works on the Hall Effect. It can be defined as when a magnetic field is brought close to the current carrying conductor then a potential difference is developed across the given conductor. Using this property a Hall sensor is used to detect the magnetic field and gives output in terms of voltage.

3.4.18 Infrared sensors (IR)

An infrared sensor is a sensor which is used to sense certain characteristics of its surroundings by either emitting or detecting infrared radiation. It is also capable of measuring the heat being emitted by the objects. They are now used in a variety of IoT projects, especially in Healthcare as they make monitoring of blood flow and blood pressure simple. They are even used in a wide array of regular smart devices such as smartwatches and smartphones as well.

3.4.19 Biosensors

A Biosensor is an analytical device that detects changes in Biological processes and converts them into an electrical signal. Biosensors detect various biological elements such as organisms, tissues, cells, enzymes, antibodies, and nucleic acids. The main area of interest of Biosensor is the Medicine, Clinical and Diagnostics applications. Electrochemical based Biosensors are commonly used in biochemical labs and clinics to monitor and measure glucose levels as well as lactic acid. Glucometers are a type of Biosensors, which measure the concentration of glucose in blood. Apart from the desired medicine and health based applications, Biosensors have also found critical applications in several other fields like industrial processing, agriculture, food processing, pollution control etc. (See Figure 3.7).

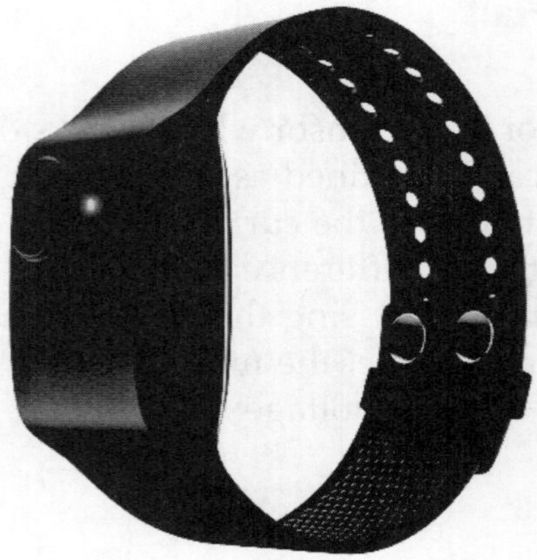

Figure 3.7 A Biosensor

3.4.20 Micro and Nanosensors

Microsensors (sometimes also called MEMS) are the miniaturized version of the conventional macrosensors with improved performance and reduced cost. Silicon micromachining technology has helped the development of many microsensors and continues to be one of the most active research and development topics in this area.
Vision microsensors have found applications in medical technology. A fiberscope of approximately 0.2 mm in diameter has been developed to inspect flaws inside tubes. Another example is a microtactile sensor, which uses laser light to detect the contact between a catheter and the inner wall of blood vessels during insertion that has sensitivity in the range of 1 mN. Similarly, the progress made in the area of nanotechnology has inspired the development of nanosensors. These are relatively new sensors that take one step further in the direction of miniaturization and are expected to open new ways for sensing applications.
All the above discussed sensors are included in a variety of devices and solutions. The trend is moving towards multi-sensor platforms that incorporate several sensing elements. For example, the standard for the next-generation of personalized self-tracking products appears to be some mix of an accelerometer, GSR sensor, temperature sensor, and heart rate sensor (from which heart rate variability may be calculated).

Let us see the various types of sensors that are available in the market and discuss their functionality, working, applications etc. You need to select the desired sensor based on your project or application.

IR LED

It is also called as IR Transmitter. It is used to emit Infrared rays. The range of these frequencies are greater than the microwave frequencies. The rays generated by an infrared LED can be sensed by Photodiode. The pair of IR LED and photodiode is called IR Sensor.

Photo Diode (Light Sensor)

It is a semiconductor device which is used to detect the light rays and mostly used as IR Receiver. Using a photodiode you can build a basic automatic street lamp which glows when the sunlight intensity decreases.

LDR (Light Dependent Resistor)

It is the resistor that depends upon the light intensity. It works on the principle of photoconductivity which means the conduction due to the light. When light falls on the LDR, its resistance decreases and acts similar to a conductor.

Thermistor (Temperature Sensor)

It is a temperature sensitive resistor that changes its physical resistance with the change in temperature. When the temperature increases the resistance decreases. So, the thermistor's resistance can be varied with the rise in temperature which causes more current flow through it. This change in current flow can be used to determine the amount of change in temperature.

Thermocouple (Temperature Sensor)

These are voltage devices that indicate temperature measuring with a change in voltage. As temperature goes up, the output voltage of the thermocouple rises.

Strain Gauge (Pressure/Force Sensor)

A strain gauge is used to detect pressure when a load is applied. It works on the principle of resistance, as the resistance is directly proportional to the length of the wire and is inversely proportional to its cross-sectional area. The same principle is applied here to measure the load. On a flexible board, a wire is arranged in a zig-zag manner so, when the pressure is applied to that particular board, it bends in a direction causing the change in overall length and cross-sectional area of the wire. This leads to change in resistance of the wire. The resistance thus obtained is very minute (few ohms) which can be determined with the help of the wheatstone bridge. The strain gauge is placed in one of the four arms in a bridge with the remaining values unchanged. Therefore, when the pressure is applied to it as the resistance changes the current passing through the bridge varies and pressure can be calculated. Strain gauges are majorly used to calculate the amount of pressure that an airplane wing can withstand and it is also used to measure the number of vehicles allowable on a particular road etc.

Load Cell (Weight Sensor)

Load cells are similar to strain gauges which measure the physical quantity like force and give the output in form of electrical signals. When some tension is applied on the load cell it structure varies causing the change in resistance.

Potentiometer

A potentiometer is used to detect the position. It generally has various ranges of resistors connected to different poles of the switch. A potentiometer can be either rotary or linear type.

Encoder

To detect the change in the position an encoder can also be used. It has a circular rotatable disk-like structure with specific openings in between such that when the IR rays or light rays pass through it only a few light rays get detected.

Accelerometer (Tilt Sensor)

An accelerometer sensor can sense the tilt or movement of it in a particular direction. It works based on the acceleration force caused due to the earth's gravity.

Microphone (Sound Sensor)

Microphone can be seen on all the smartphones or mobiles. It can detect the audio signal and convert them into small voltage (mV) electrical signals. A microphone can be of many types like condenser microphone, crystal microphone, carbon microphone etc., each type of microphone work on the properties like capacitance, piezoelectric effect, resistance respectively.

Proximity sensor

A device that detects the presence or absence of a nearby object, or properties of that object, and converts it into signal which can be easily read by user or a simple electronic instrument without getting in contact with them.

Photoelectric Sensors

Photoelectric sensor is made up of light-sensitive parts and uses a beam of light to detect the presence or absence of an object. It is an ideal alternative of inductive sensors. And used for long distance sensing or to sense non-metal object.

3.5 CRITERIA TO CHOOSE A SENSOR

A number of static and dynamic factors must be considered in selecting a suitable sensor to measure the desired physical parameter. Following is a list of typical factors:

a. **Range:** Difference between the maximum and minimum value of the sensed parameter. It indicates the limits of the input in which it can vary.
b. **Resolution:** The smallest change the sensor can differentiate.
c. **Accuracy:** The accuracy of the sensor is a key factor in selecting a sensor. It is the difference between the measured value and the true value.
d. **Precision:** Ability to reproduce repeatedly with a given accuracy.
e. **Sensitivity:** Sensitivity is a relationship between input physical signal and output electrical signal. It is the ratio of change in output of the sensor to unit change in input value that causes change in output.

f. **Ruggedness:** It is a measure of the durability when the sensor is used under extreme operating conditions.
g. **Linearity:** Percentage of deviation from the best-fit linear calibration curve. It is specified in terms of percentage of non-linearity which indicates deviation of curve of actual measurement from the curve of ideal measurement.
h. **Hysteresis:** The hysteresis is defined as the maximum difference in output at any measurable value within the sensor's specified range when approaching the point first with increasing and then with decreasing the input parameter.
i. **Response time:** The time lag between the input and output.
j. **Bandwidth:** Frequency at which the output magnitude drops.
k. **Resonance:** The frequency at which the output magnitude peak occurs.
l. **Operating temperature:** The range in which the sensor performs as specified.
m. **Signal-to-noise ratio:** Ratio between the magnitudes of the signal and the noise at the output.
n. **Type of Sensing:** The parameter that is being sensed like temperature or pressure.
o. **Power Consumption:** The power consumed by the sensor will play an important role in defining the total power of the system.
p. **Cost:** Depending on the cost of application, a low cost sensor or high cost sensor can be used.
q. **Repeatability:** It is the ability of the sensor to produce same output for different applications with same input value.
r. **Stability:** It is the ability of the sensor to produce the same output for constant input over a period of time.

3.6 ACTUATORS

Actuators convert information or energy from sensors into action by transmitting it to another power mechanism or system, such as heating or cooling a room (See Figure 3.8). No human intervention need be involved in the decision-making process. Actuators are basically the muscle behind a mechatronics system that accepts a control command (mostly in the form of an electrical signal) and produces a change in the physical system by generating force, motion, heat, flow, etc. Normally, the actuators are used in conjunction with the power supply and a coupling mechanism. The power unit provides either AC or DC power at the rated voltage and current. The coupling mechanism acts as the interface between the actuator and the physical system (See Figure 3.9). Typical mechanisms include rack and pinion, gear drive, belt drive, lead screw and nut, piston, and linkages.

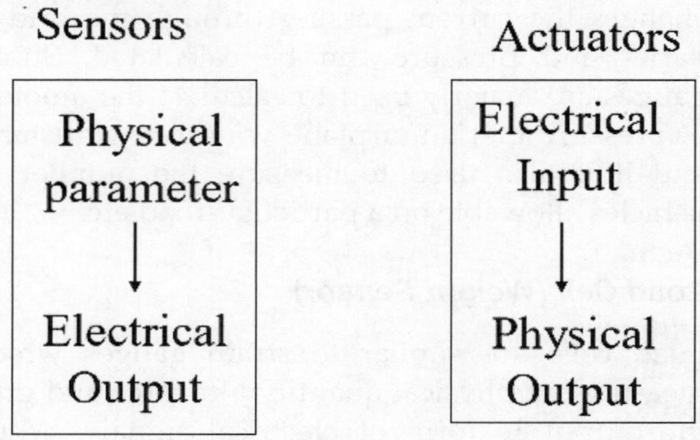

Figure 3.8 Sensor and Actuators

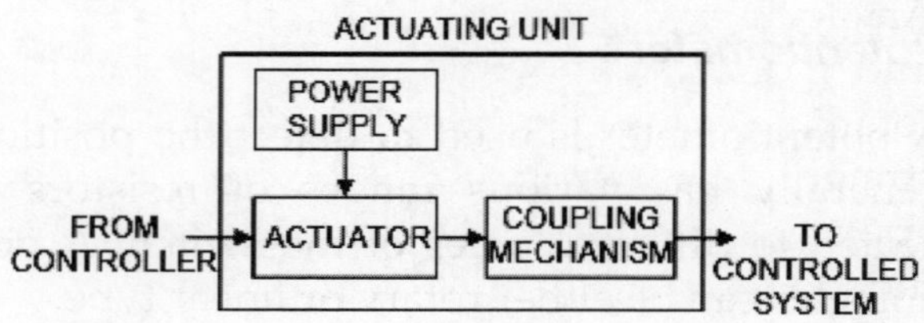

Figure 3.9 A Typical Actuating Unit

☞ *An actuator is a device that coverts an input energy into motion or mechanical energy.*

3.7 CLASSIFICATION OF ACTUATORS

An actuator is a type of motor for moving or controlling a mechanism or system. (See Figure 3.10) It is operated by a source of energy, typically electric current, hydraulic fluid pressure, or pneumatic pressure, and converts that energy into motion. An actuator is the mechanism by which a control system acts upon an environment. Actuators can be classified based on the type of energy. They are essentially of *Electrical, Electromechanical, Electromagnetic, Hydraulic,* or *Pneumatic type*. The new generations of actuators include *Smart Material Actuators, Micro-actuators,* and *Nanoactuators*.

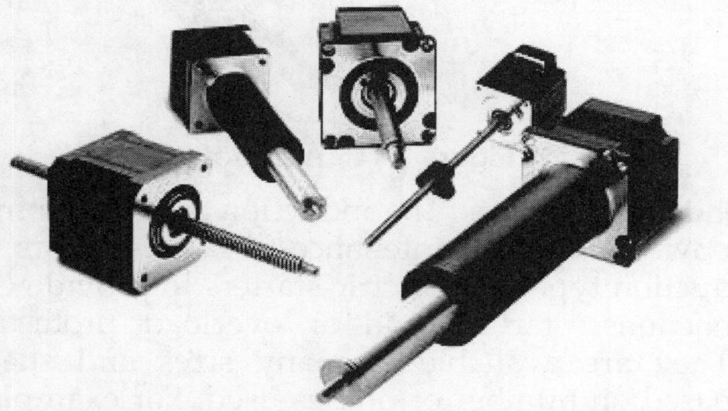

Figure 3.10 Different types of Actuator

Actuators can also be classified as binary and continuous based on the number of stable-state outputs. A relay with two stable states is a good example of a binary actuator. Similarly, a stepper motor is a good example of continuous actuator. When used for a position control, the stepper motor can provide stable outputs with very small incremental motion.

An actuator is something that converts energy into motion. Two basic motions are linear and rotary. Linear actuators convert energy into straight line motions, typically for positioning applications, and usually have a push and pull function. Some linear actuators are unpowered and manually operated by use of a rotating knob or handwheel. Rotary actuators convert energy to provide rotary motion.

An actuator requires a control signal and source of energy. An actuator typically is a mechanical device that takes energy usually energy that is created by air, electricity or liquid and converts it into some kind of motion. When the control signal is received, the actuator responds by converting the energy into mechanical motion. That motion can be in virtually any form, such as blocking, clamping or ejecting. Actuators typically are used in manufacturing or industrial applications and might be used in devices such as motors, pumps, switches and valves for *on* and *off* control, to control pressure, and to regulate flow.

3.7.1 Electrical Actuators

Electrical Actuator is an electromechanical device that converts electrical energy into mechanical energy. Most electric actuators operate through the interaction of magnetic fields and current-carrying conductors to generate force. Electrical switches are the choice of actuators for most of the on-off type control action. There are many designs of electric actuators and this depends on their function in the engine that they are installed in. Since no oil is involved, electrical actuators are considered to be one of the cleanest and readily available forms of actuators. Electric actuators are found in applications as diverse as industrial fans, blowers and pumps, machine tools, household appliances, power tools, and disk drives. (See Figure 3.11).

Figure 3.11 Electrical Actuator

3.7.2 Electromechanical Actuators

The most common electromechanical actuator is a motor that converts electrical energy to mechanical motion. (See Figure 3.12). Motors are the principal means of converting electrical energy into mechanical energy in industry. Broadly they can be classified as *DC Motors, AC Motors, Stepper Motors,* and *Servo Moter*:

Figure 3.12 A Motor

DC Motors

DC motors, move at variable speeds. In DC motors, the coil of wire (rotor) assembly rotates in an attempt to align itself with the stator assembly but is prevented by a part known as the commutator. At the precise moment, the commutator switches the rotor field while the stator assembly remains stationary. This provides the means to control speed and positioning. (See Figure 3.13).

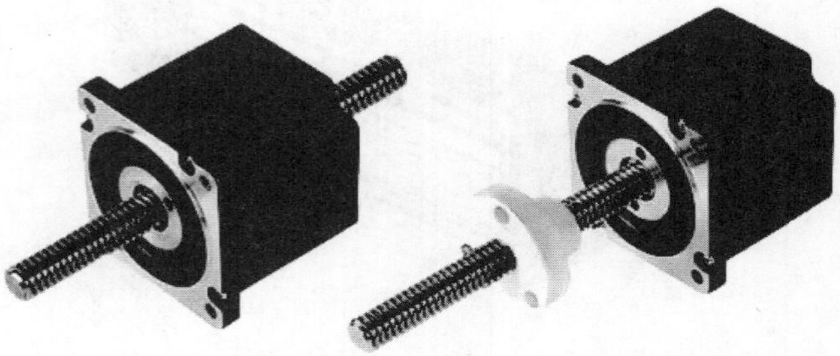

Figure 3.13 DC Motor

AC Motors

AC motors, which commonly move at a constant speed. AC motors are the most popular since they use standard AC power, do not require brushes and commutator, and are therefore less expensive. The speed of an AC motor is determined by the frequency of voltage applied by the number of magnetic poles. AC motors can be further classified as the *Induction Motors, Synchronous Motors,* and *Universal Motors* according to their physical construction. (See Figure 3.14).

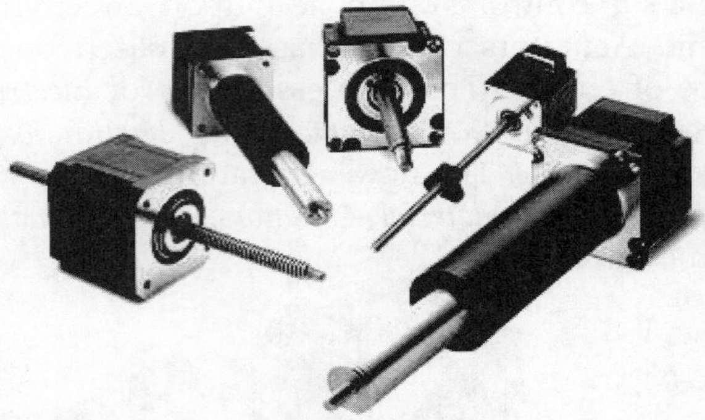

Figure 3.14 AC Motor

Induction Motors The induction motor is simple, powerful, and maintenance free. AC Motors (induction type) use electric starters to provide connections, startup, and/or overload protection. They are available in many sizes and shapes based on number of phases used. For example, a three-phase induction motor is used in large-horsepower applications, such as pump drives, steel mill drives, hoist drives, and vehicle drives. The two-phase servomotor is used extensively in position control systems. Single-phase induction motors are widely used in many household appliances.

Synchronous Motors The synchronous motor is one of the most efficient electrical motors in industry, so it is used in industry to reduce the cost of electrical power. In addition, synchronous motors rotate at synchronous speed, so they are also used in applications that require synchronous operations.

☞ *Within the AC motor are the stator assembly and the rotor assembly. If the AC motor is an induction motor, the rotor rotates slower than the stator's field. If it is a synchronous motor, the rotor and the stator move in synchronization.*

Universal Motors The universal motors operate with either AC or DC power supply. They are normally used in fractional horsepower application. The DC universal motor has the highest horsepower-per-pound ratio, but has a relatively short operating life.

Stepper Motors

Stepper motors (DC motor) are electromechanical, converting a digital pulse into rotational movement or displacement. With the rapid progress in low cost and high frequency solid-state drives, they are finding increased applications. The stepper motors are used widely in industrial control applications and horsepower applications. Stepper motors are not good for varying loads and are typically not energy efficient, they are great for constant loads and positional accuracy. (See Figure 3.15).

Figure 3.15 Stepper Motor

Servo Motors

Servo motors (DC motor) are extremely high performing with few weaknesses. Servos provide speed control and position accuracy due to its feedback device, are small, and priced relatively low. (See Figure 3.16).

Figure 3.16 Servo Motor

3.7.3 Electromagnetic Actuators

The solenoid is the most common electromagnetic actuator. A DC solenoid actuator consists of a soft iron core enclosed within a current carrying coil. When the coil is energized, a magnetic field is established that provides the force to push or pull the iron core. AC solenoid devices are also encountered, such as AC excitation relay. (See Figure 3.17).

Another important type is the electromagnet. The electromagnets are used extensively in applications that require large forces.

Figure 3.17 Electromagnetic Actuators

3.7.4 Hydraulic Actuators

Hydraulic and Pneumatic actuators are normally either rotary motors or linear piston/cylinder or control valves. They are ideally suited for generating very large forces coupled with large motion. (See Figure 3.18).

Hydraulic actuators consist of a cylinder or fluid motor that utilizes hydraulic power to facilitate mechanical process. Hydraulic motors output linear, rotary, or oscillating motion but acceleration is limited. They can produce very large forces coupled with large motion in a cost-effective manner. Hydraulic actuators can be operated manually, such as a hydraulic car jack, or they can be operated through a hydraulic pump, which can be seen in construction equipment such as cranes or excavators. The disadvantage with the hydraulic actuators is that they are more complex, typically inefficient, and require more than usual maintenance.

Figure 3.18 Hydraulic Actuator

3.7.5 Pneumatic Actuators

Pneumatic actuators work on the same concept as hydraulic actuators except compressed gas is used instead of liquid. Energy, in the form of compressed gas, is converted into linear or rotary motion. These are used in applications in which positional accuracy is not a requirement. The disadvantage with pneumatic actuator are they take up a lot of space, create a lot of noise and are difficult to transport once installed in a place. (See Figure 3.19).

Figure 3.19 Pneumatic Actuator

3.7.6 Smart Material Actuators

Unlike the conventional actuators, the smart material actuators typically become part of the load bearing structures. This is achieved by embedding the actuators in a distributed manner and integrating into the load bearing structure that could be used to suppress vibration, cancel the noise, and change shape. Of the many smart material actuators, Shape Memory Alloys, Piezoelectric (PZT), Magnetostrictive, Electrorheological Fluids, and Ion Exchange Polymers are most common.

Shape Memory Alloys

Shape Memory Alloys (SMA) are alloys of nickel and titanium that undergo phase transformation when subjected to a thermal field. When cooled below a critical temperature, their crystal structure enters martensitic phase. In this state the alloy is plastic and can easily be manipulated. When the alloy is heated above the critical temperature the phase changes to austenitic phase. Here, the alloy resumes the shape that it formally had at the higher temperature. For example, a straight wire at room temperature can be made to regain its programmed semicircle shape when heated that has found applications in orthodontics and other tensioning devices.

Piezoelectric

The PZT actuators are essentially piezocrystals with top and bottom conducting films. When an electric voltage is applied across the two conducting films, the crystal expands in the transverse direction. When the voltage polarity is reversed, the crystal contracts thereby providing bidirectional actuation.

Magnetostrictive

Magnetostrictive material is an alloy of terbium, dysprosium, and iron that generates mechanical strains up to 2000 microstrain in response to applied magnetic fields. They are available in the form of rods, plates, washers, and powder.

Ion exchange polymers

Ion exchange polymers exploit the electro-osmosis phenomenon of the natural ionic polymers for purposes of actuation. When a voltage potential is applied across the cross-linked polyelectrolytic network, the ionizable groups attain a net charge generating a mechanical deformation. These types of actuators have been used to develop artificial muscles and artificial limbs.

3.7.7 Microactuators

Microactuators, also called Micromachines Microelectromechanical System (MEMS), and microsystems are the tiny mobile devices being developed utilizing the standard microelectronics processes with the integration of semiconductors and machined micromechanical elements.

3.8 MICROCONTROLLER

A Microcontroller is a small computer on a single integrated circuit containing electronic computing unit and logic unit (combinedly known as CPU), Memory (Program Memory and Data Memory), I/O Ports (Input / Output Ports) and few other components integrated on a single chip. The CPU (Central Processing Unit) in a microcontroller performs the arithmetic, logic, math and data-oriented function. (See Figure 3.20).

Figure 3.20 A Microcontroller

☞ *Microcontroller is like a mini computer with a CPU along with RAM, ROM, serial ports, timers, and IO peripherals all embedded on a single chip.*

Microprocessors and microcontrollers are widely used in embedded system products. Microcontrollers are designed for embedded applications for specific tasks that require a certain degree of control in contrast to the microprocessors used in personal computers or other general purpose applications consisting of various discrete chips. A printer is an example of embedded system since the processor inside it performs only one task ; namely, getting the data and printing it.

Microcontroller is also called as a Computer-on-a-Chip or a Single-Chip-Computer. Since the Microcontroller and its supporting circuitry are often embedded in the device it controls, a Microcontroller is also called as an Embedded Controller.

Most modern Microcontrollers might contain even more peripherals like SPI (Serial Peripheral Interface), I2C (Inter Integrated Circuit), ADC (Analog to Digital Converter), DAC (Digital to Analog Converter), CAN (Controlled Area Network), USB (Universal Serial Bus), and many more.

There is a wide range of microcontrollers available in the market. Various companies like Atmel, ARM, Microchip, Motorola, Philips, Texas Instruments, Renesas, Freescale, NXP Semiconductors, etc. manufacture different kinds of microcontrollers with different kinds of features.

☞ *The first microcontroller was developed in 1971 by Texas Instruments and is called TMS 1000. It was made available for commercial use in 1974.*

3.8.1 Feature of Microcontrollers

a. Microcontroller has all the required peripherals on the same chip as the CPU. The integration of features like ADC, DAC etc. on the same chip as the CPU makes it more efficient and cheaper than to use a separate ADC Chip.
b. Developing a computer controlled system involves design of the hardware and also writing an efficient software program. Since a Microcontroller has all the hardware, that are required to make a computer controlled system on a single chip, using a Microcontroller will drastically reduce the efforts and time spent on hardware design and wiring.
c. Microcontrollers may be dedicated to one task and run one specific program. The program is stored in ROM and generally does not change. Also, microcontroller is a low-power device. A battery-operated microcontroller might consume as little as 50 mill watts.

☞ *Microcontrollers may be embedded inside some other device so that they can control the features or actions of the product therefore microcontroller is also know as embedded controller.*

3.8.2 Advantages of Microcontroller

a. A microcontroller is meant to be more self-contained and independent, and functions as a tiny, dedicated computer.
b. No need for any external interfacing of basic components like Memory, I/O Ports, etc.
c. Microcontrollers doesn't require complex operating systems as all the instructions must be written and stored in the memory.
d. All the Input/Output ports are programmable.
e. Integration of all the essential components reduces the cost, design time and area of the product (or application).

f. The great advantage of microcontrollers, as opposed to using larger microprocessors, is that the parts-count and design costs of the item being controlled can be kept to a minimum.
g. They are typically designed using CMOS (Complementary Metal Oxide Semiconductor) technology, an efficient fabrication technique that uses less power and is more immune to power spikes than other techniques.

3.8.3 Disadvantages of Microcontrollers

a. Microcontrollers are not known for their computation power.
b. The amount of memory limits the instructions that a microcontroller can execute.
c. No Operating System and hence, all the instruction must be written.
d. Less flexibility, because all components are integrated into the one chip.
e. MCUs tend to be application specific so the choice may be limited.

☞ *Microcontrollers are remarkably inexpensive yet offer tremendous performance.*

3.9 CLASSIFICATION OF MICROCONTROLLERS

Microcontrollers can be classified based on bus width, memory structure, instruction set and number of Input/Output pins.

3.9.1 Bus Width

Bus width indicates the size of the data bus. Higher bus widths often result in better performance. Microcontrollers come in 8 bit, 16 bit, 32 bit and 64 bit. Some most advanced microcontrollers have bits more than 64 which are capable of executing particular functions in the embedded systems. Based on bit configuration, the microcontroller is further divided into following categories:

8-bit Microcontroller

This type of microcontroller is used to execute smaller arithmetic and logical operations like addition, subtraction, multiplication division, etc. For example, Intel 8031 and 8051 are 8 bits microcontroller.

16-bit Microcontroller

This type of microcontroller is used to perform arithmetic and logical operations where higher accuracy and performance is required. In contrast to 8 bit microcontroller, 16 bit microcontroller executes program with higher precision and accuracy. For example, Intel 8096 is a 16-bit microcontroller.

32-bit Microcontroller

This type of microcontroller is generally used in automatically controlled appliances like automatic operational machines, medical appliances, robotics etc., where high durability and reliability is required.

3.9.2 Memory Structure

Microcontrollers need memory (RAM, ROM, EPROM, EEPROM, flash memory, etc.) to store programs and data. Based on the memory configuration, the microcontroller is further divided into two types i.e., embedded memory microcontroller and external memory microcontrollers.

Embedded Memory Microcontroller

In embedded memory microcontroller the data and program memory is embedded into the IC. For example, 8051 having program & data memory, I/O ports, serial communication, counters and timers and interrupts on the chip is an embedded microcontroller.

External Memory Microcontroller

External memory microcontrollers do not have program memory embedded on them and require an external chip for the same. For example, 8031 has no program memory on the chip is an external memory microcontroller. Now a day, all microcontrollers are embedded memory microcontrollers.

3.9.3 Instruction set

Based on the instruction set configuration, the microcontroller is classification into two categories CISC or RISC.

CISC

CISC stands for complex instruction set computer. It allows the user to insert a single instruction as an alternative to many simple instructions. The emphasis is on building complex instructions directly into the hardware. Majority of microcontrollers follow CISC architecture.

RISC

RISC stands for Reduced Instruction Set Computers. It reduces the operational time by shortening the clock cycle per instruction.

3.9.4 Number of Input/Output Pins

Microcontrollers vary according to the number of input-output pin sizes. One can choose a specific microcontroller as per the requirement of application.

☞ *Microcontrollers were originally programmed only in assembly language, but various high-level programming languages, such as C, Python and JavaScript, are now also in common use to target microcontrollers and embedded systems.*

3.10 COMPONENTS OF MICROCONTROLLER

Microcontroller consists of built in components including EPROM, EEPROM, RAM, ROM, timers, I/O ports and reset button. RAM is used for data storage while ROM is used for program and other parameters storage. Different components of a Microcontroller are discussed below:

3.10.1 CPU

Central Processing Unit or CPU is the brain of the Microcontroller. It behaves like a bridge that communicates with different components and activities happening inside the single chip. It consists of an Arithmetic Logic Unit (ALU) and a Control Unit (CU). ALU is responsible for timing of the communication process between the CPU and its peripherals. A CPU reads, decodes and executes instructions to perform Arithmetic, Logic and Data Transfer operations.

3.10.2 Memory

Similar to microprocessor, microcontroller comes with memory spaces such as RAM and ROM which help in storing the program source code. These memory spaces are very small as compared to desktop computers. Any Computational System requires two types of Memory:

Program Memory

Memory contains the program i.e., the instructions to be executed by the CPU. It is usually implemented as Read Only Memory or ROM, where the Program written in to it will be retained even when the power is down or the system is reset. The ROM used is normally the EEPROM (Electrically Erasable and Programmable ROM).

Data Memory

Data Memory in a Microcontroller is responsible for storing values of variables, temporary data, intermediate results and other data for proper operation of the program. Data Memory is required to store temporary data while executing the instructions. Usually, Program Memory is a Read Only Memory or ROM and the Data Memory is a Random Access Memory or RAM. Data Memory is sometimes called as Read Write Memory.

3.10.3 Input and Output Ports

The interface for the Microcontroller to the external world is provided by the I/O Ports or Input/Output Ports. Input Ports provide a gateway for passing on the data from the outside world with the help of sensors. Inputs device like Switches, Keypads, etc. provide information from the user to the CPU in the form of Binary Data. The CPU, upon receiving the data from the input devices, executes appropriate instructions and gives response through output devices like LEDs, displays, printers, etc. Generally, all ports in microcontrollers have dual functionality i.e., they can act as both input and output port.

3.10.4 System Bus

A System bus is a group of connecting wire that connect the CPU with other peripherals like Memory, I/O Ports and other supporting components.

3.10.5 Timers and Counters

Timers and Counters are very handy in achieving different tasks including pulse generation, frequency generation, measuring, clock function and modulation. Timer is used to provide a delay and counter which is used to count incoming pulses. Timer and counters functions are synchronized with microcontroller clock, used for measuring time intervals between two events and can count up to 255 count for 8 bit microcontroller and 65535 for 16 bit microcontroller.

3.10.6 Serial Port

One of the important requirement of a Microcontroller is to communicate with other device and peripherals (external). Serial Port proves such interface through serial communication. There are several serial ports available in the microcontroller which are used to connect peripherals serially with the microcontroller.

3.10.7 Interrupt Control

Interpret control is used to put a delay in the running program. Interrupts can be external, internal, hardware related or software related.

3.10.8 ADC (Analog to Digital Converter)

Analog to Digital Converter or ADC is a circuit that converts Analog signals to Digital Signals. The ADC Circuit forms the interface between the external Analog Input devices and the CPU of the Microcontroller. Almost all sensors are analog devices and the analog data from these sensors must be converted in to digital data for the CPU to understand.

3.10.9 DAC (Digital to Analog Converter)

DIgital to Analog Converter or DAC is a circuit, that works in contrast to an ADC i.e., it converts Digital Signals to Analog Signals. DAC forms the bridge between the CPU of the Microcontroller and the external analog devices.

3.11 TYPES OF MICROCONTROLLERS

3.11.1 Microcontroller 8051

8051 microcontroller is an 8-bit family of microcontroller is developed by the Intel in the year 1981. This is one of the popular families of microcontroller being used all across the world. 8051 microcontroller is a 40 pin 8 bit microcontroller. The CPU can also work for 8 bits of data at a time. In case the data is bigger than 8 bits, then it has to be broken into parts so that the CPU can process easily. 8051 consists of 5 interrupts including External interrupt 0, external interrupt 1, Timer interrupt 0, timer interrupt 1 and Serial port interrupt. It also consists of four 8 bits programmable ports. (See Figure 3.21).

It is divided into two category. They are Program Memory and Data Memory. Program Memory stores the program being executed whereas Data Memory temporarily stores the data and the results. The 8051 has been in use in a wide number of devices, mainly because it is easy to integrate into a device. Microcontrollers are mainly used in energy management, touch screen, automobiles, and medical devices. Portable electronics such as cell phones, media players and gaming devices are examples of microcontroller-based touch screens. Other applications of 8051 Microcontroller are TVs, Home Security Systems, Garage Door Openers, Defense Systems, Medical Equipment, Robotics, Remote Sensing etc.

Features of 8051 Microcontroller

- It is 8 bit Microcontroller.
- It has 128 bytes of on chip RAM.
- The data memory can be expanded up to 64kb.
- It has 4 parallel I/O port: port0, port1, port2, port3. Each port is 8-bit directional I/O port. Each port is bit/byte addressable.
- It has on chip oscillator and CLK generator circuit with operating frequency 12MHz.

It is a CISC based Microcontroller with Harvard Architecture (separate program and data memory).

Figure 3.21 8051 Microcontroller

1.2 AVR Microcontroller

'R microcontroller was developed in the year 1996 by Atmel Corporation. The structural sign of AVR was developed by the Alf-Egil gen and Vegard Wollan. The AVR microconllers are modified harvard RISC architecture :h separate memories for data and program d speed of AVR is high when compare to 8051 d PIC. The AVR stands for Alf-Egil Bogen and gard Wollan's RISC processor. There are many 'R family microcontrollers, such as ATmega8, 'mega16 and ATmega328 etc. There are many plications of AVR microcontroller; they are ed in home automation, touch screen, automoes, bio-medical devices, robotics, and defense e Figure 3.22). AVR Microcontrollers are ssified into three types:

TinyAVR: Less memory, small size, suitable only for simpler applications.
MegaAVR: These are the most popular ones having good amount of memory (up to 256 KB), higher number of inbuilt peripherals and suitable for moderate to complex applications.
XmegaAVR: Used commercially for complex applications, which require large program memory and high speed.

tures of AVR Microcontroller:

16KB of In-System Programmable Flash
512B of In-System Programmable EEPROM
16-bit Timer with extra features
Multiple internal oscillators.
Internal, self-programmable instruction flash memory up to 256K.

Figure 3.22 AVR Microcontroller

- Optional boot code section with independent lock bits for protection.
- Universal serial interface (USI) for two/three-wire synchronous data transfer.
- Low-voltage devices operating down to 1.8v
- 10-bit A/D Converters, with multiplex of up to 16 channels

3.11.3 PIC Microcontroller

Peripheral Interface Controller (PIC) is microcontroller developed by a Microchip, PIC microcontroller is fast and simple to implement program when you contrast other microcontrollers like 8051. It is controlled by the software. They could be programmed to complete many task and control a generation line and many more. PIC microcontrollers are finding their way into new applications like smart phones, audio accessories, video gaming peripherals and advanced medical devices. There are many PICs, started with PIC16F84 and PIC16C84. But these were the only affordable flash PICs. Microchip has recently introduced flash chips with types that are much more attractive, such as 16F628, 16F877 and 18F452. The 16F877 is around twice the price of the old 16F84, but has eight times the code size, much more RAM, much more I/O pins, a UART, A/D converter and a lot more. (See Figure 3.23).

Features of PIC Microcontroller:

- It is a RISC design.
- Its code is extremely efficient, allowing the PIC to run with typically less program memory than its larger competitors.
- It is low cost, high clock speed.

Figure 3.23 PIC Microcontroller

- The performance of the PIC microcontroller is very fast because of using RISC architecture. However, the length of the program is high due to using RISC architecture.
- When comparing to other microcontrollers, power consumption is very less and programming is also very easy.
- Interfacing of an analog device is easy without any extra circuitry
- PIC microcontroller supports Harvard architecture.
- Special purpose registers are also incorporated on chip hardware.
- Serial port or USB port is used to connect the computer with the microcontroller.

3.11.4 ARM Microcontroller

The ARM microcontroller stands for Advance Risk Machine. It is one of the extensive and most licensed processor cores in the world. The first ARM processor was developed in the year 1978 by Cambridge University, and the first ARM RISC processor was produced by the Acorn Group of Computers in the year 1985. ARM processors are widely used in customer electronic devices such as smart phones, tablets, multimedia players and other mobile devices, such as wearables. Because of their reduced to instruction set, they need fewer transistors, which enable a smaller die size of the integrated circuitry (IC). The ARM processors, smaller size reduced difficulty and lower power expenditure makes them suitable for increasingly miniaturized devices. (See Figure 3.24).

The ARM Cortex series of cores encompasses a very wide range of scalable performance options offering designers a great deal of choice and the opportunity to use the best-fit core for their application without being forced into a one-size-fits-all solution. The Cortex portfolio is split broadly into three main categories:

- Cortex-A application processor cores for a performance-intensive systems.
- Cortex-R high-performance cores for real-time applications.
- Cortex-M microcontroller cores for a wide range of embedded applications.

Figure 3.24 ARM Microcontroller

Features of ARM Microcontroller:

- ARM Processors (or Microcontrollers) are based on the Reduced Instruction Set Computer (RISC) architecture.
- ARM processors are available from small microcontrollers like the ARM7 series to the powerful processors like Cortex- A series that are used in today's smart phones.
- ARM based microcontrollers are advanced set of processors and hence for beginners, it might be a little difficult to understand.
- An ARM makes at 32-bit and 64-bit RISC multi-core processors.
- RISC processors are designed to perform a smaller number of types of computer instructions so that they can operate at a higher speed, performing extra millions of instructions per second (MIPS).
- Incorporate features of Berkeley RISC design - a large register file - a load/storearchitecture - uniform and fixed length instruction field - simple addressing mode.
- Based on Von Neumaan Architecture or Harvard Architecture.

3.11.5 Renesas Microcontroller

Renesas is latest automotive microcontroller family that offers high performance feature with exceptionally low power consumption over a wide and versatile extend of items. This microcontroller offers rich functional security and embedded safety characteristics required for new and advanced automotive applications. The core structure of microcontroller CPU support high reliability and high performance requirements.

The Renesas microcontroller offering low power, high performance, modest packages and the largest range of memory sizes combined together with characteristics rich peripherals. (See Figure 3.25).

Figure 3.25 Renesas Microcontroller

Renesas offers the most versatile microcontroller families in the world for example, RX family offers a many types devices with memory variants from 32K flash/4K RAM to an incredible 8M flash/512K RAM.

Application of Renesas Microcontroller are Industrial automation, Communication applications, Motor control applications, Test and measurement, Medical applications.

Features of the RX Microcontrollers:

- Low power consumption is realized using multi-core technology.
- Support for 5V operation for industrial and appliance designs.
- Scalability from 48 to 145 pins and from 32KB to 1MB flash memory, with 8KB of data flash memory included.
- Integrated safety feature.

3.12 APPLICATION OF MICROCONTROLLER

If a device or an application involves measuring, storing, calculating, controlling or displaying information, then device contains a Microcontroller in it. Microcontrollers are used in automatically controlled products and devices, such as automobile engine control systems, implantable medical devices, remote controls, office machines, appliances, power tools, toys and other embedded systems. By reducing the size and cost compared to a design that uses a separate microprocessor, memory, and input/output devices, microcontrollers make it economical to digitally control even more devices and processes.

a. In Automobiles Industry Microcontroller is used in cars for the purpose of engine control.
b. Consumer Electronics such as Digital Cameras, Video Camcorders, CD and DVD Players, Washing Machines, Ovens, etc., are loaded with Microcontrollers.
c. Microcontrollers are also used in test and measurement equipment like Multimeters, Oscilloscopes, Function Generators, etc.
d. Microcontrollers are also used in Printers, Routers, Modems, Keyboards, etc.
e. Microcontrollers are widely used in Light sensing and controlling devices like LED.
f. It is used in Temperature sensing and controlling devices like microwave oven, chimneys.
g. It is also used in fire detection and safety devices like Fire alarm.

3.13 EMBEDDED SYSTEM

An Embedded System is a combination of Hardware and Software. An embedded system can be an independent system or it can be a part of a large system. It is a microcontroller or microprocessor based system which is designed to perform a specific task. It is more of an application oriented system i.e., it is dedicated to perform a single task (See Figure 3.26). For example, a fire alarm is an embedded system; it will sense only smoke.

Starting from consumer electronics like Digital Cameras, DVD Players to high end and advanced systems like Flight Controllers and Missile Guidance Systems, embedded systems are popular and became an important part of our life.

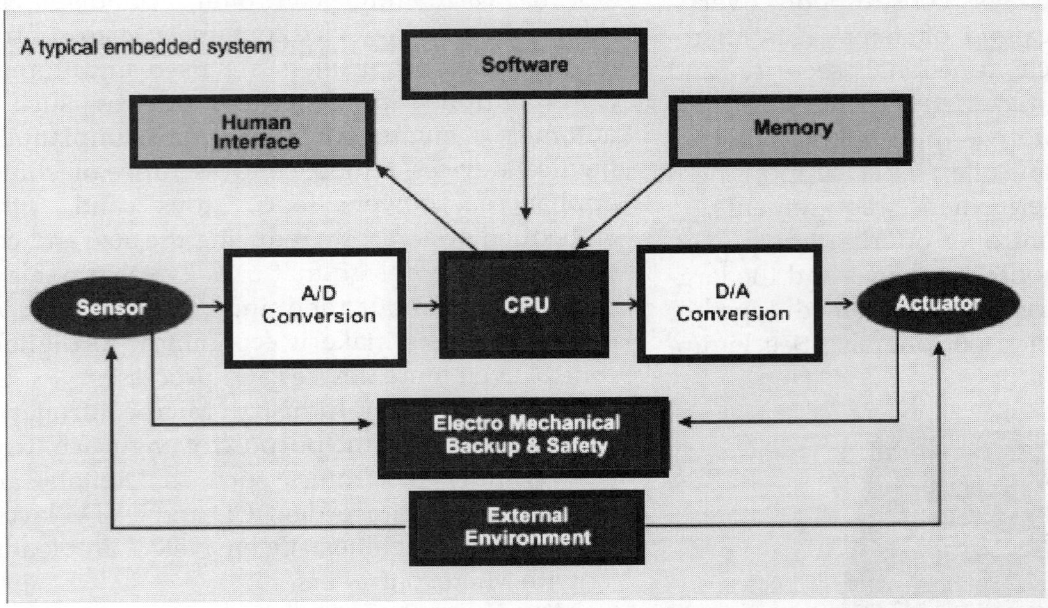

Figure 3.26 A typical Embedded System

☞ *An embedded system as a Microcontroller based is software driven, reliable, real-time control system.*

3.13.1 Components of Embedded System

An Embedded System consists of four main components. They are the Processor (Microprocessor or Microcontroller), Memory (RAM and ROM), Peripherals (Input and Output) and Software (Main program). Many Embedded Systems, usually small to medium scaled systems, generally consists of a Microcontroller as the main processor. With the help of a Microcontroller, the processor, memory and few peripherals will be integrated in to a single device.

Processor

The heart of an Embedded System is the Processor. Based on the functionality of the system, the processor can be anything like a General Purpose Processor, a Single Purpose Processor, an Application Specific Processor, a Microcontroller or an FPGA.

Memory

Memory is another important part of an embedded system. It is divided in to RAM and ROM. Memory in an Embedded System ROM stores the main program and RAM stores the program variables and temporary data.

Peripherals

In order to communicate with the outside world or control the external devices, an Embedded System must have Input and Output Peripherals. Some of these peripherals include Input / Output Ports, Communication Interfaces, Timers and Counters, etc.

Software

All the hardware work according to the software (main program) written. Software part of an Embedded System includes initialization of the system, controlling inputs and outputs, error handling etc. It has Real Time Operating System (RTOS) that supervises the application software and provide mechanism to let the processor run a process as per scheduling by following a plan to control the latencies.

3.13.2 Characteristics of an Embedded Systems

The important characteristics of an embedded systems are speed, size, power, reliability, accuracy, adaptability. Therefore, when the embedded system performs the operations at high speed, then it can be used for real-time applications. Different characteristics of Embedded system are discussed below:

a. An embedded system usually performs a specialized operation and does the same repeatedly.
b. It must be of a size to fit on a single chip, must perform fast enough to process data in real time and consume low power to extend battery life.
c. Many embedded systems must continually react to changes in the system's environment and must compute certain results in real time without any delay.
d. Dedicated to one task and run one specific program. The program is stored in ROM and generally does not change.
e. Mobile embedded systems are used in portable embedded devices like cell phones, mobiles, digital cameras, mp3 players and personal digital assistants, etc. The basic limitation of these devices is the other resources and limitation of memory.

3.14 REAL TIME EMBEDDED SYSTEM

A real time embedded system is a type of computer system with timing constraints i.e. a system which responds to external events or input stimuli in a timely fashion (within finite and specified time).

The two important characteristics of any real time embedded system are the real time embedded system must generate correct computational responses to the events (functional constraints) and the responses or results must be produced within a predefined time (timing constraints).

3.14.1 Types of Real Time Systems

Real Time Systems are classified into two types. They are:

a. Hard Real Time Systems
b. Soft Real Time Systems

Hard Real Time Systems

In Hard Real Time Systems, there is no flexibility in timing constraints i.e. they must meet all the deadlines, failing to do will result in a catastrophic consequences. A hard real time system must produce accurate responses to the events within specified time period. If either of them are not achieved i.e. if the response isn't accurate or if the response isn't delivered in right time, the result will be extremely catastrophic, like loss of life. For example, flight control systems, missile guidance systems, weapons defense system, etc.

Soft Real Time Systems

On the other hand, Soft Real Time Systems have some relaxation in meeting the deadlines i.e. the degree of tolerance is non-zero. A Soft Real Time System must produce response to an event within the deadline but with some flexibility in meeting the deadlines. Even if the response isn't delivered in the deadline (but delivered in acceptable limit), the result won't be catastrophic or failure in the system but will cost a delay in propagation. For example, set top boxes, DVD players, weather monitoring systems etc.

3.15 MICROPROCESSOR

A microprocessor is an *Integrated Circuit* (IC) that contains the Central Processing Unit (CPU) (See Figure 3.27). For a microprocessor to work, it needs a bunch of supporting hardware that can be found on a mother board. The hardware includes memory, ICs for peripheral devices, etc. The main task of a microprocessor is to accept data as input from input devices then process this data according to the instructions and provide the result of these instructions as output through output devices.

In the world of personal computers, the terms microprocessor and CPU are used interchangeably. A microprocessor (sometimes abbreviated µP) is a digital electronic component with miniaturized transistors on a single semiconductor Integrated Circuit (IC). One or more microprocessors typically serve as a Central Processing Unit (CPU) in a computer system or handheld device. Some examples of microprocessor are Pentium, i3, i5, i7, i9 etc.

Figure 3.27 Microprocessor

3.16 EVOLUTION OF MICROPROCESSOR

The first microprocessor was the Intel 4004, introduced in 1971. The 4004 was not very powerful; it was primarily used to perform simple mathematical operations in a calculator. The 4004 contained only 2300 transistors and performed 60,000 calculations per second.

☞ *Intel 4004, a 4-bit CPU released by Intel Corporation in 1971, is considered as the first commercial microprocessor.*

Figure 3.28 Intel Core i5 processor

Figure 3.29 Core i7 processor

It was quickly succeeded by the 8008, which was twice as powerful. In 1978, Intel released the 16-bit 8086 processor. The 8088, also a 16-bit chip, followed less than a year later. The 8088 incorporated technologies designed to make it backward-compatible with the 8-bit chips that were still in wide use at the time. IBM chose the 8088 chip to power their original Personal Computer. And so it was that IBM, Intel, and a little startup company called Microsoft brought computing to the masses. In the early 1990's, Intel released the i386 processor. The 386 was the first commercially available 32-bit microprocessor. For the first time, it made multitasking (running more than one program at a time) possible on desktop computers. The i486 added an onboard math co-processor, improved data transfer, and an onboard memory cache, all of which were stunning advances in technology in that era. The Intel Pentium processor, released in 1993, was the first commercially available microprocessor capable of executing two instructions for every clock cycle. Later releases in the Pentium line revolutionized everything from the way data is moved about on the chips, to the way that multimedia content is handled. Those improvements have since been eclipsed, however, by Intel's line of multi-core, 64-bit processors, such as the popular Core(tm) series.

Today Intel has many major brands for mainstream consumer PC's, Core(tm) 2, Core(tm) i7 and Core(tm) i5. The Core 2 family was introduced in 2006 and is available in dual core (Core 2(tm) Duo) as well as quad core (Core 2(tm) Quad) configurations. Intel's Core 2 processors are offered with varying clock speeds, cache sizes and bus speeds. The Core i7 and Core i5 are based on what is known as the Nehalem architecture and are very different from the Core 2 based processors. (See Figure 3.28 and 3.29).

3.17 MAJOR PARTS OF MICROPROCESSOR

The major parts of a microprocessor are: (See Figure 3.30)

a. Arithmetic Logical Unit (ALU)

b. Control Unit (CU)

These are further elaborated as follows:

Arithmetic and Logic unit (ALU): The Arithmetic Logic Unit (ALU) of a computer system is the place where the actual execution of instructions takes place during the processing operation. To be more precise, all calculations are performed and all comparisons including logical are made in the ALU.

Control unit: Control Unit is responsible for controlling the entire functioning of the ALU. It receives instructions from the main memory and executes them after decoding. The timing and control signals are generated by this unit and sent to other units for execution of the program. It also transfers data between memory and input/output devices.

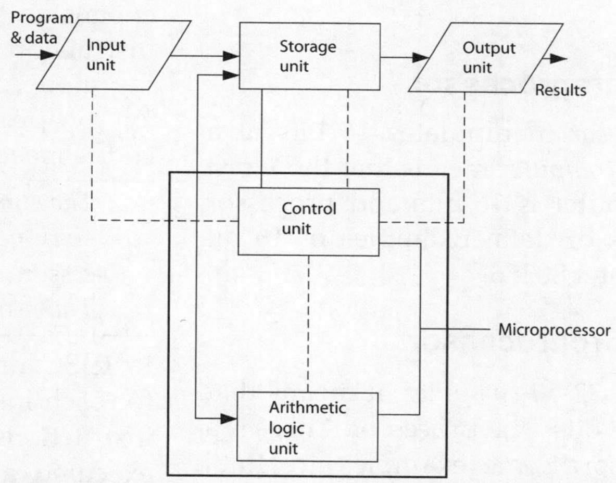

Figure 3.30 Major Parts of Microprocessor shown in thick black lined block

☞ *A **microprocessor** contains a Control Unit and an Arithmetic and Logic Unit (ALU). When main memory is added to a microprocessor, it forms a CPU.*

3.18 CHARACTERISTICS OF MICROPROCESSOR

Three basic characteristics of microprocessor are discussed below:

Instruction Set : The set of instructions that the microprocessor can execute are called instruction set.

Word Length : The number of bits that a computer can manipulate or process at a time is called its *word length*. The commonly used word lengths are: 8, 16, 32 or 64 bits. It is a measure of the computing power of a computer. Computers with longer word lengths are more powerful. When you talk of a 32-bit computer, it means that its word length is 32 bits.

Clock Speed : In a computer, *clock speed* means the number of pulses per second generated by an oscillator that sets the number of times the processor processes and operates on data in a second. Clock speed is a measure of how quickly a computer completes basic computations and operations. Clock speed is generally measured in MHz (megahertz or million pulses per second) and GHz (gegahertz or billion pulses per second).

3.19 CLASSIFICATION OF MICROPROCESSORS

Microprocessors are classified into different types on the basis of the number of bits of operations at a time. Based on bits of operation at a time, microprocessors are also classified into the following types:

3.19.1 8-Bit Microprocessor

An *8-bit microprocessor* can handle a combination of 8-bits at a time. These bits are formed by 0s and 1s such as 10011000, 01110001, etc. The most popular 8-bit microprocessor was Intel 8085. But such processors are now superceded by more powerful ones.

3.19.2 16-Bit Microprocessor

A *16-bit microprocessor* manipulates 16 bits at a time. Thus, a *16 bit computer* means that the word length of this computer is 16 bits and processor manipulates 16 bits of data. Examples of 16 bit microprocessor is Intel 80286.

3.19.3 32-Bit Microprocessor

When you talk of a *32-bit computer*, it means that its word length is 32 bits. The processor it uses is a 32-bit microprocessor. Some examples are Intel 80386, 80486, Intel Pentium, Celeron, AMD Sempron, etc. These types of microprocessors are widely used in PCs.

3.19.4 64-Bit Microprocessor

64-bit microprocessors are used in powerful workstations and mini computers. An important 64-bit microprocessor based computer is DEC's Alpha Server. 64-bit microprocessors are mostly used in servers, minicomputers and high-end workstations. An example of 64-bit microprocessor is AMD Athlon. Operating systems such as Windows 7, Windows 8, Windows 10, Linux, BSD and Mac OS X also run on 64-bit microprocessor. These operating systems fully utilize the capabilities of such processors.

Based on the instruction set, microprocessors a also classified into:

a. CISC (Complex Instruction Set Computin These types of processors are used in deskto laptops and high end servers used in busine
b. RISC (Reduced Instruction Set Computir These types of processors are commonly us in ovens, air conditioners, etc.
c. EPIC (Explicitly Parallel Instruction Comp ing): It is a computer architecture t combines the best feature of RISC and CISC

3.20 CISC

CISC stands for Complex Instruction Set Co puter. CISC computers are designed with a f set of computer instructions as needed to g processing capabilities in the most efficient w However, CISC processors are very complex a expensive to produce but they have large siz instruction sets and different variety of addre ing modes. Therefore, such processors make job of programmers easy in writing comp codes speedily.

☞ *The Cyrix 6x86 supporting CISC architecture sixth-generation, 32-bit x86-compatible microp cessor. It was manufactured by IBM and S Thomson.*

In CISC processor, a microprogram is execu for each instruction using the sequence of mic instructions. When a micro-instruction executed, a set of control signals are produced the execution of instruction. For each mic instruction, there is a microcode which is stored the ROM. Thus, the availability of micro-code i ROM enables checking of micro-instruction to carried out more easily. If there is an error in a micro-instruction then the designer can chan that micro-instruction in the ROM easily rat than changing the whole program instruction.

A CISC processor has the following properties

a. CISC processors have relatively large instru tion sets.
b. CISC machines have variable-length instru tion formats.
c. Many addressing modes are used in C machines
d. The CISC machines use microprogramming

e. CISC machines are more complex and less efficient.
f. Small numbers of general-purpose registers are employed in CISC machines.

☞ *The micro-instructions of a microprogram in CISC based PC system are executed one by one, and in turn, the necessary control signals are produced in steps for the execution of an instruction.*

3.21 RISC

RISC refers to Reduced Instruction Set Computer. It is the opposite of CISC (Complex Instruction Set Computer). In this type of microprocessor, most of the instructions for computer processing are relatively simple and computers are designed to handle those simple instructions extremely fast.

☞ *The term RISC was coined by David Patterson. He is also known as one of the innovators of the Redundant Arrays of Independent Disks (RAID) and Network of Workstations (NOW).*

RISC microprocessors are used extensively in high-end workstations and other expensive computer systems. Popular RISC microprocessor families include Sun Microsystems' SPARC (Scalar Processor ARChitecture), Intel's i860, and Motorola's 88000. A RISC processor has the following properties:

a. RISC microprocessors have relatively small instruction sets
b. RISC machines have fixed and easily decoded instruction formats.
c. Few addressing modes are used in RISC machines
d. Hardwired controls are used in RISC machines
e. RISC machine is 5 to 10 times faster than a CISC machine.
f. Several general-purpose registers are employed in RISC machines.

☞ *Software packages developed for RISC microprocessors provide a larger but simpler instruction set than software developed for CISC systems.*

3.22 EPIC

EPIC (Explicitly Parallel Instruction Computing) is a computer architecture that combines the best feature of RISC and CISC. A EPIC processor has the following properties:

a. EPIC does not use fixed with instruction, rather aims at parallel processing of instructions.
b. Programs must be written using sequential semantics with explicitly laid out parallelism.
c. It uses a bundle of complex instructions that in addition to basic instruction also contain information on how to run the instruction in parallel with other instructions.

3.23 ARCHITECTURE OF MICROPROCESSOR

The architecture of microprocessor chip is a description of the physical layout of the various elements that form it. It directly affects how information and electrical current flows throughout the chip. A microprocessor can either have a CISC, or complex instruction set computer, architecture or a RISC, or reduced instruction set computer, architecture. The CISC architecture is more complex and has the ability to perform complex commands. The RISC architecture is simpler, smaller and faster. Microprocessor architecture has evolved from single core processors to multicore processors. Processors with two or more cores are faster because they can process multiple pieces of information simultaneously. The basic components of microprocessor architecture include:

3.23.1 CPU

The CPU ("Central Processing Unit," synonymous with "microprocessor," or even simply "processor") is often referred to as the "brain" of the computer. It does the bulk of the processing and co-ordinates all of the other pieces of hardware so your computer works as it should do.

A microprocessor is a computer processor which incorporates the functions of a computer's central processing unit (CPU) on a single integrated circuit (IC), or at most a few integrated circuits. A microprocessor is a controlling unit of a micro-computer, fabricated on a small chip capable of performing Arithmetic Logical Unit (ALU) operations and communicating with the other devices connected to it. The central processing unit is responsible for handling instructions passed to it by programs and input devices. The Arithmetic Logic Unit handles the arithmetic and logic functions. The Control Unit is responsible for processing instructions that come from the computer's memory and activating the other components of the computer.

3.23.2 Input/Output Devices

Inputting refers to the process of entering data into the computer. Outputting refers to the process of showing the information or data to the user. Input-output devices are also called as peripherals. The data is retrieved from memory or taken from an input device and the result of processing is stored in the memory or delivered to an appropriate output device, all as per the instructions.

☞ *Input/output instructions are the instructions used for interacting with user, i.e., getting data from the user or showing data to the user through monitor or printer.*

3.23.3 Memory

It stores both the instructions to be executed (i.e., the program) and the data involved. It usually consists of both RAMs (Random Access Memories) and ROMS (Read Only Memories).

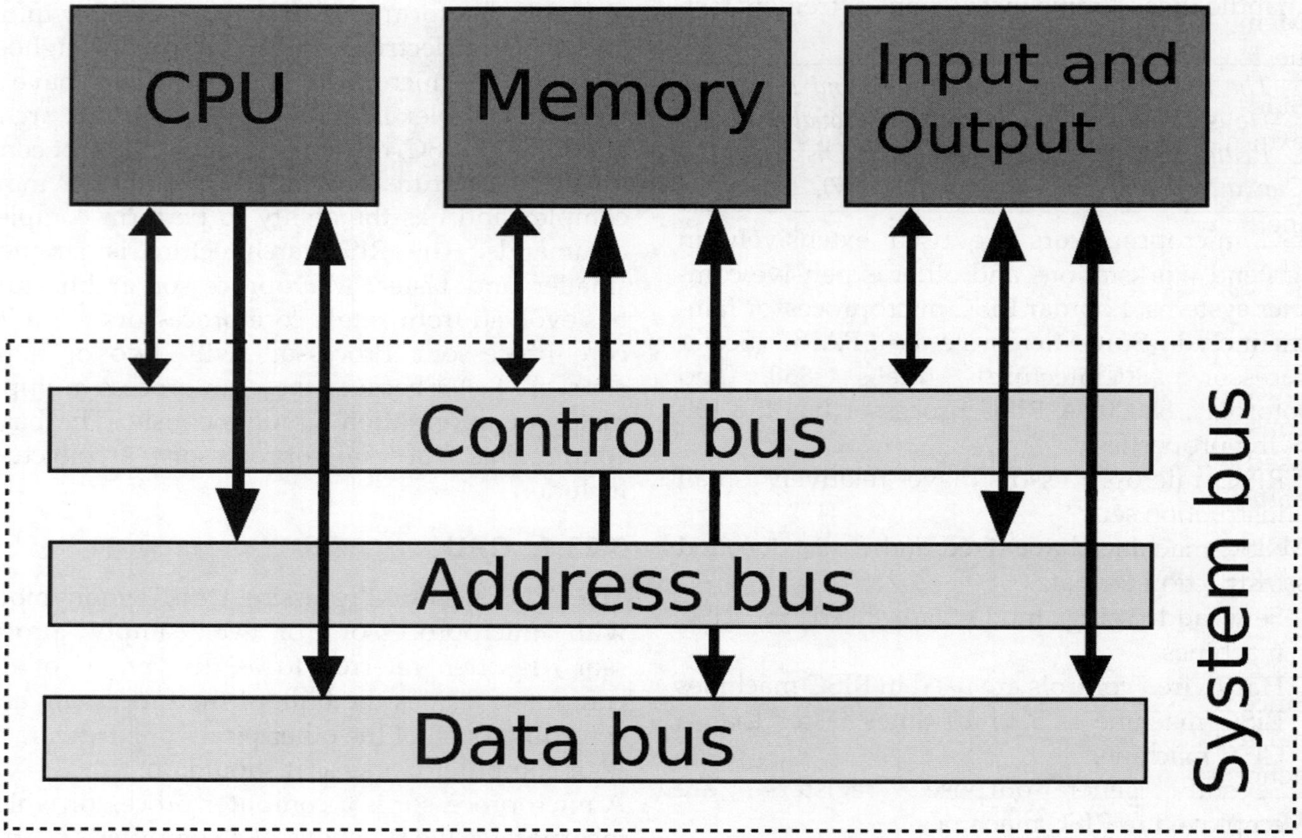

Figure 3.31 Architecture of Micoprocessor

3.24 MICROPROCESSOR vs MICROCONTROLLER

The main reason for the development of microcontroller is to overcome the only drawback of the microprocessor. Even though microprocessors are powerful devices, they require external chips like RAM, ROM, Input/Output ports and other components in order to design a complete working system. This made it economically difficult to develop computerized consumer appliances on a large scale as the system cost is very high.

Table 3.1 Comparison of Microprocessor and Microcontroller

Microprocessor	Microcontroller
Microprocessor assimilates the function of a Central Processing Unit (CPU) on to a single Integrated Circuit (IC).	Microcontroller can be considered as a small computer which has a processor and some other components in order to make it a computer.
Microprocessors are mainly used in designing general purpose systems from small to large and complex systems like super computers.	Microcontrollers are used in automatically controlled devices.
Microprocessor is heart of computer system.	Microcontroller is a heart of embedded system.
Memory and I/O components have to be connected externally.	Micro controller has external processor along with internal memory and I/O components.
Since memory and I/O has to be connected externally, the circuit becomes large.	Since memory and I/O are present internally, the circuit is small.
Cannot be used in compact systems and hence inefficient.	Can be used in compact systems and hence it is an efficient technique.
The overall cost of a system built using a microprocessor is high. This is because of the requirement of external components.	Cost of a system built using a microcontroller is less as all the components are readily available.
Due to external components, the entire power consumption is high. Hence it is not suitable to used with devices running on stored power like batteries.	Since external components are low, total power consumption is less and can be used with devices running on stored power like batteries.
Most of the microprocessors do not have power saving features.	Most of the microcontrollers have power saving modes like idle mode and power saving mode. This helps to reduce power consumption even further.
Since memory and I/O components are all external, each instruction will need external operation, hence it is relatively slower.	Since components are internal, most of the operations are internal instruction, hence speed is fast.
Microprocessor have less number of registers, hence more operations are memory based.	Microcontroller have more number of registers, hence the programs are easier to write.

(Conti...)

Microprocessors are based on von Neumann model/architecture where program and data are stored in same memory module.	Microcontrollers are based on Harvard architecture where program memory and Data memory are separate.
Computational capacity of microprocessor is very high. Hence can perform complex tasks.	Less computational capacity when compared to microprocessors. Usually used for simpler tasks.
Microprocessors have integrated Math Coprocessor. Complex mathematical calculations which involve floating point can be performed with great ease.	Microcontrollers do not have math coprocessors. They use software to perform floating point calculations which slows down the device. However, some recent designs do include an FPU and DSP optimized features.
The main task of microprocessor is to perform the instruction cycle repeatedly. This includes fetch, decode and execute.	In addition to performing the tasks of fetch, decode and execute, a microcontroller also controls its environment based on the output of the instruction cycle.

REVIEW QUESTIONS WITH ANSWERS

1. Multiple Choice Questions

1. Sensors can be:
   a. Temperature b. Light
   c. Motion d. All of the above
2. Actuators can be:
   a. Displays b. Motors
   c. Sound d. All of the above
3. Examples of sensors are:
   a. Gas sensor b. Water quality sensor
   c. Moisture sensor d. All of these
4. Different kinds of signals are:
   a. Mechanical, Thermal b. Magnetic, Electric
   c. Chemical, Radiation d. All of the above
5. ________ actuators use pressurized oil that is incompressible.
   a. Hydraulic b. Pneumatic
   c. Both (a) and (b) d. None of these
6. A microcontroller sometimes abbreviated as:
   a. μC b. uC
   c. MCU d. All of the above
7. The components that are present on a typical Microcontroller IC are:
   a. CPU b. Memory
   c. I/O ports and timers d. All of these
8. Tagging Things:
   a. RFID and NFC b. Digital watermarking
   c. QR codes d. All of the above
9. Actuators include:
   a. Motors, gears b. Pumps, pistons
   c. Valves, and switches d. All of the above
10. Add, Subtract, Divide, Multiply and Logic operations are performed by:
    a. Registers b. Control Unit
    c. ALU d. None of these
11. Logical operations in a computer are done by:
    a. Registers b. Control unit
    c. ALU d. None of the above
12. A microprocessor works using digit(s):
    a. 1 b. 0
    c. 0 and 1 d. All of the above
13. Characteristics of RISC:
    a. Pipelining b. Hardwired control
    c. Instructions executes in one clock cycle d. All of the above
14. Characteristic(s) of microprocessor:
    a. Instruction set b. Clock speed
    c. Word Length d. All of the above
15. _______ sensors produce digital outputs that can be directly interfaced with the digital controller.
    a. Digital b. Analog
    c. Both (a) and (b) d. None of the above

16. A microcontroller:
    a. Saves cost
    b. Saves power consumption
    c. Makes the circuit compact
    d. All of the above
17. Application area of 8051 Microcontroller:
    a. Medical Equipment
    b. Aeronautical and Space
    c. Defense Systems
    d. All of the above

2. State True or False for the following:

1. A sensor is not a machine.
2. IoT devices and systems include sensors that track and measure activity in the world.
3. A sensor may not be a transducer.
4. Sensor is input devices while the actuator is output devices.
5. Electrical switches are the choice of actuators for most of the on-off type control action.
6. Most electronic devices we use today have microcontroller in them of some form or another.
7. A microcontroller is designed for a very specific task to control a particular system.
8. A microcontroller is a true device that fits the computer-on-a-chip idea.
9. Microcontrollers have math coprocessors to perform floating point calculations.
10 The IC of a microcontroller has memory RAM integrated on it along with some other components like I/O devices and timers.
11. Microcontrollers are used to handle real time tasks as they are single programmed, self sufficient and task oriented devices.
12. The clock speed of the microprocessor is quite high as compared to the microcontroller.
13. The microcontroller has less registers for instruction execution as compared to microprocessor.
14. Microcontrollers are used to do the same assigned task repeatedly.
15. Thermocouple is an electric temperature detector that uses thermoelectric resistance created by heat.
16. A transducer is any device which converts one form of energy into another.
17. A light bulb is a transducer for converting electrical energy into optical energy.
18. An electric motor is a transducer for conversion of electricity into mechanical energy or motion.
19. Fetching of an instruction for execution is done by the control unit.
20. RISC stands for Reduced Instruction Small Computer.
21. Flash memory is used in digital camera, cellular phones, LAN switches etc.
22. The data in digital sensors, which is used for conversion and transmission, is analog in nature.
23. A microcontroller is a computer with most of the necessary support chips on board.
24. Another name for a microcontroller is Embedded Controller.

3. Match the following:

1. Movement Sensor	a. Collect data from the environment
2. A transducer	b. Give out data to its surrounding
3. Sensors	c. Accelerometer
4. Communication interfaces	d. Energy converter
5. Tagging Things	e. Wired or wireless
6. Actuators	f. Sensor needs a power supply
7. Clock speed	g. QR codes
8. Bandwidth	h. Sensor does not need a power supply
9. Active	i. Bits processed in a single instruction
10. Passive	j. Instructions Per Second

4. Fill in the blanks:

1. ________ act as primary devices to collect data from the environment.

2. Sensors main purpose is to collect data from its surrounding and ________ give out data to its surrounding.
3. A ________ is a device which converts signals from one form to another.
4. ________ actuators use air under pressure that is most suitable for low to medium force, short stroke, and high-speed applications.
5. ________ actuators are typically installed in engines, where they open and close different valves.
6. Another name for a microcontroller is ________.
7. ________ is a highly integrated chip that contains all the components comprising a controller.
8. The first commercial microprocessor is 4-bit 4004 developed by Intel and was made available in ________.
9. ________ indicates maximum number of bits processed in a single instruction.
10. A silicon chip that contains a CPU is called ________.
11. A ________ cell converts light into electricity.
12. A ________ converts thermal energy into electrical energy.
13. The set of instructions that the microprocessor can execute are called ________.
14. Final results of processing, before releasing, to output unit are held in ________ unit.
15. ________ holds the circuitry that controls the process of executing, decoding and fetching program instructions.
16. ________ sensors produce continuous signals that are proportional to the sensed parameter

Answers

1. 1. d 2. d 3. d 4. d 5. a 6. d
7. d 8. d 9. d 10. c 11 c 12 c
13. d 14. d 15. a 16. d 17. d

2. 1. T 2. T 3. T 4. T 5. T 6. T
7. T 8. T 9. F 10. F 11 T 12 T
13. F 14. T 15. T 16. T 17 T 18. T
19. T 20. F 21. T 22. F 23. T 24. T

3. 1. c 2. d 3. a 4. e 5. g 6. b
7. j 8. i 9. h 10. f

4.

1. Sensors	2. Actuators
3. Transducer	4. Pneumatic
5. Electric	6. Embedded Controller
7. Microcontroller	8. 1971
9. Bandwidth	10. Microprocessor
11. Solar	12. Thermocouple
13. Instruction set	14. Memory
15. Control unit	16. Analog

Short Answers Questions

1. Write short notes on the following:
(a) Microcontrollers
(b) Microprocessors
(c) DC Motors
(d) Embedded System
(e) Sensor

Ans a. Microcontrollers (embedded processors) are processors (or specialized microprocessors) that have many peripherals to interact with real-world sensors and actuators. Microcontrollers are typically employed in scenarios that must have low power consumption, operate fan-less, thus must have low power dissipation. Also, often micro-controllers run relatively simpler set of instructions.

b. Microprocessors (Application processors) usually are for general-purpose applications, and rarely have many peripheral interconnect options. They target high performance applications, focus on computational power, and thus come with multiple level of caches, have very high clock speeds, have less to worry about power dissipation and power consumption. Often, they have little or no onboard RAM.

c. DC motors, which move at variable speeds. In DC motors, the coil of wire (rotor) assembly rotates in an attempt to align itself with the stator assembly but is prevented by a part known as the commutator. At the precise moment, the commutator switches the rotor field while the stator assembly remains stationary. This provides the means to control speed and positioning.

d. An embedded system can be thought of as a computer hardware system having software embedded in it. An embedded system can be an independent system or it can be a part of a large system. An embedded system is a microcontroller or microprocessor based system which is designed to perform a specific task. For example, a fire alarm is an embedded system; it will sense only smoke.

e. The sensor can be defined as a device which can be used to sense/detect the physical quantity like force, pressure, strain, light etc and then convert it into desired output like the electrical signal to measure the applied physical quantity.

2. Write short note on Thermistor.

Ans A thermistor can be used to detect the variation in temperature. It has a negative temperature coefficient that means when the temperature increases the resistance decreases. So, the thermistor's resistance can be varied with the rise in temperature which causes more current flow through it. This change in current flow can be used to determine the amount of change in temperature. An application for thermistor is, it is used to detect the rise in temperature and control the leakage current in a transistor circuit which helps in maintaining its stability. Thermistor is used to control the DC fan automatically.

3. Differentiate between Microprocessor and Microcontroller.

Ans Difference between Microprocessor and Microcontroller are:

- Microprocessor widely used in the computer system. And microcontroller is used in embedded system.
- Microprocessor is used in Personal Computers whereas Micro Controller is used in an embedded system.
- The microprocessor uses Von Neumann architecture where data and program present in the same memory module. The microcontroller uses Harvard architecture. In this module, data and program get stored in separate memory.
- Microprocessor requires external components to operate. So, the Cost of the microprocessor is higher than the microcontroller.
- Microprocessor consists of only a Central Processing Unit, whereas Micro Controller contains a CPU, Memory, I/O all integrated into one chip.
- Microprocessor uses an external bus to interface to RAM, ROM, and other peripherals, on the other hand, Microcontroller uses an internal controlling bus.
- Microprocessor is complicated and expensive, with a large number of instructions to process but Microcontroller is inexpensive and straightforward with fewer instructions to process.

4. What are the application areas of Microprocessors?

Ans Microprocessors are mainly used in devices like:

- Calculators
- Accounting system
- Games machine
- Military applications
- Computation systems

5. What are the application areas of Microcontroller?

Ans Microcontrollers are mainly used in devices like:

- Mobile phones
- Automobiles
- CD/DVD players
- Washing machines
- Security alarms
- Microwave oven
- Mp3 players
- Cameras

6. Differentiate between 8051 and AVR Controllers.

Ans Difference between 8051 and AVR Controllers are:

- 8051s are 8-bit controllers based on CISC architecture, AVRs are 8-bit controllers based on RISC architecture.

- 8051 consumes more power than AVR microcontroller.
- In 8051, we can program easily than the AVR microcontroller.
- The speed of AVR is more than the 8051 microcontroller.

7. What is transducer?

Ans Any device converting signals of one kind to signals of a different kind is a transducer i.e., a transducer is a device which converts one physical quantity to another from of physical quantity, e.g., acceleration to voltage or voltage to pressure.

8. What is sensor?

Ans A sensor is a device that is used to detect changes in any physical quantity like temperature, speed, flow, level, pressure, etc. Any changes in the input quantity will be detected by a sensor and reflected as changes in output quantity.

9. "A transducer is more general than a sensor." Comment.

Ans A sensor is a device which can quantitatively measure a certain physical quantity. A transducer is a device which converts one physical quantity to another from of physical quantity, e.g., acceleration to voltage or voltage to pressure. Therefore, a transducer can be a sensor when it is used to measure a certain physical quantity. But the transducer can also be an actuator when the (electrical) input is converted to, for example, force. So a transducer is more general than a sensor.

10. Explain Sensors and Actuators with example.

Ans *Sensors* are devices that responds to a physical quantity with a signal and *Actuators* are devices that respond to signals with physical movement (or similar action) can be considered as Transducers.

For example, a Microphone is a Sensor, which converts sound waves into electrical signals and a Loudspeaker is an Actuator, which converts electrical signals into audio signals.

11. What is Clock speed?

Ans The clock speed determines how many instructions per second the processor can execute. Usually clock speed is in MHz (Mega Hertz) or GHz (Giga Hertz).

12. Write short note on Thermocouple.

Ans Thermocouple is a temperature sensor that can detect the variation in temperature. In its construction, two different metals are joined together to form a junction. Its main principle is when the junction of two different metals are heated or exposed to high temperatures a potential across their terminals varies. So, the varying potential can be further used to measure the amount of change in temperature.

13. Discuss important features of a RISC microprocessor.

Ans **RISC (Reduced Instruction Set Computer)**

a. RISC architecture was developed by realizing that instead of using full set of instructions, only the frequently used instructions are sufficient.
b. In this architecture, the instructions are small and highly optimized.
c. RISC processors are used where execution time of the instruction should be less and cost of development is less.
d. The ARM devices are based on ARM architecture which is a subset of RISC.

14. Discuss important features of a CISC microprocessor.

Ans **CISC (Complex Instruction Set Computer)**

a. CISC architecture consists of full set of instructions that are complex, larger, have more computational power and so on.
b. A single CISC instruction can be used to execute several low-level operations, multistep operations and multiple addressing modes.
c. The execution time of these instructions is long. Intel's X86 is an example of CISC architecture.

15. Compare RISC with CISC based machines.

Ans Comparison of RISC and CISC is shown below:

RISC	CISC
1. RISC is an abbreviation for Reduced Instruction Set Computer.	CISC is an abbreviation for Complex Instruction Set Computers.
2. The examples of RISC machines is Motorola PowerPC based computer.	The examples of CISC machines are: Intel 80486, Pentium, Motorola 68030, 68040 based computers.
3. RISC microprocessors have relatively small instruction sets	CISC processors have relatively large instruction sets.
4. RISC machines have fixed and easily decoded instruction formats.	CISC machines have variable-length instruction formats.
5. Few addressing modes are used in RISC machines.	Many addressing modes are used in CISC machines.
6. Hardwired controls are used in RISC machines	The CISC machines use microprogramming.
7. RISC machine is 5 to 10 times faster than a CISC machine.	CISC machines are more complex and less efficient.
8. Several general-purpose registers are employed in RISC machines.	Small numbers of general-purpose registers are employed in CISC machines.

16. Write properties of EPIC processor.

Ans EPIC (Explicitly Parallel Instruction Computing) is a computer architecture that combines the best feature of RISC and CISC. A EPIC processor has the following properties:

- EPIC does not use fixed with instruction, rather aims at parallel processing of instructions.
- Programs must be written using sequential semantics with explicitly laid out parallelism.
- It uses a bundle of complex instructions that in addition to basic instruction also contain information on how to run the instruction in parallel with other instructions.

17. What are Advantages and Disadvantages of Microcontroller?

Ans Advantages of Microcontroller are:

- Lower cost because many elements of the processor are contained within the one chip resulting in lower chip cost.
- Lower power consumption.
- Integrating all components onto one chip enables processor to be optimised for a given application.

Disadvantages of Microcontroller are:

- Less flexibility because all components are integrated into the one chip.
- Limited performance because the size of memory is limited by what can be accommodated on the chip.
- MCUs tend to be application specific so the choice may be limited.

18. How does Microprocessor work?

Ans There are five important components in a microprocessor. They are Arithmetic and Logic Unit (ALU), Control Unit, Registers, Instruction Decoder and Data Bus. Microprocessor holds the number of instruction. Every instruction consists of multiple steps such as fetch, decode, executes and store. While running instruction in the microprocessor, it executes multiple steps as Fetch the input, Decode instruction, Execute instruction, Store result back in the memory. Here, Instruction gets fetched and input is given externally using I/O components. The microprocessor executes an instruction. The result gets stored in the externally connected memory unit.

19. What are the criteria for choosing a microcontroller?

Ans Criteria for choosing a microcontroller are:

- The first and foremost criterion in choosing a microcontroller is that it must meet the task at hand efficiently and cost effectively.
- In analyzing the needs of a microcontroller-based project, we must first see whether an 8-bit, 16-bit, or 32-bit microcontroller can best handle the computing needs of the task most effectively.
- Power consumption especially critical for battery-powered products.
- The amount of RAM and ROM on chip.
- The number of I/O pins and the timer on the chip.
- The highest speed that the microcontroller supports.

20. Write some application areas of AVR Microcontroller.

Ans Application areas of AVR Microcontroller are:

- Robotics and Embedded systems
- Bio-medical equipment
- Automobiles and security systems
- Temperature, light sensing and Fire detection devices
- Industrial automation devices

21. How Active sensors is different from Passive sensors?

Ans Active sensors are those which require an external excitation signal or a power signal. Passive sensors, on the other hand, do not require any external power signal and directly generates output response.

22. Explain Passive Transducers with example.

Ans In Passive Transducers, the energy from the input is directly converted into the output. For example, a Thermocouple is a passive transducer, where the heat energy, which is absorbed from input, is converted into electrical signals (voltage).

23. Define computer architecture.

Ans Computer architecture is defined as the functional operation of the individual hardware unit in a computer system and the flow of information among the control of units.

EXERCISE

1. Write short note on the following:
   (a) Transducers
   (b) Analog sensors
   (c) Temperature Sensor
   (d) Micro and Nanosensors
   (e) Proximity sensor
   (f) PIC Microcontroller
   (g) 64-Bit Microprocessor
2. What is an actuator? What are its types?
3. What are actuators and sensors?
4. What is electric actuator?
5. What is Actuator and how it works?
6. What is the difference between transducers, sensors, and actuators?
7. What are actuators and where do we use them?
8. What is an embedded system?
9. Discuss characteristics of an Embedded System.
10. Why there are so many microcontrollers?
11. What are the applications of microcontrollers?
12. Write short note on EPIC.
13. What is the difference between microprocessor and microcontroller?
14. How are Microcontrollers classified?
15. What is the role played by the clock speed in a computer system?
16. Write the basic characteristics used to differentiate microprocessors.
17. Differentiate between CISC and RISC.
18. Discuss the role of Microcontroller in embedded devices.
19. Differentiate between DC motor and AC motor.
20. Differentiate between Active Transducers and Passive Transducers.
21. What is the use of Stepper Motors?

22. Discuss different criteria to choose sensor.
23. Explain the working of Thermistor (Temperature Sensor).
24. What is a sensor? Explain its working with example.
25. Discuss features of 8051 Microcontroller.
27. Discuss features of AVR Microcontroller.
28. What is Hard Real Time Systems? Explain with an example.
29. What is Real Time Embedded System?
30. What do you mean by Microactuators?

CHAPTER 4

Building IoT Applications

4.1 INTRODUCTION TO ARDUINO

Arduino first and foremost is an open-source computer hardware and software company. The Arduino Community refers to the project and user community that designs and utilizes microcontroller-based development boards. These development boards are known as Arduino Modules, which are open-source prototyping platforms. The simplified microcontroller board comes in a variety of development board packages.

Arduino was created in the year 2005 by two Italian engineers David Cuartielles and Massimo Banzi with the goal of keeping in mind about students to make them learn how to program the Arduino uno microcontroller and improve their skills about electronics and use it in the real world.

Arduino is an open source electronics platform accompanied with a *hardware* and *software* to design, develop and test complex electronics prototypes and products. The hardware consists of a micro-controllers with other electronics components which can be programmed using the software to do almost any task.

For the *hardware* part of the Arduino, it consists of the physical board and also sensors and shields used to interact with the board. Arduino shields are pre-built circuit boards that are easily plugged on top of your Arduino headers to extend its capabilities. Similar to sensors, shields have various functionalities from wifi connectivity, ethernet, driving and controlling motors, camera, storage, touch screen, display, and many more. Arduino boards comes with many varieties with different functionalities which we will discuss later in the chapter. Also, Arduino boards can be purchased pre-assembled or as do-it-yourself kits.

☞ *The Arduino boards can connect with add- on modules termed as shields.*

To program your Arduino, you will require the Arduino IDE *software* that runs on regular personal computers and allows users to write programs for Arduino using C or C++. Arduino IDE makes it easy for you to write code and upload it on your Arduino board.

Advantages of Arduino

- It is an open source.
- Easy to use and perfect for beginners. There are wide varieties of library of examples and projects available online that are pre-coded for you to learn and build using the Arduino allowing beginners to get started very easily.
- It has a large community of people using and troubleshooting it. This makes it easy to help in debugging projects.
- It also comes with open supply software system feature that permits tough software system developers to use the Arduino code to merge with the prevailing programing language libraries and may be extended and changed.
- Arduino IDE is also cross-platform which means you can run it on Windows, Macintosh OSX and also Linux operating systems compared to other microcontroller systems which can only run Windows.
- The biggest advantage of Arduino is its ready to use structure. As Arduino comes in a complete package form which includes the 5V regulator, a burner, an oscillator, a micro-controller, serial communication interface, LED and headers for the connections.
- Also, Arduino has many variations of low cost boards and peripherals for you to choose from to allow you to pick one that suits your project the most

Disadvantages of Arduino

- Requires effort to accomplish some tasks such as scheduling and database storage.

- If you need more processing power and working memory than you have to switch from Arduino environment.

4.2 TYPES OF ARDUINO BOARDS

There are many electronic boards out there, an Arduino is based on a microcontroller which is a simple easy to use computer designed for beginners to run one program at a time, over and over again. If you want a simple easy to use board to handle simple repetitive tasks like reading the weather, opening a door, driving a simple robot, turning on an LED, etc. an Arduino would be perfect.

☞ *LEDs are small, powerful lights that are used in many different applications.*

There are many variations from official Arduino boards including Arduino Uno, Arduino Mega, Arduino Leonardo, Arduino Micro and many more to Arduino compatible boards each with different capabilities and price points. Each board has its own features and was built to suit different level of applications. The different types of Arduino boards that are used for beginners are:

4.2.1 Arduino Uno

The Arduino Uno (See Figure 4.1) is one kind of microcontroller board based on ATmega328, and Uno is an Italian term which means one. The ATmega328 is one kind of single-chip microcontroller formed with Atmel within the megaAVR family. The architecture of this Arduino Uno is a customized Harvard architecture with 8 bit RISC processor core. The features of Arduino Uno ATmega328 includes the following:

- The operating voltage is 5v. You can connect an external power source of upto 12v.
- Digital input/output pins are 14 Analog input/output pins are 6 (labeled A0 through A5). This sort of pins allows you to connect hardware to your Arduino Uno board externally. These pins are used as a key for extending the computing capability of the Arduino Uno into the real world.
- DC Current for each input/output pin is 40 mA and DC Current for 3.3V Pin is 50 mA. A 3.3 volt supply generated by the on-board regulator. Maximum current draw is 50 mA.
- GND are Ground pins.
- Flash Memory is 32 KB for storing your code. SRAM is 2 KB.
- CLK Speed is 16 MHz, which is fast enough for most applications and does not speeds up the microcontroller.
- An easy USB interface allows interface with USB as this is like a serial device.

The Arduino Uno board can be built with power pins, analog pins, ATmegs328, ICSP header, Reset button, power LED, digital pins, test led 13, TX/RX pins, USB interface, an external power supply. It contains everything needed to support the microcontroller; simply connect it to a computer with a USB cable or power it with a AC-to-DC adapter or battery to get started. The Arduino UNO board description is discussed below.

USB plug/connector

It is used to load a program from the Arduino IDE onto the Arduino board. The board can also be powered through this port. USB interface chip converts signals in the USB level to a level that an Arduino UNO board understands.

Power Supply/External power

Every Arduino board needs a way to be connected to a power source. The Arduino Uno can be powered via the USB connection or with an external power (non-USB) supply. The external power supplies mainly include AC to DC adapter otherwise a battery. The adapter can be connected to the Arduino Uno by plugging into the power jack of the Arduino board. Similarly, the battery leads can be connected to the Vin pin and the GND pin of the POWER connector. Vin pin is the input voltage to the Arduino board when it's using an external power source. Where as, GND pin is Ground pin. The recommended voltage for most Arduino models is between 6 and 12 Volts. If using more than 12V, the voltage regulator may overheat and damage the board. The voltage regulator controls the amount of voltage given to the Arduino board and stabilize the DC voltages used by the processor and other elements.

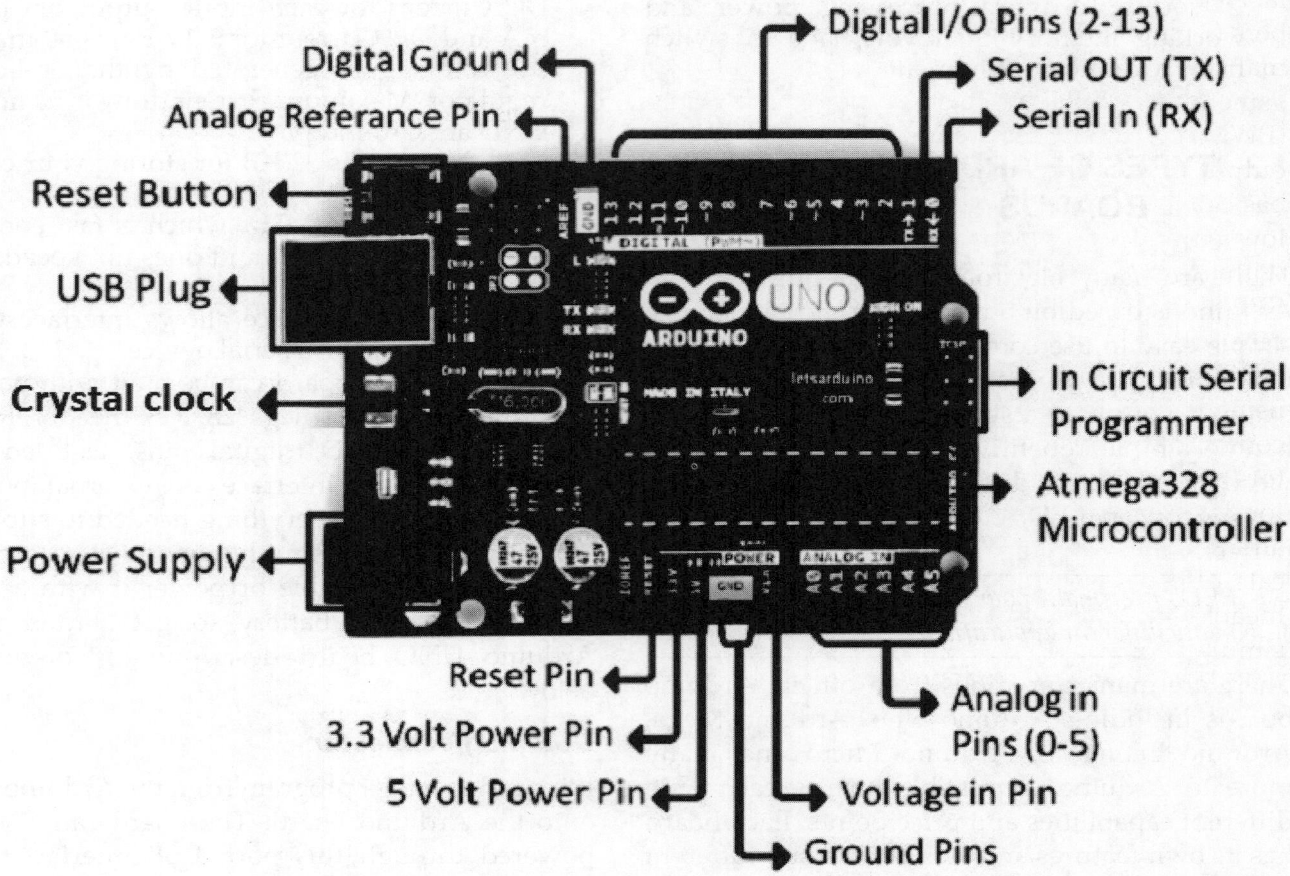

Figure 4.1 Arduino Uno

Input and Output (I/O) Pins

The pins on your Arduino are the places where you connect wires to construct a circuit. The Arduino has several different kinds of pins, each of which is labeled on the board and used for different functions. (See Figure 4.2).

Digital and Analog Pins: Each of the 14 (0 through 13) digital pins including digital pins like TX (1) and RX (0) and 6 (A0 through A5) analog pins on the Uno can be used as an input or output, under software control with the help of the functions like pinMode(), digitalWrite(), and digitalRead(). Digital pins can be used for both digital input (like telling if a button is pushed) and digital output (like powering an LED). They operate at 5 volts. Where as, analog pins can read the signal from an analog sensor (like a temperature sensor) and convert it into a digital value that you can read.

☞ *The Arduino UNO board has 14 digital I/O pins of which 6 provide PWM (Pulse Width Modulation) output.*

GND: Short for 'Ground'. There are several GND pins on the Arduino, any of which can be used to ground your circuit.

Serial Pins: Some of the pins have special functions like pins 0 & 1, which acts as a transmitter and receiver respectively. TX and RX indicates the data being transmitted or received over the USB communication.

External Interrupt Pins: The external interrupt pins of the board are 2 & 3, and these pins can be connected to activate an interrupt over a low value, a rising or falling edge, or a change in value.

PWM (Pulse-Width Modulation) Pins: You may have noticed the some of the digital pins are labeled with tilde (~) symbol next to the pin numbers (3, 5, 6, 9, 10, and 11). These pins act as normal digital pins, but can also be used for something called Pulse-Width Modulation (PWM) i.e., these pins are used to simulate analog output (like fading an LED in and out). PWM is basically, a square wave with a varying high and low time. These pin provide 8-bit PWM output with the analogWrite() function.

SPI (Serial Peripheral Interface) Pins: The SPI pins are 10, 11, 12, 13 namely SS, MOSI, MISO, SCK. These pins support SPI communication using the SPI library. SPI bus is a system for serial communication, which uses up to four conductors. One conductor is used for data receiving, one for data sending, one for synchronization and one alternatively for selecting a device to communicate with. It is a full duplex connection, which means that the data is sent and received simultaneously. SPI uses the following four wires:

- **SS**: This is the slave-selection wire.
- **MOSI**: This is the master output / slave input driven by the master.
- **MISO**: This is the master input / slave output driven by the master.
- **SCK**: This is the serial clock driven by the master.

In-built LED Pin: There is a built-in LED driven by digital pin 13, called *Power LED Indicator*. When the pin is high value, the LED is on, when the pin is low, it is off. This LED should light up whenever you plug your Arduino into a power source.

TWI (2-Wire Interface) Pins: The TWI pins are SDA or A4, & SCL or A5, which can support the communication of TWI with the help of Wire library.

AREF (Analog Reference Voltage) Pin: The reference voltage is for the analog inputs with analogReference() function. It is sometimes used to set an external reference voltage (between 0 and 5 Volts) as the upper limit for the analog input pins.

Reset Pin: This pin is used for reset the microcontroller. Making this pin LOW, resets the microcontroller.

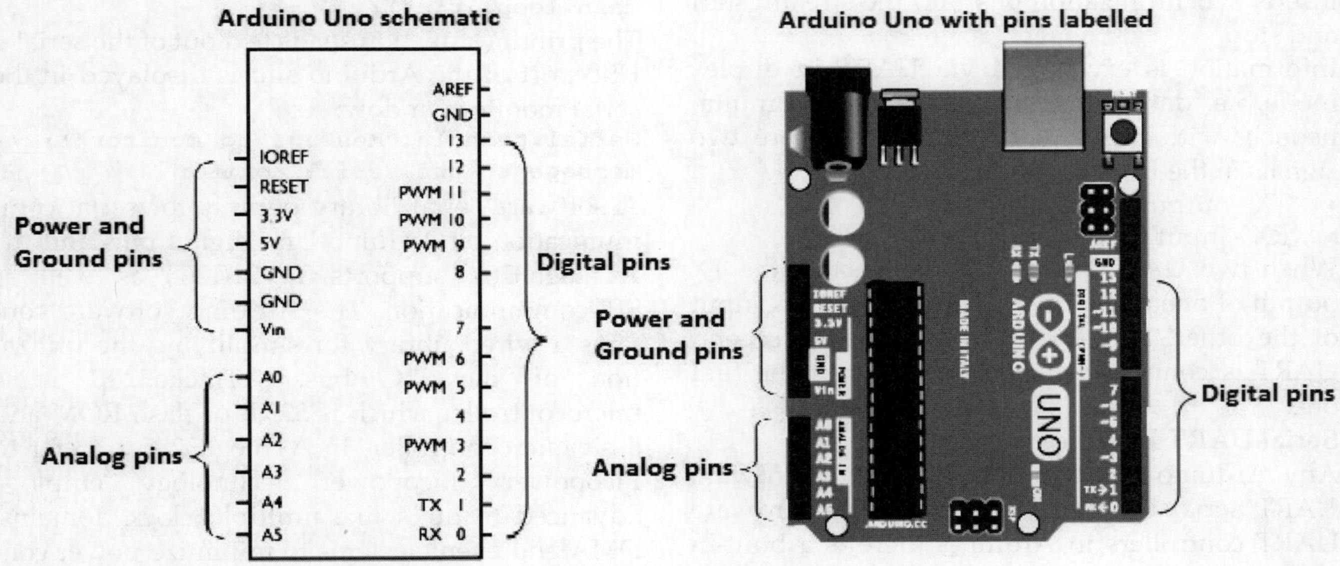

Figure 4.2 Arduino Uno schematic with pins labelled

Memory

The microcontroller has three types of memory:

- 32 KB flash (FLASH)
- 2 KB of RAM (SRAM)
- 1 KB of non-volatile memory (EEPROM)

Communication

The Arduino Uno ATmega328 offers UART TTL-serial communication, and it is accessible on digital pins like TX (1) and RX (0). The software of an Arduino has a serial monitor that permits easy data. There are two LEDs on the board like RX and TX which will blink whenever data is being broadcasted through the USB.

Serial UART interface

The UART is a Universal Asynchronous Receiver-Transmitter. UART data is transmitted by a serial code. Each bit is transmitted at regular intervals. The transmission time of one bit is determined by the transmission rate. The transmission rate is indicated in baud (bits per second). In addition to the data bits, the UART interface inserts synchronization bits into the stream: start and stop.

Information is exchanged via UART in duplex mode, i.e. data transmission can occur simultaneously with receiving. For this, there are two signals in the UART interface:

- TX - output for data transmission
- RX - input for receiving data

When two UART devices are connected, the TX output of one device is connected to the RX input of the other. And the TX signal of the second UART is connected to the RX input of the first one.

Serial UART interface in Arduino

Any Arduino board has at least one hardware UART serial interface. To work with hardware UART controllers in Arduino, there is a built-in class Serial. It is designed to control the exchange of data through the UART. Through the serial interface, data is always transmitted in binary code.

print()

Outputs data via the serial port UART in the form of ASCII characters. The function has various call forms for different formats and data types. If the argument is a char type it outputs to the port the character code.

```
char d = 83;
Serial.print(d); // displays the code 83
(symbol S)
```

If the argument is an integer type, then displays a string with a decimal number:

```
int d = 83;
Serial.print(d); // displays the string
'83'
```

println()

Outputs data through the UART serial port in the form of ASCII characters with the addition of newline characters (\ r, code 13) and (\ n, code 10). The println() function causes the invisible cursor to move to the next line in the serial monitor window. This causes the next text sent to the serial monitor window to appear on the line below the currently printed text. The \r\n at the end of this text of string moves the invisible cursor down one more line leaving a blank line between the text printed at the bottom of the loop and the text printed at the top of the loop.

```
Serial.println("Arduino now at bottom of
main loop.\r\n");
```

The println() function sends text out of the serial / USB port of the Arduino and is displayed in the serial monitor window:

```
Serial.println("Message to monitor"); //
message to the serial monitor
```

A software serial library permits for serial communication on Arduino Uno digital pins and the ATmega328p supports TWI (I2C) as well as SPI-communication. The Arduino software contains a wired library for simplifying the utilization of the I2C bus. ATmega328p is a microcontroller which is 32KB of flash ROM and 8-bit microcontroller. In ATmega328p p, refer to Picopower. Picopower technology employs advanced features like multiple clock domains, DMA and event systems to minimize power consumption.

Microcontroller

It is the black rectangular chip with pins. It is the brains of our Arduino. Each Arduino board has its own microcontroller. The microcontroller used on the UNO board is Atmega328P by Atmel (a major microcontroller manufacturer). Atmega328P is pre-programmed with bootloader. This allows you to directly upload a new Arduino program into the device, without using any external hardware programmer, making the Arduino UNO board easy to use.

Bootloader Almost all microcontroller (and microprocessor) development systems use some form of a bootloader. Often called firmware. The Arduino bootloader is one example.
Bootloader, is basically the initial piece of code which runs whenever any micro-controller is powered up or resets. It is similar to the concept of BIOS which run in our PC at the time you power up it. In case of BIOS, it waits for a user input for changing Boot options/settings. If it does not get any such inputs, it will start with the pre-installed OS.
A similar thing happens with Arduino bootloader. Whenever the Arduino is powered up or reset, it looks for external inputs (for uploading new program). If it receives no such inputs, then the processor jumps to the "user" program section to load whatever is already in program memory. This jump loads your program (or sketch).
Most of the times, bootloaders in microcontrollers are used to simplify the uploading of programs to the microcontrollers. They can also be used for initializing IO devices connected to the microcontrollers before they begin the main application program.
Optiboot bootloader is the default bootloader of the Arduino UNO. The optiboot bootloader will take 512 bytes, leaving 32256 bytes for application code. Due to its small size larger up-loadable sketch size is achieved. Like many microcontrollers, the ATmega328p dedicates a portion of its program memory for bootloading code.

☞ *Arduino bootloaders use the simple serial communication (UART) to download the hex file of program and write it in application section.*

Crystal Clock/Oscillator

The crystal oscillator helps Arduino in dealing with time issues. On each tick, the microcontroller performs one operation, for example, addition, subtraction, etc. The clock is controlled by an external 16MHz Crystal Oscillator.

Reset Button

It resets your Arduino board, i.e., start your program from the beginning. You can reset the UNO board in two ways. First, by using the reset button on the board. Second, you can connect an external reset button to the Arduino pin.

4.2.2 Arduino Leonardo

Arduino Leonardo is another entry-level board that uses the ATmega32u4 microcontroller. It is Arduino's first development board to use one microcontroller with built-in USB.

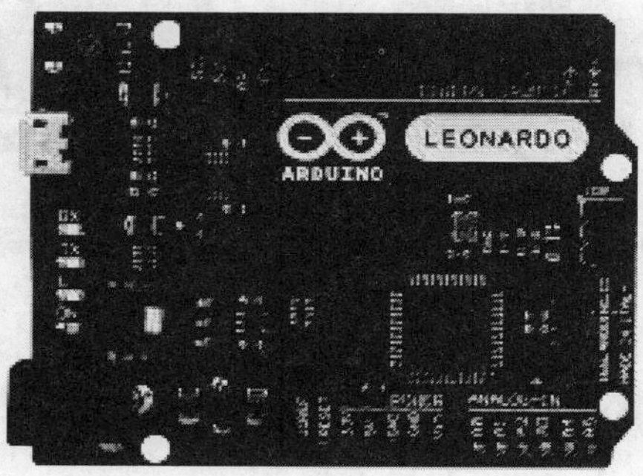

Figure 4.3 Arduino Leonardo

4.2.3 Arduino 101

The Arduino 101 is simple and has 32-bit Intel Curie microcontroller. It's a board that combines the universal appeal of Arduino with the latest technologies - like the Intel Curie module, Bluetooth LE capabilities, and a 6-axis accelerometer/gyro.

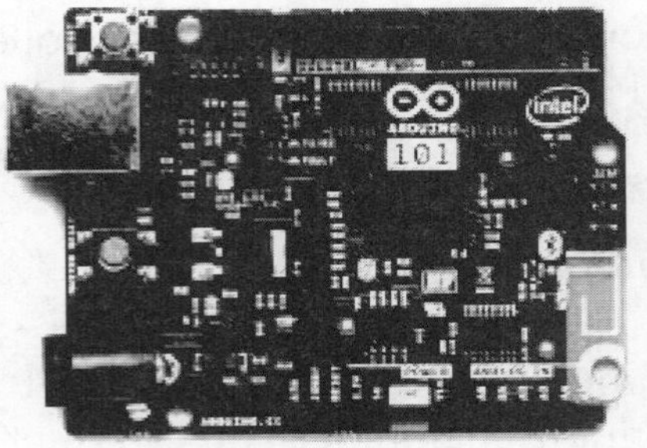

Figure 4.4 Arduino 101

4.2.4 Arduino ESPLORA

The Arduino Esplora is an Arduino Leonardo based board with integrated sensors and actuators. It uses the ATmega32u4 microcontroller. The Esplora has built-in USB communication; it can appear to a connected computer as a mouse or keyboard, in addition to a virtual (CDC) serial / COM port.

Figure 4.5 ESPLORA

4.2.5 Arduino Mini / Mini Lite

It is smallest Arduino product which is a 24-pin microcontroller without any connectors soldered. The unit features 8 analog pins and 14 digital pins. The module is based around the ATMEGA168 processor.

Figure 4.6 Arduino Mini

4.2.6 Arduino Micro

Arduino Micro is the smallest board of the family, used for interactive computing. The Micro comes with a built-in USB which makes connection with a computer. This microcontroller board is based on the ATmega32U4 .

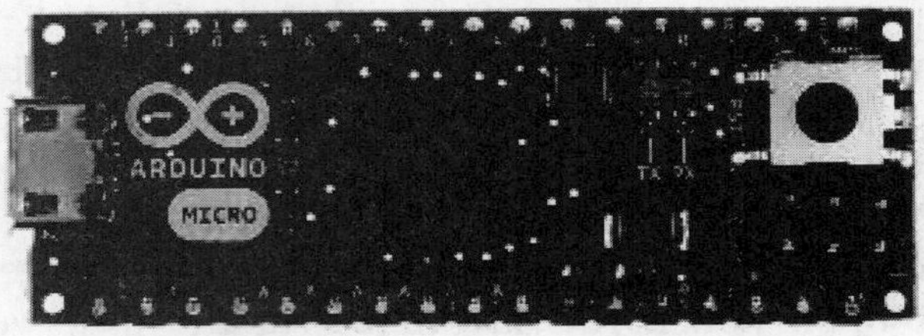

Figure 4.7 Arduino Micro

4.2.7 Arduino Nano

It is a breadboard friendly board based on the ATmega328. The Nano was the first mini breadboard-compatible board to have onboard USB. This microcontroller distinguishes itself from the others by having the USB to serial chip and connector onboard. The Nano has 8 analog pins and 14 digital pins. There is also the Arduino Nano Lite which does not include the downward facing pin headers.

Figure 4.8 Arduino Nano

4.2.8 Arduino Mega

It is based on the ATmega2560 microcontroller. It has more digital input/output pins, analog inputs, a USB connection, a power jack, and a reset button. The large number of pins make this board very handy for projects that require a bunch of digital inputs or outputs (like lots of LEDs or buttons).

Figure 4.9 Arduino Mega

4.2.9 Arduino Zero

Arduino Zero provides 32-bit extension to the platform established by Arduino Uno R3. It uses the ATSAMD21G18 microcontroller. Unlike most Arduino and Genuino boards, the Zero runs at 3.3V. The maximum voltage that the I/O pins can tolerate is 3.3V. Applying voltages higher than 3.3V to any I/O pin could damage the board.

Figure 4.10 Arduino Zero

4.2.10 Arduino M0 PRO

The Arduino M0 Pro board is equipped with Atmel Embedded Debugger (EDBG) for on-board debugging. It is based on ATSAMD21G18 microcontroller.

Figure 4.11 Arduino M0 PRO

4.2.11 Arduino Yun

The Arduino Yun uses a ATMega32U4 chip instead of the ATmega328. This extra chip allows this board to run Linux in addition to the normal Arduino operating system.

Figure 4.12 Arduino Yun

4.2.12 Arduino Industrial 101

Arduino Industrial 101 is an evaluation board for Arduino 101 LGA module. The ATmega32u4 microcontroller is integrated in the baseboard. The Arduino Industrial 101 has a number of facilities for communicating with a computer, another Arduino, or other microcontrollers.

Figure 4.13 Arduino Industrial 101

4.2.13 Arduino Tian

The Arduino Tian unleashes the power of a small computer running Linux connected to a 32-bit microcontroller.

Figure 4.14 Arduino Tian

4.2.14 Lilypad Arduino USB

The LilyPad Arduino USB is the perfect board for e-textiles and wearables projects. The LilyPad Arduino USB is a microcontroller board based on the ATmega32u4. The LilyPad Arduino USB differs from previous LilyPad boards in that the ATmega32u4 has built-in USB communication, eliminating the need for a separate USB-to-serial adapter. The LilyPad Arduino USB is programmed using the Arduino Software (IDE), our Integrated Development Environment common to all our boards and running both online and offline.

Figure 4.15 Lilypad Arduino USB

4.2.15 Lilypad Arduino main board

It is a wearable e-textile technology. Each LilyPad was creatively designed with large connecting pads and a flat back to allow them to be sewn into clothing with conductive thread. The LilyPad also has its own family of input, output, power, and sensor boards that are also built specifically for e-textiles. It uses the ATmega168V or ATmega328V, which are the lower power cersions of ATmega168 or ATmega328.

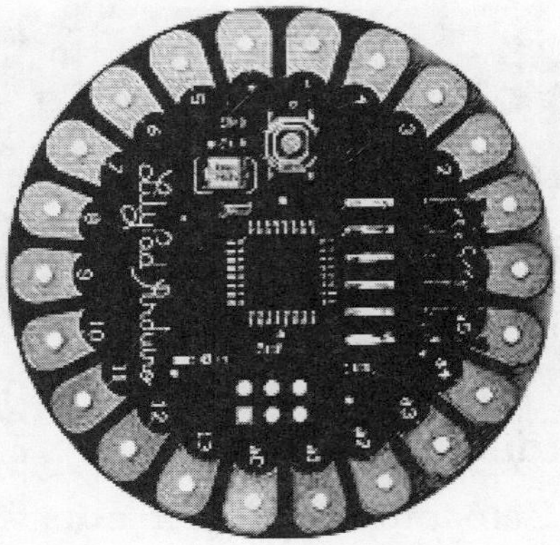

Figure 4.16 Lilypad Arduino main board

4.2.16 Arduino clones

Arduino clones devices are often available more cheaply than the genuine article and can work well in some scenarios. Arduino is an open source hardware, and anyone is free to create his/her own board. In fact, many companies make Arduino-compatible boards, building on the design to create something different and suited just for user's specific needs. They do carry the brand name Arduino, however, their names reflective of their Arduino clone status. For example, Freeduino.

4.2.17 How to power Arduino Uno?

In this section, we will discuss various ways to power up the Arduino Uno board in detail.

USB Power

USB Port is used to connect the board to your PC for programming and for powering up the Arduino board. This USB connection is important as it will be through this port where you will upload your code onto your Arduino board. The image shown in Figure 4.17 shows a USB A to B cable. You can also use a standalone 5V USB power supply (See Figure 4.18) when not connected to PC and Figure 4.19 shows an example of Arduino connected to the USB power plug.

Figure 4.17 USB A to B cable

Figure 4.18 USB power supply

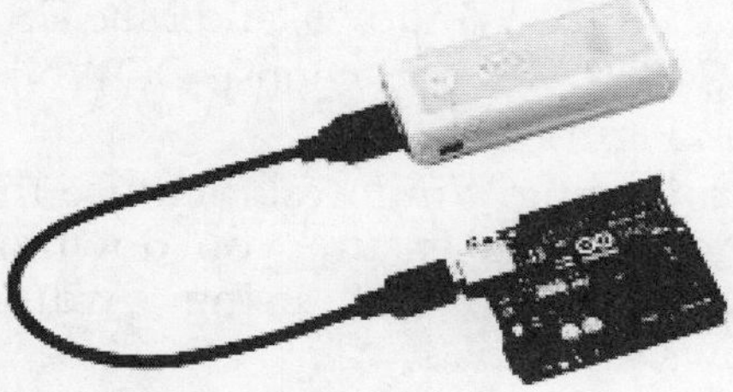

Figure 4.19 Arduino connected to the USB power plug

DC Power Jack

The DC power jack allows your Arduino board to be powered from a wall adapter so that you can supply more power to your project if needed. (See Figure 4.20).

The image in Figure 4.21 shows Arduino Uno board powered through the DC power jack using battery.

Figure 4.20 12V DC power supply

Figure 4.21 Arduino Uno board powered through the DC power jack using battery

Alternatively, you can use 9V battery with a DC barrel jack male adapter and battery connector. (See Figure 4.22 , 4.23 , and 4.24).

☞ *DC Power Barrel Jack is used for powering your Arduino with a power supply.*

Figure 4.22 9V battery

Figure 4.23 Battery connector

Figure 4.24 DC barrel jack adapter (male)

4.3 INTRODUCTION TO ARDUINO IDE

Arduino Integrated Development Environment (IDE) is an open source software that is mainly used for writing and compiling the code into the Arduino Module. The program code written for Arduino is known as a *sketch*. The software used for developing such sketches for an Arduino is commonly known as the *Arduino IDE*. It is easily available for operating systems like MAC, Windows, Linux and runs on the Java Platform that comes with inbuilt functions and commands that play a vital role for debugging, editing and compiling the code in the environment.

A range of Arduino modules available including Arduino Uno, Arduino Mega, Arduino Leonardo, Arduino Micro and many more. Each of them contains a microcontroller on the board that is actually programmed and accepts the information in the form of code. This environment supports both C and C++ languages. The most common programming approach is to use the Arduino IDE, which utilizes the C programming language. This gives you access to an enormous Arduino Library that is constantly growing.

4.3.1 Features of Arduino IDE

- The project file or the sketches for a project are saved with the file extension .ino.
- Features such as cut / copy / paste are supported in this IDE.
- There also is a facility for finding a particular word and replacing it with another by pressing the Ctrl + F buttons on the keyboard.
- The most basic part or the skeleton of all Arduino code will have two functions.

4.3.2 How to download and Install Arduino IDE?

To install the Arduino IDE on your computer, download the appropriate version for your operating system from the Arduino website https://www.arduino.cc/. You can download the Software from Arduino main website. This software is free to download and can be found at https://www.arduino.cc/en/Main/Software.

The software is available for common operating systems like Linux, Windows, and Mac OS.

Click on SOFTWARE and choose DOWNLOADS as shown in Figure 4.25.

- If you are using Windows, then use the Windows installer to ensure you download the necessary drivers for using Arduino on Windows.
- If you are using Linux, then you may have to add your user to some groups in order to use the serial port to program Arduino. This process is described in the Arduino install guide for Linux.
- If you are using Mac OS, then you can install Arduino IDE by following the Arduino install guide for OS X.

Figure 4.25 Installation Screen 1

As we will use windows so choose the option of **Windows Installer and up**, and from next window that appears click on **JUST DOWNLOAD**, it will start downloading Arduino-1.8.12-windows.exe. However when you are downloading, it might be different as the Arduino IDE is under continuous development. (See Figure 4.26, 4.27, 4.28).

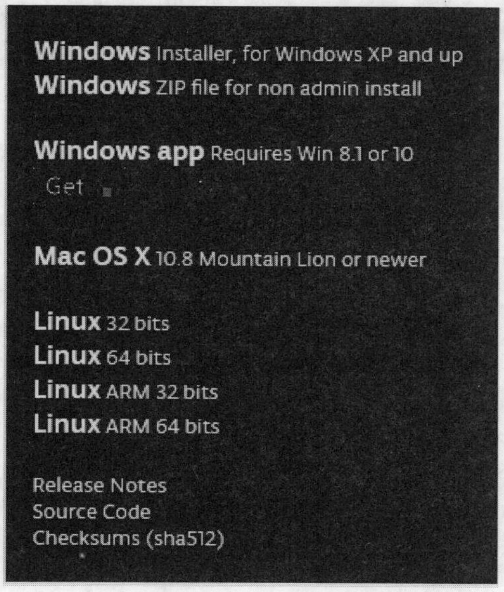

Figure 4.26 Installation Screen 2

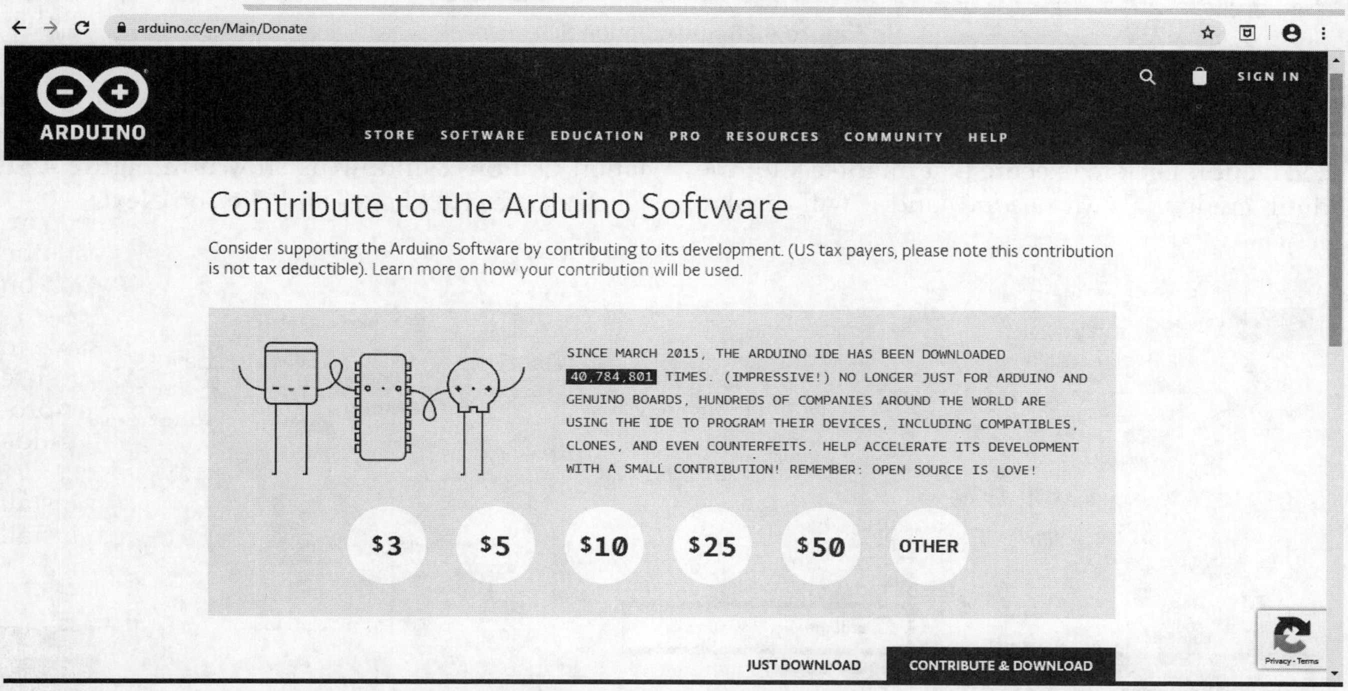

Figure 4.27 Installation Screen 3

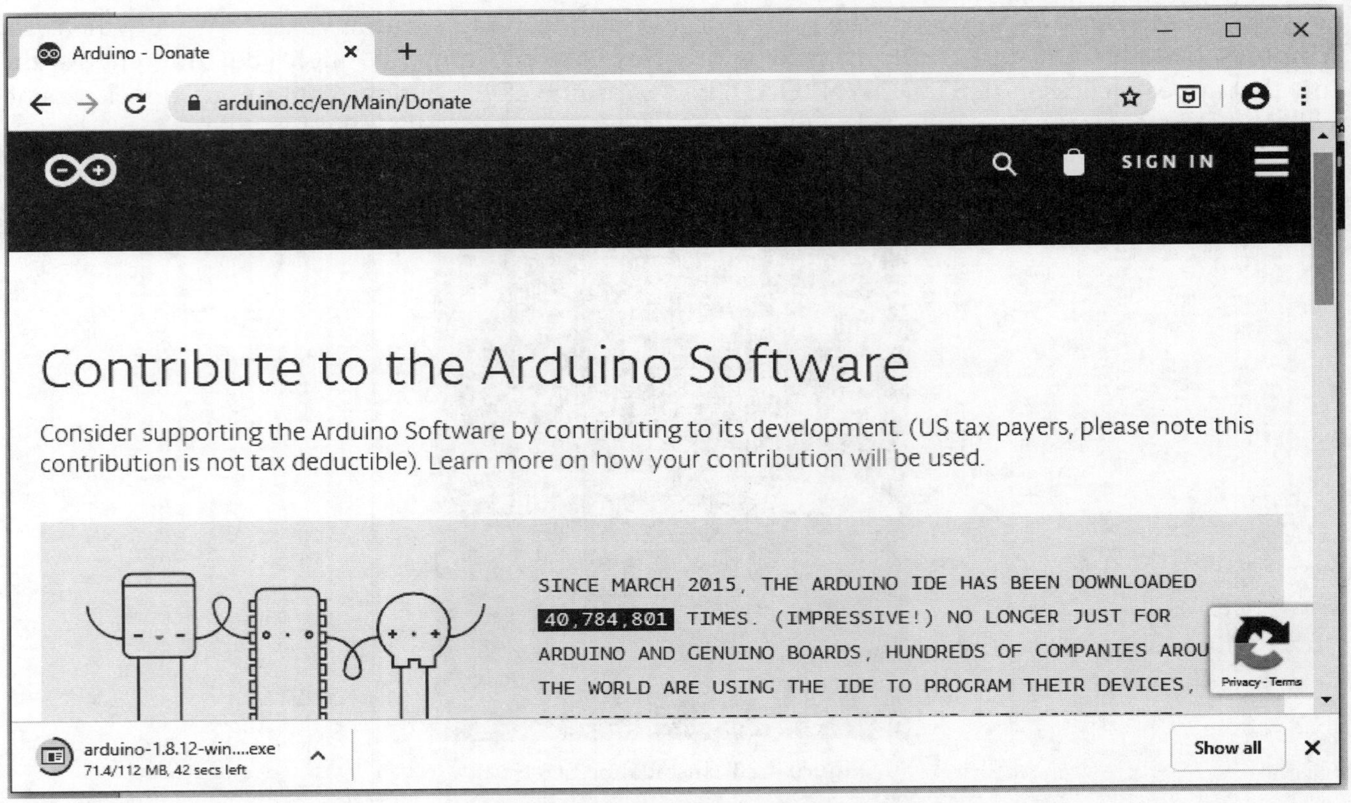

Figure 4.28 Installation Screen 4

Once download is completed, you can find the file in the Download directory as shown in Figure 4.29. Double click to execute it, it might ask for the admin credentials. (if needed) and it will display Arduino Setup Licence Agreement as shown in Figure 14.30. Click **I Agree**. It will display Installation Options window as shown in Figure 4.31. Click all the checkboxes and click on **Next**.

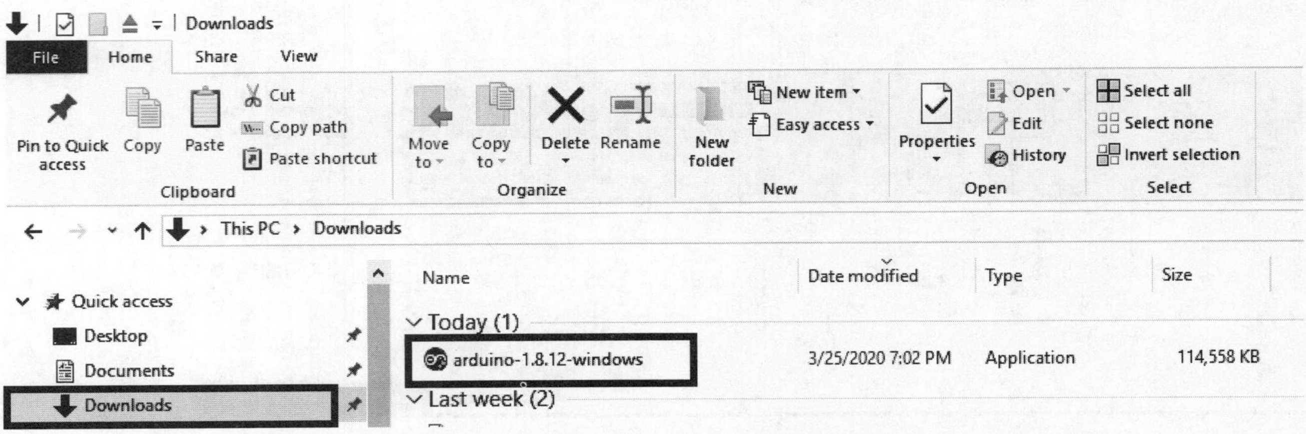

Figure 4.29 Screen showing Download directory with Arduino exe file

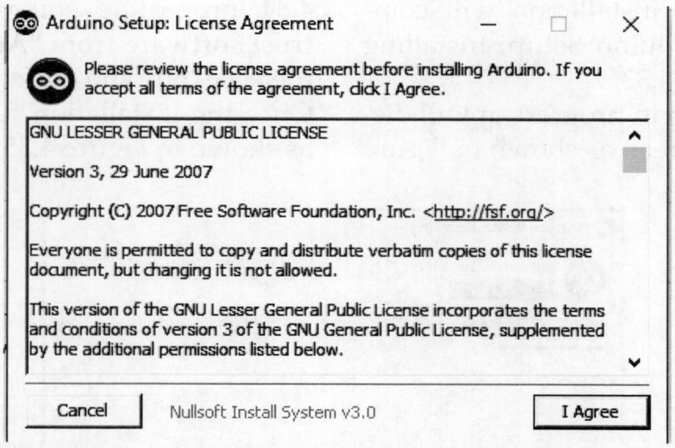

Figure 4.30 Screen showing Arduino Setup Licence Agreement

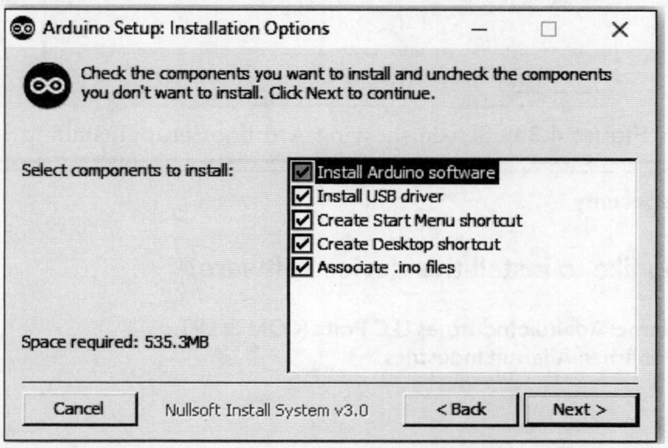

Figure 4.31 Screen showing Arduino Installation Options

It will display Arduino Setup: Installation Folder, as shown in Figure 4.32. Choose the directory where you wish the Arduino IDE to be installed.

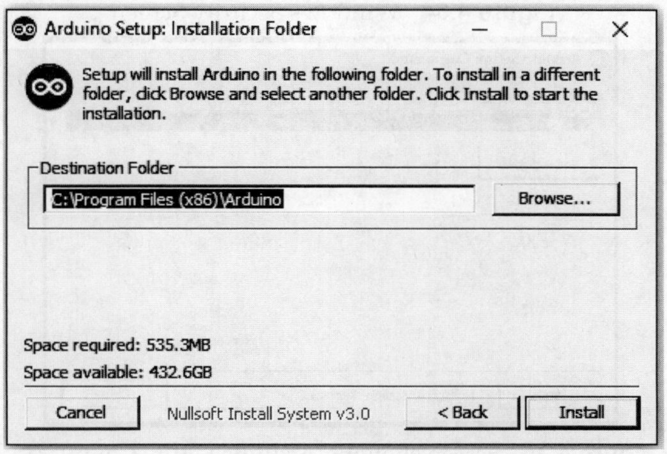

Figure 4.32 Screen showing Arduino Setup: Installation Folder

Click on **Install** and the installation will commence. It will display Arduino Setup: Installing screen as shown in Figure 4.33.

When Arduino installation in progress, it will display WIndows Security screen as shown in Figure 4.34, prompting you with the message **Always trust software from "Adafruit Industries".** Check the checkbox and click on the **Install** button.

Once the installation finishes, click on the **Close** as shown in Figure 4.35.

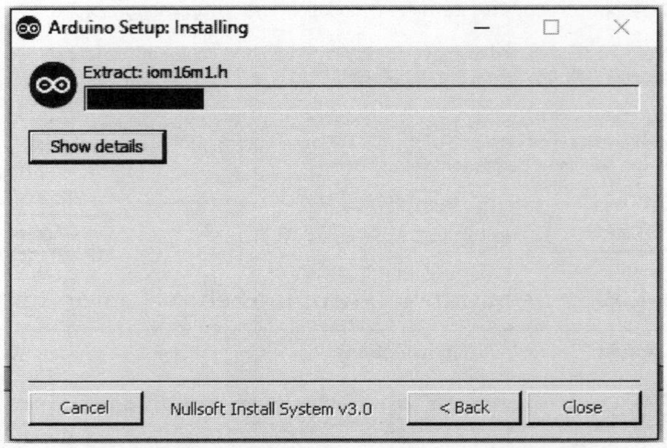

Figure 4.33 Screen showing Arduino Setup: Installing

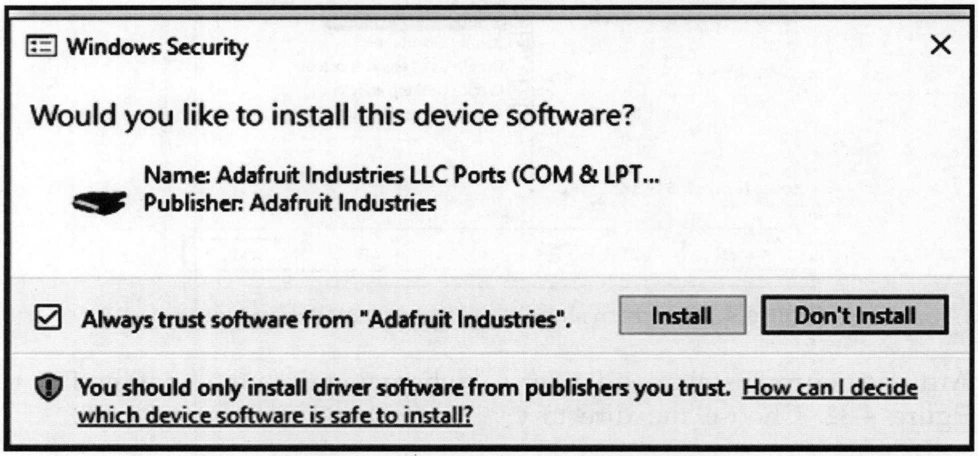

Figure 4.34 WIndows Security Screen

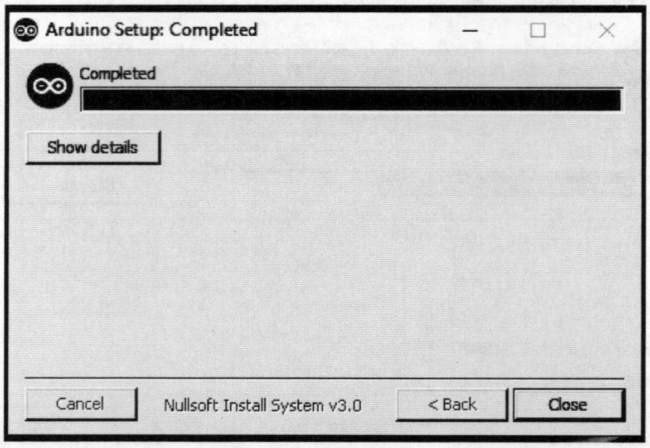

Figure 4.35 Screen showing Arduino Setup: Completed

Arduino IDE is now installed on your PC. You can now find the Arduino IDE Icon on desktop. Double click on the icon and it will display Splash screen as shown in Figure 4.36.

After few moments, the splash screen will disappear, and the Arduino IDE will appear as shown in Figure 4.37.

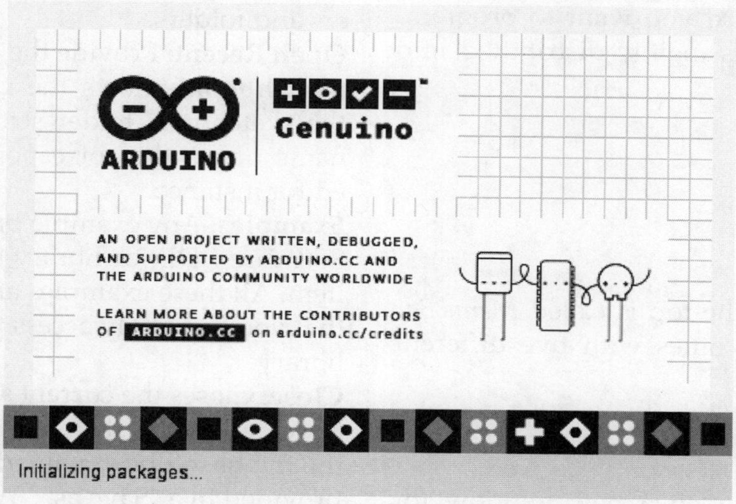

Figure 4.36 Arduino splash screen

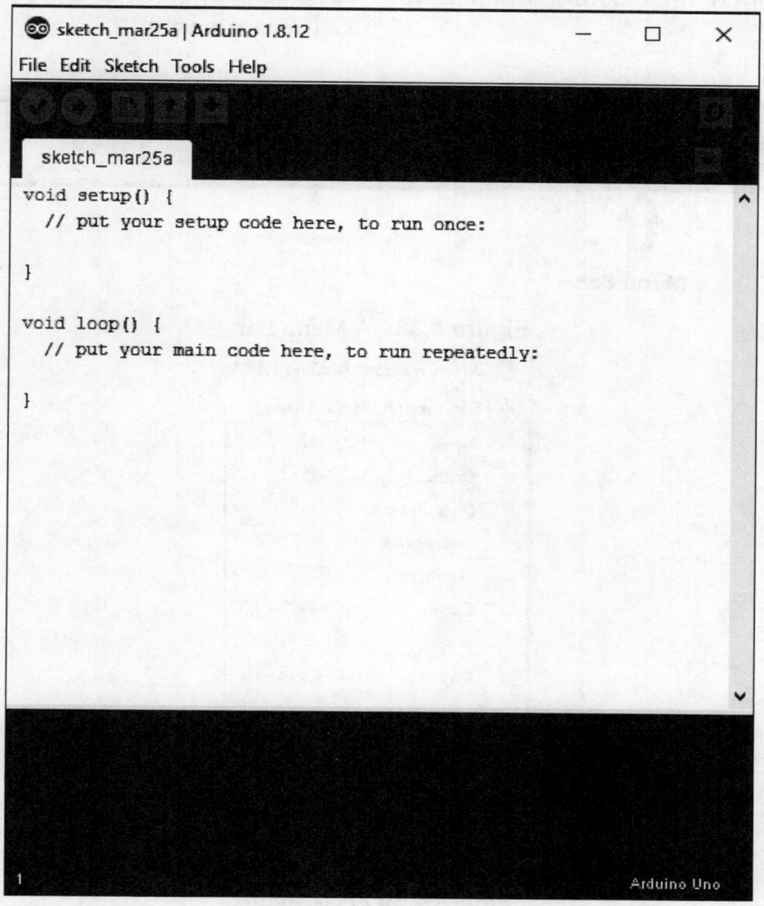

Figure 4.37 Arduino IDE

4.4 PARTS OF ARDUINO IDE

The Arduino IDE is the main text editing program used for Arduino programming. It is where you will be typing up your codes(sketches) before uploading it to the board you want to program. The IDE environment is mainly distributed into three parts:

- Menu Bar
- Text Editor
- Output Pane

4.4.1 Menu Bar

The bar appearing on the top is called *Menu Bar* (See Figure 4.38) that comes with five different options as follow:

File Menu

File menu is used to open a new window for writing the code or open an existing one. (See Figure 4.39).

New: Creates a new instance of the editor, with the bare minimum structure of a sketch already in place.
Open: Allows you to open the pre-existed sketches by browsing through the computer drivers and folders.
Open Recent: Provide the most recent sketches.
Sketchbook: Shows the current sketches within the sketchbook folder structure; clicking on any name opens the corresponding sketch in a new editor instance.
Examples: Any example provided by the Arduino Software (IDE) or library shows up in this menu item. All these examples are arranged in a tree. So that you can easily access them by using topics or library.
Close: Closes the current sketch.
Save: Saves the sketch with the current name. If the file hasn't been named before, a name will be provided in a "Save as.." Window.
Save as...: Allows to save the current sketch with a different name.

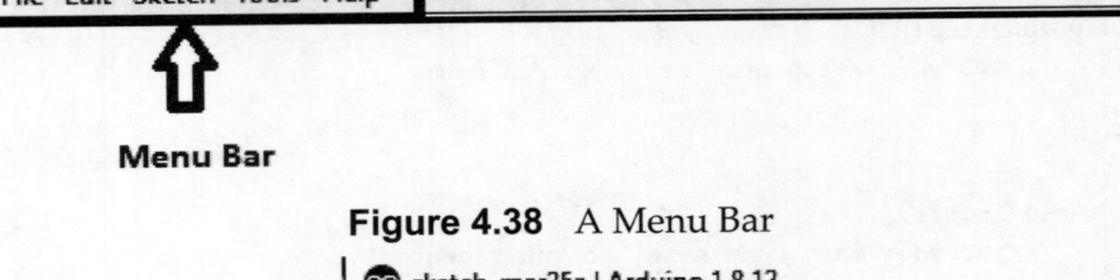

Figure 4.38 A Menu Bar

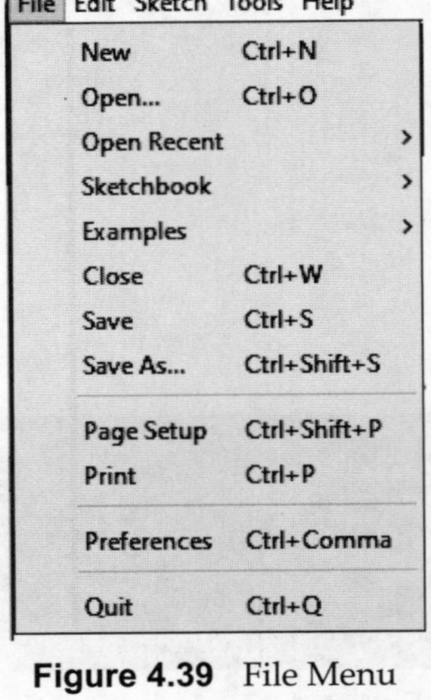

Figure 4.39 File Menu

Page Setup: It shows the Page Setup window for printing.
Print: Sends the current sketch to the printer according to the settings defined in Page Setup.
Preferences: Opens the Preferences window where you can customize the settings such as the language of the IDE interface.
Quit: Closes all IDE windows.

Edit Menu

Edit Menu is used for copying and pasting the code with further modification. (See Figure 4.40).

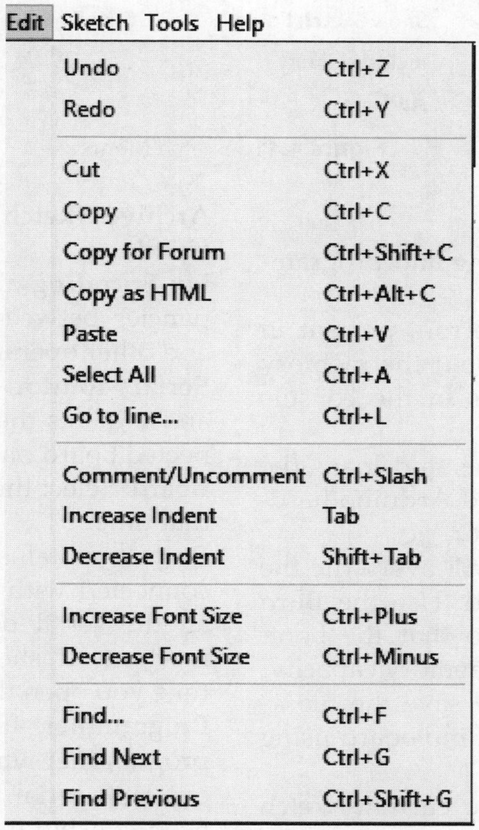

Figure 4.40 Edit Menu

Undo/Redo: You can go backwards or forward for one or more steps while editing using Undo and Redo respectively
Cut: Removes the selected text from the editor and places it into the clipboard.
Copy: Duplicates the selected text in the editor and places it into the clipboard.
Copy for Forum: Copies the code of your sketch to the clipboard in a form suitable for posting to the forum.
Copy as HTML: Copies the code of your sketch to the clipboard as HTML, suitable for embedding in web pages.
Paste: Pastes the content from the clipboard at the cursor position.
Select All: Selects and highlights the whole content of the editor i.e., the entire sketch.
Comment/Uncomment: Puts or removes the // comment marker at the beginning of each selected line.
Increase/Decrease Indent: Adds or subtracts a space at the beginning of each selected line.
Find: Opens the Find and Replace window where you can specify text to search inside the current sketch.
Find Next: Highlights the next occurrence of the specified string.
Find Previous: Highlights the previous occurrence of the specified string.

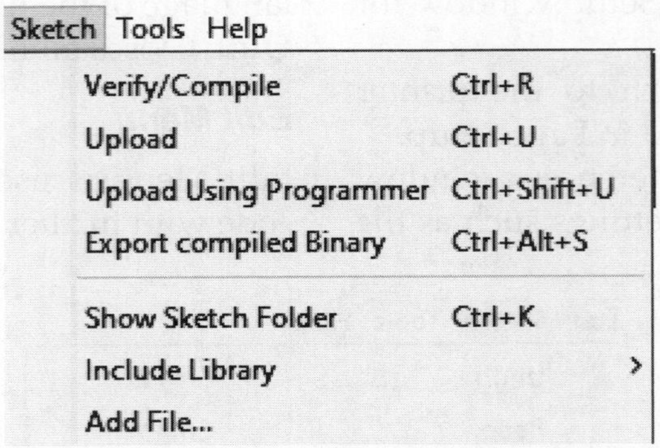

Figure 4.41 Sketch Menu

Sketch Menu

Sketch Menu is used for compiling and programming. (See Figure 4.41).

Verify/Compile: It checks the errors present in your sketch and informs you about the memory space occupied by the variables in the console area.

Upload: It automatically compiles and loads the code (binary file) into the selected Arduino hardware through the configured Port.

Upload Using Programmer: It will overwrite the bootloader present on the board. Use the Burn Bootloader tool to restore it. So that the bootloader can occupy the full flash memory capacity.

Export Compiled Binary: It will save the file as .hex file and send it to your Arduino board using other tools.

Show Sketch Folder: Opens the current sketch folder.

Include Library: Adds a library to your sketch by inserting #include statements at the start of your code. Additionally, from this menu item you can access the Library Manager and import new libraries from .zip files.

Add File...: Adds a source file to the sketch (it will be copied from its current location). The new file appears in a new tab in the sketch window.

Tools Menu

Tools Menu is mainly used for testing projects. (See Figure 4.42).

Auto Format: It will correct the indentations of the curly braces so that opening and closing curly braces line up.

Archive Sketch: It saves the current sketch as a zip file.

Fix Encoding and Reload: Fixes possible discrepancies between the editor char map encoding and other operating systems char maps.

Serial Monitor: Opens the serial monitor window and initiates the exchange of data with any connected board on the currently selected Port.

Board: Select the correct board that you are using that time.

Port: It contains all of the serial devices that are connected with your device This menu contains all the serial devices (real or virtual) on your machine. It should automatically refresh every time you open the top-level tools menu.

Programmer: It is used to select the hardware programmer while programming the board without USB serial connection. Normally you won't need this, but if you are burning a bootloader to a new microcontroller, you will use this.

Burn Bootloader: The items in this menu allow you to burn a bootloader onto the microcontroller on an Arduino board.

Help Menu

Help Menu is available from getting started to troubleshooting. (See Figure 4.43). Here you find easy access to a number of documents that come with the Arduino Software (IDE). You have access to Getting Started, Reference, this guide to the IDE and other documents locally, without an Internet connection. The documents are a local copy of the online ones and may link back to your online website.

Find in Reference: This is the only interactive function of the Help menu. It directly selects the relevant page in the local copy of the Reference for the function or command under the cursor.

The Arduino tool window is known as *Console Toolbar* shows different icons, starting from the left hand side the options are Verify/Compile, Upload, New, Open, Save and at to the extream right Serial Monitor. (See Figure 4.44).

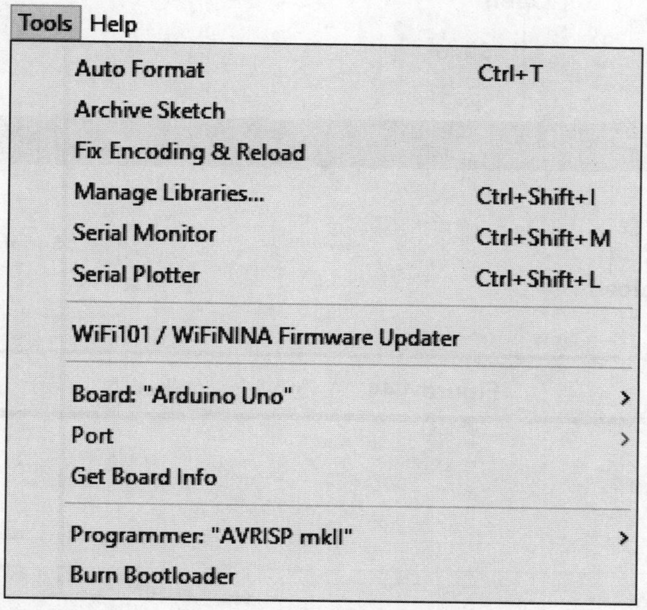

Figure 4.42 Tools Menu

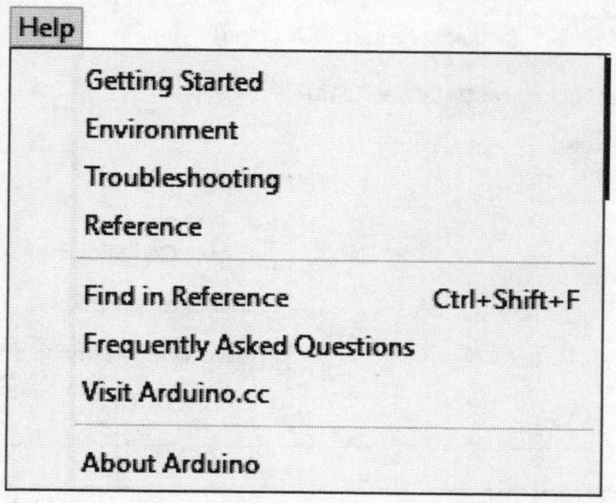

Figure 4.43 Help Menu

The arrow key will upload and transfer the required code to the Arduino board.
The dotted paper is used for creating a new file.
The upward arrow is reserved for opening an existing Arduino project.
The downward arrow is used to save the current running code.
The button appearing on the top right corner is a *Serial Monitor*. It is separate pop-up window that acts as an independent terminal and plays a vital role for sending and receiving the Serial Data.

Arduino serial monitor can be opened by clicking on the magnifying glass icon on the upper right side of the IDE. You can also go to the Tools panel and select Serial Monitor pressing Ctrl+Shift+M all at once will open the Serial Monitor. The serial monitor is used mainly for interacting with the Arduino board using the computer, and is a great tool for real-time monitoring and debugging. Your Arduino Module should be connected to your computer by USB cable in order to activate the Serial Monitor.

☞ *The serial monitor is simply an output screen, that can display the data sent by the Arduino board via USB.*

Now click on **File menu** and choose **Preferences**. It will display Preferences dialog box as shown in Figure 4.45. Now check **compilation** and **upload** options as shown in Figure 4.45.

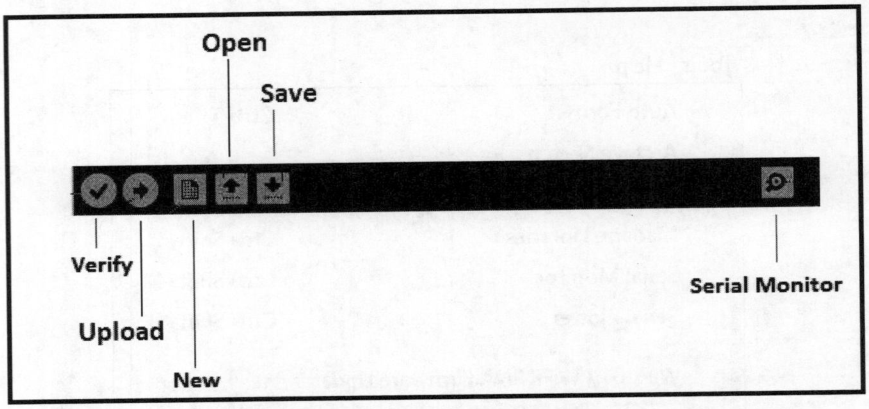

Figure 4.44 A Console Toolbar

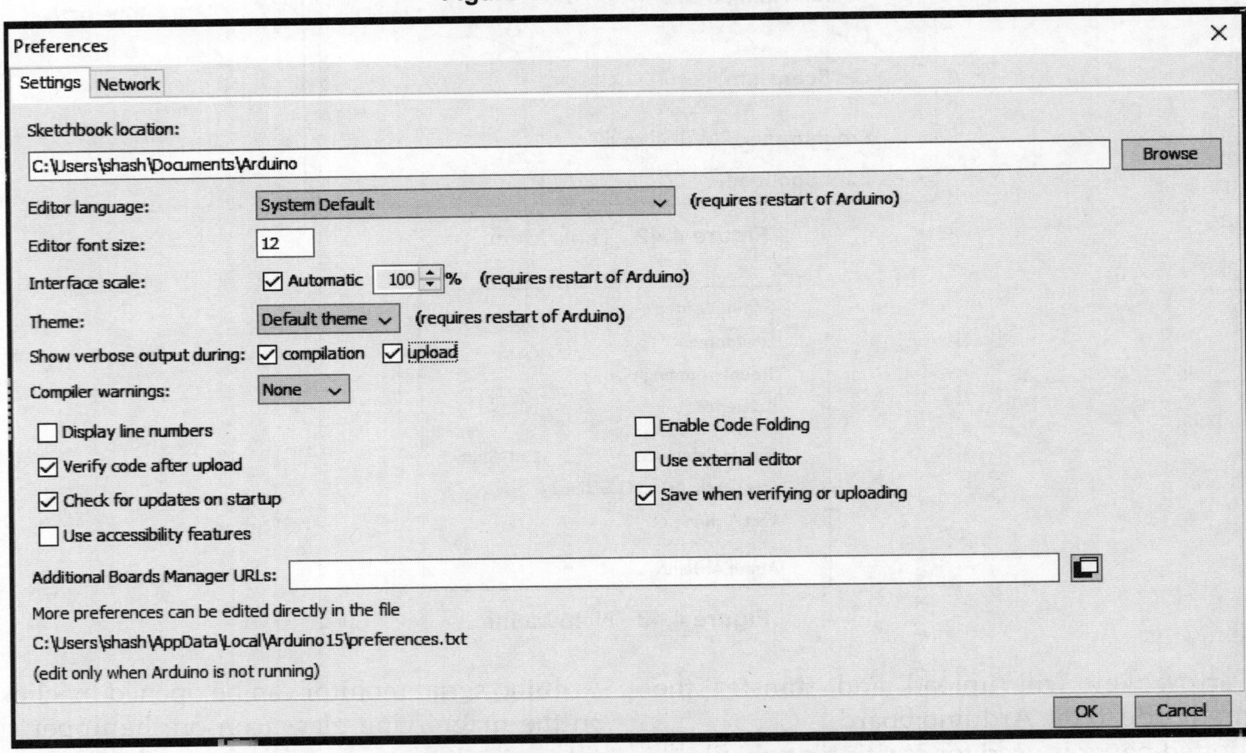

Figure 4.45 A Preferences dialog box

4.4.2 Text Editor

It is used for writing the required code. The sketch is written in the text editor and is then saved with the file extension *.ino*.

When you open the Arduino IDE, the editor window starts a new sketch. The name of the new sketch appears in the tab at the top of the editor window area, in the following format:

sketch_ mmmddx

where

mmm is a three-letter abbreviation of the month, *dd* is the two-digit numerical date, and *x* is a letter to make the sketch name unique for the day (for example, sketch_feb02a).

As you type your sketch code into the editor window, the editor will color-code different parts of the sketch code, such as making function names brown and text strings blue. This makes it easier to pick out syntax errors, and comes in handy when you are trying to debug your sketch.

After you enter the code into the editor window, choose **File > Save As** from the menu bar to save the sketch. Now you are ready to verify and compile the sketch.

☞ *Note that the recent Arduino Modules will reset automatically as you compile and press the upload button.*

4.4.3 Output Pane

The bottom of the main screen is described as an Output Pane that mainly highlights the compilation status of the running code: the memory used by the code, and errors occurred in the program. You need to fix those errors before you intend to upload the hex file into your Arduino Module.

More or less, Arduino C language works similar to the regular C language used for any embedded system microcontroller, however, there are some dedicated libraries used for calling and executing specific functions on the board. Libraries are very useful for adding the extra functionality into the Arduino Module. There is a list of libraries you can add by clicking the Sketch button in the menu bar and going to Include Library. As you click the Include Library and Add the respective library it will be on the top of the sketch with a #include sign.

On the bottom right hand corner of the window there displays the Development Board and the Serial Port in use.

☞ *Most of the libraries are pre-installed and come with the Arduino software. However, you can also download them from the external sources.*

4.5 DEVELOPMENT CYCLE

The sequence of program development is shown in the Figure 4.46 and discussed in the following sections.

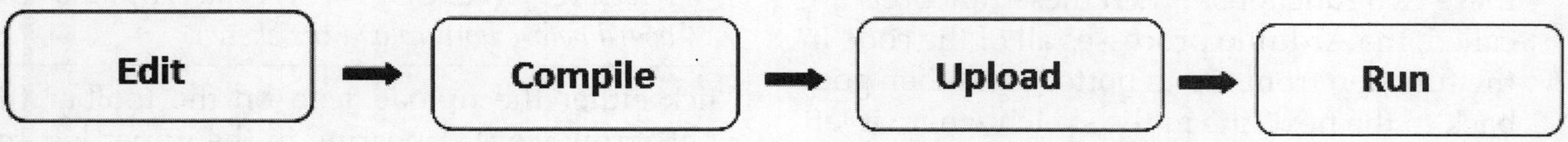

Figure 4.46 A Development Cycle

4.6 WRITING/EDITING CODE IN SKETCH

Sketch is the term used to indicate program or code written for Arduino. Each sketch contains three parts such as Variables Declaration, Initialization and Control code. Initialization is written in the setup function and Control code is written in the loop function.

☞ *Programming into the Arduino board is called as sketches.*

The sketch is saved with .ino and any operation like opening a sketch, verifying and saving can be done using the Tool menu. The sketch must be stored in the sketchbook directory.

The sketch, created on the IDE platform will ultimately generate a hex file which is then transferred and uploaded in the controller on the board. The IDE environment mainly contains two basic parts: Editor and Compiler where former is used for writing the required code and later is used for compiling and uploading the code into the given Arduino Module.

Some important things to keep in mind when writing your own code. Arduino sketches are typically broken into five parts:

a. The sketch usually starts with a header that explains what the sketch is doing, and who wrote it.

b. It usually defines global variables, where constant names are given to the different Arduino pins.
c. After the initial variables are set, the Arduino begins the setup routine. In the setup() function, you set initial conditions of variables when necessary, and run any preliminary code that you only want to run once. This is where serial communication is initiated, which is required for running the serial monitor. The setup() function must be present in the program, even if it does not contain anything.
d. From the setup() function, you go to the loop routine. This is the main routine of the sketch. This is not only where your main code goes, but it will be executed over and over, so long as the sketch continues to run.
e. Below the loop routine, there is often other functions listed. These functions are user-defined and only activated when called in the setup and loop routine. There are two required functions in an Arduino sketch or a program i.e., setup() and loop(). Other functions must be created outside the brackets of these two functions. When these functions are called, the Arduino processes all of the code in the function from top to bottom and then goes back to the next line in the sketch where it left off when the function was called.

4.7 COMPILING-DEBUGGING

The next step in the process is to compile the sketch code into the machine language code that the Arduino runs. Compile means to translate the sketch into machine language, also known as object code.

Click the verify icon on the toolbar (the checkmark icon), or choose Sketch -> Verify/Compile from the menu bar. You should see a message in the message area that the compile has completed, and the console window should show the final size of the compiled machine language code that will be uploaded to the Arduino.

If you have any typos such as incorrect punctuations, missing punctuations, misspellings, and wrong capitalizations in the sketch code that cause the compile process to fail, you will see an error message in the message area. The Arduino IDE also highlights the line of code that generated the error, making it easier for you to pick out the problem. Also, a more detailed error message appears in the console window area to help even more.

After you get the sketch to compile without any errors, the next step is to upload it to your Arduino.

4.8 UPLOADING AND RUNNING A FILE

In order to upload the sketch, you need to select the relevant board you are using and the ports for that operating system. Using the Arduino IDE click Tools > Serial Port menu bar option to set which serial port your Arduino is connected to. After you set that, you should be able to easily upload your compiled sketches.

☞ *There are few settings need to confirm such as selecting right COM Port and Arduino Uno board before you upload the sketch.*

Click either the upload icon on the toolbar (the right arrow icon) appearing in the upper left corner, or select **File -> Upload** from the menu bar in the Arduino environment for writing the code to the Arduino. Before the upload starts, the Arduino IDE recompiles the sketch code.

When the upload completes, you should see a message in both the Arduino IDE message area and console window indicating that the upload was completed. If anything goes wrong, you will see an error message that appears in the message area and the console window.

If all goes well, you are ready to start running your sketch on the Arduino. Run means Arduino sketch is executed. When the upload process completes, the bootloader automatically reboots the Arduino and runs your program code.

☞ *After writing the code automatic reset will be done so, the physical pressing of the reset button is not required.*

4.9 ROLE OF SERIAL MONITOR

Unlike other software programming platforms, Arduino does not have an onboard debugger. Users can either use third-party software, or they can utilize the serial monitor to print Arduino's active processes for monitoring and debugging.

The serial monitor allows your computer to connect serially with the Arduino. This is important because it takes data that your Arduino is receiving from sensors and other devices and displays it in real-time on your computer. Having this ability is invaluable to debug your code and understand what number values the chip is actually receiving.

You can view the output from the serial port on your Arduino using the serial monitor built in to the Arduino IDE. To access serial monitor goto the **Tools menu** and select **Serial Monitor** from the menu bar, or click the **serial monitor icon** (the magnifying glass icon) on the toolbar. The serial monitor window appears and displays the output received from the Arduino.

4.10 ROLE OF SERIAL PLOTTER

Arduino Serial Plotter is another component of the Arduino IDE, which allows you to generate a real-time graph of your serial data. The serial plotter makes it much easier for you to analyze your data through a visual display. You are able to create graphs, negative value graphs, and conduct waveform analysis. This feature helps a lot to understand the data variation in different conditions. For example, it helps you to understand the behavior of sensors in different situations. Above all, it is useful in code troubleshooting.

To access the serial plotter in the Arduino IDE go to the **Tools menu** and select the **Serial Plotter** option. This will enable you to see the graph of data.

Features of Serial plotter:

- It can plot multiple graphs.
- It is an offline tool to visualize the data in the form of graphs.
- It can support negative value graphs.
- It can Auto-resize graph.
- Different colours can be assigned for every variable.

☞ *Baud rate in Arduino IDE is the number of signals transitions that occur in one second.*

4.11 LED PROGRAMMING

Before you start with the programming you should have a basic knowledge of new electronic components needed to implement different projects. Now lets begin playing with our LED adventure. You need an Arduino board, a breadboard , an LED, a resistor and jumper wires. (See Figure 4.47).

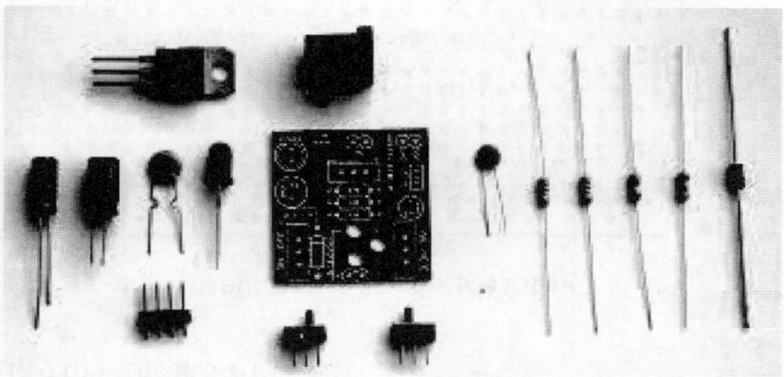

Figure 4.47 Electronic components to implement different projects

4.11.1 Arduino board

There are many electronic boards you have already seen, but Arduino uno is simple, easy to use board to handle simple repetitive tasks like turning on an LED, etc. It is based on a microcontroller which is a simple easy to use computer designed for beginners. (See Figure 4.48).

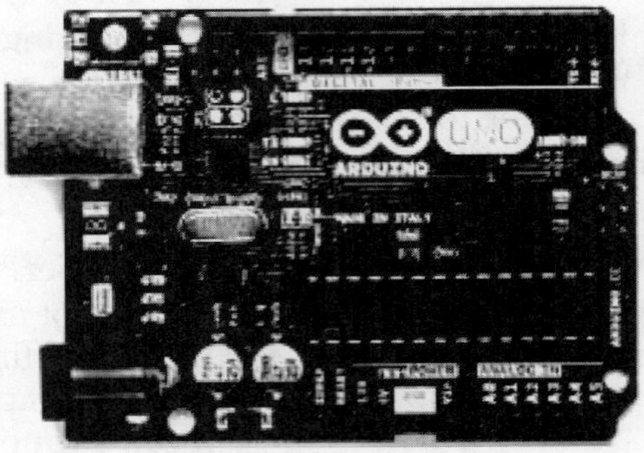

Figure 4.48 An Arduino Uno board

4.11.2 Breadboard

A breadboard is a circuit board that is used to make temporary circuits and prototyping as shown in Figure 4.49. *Prototyping* is the process of testing out an idea by creating a preliminary model from which other forms are developed or copied. A breadboard generally consists of lots of holes so that wires can easily be pushed in. In order to form a circuit, wires are inserted simply inside the holes. An advantage of using a breadboard is that the positions of the wires can be changed if they are placed in a wrong order. Also, connections of the breadboard are mostly temporary and the elements can further be reassembled and reused without any damage.

Standard wires cannot be used for breadboard as they get damaged easily and hence they require single core plastic coated wires that have 0.6mm diameter. Standard wires if used can also lead to damage of the board.

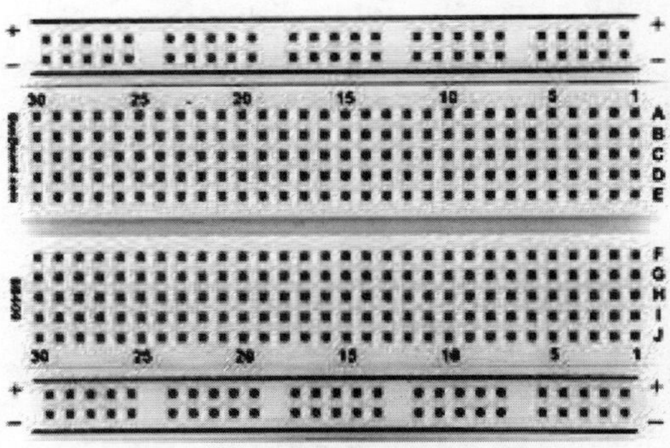

Figure 4.49 A breadboard

4.11.3 LED

Light Emitting Diode or simply LED is one of the most commonly used sources of light now-a-days. They do many different jobs in all kinds of devices. For instance, they are widely used for displaying the time and many other types of data on screens in certain display devices. It is also used in applications such as digital clocks, transmit information from remote controls, light up watches, illuminate a traffic lights, incandescent bulbs, and tell you when your appliances are turned on. (See Figure 4.50).

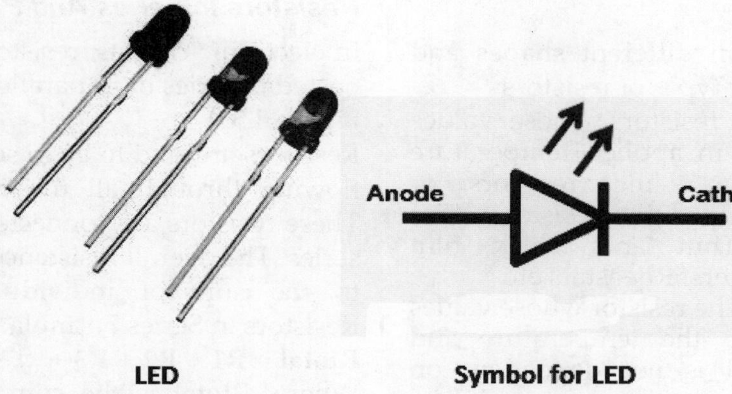

Figure 4.50 LED's and electrical symbol for an LED

Advantages of LED

- Small size and low cost.
- Long life time and high energy efficiency.
- Low temperature and generate very little heat.
- Available in many colours and are eco-friendly.
- High switching speed and luminous intensity.

Disadvantages of LED

- Ambient temperature dependence of radiant output power and wavelength of the LED.
- Sensitivity to damages by excess voltage and/or excess current.

4.11.4 Resistor

A resistor is an electrical component that limits or regulates the flow of electrical current in an electronic circuit. Resistors can also be used to provide a specific voltage for an active device such as a transistor. All other factors being equal, in a direct-current (DC) circuit, the current through a resistor is inversely proportional to its resistance, and directly proportional to the voltage across it. This is the well-known *Ohm's Law*. Resistance is the property of opposing the flow of electrons, in a conductor or a semiconductor. A Resistor is an electronic component which has the property of resistance. The units of resistance is Ohms, which is indicated by Ω omega. The formula for resistance is R = V/I, where V is Voltage and I is Current.

In alternating-current (AC) circuits, this rule also applies as long as the resistor does not contain inductance or capacitance. The most common schematic symbol for a resistor is a zig-zag line. Resistors can be fabricated in a variety of ways. (See Figure 4.51).

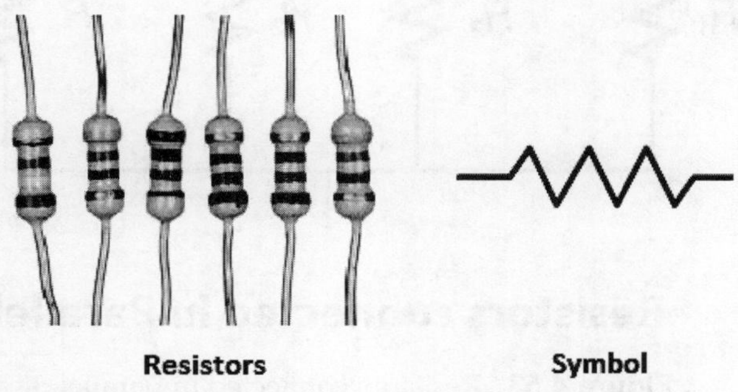

Figure 4.51 Resistors and symbol for resistor

Types of Resistors

Resistors are available in different shapes and sizes. There are two basic types of resistors:

- **Linear resistor**: The resistors whose values change with change in applied temperature and voltage are known as linear resistors. For example, Carbon composition resistors, Wire wound resistors, Thin and Thick film resistors, Potentiometers, Rheostats etc.
- **Non-linear resistor**: The resistor whose values change according to the temperature and voltage applied and is not dependent on Ohm's law. For example, Thermisters, Varisters, Photo resistors etc.

Resistors are used in digital multi-meter, amplifiers, telecommunication, oscillators, modulators, demodulators, and transmitters etc. Photo resistors find application in flame detectors, burglar alarm, in photographic devices, etc.

Resistors In Series And Parallel

In electronic circuits, resistors are very often connected in series or in parallel. (See Figure 4.52 and Figure 4.53).

Resistors are said to be in series when the current flowing through all the resistors is the same. These resistors are connected from head to tail in series. The overall resistance of the circuit is equal to the sum of individual resistance values. Resistors in Series Formula:

Rtotal = R1 + R2 + R3 + ...+Rn

Where, Rtotal is the sum of all the individual resistances.

Resistors in parallel share the same voltage at their terminals. Resistors in Parallel Formula:

1Rtotal=1R1 + 1R2 +..+ 1Rn

Where, 1Rtotal is the sum of all the individual resistances.

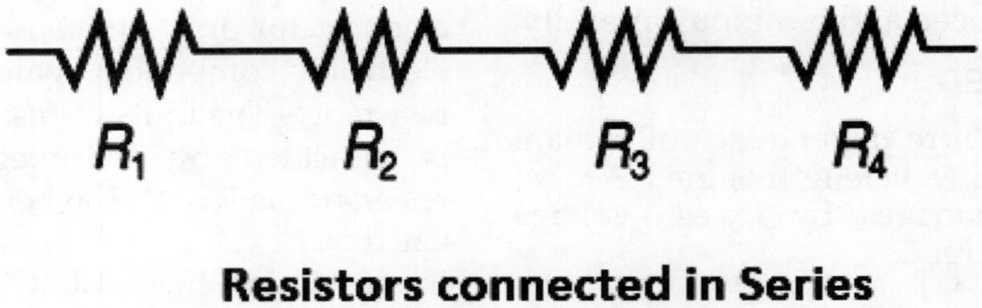

Figure 4.52 Resistors connected in series

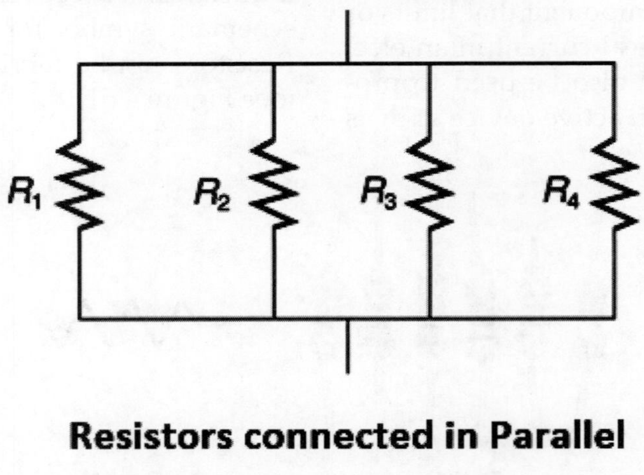

Figure 4.53 Resistors connected in parallel

4.11.5 Jumper wires

Jumper wires are simply wires that have connector pins at each end, allowing them to be used to connect two points to each other without soldering. Jumper wires are typically used with breadboards and other prototyping tools in order to make it easy to change a circuit as needed.

Jumper wires come in a variety of colors, the colors don't actually mean anything. This means that a red jumper wire is technically the same as a black one. But the colors can be used to differentiate between types of connections, such as ground or power.

Jumper wires typically come in three versions: *male-to-male*, *male-to-female* and *female-to-female*. The difference between each is in the end point of the wire. Figure 4.54, 4.55 and 4.56 shows different versions of jumper wires.

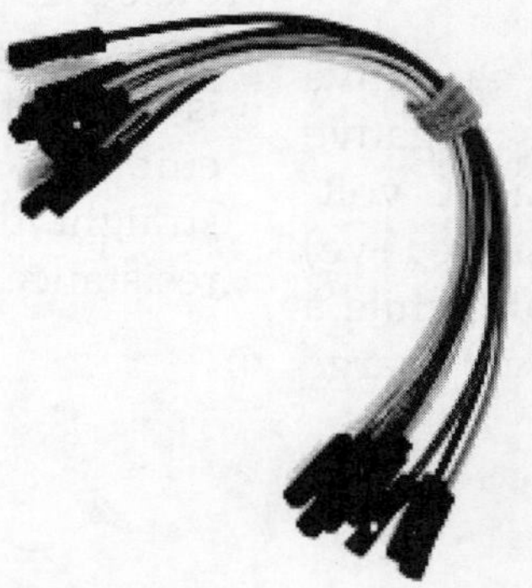

Figure 4.54 Male-to-male jumper cables

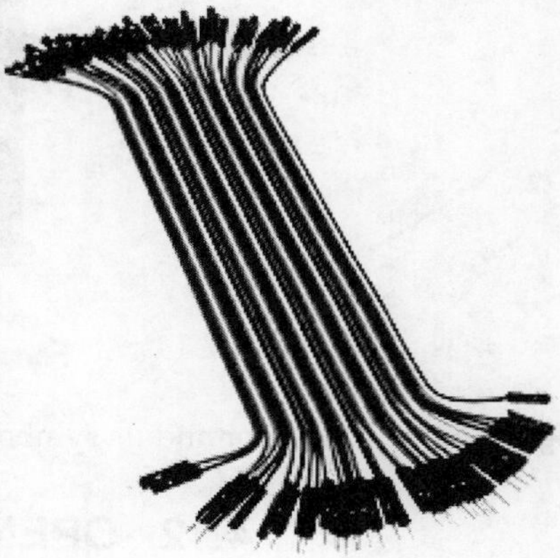

Figure 4.55 Female-to-female jumper cable

Figure 4.56 Male-to-female jumper cable

4.11.6 Capacitor

A capacitor is a device that stores electrical energy in an electric field. It is a passive electronic component with two terminals. The effect of a capacitor is known as *capacitance*. Each capacitor is built to have a specific amount of capacitance. The capacitance of a capacitor tells you how much charge it can store, more capacitance means more capacity to store charge. The standard unit of capacitance is called the farad, which is abbreviated F. (See Figure 4.57).

There are two types of electrical charge, a positive charge in the form of protons and a negative charge in the form of electrons. When a DC voltage is placed across a capacitor, the positive (+ve) charge quickly accumulates on one plate while a corresponding and opposite negative (-ve) charge accumulates on the other plate. The flow of electrons onto the plates is known as the capacitors charging current which continues to flow until the voltage across both plates (and hence the capacitor) is equal to the applied voltage Vc. At this point the capacitor is said to be "fully charged" with electrons.

When used in a direct current or DC circuit, a capacitor charges up to its supply voltage but blocks the flow of current through it because the dielectric of a capacitor is non-conductive and basically an insulator. However, when a capacitor is connected to an alternating current or AC circuit, the flow of the current appears to pass straight through the capacitor with little or no resistance.

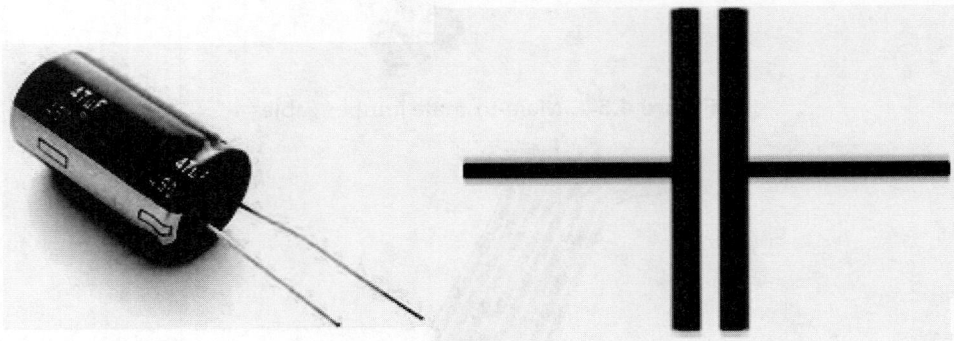

Capacitor **Symbol**

Figure 4.57 Capacitor and its symbol

4.11.7 Designing simple LED circuit

Now let us consider designing simple LED circuit which makes the LED to glow using a power supply through a resistor for controlling the power to LED. Connect the external power supply through binding posts or directly from voltage source using jumping wires. Then, connect these jumper wires to the LED through a resistor. Now, switch ON the power supply and thus the LED glows.

4.12 OPEN YOUR FIRST SKETCH

The Arduino programmer comes with a many example of sketches preloaded. This is great because even if you have never programmed anything in your life, you can load one of these sketches and get the Arduino to do something.

Let's work with our very first Arduino sketch/program. But before that connect the Arduino Uno or compatible clone to the PC with USB cable as shown in Figure 4.58.

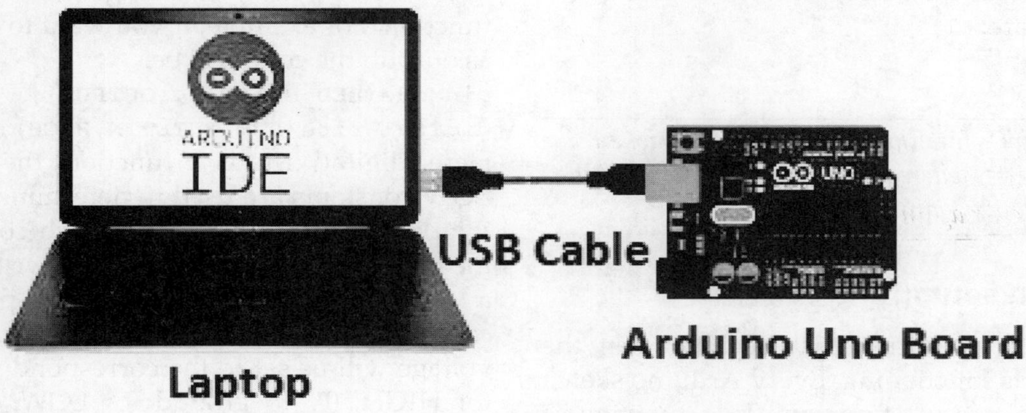

Figure 4.58 Arduino Uno connected to the laptop with USB cable

Once connected and when your PC/laptop is powered on, the power LED on the Arduino Uno board will glow, indicating that the board is in ON state. To check whether Windows OS identifies the board open up the Control Panel and open the Device Manager window. Check the Ports (COM and LPT) section to know that at what port Arduino board is connected. Now, click **Tools->Board** and choose the right board which you are using from the list of available boards.

Select the serial device of the board from the **Tools->Port**. This is likely to be COM3 or higher (COM1 and COM2 are usually reserved for hardware serial ports). To find out, you can disconnect your board and re-open the menu; the entry that disappears should be the Arduino board. Reconnect the board and select that serial port.

You know that Pin 13 of Arduino Uno board is connected to a built-in LED. Let's load the blink example belongs to built-in example project. This program will blink onboard LED with the delay of 1 second. Open the Arduino software you have downloaded by double clicking on the Arduino icon.

`Click File -> Example -> Basics -> Blink`

It will open an example program Blink.ino as shown in Figure 4.59. The blink example basically sets pin D13 as an output and then blinks the test LED on the Arduino board *on* and *off* every second.

```
// the setup function runs once when you press reset or power the board
void setup() {
  // initialize digital pin LED_BUILTIN as an output.
  pinMode(LED_BUILTIN, OUTPUT);
}
// the loop function runs over and over again forever
void loop() {
  digitalWrite(LED_BUILTIN, HIGH); // turn the LED on (HIGH is the voltage level)
  delay(1000);                     // wait for a second
  digitalWrite(LED_BUILTIN, LOW);  // turn the LED off by making the voltage LOW
  delay(1000);                     // wait for a second
}
```

Figure 4.59 LED blink program

The program in Arduino consists of two functions. These are:

a. void setup()
b. void loop()

☞ *The setup() function is called once, when the sketch starts, whereas the loop() function is called over and over again repeatedly.*

4.12.1 void setup()

This is the first routine that begins when the Arduino starts functioning. Every Arduino sketch must have a setup() function. This function is executed only once throughout the entire program functioning. The setup() function contains the initialization of every pin you intend use in your project for input or output. It is also used to initialize classes and variables.
Here, the pin is the no. of the pin that is to be defined. INPUT/OUPUT correspond to the mode in which the pin is to be used.

☞ *The first few lines of the Blink sketch are a comment. Everything between the /* and */ is ignored by the Arduino when it runs the sketch. Also // is another style for short, single-line comments. These start with // and continue to the end of the line.*

4.12.2 void loop()

This function is the next important function in the Sketch. It consists of that part of the code that needs to be continuously executed in a loop over and over again. The loop describes the main logic of your circuit.

☞ *The use of the term **void** means that the function doesn't return any values.*

Making Pins As Input or Output

The digitalRead and digitalWrite commands are used for addressing and making the Arduino pins as an input and output respectively. These commands are text sensitive i.e., you need to write them down the exact way they are given like digitalWrite starting with small 'd' and write with capital 'W'. Writing it down with Digitalwrite or digitalwrite won't be calling or addressing any function. For example, if you want to use Pin D13 as output, the code will be:

```
pinMode(LED_BUILTIN, OUTPUT);
digitalWrite(LED_BUILTIN,HIGH);
```

Here, digitalWrite is a function, the HIGH and LOW constants are used to determine the state of the pins in these functions, which correspond to the high and low signal level that writes a high or a low value to a digital pin. If the pin has been configured as an OUTPUT with pinMode(), its voltage will be set to the corresponding value 5V for HIGH, 0V to ground for LOW. This allows turn things on and off and making LED blink.
Similarly, if there is a need for delay in the sketch then there is another function delay() that creates a delay in the execution of the code. This creates a delay in the execution of the program for the time period specified (in milliseconds).

☞ *There are 1000 milliseconds in a second.*

Now to check your board with an blinking led, compile the Blink led program Click the verify icon on the toolbar (the checkmark icon), or choose Sketch-> Verify/Compile from the menu bar. If the compile is successful, the message "*Done compiling.*" will appear in the status bar. (See Figure 4.60)
Now you can upload the sketch. Click either the upload icon on the toolbar (the right arrow icon) appearing in the upper left corner, or select File ->Upload from the menu bar in the Arduino environment for writing the code to the Arduino. Before the upload starts, the Arduino IDE recompiles the sketch code. If the upload is successful, the message "*Done uploading.*" will appear in the status bar.
Notice that the surface mount status LED connected to pin 13 on the Arduino will start to blink. You can change the rate of the blinking by changing the length of the delay and pressing the Upload button again.
You know that the Arduino board is connected to a computer via USB, where it connects with the Arduino development environment (IDE). The user writes the Arduino code in the IDE, then uploads it to the microcontroller which executes the code, interacting with inputs and outputs

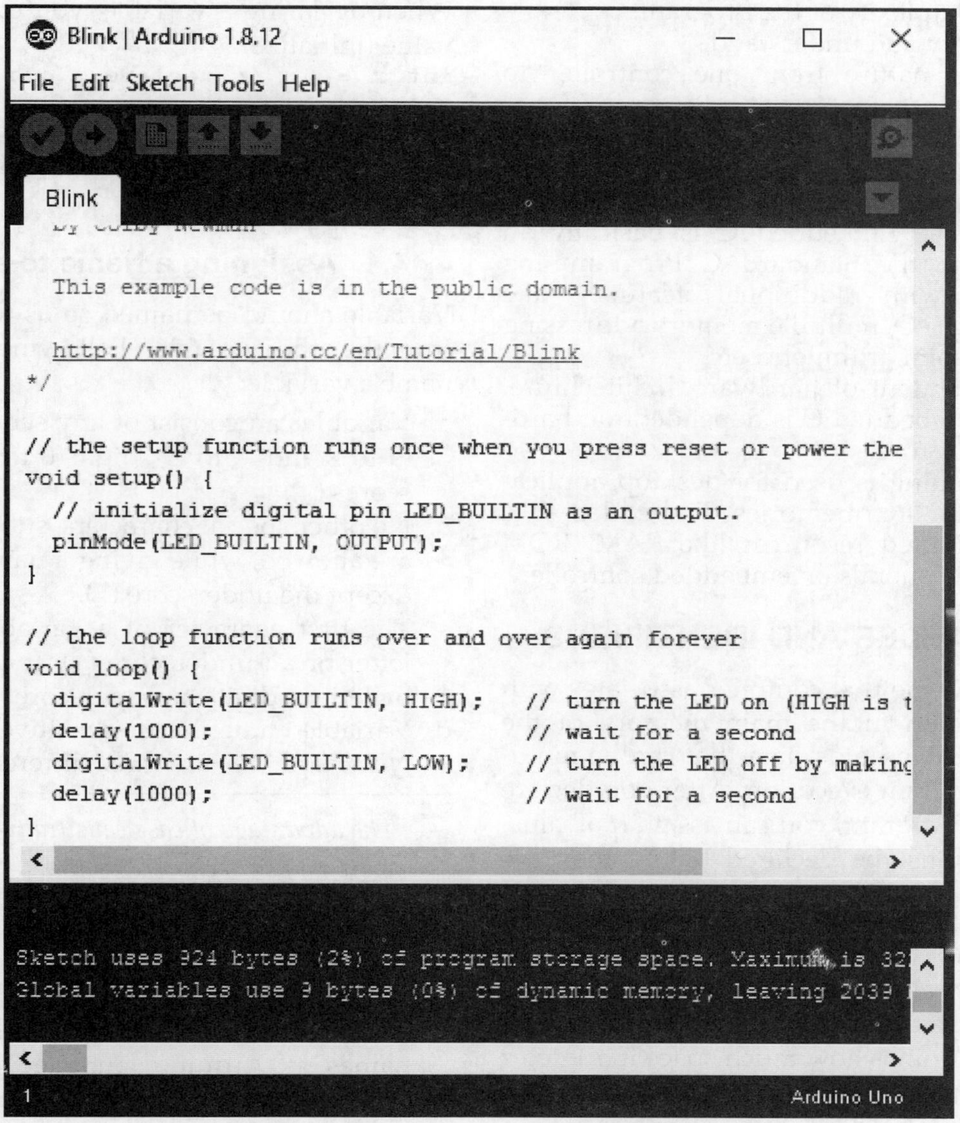

Figure 4.60 The the message - Done compiling

such as sensors, motors, and lights. So, user can write their own code or use thousands of Arduino code examples available online.

4.13 EMBEDDED 'C' LANGUAGE BASICS

C is a high-level programming language intended for system programming. Embedded C is an extension that provides support for developing efficient programs for embedded devices. The embedded C programming language uses the same syntax and semantics as the C programming language. We use Embedded C to write Arduino programs. Embedded C finds applications in cases where the coding is very near to the hardware. This means that the language directly communicates with the hardware.

In day-to-day life you used many electronic devices such as mobile phone, washing machine, digital camera, etc. These all device working is based on microcontroller that are programmed by embedded C.

Features of embedded C

- Easy to understand.
- High Reliability.
- Less development time.

- Reduces complexity of the program.
- Easy to verify and understand.
- Portable in nature from one controller to another.

Difference between C and Embedded C

- Both C and Embedded C are ISO Standards that have almost same syntax, datatypes, functions, etc. Embedded C is basically an extension to the Standard C Programming Language with additional features like Addressing I/O, multiple memory addressing and fixed-point arithmetic, etc.
- C is independent of hardware architechture. Where as embedded C is dependent on hardware architecture.
- C programming is used for desktop application, OS and PC memories. Embedded C is used for limited resources like RAM, ROM and I/O peripherals on embedded controller.

4.14 VARIABLES AND IDENTIFIERS

A *variable* is a name that compiler associates with a storage location in the main memory of the computer. Variable holds data that can be modified during program execution. After you declare a variable in a program, you can assign it a value. All variables must be declared before they are used.

```
int j; //declare a variable with the name j of type int
```

You assign a value to a variable using the equal sign (called the assignment operator). The type of a variable determines how much space it occupies in the storage and how the bit pattern stored is interpreted.

The statement:

```
j = 5 + 10;
```

means "add the value 5 with 10 and assign the result to a variable called `j`." You know that "5" and "10" are integer values, "+" and "=" are operators, a semicolon ";" determines the end of the statement and `j` is a variable which can take different values.

The numbers 5 and 10 are constants because they have the same value no matter where they appear in a program. The alphabet `j`, is the name given to the variable which will be able to represent different values at different time in the same program.

When declaring a variable, you can set its initial value (initialize).

```
int x = 0; // declare a variable x with initial value 0
int total = 0; // the integer value named total is defined and assigned a value of zero (0)
```

4.14.1 Assigning a Name to a Variable

Variable should be named so as to distinguish it from the other variables. Following are the *rules* to name a variable:

a. Variable can consist of any sequence of letters (a to z and A to Z), digits(0 to 9), and underscores (_).
b. No other special characters, such as +, $, –, etc., are allowed, while giving a name to a variable except the underscore (_).
c. The first character of a variable should be a letter or an underscore (_). It can be followed by letters, digits or underscore.
d. Variable name is case-sensitive. That is, *Num*, *NUM* and *num* are three different variables.

☞ *The advantage of case sensitivity is that you have more names to choose from.*

e. Reserved words called *keywords* convey specific meaning to the compiler of language and cannot be used as names of identifiers or variables. Variables may not have the same names as Arduino language keywords, e.g. you can not have a variable named int.
f. Variables must have unique names i.e. you can not have two variables with the same name.

☞ *A variable is an identifier that is used to represent some specified type of information within a designated portion of a program.*

Identifiers are the names given to program elements, such as variables, functions and arrays, etc. Identifiers are also the names of objects, which can take different values but only one value at a time.

Once a type or value is assigned to an identifier, it cannot be changed during the execution of the program. For example, if an integer variable is named as 'x' then 'x' will always remain an integer variable which can hold varying integer values only.

4.15 KEYWORDS

At the time of designing compiler of a programming language such as C, some words are reserved to do specific tasks. Such words are called *keywords* or *reserved words*.

They are standard and predefined in the Embedded C. These keywords must be defined before writing the main program. The embedded C additional keywords are given below:

sbit: "sbit" is used for declaring the single PIN of the microcontroller.

bit: "bit" is used for checking status of the variable.

SFR (Special Function Register): "SFR" is used for accessing a SFR register by another name. All the SFR registers must be declared with capital letters.

volatile: The variable that declares with the volatile keyword value can not be changed unexpectedly.

macro: The macro is a name used to declare the block of statements as pre-processor directive. The macros are represented by the #define.

4.16 BUILT-IN DATA TYPES

The kind of data that the variable may hold in a programming language is referred to as data types. There are various types of data, such as *integer, character, real, string,* etc., that a variable may contain in a programming language. All such types are named as *data type*. Anything enclosed in a 'single quotes' represents character data. Numbers without fractions represents integer data. Number with fractions represents real (float) data. Anything enclosed in "double quotes" represents a string.

There are two reasons for distinguishing among different data types. These are:

- The compiler which translates a program into object code (0 and 1 form) can use the proper internal representation for each data type.
- The programmer while designing a program may use the correct operators to operate on each type of data.

The fundamental data types in C are char, int, float and double. Some of these data types may be modified by keywords short, long, signed, and unsigned. The modifiers short and long specify the amount of storage allocation to the fundamental type they modify. The modifiers signed and unsigned specify whether the most significant bit represents a sign bit or not. C language also supports derived data types such as pointer reference types, array and struct.

A character variable occupies one byte of space in memory in which the character constant, such as 'b' or 'x' can be stored. The type name for a character is *char*.

int is another type of numerical variable and stores positive or negative integers.

☞ *The data type int should not be used to hold fractions or real numbers.*

To store a fraction, you need a floating point type of data variable, called data type *float*.

A *double* data type can store a floating point value with a greater accuracy than a *float* type.

There are two kinds of variables, signed and unsigned. Signed variables can have a positive or negative value, so you can store negative numbers. Unsigned variables can only store positive numbers. Unsigned variables are useful if you know in advance that there will never be a negative value for that variable. For example, the number of students in a class can never be less than zero, so an unsigned variable should be used. By default, variables are signed.

The following section provides all the data types that you will use during Arduino programming:

4.16.1 void

The void keyword is used only in function declarations. It indicates that the function is expected to return no information to the function from which it was called.

```
void loop () {
    // rest of the code
}
```

4.16.2 boolean

A Boolean holds one of two values, true or false. Each Boolean variable occupies one byte of memory.

```
boolean val = false; // declaration of variable with type boolean and initialize it with false
boolean state = true; // declaration of variable with type boolean and initialize it with true
```

4.16.3 char

A data type that takes up one byte of memory stores a character value. Character literals are written in single quotes like this: 'A' and for multiple characters, strings use double quotes: "ABC". Characters are stored as numbers. This means that it is possible to do arithmetic on characters, in which the ASCII value of the character is used (e.g. 'A' + 1 has the value 66, since the ASCII value of the capital letter A is 65).

```
char chr_a = 'a'; //declaration of variable with type char and initialize it with character a
char chr_c = 97;//declaration of variable with type char and initialize it with character 97
```

4.16.4 unsigned char

An unsigned char is an unsigned data type that occupies one byte of memory. The unsigned char data type encodes numbers from 0 to 255.

```
unsigned char chr_y = 121; // declaration of variable with type Unsigned char and initialize it with character y
```

4.16.5 byte

A byte stores an 8-bit unsigned number, from 0 to 255.

```
byte m = 25 ;//declaration of variable with type byte and initialize it with 25
```

4.16.6 int

Integers are the primary data-type for number storage. int stores a 16-bit (2-byte) value. This yields a range of -32,768 to 32,767. The int size varies from board to board. On the Arduino Uno, for example, an int stores a 32-bit (4-byte) value.

```
int counter = 32 ;// declaration of variable with type int and initialize it with 32
```

4.16.7 unsigned int

An unsigned ints (unsigned integers) are the same as int in the way that they store a 2 byte value. Instead of storing negative numbers, however, they only store positive values, yielding a useful range of 0 to 65,535

```
unsigned int counter = 60 ; // declaration of variable with type unsigned int and initialize it with 60
```

4.16.8 word

A word can store an unsigned number of at least 16 bits (from 0 to 65535).

```
word w = 1000 ;//declaration of variable with type word and initialize it with 1000
```

4.16.9 long

The long variables are extended size variables for number storage, and store 32 bits (4 bytes), from -2,147,483,648 to 2,147,483,647.

```
long velocity = 102346 ;//declaration of variable with type long and initialize it with 102346
```

4.16.10 unsigned long

Unsigned long variables are extended size variables for number storage and store 32 bits (4 bytes). Unlike standard longs, unsigned longs will not store negative numbers.

```
unsigned Long velocity = 101006 ;// declaration of variable with type unsigned long and initialize it with 101006
```

4.16.11 short

A short is a 16-bit data-type. On all Arduinos (ATMega and ARM based), a short stores a 16-bit (2-byte) value. This yields a range of -32,768 to 32,767.

```
void setup() {
  float average;
  Serial.begin(9600);
  average = 12.3299;
  Serial.println(average);
  Serial.println(average, 4);
}
void loop() {
}
```

Figure 4.61 Printing a float Value

short val = 13 ;//declaration of variable with type short and initialize it with 13

4.16.12 float

Data type for floating-point number is a number that has a decimal point. Floating-point numbers are often used to approximate the analog and continuous values because they have greater resolution than integers. They are stored as 32 bits (4 bytes) of information.

float num = 12.3299;//declaration of variable with type float and initialize it with 12.3299

To print or send a floating point value to the Arduino serial monitor window, the println() function can be used. A second parameter can be passed to the println() function to specify the number of decimal places that must be printed as shown in sketch given in Figure 4.61.

The above sketch assigns a value of 12.3299 to the average floating point variable. When the value of the variable is sent to the serial monitor window, you can see that println() automatically rounds the number off to two decimal places.

The second time that println() is used to send the value of the variable to the serial monitor window, the number of decimal places is specified as 4. This is done by passing a second parameter value of 4 to the println() function.

4.16.13 double

On the Uno and other ATMEGA based boards, double precision floating-point number occupies four bytes. That is, the double implementation is exactly the same as the float, with no gain in precision.

double num = 45.352 ;// declaration of variable with type double and initialize it with 45

4.16.14 String

In pure C, you don't have the data type String, but in C for Arduino, you do. It is a particular structure of data, namely a class, that provides a nice way to use and work with strings of text. It comes with methods/functions to easily concatenate strings, split strings, and much more. Be careful of the capital "S" at the beginning of String. Let's look at a basic program using the string data type as shown in Figure 4.62.

```
// Demo of String data type
String myString = "Hello, How are you?";
void setup() {
  Serial.begin(9600);
  Serial.print(myString);
}
void loop() {
}
```

Figure 4.62 Demo of String data type

The output is a plain text that you assigned to your String variable, myString.

4.16.15 string

It stores text strings in an array of char which are the same as the strings used in C programming. A string is an array of char variables. It is a special array that has one extra element at the end of the string which always has the value of 0 (zero). This is known as a "null terminated string". Be careful of the "s" in lower case at the beginning of string. All of the following are valid declarations for strings.

```
char Str1[10];
char Str2[6] = {'h', 'e', 'l', 'l', 'o'};
char my_str[] = "Hello";
```

☞ *Characters are written between single quotes where as strings are written between double quotes.*

4.16.16 array

An array is a collection of variables that are accessed with an index number.

4.16.17 size_t

size_t is a data type capable of representing the size of any object in bytes. Examples of the use of size_t are the return type of sizeof() and Serial.print().

4.17 VARIABLE SCOPE

The *scope* of a variable refers to the extent to which different parts of a program have access to the variable - in other words, the variable is *visible*.

Scope also affects a variable's *lifetime*, i.e., how long the variable persists in memory, or in other words when the variable's storage is allocated and deallocated.

A variable can be declared in any part of the program, but it determines which blocks of the program can use it. A scope is a region of the program and there are three places where variables can be declared. They are:

- Inside a function or a block, which is called local variables.
- In the definition of function parameters, which is called formal parameters
- Outside of all functions, which is called global variables.

4.17.1 Local Variables

Variables that are declared inside a function or block are local variables. They can be used only by the statements that are inside that function or block of code. Local variables are not known to function outside their own. Following is the example using local variables as shown in Figure 4.63.

```
// Demo of local variable
void setup () {
  // empty block, initial settings are not required
}
void loop () {
  int x , y ;
  int z ; //Local variable declaration
  x = 0;
  y = 0; //actual initialization
  z = 10;
}
```

Figure 4.63 Demo of local variable

In the above sketch the variable z is only available in the loop() function.

☞ *A local variable is one that is defined within a function. The scope of a local variable is limited to the function in which it is defined.*

4.17.2 Global Variables

Global variables are defined outside of all the functions, usually at the top of the program. The global variables will hold their value throughout the life-time of your program. Variables declared at the beginning of the program, prior to the void setup() function, are considered global and are available anywhere in the program.

A global variable can be accessed by any function. That is, a global variable is available for use throughout your entire program after its declaration.

The following example uses global and local variables as shown in Figure 4.64.

```
// Demo of global and local variables
float c = 0; //Global variable declaration
void setup () {
}
void loop () {
  int x , y ;
  int z ; //Local variable declaration
  x = 0;
  y = 0;
  z = 10;
}
```

Figure 4.64 Demo of global and local variables

In the above sketch variable *c* is available to all functions.

4.18 COMMENT

Commenting sketches allows you to write your own text notes along with the code of the sketch.

4.18.1 Multi-line Comments

The first line starting with the characters /* and ending with the characters */ is the *comment.* Comments are important because they help in documenting a program. Comments should be written so that the logic of a program is understood easily. You may type as many lines as you wish between these two sets of characters i.e., (/*, */) for writing comments. Note that the compiler ignores comments, and does not take any action.

4.18.2 Single Line Comments

The double forward slash (//) is used to create a single line comment. All text to the right of the double forward slash on the same line will be a comment and will be ignored by the compiler.

```
// single-line: this text is ignored until the end of the line
// the delay slows down the printing of the numbers
delay(1000); // 1 second delay between printing
```

4.19 PREPROCESSOR DIRECTIVE

A Preprocessor Directive in Embedded C is an indication to the compiler that it must look in to this file for symbols that are not defined in the program. In Embedded C Programming, you usually use the preprocessor directive to indicate a header file specific to the microcontroller, which contains all the SFRs and the bits in those SFRs.

In Embedded C, Preprocessor Directives are usually represented using #include or #define.

4.19.1 The #include directive

The #include directive instructs the compiler to include in the program code text from a file, the name of which follows the directive. For example,

```
#include "Arduino.h"
```

In this case, the Arduino.h file will be included, containing the standard constants and variables of the Arduino language. In normal programs, it is added automatically, and for the library it must be specified explicitly.

4.19.2 The #define directive

The #define directive (also known as *symbolic constant*) determine the identifier and sequence of characters that is substituted for the identifier, each time it appears in the text of the program.

> *#define statement must not end with semicolon and no blank space between the pound(hash) sign '#' and the word define is permitted.*

Symbolic constants are defined using *#define* as given below:

```
#define <symbolic constant name> <value>
```

For example, if in your programs you write:

```
#define LED_PIN 13 // the number of the LED output is 13
```

Then every time the name LED_PIN appears in the program, it will be substituted the symbols 13 during the translation.

Note that after the #define directive, the semicolon is not set, because it is a pseudo operator. It does not do anything. The directive specifies constants, so the names for it are assumed to be written in uppercase with a separator _ (underscore).

> *With a symbolic constant, you need to make a change only in the place where the constant is defined (i.e., in the #define declaration).*

In Embedded C Programming, you usually use the preprocessor directive to indicate a header file specific to the microcontroller, which contains all the SFRs and the bits in those SFRs.

> *In case of 8051, Keil Compiler has the file reg51.h, which must be written at the beginning of every Embedded C Program:*
> ```
> #include<reg51.h>
> //Preprocessor Directive
> ```

4.20 OPERATORS

An *operator* operates on variables and perform an action in a program. It consists of words or symbols. For instance, the arithmetic operators (+) and (–) cause us to add or subtract two numbers respectively.

> *Operators are essential to form expressions and to perform arithmetical and logical operations on variables.*

You need operators to do arithmetic operations, such as addition, subtraction, etc. Similarly, to perform relational comparison, you need relational operators like >, <, <=, >=, etc. The programming language C supports the bitwise operations and increment/decrement operations. You will see how to use these operators to form expressions and how to use them in various statements. Operators in C language may be classified as:

- Arithmetic operators
- Relational (Comparison) operators
- Logical (Boolean) operators
- Assignment operators
- Pointer operators
- Special operators
- Bitwise operators

4.20.1 Arithmetic Operators

An arithmetic operator is a symbol which performs an arithmetic operation namely, *addition*, *subtraction*, etc. The data on which such operations are carried out may be a variable or a constant.

The operator thus operates on an operand. For instance, in the expression:

```
sum = a + b;
```

the + symbol is *operator* and the a,b are the *operands*. C supports the arithmetic operators as given in Table 4.1.

Table 4.1 Arithmetic Operators

Operator	Symbol	Form	Operation
Addition	+	x + y	y is added to x
Subtraction	–	x – y	y is subtracted from x
Multiplication	*	x * y	x times y
Division	/	x / y	x divided by y
Remainder	%	x % y	remainder of x divided by y

Addition

To add numbers on the Arduino, we use the addition operator (+). For example,

```
int x = 7;
int y = 2;
int sum;
sum = x + y;
```

In the above code, three variables are defined. Variables *x* and *y* are each assigned a value when they are defined. The *sum* variable is defined, but not initialized, so contains any random number.

After the statement shown below has been executed, sum will contain the value 9 i.e., the result of the addition of variable x and y.

You can also add two constant values and store the result in a variable as shown below.

```
int sum;
sum = 7 + 2;
```

The result stored in sum after execution of the addition statement i.e., 9.

Constant values and variables can also be added together and the result stored in a variable as shown here.

```
int x = 7;
int sum;
sum = x + 2;
```

After execution of the addition, sum will contain 27.

Subtraction

The subtraction operator subtracts one number from another using the minus sign (-) .For example,

```
int x = 7;
int y = 2;
int sub;
sub = x - y;
```

After the statements shown above has been executed, sub will contain the value 5 i.e., the result of the subtraction of variable x and y.

Multiplication

Multiplication is done by using the multiplication operator (*). For example,

```
int x = 7;
int y = 2;
int multi;
multi = x * y;
```

After the statements shown above has been executed, multi will contain the value 14 i.e., the result of the multiplication of variable x and y.

Division

The division operator (/) is used to perform division in the Arduino. For example,

```
int x = 7;
int y = 2;
int divi;
divi = x / y;
```

After the statements shown above has been executed, divi will contain the value 3 i.e., the result of the division of variable x and y.

The following examples will demonstrate what happens when a result with a fractional part is stored in a floating point variable.

```
float x = 7.0;
float y = 2.0;
float divi;
divi = x / y;
```

The result now contained in the divi variable is 3.5.

Remainder (Modulo Division)

The remainder operator (or modulo operator) is used to find the remainder after the division of two numbers. The percentage sign (%) is used as the modulo operator. For example,

```
int x = 7;
int y = 2;
int remain;
remain = x % y;
```

After the statements shown above has been executed, remain will contain the value 1 i.e., the result of the modulo division of variable x and y.

The following sketch called arithmetic demonstrates all of the above arithmetic operators.

```
void setup() {
  int x = 7;
  int y = 2;
  int result;
  float result_fl;

  Serial.begin(9600);

  Serial.print("Addition (7 + 2): ");
  result = x + y;
  Serial.println(result);

  Serial.print("Subtraction (7 - 2): ");
  result = 7 - 2;
  Serial.println(result);

  Serial.print("Multiplication (7 * 2): ");
  result = 7 * 2;
  Serial.println(result);

  Serial.print("Int Division (7 / 2): ");
  result = 7 / 2;
  Serial.println(result);

  Serial.print("Float Division (7.0 / 2.0): ");
  result_fl = 7.0 / 2.0;
  Serial.println(result_fl);

  Serial.print("Remainder (7 % 2): ");
  result = 7 % 2;
  Serial.println(result);
}
void loop() {
}
```

Figure 4.65 Demo of arithmetic operators

The sketch given in Figure 4.65 contains print() and println() functions. print() is called when the invisible cursor must stay on the same line so text printed in the println() statement that follows will be printed on the same line as well. println() is used when text must be printed and then the invisible cursor moved to the next line so that the next print() statement will print text on a new line.

☞ *All the arithmetic operators are binary operators, since they operate on two operands at a time.*

The multiplication, division, and remainder operators are called *multiplicative* operators and have a higher precedence than the additive operators (addition and subtraction). These operators require two operands to operate upon.

☞ *The – operator is an unary operator when operates on one operand say – x. Unary operators take just a single operand. The operand can be any integer or floating point value.*

☞ *(*) and (/) have a higher precedence than (+) and (–) operators.*

Unlike other arithmetic operators which accept both integers and floating point operands, the remainder operator or *modulo operator* accepts integer operands only. The resulting value after the operation is the remainder of the first operand divided by the second operand. The remainder value is also an integer value. For example, in the expression given below, the variable *answer* will be assigned the value 3, since that is the remainder when 13 is divided by 5.

```
answer = 13%5
```

☞ *The / operation for integers gives the quotient after division. Thus if you write 7 / 3 the answer would be 2. The % operation gives the remainder obtained in integer division. Thus 7 % 3 is 1. The operator used for division of floating point number is division operator (/). Thus 7.0 / 3.0 would give 2.333333.*

Increment (++) and decrement (--)

The increment and decrement operators are represented by ++ and –– signs respectively. These operators increment or decrement a value by 1. These characters can either precede or follow a variable. If you write i++, this first increments i by 1 and then evaluates to the equivalent of i + 1, while ++i first evaluates to the value of i and then increments i. Notice that the ++ symbol appears after the variable name with the post-increment operator and before the variable name in the pre-increment operator.

```
a = a + 1;
```

you may use the expression:

```
++a;
```

Similarly, the expression

```
a = a - 1;
```

is the same as the expression

```
--a;
```

For example, in the first case (++x), the x variable will be first incremented by 1, then used in expression. Otherwise, the variable will be first used in expression, then incremented by 1. The same applies to the decrement operation. For example, instead of using the following expression to increment a counter:

```
x = 2;
y = ++x;  // x now contains 3, y contains
3
y = x++;  // x contains 4, but y still
contains 3

x = 2;
y = --x;  // x now contains 1, y contains
1
y = x--;  // x contains 0, but y still
contains 1
```

Precedence of Arithmetic Operators

Table 4.2 shows the precedence or the preferences that the various arithmetic operators get and their associativity. *Associativity* means that in the same expression if you have two operators of the same precedence, they are evaluated from left to right. But the *increment* and *decrement* operators are evaluated from right to left.

Table 4.2 Precedence of Arithmetic Operators

Operator	Associativity	Precedence
++ or – –	Right to left	Highest
—	Left to right	↑
* / %	Left to right	
+ –	Left to right	Lowest

You can always use parentheses to change the order of calculations. For example:

```
2 + 8/2 is equal to 6
(2 + 8)/2 is equal to 5
```

The expression 2 + 8/2 is evaluated as 6 since the division is done first; while the expression:

```
(2 + 8)/2
```

is evaluated as 5 because the addition, between the parentheses, is done first.

In arithmetic operations with different types of data, data types are automatically converted. But it is better to always use an explicit transformation.

```
int x; // variable int
char y; // char variable
int z; // variable int
z = x + (int) y; // the variable y is
explicitly converted to int
```

4.20.2 Relational and Logical Operators

Relational operators are used in comparisons for the purpose of comparing two variables which can be integers (int) or floating point numbers (float). If an expression evaluates to true, a 1 is returned. Otherwise, a 0 is returned.

The logical operators, such as AND (&&), OR (||), etc. are used to connect relational expressions together using the rules of Boolean Algebra. Both these types of expressions give true or false results. Here, false is zero, while any non-zero number is true.

☞ *The logical or relational expressions give the value "1" for TRUE result and the value "0" for FALSE result.*

Table 4.3 shows the relational and logical operators. They have *lower* precedence than arithmetic operators, such as +, –, etc. This means that the expression:

```
100 > 90 + 9
```

is equivalent to the expression

```
100 > (90 + 9)
```

This is because in both cases the addition is evaluated first. However, you will make less mistakes, if you use parentheses or the brackets ( ).

Table 4.3 Relational and Logical Operators

Operator	Action
Relational Operators:	
>	Greater than
<	Less than
>=	Greater than or equal
<=	Less than or equal
==	Equal
!=	Not equal
Logical Operators:	
&&	AND
||	OR
!	NOT

The Arduino programming language has six relational operators listed below:

Greater Than >

Greater than > operators test the relationship between values. Here is another example using the same operator to compare the contents of two variables.

```
int x = 5;
int y = 9;
Serial.println(x > y);
```

The relational operator asks the question "Is x greater than y?". The result of the comparison will be 0 (false), because the value that variable x contains is not greater than the value that variable y contains.

Less Than <

Here, you use the less than relational operator to compare the contents of the same two variables.

```
int x = 5;
int y = 9;
Serial.println(x < y);
```

The relational operator asks the question "Is x less than y?". The output of this sketch will be 1 (true) because the value that variable x contains is less than the value that variable y contains.

The following sketch uses the greater than (>) relational operator and the less than (<) relational operator to compare two numbers as shown in Figure 4.66.

In the above sketch 5 > 9 is 0 i.e., (false) and 5 < 9 is 1 i.e., true.

Greater Than or Equal To >=

This operator is same as the greater than operator, but it also checks if the two values being compared are equal to each other. For example,

```
int x = 5;
int y = 9;
Serial.println(x >= y);
```

In the above sketch 5 >= 9 is 0 i.e., (false)

```
int x = 9;
int y = 9;
Serial.println(x >= y);
```

In the above sketch 9 >= 9 is 1 i.e., (true)

Less Than or Equal To <=

This operator is same as the less than operator, but it also checks if the two values being compared are equal to each other.

```
int x = 9;
int y = 9;
Serial.println(x <= y);
```

In the above sketch 9 <= 9 is 1 i.e., (true)

Equal To ==

The equal to relational operator will only evaluate to true (1) if both values being compared are equal, otherwise it will evaluate to false (0).

```
int x = 9;
int y = 9;
Serial.println(x == y);
```

In the above sketch 9 == 9 is 1 i.e., (true)

Not Equal To !=

The not equal to relational operator will only evaluate to true if the two values being compared to each other are not equal to each other, otherwise it will evaluate to false.

```
int x = 9;
int y = 9;
Serial.println(x != y);
```

In the above sketch 9 != 9 is 0 i.e., (false)

```
void setup() {
  Serial.begin(9600);

  Serial.print("Is 5 greater than 9? ");
  Serial.println(5 > 9);

  Serial.print("Is 5 less than 9? ");
  Serial.println(5 < 9);
}
void loop() {
}
```

Figure 4.66 Demo of Relational operator

The three logical operators are AND (&&), OR (| |), and NOT (!)

The AND Logical Operator (&&)

The AND Logical Operator (&&) returns true only if both operands are true.

The OR Logical Operator (||)

The OR Logical Operator (| |) returns true if either operand is true. The OR logical operator is written in sketches as two vertical pipe symbols (| |) found on the same key as the backslash (\). Pressing Shift + \ (Shift and back slash keys) will type the vertical pipe character.

The NOT Logical Operator (!)

The NOT Logical Operator (!) returns true if the operand is false. For example,

```
if (year % 4 == 0 && year % 100 != 0 ||
year % 400 == 0) {
  return 1; // It is a leap year
}
else {
  return 0; // not a leap year
}
```

Precedence of Relational and Logical Operators

Table 4.4 shows the relative precedence of the relational and logical operators.

Table 4.4 Precedence of Relational and Logical Operators

Operator	Associativity	Precedence
!	Right to left	Highest
> >= < <=	Left to right	↑
== !=	Left to right	
&&	Left to right	
||	Left to right	Lowest

In order to see how the precedence helps in evaluating an expression, study the following expression:

```
a == b && x == y || m == n
```

This expression is evaluated as TRUE if one of the following conditions are met:

a If a == b is evaluated as TRUE, and x == y is evaluated as TRUE, or

b If m == n is evaluated as TRUE.

This means that the operator AND (&&) is evaluated before the operator OR (||) because the operator && is having higher precedence than the operator ||.

4.20.3 Assignment Operators

The assignment operator is represented by the equal sign (=). The variable appearing on the left side of = sign and it is assigned the value appearing on the right side of this sign. The assignment statement takes the following format:

```
variable_name = expression;
```

The expression can be a single variable or literal, or a combination of variables, literals, and operators.

In Arduino, shortcuts are possible. For example, in place of the following statement:

```
a = a+b;
```

you may use the shorthand form as given below:

```
a += b;
```

> ☞ *The combination "+=" includes adding the value of b to a and then assigning a + b to a. It is called the combined operator.*

Many similar assignments can be made as mentioned below:

x −= y; is the same asx = x−y;
x *= y; is the same as x = x*y;
x /= y; is the same as x = x/y;
x %= y; is the same asx = x%y;

4.20.4 Pointer Operators

A pointer is a variable that contains the address of a memory cell. A pointer refers to the beginning of a block of memory that contains a variable or function. The pointer operators are the *address-of* operator (&) and the indirection operator (*). The pointer or *indirection* operator is used to get the contents of the address operand pointing to a particular memory element or cell. The & operator returns the address of the variable. For example, if you declare an integer variable by the statement:

```
int salary;
```

then the pointer "&salary" returns the address of the variable "salary" where the *variable salary* is stored in the main memory of the computer. Similarly, if you declare an integer pointer with the statement given below:

```
int *pntr;
```

then you may assign the address "&salary" to the pointer variable *pntr* using the statement:

```
pntr = &salary;
```

4.20.5 Bitwise Operators

Using the programming language C, you will get access to every bit of data available in the main memory. This would enable us to perform machine level operations.

> ☞ *A bit is the smallest possible unit of data storage, and it can have only one of the two values 0 and 1.*

In order to understand the bitwise operators, let us consider first the SHIFT operations. There are two types of shift operators that shift the bits in any integer variable by a specified number of positions. The '>>' operator shifts bits to the right, and the '<<' operator shifts bits to the left.

Right Shift Operator '>>'

You know that the decimal number 8 is represented in binary form as:

```
1000
```

Similarly, the decimal number 4 is represented as:

```
100
```

If you represent data in a computer using 8 bits form, then decimal digits 8 and 4 will be represented by 00001000 and 00000100, respectively. The only difference are between these two numbers that the "1" in the second number is shifted one bit to your right. If the variable "a" holds the value "8", then you can shift it right one position, by the statement:

```
a >> 1
```

In this expression new number when converted to decimal value would be evaluated as "4". You can shift a number by several bits. For example, you can change "8" into "2" by shifting the digit '1' by two bits to the right by using the expression

```
a >> 2
```

In general, the right shift operator is used in the form:

```
variable >> number-of-bits
```

Left Shift Operator '<<'

The left shift operator shifts bits to the left for a specified number of bit positions. The expression takes the form:

```
variable << number-of-bits
```

Table 4.5 shows the bitwise operators and their meaning.

Table 4.5 Bitwise Operators and their Meaning

Bitwise Operator	Meaning
&	Bitwise AND
¦	Bitwise OR
^	Bitwise XOR
~	1's complement
>>	Right shift
<<	Left shift

Precedence of operators decides the order in which different operators are applied. *Associativity* of operators decides the order in which multiple occurrences of the same level operator are applied. Table 4.6 shows the precedences and the associativity of various operators available in C.

Table 4.6 Precedence of Operators used in 'C'

Operator	Associativity	Precedence
() [] -> .	Left to right	Highest
! ~ ++ -- - & *	Right to left	
* / %	Left to right	
+ –	Left to right	
<< >>	Left to right	
< <= > >=	Left to right	
== !=	Left to right	
&	Left to right	
^	Left to right	
¦	Left to right	
&&	Left to right	
¦¦	Left to right	
?:	Right to left	
= += -= *= /=	Right to left	
,	Left to right	Lowest

4.21 EXPRESSION

An expression is a combination of operators, numbers and names that work together to carry out the computation. The following are some of the examples demonstrating expressions:

`5 + j`	A constant plus a variable
`(5 * j) + 6`	A constant times a variable plus a constant value 6

The building blocks of expressions include variables, constants, etc. The building blocks may by themselves be the expressions, or they can be combined with other operators to form more complex expressions. Following are some basic operators which are used to create an expression:

`+`	Addition
`-`	Subtraction
`*`	Multiplication
`/`	Division
`%`	Remainder

4.22 CONSTANT AND LITERALS

Constant (literals) is a value, written into a program instruction, that does not *change* during the execution of a program. A literal constant is a value that is typed directly into the source code, wherever it is needed. For example, in a program, a *name* may be assigned to a data item. If it remains the same, throughout the program execution, then we say that the value of *name* is a constant.

For example, here, numbers are directly used in a calculation and are not assigned to a variable.

```
sum = 10 + 7 // contains the constants 10
and 7.
```

There are *three* types of constants:

- String constant
- Numeric constant
- Character constant

These are discussed further.

4.22.1 String Constant

A string constant or literal is a sequence of alphanumeric characters enclosed in double quotation marks. The maximum length of a string constant is limited to 255 characters. Each string constant is automatically added with a terminating character '\0'. Thus the string "abc" will actually be represented as "abc\0" in the memory and its size is 4 characters. For example,

```
const char Message_1[] = "Press any key";
// Message 1 for LCD
```

4.22.2 Numeric Constant

Numeric constant (literal) has a constant value in numbers. The value of the constant can be positive or negative numeral. There are four types of numeric constants. These are *Integer constant, Floating-point constant*, *Octal constant* and *Hex constant.*

Integer Constant

Integer constants are whole numbers (0, 1, – 1, 2, – 2, 3, – 3, etc.) and should not have any fractional or decimal part. Integer constants are numbers that are used directly in a sketch, like 123. By default, these numbers are treated as *int*. The following are examples of valid integer constants:

```
const int MINIMUM = -100; // Declare
constant MINIMUM
```

Floating-Point Constant

A floating-point constant has a real value. It may be written in two forms called the *fraction* form, such as 0.3 and the other as *exponent* form such as 3.7e12 or 3.7E12.

```
const float T_MAX = 32.60; // Declare
temperature T_MAX
```

Octal Constant

Octal numbers are the integer numbers with a base 8. The digits allowed in this system are 0 to 7 and preceded by a minus or plus sign. An octal constant is written by preceding the value with digit zero (0).

Hex Constant

Hexadecimal numbers are integer numbers to the base 16. The digits allowed in this system are 0 to 9 and letters A to F and preceded by a minus or plus sign. A hex a decimal constant is normally represented by 0*x* or 0X.

4.22.3 Character Constant

Character constant is either a single alphabet or a single digit, or a single special symbol enclosed within a pair of single quotation mark. In the following example, a constant named I_CLASS is declared as A character

```
const char I_CLASS = 'A'; // Declare
constant I_CLASS
```

The *const* keyword stands for constant. It is a variable qualifier that modifies the behavior of the variable, making a variable "read-only". This means that the variable can be used just as any other variable of its type, but its value cannot be changed.

4.23 CONDITIONAL STATEMENTS AND LOOPS

Control statements allow you to change the sequence of instructions for execution. Control statements are of the following two types:

- Conditional branching
- Looping

Conditional branching, a program is to decide whether or not to execute the next statement(s) based on the resultant value of the current expression. For example, go to IInd year, if you pass I[st] year exams, else repeat I[st] year.

Looping, the program performs a set of steps or operations repeatedly till a given condition is obtained. Looping for example, add 1 to number x till current value of x becomes 100 is also called *iteration.*

☞ *Iteration is a process of executing a statement or a set of statements repeatedly, until some specific condition is specified.*

In some programs, you may need to change the sequence of execution of instructions according to specified conditions. For example, you may need to use a simple condition like:

"If it is cold then put your coat on."

In this statement, the resultant action is taken if the condition evaluated is *true* (i.e., the weather is cold). The conditions could be multiple also, as in the following conversation:

"Ok then, if I come back early from work, I'll see you tonight; else if it is too late I'll make it tomorrow; else if my brother arrives tomorrow we can get together on Tuesday; else if Tuesday is a holiday then let it be on Wednesday; else I'll call you up to arrange for the next meeting!"

Such multiple choice conditions can be easily handled, if a programmer is able to write the correct code. There are control structures that can handle even more complex conditions and give the right decisions.

4.24 DECISION MAKING USING RELATIONAL OPERATORS

4.24.1 The *if* Statement

The *if* statement is a control statement that tests a particular condition. Whenever, the evaluated condition comes out to be *true,* then that action or the set of actions are carried out. Otherwise, the given set of action(s) are ignored. The syntax for this statement is:

```
if(expression)
    statement(s);
```

The *expression* must be enclosed within parentheses( ). If expression evaluates to a non-zero value, the condition is considered to be *true* and the next *statement(s)* following the closing parentheses is/are executed.

☞ *The if statement also allows answer for the kind of either–or condition by using an else clause.*

4.24.2 if-else Statement

The *if* statement by itself will cause the execution of a single statement, or a group of statements when enclosed in pair of braces, provided the condition following *if* is *true*. However, you can also execute one group of statements if the condition is *true* and another group of statements if the condition is *false*. This is the purpose of the *else* statement added along with *if* statement. The syntax is shown in Figure 4.67.

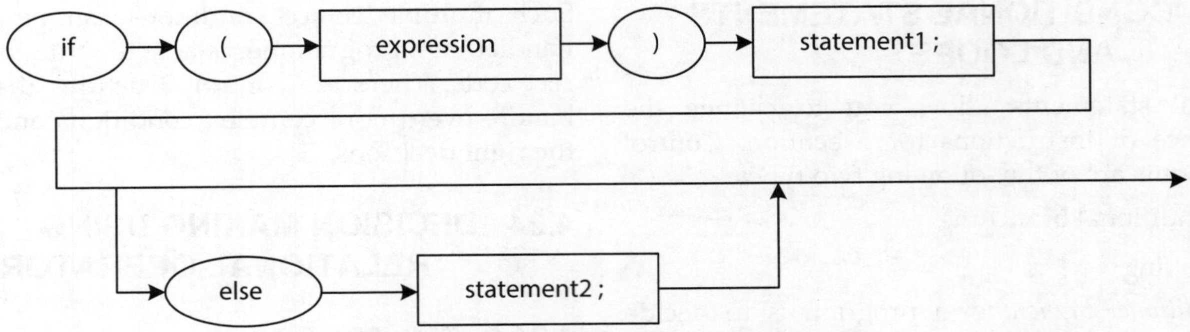

Figure 4.67 The syntax of an *if...else* statement

The format of the *if–else* statement is as follows:

```
if(expression)
    statement_1;
else
    statement_2;
```

When the expression within the parentheses in the set of statements evaluates to a non-zero value, the condition is considered to be *true* and statement_1 is executed; otherwise, statement_2 is executed. Note that statement_1 is terminated by a *semicolon*. For example, the sentence, "if the light is red, stop, otherwise go" would be written as:

```
if (light == "red")
    stop;
else
    go;
```

Note the semicolon (;) after the word stop.

Another example, if the value of the variable *a* is smaller than the value of variable *b*, switch on the LED, else switch it off.

```
int a;
int b;
int ledState;
if (a < b) {
  ledState = 1;
}
else {
  ledState = 0;
}
```

4.24.3 The Conditional Operator (?:)

The conditional operator (?:) helps in building a simple conditional expression in the following form:

```
variable = expression_1 ? expression_2 :
           expression_3;
```

This form emulates the *if* statement as mentioned below:

```
if expression_1 is True Then
 variable = expression_2
else
 variable = expression_3
```

Note that, in both cases, expression_1 is a relational or a logical expression. If expression_1 is evaluated as TRUE, then the variable is assigned the value of expression_2; otherwise, it is assigned the value of expression_3.

For example,

```
b=a>25 ? 100 : 99;
```

In the above sketch, the value of the variable "*b*" is determined according to whether or not the value of the variable "*a*" is greater than 25.

4.24.4 Nested *if-else* Statement

A single *if* statement allows the program to select one out of the two given statements. However, you may need to specify several conditions and take one out of them. This type of program flow requires a construct called a *nested if* statement. The conditions and their associated statements can be arranged in a nested *if* construct that takes the following form:

```
if (condition1)
    statement1;
else if (condition2)
    statement2;
else if (condition3)
    statement3;
...
else
    statement;
```

Figure 4.68 shows the logic for evaluating the smallest of the three numbers a, b and c.

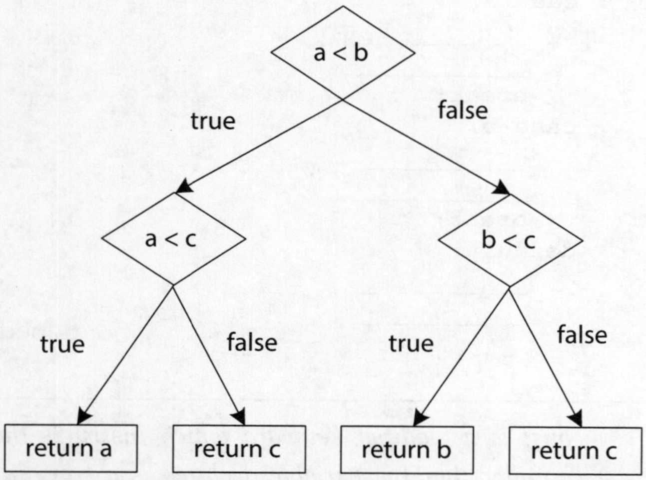

Figure 4.68 Logic of nested *if* statement, to find smallest of a, b and c

The conditions are evaluated from top to bottom, and whenever an evaluated condition is *true*, the corresponding statement(s) are executed and the rest of the statements are skipped. The arrangement of statements in this manner is called *if-else-if* ladder.

4.24.5 The *switch* Statement

Instead of using the *if-else-if* ladder, the *switch* statement can be used for handling multiple choices. The general form of the switch construct is:

```
switch(variable)
{
  case constant1:
    statement(s);
    break;
  case constant2:
    statement(s);
    break;
  case constant3:
    statement(s);
    break;
  ...
  default:
    statement(s);
}
```

The switch control statement begins with the *switch* keyword followed by one block which contains the different cases. Each case handles the statements corresponding to an option (a satisfied condition) and ends with the *break* statement which transfers the control out of the switch structure to the original program. Note that the variable between the parentheses following the switch keyword is used to test the conditions and is called as the control variable. If result is evaluated as "constant1", the "*case* constant1:" is executed. If the value evaluated as "constant2", the "*case* constant2:" is executed, and so on. If the value of the variable does not correspond to any *case,* the default case is executed.

The '*break*' statement is important to transfer the control out of the switch statement. A failure to add the break statement at the end of each case will lead to the execution of the steps in the next case conditions till a '*break*' or the closing brace is encountered. This is called '*fall through execution*'. For example, switch() allows you to compare a variable with several constants and execute a block in which the variable is equal to a constant.

```
switch (x) {
  case 2:
    // code is executed if x = 2
    break;
  case 4:
    // code is executed if x = 4
    break;
  default:
     // code is executed if none of the
previous values match
    break;
}
```

☞ *The control variable of the switch construct can only be of the type int, long, or char.*

☞ *The block of statements under default is executed when none of the cases match the value of the expression.*

4.24.6 Wrong switch-case Expressions

The following program structure shows the wrong way of constructing the switch-case loop.

(a) The case label must not be a floating point number. Case labels should always be integer constants or character constants.

```
switch (value)  {  /*  wrong  */
 case '12.13':
            ___________
            ___________
            break;
 case '10.11 22':
            ___________
            break;
default:
            ___________
            ___________
}
```

(b) The case label must not be a string.

```
switch (value) { /* wrong */
 case "beautiful":
            ___________
            break;
 case "ugly":
            ___________
            ___________
            break;
 default :
            ___________
            ___________
}
```

(c) The case label cannot be another variable but can be a constant variable.

```
int a = 3, b = 5;
switch (value) { /* wrong */
 case a:
            ___________
            ___________
            break;
 case b:
            ___________
            ___________
            break;
 default:
            ___________
            ___________
}
```

```
const int a = 3, b = 5;
switch (value) { /* right */
 case a:
            ___________
            ___________
            break;
 case b:
            ___________
            ___________
            break;
 default:
            ___________
            ___________
}
```

☞ *const is a modifier keyword which instructs the compiler that the variable declared is a constant and will not be changed during execution. Attempts to change the value of a const variable will produce an error. These variables can be used to declare predefined constants. e.g.*
const float pi = 3.14;
const char fail = 'F';

(d) The case label cannot be an expression.

```
switch (expression) { /* wrong */
case 'a*b':
            ___________
            ___________
            break;
case 'a+b':
            ___________
            ___________
            break;
default:
            ___________
            ___________
}
```

4.25 LOGICAL CONNECTIVES

These are used when you want to combine multiple conditions. For example, if you want to check whether the value coming from a sensor is between 5 and 10, you would write this:

```
if ( (sensor >= 5) && (sensor <=10) )
```

The detection of the event occurs in the construction:

```
if ( (buttonPrevState == HIGH) && (but-
tonState == LOW) )
```

&& is a logical AND, produced over conditional expressions. As a result of its application, the condition will be worked out true if both expressions are true. In this case, the block of the if statement will be executed if the previous state of the button = HIGH and the current state of the button = LOW simultaneously.

4.26 LOOPS

The Loop or iteration construct, directs a program to perform a set of operations again and again until a specified condition is achieved. This condition causes the termination of the loop. Programming language C contains three statements for looping:

- The *while* loop
- The *do... while* loop
- The *for* loop

The *while* and *do-while* loop constructs are more suitable in situations where prior knowledge of the terminating condition is not known. *while* loop evaluates a test expression before allowing entry into the loop, whereas *do-while* loop is executed at-least *once* before it evaluates the test expression which is available at the end of the loop.

The *for* loop construct is appropriate when in advance it is known as to how many times the loop will be executed.

The control statement may be given in the starting of the looping construct or in the end. Depending upon whether the control statement is given at the Entry or Exit of the looping construct, looping constructs are classified into following two types.

- Entry-controlled loop
- Exit-controlled loop

In Entry-controlled loop, the control statement (test condition) is given at the entry of the loop, if it evaluates to *true* then only the compiler reads and executes the body of the loop, otherwise it exits the loop and executes next statement in sequence.

In Exit-controlled loop, first the loop body is executed and then the test condition is tested. If it evaluates to *true*, then only the next iteration takes place. As condition is tested after execution of loop body. So, even if condition is false, the loop body gets executed once.

Each of these control loop statements are discussed, further.

4.26.1 *while* Loop

The while loop is an Entry-controlled loop. *while* loop construct contains the condition first. If the condition is satisfied, the control executes the statements following the while loop else, it ignores these statements. The general form of while loop is:

```
while(condition)
{
  statement1;
  statement2;
  ....
}
```

☞ *The condition in the program is evaluated first. The block of statements following the word while are executed repeatedly until the value of the expression laying down the condition is false (See Figure 4.69).*

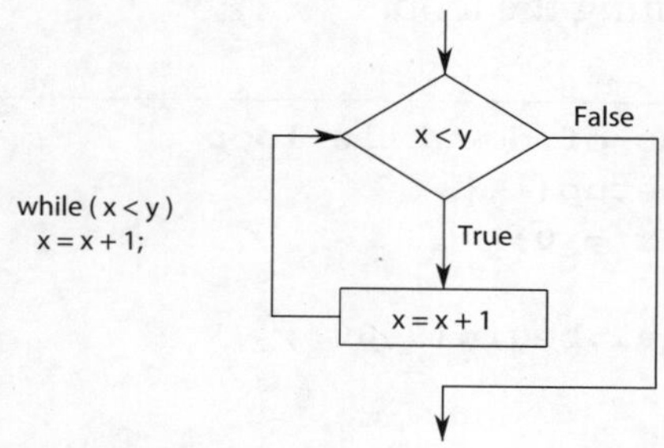

Figure 4.69 Flow control of a while loop

You should also take care of the initializing and incrementing steps when using *while* construct.

For example, consider the following program segments as shown in Figure 4.70.

```
//Demo of while loop
void setup() {
  int x = 0; // Set initial value

  Serial.begin(9600);

  while (x < 10) {
    Serial.print("x = ");
    Serial.println(x);
    x++;
  }
}
void loop() {
}
```

Figure 4.70 Demo of while loop

In this case, the statements within the curly braces { } following *while* statement are executed so long as the current value of *x* is less than 10.

4.26.2 *do–while* Loop

do-while loop construct is another method used in C programming. *do-while* loop ensures that the program is executed at least once and checks whether the condition at the end of the *do-while* loop is *true* or *false*. As long as the test condition is *true*, the statements will be repeated. The control will come out from the loop, only when the test condition is *false*. do-while loop is an exit-controlled loop. The given instructions are first executed and then given condition is checked while exiting the loop.

The do-while loop has the following form:

```
do
{
statement1;
statement2;
.....
}
while(condition);
```

The blocks of statements with in double braces {} following the word *do* are executed at least once. Then the condition is evaluated. If the condition is *true*, the block of statements are executed again until the value of condition tested is *false*.

For example, consider the following program segment as shown in Figure 4.71.

```
// Demo of do-while loop
void setup() {
  int x = 0;

  Serial.begin(9600);

  do {
    Serial.print("x = ");
    Serial.println(x);
    x++;
  } while (x < 10); // Check condition
}
void loop() {
}
```

Figure 4.71 Demo of do-while loop

Here, the statements after *do* are executed at least once. Then the condition ($x < 10$) is tested. So the loop is executed nine times. After that, the value of x becomes 10 and the control comes out of the loop.

Even if the value of x is 10 or more before the first statement do, the block of statements within the braces { } would be executed once and then only the condition would be tested. Thereafter, the control may come out of the loop, if the tested condition is false. In case, the tested condition never becomes false, then the program goes into endless loop execution. It will be an infinite loop and control will never come out of the loop.

4.26.3 *for* Loop

The *for* loop construct is used to execute a set of statements for a given number of times. The for loop is an entry-controlled loop. A for loop executes statements a predetermined number of times. The control expression for the loop is initialized, tested and manipulated entirely within the for loop parentheses.

The syntax is:

```
for(initial condition; test condition;
   incrementer or decrementer)
 {
   statement1;
   statement2;
 }
```

☞ *The three parts of the loop expression in a for loop construct are the initial expression, the test expression, and the incrementer or decrementer expression.*

The *for* loop construct requires to specify three characteristics. These are:

a. The initial value of the loop counter;
b. Testing the loop counter value to determine whether its current value has reached the number of repetitions desired.
c. Increasing or decreasing the value of loop counter by a specified number, each time the program segment is executed (See Figure 4.72).

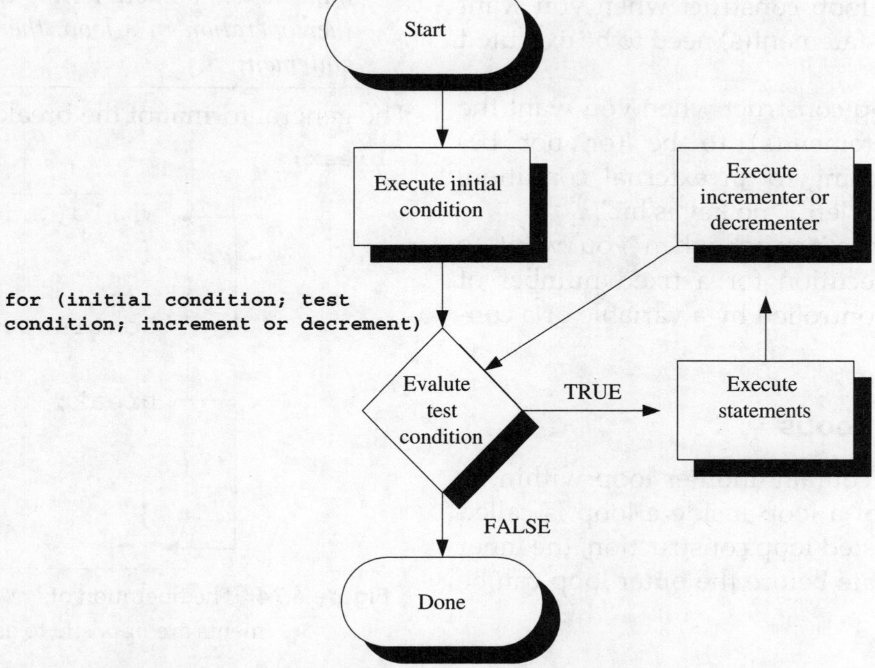

Figure 4.72 A schematic representation of *for* loop construct

```
// Demo of for loop
void setup() {
  Serial.begin(9600);

  for (int x = 0; x < 10; x++) {
    Serial.print("x = ");
    Serial.println(x);
  }
}
void loop() {
}
```

Figure 4.73 Demo of for loop

For example, consider the program segment as shown in Figure 4.73.

This sketch outputs the numbers 0 to 9.

If one enters the *for* loop as follows:

```
for(;;)
```

Then, the *for* loop is valid but it will execute the loop *indefinitely* because there is no condition to be checked to terminate this loop. This loop can be terminated by other means.

Use a different loop construct according to the following recommendations:

- Use a *do-while* loop construct when you want the associated statement(s) need to be executed at least once.
- Use a *while* loop construct when you want the associated statement(s) to be (or not be) executed according to an external condition, such as "no data left", "no key is hit".
- Use a *for* loop construct when you want to control the execution for a fixed number of times. This is controlled by a variable or a constant value.

4.26.4 Nested Loops

A loop may also contain another loop within its body. This form of a loop inside a loop is called *nested loop*. In a nested loop construction, the inner loop must terminate before the outer loop can be ended.

4.26.5 Infinite Loops

It is the loop having no terminating condition, so the loop becomes infinite.

☞ *An infinite loop is one that never terminates.*

4.27 THE *break* STATEMENT

The *break* statement causes an immediate *exit* from the innermost loop structure. The *break* statement can also be used with *switch* case structure, that you studied earlier. (See Figure 4.74).

☞ *If you need to come out of a running program immediately without letting it to perform any further operation in a loop, then you can use break statement.*

The general format of the break statement is:

```
break;
```

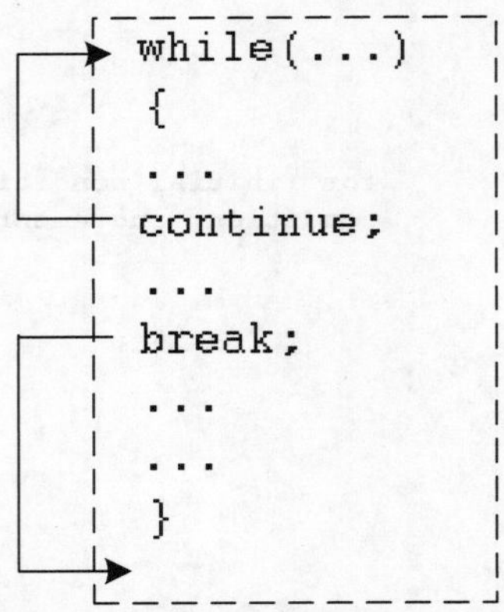

Figure 4.74 The operation of *break* and *continue* statements are opposite to each other

4.28 THE *continue* STATEMENT

The *continue* statement forces the next iteration of the loop to take place, skipping any statement(s)

following the continue statement in the body of the loop. (See Figure 4.74). The syntax of the *continue* statement is :

```
continue;
```

☞ *Continue statement is not used with switch statement.*

4.29 ARRAYS

An array is a consecutive group of memory locations that are of the same type. To refer to a particular location or element in the array, you specify the name of the array and the position number of the particular element in the array. A list of variables can be accessed via an index. For example, if you want to store different levels of brightness to be used when fading an LED, you could create six variables called light01, light02, and so on.

```
int light[6] = {0, 20, 50, 75, 100};
```

Figure 4.75 shows the difference between using individual variable and an array of memory locations with a common name. Variables are like individual folders, whereas an array is like a single folder with many compartments. Array names follow the same conventions as other variable names.

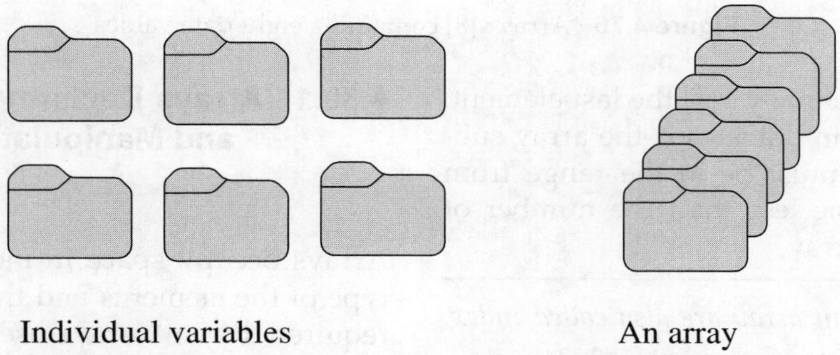

Figure 4.75 Illustration of individual variables and an array

4.30 ARRAY DECLARATION

Like variables array must be declared in the program before it is used for storing information. To set up an array, you need to declare both the name of the array and the number of cells or size of this array. The declaration of an array say *x* is as follows:

```
double x[8];
```

This declaration instructs the compiler to associate eight memory cells with the name *x*. These memory cells containing different values of *x* will be adjacent to each other and can hold double precision numerical values.

☞ *When you declare an array, the brackets along with the variable, such as x[8], indicates to the compiler that you are declaring an array and the compiler sets aside a block of memory large enough to hold the entire array.*

In order to manipulate data stored in an array, you refer each individual element of the array by specifying the array *name* and identify the element desired by a *subscript*. A subscript is a number in brackets that follows an array's name. This number can identify the number of individual elements of the array. For example, the subscripted variable *x*[0] may be used to give reference the initial or 0th element of the array *x*, *x*[1]

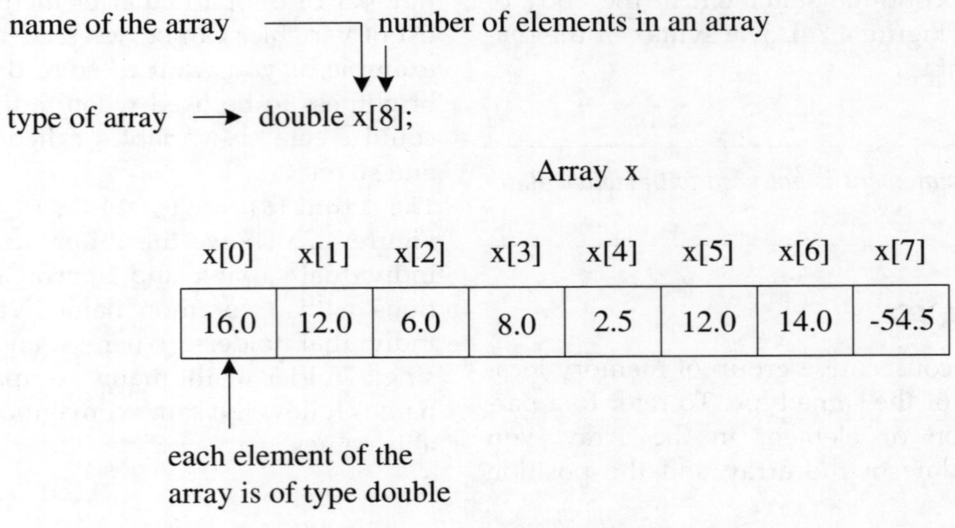

Figure 4.76 Array x[8] containing eight data values

the next element, and finally $x[7]$ the last element. The integer enclosed in brackets is the array subscript, and its value must be in the range from zero to seven, i.e., one less than the number of memory cells in the array.

☞ *The subscripts of an array are also called index. The index set consists of integer 0, 1, 2, 3 ... etc.*

Let x be the array shown in Figure 4.76. The first element is $x[0]$, the second element of the array is $x[1]$ and finally $x[7]$ is the last element of the array x, containing 8 memory locations.

☞ *Remember that array element starts with 0 not 1. Also remember that the last element is one less than the number of elements in the declaration of array. For example, an array with 10 elements contains elements 0 to 9.*

☞ *One drawback of arrays is that the specified memory space is reserved in advance in consecutive order. This leads to wastage of storage space if all the reserved memory locations are not assigned values, i.e., some elements of arrays are left unused.*

4.30.1 Arrays Declaring and Manipulating

Arrays occupy space in memory. To specify the type of the elements and the number of elements required by an array, use a declaration of the form:

type arrayName [arraySize];

The compiler reserves the appropriate amount of memory. The arraySize must be an integer constant greater than zero. For example:

```
int age [5]; // an array of 5 variables
of type int
float weight [10]; // an array of 10
float variables
```

When declaring, arrays can be initialized:

```
int ages [5] = {16, 23, 27, 42, 48};
```

You can refer to array variables as follows:

```
x = age [3]; // x is assigned a value
from the 3 element of the array
ages [4] = 35; // 4 array element is set
to 35
```

Note that the numbering of array elements is always start from zero.

The following program declares a 10-element integer array n.

```
// Demo of array declaration
int n[10]; // n is an array of 10 integers
void setup () {
}
void loop () {
  for (int i = 0; i < 10; ++i ) // initialize elements of array n to 0
  {
    n[i] = 0; // set element at location i to 0
    Serial.print (i) ;
    Serial.print ('\r') ;
  }
  for (int j = 0; j < 10; ++j ) // output each array element's value
  {
    Serial.print (n[j]) ;
    Serial.print ('\r') ;
  }
}
```

Figure 4.77 Demo of array declaration

The elements of an array can also be initialized in the array declaration by following the array name with an equal-to sign and a brace-delimited comma-separated list of initializers. The program uses an initializer list to initialize an integer array with 10 values (line a) and prints the array in tabular format

```
// Array initiazation, n is an array of 10 integers
int n[10] = { 32, 27, 64, 18, 95, 14, 90, 70, 60, 37 };
void setup () {
}
void loop () {
  for (int i = 0; i < 10; ++i ) {
    Serial.print (i) ;
    Serial.print ('\r') ;
  }
  for (int j = 0; j < 10; ++j ) // output each array element's value
  {
    Serial.print (n[j]) ;
    Serial.print ('\r') ;
  }
}
```

Figure 4.78 Demo of Array initialization

The elements of an array represent a series of values to be used in a calculation. The program sums the values contained in the 10-element integer array a.

```
const int arraySize = 10; // constant variable indicating size of array
int a[arraySize] = { 87, 68, 94, 100, 83, 78, 85, 91, 76, 87 };
int total = 0;
void setup () {
```

(cont...)

```
}
void loop () {
  // sum contents of array a
  for (int i = 0; i < arraySize; ++i)
    total += a[ i ];
  Serial.print ('Total of array elements : ') ;
  Serial.print(total) ;
}
```

Figure 4.79 Demo of const variable

4.31 STRINGS

Strings are used to store text. They can be used to display text on an LCD or in the Arduino IDE Serial Monitor window. Strings are also useful for storing the user input. For example, the characters that a user types on a keypad connected to the Arduino.

There are two types of strings in Arduino programming:

- Arrays of characters, which are the same as the strings used in C programming.
- The Arduino String, which lets us use a string object in a sketch.

4.31.1 String Character Arrays

An array is a consecutive series of same type of variable stored in memory. A string is an array of char variables. A string is a special array that has one extra element at the end of the string, which always has the value of 0 (zero). This is known as a "null terminated string".

```
char string1[] = "Arduino"; // 7 chars + 1 null char
char string2[8] = "Arduino"; // 7 chars + 1 null char
```

Following example shows how to make a string and print it to the serial monitor window:

```
/ Demo to print string on serial monitor
void setup() {
  char my_str[6]; // an array big enough for a 5 character string
  Serial.begin(9600);// set up serial library baud rate to 9600
  my_str[0] = 'H'; // the string consists of 5 characters
  my_str[1] = 'e';
  my_str[2] = 'l';
  my_str[3] = 'l';
  my_str[4] = 'o';
  my_str[5] = 0; // 6th array element is a null terminator
  Serial.println(my_str);
}
void loop() {
}
```

Figure 4.80 Demo to print string on serial monitor

The above example shows that a string is made up of; a character array with printable characters and 0 as the last element of the array to show that this is where the string ends. The string can be printed out to the Arduino IDE Serial Monitor window by using Serial.println() and passing the name of the string.

This same example can be written in a more convenient way as shown below:

```
//Demo to print string on serial monitor in more convenient way
void setup() {
  char my_str[] = "Hello";
  Serial.begin(9600);
  Serial.println(my_str);
}
void loop() {
}
```

Figure 4.81 Demo to print string on serial monitor in more convenient way

In this sketch, the compiler calculates the size of the string array and also automatically null terminates the string with a zero. An array that is six elements long and consists of five characters followed by a zero is created exactly the same way as in the previous sketch.

4.32 FUNCTIONS

A *function* is a routine, or set of instructions, that performs a specific task and can be processed independently. When the program passes control to a function, the function performs that task and *returns* control to the instruction following the *calling* instruction. The function may perform a stand-alone task, such as initializing a set of variables, or it may accepts values (arguments) from the calling instruction, process them and pass the results back when finished.

The most important reason to use functions is to make program handling easier as only a small part of the program is dealt with at a time. Another reason of using a function is to reduce the size of the program and to make program more readable and understandable.

Functions allow structuring the programs in segments of code to perform individual tasks.

- The complexity of the entire program can be divided into simple subtasks. Functions help the programmer stay organized. Often this helps to conceptualize the program.
- The subprograms (which are in the form of functions) are easier to write, understand and debug.
- This also reduces chances for errors in modification, if the code needs to be changed.
- Functions make the whole sketch smaller and more compact because sections of code are reused many times.
- They make it easier to reuse code in other programs by making it modular, and using functions often makes the code more readable.
- A library of functions can be designed and tested for use of every programmer.

4.33 CLASSIFICATION OF FUNCTIONS

There are two required functions in an Arduino sketch or a program i.e., setup() and loop(). Other functions must be created outside the brackets of these two functions.

Functions are of two types:

a. Built-in functions or Library functions
b. User-defined functions

4.33.1 Standard Library of C function in Arduino IDE

Many of the operations, like calculating the square root of a number, getting tangent value of an angle, etc., are frequently used by many programmers. Writing a program to find them every time in each program is not necessary. Such operations are programmed and stored in C library, so that they can be called by any other program in the form of functions. These functions are called *library functions* or *built-in functions*. A library of functions can be designed and tested for use of every programmer.

Digital I/O

digitalRead() reads the value from a digital pin. Accepts a pin number as a parameter, and returns the HIGH or LOW constant.

digitalWrite() writes a HIGH or LOW value to a digital output pin. You pass the pin number and HIGH or LOW as parameters.

pinMode() sets a pin to be an input, or an output. You pass the pin number and the INPUT or OUTPUT value as parameters.

Analog I/O

analogRead() reads the value from an analog pin. The name of the analog input pin to read from (A0 to A5 on most boards).
analogReference() configures the value used for the top input range in the analog input, by default 5V in 5V boards and 3.3V in 3.3V boards.
analogWrite() writes an analog value (PWM wave) to a pin. Can be used to light a LED at varying brightnesses or drive a motor at various speeds.
analogReadResolution() lets you change the default analog bits resolution for analogRead(), by default 10 bits. Only works on specific devices (Arduino Due, Zero and MKR).
analogWriteResolution() lets you change the default analog bits resolution for analogWrite(), by default 10 bits. Only works on specific devices (Arduino Due, Zero and MKR).

☞ *analogRead() method in Arduino UNO returns value range 0-1023 and analogWrite() method in Arduino UNO accepts value range 0-255.*

Time functions

delay() pauses the program for a number of milliseconds specified as parameter. Note that there are 1000 milliseconds in a second.
delayMicroseconds() pauses the program for a number of microseconds specified as parameter. Note that there are a thousand microseconds in a millisecond and a million microseconds in a second.
micros() the number of microseconds since the start of the program. Resets after approximately 70 minutes due to overflow.
millis() the number of milliseconds since the start of the program. Resets after approximately 50 days due to overflow.

Math functions

abs() calculates the absolute value of a number
constrain() constrains a number to be within a range.
map() re-maps a number from one range to another. It uses integer math so will not generate fractions. The function also handles negative numbers well.
max() calculates the maximum of two numbers.
min() calculates the minimum of two numbers.
pow() calculates the value of a number raised to a power. pow() can be used to raise a number to a fractional power.
sq() calculates the square of a number i.e., the number multiplied by itself.
sqrt() calculates the square root of a number.
cos() calculates the cosine of an angle (in radians). The result will be between -1 and 1.
sin() calculates the sine of an angle (in radians). The result will be between -1 and 1.
tan() calculates the tangent of an angle (in radians). The result will be between negative infinity and infinity.

character function

isAlpha() checks if a char is alpha (a letter).
isAlphaNumeric() checks if a char is alphanumeric (a letter or number).
isAscii() checks if a char is an ASCII character.
isControl() checks if a char is a control character.
isDigit() checks if a char is a digit (that is a number).
isGraph() checks if a char is a printable ASCII character, and contains content. Note that (space is printable but has no content).
isHexadecimalDigit() checks if a char is an hexadecimal digit (A-F, 0-9).
isLowerCase() checks if a char lower case (that is a letter in lower case).
isPrintable() checks if a char is a printable ASCII character, that is any character that produces an output, even a blank space.
isPunct() checks if a char is a punctuation (a comma, a semicolon, an exclamation mark etc).
isSpace() checks if a char is a white-space character. Returns true if the argument is a space, form feed ('\f'), newline ('\n'), carriage return ('\r'), horizontal tab ('\t'), or vertical tab ('\v').
isUpperCase() checks if a char is upper case.
isWhitespace() checks if a char is a space character or an horizontal tab ('\t').

Random numbers generation

random() generate a pseudo-random number.
randomSeed() initialize the pseudo-random number generator with an arbitrary initial number.

Bits and Bytes

bit() computes the value of a bit.
bitClear() clears (sets to 0) a bit of a numeric variable. Accepts a number, and the number of the bit starting from the right.
bitRead() reads a bit of a number. Accepts a number, and the number of the bit starting from the right.
bitSet() sets to 1 a bit of a number. Accepts a number, and the number of the bit starting from the right.
bitWrite() writes 1 or 0 to a specific bit of a number Accepts a number, the number of the bit starting from the right, and the value to write (0 or 1).
highByte() extracts the high-order (leftmost) byte of a word (or the second lowest byte of a larger data type).
lowByte() extracts the low-order (rightmost) byte of a word.

Interrupts

noInterrupts() disables interrupts.
interrupts() re-enables interrupts after they have been disabled.
attachInterrupt() allow a digital input pin to be an interrupt. Different boards have different allowed pins.
detachInterrupt() disables an interrupt enabled using attachInterrupt().

Communication

Serial.begin() Everything begins with the Serial.begin() function. This function in the setup() routine is executed only once, that is, when the Arduino is starting.
Serial.print() and Serial.println() behave almost identically: they write something to the serial output, but the *ln* version also adds a carriage return and a newline. The syntax of this function is Serial.print(val) or Serial.print(val,format).

Advanced I/O

pulseIn() reads a pulse (either HIGH or LOW) on a pin.
pulseInLong() is same as pulseIn(), except it is implemented differently and it can't be used if interrupts are turned off. It is better at handling long pulse.
shiftIn() shifts in a byte of data one bit at a time. Starts from either the most (i.e. the leftmost) or least (rightmost) significant bit.
shiftOut() shifts out a byte of data one bit at a time. Starts from either the most (i.e. the leftmost) or least (rightmost) significant bit.
tone() sends a square wave on a pin, used for buzzers/speakers to play tones. You can specify the pin, and the frequency. It works on both digital and analog pins.
noTone() stops the tone() generated wave on a pin.

String functions

String() defines a String object.
charAt() gets a character at a specified index.
compareTo() compares two Strings.
concat() appends one String to another String.
endsWith() gets the last character in the String.
equals() compares two Strings.
equalsIgnoreCase() compares two Strings, but ignore case differences.
getBytes() copies a String into a byte array.
indexOf() gets the index of a specified character.
lastIndexOf() gets the index of the last occurrence of a specified character.
length() finds number of characters in the String, excluding the null character.
replace() replaces one given character with another given character.
setCharAt() changes the character at a specific index.
startsWith() checks the String begin with a specified sequence of characters.
substring() finds a substring within a String.
toCharArray() changes from String to character array.
toLowerCase() changes all characters to lower case.
toUpperCase() changes all characters to upper case.

trim() removes all whitespace characters from a String.

4.33.2 User-Defined Functions

Apart from the library functions that are built in C, users can also define and write small programs as functions to do a task relevant to their programs. Such functions are called *user-defined functions*. These functions should be codified by the user, so that such functions can perform the task as desired by the user.

Types of User-Defined Functions

The user-defined functions may be classified as the following three types. Each type is based on the formal *arguments* or *parameters* passed to the functions and the usage of return statement. These types are:

a. A function is invoked or called without *passing* any formal argument from the calling portion of a program and also the function *does not return* any value to the calling function.
b. A function is invoked by the calling program and formal arguments are *passed* from the calling program but the function does not return any values to the calling program.
c. A function is invoked with formal arguments from the calling portion of a program and the function *returns* value(s) to the calling program.

4.34 PROTOTYPE OF A FUNCTION

The prototype tells the compiler in advance about some characteristics of a function used in a program. A function prototype takes the form:

```
type function_name(type argument_1,
       type argument_2,....);
```

It has three main components. These are:

- Function type
- Function name
- Arguments

Function type

The function "type" is the type of the returned value. If the function does not return a value, the type is defined as *void*.

Function name

The function name is any legal identifier followed by the parentheses without any spaces in between.

Arguments

The arguments (or parameters) are given inside the parentheses, preceded by their types and separated by commas. If the function does not use any parameters, the word *void* is used inside the parentheses. Here are some examples for prototypes of the built-in functions.

```
int getchar(void);
double pow(double x, double y);
```

The first function `int getchar(void);` returns an integer value and does not take any arguments.

The second function `double pow(double x, double y);` takes two double arguments (the value of *x* and the value of *y*) and returns a value of the type double.

A function is declared outside any other functions, above or below the loop function. You can declare the function in two different ways:

The first way is just writing the part of the function called a function prototype above the loop function, which consists of:

- Function return type
- Function name
- Function argument type, no need to write the argument name

```
// Demo of function declaration
int sum_func (int x, int y) // function declaration
{  int z = 0;
  z = x + y ;
  return z; // return the value
}
```

(cont...)

```
void setup () {
  // group of statements
}
void loop () {
  int result = 0 ;
  result = sum_func (5, 6) ; // function call
}
```

Figure 4.82 Demo of function declaration

The second part, which is called the function definition or declaration, must be declared below the loop function, which consists of:

- Function return type
- Function name
- Function argument type
- The function body

A function definition has a name, a parentheses pair containing zero or more parameters and a body. For each parameter, there should be a corresponding declaration that occurs before the body. Any parameter not declared is taken to be an integer (int) by default. For good programming, one should declare all parameters.
The following example demonstrates the declaration of function using the second method.

```
// Demo of function declaration
int sum_func (int, int ); // function prototype
void setup () {
  // group of statements
}
void loop () {
  int result = 0;
  result = sum_func (5, 6); // function call
}
int sum_func (int x, int y) { // function declaration
  int z = 0;
  z = x + y ;
  return z; // return the value
}
```

Figure 4.83 Demo of function declaration

The second method just declares the function above the loop function.
Function prototype must be followed by a semicolon (;).

4.35 FORMAL PARAMETER LIST

You can pass many different arguments to a function. If the function takes multiple arguments, the arguments listed in the function call are assigned to the function parameters in specific order. The first argument is assigned to the first parameter, the second argument to the second parameter, and so on.

The parameters that appears in a function call statement are *actual arguments*. The arguments that appear in function definition are *formal arguments,* that is the function creates its own copy of argument values (dummy arguments) and then uses them. The formal arguments may be declared by the same or different names in the calling portion of the program and the called function but the data type should be same in both blocks.

☞ *The argument that is passed is often called an* ***actual argument*** *and while the received copy is called a* ***formal argument*** *or formal parameter.*

4.36 RETURN TYPE

The return() statement has two purposes.

a. Executing it immediately and transferring control from the function back to the calling program.
b. Whatever is inside the parentheses following return is returned as a value to the calling program.

Note that an array or a function can not be specified as a *return* type. A function that does not return a value should declare a return type of *void*. A function without an explicit return value by default is assumed to return a value of type *int*.

☞ *A return statement would terminate the function being currently executed. Program control is returned to the function from which the new-terminated function was called.*

There are two forms of the *return* statement. These are:

```
return;
return expression;
```

A return statement is not strictly necessary in a function that declares a return type of *void*. It is used primarily to effect a premature termination of the function. The *return* statement is similar to the use of the *break* statement inside a loop. An implicit return is effected upon completion of a function's final statement.

The second form of the return statement specifies the function result. It may be an arbitrarily complex expression. It may also contain a function call.

☞ *A value returning function —that is, a function not declared to have a return type of void— must return a value. If the type of the value returned does not exactly match the formal return type, then an implicit conversion if possible, is applied. If no implicit conversion is possible, an error is generated.*

When a function returns an integer value, i.e., a value of the type *int*, you call it an integer function. But if a function that returns a value of a type other than *int*, for example, type *float*, then such a function is known as non-integer function.

The sketch calculates the area of a circle from a radius value of the circle.

```
//Program to calculate the area of a circle
void setup() {
  float area;
  Serial.begin(9600); // calculate the area of a circle with radius of 9.2
  float r = 9.2;
  area = CircleArea(r);
  Serial.print("Area of circle is: "); // print area to 4 decimal places
  Serial.println(area, 4);
}
void loop() {
}
// calculate the area of a circle
float CircleArea(float radius)
{
  float result;
  const float pi = 3.14;
  result = pi * radius * radius;
  return result;
}
```

Figure 4.84 Program to calculate the area of a circle

4.37 FUNCTION CALL

A user-defined function is invoked or called from the main program simply by using the name of the function, including the parentheses followed by a semicolon

☞ *The parentheses are necessary so that compiler knows that you are referring to a function and not a variable that you forgot to declare. The semicolon indicates to the compiler that you are calling a function.*

4.38 POINTERS

A pointer is a special type of variable holding the address of character variables. In other words, the pointer points to another variable. The storage and retrieval of data using the memory address of a variable (i.e. a pointer) is faster than that of using variable. To declare and refer to a pointer type variable, two special unary operators are used namely, * and &. It is declared as follows:

```
type_of_variable *pointer_name;
```

In order to assign the address of a variable to a pointer, it is necessary to use the '=' character and write variable name preceded by the '&' (ampersand) character.

In the following example, the pointer 'multiplex' is declared and assigned the address of the first out of eight LED displays:

```
unsigned int *multiplex; // Declare name
and type of pointer multiplex
multiplex = &display1; // Pointer multi-
plex is assigned the address of variable
display1
```

To change the value of the pointed variable, it is sufficient to write the '*' character in front of its pointer and assign it a new value.

```
*multiplex = 6; // Variable display1 is
assigned the number 6
```

4.39 INTERFACING SENSOR

4.39.1 Working of Digital and Analog pins

The pins on the Arduino board can be configured as either inputs or outputs. It is important to note that a majority of Arduino analog pins, may be configured, and used, in exactly the same manner as digital pins.

4.39.2 Pins Configured as INPUT

Arduino pins are by default configured as inputs, so they do not need to be explicitly declared as inputs with pinMode() when you are using them as inputs. Pins configured this way are said to be in a high-impedance state. Input pins make extremely small demands on the circuit that they are sampling, equivalent to a series resistor of 100 megaohm in front of the pin.

This means that it takes very little current to switch the input pin from one state to another. This makes the pins useful for such tasks as implementing a capacitive touch sensor or reading an LED as a photodiode.

4.39.3 Pull-up Resistors

Pull-up resistors are often useful to steer an input pin to a known state if no input is present. This can be done by adding a pull-up resistor (to +5V), or a pull-down resistor (resistor to ground) on the input. A 10K resistor is a good value for a pull-up or pull-down resistor.

☞ *Pull-down resistors are used in electronic logic circuits to ensure that inputs to Arduino settle at expected logic levels if external devices are disconnected or are at high-impedance.*

Using Built-in Pull-up Resistor with Pins Configured as Input

The built-in pull-up resistors are accessed by setting the pinMode() as INPUT_PULLUP. This effectively inverts the behavior of the INPUT mode, where HIGH means the sensor is OFF and LOW means the sensor is ON. The value of this pull-up depends on the microcontroller used. When connecting a sensor to a pin configured with INPUT_PULLUP, the other end should be connected to the ground.

4.39.4 Pins Configured as OUTPUT

Pins configured as OUTPUT with pinMode() are said to be in a low-impedance state. This means that they can provide a substantial amount of current to other circuits. Attempting to run high current devices from the output pins, can damage or destroy the output transistors in the pin, or damage the entire chip. For this reason, it is a good idea to connect the OUTPUT pins to other devices through 470Ω or 1k resistors, unless maximum current drawn from the pins is required for a particular application.

4.39.5 pinMode() Function

The pinMode() function is used to configure a specific pin to behave either as an input or an output. It is possible to enable the internal pull-up resistors with the mode INPUT_PULLUP. Additionally, the INPUT mode explicitly disables the internal pull-ups.

Syntax

```
void setup () {
   pinMode (pin , mode);
}
```

pin-the number of the pin whose mode you wish to set

mode-INPUT, OUTPUT, or INPUT_PULLUP.

For example,

```
//Demo of pinMode()
int button = 5 ; // button connected to pin 5
int LED = 6; // LED connected to pin 6
void setup () {
  pinMode(button , INPUT_PULLUP);
  // set the digital pin as input with pull-up resistor
  pinMode(button , OUTPUT); // set the digital pin as output
}
void loop() {
  if (digitalRead(button ) == LOW) // if button pressed
  {
    digitalWrite(LED, HIGH); // turn on led
    delay(500); // delay for 500 ms
    digitalWrite(LED, LOW); // turn off led
    delay(500); // delay for 500 ms
  }
}
```

Figure 4.85 Demo of pinMode()

4.39.6 digitalWrite() Function

The digitalWrite() function is used to write a HIGH or a LOW value to a digital pin. If the pin has been configured as an OUTPUT with pinMode(), its voltage will be set to the corresponding value: 5V (or 3.3V on 3.3V boards) for HIGH, 0V (ground) for LOW. If the pin is configured as an INPUT, digitalWrite() will enable (HIGH) or disable (LOW) the internal pullup on the input pin. It is recommended to set the pinMode() to INPUT_PULLUP to enable the internal pull-up resistor.

Syntax

```
void loop() {
   digitalWrite (pin,value);
}
```

pin- the number of the pin whose mode you wish to set

value- HIGH, or LOW

For example,

```
//Demo of digitalWrite()
int LED = 6; // LED connected to pin 6
void setup () {
```

(cont...)

```
  pinMode(LED, OUTPUT); // set the digital pin as output
}
void loop() {
  digitalWrite(LED, HIGH); // turn on led
  delay(500); // delay for 500 ms
  digitalWrite(LED, LOW); // turn off led
  delay(500); // delay for 500 ms
}
```

Figure 4.86 Demo of digitalWrite()

4.39.7 analogRead() Function

Arduino is able to detect whether there is a voltage applied to one of its pins and report it through the digitalRead() function. There is a difference between an on/off sensor (which detects the presence of an object) and an analog sensor, whose value continuously changes. In order to read this type of sensor, you need a different type of pin.

In the lower-right part of the Arduino board, you will see six pins marked "Analog In". These special pins not only tell whether there is a voltage applied to them, but also its value. By using the analogRead() function, you can read the voltage applied to one of the pins.

Syntax

`analogRead(pin);`

pin!- the number of the analog input pin to read from (0 to 5 on most boards, 0 to 7 on the Mini and Nano, 0 to 15 on the Mega)

For example,

```
//Demo of analogRead()
int analogPin = 3;//potentiometer wiper (middle terminal)
// connected to analog pin 3
int val = 0; // variable to store the value read
void setup() {
  Serial.begin(9600); // setup serial
}
void loop() {
  val = analogRead(analogPin); // read the input pin
  Serial.println(val); // debug value
}
```

Figure 4.87 Demo of analogRead()

4.39.8 analogReference() Function

Configures the reference voltage used for analog input (i.e., the value used as the top of the input range).

Syntax

`analogReference (type);`

type - can use any type of the follow (DEFAULT, INTERNAL, INTERNAL1V1, INTERNAL2V56, EXTERNAL)

The options are explained below:

DEFAULT: The default analog reference of 5 volts (on 5V Arduino boards) or 3.3 volts (on 3.3V Arduino boards).

INTERNAL: An built-in reference, equal to 1.1 volts on the ATmega168 or ATmega328 and 2.56 volts on the ATmega8 (not available on the Arduino Mega).

INTERNAL1V1: A built-in 1.1V reference (Arduino Mega only).

INTERNAL2V56: A built-in 2.56V reference (Arduino Mega only).

EXTERNAL: The voltage applied to the AREF pin (0 to 5V only) is used as the reference.

Pulse Width Modulation (PWM)

Pulse Width Modulation or PWM is a common technique used to vary the width of the pulses in a pulse-train. PWM has many applications such as controlling servos and speed controllers, limiting the effective power of motors and LEDs.

Basic Principle of PWM

There are various terms associated with PWM:

a. **On-Time**: Duration of time signal is high.
b. **Off-Time**: Duration of time signal is low.
c. **Period**: It is represented as the sum of on-time and off-time of PWM signal.
d. **Duty Cycle**: It is represented as the percentage of time signal that remains on during the period of the PWM signal.

4.39.9 analogWrite() Function

The analogWrite() function writes an analog value (PWM wave) to a pin. It can be used to light a LED at varying brightness or drive a motor at various speeds. After a call of the analogWrite() function, the pin will generate a steady square wave of the specified duty cycle until the next call to analogWrite() or a call to digitalRead() or digitalWrite() on the same pin. The frequency of the PWM signal on most pins is approximately 490 Hz. On most Arduino boards (those with the ATmega168 or ATmega328), this function works on pins 3, 5, 6, 9, 10, and 11.

You do not need to call pinMode() to set the pin as an output before calling analogWrite().

Syntax:

```
analogWrite ( pin , value ) ;
```

value: the duty cycle between 0 (always off) and 255 (always on).

For example,

```
//Demo of analogWrite()
int ledPin = 9; // LED connected to digital pin 9
int analogPin = 3; // potentiometer connected to analog pin 3
int val = 0; // variable to store the read value
void setup() {
  pinMode(ledPin, OUTPUT); // sets the pin as output
}
void loop() {
  val = analogRead(analogPin); // read the input pin
  analogWrite(ledPin, (val / 4)); // analogRead values go from 0 to 1023,
  // analogWrite values from 0 to 255
}
```

Figure 4.88 Demo of analogWrite()

☞ *A potentiometer is a simple electro-mechanical transducer. It converts rotary or linear motion from the input operator into a change of resistance.*

To generate random numbers, you can use Arduino random number functions. You have two functions

a. randomSeed(seed)
b. random()

4.39.10 randomSeed(seed)

The function randomSeed(seed) resets Arduino's pseudorandom number generator. Although the distribution of the numbers returned by random() is essentially random, the sequence is predictable. You should reset the generator to some random value. If you have an unconnected analog pin, it might pick up random noise from the surrounding environment. These may be radio waves, cosmic rays, electromagnetic interference from cell phones, fluorescent lights and so on.

For example,

```
randomSeed(analogRead(5)); // randomize
using noise from analog pin 5
```

4.39.11 random()

The random() function generates pseudo-random

```
// Demo of random()
long randNumber;
void setup() {
  Serial.begin(9600);
  // if analog input pin 0 is unconnected, random analog
  // noise will cause the call to randomSeed() to generate
  // different seed numbers each time the sketch runs.
  // randomSeed() will then shuffle the random function.
  randomSeed(analogRead(0));
}
void loop() {
  // print a random number from 0 to 299
  Serial.print("random1=");
  randNumber = random(300);
  Serial.println(randNumber); // print a random number from 0to 299
  Serial.print("random2=");
  randNumber = random(10, 20);// print a random number from 10 to 19
  Serial.println (randNumber);
  delay(50);
}
```

Figure 4.89 Demo of random()

numbers. As shown in Figure 4.89.

Syntax

```
long random(max) // it generate random numbers from 0 to max
long random(min, max) // it generate random numbers from min to max
```

4.40 INTERRUPT

Interrupts are very useful in Arduino programs as it helps in solving timing problems.

For example, the main program is running and performing some function in a circuit. However, when an interrupt occurs the main program halts while another routine is carried out. When this routine finishes, the processor goes back to the main routine again.

4.40.1 Types of Interrupts

There are two types of interrupts

a. Hardware Interrupts
b. Software Interrupts

Hardware Interrupts

They occur in response to an external event, such as an external interrupt pin going high or low. A hardware interrupt is a signal that reports some event. Upon its arrival, the execution of the program is suspended, and control passes to the interrupt handler. After processing, the control returns to the interrupted program code. The timer interrupt signal is generated cyclically, with a specified period time. It is formed by a hardware timer - a counter with logic, which resets its code when it reaches a certain value.

Software Interrupts

They occur in response to an instruction sent in software. The only type of interrupt that the 'Arduino language' supports is the attachInterrupt() function.

4.41 INTERFACING LED

Led brightness can be varied by applying a variable voltage to it. Suppose if led max voltage requirement is 2 volts. If you supply varying voltage suppose 0.9 volts or 1.5 volts you can fade led. At 2 volts led will glow with full intensity/brightness and at 1 volt the led brightness will be half.

```
//Program for fading led with light sensor
int sensor=A0;
int output=9;
void setup()
{
pinMode(output, OUTPUT);
}
void loop()
{
int reading=analogRead(sensor);
int bright=reading/4;
delay(500);
analogWrite(output, bright);
}
```

Figure 4.90 Program for fading led with light sensor

```
// Dimming LED
int ledPin = 11;     // LED connected to digital pin 11
void setup()  {
  // nothing happens in setup
}
void loop()  {
  // fade in from min to max in increments of 5 points:
  for (int fadeValue = 0 ; fadeValue <= 255; fadeValue += 5) {
    // sets the value (range from 0 to 255):
    analogWrite(ledPin, fadeValue);
    // wait for 30 milliseconds to see the dimming effect
    delay(30);
  }
 // fade out from max to min in decrements of 5 points:
  for (int fadeValue = 255 ; fadeValue >= 0; fadeValue -= 5) {
    // sets the value (range from 0 to 255):
  analogWrite(ledPin, fadeValue);
    // wait for 30 milliseconds to see the dimming effect
  delay(30);
 }
 }
```

Figure 4.91 Program for dimming LED

```
//Use of RGB LED with Arduino to obtain different colours
int red_light_pin= 11;
int green_light_pin = 10;
int blue_light_pin = 9;
```

(cont...)

```
void setup() {
  pinMode(red_light_pin, OUTPUT);
  pinMode(green_light_pin, OUTPUT);
  pinMode(blue_light_pin, OUTPUT);
}
void loop() {
  RGB_color(255, 0, 0); // Red
  delay(1000);
  RGB_color(0, 255, 0); // Green
  delay(1000);
  RGB_color(0, 0, 255); // Blue
  delay(1000);
 }
void RGB_color(int red_light_value, int green_light_value, int blue_light_value)
 {
  analogWrite(red_light_pin, red_light_value);
  analogWrite(green_light_pin, green_light_value);
  analogWrite(blue_light_pin, blue_light_value);
}
```

Figure 4.92 Program to use RGB LED with Arduino to obtain different colours

In the following program, you are going to interface RGB (Red Green Blue) LED with Arduino Uno. If you want RED to be On, you need to power the RED LED pin and ground the common negative. The same goes for all the LEDs. Remember that LED will be off when ground terminal of respective color is high and LED will glow when ground terminal of respective color is Low.

```
//Single RGB LED interfacing with Arduino Uno
void setup() {
    pinMode(2, OUTPUT);
    pinMode(3, OUTPUT);
    pinMode(4, OUTPUT);
}
void loop() {
  digitalWrite(2, LOW);
  delay(500);
  digitalWrite(2, HIGH);
  delay(500);
  digitalWrite(3, LOW);
  delay(500);
  digitalWrite(3, HIGH);
  delay(500);
  digitalWrite(4, LOW);
  delay(500);
  digitalWrite(4, HIGH);
  delay(500);
}
```

Figure 4.93 Program for single RGB LED interfacing with Arduino Uno

```
# Program to blink two LED on Arduino board with dely of 0.5 seconds
int led1=13;
int led2=12;
int i=0;
void setup()
{
  pinMode(13,OUTPUT);
  pinMode(12,OUTPUT);

}
void loop()
{
  for(i=0;i<=5;i++)
  {
  digitalWrite(13,HIGH);
  delay(50);
  digitalWrite(13,LOW);
  delay(50);
  }
  for(i=6;i<=10;i++)
  {
  digitalWrite(12,HIGH);
  delay(50);
  digitalWrite(12,LOW);
  delay(50);
  }
}
```

Figure 4.94 Program to blink two LED on Arduino board with dely of 0.5 seconds

```
//Blinking LEDs - test program to run 5 LEDs in a pattern of blinks
int led1 = 0;
int led2 = 1;
int led3 = 2;
int led4 = 3;
int led5 = 4;
// the setup routine runs once when you press reset:
void setup() {
  // initialize the digital pin as an output.
  pinMode(led1, OUTPUT);
  pinMode(led2, OUTPUT);
  pinMode(led3, OUTPUT);
  pinMode(led4, OUTPUT);
  pinMode(led5, OUTPUT);
}
// the loop routine runs over and over again forever:
void loop() {
  digitalWrite(led1, HIGH);   // turn the LED on (HIGH-voltage level)
  delay(50);                  // wait for 1/2 a second
  digitalWrite(led1, LOW);    // turn the LED off (LOW-voltage level)
```

(cont...)

```
  digitalWrite(led2, HIGH);     // turn the LED on (HIGH-voltage level)
  delay(50);                    // wait for 1/2 a second
  digitalWrite(led2, LOW);
  digitalWrite(led3, HIGH);
  delay(50);
  digitalWrite(led3, LOW);
  digitalWrite(led4, HIGH);
  delay(50);
  digitalWrite(led4, LOW);
  digitalWrite(led5, HIGH);
  delay(50);
  digitalWrite(led5, LOW);
  delay(1000);
}
```

Figure 4.95 Program for blinking LEDs in pattern

```
//LED Chaser
int pinsCount=10;                        // declaring the integer variable pinsCount
int pins[] = {2,3,4,5,6,7,8,9,10,11};        // declaring the array pins[]

void setup() {
  for (int i=0; i<pinsCount; i=i+1){    // counting the variable i from 0 to 9
   pinMode(pins[i], OUTPUT); //initialising the pin at index i of the array of pins
as OUTPUT
  }
}
void loop() {
  for (int i=0; i<pinsCount; i=i+1){     // chasing right
    digitalWrite(pins[i], HIGH);         // switching the LED at index i on
    delay(100);                       // stopping the program for 100 milliseconds
    digitalWrite(pins[i], LOW);          // switching the LED at index i off
  }
  for (int i=pinsCount-1; i>0; i=i-1){ // chasing left (except the outer leds)
    digitalWrite(pins[i], HIGH);         // switching the LED at index i on
   delay(100);                     // stopping the program for 100 milliseconds
    digitalWrite(pins[i], LOW);          // switching the LED at index i off
  }
}
```

Figure 4.96 Program for LED chaser in left and right

```
// Dual LED chaser
// One led moves from left to right
// while the second LED moves from right to left.
#define SPEED_MS  100
void setup() {
  // set up pins 2 to 13 as outputs
  for (int i = 2; i <= 13; i++) {
    pinMode(i, OUTPUT);
  }
}
```

(cont...)

```
uint16_t chase2 = 13; // keeps track of second LED movement
void loop() {
  // move first LED from left to right and second from right to left
  for (int i = 2; i < 13; i++) {
    allLEDsOff();
    digitalWrite(i, HIGH);       // chaser 1
    digitalWrite(chase2, HIGH); // chaser 2
    chase2--;
    // stop LEDs from appearing to stand still in the middle
    if (chase2 != 7) {
      delay(SPEED_MS);
    }
  }
  // move first LED from right to left and second LED from left to right
  for (int i = 13; i > 2; i--) {
    allLEDsOff();
    digitalWrite(i, HIGH);       // chaser 1
    digitalWrite(chase2, HIGH); // chaser 2
    chase2++;
    // stop LEDs from appearing to stand still in the middle
    if (chase2 != 8) {
      delay(SPEED_MS);
    }
  }
}
// function to switch all LEDs off
void allLEDsOff(void)
{
  for (int i = 2; i <= 13; i++) {
    digitalWrite(i, LOW);
  }
}
```

Figure 4.97 Program for Dual LED chaser

4.42 BUTTON

The pushbutton is a component that connects two points in a circuit when you press it. The example turns on an LED when you press the button.

```
//Interfacing button
// Turn On, LED light with a Push Button
int ledPin = 13; // The pin the LED is connected to
int inputPin = 2; // The input pin (for a push button)
int inputStatus = 0; // Variable for reading the pin status
// Executes once when the arduino power button is pressed on
void setup() {
  pinMode(ledPin, OUTPUT); // Declare the LED as an output
  pinMode(inputPin, INPUT); // Declare pushbutton as input
}
```

(cont...)

```
// This method repeats forever
// This method makes a led light when button is pushed
void loop() {
// Reads incoming input value from our inputPin
  inputStatus = digitalRead(inputPin);
 // Check if the input is HIGH (pushbutton released)
  if (inputStatus == HIGH) {
    digitalWrite(ledPin, LOW); // Turn the LED off
  }
  else {
    digitalWrite(ledPin, HIGH); // Turn the LED on
  }
}
```

Figure 4.98 Program to turn On, LED light with a Push Button

4.43 SENSOR-DHT

You have two versions of the DHTxx sensor series. They look a bit similar and have the same pinout, but have different characteristics. The DHT22 is the more expensive version and has better specifications. The DHT-22 (also named as AM2302) is a digital-output, relative humidity, and temperature sensor. It uses a capacitive humidity sensor and a thermistor to measure the surrounding air, and sends a digital signal on the data pin.

You are going to use the DHT library which takes care of almost everything. Download the library first. To install it, open the Arduino IDE, go to Sketch > Include Library > Add .ZIP Library, and then select the DHTlib ZIP file that you just downloaded. The following test program/sketch will print the temperature and relative humidity values on the serial monitor.

Figure 4.99 DTH sensor

```
// DHT interface to print temperature and relative humidity values on the
// serial monitor

#include <dht.h>
#define dataPin 8 // Defines pin number to which the sensor is connected
dht DHT; // Creates a DHT object

void setup()
{
  Serial.begin(9600);
}
void loop()
{
  int readData = DHT.read22(dataPin); // DHT22
  // Printing the results on the serial monitor
  Serial.print("Temperature = ");
  Serial.println(t);
  Serial.print(" ");
  Serial.print((char)176);//shows degrees character
  Serial.println("C ");
  Serial.print((t * 9.0) / 5.0 + 32.0);//print the temperature in Fahrenheit
  Serial.print(" ");
  Serial.print((char)176);//shows degrees character
  Serial.println("F ");
  Serial.print("Humidity = ");
  Serial.println(h);
  Serial.println(" % ");
  Serial.println("");
  delay(2000); // Delays 2 seconds
}
```

Figure 4.100 Program for DHT interface to print temperature and relative humidity values

The program given in Figure 4.101 outputs the humidity and temperature, when you place your fingers on the DHT11 and you will see the readings fluctuate.

```
// Program for humidity and temperature, when you place your fingers on the DHT11
#include <dht11.h>
dht11 DHT;
//Pin 4 of Arduino to Data of DHT11
#define DHT11_PIN 4
void setup()
{
  Serial.begin(9600);
}
void loop()
{
  //humidity and temperature output
  Serial.print("Humidity is ");
```

(cont...)

```
  Serial.print(DHT.humidity, 1);
  Serial.print("\n");
  Serial.println("Temperature is ");
  Serial.println(DHT.temperature, 1);
  delay(1000);
}
```

Figure 4.101 Program for humidity and temperature when you place your fingers on the DHT11

4.44 LDR

A sensor called LDR or Light Dependent Resistor is used to detect the light intensity. The LDR gives out an analog voltage when connected to VCC (5V), which varies in magnitude in direct proportion to the input light intensity on it. That is, the greater the intensity of light, the greater the corresponding voltage from the LDR will be. Since the LDR gives out an analog voltage, it is connected to the analog input pin on the Arduino.

Figure 4.102 LDR sensor

```
// Program that automatically turn lights on when an LDR sensor detects darkness
and turn lights off when LDR sensor brightness
const int ledPin = 13;
const int ldrPin = A0;
void setup() {
  Serial.begin(9600);
  Serial.begin(9600);
  pinMode(ledPin, OUTPUT);
  pinMode(ldrPin, INPUT);
}
void loop() {
  int ldrStatus = analogRead(ldrPin);
  if (ldrStatus <= 200) {
    digitalWrite(ledPin, HIGH);
    Serial.print("Its DARK, Turn on the LED : ");
    Serial.println(ldrStatus);
  } else {
    digitalWrite(ledPin, LOW);
    Serial.print("Its BRIGHT, Turn off the LED : ");
    Serial.println(ldrStatus);
  }
}
```

Figure 4.103 Program that automatically turn lights on or off

In the program given in Figure 4.104 you will interface Buzzer with LDR and LED. When light shines on LDR; the buzzer will give alarm and the LED will flash.

```
// Program to interface Arduino - Buzzer with LDR and LED
const int ledPin = 13;
const int buzzerPin = 12;
const int ldrPin = A0;
void setup () {
  Serial.begin(9600);
  pinMode(ledPin, OUTPUT);
  pinMode(buzzerPin, OUTPUT);
  pinMode(ldrPin, INPUT);
}
void loop() {
  int ldrStatus = analogRead(ldrPin);
  if (ldrStatus >= 400) {
    tone(buzzerPin, 100);
    digitalWrite(ledPin, HIGH);
    delay(100);
    noTone(buzzerPin);
    digitalWrite(ledPin, LOW);
    delay(100);
    Serial.println("ALARM ACTIVATED");
  }
  else {
    noTone(buzzerPin);
    digitalWrite(ledPin, LOW);
    Serial.println("ALARM DEACTIVATED");
  }
}
```

Figure 4.104 Program to interface Arduino Buzzer with LDR and LED

4.45 MQ135

You see different gasses being emitted in atmosphere such as home appliances like air conditioner and industrial chimneys. Monitoring of these gasses is very important with safety point of view. Gas Sensors are very helpful in accomplishing this task. Small nose like sensor spontaneously respond to the alteration of gas concentration and keep our systems updated for special tasks. M135 is one of the commonly used gas sensors in MQ sensor series. In this code, you will learn how MQ135 gas sensor interfacing with Arduino Uno.

Figure 4.105 MQ135 sensor

```
// Program for MQ135 gas sensor interfacing with Arduino Uno
void setup()
{
  Serial.begin(9600); // sets the serial port to 9600
  pinMode(13, OUTPUT);
  pinMode( 3, INPUT);
}
void loop()
{
  sensorValue = analogRead(0); // read analog input pin 0
  digitalValue = digitalRead(2);
  if (sensorValue > 400)
  {
    digitalWrite(13, HIGH);
  }
  else
    digitalWrite(13, LOW);
  Serial.println(sensorValue, DEC); // prints the value read
  Serial.println(digitalValue, DEC);
  delay(1000); // waits for 1 sec for next reading
}
```

Figure 4.106 Program for MQ135 gas sensor interfacing with Arduino Uno

4.46 IR

An Infrared sensor(IR) is an electronic device, that emits in order to sense some aspects of the surroundings. An IR sensor can measure the heat of an object as well as detects the motion.

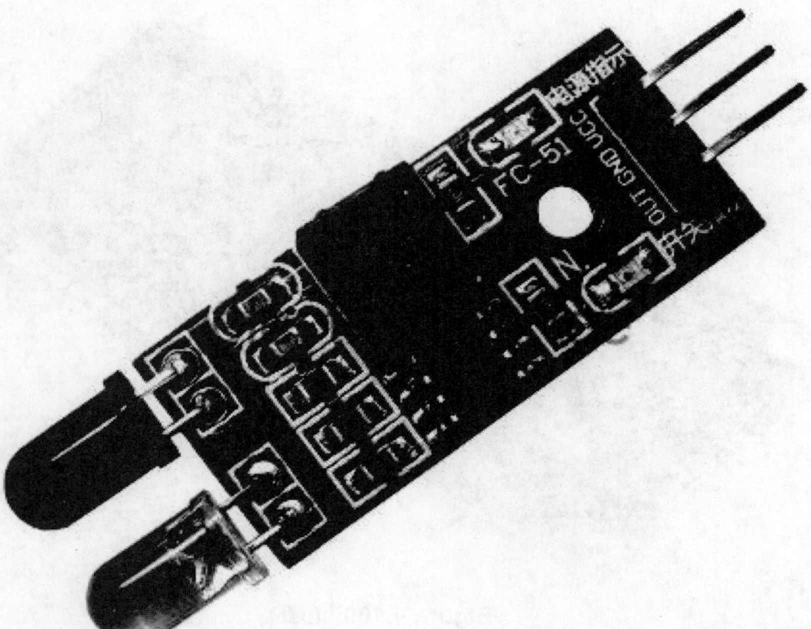

Figure 4.107 IR sensor

```
// Program for interfacing IR sensor
const int IR_Sensor = 2;
void setup() {
  // initialize the digital pin as an output.
  // Pin 13 has an LED  on  Arduino boards:
  pinMode(13, OUTPUT);
  //Pin 2 is connected to the output of IR_Sensor
  pinMode(IR_Sensor, INPUT);
}
void loop() {
  if (digitalRead(IR_Sensor) == HIGH)    //Check the sensor output
  {
    digitalWrite(13, HIGH);    // set the LED on
  }
  else
  {
    digitalWrite(13, LOW);     // set the LED off
  }
  delay(1000);                // wait for a second
}
```

Figure 4.108 Program for interfacing IR sensor

4.47 DISPLAY DATA ON LCD

An LCD is short for Liquid Crystal Display. It is basically a display unit which uses liquid crystals to produce a visible image. The LCD uses the property of light monitoring of liquid crystal and they do not emit the light directly.

Figure 4.109 LCD

```
// Printing message on LCD
#include<LiquidCrystal.h>
LiquidCrystal lcd (5, 4, 3, 2, 1, 0);  // sets the interfacing pins
void setup ()
{
  lcd.begin(16, 2);  // initializes the 16x2 LCD
}
void loop ()
{
  lcd.setCursor (0, 0);              //sets the cursor at row 0 column 0
  lcd.print ("Learning Arduino"); // prints Learning Arduino
  lcd.setCursor (0, 1);            //sets the cursor at row 0 column 1
  lcd.print ("16X2 LCD");         // prints 16X2 LCD
}
```

Figure 4.110 Printing message on LCD

4.48 INTERFACING SOUND SENSOR

The sound sensor is a small board that combines a microphone (50Hz-10kHz) and some processing circuitry to convert sound waves into electrical signals. These sound sensors are inexpensive, easy to interface with and are able to detect sounds of voice, claps or door knocks.

This electrical signal is fed to on-board high precision comparator to digitize it and is made available at OUT pin. The module has a built-in potentiometer for sensitivity adjustment of the OUT signal.

You can set a threshold by using a potentiometer; So that when the amplitude of the sound exceeds the threshold value, the module will output LOW otherwise HIGH. The module has a built-in potentiometer for calibrating the digital output (OUT).

By turning the knob of the potentiometer, you can set a threshold. So that when the sound level exceeds the threshold value, the Status LED will light up and the digital output (OUT) will output LOW.

Now to calibrate the sensor, start clapping near the microphone and adjust the potentiometer until you see the Status LED on the module blink in response to your claps. The following example detects claps and prints message on the serial monitor.

```
// Interface Sound Sensor with Arduino and Control Devices With a Clap.
// Variable to store the time when last event happened
unsigned long lastEvent = 0;

void setup() {
  pinMode(sensorPin, INPUT);  // Set sensor pin as an INPUT
  Serial.begin(9600);
}
void loop() {
  // Read Sound sensor
  int sensorData = digitalRead(sensorPin);
  // If pin goes LOW, sound is detected
  if (sensorData == LOW) {
    // If 25ms have passed since last LOW state, it means that
    // the clap is detected and not due to any spurious sounds
```

(cont...)

```
    if (millis() - lastEvent > 25) {
      Serial.println("Clap detected!");
    }

    // Remember when last event happened
    lastEvent = millis();
  }
}
```

Figure 4.111 Program to Interface Sound Sensor

4.49 INTERFACING KEYPAD

Keypad is used as an input device to read the key pressed by the user and to process it. They do come in may sizes 4X3, 4X4, 4X1 etc. Regardless of their size, they all work in the same way. The 4X3 keypad consists of 4 rows and 3 columns, same way 4x4 keypad consists of 4 rows and 4 columns. Switches are placed between the rows and columns. In order to determine which key was pressed, you need to continuously scan rows & columns. A key press establishes a connection between the corresponding row and column, between which the switch is placed.

In order to determine the key pressed on the Keypad, you have use a special library called, well "Keypad". You should first download this library from this link and place it in Arduino/libraries directory (C:\Program Files (x86)\Arduino\libraries. To install the library navigate to the Sketch > Include Library > Manage Libraries. Wait for Library Manager to download libraries index and update list of installed libraries.

Filter your search by typing "keypad". There should be a many entries. Look for Keypad by Mark Stanley, Alexander Brevig. You have to scroll a little bit. Click on that entry, and then select **Install**.

The program in Figure 4.112 interface keypad with Arduino board and display the key pressed on Serial monitor.

Figure 4.112 4X3 Keypad

Figure 4.113 4X4 Keypad

```
//Interfacing keypad Code for 4X3 Keypad
#include <Keypad.h>
const byte ROWS = 4; //four rows
const byte COLS = 3; //three columns
char keys[ROWS][COLS] = {
```

(cont...)

```
    {'1','2','3'},
    {'4','5','6'},
    {'7','8','9'},
    {'*','0','#'}
};
byte rowPins[ROWS] = {9, 8, 7, 6}; //connect to the row pinouts of the keypad
byte colPins[COLS] = {5, 4, 3}; //connect to the column pinouts of the keypad

//Create an object of keypad
Keypad keypad = Keypad( makeKeymap(keys), rowPins, colPins, ROWS, COLS );

void setup(){
  Serial.begin(9600);
}

void loop(){
  char key = keypad.getKey();// Read the key

  // Print if key pressed
  if (key){
    Serial.print("Key Pressed : ");
    Serial.println(key);
  }
}
```

Figure 4.114 Program for interfacing keypad Code for 4X3 Keypad

The aim of this simple project is to explain how to interface a 4X4 Matrix Keypad to Arduino, how the Arduino Keypad Interface works and how to determine the key pressed on the keypad and display it on the 16*2 LCD Display. Note that in the code, given in Figure 4.115 the keys of the 4X4 Matrix keypad are mapped with digits from 0 to 9, symbols * and # and alphabets A, B, C and D.

```
//Interfacing keypad Code for 4X4 Keypad
const byte ROWS = 4; //four rows
const byte COLS = 4; //four columns

char keys[ROWS][COLS] = {
  {'1','2','3','A'},
  {'4','5','6','B'},
  {'7','8','9','C'},
  {'*','0','#','D'}
};
byte rowPins[ROWS] = {9, 8, 7, 6}; //connect to the row pinouts of the keypad
byte colPins[COLS] = {5, 4, 3, 2}; //connect to the column pinouts of the keypad

//Create an object of keypad
Keypad keypad = Keypad( makeKeymap(keys), rowPins, colPins, ROWS, COLS );
```

(cont...)

Module 4: M4–R5

```
void setup(){
  Serial.begin(9600);
}

void loop(){
   char key = keypad.getKey();// Command getKey() is used to check which key is
pressed, if any.

  // Print if key pressed
  if (key){
    Serial.print("Key Pressed : ");
    Serial.println(key);
  }
}
```

Figure 4.115 Program for interfacing keypad Code for 4X4 Keypad

4.50 SERIAL COMMUNICATION

Serial communication is the process of sending data from one device to another device sequentially. In serial communication the data bits are send serially from one device to another device providing faster means of communication.

4.50.1 Interfacing HC-05 (Bluetooth module)

The HC-05 module is a Bluetooth SPP (Serial Port Protocol) module, which means it communicates with the Arduino via the Serial Communication. Bluetooth is a technology for wireless communication. It is designed to replace cable connections. It uses serial communication to communicate with devices. HC05 module is a Bluetooth module using serial communication, mostly used in electronics projects. It communicates with microcontrollers using serial communication (USART). Usually, it connects small devices like mobile phones, PDAs and TVs using a short-range wireless connection to exchange documents. HC-05 can be set as master as well slave which enables making a communication between two separate Arduino Boards. This Module has two types of operation modes discussed below:

a. AT Command Mode
b. Connection Mode

The AT command mode is a module whenever the set of commands is used for the setup and configure the module. In this mode, the modules are not identified by the other Bluetooth devices. This type of mode will take the pin to high and the commands are sent to the module serially like string.

The connection mode is the device which can connect directly to the other device. You can identify this device on other devices and it can connect with the help of the passkey which should be entered and the passkey is a default which is "1234". In the connection mode, you cannot change configuration serially but you can only communicate with it.

Advantages of Bluetooth Module

a. The Bluetooth modules are standardized protocol because they can connect with the same Bluetooth as well as with the different Bluetooth projects model.
b. The Bluetooth module can connect automatically with another Bluetooth device at a range of 30 feet.
c. Low energy consumption and are inexpensive.

Connecting Phone to HC-05 Bluetooth Module

a. Make the connections and power on the Bluetooth Module. If this is the first time you are using your Bluetooth Module, then the LED will blink rapidly. In order to pair the module with your phone, open Bluetooth Settings in your phone and connect to "HC-05" with pin "1234". If 1234 doesn't work, try "0000".

b. Once the Bluetooth Module is paired with your phone, you can start using the App. Open the Bluetooth Controller App and click on scan. A list of Bluetooth Devices will appear on the screen. Select HC-05.
c. Now, select Set Keys option in the app and enter the following information:

Key Name	Data of Key
LED ON	1
LED OFF	0

d. After entering this information, save it by clicking on OK. Now, on the home screen of the app, you can see two buttons (or slots) with titles "LED ON" and "LED OFF". If you click on LED ON, '1' will be transmitted over Bluetooth Communication to the HC-05 Module, which then transmits it to Arduino.
e. In case you click on LED OFF, '0' will be transmitted. Arduino then turns ON or OFF the LED based on the received data.

In the example given in Figure 4.116 you will transmit data from Smartphone via Bluetooth to the Arduino Uno and display it on Serial Monitor of PC. Download and install a Bluetooth terminal application on your phone and use it to connect to the HC-05 Bluetooth module.

```
//Sketch for displaying data received via bluetooth on Serial Monitor

#include<SoftwareSerial.h>
// Create object named bt of the class SoftwareSerial
SoftwareSerial bt(2,3); // (Rx,Tx)
void setup() {
  bt.begin(9600); // Define baud rate for software serial communication
  Serial.begin(9600); // Define baud rate for serial communication
}

void loop() {

    if (bt.available()) // If data is available on serial port
    {
     Serial.write(bt.read()); // Print character received on to the serial monitor
    }
}
```

Figure 4.116 Sketch for displaying data received via bluetooth on Serial Monitor

4.51 INTERFACING RELAY MODULE

The example shown in Figure 4.117 demonstrate how to control a AC light with Arduino using relay module. AC is alternating current 220v (India) which powers the AC lights. Arduino cannot control high volt *n* amp, but a relay can do this job, which is the sole design of it. So you are using relay as switch to control high power devices.

A relay is an electrically operated switch to control high power/voltage or AC household devices using low-power signals from a microcontroller, etc. Many relays use an electromagnet to operate a switching mechanism mechanically, but other operating principles are also used. Relays are used where it is necessary to control a high power/voltage circuit by a low-power signal (with complete electrical isolation between control and controlled circuits), or where several circuits must be controlled by one signal.

4.50.1 Control and Handle 220V AC supply

Program in Figure 4.117 shows controlling AC Light Using Arduino With Relay Module.

```
//Program for controlling AC Light Using Arduino With Relay Module
#define RELAY1  7
void setup()

{
  Serial.begin(9600);
  pinMode(RELAY1, OUTPUT);
}
void loop()
{
  digitalWrite(RELAY1, 0);          // Turns ON Relays 1
  Serial.println("Light ON");
  delay(1000);                     // Wait 1 seconds
  digitalWrite(RELAY1, 1);          // Turns Relay Off
  Serial.println("Light OFF");
  delay(1000);
}
```

Figure 4.117 Program for controlling AC Light Using Arduino With Relay Module

Figure 4.118 Relay Module

REVIEW QUESTIONS WITH ANSWERS

1. Multiple Choice Questions

1. All code in an Arduino sketch is processed from:
   a. Top to bottom b. Bottom to top
   c. Any order d. None of these
2. Almost all statements written in the Arduino language must end with a:
   a. Comma (,) b. Colon (:)
   c. Semicolon(;) d. Fullstop(.)
3. Which of the following statement is true about a sketch?
   a. It is a the name that Arduino uses for a program.
   b. It's the unit of code that is uploaded to and run on an Arduino board.
   c. Both (a) and (b)
   d. None of these
4. Advantage(s) of the Arduino:
   a. Easy to learn
   b. Huge community
   c. Many third-party libraries
   d. All of the above
5. Full form of GPIO is:
   a. Ground Pin Input/Output
   b. General Pin Input/Output
   c. General Purpose Input/Output
   d. None of these
6. The setup() defines:
   a. Pin functionality using the pinMode function
   b. Initial state of pins
   c. Initialize classes and variables
   d. All of the above

7. The SPI pins are:
   a. pins 10 (SS), 11 (MOSI)
   b. 12 (MISO), 13 (SCK)
   c. Both (a) and (b)
   d. None of these
8. Some of the compile errors are:
   a. Missing semicolons or parentheses
   b. Missing variable initializations
   c. Misspellings & wrong capitalizations
   d. All of the above
9. Which of the following statement(s) are true about serial communication?
   a. Serial communication is the process of sending data from one device to another device sequentially.
   b. In serial communication the data bits are send serially from one device to another device.
   c. Provides faster means of communication.
   d. All of the above
10. The HC-05 module can be operated in:
    a. Slave mode
    b. Master mode
    c. Both (a) and (b)
    d. None of these
11. The default method(s) in Arduino program is/are:
    a. Only loop()
    b. Only setup()
    c. setup() and loop()
    d. Can be either setup() and loop()
12. Which symbol is used in Arduino to calculate Modulo?
    a. #
    b. $
    c. %
    d. !

2. State True or False for the following:

1. The sketch usually starts with a header that explains what the sketch is doing, and who wrote it.
2. The BareMinimum sketch, can be found at: File --> Examples --> 1.Basic --> BareMinimum.
3. Arduino uses serial USB interface to transfer user program/sketch from PC to Arduino board.
4. Arduino board is a simple and easy to use electronic prototyping platform.
5. setup() function runs in a loop over and over again.
6. There are 1000 milliseconds in a second.
7. The digitalRead and digitalWrite commands are used for addressing and making the Arduino pins as an input and output respectively.
8. The digitalRead and digitalWrite commands are case insensitive.
9. The Arduino Uno power supply can be done with the help of a USB cable only.
10 The Uno has 6 analog inputs, labeled A0 through A6.
11. The Arduino software includes a serial monitor which allows simple textual data to be sent to and from the Arduino board.
12. The RX and TX LEDs on the board will flash when data is being transmitted via the USB-to-serial chip and USB connection to the computer.
13. A low level on this pin causes the microcontroller to reset.
14. The HIGH and LOW constants are used to determine the state of the pins.
15. Every electrical and electronics projects circuit can be designed on breadboard.
16. A subscript must be an integer or integer expression in an array.
17. The *while* and *for* loops test the termination condition at the bottom of the loop, but the do-while tests the termination condition at the top.
18. The logical NOT operator is a unary.
19. Arduino program statement for generating one second delay is delay(100);.
20. Arduino IDE consists of two functions setup() and build().
21. analogRead() method in Arduino UNO returns value range 0-1023.
22. analogWrite() method in Arduino UNO accepts value range 0-255.
23. setup() function is called once in Arduino program.
24. Single line comment is written using //.

3. Match the following:

1. Arduino program	a. Microcontroller
2. Short pin	b. It contains syntax errors
3. ATmega328	c. //
4. Compile errors	d. Ground
5. Reset button	e. Sketch
6. Verify option	f. Reupload the code
7. Quit	g. Compile the sketch
8. Comment	h. Connector pins
9. Circuit boards	i. Closes all IDE windows
10. Jumper wires	j. Solderless breadboards

4. Fill in the blanks:

1. The main code, also known as a _______.
2. The ________ will actually help to debug the written Sketches where you can get a hold of how your program is operating.
3. _________ function defines the initial state of the Arduino upon boot and runs only once.
4. The _________ function configures a pin as either an input or an output.
5. The _________ functions outputs a value on a pin.
6. The _________ function causes the Arduino to wait for the specified number of milliseconds before continuing on to the next line.
7. PWM is basically, a ______ wave with a varying high and low time.
8. The Arduino board can be powered through an AC-to-DC adapter or a _______.
9. The digital output has only ______ states.
10. ______ means this pin is at zero voltage with respect to the power supply and ground plane of the circuit board.
11. The _______ pins allows the Arduino to read signals from an analog sensor like a light sensor and convert it into a digital value.
12. _______ is defined as the rate at which highs and lows must be sampled to decode the signal.
13. A ________ is a circuit board that is used to make temporary circuits.
14. The most common eminent source of light available in electronic components are ________.
15. The resistance is measured in ________.
16. The ________ define a function block or expressions.
17. ________ board of Arduino family can be used to sewn into clothing.
18. The founder of Arduino project is ___________.
19. In ATmega328p, p stands for __________.
20. AnalogWrite method is used for ________ pins in Arduino.

Answers

1. 1. a 2. c 3. d 4. d 5. c 6. d 7. c 8. d 9. d 10. c 11 c 12 c

2. 1. T 2. T 3. T 4. T 5. F 6. T 7. T 8. F 9. F 10. F 11 T 12 T 13. T 14. T 15. T 16. T 17. F 18. T 19. F 20. F 21. T 22. T 23. T 24. T

3. 1. e 2. d 3. a 4. b 5. f 6. g 7. i 8. c 9. j 10. h

4.

1. Sketch	2. Serial Monitor
3. setup()	4. pinMode()
5. digitalWrite()	6. delay()
7. square	8. battery
9. two	10. GND
11. analog	12. Baud rate
13. breadboard	14. Light Emitting Diodes
15. ohms	16. braces {}
17. Lilypad	18. Massimo Banzi
19. Picopower	20. PMW

Short Answers Questions

1. Write short notes on the following:

(a) Resistor
(b) Breadboard
(c) VIN
(d) Servo Motor
(e) DC motor

Ans a. A resistor is a passive electrical component with the primary function to limit the flow of electric current.

b. A breadboard is a temporary circuit board for testing and prototyping circuits, no soldering is done on the board, this mean it is faster and easier to prototype circuits.

c. The input voltage to the Arduino/Genuino board when it is using an external power source (as opposed to 5 volts from the USB connection or other regulated power source). We can supply voltage through this pin, or, if supplying voltage via the power jack, access it through this pin.

d. A Servo Motor is a small device that has an output shaft. This shaft can be positioned to specific angular positions by sending the servo a coded signal. As long as the coded signal exists on the input line, the servo will maintain the angular position of the shaft. If the coded signal changes, the angular position of the shaft changes. Servos are extremely useful in robotics.

e. A DC motor (Direct Current motor) is the most common type of motor. DC motors normally have just two leads, one positive and one negative. If you connect these two leads directly to a battery, the motor will rotate. If you switch the leads, the motor will rotate in the opposite direction.

2. What is the use of setup() function?

Ans The setup() function is called when a sketch starts. Use it to initialize variables, pin modes, start using libraries, etc. The setup() function will only run once, after each powerup or reset of the Arduino board.

3. What is text editor? What is its file extension?

Ans It is used for writing the required code. The sketch is written in the text editor and is then saved with the file extension *.ino*.

4. What is Pulse Width Modulation?

Ans Pulse Width Modulation or PWM is a common technique used to vary the width of the pulses. PWM has many applications such as controlling servos and speed controllers, limiting the effective power of motors and LEDs.

5. What are Libraries?

Ans Libraries are simply a collection of code that helps us to interface the hardware with any peripheral devices such as sensors, modules, shields, etc. easily. We can use built-in functions of the libraries to make a coding project much more comfortable.

6. What is the purpose of the /* and */ character pairs?

Ans This sequence of characters marks the start and end of a multiline comment in a program.

7. Discuss the role of PWM pins in Arduino UNO.

Ans PWM stands for Pulse Width Modulation technique, is used to convert the digital signal into an analog by varying the width of the Pulse. The PWM pins are used for giving the desired analog output. They are used to set the LED brightness or to run Stepper or Servo Motor or anything which require analog inputs .

Digital control is used to create a square wave, a signal switched between on and off. This on-off pattern can simulate voltages in between full on (5 Volts) and off (0 Volts) by changing the portion of the time the signal spends on versus the time that the signal spends off. The duration of "on time" is called the pulse width. To get varying analog values, we change, or modulate, that pulse width. If we repeat this on-off pattern fast enough with an LED for example, the result is as if the signal is a steady voltage between 0 and 5v controlling the brightness of the LED.

8. What is an Infrared sensor?

Ans An Infrared sensor is an electronic device, that emits in order to sense some aspects of the surroundings. An IR sensor can measure the heat of an object as well as detects the motion. These types of sensors measures only infrared radiation, rather than emitting it that is called as a passive IR sensor.

9. Can an IR sensor detect humans?

Ans Yes, the Passive Infrared (PIR) sensor is used to detect the presence of human.

10. What is the use of break and continue?

Ans The break and continue statements are often used within loops structures. A break statement sends program control to the statement that immediately follows the closing brace of the loop body. The continue statement immediately sends program control to the test conditions of the loop.

11. What is bootloader?

Ans Bootloader, is basically the initial piece of code which runs whenever any microcontroller is powered up or resets. It can be used to setup the microcontroller or provide limited ability to update the main program's code.

12. How setup() is different from loop()?

Ans setup() is called once in the program when a sketch starts after power-up. It is used to initialize variables, input and output pin modes, and other libraries needed in the sketch.

loop() is used after setup() been called, function loop() is executed repeatedly in the main program. It controls the board until the board is powered off or is reset.

13. How many digital pins are there on the UNO board?

Ans It has 14 digital pins input/output pins of which 6 can be used as PWM output.

14. What is the application area of LilyPad board?

Ans LilyPad was creatively designed with large connecting pads and a flat back to allow them to be sewn into clothing with conductive thread.

15. What is difference between Verify/Compile and Upload?

Ans **Verify/Compile**: It checks the errors present in your sketch and informs you about the memory space occupied by the variables in the console area.

Upload: It automatically compiles and loads the code (binary file) into the selected Arduino hardware through the configured Port.

16. What is outpane?

Ans The bottom of the main screen is described as an Output Pane that mainly highlights the compilation status of the running code: the memory used by the code, and errors occurred in the program. We need to fix those errors before we intend to upload the hex file into our Arduino Module.

17. What is the role of Serial Monitor?

Ans The Serial Monitor allows your computer to connect serially with the Arduino. This is important because it takes data that our Arduino is receiving from sensors and other devices and displays it in real-time on our computer.

18. What is serial plotter?

Ans Arduino Serial Plotter is another component of the Arduino IDE, which allows us to generate a real-time graph of our serial data. The serial plotter makes it much easier for us to analyze our data through a visual display.

19. What is the use of modulo operator?

Ans The remainder operator (or modulo operator) is used to find the remainder after the division of two numbers. The percentage sign (%) is used as the modulo operator.

20. What is the function of keyword *void* in function declaration?

Ans void may be used to declare functions that do not return a value. Thus, functions with no return value will have a new type void.

21. Differentiate between local and global variables.

Ans A *local variable* is one that is defined within a function. The scope of a local variable is limited to the function in which it is defined. The life of local variable is limited to the function. *Global variable* is defined outside the function block. The scope of global variable is throughout the program. The life of global variable is throughout the program.

22. What do you mean by function prototyping? What are its advantages?

Ans A function prototype is a declaration of a function that tells the program about the type of the value returned by the function and the number and type of each argument.
The advantage of function prototyping is that it enables a compiler to compare each use of function with the prototype to determine whether the function is invoked properly or not. The number and types of arguments can be easily compared and any wrong number or type of the argument is reported.

23. What is the role of Serial.begin()?

Ans Everything begins with the Serial.begin() function. This function in the setup() routine is executed only once, that is, when the Arduino is starting.

24. What is the purpose of crystal oscillator?

Ans The crystal oscillator helps Arduino in dealing with time issues. On each tick, the microcontroller performs one operation, for example, addition, subtraction, etc. The clock is controlled by an external 16MHz Crystal Oscillator.

25. What is SPI (Serial Peripheral Interface) Pins?

Ans The SPI pins are 10, 11, 12, 13 namely SS, MOSI, MISO, SCK. These pins support SPI communication using the SPI library. SPI bus is a system for serial communication, which uses up to four conductors. One conductor is used for data receiving, one for data sending, one for synchronization and one alternatively for selecting a device to communicate with. It is a full duplex connection, which means that the data is sent and received simultaneously. SPI uses the following four wires:

26. What is the use of Serial Pins?

Ans Serial Pins are the pins have special functions like pins 0 & 1, which acts as a transmitter and receiver respectively. TX and RX indicates the data being transmitted or received over the USB communication.

27. What is difference between tone() and noTone()?

Ans **tone()** sends a square wave on a pin, used for buzzers/speakers to play tones. You can specify the pin, and the frequency. It works on both digital and analog pins.
noTone() stops the tone() generated wave on a pin.

28. What is an HC-05 Bluetooth Module? What are its advantages.

Ans HC-05 Bluetooth is a wireless communication protocol; it is used in two devices as a sending and receiving the information. The HC-05 Bluetooth modules are easy to use and simple, its price is low and these types of modules are interfaced with the Arduino, Rasberry Pi, and Microcontroller through the serial UART interface.

29. What is the SI Unit of Resistor?

Ans The SI unit of resistor is Ohm.

30. What is the use of delay() function?

Ans It accepts a single integer (or number) argument. This number represents the time (measured in milliseconds).

31. What is the use of micros() function?

Ans The micros() function returns the number of microseconds from the time, the Arduino board begins running the current program.

32. What is difference between entry controlled loop and exit controlled loop?

Ans In an entry-controlled loop, the loop control condition is evaluated at the entry point of the loop. However, in an exit-controlled loop, the loop control condition is evaluated at the exit point of the loop.
If the loop control condition is false in the

beginning, the entry-controlled loop is never executed, however, the exit-controlled loop would be executed at least once.

33. What is ISR? Can we pass any parameter and return a value from the ISR?

Ans ISR refers to the Interrupt Service Routines. These are procedures stored at specific memory addresses which are called when a certain type of interrupt occurs.

ISR returns nothing and not allow to pass any parameter. An ISR is called when a hardware or software event occurs, it is not called by the code, so that's the reason no parameters are passed into an ISR.

34. What is the difference between Bit Rate and Baud Rate?

Ans

Bit Rate	Baud Rate
Bit rate is the number of bits per second.	Baud rate is the number of signal units per second.
It determines the number of bits traveled per second.	It determines how many times the state of a signal is changing.
Cannot determine the bandwidth.	It can determine how much bandwidth is required to send the signal.
This term generally used to describe the processor efficiency.	This term generally used to describe the data transmission over the channel.

35. Write short note on Global Variables and Local Variables.

Ans Global Variables: Global Variables, as the name suggests, are Global to the program i.e. they can be accessed anywhere in the program.

Local Variables: Local Variables, in contrast to Global Variables, are confined to their respective function.

36. What is Main Function?

Ans Every C or Embedded C Program has one main function, from where the execution of the program begins.

37. What is a difference between unsigned int and signed int in C?

Ans A signed integer can store both the positive and negative values. An unsigned integer can only store the positive value.
For example,
Assuming the size of the integer is 2 bytes.
signed int -32768 to +32767
unsigned int 0 to 65535

38. What does the keyword const mean?

Ans A const is only a qualifier, it changes the behavior of a variable and makes it read-only type. When we want to make an object read-only type, then we have to declare it as const.
const int iData = 0

39. Discuss Arduino Uno Board Power Supply.

Ans The Arduino Uno power supply can be done with the help of a USB cable or an external power supply. The external power supplies mainly include AC to DC adapter otherwise a battery. The adapter can be connected to the Arduino Uno by plugging into the power jack of the Arduino board. Similarly, the battery leads can be connected to the Vin pin and the GND pin of the POWER connector. The suggested voltage range will be 7 volts to 12 volts.

40. What is baud rate? Explain with an example.

Ans The term baud rate is used to denote the number of bits transferred per second (bps). The following code will make Arduino send hello world when it starts up.

```
void setup() {
  Serial.begin(9600); //set up serial library baud rate to 9600
```

(cont...)

```
  Serial.println("hello world"); //print hello world
}
void loop() {
}
```

Figure 1 Program for Q40

41. Write a code to print all integers from 0 to 99 using for loop.

Ans

```
//print all integers from 0 to 99 using for loop
void setup() {
  Serial.begin(9600);
  for (int x = 0; x < 100; x++) {
    Serial.print("x = ");
    Serial.println(x);
  }
}
void loop() {
}
```

Figure 2 Program for Q41

42. Write a code to print odd numbers from 1 to 99 using for loop.

Ans

```
//print odd numbers from 1 to 99
void setup() {
  Serial.begin(9600);
  for (int i = 0 ; i < 50 ; i = 2 * i + 1) {
    Serial.print("i = ");
    Serial.println(i);
  }
}
void loop() {
}
```

Figure 3 Program for Q42

43. Write a code to print odd numbers from 99 to 1 using for loop.

Ans

```
//print odd numbers from 99 to 1
void setup() {
  Serial.begin(9600);
  for (int i = 50 ; i > 0 ; i = 2 * i - 1) {
    Serial.print("i = ");
    Serial.println(i);
  }
}
void loop() {
}
```

Figure 4 Program for Q43

44. Write a program to interface LED on pin no. 8 and blink with the delay of 1 sec.

Ans.

```
void setup() {
  pinMode(8, OUTPUT);
}
void loop() {

  digitalWrite(8, HIGH);
  delay(1000);
  digitalWrite(8, LOW);
  delay(1000);
}
```

Figure 5 Program for Q44

45. Explain anatomy of an Arduino Uno with diagram.

Ans Anatomy of Arduino Uno is given in Figure 6.

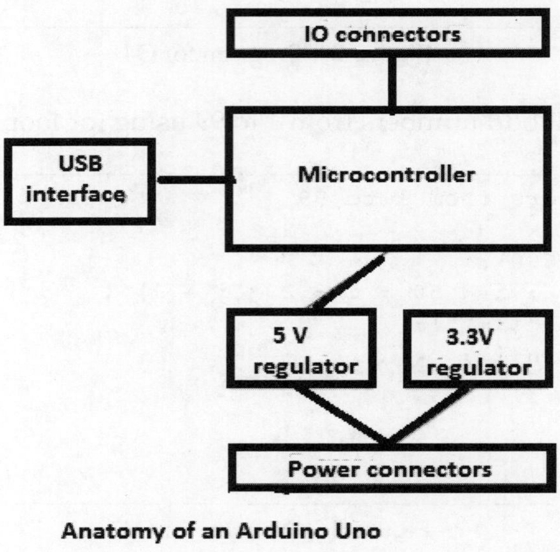

Figure 6 An Arduino Uno anatomy

46. Write a code so that the LED is *on* for 100 milliseconds and *off* for 1000.

Ans.

```
/*
   Blink
  Turns on an LED on for 100 milliseconds, then off for 1000 milliseconds,
repeatedly.
*/
// the setup function runs once when you press reset or power the board
void setup() {  // initialize digital pin 13 as an output.
   pinMode(13, OUTPUT);
}// the loop function runs over and over again
```

(cont...)

```
void loop() {
  digitalWrite(13, HIGH); // turn the LED on (HIGH is the voltage level)
  delay(100); // wait for 100 milliseconds
  digitalWrite(13, LOW); // turn the LED off by making the voltage LOW
  delay(1000); // wait for 1 second
}
```

Figure 7 Program for Q46

47. Write a program to interface LEDs on pin number 11, 12, and 13 and blink alternatively at delay of 1 second.

Ans.

```
// Multiple LED blinking with dely of 1 sec.
int led = 13;
int led2 = 12;
int led3 = 11;
// the setup routine runs once when you press reset:
void setup() {
  // initialize the digital pin as an output.
  pinMode(led, OUTPUT);
  pinMode(led2, OUTPUT);
  pinMode(led3, OUTPUT);
}
// the loop routine runs over and over again forever:
void loop() {
  digitalWrite(led, HIGH);   // turn the LED on (HIGH is the voltage level)
  delay(1000);               // wait for a second
  digitalWrite(led, LOW);    // turn the LED off by making the voltage LOW
  delay(1000);
  { digitalWrite(led2, HIGH);
    delay(1000);
    digitalWrite(led2, LOW);
    delay(1000);
  }
  { digitalWrite(led3, HIGH);
    delay(1000);
    digitalWrite(led3, LOW);
    delay(1000);
  }// wait for a second
}
```

Figure 8 Program for Q47

48. Write a program to blink default Light Emitting Diode (LED) on Arduino board with delay of 2 seconds.

Ans.

```
// Program for default LED blinking with dely of 2 sec.
int led = 13;
// the setup routine runs once when you press reset:
```

(cont...)

```
void setup() {
  // initialize the digital pin as an output.
  pinMode(led, OUTPUT);
}
// the loop routine runs over and over again forever:
void loop() {
  digitalWrite(led, HIGH);    // turn the LED on (HIGH)
  delay(2000);                // wait for 2 second
  digitalWrite(led, LOW);     // turn the LED off (LOW)
  delay(2000);
  }// wait for 2 second
}
```

Figure 9 Program for Q48

49. Write a program to interface LCD and keypad with Arduino board and display the key pressed from keypad on LCD.

Ans.

```
// Arduino  4X4  Keypad Interface

#include <Keypad.h>
#include <LiquidCrystal.h>

const byte ROWS = 4; //four rows
const byte COLS = 4; //four columns
//define the symbols on the buttons of the keypads
char hexaKeys[ROWS][COLS] = {
                              {'1','2','3','A'},
                              {'4','5','6','B'},
                              {'7','8','9','C'},
                              {'*','0','#','D'}
                                                  };
byte rowPins[ROWS] = {0, 1, 2, 3}; //connect to the row pinouts of the
keypad
byte colPins[COLS] = {4, 5, 6, 7}; //connect to the column pinouts of the
keypad

//initialize an instance of class NewKeypad
Keypad customKeypad = Keypad( makeKeymap(hexaKeys), rowPins, colPins, ROWS,
COLS);
LiquidCrystal lcd(13, 12, 11, 10, 9, 8);

void setup()
{
  lcd.begin(16, 2);
  lcd.print("KEY PRESSED");
  delay(2000);
  lcd.clear();
  lcd.setCursor(0, 0);
}
```

Figure 10 Program for Q49

50. Write a program to interface LCD with Arduino board and display "Hello World" on it.

Ans.

```
// Arduino Code to print "Hello World!" message on the LCD.
// include the library code:
#include <LiquidCrystal.h>

// Creates an LCD object. Parameters: (rs, enable, d4, d5, d6, d7)
LiquidCrystal lcd(12, 11, 5, 4, 3, 2);

void setup()
{
  // set up the LCD's number of columns and rows:
  lcd.begin(16, 2);
  // Clears the LCD screen and moves the cursor to the upper left corner.
  lcd.clear();
}

void loop()
{
  // Print a message to the LCD.
  lcd.print(" Hello world!");

  // set the cursor to column 0, line 1
  // (note: line 1 is the second row, since counting begins with 0):
  lcd.setCursor(0, 1);
  // Print a message to the LCD
  lcd.print(" Message printed");
}
```

Figure 11 Program for Q50

51. Write a program to interface keypad with Arduino board and determine the key pressed on the keypad and display it on the 16X2 LCD Display.

Ans.

```
#include <Keypad.h>
#include <LiquidCrystal.h>

const byte ROWS = 4; //four rows
const byte COLS = 4; //four columns
//define the symbols on the buttons of the keypads
char hexaKeys[ROWS][COLS] = {
                              {'1','2','3','A'},
                              {'4','5','6','B'},
                              {'7','8','9','C'},
                              {'*','0','#','D'}
                                               };
byte rowPins[ROWS] = {0, 1, 2, 3}; //connect to the row pinouts of the
keypad
byte colPins[COLS] = {4, 5, 6, 7}; //connect to the column pinouts of the
keypad
```

(cont...)

```
//initialize an instance of class NewKeypad
Keypad customKeypad = Keypad( makeKeymap(hexaKeys), rowPins, colPins, ROWS,
COLS);
LiquidCrystal lcd(13, 12, 11, 10, 9, 8);

void setup()
{
  lcd.begin(16, 2);
  lcd.print("KEY PRESSED");
  delay(2000);
  lcd.clear();
  lcd.setCursor(0, 0);
}
```

Figure 12 Program for Q51

52. Write a program that Lights multiple LEDs in sequence, then in reverse.

Ans.

```
// Lights multiple LEDs in sequence, then in reverse.
int timer = 100;      // The higher the number, the slower the timing.
int ledPins[] = {
  2, 7, 4, 6, 5, 3
};       // an array of pin numbers to which LEDs are attached
int pinCount = 6;  // the no. of pins (i.e. the length of the array)

void setup() {
  // the array elements are numbered from 0 to (pinCount - 1).
  // use a for loop to initialize each pin as an output:
  for (int thisPin = 0; thisPin < pinCount; thisPin++) {
    pinMode(ledPins[thisPin], OUTPUT);
  }
}

void loop() {
  // loop from the lowest pin to the highest:
  for (int thisPin = 0; thisPin < pinCount; thisPin++) {
    // turn the pin on:
    digitalWrite(ledPins[thisPin], HIGH);
    delay(timer);
    // turn the pin off:
    digitalWrite(ledPins[thisPin], LOW);
  }
  // loop from the highest pin to the lowest:
  for (int thisPin = pinCount - 1; thisPin >= 0; thisPin--) {
    // turn the pin on:
    digitalWrite(ledPins[thisPin], HIGH);
    delay(timer);
    // turn the pin off:
    digitalWrite(ledPins[thisPin], LOW);
  }
}
```

Figure 13 Program for Q52

53. Write a program to interface Buzzer and LED, if we keep some fuels which have harmful gases CO_2, NO_2 etc. the RED LED will glow and the buzzer starts ringing else if it is good quality air around, then green LED will glow.

Ans.

```
// Program to interface Buzzer and LED
// Take the threshold value as 150
int sensorThres = 150;

void setup() {
  pinMode(redLed, OUTPUT);
  pinMode(greenLed, OUTPUT);
  pinMode(buzzer, OUTPUT);
  pinMode(smokeA0, INPUT);
  Serial.begin(9600);
}
void loop() {
  int analogSensor = analogRead(smokeA0);
  Serial.print("Pin A0: ");
  Serial.println(analogSensor);
  // Checks if it has reached the threshold value
  if (analogSensor > sensorThres)
  {
    digitalWrite(redLed, HIGH);
    digitalWrite(greenLed, LOW);
    tone(buzzer, 3000, 300);
  }
  else
  {
    digitalWrite(redLed, LOW);
    digitalWrite(greenLed, HIGH);
    noTone(buzzer);
  }
  delay(100);
}
```

Figure 14 Program for Q53

54. Write a program to run pattern(s) on LEDs connected at pin 3, 4, 5.
Pattern example:
on, on, on
on, off, off
off, on, off
off, off, on
off, off, off

Ans.

```
// Program to run pattern(s) on LEDs connected at pins 3, 4. 5
// Defining LEDs
int redLED = 3;
int greenLED = 4;
int blueLED = 5;
int del = 1000; // Milliseconds of delay
void setup() {
```

(cont...)

```
  // Making the LEDs outputs
  pinMode(redLED,OUTPUT);
  pinMode(greenLED, OUTPUT);
  pinMode(blueLED, OUTPUT);
}
void loop() {
  // blink in pattern on, on, on
  Serial.print("Blink in pattern");
  digitalWrite(redLED,HIGH);
  digitalWrite(greenLED,HIGH);
  digitalWrite(blueLED,HIGH);
  delay(del);

  // blink in pattern on, off, off
  digitalWrite(redLED,HIGH);
  digitalWrite(greenLED,LOW);
  digitalWrite(blueLED,LOW);
  delay(del);

  // blink in pattern off, on, off
  digitalWrite(redLED,LOW);
  digitalWrite(greenLED,HIGH);
  digitalWrite(blueLED,LOW);
  delay(del);

 // blink in pattern off, off, on
  digitalWrite(redLED,LOW);
  digitalWrite(greenLED,LOW);
  digitalWrite(blueLED,HIGH);
  delay(del);

  // blink in pattern off, off, off
  digitalWrite(redLED,LOW);
  digitalWrite(greenLED,LOW);
  digitalWrite(blueLED,LOW);
  delay(del);
}
```

Figure 15 Program for Q54

55. Write a program to run pattern for Multiple LEDs Pattern Generation using Arduino Uno. Note that 12 LEDs are connected on digital pins of Arduino from pin no 2 - 13. All LEDs ground are shorted with Arduino ground. Pattern example:
Patten 1 : Turning *on* all LEDs in increasing order and turning *off* in decreasing order.
Pattern 2: Turning *on* one led at a time in increasing and decreasing order.
Pattern 3: Turning *on* all even number LEDs and then odd number LEDs.

Ans.

```
const int led1 = 2;
const int led2 = 3;
const int led3 = 4;
const int led4 = 5;
```

(cont...)

```
const int led5 = 6;
const int led6 = 7;
const int led7 = 8;
const int led8 = 9;
const int led9 = 10;
const int led10 = 11;
const int led11 = 12;
const int led12 = 13;
int a = 2;

void setup()
{
  pinMode(led1, OUTPUT);
  pinMode(led2, OUTPUT);
  pinMode(led3, OUTPUT);
  pinMode(led4, OUTPUT);
  pinMode(led5, OUTPUT);
  pinMode(led6, OUTPUT);
  pinMode(led7, OUTPUT);
  pinMode(led8, OUTPUT);
  pinMode(led9, OUTPUT);
  pinMode(led10, OUTPUT);
  pinMode(led11, OUTPUT);
  pinMode(led12, OUTPUT);
}

void loop()
{
  //pattern 1
 // Turning on all LEDs in increasing order and turning off in decreasing
order
  for (a = 2; a <= 13; a++)
  {
    digitalWrite(a, HIGH);
    delay(50);
  }
  for (a = 13; a >= 2; a--)
  {
    digitalWrite(a, LOW);
    delay(50);
  }
  //pattern 2
  //Turning on one led at a time in increasing and decreasing order
  for (a = 2; a <= 13; a++)
  {
    digitalWrite(a, HIGH);
    delay(50);
    digitalWrite(a, LOW);
  }
```

(cont...)

```
  for (a = 13; a >= 2; a--)
  {
    digitalWrite(a, HIGH);
    delay(50);
    digitalWrite(a, LOW);
  }
  //pattern 3
  //Turning on all even number LEDs and then odd number LEDs.
  for (a = 2; a <= 13; a++) {
    if ((a % 2) == 0) {

      digitalWrite(a, HIGH);
      delay(50);
    }
  }

  for (a = 13; a <= 2; a--) {
    if ((a % 2) == 1) {
      digitalWrite(a, HIGH);
      delay(50);
    }
  }

  //turning OFF ALL LEDs
  for (a = 13; a >= 2; a--)
  {
    digitalWrite(a, LOW);
    delay(50);
  }
}
```

Figure 16 Program for Q55

56. Write a program for Sequential LED ON-OFF.

Ans.

```
//Sketch for Sequential LED ON-OFF
void setup() {
  //set gpio pin {0,1,2,3} as output
  pinMode(0, OUTPUT);
  pinMode(1, OUTPUT);
  pinMode(2, OUTPUT);
  pinMode(3, OUTPUT);
}

void loop() {
  //turn LED ON one by one
  for (int i = 0; i < 4; i++) {
    digitalWrite(i, HIGH);
    delay(1000);
  }
```

(cont...)

```
  //turn LED OFF one by one
  for (int i = 3; i >= 0; i--) {
    digitalWrite(i, LOW);
    delay(1000);
  }
}
```

Figure 17 Program for Q56

57. Write a program/sketch for controlling LED using switch.

Ans.

```
//Sketch for controlling LED using switch

int pushButton = 2;
int LED = 13;

void setup() {
  // make the pushbutton's pin as input:
  pinMode(pushButton, INPUT_PULLUP);
  //configure pin as input with pullup enabled
  pinMode(LED, OUTPUT);
  //configure pin as output
}
void loop() {
  // read the input pin:
  int buttonState = digitalRead(pushButton);
  digitalWrite(LED, (!(buttonState)));
 //turn led on when switch pressed
  delay(10);        // delay in between reads for stability
}
```

Figure 18 Program for Q57

58. Write a program that automatically turn lights on when an LDR sensor detects darkness.

Ans.

```
//Program that automatically turn lights on when an LDR sensor detects
darkness.
int sensorPin = A0; // select the input pin for LDR
int sensorValue = 0; // variable to store the value coming from the sensor
void setup() {
  Serial.begin(9600); //sets serial port for communication
}
void loop() {
  sensorValue = analogRead(sensorPin); // read the value from the sensor
  Serial.println(sensorValue); //prints the values coming from the sensor
on the screen
  delay(100);
}
```

Figure 19 Program for Q58

59. Write a program to interface LDR and LED with Arduino board. Whenever there is sufficient light falls on LDR the LED is off and when there is dark around LDR the LED is put on.

Ans.

```
const int ledPin = 13;
const int ldrPin = A0;
void setup() {
  Serial.begin(9600);
  pinMode(ledPin, OUTPUT);
  pinMode(ldrPin, INPUT);
}
void loop() {
  int ldrStatus = analogRead(ldrPin);
  if (ldrStatus <= 200) {
    digitalWrite(ledPin, HIGH);
    Serial.print("Its DARK, Turn on the LED : ");
    Serial.println(ldrStatus);
  } else {
    digitalWrite(ledPin, LOW);
    Serial.print("Its BRIGHT, Turn off the LED : ");
    Serial.println(ldrStatus);
  }
```

Figure 20 Program for Q59

60. Write a program to interface DHT sensor and LED. Put your hand on the LM35 (a temperature sensor) and that should push the temperature higher than 25 degrees and the LED will light.

Ans.

```
// Program to switch on LED once the temperature rises above 25 degrees
#define lm35Pin A2
#define ledPin 12

//this sets the ground pin to LOW and the input voltage pin to high
void setup()
{
Serial.begin(9600);
pinMode(ledPin, INPUT);
digitalWrite(ledPin,0);
}

//main loop
void loop()
{
  int rawvoltage= analogRead(lm35Pin);//Read Temperature
  float millivolts= (rawvoltage/1024.0) * 5000;
  float celsius= millivolts/10;
  Serial.print(celsius);
  Serial.print(" degrees Celsius, ");
```

(cont...)

```
if(celsius >25)
{
  digitalWrite(ledPin,1);
}
else
{
  digitalWrite(ledPin,0);
}
delay(1000);

}
```

Figure 21 Program for Q60

61. Write a program to interface LM35 is a temperature sensor which measures the temperature of surroundings and displaying it on the serial monitor of Arduino.

Ans.

```
const int lm35_pin = A1;  //LM35 O/P pin
void setup() {
  Serial.begin(9600);
}
void loop() {
  int temp_adc_val;
  float temp_val;
  temp_adc_val = analogRead(lm35_pin);  //Read Temperature
   temp_val = (temp_adc_val * 4.88); // Convert adc value to equivalent
voltage
  temp_val = (temp_val/10); //LM35 gives output
  Serial.print("Temperature = ");
  Serial.print(temp_val);
  Serial.print(" Degree Celsius\n");
  delay(1000);
}
```

Figure 22 Program for Q61

62. Write a program to print "Hello World" on serial monitor.

Ans.

```
// Program to print "Hello World" on serial monitor
void setup() {
 Serial.begin(9600); }
void loop() {
 Serial.print("Hello World");
 delay(1000); }
void setup() {
  Serial.begin(9600);
}
void loop() {
  Serial.print("Hello World");
  delay(1000);
  }
```

Figure 23 Program for Q62

EXERCISE

1. Write short notes on the following:
   (a) Bootloader
   (b) Serial UART interface
   (c) Serial.print()
   (d) Arduino Nano board
   (e) random()
   (f) Nested Loops
   (g) Preprocessor Directive
2. What is Arduino?
3. What are the benefits of using Lilypad Arduino?
4. What are the limitations of using Arduino?
5. What is an Arduino UNO board?
6. What are the advantages of Arduino?
7. Discuss different types of Interrupts in Arduino programs.
8. Write short note on External Interrupt Pins.
9. What is the use of Reset Button?
10. What is the difference between a function definition and a function prototype?
11. What do you mean by a built-in function? Explain with an example.
12. Write short notes on Actual parameters.
13. What do you understand by a function. List out the advantages and disadvantages.
14. What is the purpose of the keyword *void* in function declaration?
15. What is the advantage of using function prototypes in a program?
16. What is the purpose of return() statement?
17. What is the purpose of using functions? Differentiate declaration and definition of a function.
18. What is the difference between a String and an array of characters?
19. Discuss the use of arrays and how they initialized at the time of declaration?
20. In what way does an array differ from an ordinary variable?
21. What do you mean by subscripts? How are they written?
22. What three constructs are supported by C programming language?
23. What is the difference between *while* and *do-while* loop?
24. What do you mean by infinite loop?
25. Write short note on switch statement.
26. What is the use of abs() and pow()?
27. What is the use of Pull-down resistors?
28. What is the role of logical operators AND (&&), OR (| |), and NOT (!)?
29. How digitalRead() is different from digitalWrite()?
30. Why is it suggested to put a break statement after the last case statement in a switch even though it is not needed synthetically?
31. What do you understand by the term actual and formal parameters for a function?
32. Write a code so that the LED turns on when the sketch starts and stays on.
33. Write a C program to depict an IoT uses where LED is switched ON once the button is pressed and released and next time button is pressed and released the LED is switched OFF.
34. Write a C program to interface DHT sensor and LED. The program will switch ON LED once the temperature rises above 25 degrees.
35. Write a program to run pattern(s) on LEDs connect at pins 10, 11, 12, 13.
    Pattern example:

on, off, off, off	on, on, off, off
off, on, off, off	off, on, on, off
off, off, on, off	off, off, on, on
off, off, off, on	

36. Write a program to interface buzzer with Arduino board to buzz on/off with the delay of 1 sec.
37. Write a program to interface LED and Buzzer with Arduino board, so that buzzer is put on whenever LED is on and Buzzer is put off when LED is off.
38. Write a program to interface Button and LED, so that LED blinks/glow when button is pressed.
39. Write a program to interface Button, Buzzer and LED, whereever the button is pressed the buzzer gives beep for 100 ms an LED status is toggled.

40. Write a program to interface LDR and LED with Arduino board. Whenever there is sufficient light falls on LDR the LED is off and when there is dark around LDR, the LED is put on.

41. Write a program to interface any analog (pollution) sensor and display the values read on Serial monitor.

42. Write a program to interface LCD with Arduino board and display "Hello World" on it.

43. Write a program to interface keypad with Arduino board and display the key pressed on Serial monitor.

44. Write a program to interface LCD and keypad (4X4) to exhibit the functionality of a basic calculator.

45. Write a program to interface LEDs at pins 10, 11, 12, 13 and button 7. The press of button changes the pattern of LED glow. (Considering four pattern of LED glow.

46. Write the output of the following program segments:

(a)

```
void setup() {
  Serial.begin(9600);
}
void loop() {
  Serial.print("Hello World");
  delay(1000);
}
```

Figure 24 Program for Q46(a)

(b)

```
int myValue = 0;
void setup() {
  Serial.begin(9600);
}
void loop() {
  myValue = random(100);
  Serial.print("The Value is: ");
  Serial.println(myValue);
  delay(1000);
}
```

Figure 25 Program for Q146(b)

(c)

```
int z;
void setup() {
}
void loop()
{
  z = calculate(2, 3);
}
float calculate(int x, int y)
{
  return (x + y);
}
```

Figure 26 Program for Q46(c)

(d)

```
void setup() {
  char my_str[] = "Hello";
  Serial.begin(9600);
  Serial.println(my_str);
}
void loop() {
}
```

Figure 27 Program for Q46(d)

(e)

```
int z; int a; int b;
void setup() {
  Serial.begin(9600);
}
void loop()
{
  a = random(100);
  b = random(100);
  z = calculate(a, b); //Adding 2 Numbers
  //Write Values to Serial Monitor
  Serial.print(a);
  Serial.print(" + ");
  Serial.print(b);
  Serial.print(" = ");
  Serial.println(z);
  delay(1000);
}
float calculate(int x, int y)
{
  return (x + y);
}
```

Figure 28 Program for Q46(e)

(f)

```
int x; int sum = 0; float average = 0;
void setup() {
  Serial.begin(9600);
} void loop() {
  sum = 0;
  for (int i = 0; i < 100; i++)   {
    x = random(100);
    sum = sum + x;
  }
  average = sum / 100;
  Serial.print("Sum = ");
  Serial.print(sum);
  Serial.print("Average = ");
  Serial.println(average);
  delay(1000);
}
```

Figure 29 Program for Q46(f)

(g)

```
//printing all integers from 0 to 99 using while loop:
void setup() {
  int x = 0; // Set initial value
  Serial.begin(9600);
  while (x < 100) {
    Serial.print("x = ");
    Serial.println(x);
    x++;
  }
}
void loop() {
}
```

Figure 30 Program for Q46(g)

CHAPTER 5

Security and Future of IoT Ecosystem

5.1 INTRODUCTION

IoT security is the technology area concerned with safeguarding of connected devices and networks in the Internet of Things (IoT). IoT involves adding Internet connectivity to a system of interrelated computing devices, mechanical and digital machines, objects, animals and/or people. Each "thing" is provided a unique identifier and the ability to automatically transfer data over a network. Allowing devices to connect to the Internet opens them up to a number of serious vulnerabilities if they are not properly protected. *Vulnerabilities* are weaknesses in a system or its design that allow an intruder to execute commands, access unauthorized data, and/or conduct denial-of-service attacks. *Denial-of-service (DoS)* attack is an attempt to make a machine or network resource unavailable to its intended users. Due to low memory capabilities and limited computation resources, the majority of devices in IoT are vulnerable to resource disable attacks.

5.2 SECURITY

Security means preventing safeguarding connected devices and networks in the Internet of things (IoT) falling in the hands of unauthorized people. The sender of data may wish to be assured that only the intended party actually receives designated data. The receiver must authenticate first that it is the one who is authorized to receive data and thereafter the sender exchanges data. Vulnerabilities can be found in variety of areas in the IoT systems. IoT device security must protect systems, networks, and data from a broad spectrum of IoT security attacks, which target four types of vulnerabilities:

- Communication attacks, which put the data transmitted between IoT devices and servers at risk. Cryptography is technique of securing information and communications through use of codes so that only those person for whom the information is intended can understand it and process it. Thus preventing unauthorized access to information.
- Lifecycle attacks, which put the integrity of the IoT device as it changes hands from user to maintenance. Owner-ship of a device changes during the lifetime of the device from the manufacturer, supplier, retailer, and consumer. The result of this effect could be in the form of loss of life or property. To get rid of such attacks, passwords should be changed frequently. Also, security services are offered for protecting against lifecycle attacks.
- Attacks on the device software, are actions taken to harm a system or disrupt normal operations by exploiting vulnerabilities using various techniques and tools.
- Physical attacks, which target the chip in the device directly. Physical access to IoT devices can introduce risk if those devices are not hardened against physical attack. Such an attack may not be intended to damage the device, but rather to extract information. Simply removing a microSD memory card to read its contents can give an attacker private data, as well as information such as embedded passwords that may allow access to other devices.

A robust IoT security binder allows developers to protect their devices from all types of vulnerabilities while deploying the security level that best matches their application needs. Security vulnerabilities begin from implementation flaws, design flaws, or failure to properly install and use security features. Cryptography technologies are used to fight communication attacks.

☞ *The collection of tools designed to protect data and prevent hackers is known as* ***computer security****.*

5.3 CYBER SECURITY

Cyber security deals with the security of information technology. It also refers to protecting computers, networks, programs and data from unauthorized users.

The information stored in the cyber environment and user's assets is connected to computer devices, applications, services and telecommunications systems. Cyber Security is also used to protect your Internet and network based digital equipment and information from unauthorized access. Its purpose is to defend the assets against all threat actors throughout the entire life cycle of a cyber-attack.

There is a need for Internet users to understand how to protect themselves from online fraud and identity theft.

5.3.1 Securing your PC

Computer has become an essential part of our daily lives. You get almost everything done online via PC or laptop. You can secure your PC from virus and spyware in the following ways:

Creating Strong and Unique Password

Password is the most common form of computer security. Passwords give the first line of protection against any unauthorized access to your computer. Never use default passwords, and make sure that each strong password uses a mix of upper and lowercase letters, numbers, and special characters. The stronger your password, the more protected your computer is from hackers and malicious software.

Keep Windows and devices Updated

Choose an Operating System based on its security and vulnerability. Make sure you update your Operating System with security updates. Windows has a built-in firewall that protects your PC from unwanted attention via the Internet. Also make sure to check manufacturer's websites regularly to see if patches have been released. Manufacturers issue patches and updates for vulnerabilities as they are discovered. If you find any, update your device. Rather you should enable automatic updates, it is necessary as this is the way new security patches are installed on your devices.

Use 2FA

Two-factor authentication (2FA) is another protective layer of security that requires the user to enter a one-time code after entering their password. So, if you have, you must use it in your device.

☞ *Authorization is the process of determining how an authenticated user is permitted to use specific resources. An authorization mechanism automatically enforces a management policy regarding resource object use.*

Install, update and use anti-virus software

Install antivirus software, which detects malicious programs like ransomware, virus etc., as they arrive, and prevents unauthorized applications from executing.

Encrypt your Connection to the Internet

One of the best encryption tools is VPN. A VPN encrypts your Internet connection and keeps your online activities safe; by using a VPN, you ensure that your computer or laptop is safe while connected to the Internet.

☞ *Encryption is the process of taking data and modifying it so that it cannot be read by untrusted users.*

Disable UPnP

UPnP is the protocol that enables networked devices to discover other networked devices. Though it is important for interoperability, and allow devices to be tracked. You should, turn off all default settings or features that you don't need on all of your devices.

Securing IoT with logz.io

One valuable resource used for securing IoT is the data coming out of these internet-connected devices. IoT devices create lots of data, such as logs and metrics, that can be monitored and analyzed to not only monitor performance but also preemptively discover and troubleshoot vulnerabilities and other security issues.

Preventing the next big attack means implementing best practices and using the right tool set. Logz.io security analytics, for example, enables users to identify potential threats based on what is happening both inside the system and in the world outside the corporate network. Capabilities such as threat detection and correlation rules enable users to monitor IoT devices and identify attack patterns as they are taking place.

5.3.2 Securing your Mobile

Smart phones, tablets, and other mobile devices have become a necessary part of many people's lives. Here are some simple steps to keep you and your devices safe and secure.

- Protect your device physically by choosing a strong password, using the auto-lock feature, and by not sharing your device with others. Passwords become weak links when they are shared among colleagues, stolen, written down or created in such a way that they can be easily guessed. For example, users will try to create memorable passwords by using their names, dob, or social security numbers.
- Keep your data secure by regularly backing up and syncing, staying up-to-date with patches and doing operating system updates, and not overriding any software or security features.
- Safeguard your Personally Identifiable Information (PII) like Social Security numbers, passwords, and account numbers. Do not share this information via text; make sure any mobile shopping or banking is done over a secure connection, and disable geotagging.
- Protect your device from malware by being cautious about installing apps.
- Try to use private data connection and switch off Wi-Fi on your mobile phone whenever you are in public place.

5.4 NEED OF SECURITY IN IoT

We all live in a digital era world which is networked together, from Internet banking to government infrastructure, where data is stored on computers and other devices. A portion of that data can be sensitive information, whether that be intellectual property, financial data, personal information, or other types of data for which unauthorized access could have negative concerns that hacks and other security attacks could endanger the global economy.

There are critical vulnerabilities and security loopholes found in IoT solutions which could be control by hackers to carry out number of criminal activities, including monitoring live feeds, changing device settings and authorizing other users to remotely view and control devices.

IoT security hacks can happen in any industry, from smart home to a manufacturing plant to a connected car. In Internet-connected cars hackers can carry out any number of malicious activities, including taking control of the entertainment system, unlocking the doors or even shutting down the car in motion.

Wearables also can become a source of threat to your privacy, as hackers can use the motion sensors embedded in smartwatches to steal information you're typing, or they can gather health data from smartwatch apps or health tracker devices you might be using.

Home control hubs have been found to be vulnerable, allowing attackers to tamper with heating, lighting, power and door locks, other cases involve industrial control systems being hacked via their wireless network and sensors.

Organization transmit sensitive data across network and other devices, cyber security to protect that information and the systems used to process or store it.

The IoT allows billions of devices, peoples, and services to connect with others and exchange information. Due to the increased usage of IoT devices, the IoT networks are prone to various security attacks. The deployment of efficient security and privacy protocols in IoT networks is extremely needed to ensure Confidentiality, Integrity, and Availability among others. These three goals from the Confidentially, Integrity, Availability (CIA) triad, the basis of all security programs. This is also referred to as the AIC (availability, Integrity, and Confidentiality) triad to avoid the confusion with the Central Intelligence Agency. The elements are considered the three most crucial components of security. In this context, *confidentiality* is a set of rules that limits access to information, *integrity* is the assurance that the information is trustworthy and accurate, and *availability* is a guarantee of reliable access to the information by authorized people.

5.4.1 Confidentiality

As IoT data travels through multiple hops in a network, a proper encryption mechanism is required to ensure the condentiality of data. It is equivalent to privacy and avoids the unauthorized disclosure of information. It involves the protection of data, providing access for those who are allowed to see it while disallowing others from learning about its content. Data encryption is a good example to ensure confidentiality.

5.4.2 Integrity

It refers to the methods for ensuring that data is real, accurate and safeguard from unauthorized user modification. The information has not be altered in an unauthorized way, and that source of the information is genuine. Due to a diverse integration of services, devices and network, the data stored on a device is vulnerable to privacy violation by compromising nodes existing in an IoT network. The IoT devices susceptible to attacks may cause an attacker to impact the data integrity by modifying the stored data for malicious purposes.

5.4.3 Availability

It is the guarantee of reliable and constant access to your sensitive data by authorized people. The attacks on IoT devices may block the provision of services through the conventional denial-of-service attacks.

5.5 TYPES OF CYBER ATTACKS

A cyber-attack is and exploitation of computer systems and networks. It uses malicious code to alter computer code, logic or data and lead to cybercrime, such as information and identity theft.

Cyber-attacks can be classified into the following categories:

5.5.1 Web-based attacks

These are the attacks which occur on a websites or web applications. Some of the important web-based attacks are:

Injection attacks

Injection attacks are amongst the oldest and most dangerous web application attacks. Injection injects application code which can execute operating system commands as the user running the web application. They can result in data theft, data loss, loss of data integrity, Denial of Service, as well as full system compromise. Injection is a major problem in web security. Injection attacks, particularly SQL injections (SQLi attacks) and Cross-site Scripting (XSS) are the most common injection attacks.

DNS Spoofing

DNS spoofing, also referred to as DNS cache poisoning, is a form of computer security hacking in which corrupt Domain Name System data is introduced into the DNS resolver's cache, causing the name server to return an incorrect result record, e.g., an IP address. This results in traffic being diverted to the attacker's computer (or any other computer). Since DNS servers cache the DNS translation for faster, more efficient browsing, attackers can take advantage of this to perform DNS spoofing. If an attacker is able to inject a forged DNS entry into the DNS server, all users will now be using that forged DNS entry until the cache expires. DNS cache poisoning can also sometimes be quite difficult to spot. If the malicious website is very similar to the website it is trying to establish, some users may not even notice the difference. The code for DNS cache poisoning is often found in URLs sent via spam emails. These emails attempt to frighten users into clicking on the supplied URL, which in turn infects their computer. To prevent DNS poisoning, users should never click on a link they don't recognize, and regularly scan their computer for malware.

☞ *Spam is flooding the Internet with many copies of the same message. The most common form of spam is unwanted e-mail.*

Session Hijacking

Hijackers take control of various parts of your web browser, including your home page, search pages, and search bar. They may also redirect you to certain sites which is configured to return a malicious IP address. Some will even redirect you to their own search engine when you attempt a search.

Phishing

It is an attempt of acquiring sensitive information such as usernames, passwords, and credit card details, by hacker in an electronic communication. Phishing is carried out either by email spoofing (creation of email messages with a forged sender address) or instant messaging (online chat which offers real-time text transmission over the Internet), and it directs users to enter the details at a fake website which appears to be identical to the legitimate one.

Few tips to identify the phishing are as follows:

- Do not trust the display name.
- Look at the content of the email, but do not click it.
- Do not give away any personal information.
- **Check for spelling mistakes:** Brands are serious about email, and you do not find any major spelling mistakes or poor grammar.
- **See the salutation:** Legitimate businesses use a personal salutation with first and last name. Lack of details about the signer or company's contact number suggests a phish, as legitimate businesses always provide contact details.
- **Do not click on attachments:** They may contain viruses and malware which damages the files present on your computer.

Brute force

A *brute force* attack (also known as brute force cracking) is an attempt to crack a password or username or find a hidden web page, or find the key used to encrypt a message, using a trial and error approach and hoping, eventually, to guess correctly. Attackers let a computer do the work trying different combinations of usernames and passwords, for example until they find one that works. The most basic brute force attack is a dictionary attack, where the attacker works through a dictionary of possible passwords and tries them all. Dictionary attacks start with some assumptions about common passwords to try to guess from the list in the dictionary. These kinds of brute force attacks are known as an *exhaustive key* search, where the computer tries every possible combination of every possible character to find the right combination. Goals of a brute force attack include:

- Theft of personal information such as passwords, passphrases and other information used to access online accounts and network resources.
- Collect credentials to sell to third parties.
- Provide phishing links to user or spread fake content.
- Defacement of websites and other information in the public domain that could damage the reputation of the organization.
- Redirect domains to sites holding malicious content.

Brute force attacks typically depend on weak passwords and careless network administration. Utilizing strong passwords, allowing a limited number of login attempts and enabling two-factor authentication can help to prevent brute force attacks.

5.5.2 System-based attacks

These are the attacks which are intended to compromise a computer or a computer network. Some of the important system-based attacks are:

Virus

A computer virus is a kind of malware program, which, when executed, gets replicated by inserting copies of itself into other computer programs, data files of the hard drive. When the replication process of virus gets succeeded, the affected areas are called as "*infected*".

Computer viruses can be considered as small software programs which are designed to spread from one computer to another through an interface program.

Computer viruses can spread through many ways, which are:

- Email
- Removable hardware such as pendrives.
- Downloading
- By attaching itself to file or boot records, etc.

Damages caused by virus:

- It gives you fake pop ups which tell you to buy non-existent antivirus software.
- Some can monitor what you are doing.
- Slows down your computer performance
- Steals files and other sensitive information such as passwords, or bank account details, credit card number etc. from your computer.

Worm

A worm is a destructive program that is designed to corrupt database either all at once or over a period of time. After the worm code is written, it is hidden within an existing program, and once that program is loaded into the computer, the worm replicates by attaching copies of itself to other programs in the system. The purpose of the worm can range from a simple prank that pops up a strange message on the screen out of the blue, to the actual destruction of programs and data that may be set to occur at any time in the future.

A virus is similar to a worm, which is also a destructive program, however, the virus always attaches itself to other programs, whereas the worm may not. Worms are less harmful than viruses. They do not require any carrier program and spread by duplicating themselves. They are merely found in the network environment.

The characteristics of a worm are as follows:

- It is self-contained.
- It can replicate.
- It is activated by creating process.

How do worms spread?

Worms are autonomous agents which are capable of propagating themselves without the use of other program or intervention or action by a user.

Damage caused by worm

- Disrupt services.
- Creates system management problems.
- It can scan for passwords and send information back to attacker.

Different types of computer worm

- **Email Worms:** It spreads through infected email messages as an attachment or a link.
- **Instant Messaging Worms:** It spreads by sending links to the contact list of instant messaging applications.
- **Internet Worms:** It scans all available network resources by using local operating system services; it will connect and gain access to computer if it is found to be vulnerable.
- **IRC Worm:** It spreads through IRC chat channels by sending infected files or links of infected websites to other users in the same channel.

☞ *Worm is a program made to replicate automatically. A worm replicates continuously until the entire hard disk space and memory are eaten up and it may do so without any user intervention.*

Trojan horse

A trojan horse is a program that invades a computer system by secretly attaching itself to a valid program downloaded into the computer. It may be used to locate password information, or it may alter an existing program to make it easier to gain access to it.

☞ *Trojan Horse is a program that appears to do something useful but actually delivers a harmful effect, such as opening up a security hole, spreading itself via e-mail, or deleting or damaging files. It has no way to replicate automatically.*

Types of Trojan Horses

Trojans are classified according to the type of actions:

- **Backdoor:** It gives remote control to the malicious users of an infected computer.
- **Exploit:** These are the programs which contain data or code that takes an advantage of a vulnerability within application software which is running on your computer.
- **Rootkit:** These are designed to conceal certain objects or activities in your system. It prevent malicious programs from getting detected.
- **Trojan-Banker:** It is designed to steal your account data for online banking systems, e-payment systems, and credit or debit cards.
- **Trojan-DDoS:** It conducts DoS (Denial of Service), which is done by sending multiple requests from your computer and several other infected computers; the attack then overburdens the target address which leads to problem.
- **Trojan-Downloader:** It automatically downloads and installs new versions of malicious programs onto your computer.

- **Trojan-Dropper:** It is used by hackers to install Trojans and/or viruses for preventing the detection of malicious programs.

How do Trojan Horses spread?

They generally spread through e-mail.

Limitations

Since Trojan Horse malware is not technically viral, it cannot self-replicate and requires a user interaction to function.

Protection against Trojans

By installing anti-malware software on PCs, laptops, Macs, tablets, and smartphones, one can get protection against Trojans.

Backdoors

This is a program that sends information back to its creator about the infected system, making it easy for that person to hack into the infected system and take control of it or read sensitive data.

☞ *It gives remote control to the malicious users of an infected computer.*

Bots

A bot short for "robot" and also called an Internet bot is an automated program that runs over the Internet. Bots are automated, means they run according to their instructions without a human user to start them up. Bots often imitate or replace a human user's behavior. Typically they do repetitive tasks, and they can do them much faster than human users could.

Some bots are useful, one of the best examples of a good bot is a search engine spider that index content for a search engine. Other bots are "bad" and are programmed to break into user accounts, scan the web for contact information for sending spam, or perform other malicious activities.

While most bots are used for productive purposes, some are considered malware, since they perform undesirable functions. For example, spambots capture email addresses from website contact forms, address books, and email programs, then add them to a spam mailing list. Site scrapers download entire websites, enabling unauthorized duplication of a website's contents. DoS bots send automated requests to websites, making them unresponsive. Botnets, which consist of many bots working together, may be used to gain unauthorized access to computer systems and infect computers.

Bots can be of following types:

- **Chatbots**: These bots are scripts that look for certain text patterns submitted by chat room participants and respond with automated actions. For example, a chat bot might warn a user if his language is inappropriate.
- **Web crawlers**: Bots that scan content on webpages all over the Internet. Web crawlers are used by search engines to scan websites on a regular basis. These bots "crawl" websites by following the links on each page.
- **Social bots**: Bots that operate on social media platforms.
- **Malicious bots**: Bots that scrape content, spread spam content, or carry out credential stuffing attacks. Malicious bots are typically blended threats that come as part virus/worm and are used in a identity theft or to launch denial of service attacks.

5.6 IoT AND CYBER SECURITY CHALLENGES

A number of challenges prevent the securing of IoT devices and ensuring end-to-end security in an IoT environment. Because the idea of networking appliances and other objects is relatively new, security has not always been considered top priority during a product's design phase. Additionally, because IoT is a founding market, many product designers and manufacturers are more interested in getting their products to market quickly, rather than taking the necessary steps to build security in from the start. From a manufacturer's viewpoint, building security in; from the start can be costly, slow down development and cause the device not to function as it should.

In India, there are many challenges related to cyber security. With the increased of cyber-attack, every organization needs a security analyst who makes that their system is secured. These security analysts face many challenges related to cyber security such as securing confidential data of government organizations, securing the private organization servers, etc.

The important cyber security challenges are as follows:

5.6.1 Blockchain Revolution

Blockchain is the technology of Digital Crypto-Currency Bitcoin. Blockchain was invented by a person (or group of people) using the name 'Satoshi Nakamoto' in 2008 to serve as the public transaction ledger of the cryptocurrency bitcoin. It is a distributed database of records of all transactions that have been executed and shared among participating parties. Each transactions verified by the majority of participants of the system. It contains every single record of each transaction. Bitcoin is the most popular cryptocurrency example of the blockchain.

Bitcoin is a crypto-currency and digital payment system invented by Satoshi Nakamoto. It means they can used like a currency which can be used to buy things online. These are similar to digital cash that exist as bits on people's computers. Bitcoins exist only in the cloud, like Paypal. Even though they are virtual, rather than physical, they are used like cash when transferred between people through the web.

Blockchaing technology can be integrated into multiple areas. The primary use of blockchains is as a distorted ledger for cryptocurrencies. It shows great across a wide range of business applications like banking, finance, government, healthcare, Insurance, media and entertainment, retail etc.

Blockchain network is way better than the traditional methods of saving records on papers. The details of every transaction are stored across the network, which makes it difficult for hackers to hinder with the security. This is the reason why industries such as finance, banking etc., where the data shared is sensitive, are turning to blockchain technology for a solution.

A piece of data that is shared via blockchain technology is complete in itself, accurate and consistent with all the members. The distributed structure of blockchain makes it possible for users to control and access details about the transactions.

5.6.2 Ransomware Evolution

In 1996, ransomware was known as cryptoviral extortion, introduced by Moti Yung and Adam Young from Columbia University. Ransomware is a type of malicious software that blocks access to a computer system or data, usually by encrypting it, until the victim pays a fee to the attacker. In many cases, the ransom demand comes with a deadline. If the victim does not pay in time, the data is gone forever. The two most common types of ransomware are encryptors and screen lockers. *Encryptors* encrypt data on a system, making the content useless without the decryption key. *Screen lockers*, on the other hand, simply block access to the system with a lock screen stating that the system is encrypted.

There are several different ways that ransomware can infect your computer. One of the most common methods today is through malicious spam, which is unsolicited email that is used to deliver malware. Malspam uses social engineering in order to trick people into opening attachments or clicking on links by appearing as it is from a trusted institution.

Insecure devices can also be directly targeted by ransomware or other malware, for example, to be used for cryptocurrency mining or as DDoS (Distributed Denial of service) attack drones in a botnet (Mirai).

5.6.3 IoT Threats

Wireless communication networks are highly prone to security threats. The major applications of wireless communication networks are in military, business, healthcare, retail, and transportations. These systems use wired, cellular, or adhoc networks. Wireless sensor networks, actuator networks, and vehicular networks have received a great attention in society and industry. In recent years, the Internet of Things (IoT) has received considerable research attention. The IoT is considered as future of the Internet. The IoT allows billions of devices, peoples, and services to connect with others and exchange information. Although the IoT provides huge benefits, it is prone to various security threats in your daily life. The majority of the security threats are related to leakage of information and loss of services. In IoT, the security threats are affecting the physical security risk also. The deployment of efficient security and privacy protocols in IoT networks is extremely needed to ensure confidentiality, authentication, access control, and integrity, among others. In fact, in IoT environments, devices should be protected against any threats that can affect their functionality. It is challenging to implement and use a strong security mechanism due to resource constraints in terms of IoT computational capabilities, memory, and battery power. Some security threats in the IoT are as follows:

- To ensure the security of data in IoT environment, end-to-end data protection should be provided in a complete network of data to manage information privacy in full data life cycle.
- Data is collected from different devices connected to each other and instantly shared with other devices. The interconnection and communication among the devices in the IoT adjust according to the situation. Therefore, the devices must be capable of maintaining security level.
- Most of the security and privacy concerns are invoke by misconfiguration of users. So, it necessary to select security and privacy policies that may apply automatically.

5.6.4 AI Expansion

The bots can download a complimentary copy of AI and Machine Learning in your Organization to learn about the ways in which AI and machine learning are being applied IT operations and security.

5.6.5 Serverless Apps Vulnerability

Serverless apps, the latest aspect of virtual computing, enable a new degree of granularity in computing functions. Serverless apps can save time and reduce costs. For example, some providers have recently reduced the billing iteration to seconds, which will have a substantial impact on growth. Billing for functions in seconds, instead of using containers or virtual machines that require minutes or hours.

Serverless apps that are quickly implemented or rapidly deployed can use an inappropriate privilege level, leaving the environment open to a privilege rise attack. Similarly, the speed of deployment can result in a function depending on packages pulled from external repositories that are not under the organization's control and have not been properly evaluated.

There are other risks by looking at the URL, You can tell if the request is going to a serverless environment. As a result, it might be possible for an attacker to disrupt or disable the infrastructure from the outside, affecting a large number of organizations. Also, the data is not on the same server that executes the function, it must transit some network and may be at risk of interception or manipulation.

5.7 PRIVACY FOR IoT ENABLED DEVICES

It's a reality today that Internet connected devices are everywhere from our fitness trackers to our vehicles and appliances. These devices track our sleep patterns, enable us to set our coffee machines or put on our AC remotely.

Not only IoT has changed our personal lives and habits, it has a great impact on industries such as manufacturing, energy production, agriculture, mining, and construction. For example, thermometers, are now enabled with sensors which collect data and change it into electrical outputs, and actuators, which take data and convert it into energy. The data that is collected, monitored, and analyzed is then controlled to optimize processes, saving businesses money and time.

In the healthcare field, the developments brought about by IoT are amazing. It allows many medical devices such as heart monitoring, asthma monitoring, and diagnosing and treating certain kinds of cancer to connect to the Internet for performing different procedures. There are even sensors that allow doctors to track whether or not patients are taking their medications as prescribed using a smartphone app.

Though these IoT devices are beneficial, they do create significant security challenges. IoT devices present some major security concerns, which are outlined below:

5.7.1 Difficult to Encrypt

Typically, IoT devices are basically single-purpose computers built without a lot of memory or processing power that run on weak hardware. This makes encrypting them more difficult, which in turn makes these devices easy target for many different kinds of attacks.

5.7.2 Lack of Experience

Many inexperienced manufacturers are coming on the IoT field. IoT devices are more challenging to program than traditional software. They require programmers to know more about kernel and OS internals than regular programmers often do.

5.7.3 Lack of Standards

The standards and best practices for IoT devices are currently still under development. Organizations like The National Institute of Standards and Technology (NIST) and The Internet of Things Security Foundation (IoTSF) are working on developing baseline security standards, but these are not yet complete.

5.7.4 Third party IoT vulnerabilities

One of the main issues in IoT security is the heavily dependent of IoT devices on third-party components for communication capabilities, cryptographic capabilities, the Operating System itself etc. The fact that third-party libraries are commonly used across devices, combined with difficulty to secure them, makes the spot for hackers to look for IoT vulnerabilities and exploit many IoT devices through such third-party component. Many third-party components are delivered in binary form, with no source code available. Even when the source code is available, it's often hard to examine and asses the security level or vulnerabilities inside it.

5.8 MAJOR IoT LEAKS

Below are a few examples of problems that the vulnerabilities in improperly secured IoT devices have already caused.

5.8.1 Mirai

Cybercriminals can control the power of your IoT devices. A botnet called mirai used IoT devices to launch numerous DDoS attacks against entities such as KrebsOnSecurity, the French Internet host OVH, and the US's Dyn DNS provider. A botnet can combine the processing power of small devices to launch a large-scale cyberattack. The attacks infiltrated the network through consumer IoT devices, including IP cameras and routers. Thereafter, Domain Name System (DNS) service provider Dyn's network was targeted, making a number of websites, including Amazon, Netflix, Twitter and The New York Times, unavailable for hours.

5.8.2 Hackable Cardiac Devices

IoT is setting huge advances in healthcare. Some of these advances, such as the radio-controlled implantable cardiac devices developed by St. Jude Medical, are incredibly invasive. These devices were built with a vulnerability that allows attackers to access and reprogram them this could enable an attacker to administer inappropriate levels of pacing, potentially causing patients to die.

5.8.3 Casino Fish Tank Hack

An Internet connected fish tank was hacked via its thermostat at an unnamed US casino in 2017. The large aquarium, brimming with exotic fish and saltwater plants contained a vulnerability that allowed attackers to steal data from the casino's database.

5.8.4 VPNFilter malware

Cybercriminals sometimes access your home network though your router. It happened in 2018. The VPNFilter malware - short for malicious software - infected over half a million routers in more than 50 countries. VPNFilter is able to install malware onto devices and systems connected to your router - the hardware that allows communication between your connected devices and the Internet. It can also collect information passing through your router. And it can block network traffic and steal your passwords.

If both manufacturers and users begin to implement better practices in these technologies in initial stages, a great deal of future damage can be avoided.

5.9 SECURITY FOR CONSUMER DEVICES

The rapid growth of the IoT has led to greater security and privacy risks. Many such risks are apply to device vulnerabilities that arise from cybercrime by hackers and improper use of system resources. The IoT needs to be built in such a way as to ensure easy and safe usage control. Consumers need confidence to fully utilize the IoT in order to enjoy its benefits and avoid security and privacy risks. IoT presents a variety of potential security risks that could be exploited to harm consumers by:

- Enabling unauthorized access and misuse of personal information.
- Facilitating attacks on other systems.
- Creating risks to personal safety.

It is important to balance optimised and personalised service with the desire for privacy. One method of reconciling these competing objectives is to ensure the consent of the consumer to their data to be collected, stored, and shared. However, this brings about a number of challenges. Consent has traditionally been based on a system of transparency: a provider of a service should make clear what data is collected and what it is to be used for. There should be widespread agreement that companies developing IoT products should implement reasonable security. Companies should build security into their devices at the outset, rather than afterward. As part of the security by design process, companies should consider:

- Conducting a privacy or security risk assessment.
- Minimizing the data they collect and retain; and testing their security measures before launching their products. Also, companies should train all employees about good security, and ensure that security issues are addressed at the appropriate level of responsibility within the organization.
- Companies should retain service providers that are capable of maintaining reasonable security and provide reasonable oversight for these service providers.
- When companies identify significant risks within their systems, they should implement a defense-in depth approach, in which they consider implementing security measures at several levels.
- Companies should consider implementing reasonable access control measures to limit the ability of an unauthorized person to access a consumer's device, data, or even the consumer's network.
- Finally, companies should continue to monitor products throughout the life cycle and, to the extent feasible, patch known vulnerabilities.

Consumers must be made aware of the dangers of IoT systems and provided steps they can take to stay secure, such as updating default credentials and applying software updates. Consumers can also play a role in requiring device manufacturers to create secure devices, and refusing to use those that don't meet high security standards. Likewise, manufacturers should also be aware that failing to manage the security of their devices and the data collected by them will eventually lead to exposure of their customer's private information which will in turn lead to the reduced consumer confidence and (potentially) fewer sales.

5.10 SECURITY LEVELS

The IoT is facing various types of attacks including active attacks and passive attacks that may easily disturb the functionality and abolish the benefits of its services. Different types of attack, nature/behavior of attack and threat level of attacks are discussed in this section.

Modification of messages being transmitted, capturing authentication sequences and obtaining extra privileges, creation of false messages etc., are a few *active attacks*. Active attacks are difficult to prevent because they require protection of all communication facilities and paths at all times. But one can detect and recover from the disruptions caused by them. These active attacks are classified into two further categories that are *internal attacks* and *external attacks*. Such vulnerable attacks can prevent the devices to communicate smartly. Hence the security constraints must be applied to prevent devices from malicious attacks.

In a *passive attack*, an intruder just senses the node or may steal the information but it never attacks physically. However, the active attacks disturb the performance physically.

Different levels of attacks are categorized into four types according to their behavior and propose possible solutions to threats/attacks.

- **Low-level attack**: If an attacker tries to attack a network and his attack is not successful.
- **Medium-level attack**: If an attacker/intruder or an eavesdropper is just listening to the medium but do not alter the integrity of data.
- **High-level attack**: If an attack is carried on a network and it alters the integrity of data or modifies the data.
- **Extremely High-level attack**: If an intruder/attacker attacks on a network by gaining unauthorized access and performing an illegal operation, making the network unavailable, sending bulk messages, or jamming network.

☞ *An eavesdropper can silently sense the transmission medium and can modify the data if encryption is not applied and steal the information that is being transmitted. For example in medical environment, privacy of a patient may be leaked by eavesdropping.*

5.11 PROTECTING IoT DEVICES

Security needs to be built in as the foundation of IoT systems, with rigorous validity checks, authentication, data verification, and all the data needs to be encrypted. IoT security methods vary depending on your specific IoT application and your place in the IoT ecosystem. For example, IoT manufacturers - from product makers to semiconductor companies - should concentrate on building security in from the start, making hardware tamper-proof, building secure hardware, ensuring secure upgrades, providing firmware updates/patches and performing dynamic testing. A security solution for embedded devices must ensure the device firmware has not been tampered with, it must secure the data stored by the device, secure communication and it must protect the device from cyber-attacks. A solution developer's focus should be on secure software development and secure integration.

Common IoT security measures include:

- Incorporating security at the design phase. IoT developers should include security at the start of any consumer, enterprise or industrial-based device development.
- Hardcoded credentials should never be part of the design process. An additional measure developers can take is to require credentials be updated by a user before the device functions. If a device comes with default credentials, users should update them using a strong password or multifactor authentication or biometrics where possible.

  Also, you need to keep the softwares used for computer networks, servers, laptops, desktops, wireless routers, network switches and any other devices up-to-date, particularly with the latest manufacturer security updates. Authentic updates safeguard your devices against any security threat.
- **PKI and digital certificates**: Public key infrastructure (PKI) and digital certificates play critical roles in the development of secure IoT devices, providing the trust and control needed to distribute and identify public encryption keys, secure data exchanges over networks and verify identity.
- **API security**: Application performance indicator (API) security is essential to protect the integrity of data being sent from IoT devices to back-end systems and ensure only authorized devices, developers and apps communicate with APIs.
- **Integrating teams**: Along with training, integrating disparate and regularly siloed teams can be useful. For example, having programing developers work with security specialists can help ensure the proper controls are added to devices during the development phase.
- **Identity management**: Providing each device with a unique identifier is critical to understanding what the device is, how it behaves,

the other devices it interacts with and the proper security measures that should be taken for that device.

- **Hardware security**: Securing IoT devices is a real challenge. Endpoint hardening includes making devices tamper-proof or tamper-evident. This is especially important when devices will be used in harsh environments or where they will not be monitored physically. Also, IoT devices are highly diversified, with a wide variety of operating systems (real-time operating systems, Linux-based or bare-metal), communication protocols and architectures. Along with high diversity there is issues of low resources and lack of industry standards and regulations.
- **Strong encryption**: It is critical to securing communication between devices. Data at rest and in transit should be secured using cryptographic algorithms. This includes the use of key lifecycle management. Microsoft has added BitLocker encryption and Secure Boot technology to the Windows 10 IoT which is Microsoft's Operating System for IoT devices and platforms like the Raspberry Pi. *BitLocker* is an encryption technology that can code entire disk volumes, and it has been featured in Windows operating systems. This can be crucial to secure on-device data. *Secure Boot* is a security standard developed by members of the PC industry to help make sure that your PC boots using only software that is trusted by the PC manufacturer. Its implementation can prevent device hijacking.
- **Network security**: The fact that IoT devices can be easily exploited makes them a very good target for attackers, aiming to use the weak IoT device as an entry point to the entire enterprise network, without being caught. Protecting an IoT network includes ensuring port security, disabling port forwarding and never opening ports when not needed; using anti-malware, firewalls and intrusion detection system/intrusion prevention system; blocking unauthorized IP addresses; and ensuring systems are patched and up-to-date. You need to have the usual security technologies in place such as anti-virus, anti-malware, firewalls, encryption along with ransomware protection. There are softwares to monitor the network data flow, flags suspicious files, and analyzes them for destructive or malicious intention.
- **Network access control**: NAC can help identify and inventory IoT devices connecting to a network. This will provide a baseline for tracking and monitoring devices.
- IoT devices that need to connect directly to the Internet should be segmented into their own networks and have access to enterprise network restricted. Network segments should be monitoring for anomalous activity, where action can be taken, should an issue be detected.
- **Security gateways**: Acting as an intermediary between IoT devices and the network, security gateways have more processing power, memory and capabilities than the IoT devices themselves, which provides them the ability to implement features such as firewalls to ensure hackers cannot access the IoT devices they connect.
- Patch management/continuous software updates. Providing means of updating devices and software either over network connections or through automation is critical. Having a coordinated disclosure of vulnerabilities is also important to updating devices as soon as possible.
- IoT and operational system security are new to many existing security teams. It is critical to keep security staff up to date with new or unknown systems, learn new architectures and programming languages and be ready for new security challenges. C-level and cybersecurity teams should receive regular training to keep up with modern threats and security measures.
- Consumer education: Consumers must be made aware of the dangers of IoT systems and provided steps they can take to stay secure, such as updating default credentials and applying software updates. Consumers can also play a role in requiring device manufacturers to create secure devices, and refusing to use those that don't meet high security standards.

- **Embedded system security**: Embedded system security is a strategic approach for protecting software running on embedded systems from attack.
- **Holistic security**: Holistic security is an approach that seeks to integrate all the elements designed to safeguard an organization, considering them.
- **IoT policy**: An Internet of Things policy is a document that provides a comprehensive guide designed to help an organization deal with

5.12 FUTURE IoT ECO SYSTEM

The IoT is considered as future of the Internet. In future, the IoT will completely change our living styles and business models. It will permit people and devices to communicate anytime, anyplace, with any device under ideal conditions using any network and any service. The usage of IoT in different applications is expected to rise rapidly in the coming years. The IoT allows billions of devices, peoples, and services to connect with others and exchange information. Due to the increased usage of IoT devices, the IoT networks are prone to various security attacks. The deployment of efficient security and privacy protocols in IoT networks is extremely needed to ensure confidentiality, authentication, access control, and integrity, among others. The main goal of IoT is to create Superior world for human beings in future. The IoT is a concept that depicts future where the physical objects connected to Internet communicate with each other and identify themselves for other devices. The IoT system consists of smart objects, smartphones, tablets and intelligent devices etc. Such systems use RFID, Quick Response (QR) codes or wireless technology to perform communication between different devices. The application of RFID technology to logistics enables industry to forecast information, identify future trends, estimate the probability of an accident, and allow for the early adoption of remedial measures. This can improve enterprises ability to respond to the market and maintain risk aware supply.

5.13 NEED OF POWERFUL CORE FOR BUILDING SECURE ALGORITHM

To protect the privacy of users and prevent IoT data breaches, encrypt the data at rest and in-transit between IoT devices and back-end systems by using standard cryptographic algorithms and fully-encrypted key lifecycle management processes to boost the overall security of user data and privacy. Strong encryption is critical to securing communication between devices. Data at rest and in transit should be secured using cryptographic algorithms. This includes the use of key lifecycle management.

5.13.1 What is Cryptography?

Cryptography is the science of information security. It is closely related to the disciplines of cryptology (it is the mathematics, such as a number theory and the application of formulas and algorithms) and cryptanalysis (it refers to the study of ciphers, ciphertext with a view to finding weaknesses in them that will permit retrieval of the plain text from the ciphertext, without necessarily knowing the key or the algorithms). Cryptography includes techniques such as microdots, merging words with images, and other ways to hide information in storage or transit. However, cryptography is most often associated with scrambling plain text (ordinary text) into ciphertext (a process called encryption), then back again (known as decryption). Individuals who practice this field are known as cryptographers.

5.13.2 Cryptographic Algorithms

Cryptographic algorithms!are used for important tasks such as data encryption, authentication, and digital signatures. Cryptographic algorithms!are being applied in an increasing number of devices to satisfy their high security requirements. Many of these devices require high-speed operation and include specialized hardware encryption and/or decryption circuits for the selected cryptographic algorithm. Cryptographic algorithms!are the most frequently used privacy protection method in the IoT domain.

Cryptographic techniques allow a sender to disguise data so that an intruder can gain no information from the intercepted data. Cryptography involves two corresponding processes. These processes are described as under:

(a) *Encryption:* It is the process of taking data and modifying it so that it cannot be read by untrusted users.

(b) *Decryption:* It is the process of taking encrypted data and rendering it readable for trusted users.

Cryptography is broadly classified into two categories:

- **Symmetric key Cryptography**: An encryption system in which the sender and receiver of a message share a single, common key that is used to encrypt and decrypt the message.
- **Asymmetric key Cryptography (popularly known as public key cryptography):** The encryption process where different keys are used for encrypting and decrypting the information. Keys are different but are mathematically related, such that retrieving the plain text by decrypting ciphertext is feasible. Public-key or asymmetric-key encryption algorithms use a pair of keys, a public key associated with the creator/sender for encrypting messages and a private key that only the originator knows for decrypting that information.

5.13.3 Securing Data with Cryptographic Algorithms

Literally thousands of different cryptographic algorithms have been developed over the years. Cryptographic algorithms can be classified as follows:

- Encryption algorithms that are used to encrypt data and provide confidentiality. To safeguard your information and data shared over the Internet it is important to use strong encryption algorithms.
- Signature algorithms that are used to digitally sign data to provide authentication. A digital signature is merely a means of signing data to authenticate that the message sender is really the person he or she claims to be. Digital signatures can also provide for data integrity along with authentication and nonrepudiation. Digital signatures generally use both signature algorithms and hash algorithms. When a message is encrypted with a user's private key, the hash value that is created becomes the signature for that message. Signing a different message will produce a different signature. Each signature is unique, and any attempt to move the signature from one message to another would result in a hash value that would not match the original; thus, the signature would be invalidated.
- Hashing algorithms that are used to provide data integrity. In addition to cryptographic algorithms that are used to ensure the confidentiality of communications, a specific family of algorithms is used to guarantee the integrity of exchanges. These are known as cryptographic hash functions.

  Hashing is a technique in which an algorithm (also called a hash function) is applied to a portion of data to create a unique digital fingerprint that is a fixed-size variable. If anyone changes the data by one binary digit, the hash function will produce a different output (called the hash value) and the recipient will know that the data has been changed. Hashing can ensure integrity and provide authentication as well.

  In order to be effective, a hash function should be combined with other cryptographic primitives in a protocol. It would be easy for an attacker to recalculate a correct hash for a message which he or she had modified; however, if a message and the associated hash are encrypted by the sender, then an attacker would be unable to correctly modify the encrypted value of the message hash.

Algorithms (ciphers) are also categorized by the way they work at the technical level (*Stream ciphers* and *Block ciphers*). This categorization refers to whether the algorithm is applied to a stream of data, operating on individual bits, or to an entire block of data. Stream ciphers provide faster encryption and decryption capability than block ciphers, because they work on smaller units of data and can be used in both symmetric (Same key can encrypt & decrypt) and asymmetric (Different key required for reverse operation) key cryptosystems. The key is generated as a keystream, and this is combined with the plain text to be encrypted. *Block ciphers* take a block of plain text and turn it into a block of cipher text. The drawback to this type of system is that if the key is discovered, all messages can be decrypted. Block ciphers are mostly used in symmetric key encryption.

There are two types of stream ciphers:

Synchronous stream ciphers

In a synchronous stream cipher, the keystream is generated independently of the plaintext and ciphertext messages. The keystream is then applied to the plaintext for encryption (or ciphertext for decryption). For encryption and decryption to work, both the sender and the recipient must use the same key, and at the same position within the keystream. If the keystream is altered, the decryption process will fail.

Synchronous stream ciphers are useful when the transmission error rate is high, as single-digit corruption of alteration of the message only affects a single digit of the decrypted plaintext.

Asynchronous Stream Ciphers

Asynchronous stream ciphers, otherwise known as self-synchronizing stream ciphers, can self-correct the output stream when there are limited errors in the transmission. When a recipient detects an error in the transmission, an automatic re-synchronizing process with the keystream generator occurs.

5.14 EXAMPLES OF NEW TRENDS

Today, you are totally dependent on technologies. Artificial Intelligence (AI) and Internet of Things (IoT) are among the technologies that have great scope and prospects for the future.

Artificial Intelligence permits machines to learn, think, act, and react like humans. It helps machines to analyze and study the ancient information, perceive patterns and make real-time decisions. AI also enables machines to learn from experience. Artificial Intelligence and Machine Learning have started changing the world and humankind is experiencing a phase of paradigm shift into a future of technological advancement. AI algorithms are being used in Climate modelling to predict the weather conditions well in advanced. Machine Learning and robotic automation are now a part of industrial setups and manufacturing units. Companies are using predictive data analytics to understand consumer behaviour which is helping them in overall growth of their business.

IoT is an advanced automation and analytics system which deals with artificial intelligence, sensor, networking, electronic, cloud messaging etc. to deliver complete systems for the product or services. The system created by IoT has greater transparency, control, and performance. IoT makes things smart and enhances life through the use of data. For example, if you have a coffee machine whose beans have going to end, then the coffee machine itself order the coffee beans of your choice from the retailer.

5.15 ARTIFICIAL INTELLIGENCE (AI)

Artificial Intelligence is one of the emerging technologies that try to simulate human reasoning in AI systems. You are already using AI in your day-to-day lives for example a virtual assistant such as Siri, Google Assistant or Cortana all are our digital personal assistants. They help you find useful information when you ask for it using your voice. This is a simple example of Artificial Intelligence.

John McCarthy defined the term Artificial Intelligence in the year 1950. It is a concept that refers to a computer ability to perform tasks and make decisions that require some level of human intelligence.

AI systems will typically demonstrate at least some of the following behaviours associated with human intelligence: planning, learning, reasoning, problem solving, knowledge representation, perception, motion, and manipulation and, to a lesser extent, social intelligence and creativity.

Al is a vast subject and its field of study includes many theories, methods and technology. There are many major subfields under it:

- **Machine Learning**: Machine Learning is an application of Artificial Intelligence (AI) that provides systems the ability to automatically learn and improve from experience without being explicitly programmed.

- **Neural networks**: A computer system modelled on the human brain and nervous system. These are brain-inspired networks of interconnected layers of algorithms, called neurons, that feed data into each other, and which can be trained to carry out specific tasks.
- **Deep learning**: A machine learning technique that teaches computers to learn by example.
- **Computer vision**: Computer vision system is a technology of obtaining models to control information from visual data. For example, a spying aeroplane takes photographs which are used to figure out spatial information or map of the areas.
- **Natural language processing**: It is possible to interact with the computer that understand human language.

5.15.1 Applications of AI

AI is used in applicable in many aspects such as Finance, Medical, Entertainment, Pattern recognition, and Data mining. Some important applications of AI are listed below:

- **Gaming**: It plays an important role in designing strategic games such as chess, tic-tac-toe etc. These are the logical games in which the system can determine the various available options based on the information fed.
- **Natural Language Processing**: It is possible to interact with the computer that understand human language.
- **Expert System**: Expert systems are developed to solve complex problems by the knowledge of reasoning, which is represented primarily using if-then rules rather than conventional procedural code.
- **Vision System**: Computer vision system is a technology of obtaining models to control information from visual data. For example, a spying aeroplane takes photographs which are used to figure out spatial information or map of the areas.
- **Speech Recognition**: Some intelligent systems are capable of hearing and comprehending the language in terms of sentences and their meanings while a human talks to it. Applications use artificial intelligence to optimize speech recognition functions. Examples include intelligent personal assistants, e.g. Amazon's Alexa or Apple's Siri.
- **Handwriting Recognition**: The software reads the text written on paper by a pen or on screen by a stylus. It can recognize the shapes of the letters and convert it into editable text.
- **Intelligent Robotics**: It is able to perform the tasks by a human. They have sensors to detect physical data from the real world such as light, heat, temperature, movement, sound. In addition, they are capable of learning from their mistakes and they can adapt to the new environment.

5.15.2 Advantages of AI

Reduction in Human Error

AI would have a low error rate compared to humans, if coded properly. They would have incredible precision, accuracy, and speed.

Takes risks instead of Humans

AI Robot are not affected by adverse environments, thus able to complete dangerous tasks, such as going to mars, defuse a bomb, explore the deepest parts of oceans, mining for coal and oil. It can also be used effectively in any kind of disaster.

Available 24x7

Using AI you can make machines work 24x7 without any breaks and they don't even get bored, unlike humans. Educational Institutes and Helpline centers are getting many queries and issues which can be handled effectively using AI.

Helping in Repetitive Jobs

In your day-to-day work, you will be performing many repetitive works like sending a thanking mail, verifying certain documents for errors and many more things. Using Artificial Intelligence you can productively automate these common tasks. In banks, you often see many verifications of documents to get a loan which is a repetitive task for the owner of the bank. Using AI Cognitive Automation the owner can speed up the process of verifying the documents by which both the customers and the owner will be benefited.

Digital Assistance

Some of the highly advanced organizations use digital assistants to interact with their users, this helps them to save time and the need for human resources. Artificial Intelligence is widely employed by financial institutions and banking institutions and helps to organize and manage data. Also, detection of fraud uses AI in a smart card-based system.

The digital assistants also used in many websites to provide things that users want. You can chat with them about what you are looking for. Also, applications such as Siri, Cortana, and Google are frequently used in our daily routine whether it is for searching a location, making a phone call, replying to a mail etc.

Needs no breaks

Using AI machines are programmed for long hours and can continuously perform without getting bored or distracted. The machine does not get tired, even if it has to work for consecutive hours. This is a major benefit over humans, who need a rest from time to time to be efficient.

Faster Decisions

The complete absence of emotions from a machine makes it more efficient as they are able to take decisions faster than a human and carry out actions quickly. The integration of AI tools in the healthcare sector has improved the efficiency of treatments by minimizing the risk of false diagnosis.

New Inventions

AI is powering many inventions in almost every domain which will help humans solve the majority of complex problems. Nowadays, medical professionals are trained with artificial surgery simulators. It uses application which helps in detecting and monitoring neurological disorders and stimulate the brain functions. This also helps in the radiosurgery. Radiosurgery is used in operating tumors and help in the operation without damaging the surrounding tissues.

5.15.3 Disadvantages of AI

High Costs of Creation

Apart from the installation cost, AI hardware and software need to be updated to meet the latest requirements. Also, repairing and maintenance cost is very high.

Making Humans Lazy

AI is automated and do all human work making human lazy. Machines are able to think faster than humans and they can be easily put into multitasking.

Unemployment

AI machines can predict what a user will search, ask, type. They can also recommend some actions according to the user's needs. They are replacing people in many tasks for example, many robots have taken jobs in the assembly line, driverless cars that could replace millions of human drivers etc. As AI is replacing the majority of the repetitive tasks and other works with robots, human interference is becoming less which will cause a major problem in the employment standards.

No Emotions

No matter how smart a machine becomes, it can never replicate a human. Machines don't possess emotions and moral values. Because of this, don't have their own judgment making skills. They do what they are told to do and therefore the judgment of right or wrong is nil for them. If they encounter a situation that is unfamiliar to them then they perform incorrectly or else break down in such situations.

Lacking Out of Box Thinking

Machines can perform only those tasks which they are designed or programmed to do, so they cannot work outside of what they were programmed for. Though they help in designing and creating, they can't match the power of a human brain. Humans can generate ideas, can think out of the box.

5.15.4 Types of AI

Artificial Intelligence can be divided in to following types based on capabilities and functionally of AI.

Weak or Narrow AI

Narrow AI is a type of AI which is able to perform a dedicated task with intelligence. It cannot perform beyond its field or limitations, as it is only trained for specific task. Hence it is also known as weak AI. Apple Siri is a good example of Narrow AI, but is operates with a limited pre-defined range of functions. Some examples of Narrow AI are playing chess, speech recognition and image recognition.

General AI

General AI is as type of intelligence which could perform any intellectual task with efficiency like a human. The general AI systems which could be smarter and think like a human by its own. Currently, there is no such system exist which could come under general AI and can perform any task as human. As systems with general AI are still under research, and it will take lots of efforts to develop such systems.

Super AI

Super AI is a level of Intelligence of systems at which machines could surpass human intelligence, and can perform any task better than human. The key characteristics of strong AI include the ability to think, solve the puzzle, learn and communicate by its own. It is still a hypothetical concept of Artificial Intelligence. Development of such system in real is still world changing task.

There are many ways AI can be achieved some of them are as follows:

- **Machine Learning**: It is a method where the target is defined and the steps to reach that target is learned by the machine itself by training. For example, to identify a simple object such as an apple or orange. The target is achieved not by clearly specifying the details about it but it is just as you teach a child by showing multiple different pictures of it and therefore allowing the machine to define the steps to identify it like an apple or orange.
- **Natural Language Processing**: It is broadly defined as the automatic manipulation of natural language, like speech and text, by software. One of the well-known examples of this is email spam detection as you can see how it has improved in your mail system.
- **Vision**: Machine vision captures and analyses visual information using a camera, analog-to-digital conversion and digital signal processing. It can be compared to human eyesight but it is not bound by the human limitation which can enable it to see through walls. It is usually achieved through machine learning to get the best possible results so you could say that these two fields are interlinked.
- **Robotics**: It is a field of engineering focused on the design and manufacturing of robots. They are often used to perform tasks that are difficult for humans to perform or perform consistently. Examples include car assembly lines, in hospitals, office cleaner, serving foods, patrolling farm areas and even as police officers.
- **Autonomous Vehicles**: This area of AI has gathered a lot of attention. The list of vehicles includes cars, buses, trucks, trains, ships etc.

5.16 MACHINE LEARNING (ML)

Machine learning is a method of data analysis that automates construction of analytical models, based on the idea that systems can learn from data, identify patterns and make decisions with minimal human intervention. So it is a method where the target is defined and the steps to reach that target is learned by the machine itself by training.

5.16.1 Elements of Machine learning

Each form of Machine Learning has differing approaches, but they all follow the same underlying process and theory. Machine learning has three main categories:

Supervised learning

This process of teaching a machine by example is called supervised learning. A common technique for teaching AI systems is by training them using a very large number of labelled examples. These machine-learning systems are fed huge amounts of data, which has been annotated to highlight the features of interest. For example, if you are creating a machine learning model to detect pictures of dogs, it will only give result for dog images, but if you provide a new data like cat image then it will become unresponsive.

Unsupervised learning

In contrast, unsupervised learning uses a different approach. The data given to the learning algorithm is unlabeled, and the algorithm is asked to identify patterns in the input data. For example, the recommendation system of an e-commerce website where the learning algorithm discovers similar items often bought together.

Reinforcement learning

Reinforcement learning describes a class of problems where an agent operates in an environment and must learn to operate using feedback. For example, self-driving cars being rewarded to stay on the road.

5.16.2 Advantages of ML

Easily identifies trends and patterns

Machine Learning can review large volumes of data and discover specific trends and patterns that would not be apparent to humans. For instance, for an e-commerce website like Amazon, it serves to understand the browsing behaviors and purchase histories of its users to help cater to the right products, deals, and reminders relevant to them. It uses the results to reveal relevant advertisements to them.

No human intervention needed (automation)

Because of the machine learning technique, you don't need to assist your system or give it commands to follow certain instructions. To control their decision-making ability. Rather let it take its own decision by itself without your interference. Hence it helps them to develop and improve their decision-making ability by themselves and also to rectify the errors. A common example of this is anti-virus softwares; they learn to filter new threats as they are recognized. ML is also good at recognizing spam.

Continuous Improvement

As ML algorithms gain experience, they keep improving in accuracy and efficiency. This lets them make better decisions. For example, if you are designing a weather forecast application and it gives you regular weather predictions. The accuracy for that prediction depends completely on the regular error check and with improved accuracy.

Handling multi-dimensional and multi-variety data

Machine Learning algorithms are good at handling data that are multi-dimensional and multi-variety, and improving their skills in having no errors in them with the help of AI technology.

Wide Applications

ML can be helpful for those who are in the field of e-commerce or the healthcare, banking, financial sector, retail, publishing, etc. They can make use of ML to get tremendous help in their market growth and also it helps in the increase of the human work efficiency.

5.16.3 Disadvantages of ML

Data Acquisition

In the process of machine learning, a large amount of data is used in the process of training and learning and these should be inclusive/unbiased, and of good quality. During the process of machine learning with help of software development services, there are also moments when you need to wait. In that period of time new data is being generated and can be used for further process.

Time and Resources

It needs much time to let the algorithms adapt, learn and develop in order to fulfill their purpose with a considerable amount of accuracy and relevancy. It also needs huge resources to function.

Interpretation

Another major challenge is the ability to accurately interpret results generated by the algorithms. You must also carefully choose the algorithms for your purpose.

High error-susceptibility

Machine Learning is autonomous but highly susceptible to errors. Suppose you train an algorithm with data sets, the high amount of data is used and on the other hand, many algorithms are used and tested. Hence there is a huge change to experience many errors. Because when these mistakes happen, it is not easy to find out the main source for which the issue is been created and to find out that particular issue and rectifying it, takes a longer time.

Difference between Artificial Intelligence (AI) and Machine Learning (ML)

Table 5.1 Comparison of AI and ML

Artificial Intelligence	Machine Learning
Artificial Intelligence is a technology to create intelligent machines that can simulate human thinking capability and behavior.	Machine Learning is an application or subset of AI that allows machines to learn from data without being programmed explicitly.
The goal of AI is to make a smart computer system like humans to solve complex problems.	The goal of ML is to allow machines to learn from historical data without being explicitly programmed.
AI is intelligence based on language processing, perception, motion and manipulation, and social intelligence.	ML is a center of information and knowledge based on facts and data collected over time.
AI has a very wide range of scope.	Machine Learning has a limited scope.
The system makes decisions.	The system learns from data. It does not make its own decisions.
AI is working to create an intelligent system which can perform various complex tasks.	Machine learning is working to create machines that can perform only those specific tasks for which they are trained.
It is a computer program that uses its own intelligence to think and perform like a human would do.	The machine takes facts and data, analyses the data and learns from the data.
AI is being used in multiple places such as Siri, customer support using catboats, intelligent humanoid robot, Chess playing etc.	ML are used Online recommender system, Google search algorithms, Facebook auto friend tagging suggestions, etc.

5.16.4 Robotics Process Automation

Robotic Process Automation (RPA) is the use of software with Artificial Intelligence (AI) and machine learning capabilities to handle high-volume, repeatable tasks that require human to perform. These tasks can include queries, calculations and maintenance of records and transactions.

Robotic Process Automation (RPA) is the application of technology that allows employees in a company to configure computer software or a 'robot' to capture and interpret existing applications for processing a transaction, manipulating data, triggering responses and communicating with other digital systems.

Any company that uses labor on a large scale for general knowledge process work, where people are performing high-volume, high transactional process functions, will boost their capabilities and save money and time with robotic process automatic software.

Applications of RPA

Some of the applications of RPA include:

- **Customer service**: It can help companies offer better customer service by verifying e-signatures and uploading scanned documents.

- **Accounting service**: It is used for general accounting, operational accounting, transactional reporting and budgeting.
- **Financial services**: It can be used for foreign exchange payments.
- **Health care**: It can be used for handling patient records.
- **Banking**: Automation of credit card applications in bank loan processing.

5.17 AI PENETRATION TO IoT

Artificial Intelligence in IoT makes things smart and enhances life through the use of data. IoT applications are used in everyday objects with connectivity and intelligence in various domains. There are several sectors that have already started the use of AI, like healthcare, automobiles, heavy industries and etc. Here machine is used to speed up the process of doing work and give you an accurate result.

IoT is a blend of Artificial Intelligence, electronics, and software and networking, which enables more automation, analysis and integration within a system. The basic features which enable proper functioning of IoT are active engagement, integration, sensing and analyzing, connectivity and artificial intelligence.

All these IoT devices generate a lot of data that needs to be collected and mined for actionable results. This is where Artificial Intelligence comes into the picture. Internet of Things is used to collect and handle the huge amount of data that is required by the Artificial Intelligence algorithms. In turn, these algorithms convert the data into useful actionable results that can be implemented by the IoT devices.

Artificial Intelligence is the most important feature or rather an achievement of IoT is in making the world around us much smarter. It enhances the intelligence of every device around us through data collection, algorithms and networks. Artificial intelligence enables algorithm to collect data and communication among connected devices for achieving required results.

There are many different applications across multiple industries that require Artificial Intelligence and Internet of Things. Some of these are given as follows:

5.17.1 Collaborative Robots

Collaborative Robots or Cobots are highly complex machines that are designed to help humans in a shared workspace with environments ranging from office to industrial. They can be a robot arm designed to perform tasks or even a complex robot designed to fulfill tough tasks. Due to the programming of the robots, they can perform a more laborious task with extra hard work and with greater responsibility. AI Robots can be used in such situations where intervention can be hazardous. Now doctors have started performing remote surgeries through robots. Robots are often used for curing the mental diseases, they help people to fight depression.

5.17.2 Drones

Drones are aircraft without a human pilot. They are extremely useful as they can navigate unknown surroundings and reach areas hazardous for humans such as offshore operations, mines, war zones or burning buildings.

5.17.3 Smart Cities

Smart cities can be created with a network of sensors that are attached to the physical city infrastructure. These sensors can be used to monitor the city for various factors such as energy efficiency, air pollution, water use, noise pollution, traffic conditions, etc.

5.17.4 Smart Retailing

AI and IoT can be used by retailers to understand the customer behavior and then send real-time offers while the customer is in the store.

5.17.5 Automated vacuum cleaner

It is a robotic vacuum cleaner (iRobot Roomba) that uses IoT and AI to clean a room as efficiently as possible. It is a robotic vacuum cleaner that uses a set of sensors to detect obstacles, dirty spots on the floor

REVIEW QUESTIONS WITH ANSWERS

1. Multiple Choice Questions

1. What is Artificial Intelligence?
   a. Putting your intelligence into Computer
   b. Programming with your own intelligence
   c. Making a machine intelligent
   d. Putting more memory into computer
2. What is a private key?
   a. A key on your key chain
   b. A key given to the public
   c. A key NOT to be given to the public
   d. A key that opens a secret door
3. Which one is not an element of IoT?
   a. Security b. Process
   c. People d. Things
4. The device connected to the Internet of Things have to communicate automatically, not via humans. What is this called?
   a. Bot-to-Bot (B2B) b. Machine-to-Machine (M2M)
   c. InterCloud d. Skynet
5. Who created Bitcoin?
   a. Satoshi Nakamoto b. Samsung
   c. John Mcafee d. China
6. What is a blockchain?
   a. A distributed ledger on a peer-to-peer network
   b. A type of Cryptocurrency
   c. An exchange
   d. A centralized ledger
7. The poor security practices could include(s):
   a. No system hardening
   b. No mechanism for updating software
   c. Default or hardcoded passwords
   d. All of the above
8. The term "bot" comes from robot. An Internet bot may also be known as:
   a. Web robot b. WWW robot
   c. Both (a) and (b) d. None of these
9. Which statement(s) are true about a brute force attack?
   a. Crack a password or username
   b. Find a hidden web page
   c. Find the key used to encrypt a message
   d. All of the above
10. Dictionary attacks is a kind of:
    a. Injection attacks b. Brute force attack
    c. Session Hijacking d. None of the above
11. Bonet is often used to launch ________ attack.
    a. DoS b. DDoS
    c. Brute force d. Passive
12. To secure your data on IoT devices:
    a. Keep changing your passwords
    b. Update your every device
    c. Avoid using devices that are risky
    d. All of the above

2. State True or False for the following:

1. Bitcoin is the first distributed blockchain implementation.
2. You cannot access your data from any computer in the world, as long as you have an Internet connection.
3. Trojan Horses are very similar to virus in that they are computer programs that replicate copies of themselves.
4. In blockchain, each blocks is linked backward to the previous block.
5. Default or hardcoded passwords can be misused by hackers.
6. Password is the method of Authentication, Confidentiality, Integrity and Availability are basic requirements of Internet Security.
7. Firewall is hardware or software designed to keep network hackers out.
8. Firewalls cannot protect against viruses.
9. Password is the method of authentication.
10. Signature algorithms!are used to create digital signatures.
11. Hashing algorithms!are referred to as one-way hashes.
12. DNS spoofing attack is either for their own personal gain or to spread malware.
13. Mirai botnet attack was originated from IoT cameras.

14. Brute force attacks are usually used to obtain personal information such as passwords, passphrases, usernames and Personal Identification Numbers (PINS).
15. Cryptocurrency is a digital currency that uses encryption techniques to verify and secure transactions.
16. Blockchain is a growing list of records, called blocks, which are linked using cryptography.
17. Compared to supervised learning, unsupervised learning operates upon only the input data without outputs or target variables.
18. IP cameras are frequently targeted IoT devices.

3. Match the following:

1. Making a machine intelligent	a. A dictionary attack
2. It is the protection of Internet-connected system Including hardware, software and data	b. URLs sent via spam emails
3. A distributed ledger on a P2P network	c. Artificial Intelligence
4. Symmetric	d. Cybersecurity
5. Asymmetric	e. Different key required for reverse operation.
6. DNS cache poisoning	f. Same key can encrypt & decrypt.
7. Brute Force Attack	g. Making the content useless without the decryption key.
8. A ransomware	h. Trustworthy and accurate
9. Encryptors	i. Type of malware
10. Integrity	j. Blockchain

4. Fill in the blanks:

1. Passwords are used to improve the ________ of a network.
2. Bitcoin transaction are verified by network nodes and recorded in a public distribute ledger called a ___________.
3. ________ algorithms!are used for important tasks such as data encryption, authentication, and digital signatures.
4. A ________ is an automated application used to perform simple and repetitive tasks.
5. The brute force attacks are known as an ________ key search.
6. The ________ is a type of malicious software that blocks access to a computer system or data, usually by encrypting it, until the victim pays a fee to the attacker.
7. ________ listening to a conversation between two parties.
8. ________ learning is the one, where you can consider the learning is guided by a teacher.
9. ________ is designed to launch bonet attack from IoT.
10. ________ is ensuring that no one can read the message except the intended receiver.

Answers

1. 1. c 2. c 3. a 4. b 5. a 6. a 7. d 8. c 9. d 10. b 11 b 12 d

2. 1. T 2. F 3. F 4. F 5. T 6. T 7. T 8. T 9. T 10. T 11 T 12 T 13. T 14. T 15. T 16. T 17. T 18 T

3. 1. c 2. d 3. j 4. f 5. e 6. b 7. a 8. i 9. g 10. h

4. 1. Security 2. Blockchain 3. Cryptographic 4. Bot 5. Exhaustive 6. Ransomware 7. Eavesdropping 8. Supervised 9. mirai 10. Confidentiality

Short Answers Questions

1. Write short notes on the following:
(a) Malware
(b) Phishing

(c) Active Attack
(d) Vulnerability
(e) Cryptography

Ans a. Malware (malicious software) are the software programs designed to damage or do other unwanted actions on a computer system. Some examples of malware include viruses, worms, trojan horses, and spyware. Malware can cause havoc on the computer hard drive by deleting files or directory information.

b. Phishing is an attempt of acquiring sensitive information, such as usernames, passwords, and credit card details, by hacker in an electronic communication.

c. Modification of messages being transmitted, capturing authentication sequences and obtaining extra privileges, creation of false messages etc. are a few active attacks. Active attacks are difficult to prevent because they require protection of all communication facilities and paths at all times. But one can detect and recover from the disruptions caused by them.

d. Vulnerabilities are weaknesses in a system or its design that allow an intruder to execute commands, access unauthorized data, and/or conduct denial-of-service attacks.

e. Cryptography is technique of securing information and communications through use of codes so that only those person for whom the information is intended can understand it and process it. Thus preventing unauthorized access to information.

2. Define Encryption and why it is used?

Ans It is a process of converting the data of file into an unreadable format to protect the data from attack. It is being widely used in an organization to secure their data.

3. What are the key terms of Security?

Ans The key terms for security are Confidentiality, Integrity and Availability. It is also known as CIA. These three things are considered to be the most important components of the security. Confidentiality means protecting the information and the information remain between the client and organization, and not sharing the information with other people.

Integrity means the reliability and trusted data, which refers to real and accurate data.

Availability refers to access information from the specified location.

4. What is Blockchain?

Ans It is an incorruptible digital ledger of economic transactions that can be programmed to record not only financial transactions but virtually everything of value. In simple terms, it is a decentralized distributed database of immutable records that are managed by a group of computers but not owned by any single entity. It is stored as a database or a flat-file.

5. How does blockchain works?

Ans It is consists of immutable records of data called blocks with are linked using cryptography. It is nothing but a process to encrypt and secure data communication from third parties in reading private messages. Once the data has been recorded, it will not be changed. It works like a digital notary with timestamps to avoid tampering of information.

6. What do you mean by Encryption?

Ans It is a process of converting the data of file into an unreadable format to protect the data from attack. It is being widely used in an organization to secure their data.

7. How will you make your smart home more secure?

Ans To make your smart home more secure, do the following:

- Give your router a name: Don't stick with the name the manufacturer gave it - it might identify the make or model. Give it an unusual name.
- Change default usernames and passwords: Cybercriminals probably already know the default passwords that come with many IoT products. That makes it easy for them to access your IoT devices and, potentially, the information on them. So, change default usernames and passwords. Use unique, complex passwords made up of letters, numbers, and symbols.

- Keep your software up-to-date: Mobile security is important, since you may connect to your smart home through mobile devices. Your IoT device makers also may sent you updates - or you might have to visit their websites to check for them. Be sure to download updates and apply them to your device to help stay safe.

8. How will you make a password strong?

Ans A strong password must:

- Be eight characters long (characters which include uppercase A-Z, lower case a-z; numbers 0-9; symbols found on the keyboard and spaces which include ' ~ ! @ # $ % ^ & * ( ) _ - + = { } [ ] \ | : ; " ' < > , . ? /)
- Not contain user, real or company name.
- Not contain a complete word and be different from previous passwords.

9. What is difference between Trojan horse and Worm?

Ans A Trojan horse is a term used to describe malware that appears, to the user, to perform a desirable function but, facilitates unauthorized access to the user's computer system.

A computer worm is a self-replicating computer program. It uses a network to send copies of itself to other nodes and it may do so without any user intervention.

10. What is DNS spoofing?

Ans Domain Name Server (DNS) poisoning or spoofing is a type of cyber-attack that exploits system vulnerabilities in the domain name server to divert traffic away from legitimate servers and directs it towards fake ones.

11. What is Brute Force Attack?

Ans A Brute Force Attack is the simplest method to gain access to a site or server (or anything that is password protected). It tries various combinations of usernames and passwords again and again until it gets in. The longer the password, the more combinations that will need to be tested. However, if the password is weak it could merely take seconds with hardly any effort.

12. What is Ransomware?

Ans Ransomware is a form of malware that encrypts a victim's files. The attacker then demands a ransom from the victim to restore access to the data upon payment.

13. What is Botnet?

Ans Botnets consist of many bots working together, may be used to gain unauthorized access to computer systems and infect computers . For example, The attack used the Mirai IoT Botnet, taking control of over 600,000 IoT devices to flood Dyn with traffic in a massive DDoS attack. The devices seemed to be mostly routers and IP cameras. IP cameras are frequently targeted IoT devices.

14. List few tips to identify phishing.

Ans Few tips to identify the phishing are as follows:

- Do not trust the display name.
- Look at the content of the email, but do not click it.
- Do not give away any personal information.

15. Discuss goal of Brute Force Attack.

Ans Goal of Brute Force Attack are as follows:

- Theft of personal information such as passwords, passphrases and other information used to access online accounts and network resources.
- Collect credentials to sell to third parties.
- Defacement of websites and other information in the public domain that could damage the reputation of the organization.
- Redirecting domains to sites holding malicious content.

16. How IoT and AI are used to track Endangered Species?

Ans There are many animals that are endangered or going extinct in various countries So WildTrack's footprint identification technique (FIT) uses IoT and AI algorithms to identify the species, individual, age and gender of an animal from its unique footprint.

17. What is Passive Attack?

Ans Eavesdropping on or monitoring of transmissions is known as passive attack. The goal of eavesdropping is to obtain that information which is being transmitted. Passive attacks are difficult to detect (if they occur) but they can be prevented.

18. Write Pros and Cons of Symmetric cryptography algorithms.

Ans Pros: Faster than asymmetric cryptography.
Cons: Difficult to distribute and protect the shared secret key securely.

19. Write Pros and Cons of Asymmetric cryptography algorithms.

Ans Pros: Easy to manage, scalable.
Cons: Slower than symmetric cryptography.

20. List some IoT Security Weaknesses.

Ans Some IoT Security Weaknesses are:

- Weak, Guessable, or Hardcoded Passwords.
- Insecure Network Services.
- Use of Insecure or Outdated Components.
- Lack of Secure Update Mechanism.

21. What is the difference between strong and weak artificial Intelligence?

Ans The difference between strong and weak artificial Intelligence are listed below:

Weak AI	**Strong AI**
Narrow application, with very limited scope	Widely applied, with vast scope
Good at specific tasks	Incredible human-level intelligence
Uses supervised and unsupervised Learning to process data	Uses clustering and association to process data
For example Siri, Alexa, etc.	For example Advanced Robotics

22. What is the difference between IoT and AI?

Ans The difference between IoT and AI are listed below:

IoT	**AI**
IoT is a concept based on the very idea of everyday physical objects with the ability to communicate directly over the Internet.	Artificial Intelligence (AI), on the other hand, is an area of computer science to create machines to do intelligent things the way humans do, or possibly even better.
IoT is a vast network of interrelated computing devices connected to the Internet. These devices can sense, accumulate and transfer data over a network without any human interaction.	AI, on the other hand, is all about creating smart, intelligent machines that can behave and react like humans, providing them with the ability of sensing, actuation, data storage and processing.
IoT is about connecting machines and making use of the data generated from those machines.	AI is about simulating intelligent behaviour in machines of all kinds.
IoT will not work without AI.	AI is not dependable on IoT.
Applications include fitness trackers, health monitoring devices, smart wearables, smart parking etc.	Application of AI include machine learning, natural language processing, robotics, speech recognition etc.

23. List some applications of AI.

Ans Some applications of AI are:

- Natural language processing
- Chatbots
- Sales prediction
- Self-driving card
- Facial expression recognition
- Image tagging

EXERCISE

1. Write short note on the following:
(a) Botnet

(b) Machine Learning
(c) Mirai
(d) Ransomware Evolution
(e) Trojan horse
(f) DNS Spoofing
(g) Narrow AI

2. What is Artificial Intelligence?
3. Explain Cyber Attack.
4. What are the principals to identify the cyber attack?
5. What is phishing? How will you identify the phishing?
6. How will you prevent your computer from virus?
7. How are virus different from worms?
8. What is Web crawlers?
9. Explain different security levels of attacks.
10. Discuss advantages and disadvantages of ML.
11. Discuss advantages of AI.
12. What is Symmetric key Cryptography?
13. How will you secure your PC from virus and spyware?
14. How will you keep your devices safe and secure?
15. What is hashing algorithms?
16. Discuss techniques used for Cryptography.
17. Discuss some important applications of AI.
18. What is injection attacks?
19. What is Ransomware?
20. What is a Digital Certificate and Digital Signature?
21. What is Public Key Infrastructure (PKI)?
22. What is end-to-end encryption?
23. What are types of blockchain? Explain the types in short.
24. What is the difference between private and public blockchain?
25. What is cyber attack? What are the principals to identify the cyber attack?
26. Discuss few applications of RPA.

CHAPTER 6

Soft skills-Personality Development

6.1 PERSONALITY DEVELOPMENT

Its a relatively enduring pattern of thoughts, feelings, and behaviour which differentiate person from each other. It is becoming a better version of yourself and personality emerges early and continues to change in meaningful ways throughout the lifespan.

6.2 WHAT IS PERSONALITY?

Personality is the constant pattern of thinking, feeling and acting as define by "MACIONIS". It may be considered as a combination of individual thought, characteristics, behaviours, attitude or it is the product of social interaction in group life as every person living in society has different traits such as skin, color, weight, etc. because all the individuals are not alike. Every person has personality which may be god-bad, impressive – unimpressive. Personality a person develops during the socialization in a culture of a specific group or society.

Personality is derived from Latin word - "persona", meaning mask (used by actors for changing their appearance).

Robert Park and Earnest Burgess, defines Personality as the sum and organization of the traits which determine the role of the individual in the group. According to Davis, personality is a psychic phenomenon which is neither organic nor social but a combination of two.

There are two main approaches to the study of personality:

a. Psychological
   It considers personality as a certain style which is peculiar to the individual and is determined by the characteristic organization of mental trends, complexes, emotions and sentiments. The psychological approach enables a person to understand the phenomena of personality disorganization and the role of wishes, of mental conflict.
b. Sociological
   It considers personality in terms of the status of the person in the group, like how he/she consider his/her conception about his role in the group of which he/she is a member. Basically, what others think of us also plays a very important role in the formation of our personality.

So, one can say that personality is a sum of the ideas, attitudes values of a person which determine its role in society and thus form an integral part of his/her character.

One can say that, Personality is developed by the individual as a result of his participation in group life because being a member of the group he can learns certain behaviour systems and symbolic skills which determine his/her ideas, attitudes and social values.

So, the characteristics of personality are:

a. It is not related only to body structure, but it includes both the structure and dynamics.
b. It is an indivisible unit.
c. It is unique for every individual.
d. It is a persistent quality of the individual.
e. It expresses consistency and regularity.
f. It is attained.
g. It is influenced by social interaction.
h. It is defined in terms of behaviour.

6.2.1 Factors of Personality

Personality is the combination of four factors:

a. **Physical Environment**
   Environment in which we live also effect on culture and the geographical environment sometimes determines cultural variability. For example, Eskimos have a different culture

from Indians is due because Eskimos have different geography or living conditions from the latter. Man, comes to form ideas and attitudes according to the physical environment in which he lives.

Also, physical environment determines the cultural development and the culture in turn determines personality, so the relationship between personality and environment becomes clear.

"Aristotle", two thousand years ago, explains that the people living in Northern Europe were owing to a cold climate and are living with full of spirit but they are lacking in intelligence and skill, but on the other hand, people living in the natives of Asia are intelligent and inventive but are living with lack in spirit.

The people living in mountains as well in deserts are bold, hard and powerful. Huntington's told the effects of physical environment on man's attitudes and mental make-up, he told that the physical conditions are more permissive and thus they limit the factors than causative factors. They set the limits within which personality can develop. So, climate and topography determine the physical, mental traits and behaviour of a people.

b. **Heredity**

Similarities in man's personality is due to his common heredity. Every human group inherits the same general set of biological needs and capacities which explain some of our similarities in personality. Man, originates from the union of male and female germ cells into a single cell which is formed at the moment of conception.

He tends to resemble his parents in physical appearance and intelligence. A man with a good physical structure and health generally possess an attractive personality and with poor health, develops inferiority complex.

The growth of his personality is checked, rejected and hated by the society may turn him out to be a thief, dacoit, or drunkard. But he may also become a leader, or a genius. So, the nervous system and glandular system may affect the personality of an individual.

The nervous system affects the intelligence and talent of the individual. The hormones affect the growth of personality.

c. **Culture**

Personality is the subjective aspect of culture and regarded as two sides of the same coin.

Spiro said that, The development of personality and the acquisition of culture are not different processes, but are same learning process." Personality is an individual aspect of culture, whereas culture is a collective aspect of personality."

d. **Particular Experiences**

Personality can also be determined by the particular and unique experiences. There are two types of experiences one which is from continuous association with one's group, and the other arise suddenly. The people who meet daily has a major influence on personality. The personality of parents affect more a child's personality.

If the parents are kind, tolerant of boyish pranks, interested in athletics and anxious to encourage their child's separate interests the child will have a different experience and there shall be different influence on his personality than the one when the parents are unkind, quick tempered and arbitrary. In the home is fashioned the style of personality that will by and large characterize the individual throughout his life.

Characteristics of Personality

- **Unique:** Each individual personality is unique and specific.
- **Organization:** Personality is not just one or more aspects of behaviour, but it is one's total integrated behaviour.
- **Consistency or stability:** A person is recognizable from situation to situation by the consistent characteristics that are reflected in his behaviour.
- **Dynamic:** Personality of an individual remains stable to a large extent, it is not static but it is dynamic and continuously in the process of change and modification.
- **Self-consciousness:** Personality exhibits self-consciousness and it is the proud possession of human being.

- **Social:** Personality has existence only in relation to the external world. An individual's relation with his environment, his feelings, attitudes, are basic to the idea of personality.

6.3 DETERMINANTS OF PERSONALITY

There are some very important traits or determinants which affects personality. Firstly, knowing self is must, as it helps in monitoring our self continually and works as a very effective tool to improve our self consistently.

6.3.1 Self-Awareness

Anyone who is dedicated to self-improvement, personal development or the higher goal of spiritual growth needs to understand oneself because when one understands where one lacks, then he or she can focus their efforts on what to improve.

Self-awareness is the capacity that a person has to introspect, it includes gaining an understanding of and insight into one's strengths, qualities, weakness, defects, ideas, thoughts, beliefs, ideals, responses, reactions, attitude, emotions and motivations.

Psychologists break self-awareness down into two types:

a. **Public Self-Awareness:** When people are aware of how they appear to others, this is **Public Self-Awareness**. It emerges when people are at the centre of attention, such as when giving a presentation or talking to a group of friends. When we are aware that we are being watched and evaluated, we often try to behave in ways that are socially acceptable and desirable.
b. **Private Self-Awareness:** When people become aware of some aspects of themselves, in a private way this is Private Self-Awareness. For example, seeing your face in the mirror is a type of private self-awareness.

How to increase self-awareness

a. **By observing oneself:**
   - To understand our personality, we need to understand the nature of our mind.
   - The mind is made up of two parts. Conscious and sub-conscious mind.
   - The sub-conscious mind is vast and the impressions which are buried deep inside are not easy to uncover and analyse.
   - Often during the day, one's mind erupts and reacts to some events and situations negatively. So, one feels a certain amount of restlessness and emotions such as insecurity, fear or anger.
   - If one is alert and objective in one's outlook, one can follow the pathway through the window that the mind opens up.
   - As a result, through this process one begins to gain greater self-awareness as to how one's mind works and how it responds to various stimuli.
b. **Someone providing us with feedback or telling our mistake**
   It is never easy to take negative feedback from others about our actions or our life. When other people give us some feedback however stern it may be, it provides us with a clue as to how we are perceived by others. If someone has experienced pain due to our actions, it is mostly due to some personality defect in us that is causing our action to impact others adversely.
c. **Observing someone else's mistake and then introspecting**
   When one observes a situation, which involves other people, one gains a greater understanding of oneself. As one may not be emotionally involved in the situation, one is more objective and hence the ability to learn is more.
d. **Our dreams can also tell us about ourselves**
   Sometimes stronger impressions in our sub-conscious mind surface in our dreams to the extent that we are able to remember the dream and even learn about our mind.

6.3.2 Self-Analysis

In social psychology, self-assessment or Self-Analysis is the process of looking at oneself to assess aspects which are important to one's identity. Sedikides suggests "self-assessment motive will prompt people to get information to confirm their uncertain self-concept rather than their certain self-concept. People use self-assessment to enhance their certainty of their own self-knowledge.

Self-awareness helps to identify gaps in the management skills, thus it promotes skill development, assists with intuitive decision making, and aids stress management.

6.3.3 Self-Disclosure

It is a process of communication by which one person reveals information about himself or herself to another. Information which is revealed can be descriptive or evaluative, and include thoughts, feelings, aspirations, goals, failures, successes, fears, and dreams, as well as one's likes, dislikes, and favourites. Self-disclosure is an important building block for intimacy and is assessed by an analysis of cost and rewards which can be further explained by social exchange theory. Most self-disclosure occurs early in relational development, but more intimate self-disclosure occurs later.

6.3.4 Self-Esteem

Self-esteem reflects a person's overall subjective emotional evaluation of his or her own worth. It is a kind of judgment of oneself and an attitude toward the self. It encompasses of beliefs about oneself, and emotional states.

Smith and Mackie (2007) defined Self-Esteem as "The self-concept is what we think about the self; self-esteem, is the positive or negative evaluations of the self, as in how we feel about it.

6.3.5 Motivation

It is a theoretical construct which is used to explain the behaviour. It gives the reasons for people's actions, desires, and needs. Motivation can also be defined as one's direction to behaviour, or what causes a person to want to repeat a behaviour. A motive is what prompts the person to act in a certain way, or at least develop an inclination for specific behaviour.

6.3.6 Self-Discipline

It is the suppression of base desires, which is understood as a form of self-control restraint and control. Discipline is when one uses reason to determine the best course of action regardless of one's desires, which may be the opposite of excited.

6.3.7 Appearance

Appearance is how you look or present yourself to others. Personal appearance is an important aspect to reflect personality.

6.3.8 Posture

Body language or Posture, is a non-verbal form of communication which is showed through facial expressions, gestures, posture, and body movements. For example, if you want to achieve an effective personality, you will also need to improve your body language. There are many ways you can improve your body language, but like most things, it needs practice and consistency so that it will become part of you, and not just something you can do for a certain period of time. If you want to develop your personality in a positive way, you need to be aware of your own body language and make sure it adheres to what is generally perceived as positive body language.

6.3.9 Health and Hygiene

Hygiene is a set of practices which are performed for the preservation of health. According to the World Health Organization (WHO), "Hygiene is the conditions and practices which help to maintain health and prevent the spread of diseases."

It is often express as 'cleanliness', hygiene in its fullest and original meaning includes all the circumstances and practices, lifestyle issues, premises and commodities which produce a safe and healthy environment. In modern medical sciences, there are set of standards of hygiene which are recommended for different situations, and is not vary among different cultures, genders and age groups.

6.4 BUILDING A POSITIVE PERSONALITY

Every person has a unique personality which characterizes an individual. Our personalities may be perceived by others as good or bad. People see you and think of you as having a bad personality if you tend not to be socialize, you always seem grumpy and overly serious, you think more of pessimistic thoughts, and you do not look presentable with your manner of dressing. On the other hand, you are known to have a good personality if you have a cheerful disposition, you appear neat and well-groomed, and you have a desirable attitude.

You are known for who you are and what you are with the way you present yourself to people. If you keep getting feedback or remarks regarding your personality, you might as well take a self-reflection and assess yourself. Sometimes, other people can see and notice the things in you that may not seem proper and pleasing to them.

A paradigm shift in your personality may lead to the possibilities of improving your life and growing in maturity.

➔ **To develop a positive personality:**

a. **Have a Positive Outlook in Life**
   Take a self-reflection of how you envision your life and the way you deal with life and people everyday.

b. **Entertain Positive Thoughts**
   Having a generally positive outlook in life can also help develop positive thoughts. Keeping an optimistic mind also keeps one's viewpoints positive.

c. **Maintain a Positive Attitude**
   Keeping a positive attitude is another way to develop a positive personality. Build your level of courtesy toward others. Show consideration and respect for them by giving a warm smile, saying 'thank you' to show appreciation, and listening when someone is talking.

d. **Keep smiling face**
   A smile can make a big difference in a chaotic and complicated situation. A smile can be a cure for a broken relationship. A sincere smile shows that you hold no grudges against others.

6.5 ATTITUDES - MEANING AND MAINTENANCE

Attitude is a psychological construct, or its a mental and emotional entity which inheres in, or characterizes a person. It is an acquired state through experiences. It is an individual's predisposed state of mind regarding a value and it is precipitated through a responsive expression toward a person, place, thing, or event which influences individual's thought and action. An attitude is a persistent tendency which is to feel and then behave in a particular way toward some object.

It has three basic characteristics:

- It is directed toward an object for which a person has feelings, and beliefs,
- It persists unless changed in some way
- In may be positive to negative.

Attitudes have three components:

- emotional (feelings)
- Informational
- Behavioral

Attitudes, is persistent so it helps employees to adapt themselves to their work environment by providing a way of interpreting things in the environment.

Attitude help people to:

- adjust to their environment
- defend their self-image
- express their values
- supply standards and frames of reference which allow them to organize and explain the world around them.

6.6 GESTURES

It is a form of non-verbal communication in which body actions communicates a particular message, either with or without speech. Gestures includes the movement of the hands, face, or other parts of the body.

It differs from physical non-verbal communication and allow individuals to communicate feelings and thoughts with body language in addition to words when they speak.

6.6.1 Importance of Personality Development

Personality refers to person's appearance, characteristics, attitude, mindset and behaviour with others.

- grooms an individual and helps him to make a mark of his/her own.
- Reduce stress and conflicts.
- encourages individuals to look at the brighter sides of life.
- develop a positive attitude in life.
- behave well with people around.
- gain recognition and acceptance from the society as well as people around.
- makes an individual disciplined, punctual and an asset for his/her organization.
- inculcate positive qualities like punctuality, flexible attitude, willingness to learn, friendly nature, eagerness to help others and so on.
- develop an impressive personality and makes you stand apart from the rest.
- improve one's communication skills.

6.7 SELF-ESTEEM

Self-esteem is crucial and is a cornerstone of a positive attitude towards living. It is very important because it affects how you think, act and even how you relate to other people. It allows you to live life to your potential.

In sociology and psychology, self-esteem reflects a person's subjective emotional evaluation of his or her own worth. It is a judgment of oneself and an attitude toward the self. It encompasses of beliefs and emotional states about oneself. Smith and Mackie (2007) defined Self-Esteem as "The self-concept is what we think about the self; self-esteem, is the positive or negative evaluations of the self, as in how we feel about it."

So, Self-Esteem is:

- a degree to which you value yourself.
- thoughts and feelings about yourself and your place in the world.

Elements of Self-Esteem are: Self-confidence, self-respect, self-acceptance and self-love. There are two basic components of self-esteem:

a. Feelings of personal competence (to accomplish and succeed in tasks).
b. Feelings of personal worth (love and friendship).

A balance of these two components is needed for healthy self-esteem.

6.8 SELF-ESTEEM IS A MUST

Self-Esteem is important because it impact on life and choices of an individual. Self-value of an individual is the source of mental health. Self-Esteem is the idea which you have about yourself like how valuable and important you think you are. It is the result of one's own evaluation based on many factors. It is how we value and perceive our value to the world. It involves self-beliefs, emotions such as accomplishment, depression, pride and humiliation as gathered or accumulated in our own mind.

Self-Esteem is important because:

a. You believe, that you are worthy of happiness and of respect.
b. It is the first step in believing in you and it builds self-confidence.
c. It has a profound effect on your thinking, emotions, happiness, desires, values, and goals.
d. You can still feel respect and be proud even if you make a mistake.
e. You never compare yourself to others.
f. Your Self-confidence is strong.
g. You have a sense of control and direction.
h. You approach towards your problems with a different perspective.
i. It allows you to make correct choices and take action.
j. It allows you to act independently.
k. It allows you to take new challenges easily and handle criticism.
l. You consider yourself a valuable person and you live for a reason.
m. It gives you the clarity to recognize your qualities.
n. It imparts strong faith in yourself.

Factors that can influence self-esteem:

- Your own thoughts and perceptions
- How other people react to you
- Experiences at home, school, work and in the community
- Illness, disability or injury

- Culture or religion
- Role and status in society
- Media messages

6.9 WHERE DOES SELF-ESTEEM COME FROM?

"You cannot rely on others for your self-esteem. You must look within to find out who you really are."

-Anika

Self- esteem develops and comes from yourself, but it is influenced by the messages, which you get about yourself from:

- Talk, support and spending time with your family.
- Your friends support and respect.
- Teachers who encourages you and are proud of your work.
- People around you when you take challenges, and develop some skills to a finer point.
- Your school mates when you play in a team, or work in a school newspaper.
- Society, like, how women are portrayed on TV and in the media, can affect how you see yourself.

"Self-esteem is not something you get over night. It is something you have to build up. It is important to know who you are so you can stick up for yourself when someone puts you down and so that it doesn't affect you as much."

-Natasha.

6.10 HEALTHY SELF-ESTEEM AND POOR SELF-ESTEEM

Self-esteem as studied till now tells you, how you see and react to different things which happen to you and around you in your life. For people having right and good self-esteem, in their life the normal up and down does not make many changes in their feelings about themselves; But, a person with low self-esteem, in their life the normal up and down does make changes and generate too much difference in their self-opinion. Self-esteem develops completely during childhood.

People with healthy self-esteem is more practical and accurate in judging the right capabilities about themselves. They have the ability to accept and value themselves in any condition or perspective. The healthy self-esteem is the outcome of a childhood experience where the child is being praised, listened, spoken respectfully, got attention, experienced success in sports or school and have trustworthy friends. All of these make a strong impact and the person has healthy self-esteem.

People with poor self-esteem, takes the present perspective to judge about themselves; like, how they are feeling about themselves. They need the opinion of others to judge their own self-esteem. They have lot of negative feelings which cripples their self-image. Low Self-Esteem adults have a childhood in which they are treated harshly or criticized, being yelled or beaten, ignored or teased, burdened with the expectations and they got an impression that a normal loss at a game is failure of them as a person.

To convert low self Esteem to Healthy one, you need to:

a. Be kind to yourself and respect yourself.
b. Do not make yourself suffer if you make mistakes.
c. Stay away from the negative self-talk.
d. Stop criticizing yourself.
e. Take help from a trusted family member or friend if you find it difficult.
f. Never compare yourself with others.
g. Tell yourself your own achievements.
h. Remind your own good qualities about you every day.
i. Read inspirational quotes and books which can give you positive side of life.
j. Enjoy, relax and have fun in your daily life.

Characteristics of people having:

Healthy Self-Esteem	Poor Self-Esteem
They feel good about themselves	They have negative feelings about themselves.
They have a positive attitude about life.	They have a negative attitude about life.

(Contd...)

Healthy Self-Esteem	Poor Self-Esteem
They feel capable of meeting life's challenge.	They are reluctant to take risks for fear of failing.
They do not need the approval and praise of others to feel good about themselves.	They need the approval and praise of others to feel good about themselves.
They do not feel any difficulty in connecting with their inner selves.	They have difficulty connecting with their inner selves.

6.11 SELF-EFFICACY/PERSONAL EFFICACY

It is the extent of one's belief in its own ability to complete the task and reach towards its goals. As, coined by **Albert Bandura**; Self-Efficacy is a person's belief in his or her ability to complete a future task or solve a future problem.

Self-Efficacy also influence individual goals, actions, successes or failures in life. If your self-efficacy in an area is much lower than your ability, you will never challenge yourself or improve. If your self-efficacy in an area is much higher than your ability, you will set goals which are too high, fail, and possibly quit.

6.11.1 Importance of Self-Efficacy

Self-efficacy impact how people feel, think, behave, and motivate themselves. People having self-efficacy can:

- See challenging problems as tasks to be solved rather than to avoid.
- Develop greater intrinsic interest.
- Focus in their activities.
- Set challenging goals.
- Demonstrate a stronger sense of commitment to them.
- Learn and achieve more than those with low self-efficacy.

6.12 SELF-MOTIVATION

It is an ability to do what needs to be done, without the influence from other people or situations. People with self-motivation can find a reason and strength to complete a task without giving up.

It is the force which drives you to do things. Self-motivation is a key life skill of personal development and an emotional intelligence.

Motivation is kind of force which pushes people to achieve their goals, feel more fulfilled and improve overall quality of life. People who are self-motivated, tend to be more organised, good time management skills, more self-esteem and confidence.

Fundamental to self-motivation is understanding what motivates you to do things. There are two main types of motivation:

- **Intrinsic:** To perform an action or task based on the expected or perceived satisfaction of performing the action or task. It includes having fun, being interested and personal challenge.
- **Extrinsic:** To perform an action or task in order to attain some sort of reward, including money, power and good marks or grades.

Skills

There are a number of skills involved in self-motivation.

These include:

- Setting high but realistic goals.
- Taking the right level of risk.
- Seeking constant feedback to work out how to improve.
- Being committed to personal or organisational goals and going the "extra mile" to achieve them.
- Actively seeking out opportunities and seizing them when they occur.

6.13 TIME MANAGEMENT

It is a kind of planning and exercising conscious control over the amount of time spent on the specific activities, to increase effectiveness, efficiency or productivity.

Time management include:

- Creating an environment conducive to effectiveness.
- Setting of priorities.
- Carrying out activity around prioritization.

It may be defined as a way of organizing and planning, how long you spend on specific activities.

6.13.1 Benefits of Time Management

- Greater productivity and efficiency
- A better professional reputation
- Less stress
- Greater opportunities to achieve important life and career goals.

Consequences in failure of Time Management:

- Missed deadlines.
- Inefficient work flow.
- Poor work quality.
- Higher stress levels.

Managing time is nothing but a fruitful utilization of available time for achieving the desired goals. In order to manage the time successfully keep aware about your goals and prioritize your activities according to that. It means you can execute a particular job at a particular time as per the urgency or nature of the job to save more time for other jobs which can be scheduled as per priority and urgency.

Time management provide you the opportunity to create a schedule which works for you, not for others. This personal attention gives you the flexibility to include the things that are most important to you.

Important of time management

Time management is important as it teaches you to manage your time effectively and make the most of it. It is important because:

- You are more efficient, as better time management can help you to do more of what you have to do faster. This does not mean cutting corners or a decrease in quality. You just do what you have to do quicker so you can do what you want to do sooner.
- You feel calmer and more in control, because learning time management skills matters will reduce the amount of unhealthy stress you feel.
- You are more fulfilled, because people often think that getting organized means time management software, lists, planners and diaries, but it goes beyond that.
- Time management starts with the choices and decisions you make based on the values you hold.
- You have more energy, as you finish the tasks on time and it often brings a level of satisfaction and energy that makes you feel good.
- You develop more qualities.
- You achieve what you want to and need to faster.

Time tips

Time is precious, as there are never more than 24 hours in a day. Some respond to this fact of life with focus and purpose whereas others freak out.

Tips for effectively managing your time:

a. **Know your goals:** Make sure you are engaging in activities which supports your business goals which are either short- and long-term. Your daily plan should revolve around working on tasks and activities that directly relate to generating income and growing your business.

b. **Prioritize Wisely:** Look at what goes into making up your day, where do your activities fit into these categories and then prioritize them according to:
   - Tasks that must !be done and do them right away.
   - Tasks that appear important, but can be delayed for one or two days.
   - Tasks that make the most "noise," but when accomplished, have little or no lasting value.
   - Low-priority work which offer the illusion of "being busy." Do them later.

c. **Just say no:** If you have to decline a request in order to attend to what's truly important and urgent, do not hesitate to do so.

d. **Plan ahead:** Never jump into the workday when you have no clear idea about what needs to get done. So, always spend time for thinking and planning your activities. You can plan:
   - End of the day, it takes maximum of 15 minutes to clear your desk and put together a list of the next day's tasks. It is a great decompression technique, and you will feel better sitting down at a clean desk in the morning.
   - Early morning by arriving a few minutes early and assemble your prioritized to-do list.

e. **Eliminate distractions.**

f. **Take care of yourself:** Be sure to get plenty of sleep and exercise, as alert mind is a high-functioning mind.

6.14 WHAT IS STRESS?

Stress is an emotional/bodily reaction to physical, psychological or emotional demands. Stress is your body's way of responding to demand or threat. Consider an example, when you sense danger - whether real or imagined your body's defences kick into high gear in a rapid, automatic process known as the "fight-or-flight" reaction, or the stress response.

The stress response is the body's way of protecting you.

A positive attitude, balance approach and relaxation exercises are some ways by which one can combat stress. When you work properly, you stay focused, energetic, and alert. In emergency situations, stress can save your life by giving you an extra strength to defend yourself. Stress can also help you to meet challenges, sharpens your concentration or drives you to study for an exam. But beyond a certain point, stress stops being helpful and starts causing major damage to your health, mood, productivity, relationships, and quality of life.

6.14.1 Causes of Stress

- Expectations of others or which we place on yourself.
- Physical environment, which include noise, movement etc.
- Internal environment such as academic pressure, frustration, social life, etc.

Ways to manage stress:

- Add balance to life.
- Don't overdo studies or play.
- Know your strength and weakness.
- Accept yourself the way you are.
- Take "time outs", especially during study.
- Expand your support network.
- Exercise regularly.

Everyone has different stress triggers. Work stress tops the list, according to surveys. Majority of workers admit to experiencing office stress, and some says work is the biggest source of stress in their lives.

So, work stress may be due to:

- Being unhappy in your job
- Having a heavy workload or too much responsibility
- Working long hours
- Unclear expectations of your work, or no say in the decision-making process
- Working under dangerous conditions
- Risk of termination
- Facing discrimination or harassment at work.

Sometimes the stress comes from inside, rather than outside. You can stress yourself out just by worrying about things. All of these factors can lead to Life stresses and is due to:

- The death of a loved one
- Divorce
- Loss of a job
- Increase in financial obligations
- Getting married
- Moving to a new home
- Chronic illness or injury
- Depression, anxiety, anger, grief, guilt, low self-esteem
- Traumatic event, such as a natural disaster, theft, rape, or violence against you or a loved one

Effects of Stress on Your Health

When you are in a stressful situation, your body launches a physical response. Your nervous system comes into action, releasing hormones which prepare you to either fight or take off. It's called the "fight or flight" response. Similarly, when you are in a stressful situation, you may notice that your heartbeat speeds up, your breathing gets faster, your muscles tense, and you start sweating. This kind of stress is short-term and temporary or acute stress, and your body usually recovers quickly from it.

But if your stress system stays activated over a long period of time also called as *chronic stress*, it can lead to serious health problems. The constant rush of stress hormones can put a lot of wear and tear on your body, causing it to age more quickly and making it more prone to illness.

Physical signs if you are suffering from acute stress:

- Headache
- Fatigue
- Difficulty in sleeping
- Upset stomach
- Irritability

Physical signs if you are suffering from chronic stress:

- Depression
- High blood pressure

- Abnormal heartbeat
- Hardening of the arteries
- Heart disease
- Heart attack
- Weight gain or loss

Sign and symptoms of Stress:

- Gritting, grinding teeth
- Stuttering
- Tremors, trembling of lips and hands
- Neck ache
- Back pain
- Muscle spasms
- Light headedness
- Frequent blushing
- Cold or sweaty hands, feet
- Dry mouth, problems swallowing
- Frequent colds, infections, herpes sores
- Unexplained or frequent "allergy" attacks
- Heartburn, stomach pain, nausea
- Excess belching, flatulence
- Difficulty breathing, frequent sighing
- Sudden attacks of life threatening panic
- Chest pain, palpitations, rapid pulse
- Increased anger, frustration, hostility
- Depression, frequent or wild mood swings

Overcome stress:

a. **One thing at a time:** Simplest and best way to start reducing your stress, which you can start from today. Focus on doing one thing at a time. Clear your desk of distractions or any distraction such as phones and e-mail notifications. Pick something to work on.
b. **Simplify your schedule:** Hectic schedule is a major cause of high stress, simplify your schedule by reducing the number of commitments in your life to just the essential ones. Schedule only a few important things each day, and put space between them.
c. **Get moving:** Do something each day to be active such as walk, hike, play a sport, go for a run.
d. **Develop one healthy habit:** Eat fruits and veggies for snacks, floss every day, Quit smoking, Cook something healthy for dinner or Drink water instead of soda.
e. Do work calming.
f. Simplify your finances. Finances can be a drain on your energy and a major source of stress in your life.
g. Have some fun
h. Get creative.
i. Be early.

6.15 ATTITUDES

It is defined as response to people, place, things or events in life. Basically, a person's viewpoint, mind set and belief makes an attitude.

Attitude is composed of three components:

a. **Cognitive component:** it is based on the information or prior knowledge which represents our thoughts, beliefs and ideas about something.
b. **Affective/emotional component:** It is based on the feelings or assumptions brought to the surface about something such as fear or hate.
c. **Behavioural components/ conative component:** it reflects how the attitude effects the way we act or behave and centres on individual acting a certain way towards something.

Consider an example, a person who is scared of an injection, then:

- Cognitive component is the fact that an injection would hurt.
- Affective/emotional component would be the feeling that he/she is scared of an injection.
- Behavioural components/conative component, would be that the person would completely avoid getting an injection.

So, attitude is mainly an evaluative statement that is either positive or negative depending upon the degree of like or dislike for the subject matter. An attitude reflects how one thinks, feels and behaves in a given situation.

6.15.1 Types of Attitudes

There are three types of attitude:

a. **Positive attitude:** Individual will pay attention to the good in people. Situation, event, etc. They will not consider a mistake or failure as a hurdle but as an opportunity. They learn from mistakes and move forward in life.
b. **Negative attitude:** Individual will ignore the good and pay attention to the bad in people, situation, events, etc. They also complain about changes, rather than adapting to the changing environment. They blame their failure on others.

c. **Neutral attitude:** individual do not give enough importance to situations or events. They ignore the problem, leaving it for someone else to solve. They do not feel the need to change.

Attitudes are formed over the years by various means like past experience, acquired from other people based on some truth or what we might consider to be the truth. Attitude can change with different situations and experience in life.

Attitudes and the Workplace

The three components of attitude can impact the workplace. The challenge in the workplace is that now these components are tired to work functions, police, procedure and organisational structure as well as the people and individuals present in the organization. Hence the impact of attitude on other is considerable.

Consider an example: employees having negative thoughts or beliefs about their manager and those thoughts or beliefs could manifest themselves in not trusting a manager resulting in atmosphere where they never want to develop a close relationship with manager (conative).

Etiquettes & Manners

Etiquettes is a code of behaviour which delineates expectations for social behaviour according to contemporary conventional norms within a society, social class, or group. Everyone like a well-behaved person. During any situation, certain words carry a tremendous amount of power forcing others to reciprocate in positive and kind manner. Words like "please", "thank you", "you are welcome" and "excuse me" while talking show your etiquettes and good manners.

Good manners involve acting appropriately in a social acceptable and respectful way by sowing respect, care and consideration for others. Manners decide the fate of your relationship with people you know and those you shall meet. Good manners include greetings, politeness, phone – dinning etiquette.

Always convey respect to those you interact with and also commands respect from those you interact with.

Good etiquettes are:

- Hold doors open for other people
- Speak polity
- Listen to another person
- Give up your seat on public transportation
- Appreciate people
- Be a good sport
- Greet people
- Groom yourself appropriately
- Extend thanks
- Be on time
- Help others.
- Don't speak loud on your cell phone.
- Turn off the phone at a dinner party.
- Keep personal conversations and arguments off social networking sites.
- Moderate your use of cameras and video at events.
- Do not lend someone a book or item unless they specifically ask for it.

Office Etiquette or office manners is about conducting yourself respectfully and courteously in the office or workplace. There are many manners which can be considered which are:

- First impressions are important. You are the ambassador of the business. Always act with honesty and dignity.
- Never eat chewing gum in presence of co-workers or while attending customers.
- Wear appropriate office attire.
- Don't display tattoo and body piercing.
- Do not cough or sneeze in anyone direction, always use tissue and say "Excuse me".
- Be respectful and courteous all times with everybody.
- Knock before entering.
- Put your cell phone on vibrate mode to prevent disturbing others.
- Be helpful and co-operative with others.
- Speak clear, slow without shouting.
- Take responsibility for your mistake, apologise and go about correcting your mistakes.
- Make new employees feel comfortable around you.
- Be always thoughtful when interacting with peers.
- Keep your work area tidy.
- If there is any conflict, do not get personal in your remarks.
- Never arrive late for a meeting.
- Do not interrupt another speaker.
- Do not dominate the meeting.
- Do not shuffle your papers.
- Never be petty or small minded in your behaviour.

6.16 COMMUNICATION, THE VITAL LIFE SKILL

"Communication", is derived from the Latin word communis which signifies "to share", that is, sharing of ideas, feelings and emotions. The art of communication is practically as old as man himself. The significance of communication can be gauged from the way that we are communicating in some structure or other each moment of our lives. While we are strolling, talking, playing, sitting, or resting, a message is being defined and transmitted. Man is a social creature and is always communicating with different people. Therefore it is critical for him to comprehend the specialty of communication and apply or alter it in a suitable way.

Man has the capacity to convey, which is a great deal more than an arrangement of certain physical properties, vocal harmonies, articulators, etc. He has the one of a kind capacity to understand ideas as far as images and symbols. It is this capacity that engages him to communicate and be alive with expressions of his feelings and emotions. Man is alive to the extent of his capacity to communicate viably and dead to the extent of the failure to do as such. From the time immemorial, the need to share or to communicate had been felt. Distinctive vehicles/bearers/channels were recognized and enhanced with the end goal of transmission of ideas, feelings and emotions.

An investigation of these channels empowers us to gain an understanding into the procedure of communication and to communicate better. How does one talk so that someone else listens and gets it? How does one tune in? How does one know whether he has been heard and understood? These are all points about communication that have at no other time been investigated or clarified.

Individuals have realized that communication is a vital part of life however until nobody has ever possessed the capacity to advise anybody how to communicate. The subject of communication had received no emphasis or study. Any consideration given to it was mechanical and the region of engineers. Yet all human tries depend completely on a full learning of the genuine basics of communication. To ace communication, one must understand it. Communication, basically, is the movement of a particle starting with one part of space to another. A particle is the thing being communicated. It can be an item, a composed message, a talked word or a thought. In its crudest definition, this is communication.

This basic perspective of communication prompts the full definition:

Communication is the consideration and action of impelling an impulse or particle from source-point across a distance to receipt point, with the intention of bringing into being at the receipt-point, a duplication and understanding of that which emanated from the source-point.

Duplication is the demonstration of repeating something precisely. Exuded signifies "approached." The equation of communication is reason, separation, and impact, with expectation, consideration and duplication with understanding.

The definition and equation of communication open the way to understand this subject. By analyzing communication into its segment parts, we can see the capacity of each and in this manner all the more clearly understand entirety.

6.16.1 Meaning and Definitions

Communication is the nervous system of a company. It keeps the individuals from the company educated about the interior and outer happenings important to an undertaking and of enthusiasm to the company. It facilitates the endeavors of the individuals towards accomplishing hierarchical destinations. It is the procedure of affecting the activity of an individual or a gathering. It is a procedure of important company among people to start, execute, finish, and on the other hand keep certain activities. Communication is, in this way, the lifeblood of a company. Without communication, a company is dead and its exceptionally presence is in threat.

Definitions:

There are a number of definitions of the term communication. A few of them are being reproduced below:

"Communication is the sum of all things, one person does when he wants to create understanding in the minds of another, it involves a systematic and continuous process of telling, listening and understanding."
Allen Louis

6.17 THE COMMUNICATION PROCESS

Communication is a method of exchanging verbal and non-verbal messages.

6.17.1 Sender/Encoder

The sender is an individual, gathering, or association who starts the communication. This source is at first in charge of the achievement of the message. The sender's encounters, demeanors, information, expertise, observations, and society impact the message. "The composed words, talked words, and non-verbal dialect chose are foremost in guaranteeing the collector translates the message as proposed by the sender" (Burnett and Dollar, 1989). All communication starts with the sender.

The initial step the sender is confronted with includes the encoding procedure. Keeping in mind the end goal to pass on significance, the sender must start encoding, which means making an interpretation of data into a message as images that speak to thoughts or ideas. This procedure deciphers the thoughts or ideas into the coded message that will be imparted. The images can tackle various structures, for example, dialects, words, or motions. These images are utilized to encode thoughts into messages that others can get it.

At the point when encoding a message, the sender needs to start by choosing what he/she needs to transmit. This choice by the sender depends on what he/she accepts about the recipients learning and suppositions, alongside what extra data he/she needs the beneficiary to have. It is essential for the sender to utilize images that are natural to the expected beneficiary. A decent route for the sender to enhance encoding their message is to rationally envision the communication from the collector's perspective.

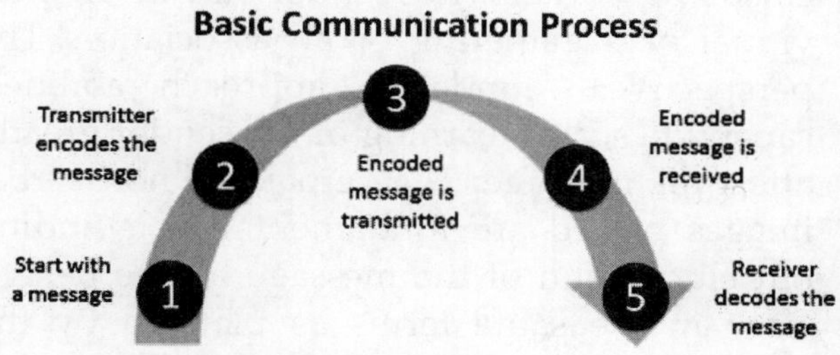

Figure 6.1 Communication Process

- It is a continuous process.
- Pre-requisite of communication is a message.
- This message must be communicated through some medium to the recipient.
- It is essential that the receiver must understand this message in same terms as intended by the sender.
- The receiver must react within a time frame.

Thus, communication is a two-way method and is inadequate without a feedback from the recipient to the sender on how well he acknowledges the message.

6.17.2 Elements of the Communication

The principle parts of communication procedure are as per the following:

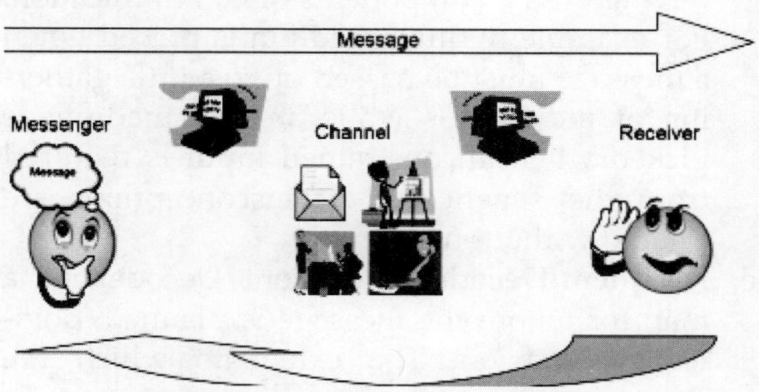

Figure 6.2 Elements of Communication

a. **Connection**: Communication is influenced by the setting in which it happens. This connection may be physical, social, ordered or social. Each discussion continues with a setting. The sender picks the message to impart inside of a connection.

b. **Sender/Encoder**: Sender/Encoder is a man who sends the message. A sender makes utilization of images (words or realistic or visual guides) to pass on the message and deliver the required reaction. For example - a preparation supervisor directing preparing for another cluster of workers. The sender may be an individual or a gathering or an association. The perspectives, foundation, approach, abilities, capabilities, and learning of the sender greatly affect the message. The verbal and non-verbal images picked are fundamental in a finding out elucidation of the message by the beneficiary in the same terms as planned by the sender.

c. **Message**: Message is a fundamental thought that the sender needs to convey. It is an indication that evokes the reaction of beneficiary. Communication procedure starts with choosing about the message to be passed on. It must be guaranteed that the essential target of the message is clear.

d. **Medium**: Medium is methods used to trade/transmit the message. The sender must pick a suitable medium for imparting the message else the message won't not be passed on to the craved beneficiaries. The decision of suitable medium of communication is crucial for making the message powerful and accurately deciphered by the beneficiary. This decision of communication medium fluctuates relying on the components of communication. For example, written medium is picked when a message must be passed on to a little gathering of individuals while an oral medium is picked when unconstrained input is required from the beneficiary as misconceptions are cleared without further ado.

e. **Recipient/Decoder**: Recipient/Decoder is a man for whom the message is planned/pointed/focused on. The extent to which the decoder comprehends the message is subordinate upon different variables for example, information of beneficiary, their responsiveness to the message, and the dependence of encoder on the decoder.

f. **Feedback**: Feedback is the primary segment of the communication process as it allows the sender to examine the adequacy of the message. It helps the sender in affirming the right understanding of message by the decoder. Input may be verbal (through words) or non-verbal (in a type of grins, moans, and so forth.). It may take composed frame additionally in a type of notices, reports, and so forth.

6.17.3 Sender/Encoder

The sender is an individual, gathering, or association who starts the communication. This source is at first in charge of the achievement of the message. The sender's encounters, demeanors, information, expertise, observations, and society impact the message. "The composed words, talked words, and non-verbal dialect chose are foremost in guaranteeing the collector translates the message as proposed by the sender" (Burnett and Dollar, 1989). All communication starts with the sender.

The initial step the sender is confronted with includes the encoding procedure. Keeping in mind the end goal to pass on significance, the sender must start encoding, which means making an interpretation of data into a message as images that speak to thoughts or ideas. This procedure deciphers the thoughts or ideas into the coded message that will be imparted. The images can tackle various structures, for example, dialects, words, or motions. These images are utilized to encode thoughts into messages that others can get it.

At the point when encoding a message, the sender needs to start by choosing what he/she needs to transmit. This choice by the sender depends on what he/she accepts about the recipients learning and suppositions, alongside what extra data he/she needs the beneficiary to have. It is essential for the sender to utilize images that are natural to the expected beneficiary. A decent route for the sender to enhance encoding their message is to rationally envision the communication from the collector's perspective.

6.17.4 Message

To begin transmitting the message, the sender uses some kind of channel (moreover called a medium). The channel is the strategies used to go on the message. Most channels are either oral or formed, however starting now visual channels are ending up being more fundamental as advancement augments. Typical stations consolidate the telephone and an arrangement of created structures, for instance, updates, letters, and reports. The ampleness of the diverse channels differs depending upon the characteristics of the communication. Case in point, when brief data is basic, oral communication channels are all the more intense in light of the fact that any hazards can be cleared up on the spot. In a situation where the message must be passed on to all around social occasion of people, created channels are frequently all the more capable. Regardless of the way that a significant part of the time, both oral and made channels should be used in light of the way that one supplements the other.

6.17.5 Medium

If a sender exchanges a message through a tasteless station, its message may not accomplish the right receiver. That is the reason senders need to recall that selecting the fitting occupy will unimaginably help with the suitability of the receiver's understanding. The sender's decision to utilize either an oral or a created channel for giving a message is affected by a couple of variables. The sender should advance or herself differing request, with the objective that they can pick the best possible channel. Is the message desperate? Is fast feedback required? Is documentation or an enduring record required? Is the substance befuddled, debatable, or private? Is the message going to some individual inside or outside the affiliation? What oral and formed communication aptitudes does the authority have? Once the sender has tended to this request, they will have the ability to pick a fruitful channel.

6.17.6 Receiver/Decoder

After the fitting channel or channels are picked, the message enters the interpreting period of the communication process. The beneficiary coordinates disentangling. At the point when the message is received and investigated, the shock is sent to the brain for interpreting, remembering the deciding objective to dole out some kind of proposing to it. It is this taking care of stage that constitutes translating. The beneficiary begins to decipher the pictures sent by the sender, making an elucidation of the message to their own specific game plan of experiences to make the pictures critical. Productive communication happens when the authority precisely deciphers the sender's message.

The receiver is the individual or individuals to whom the message is composed. The extent to which this individual welcomes the message will depend on upon different variables, which consolidate the going with: how much the individual or individuals consider the subject, their receptivity to the message, and the relationship and trust that exists amidst sender and recipient. Their experiences, perspectives, data, capacities, perceptions, and society influence all interpretations by the authority. It is similar to the sender's relationship with encoding.

6.17.7 Feedback

Feedback is the last connection in the chain of the communication process. In the wake of getting a message, the receiver reacts somehow and signals that reaction to the sender. The sign may take the type of a talked remark, a long murmur, a composed message, a grin, or some other activity. "Even a lack of response, is in a sense, a form of response" (Bovee & Thill, 1992). Without feedback, the sender can't affirm that the receiver has deciphered the message accurately.

Feedback is a key part in the communication process in light of the fact that it permits the sender to assess the viability of the message. Feedback eventually gives a chance to the sender to make remedial move to clear up a misconstrued message. "Feedback plays an important role by indicating significant communication barriers: differences in background, different interpretations of words, and differing emotional reactions" (Bovee & Thill, 1992).

6.18 OBJECTIVES OF COMMUNICATION

Below are the main objectives of communication:

- **Conveying the right message:** The main objective of communication is to pass on the right message to one side individual, i.e., to the individual for whom it is implied. The message passed on should be surely knew and acknowledged by the recipient in the right point of view. At the end of the day, it should convey the same significance, which has been passed on so that it may be translated into action effectively.

- **Coordination of exertion:** Communication is an effective tool for organizing the activities of distinctive persons occupied with maintaining a business. Coordination without communication is a remote chance. The people or gatherings come to know what others are doing and what is normal from them just through communication.
- **Good Industrial relations:** Communication grows great industrial relations as it passes on the emotions, thoughts, and sentiments what's more, perspectives of one gathering to the next gathering. The two parties – the management and the subordinates – come closer through communication. They see one another and disperse any misconception. In this way, it advances participation what's more, great modern relations.
- **Development of management skills:** Communication makes a difference managers to understand human conduct at work. Communication of realities, thoughts, suppositions, data, emotions, and so on increase the value of the knowledge of managers about different happenings, in the organization and conduct of individuals. Accordingly, communication is a procedure of learning.
- **Effectiveness of policies:** The organization defines policies and projects to manage the workforce. These should be conveyed appropriately to the individuals who are truly responsible for the execution of work to accomplish the organizational objectives.

Only effective communication can make an interpretation of the policies into activity. Effectiveness of the policies can be judged from the achievement, which without a doubt relies on an effective communication system. The above objectives of communication, lead to a boosting the morale of the general population and along these lines guarantee the success of organization.

6.19 ATTRIBUTES OF COMMUNICATION

Effective communication is key to the achievement of any organization. Keeping in mind the end goal to practice great relational abilities, you should have the capacity to understand what makes up great communication, and afterward make that some portion of your corporate society through approaches and practice.

Presentation

At the point when a message has an excessive amount of information, or when it is passed on in a way that the receiver can not see, then that message is inadequate, as per the online employment resource Mind Tools. Communication should be consolidated down to essential realities and afterward put into a structure that the beneficiary can understand with the end goal it should be powerful. When the message is received and saw, then a detailed discussion with respect to the theme can start. Individuals are sent an assortment of messages throughout the day. Keeping in mind the end goal to offer your message some help with being understood you have to figure out how to appropriately arrange it and present it.

Channels

A communication framework is just as viable as its capacity to convey the message, as indicated by the educational asset Management Study Guide. The structure of an organization profoundly affects the viability of organizational communication. By making clear communication channels that are understood and maintained by the whole organization, you can essentially build the adequacy of your organization's communication.

Completeness

As in communication, all together for a message to be effective it should be complete. While it is critical to keep your message compact, you should be sure that all pertinent information is incorporated every time you convey. Plan to have a talk with somebody by examining the current subject. This will permit you to have the capacity to introduce the majority of the information expected to get a resolution.

Medium

Effective communication is done through the privilege mediums. In the event that it is a short and brisk message, then a composed medium, for example, a notice or e-mail would be adequate.

Points that require longer and more detailed discussion should be done in individual or via telephone. Picking the wrong medium can bring about issues with message maintenance. Examining the details of an agreement in individual without utilizing a composed back up implies that the data may get lost or overlooked. Selecting the right communication medium has an impact on the viability of a communication.

6.20 CATEGORIES OF COMMUNICATION

Today's business communicators are lucky therein they need a spread of communication to decide on from. Completely different business things and other worker want to demand the employment of multiple communication channels to drive messages home efficiently. An understanding of the advantages of assorted kinds of structure communication will facilitate business individuals communicate most effectively. The significance of communication in business becomes even additional apparent once we think about the communication activities of a company with an overall purpose of view.

6.20.1 Internal Communication and External Communication

Internal communication is the process of exchanging information between the people of different level or internal participants within the organization. The difference between internal communication and external communication.

Internal Communication

a. Every business has the necessity to maintain appropriate communication with its branches, staff, and employees. This is called internal communication.
b. Internal communication is an essential feature of an organization's administrative structure.
c. In modern times, the Human Resource Department (HRD) plays a significant role in keeping internal communication.

In the new millennium, particularly in the context of globalization, business has become highly competitive. Business houses have the need to maintain good channels of internal communication. The central organization or corporate office should keep its branches well informed of new policies and policy changes. The growth in business, the future projections for business, increased specializations make a great demand on the central office to maintain an uninterrupted flow of internal communication. Employees need to be motivated and exposed to the business objectives and ethical ideas of a company so that they get an involvement in the work they do. Employees on production line should be aware of the targets so that they overcome obstacles. Even the shifting of the canteen and a re-adjustment of the lunch-breaks and tea breaks have to be informed well in advance to the employees. In turn, employees should be able to tell people at higher levels their grievances, expectations and difficulties. Effective internal communication forges a strong bond between the employees and management, promotes co-operation among different sections in an establishment. It remove's misunderstanding and aids the growth of the organization at a desirable and optimum level. Internal communication in short, ensures involvement of all the people without alienating any section.

External Communication

An organization, when it communicates with Governmental offices, different organizations, clients, customers and public it is called *outside communication*. The media utilized may be composed media like letters, reports, proposition or visual media like publications, notices video tapes or electronic media like faxes, telegrams, messages, telexes. The communication may likewise be through video chats, up close and personal gatherings, board talks or presentations, shows and such occasions.

Formal and Informal Communication

Every business organization adopts some formal channels of communication that may be upward, downward, or horizontal or all the three. They are usually in the form of notices, announcements, reports, official or demi-official letters, advertisements, etc. Formal channels are officially recognized and organized. They make the working of the organization transparent. They motivate the employees. They provide the necessary feedback. But formal channels operate with some limitations. A continuous maintenance of a formal channel is time and resource consuming. At ordinary times, they exist for their own sake without any objective, as a formality and routine. Sometimes, personal factors affect free flow of information.

Formal Communication

Such a communication is that which is associated with the formal organization structure and the official status or the position of the communicator and the receiver. It travels through the formal channels officially recognized positions in the organization chart. Formal communication is mostly in black and white.

Thus, it is a deliberate attempt to regulate the flow of communication so as to ensure that information flows smoothly, accurately and timely. Formal communication is a deliberate attempt to regulate the flow of communication so as to ensure that information flows smoothly, accurately and timely.

We frequently come across the phrase "through proper channel". It emphasizes the essence of formal channel of communication. For example, when the General Manager issues instructions (because of his senior position in the organization), it is formal communication.

The forms of formal communication are as under:

a. Departmental meetings,
b. Conference,
c. Telephone calls,
d. Company news bulletins,
e. Special interviews and special purpose publications and messages.

The main advantage of the formal communication is that the official channels enable the routine and standardized information to pass without claiming much of managerial attention. Essentially, executives and managers may devote most of their precious time on matters of utmost significance.

But at the same time, the weakness of formal communication should not go unaccounted. Communication through channel of command greatly obstructs free and uninterrupted flow of information.

Types of Formal Communication

Formal communication is of two types:

a. Vertical Communication:
   - Downward Communication
   - Upward Communication
b. Horizontal Communication

Vertical Communication

Vertical communication is of the following two types:

a. **Downward Communication:**
   The communication by top hierarchy with their subordinates is called downward communication. This communication includes orders, rules, information, policies, instructions, etc. The chief advantage of the downward communication is that the subordinates get useful timely information, which helps them in their work performance.
b. **Upward Communication:**
   This is quite the reverse of the downward communication. This flows from the subordinates to the superiors. The subject matter of this communication includes suggestions, reactions, reports, complaints, etc. This sort of communication helps the superiors in taking decisions.

Horizontal Communication

Horizontal communication takes place when two individuals of the same level exchange information. The subject matter of horizontal communication includes information, requests, suggestions, mutual problems and coordination-related information. The same level officers to solve the problems of similar nature and profit by the experience of other people use horizontal communication.

Informal Communication (Grapevine)

Informal communication is also known as "Grapevine". It is free from all sorts of formalities because it is used on informal relationships between the parties, such as friendship, membership in the same club or association.

Persons at the executive levels also use informal communication when they find it difficult to collect information from the workers. Such communication includes comments, suggestions, etc. It may be conveyed by a simple glance, gesture, smile or mere silence.

Managers and executives also favour the growth and development of informal network of communication off and on. This process, In fact, serves a very useful purpose in disseminating certain information, which, in the general interest of the organization, cannot be transmitted through the official channels.

Apart from that, it also offers the high and higher ups a clearer insight into what the subordinates think and feel. But at the same time, the weakness of the informal communication are also worth noting. It may be mentioned that this process very often tends to pass distorted, misinterpreted, and inaccurate and half- truth information and facts, depending on the circumstances and the message. But still, executives and managers cannot do away with informal communication.

6.21 COMMUNICATION STEPS

The communication procedure is the way that we share our sentiments, considerations and thoughts with other individuals and has them comprehend those emotions, contemplations and thoughts. We convey by tuning in, talking and watching, yet once in a while individuals discover the procedure of communication troublesome: it can be difficult to give others a chance to wind up included, making it imperative to see how to make effective, common communication. You may need to show signs of improvement comprehension of the communication model and process before accomplishing compelling communication.

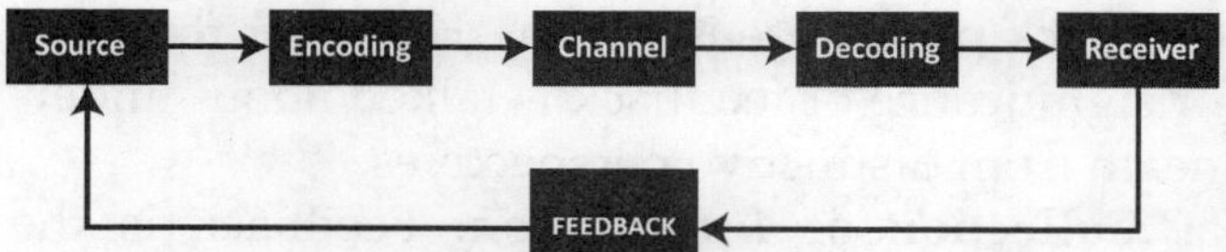

Figure 6.3 Communication Steps

The Sender has an Idea

The communicator creates or conceptualizes a thought to be sent. It is otherwise called the arranging stage subsequent to in this stage the communicator arranges the topic of communication.

The Idea becomes a Message

At the point when encoding a message, the sender needs to start by choosing what he/she needs to transmit. This choice by the sender depends on what he/she accepts about the receivers learning and suspicions, alongside what extra data he/she needs the receiver to have. It is imperative for the sender to utilize images that are commonplace to the planned receiver. A decent path for the sender to enhance encoding their message is to rationally envision the communication from the receiver's perspective.

The Message is Transmitted

In this stride, the sender really transmits the message through picked medium. In the communication cycle, the undertakings of the sender end with the transmission of the message.

The Receiver gets the Message

This stage essentially includes the gathering of sender's message by the receiver. The message can be received as hearing, seeing, feeling and so on.

The Receiver reacts and sends Feedback to the Sender

Feedback is the reaction or response of the receiver in the wake of seeing or comprehension the message. It empowers the sender to assess the adequacy of the message. It is unavoidably vital in the event of two-way communication. Without feedback, two-way communication is either insufficient or deficient. Feedback is the best way to pick up receiver's reaction and relying upon the feedback, sender can tack further steps. In organizational or business communication the feedback procedure is critical. However the need or significance of feedback is talked about underneath from distinctive perspectives:

a. **Collection of Information:** Feedback is the best way to gather information from the receiver, if the receiver doesn't send message of information (Feedback) to the sender, there is no real way to gather information from him. Thus, feedback helps the organization (Sender) to gather information from distinctive individuals (Receivers).
b. **Completion of Entire Communication Process:** Feedback is the last and critical stride of communication procedure. Through feedback, the sender can take in the response or reaction of the receiver. It is a key stride of communication without which communication procedure is inadequate. In this way, in two-way communication feedback is compulsory.
c. **Measuring the Effectiveness of Communication:** Feedback is the best way to get the reaction or response of the receiver. From it, the sender knows how well his message is comprehended and how it will be utilized by the receiver. By examining the response, positive or negative, the sender of the message can quantify to what degree communication is powerful and what are the confinements with it. In this way, in two-way communication feedback is considered to be the best way to survey the accomplishment of communication.
d. **Improving Labor-Management Relationship:** A great work administration relationship is an absolute necessity for smooth working of organizational exercises. In the event that administration trusts in two-way communication framework and grants the workers to express their sentiments, responses and conclusions on different matters, they will be highly fulfilled. In this way, management should look for feedback from representatives on diverse issues and in the meantime they should give feedback to workers. This practice will assist administration with creating a friendly climate in the organization that is fundamental for organizational achievement. In this way, feedback sets up a sound work administration relationship in the organization.
e. **Measuring the Effectiveness of Media:** We utilize distinctive kind of media to transmit messages. The receiver gets the message by the media and comprehends its significance. In the event that receiver sends his feedback to the sender, it implies that the media are fitting. Inappropriate media can't achieve the message to the receiver and in this way neglects to create any feedback. Along these lines, Feedback can be utilized as a standard of effectiveness of media.
f. **Taking Legitimate Decision:** Feedback helps the sender to take appropriate choice. On the off chance that the receiver does not send his response or reaction on certain issue, the sender can't settle on it. For instance, here and there director sends arrangements and choice or approaches to the subordinates for their examination. On the off chance that the subordinates send their choices, recommendation, grumblings, response to the directors, they can take better choices. Along these lines, feedback helps the chiefs to take legitimate and quality choices.
g. **Problem Solving:** Different sorts of issues may emerge in an organization that must be explained appropriately and opportune. Two-way communication addresses the issue and give answer for the issue. For example, if workers of an organization call for strike from the day after tomorrow it their due pay is not paid by tomorrow. Subsequent to getting the message, administration of the organization chooses to take care of their demand however does not illuminate the workers. Issue will choose to take care of their demand however does not illuminate the workers. Issue will stay, as the feedback of the administration could not reach to the representatives.

h. **Coordination among Various Departments:** There are numerous offices working in an organization to accomplish the super-ordinate objectives of the organization. For the smooth working of the exercises, these divisions must arrange and coordinate with one another. For coordination, every office must contact with other and send back reaction to any inquiry of different offices. In this way, feedback is basically required for bringing coordination among divisions.

i. **Getting the Reactions of Receiver:** Through feedback the sender can get the reactions or responses of the receiver of his message. From the reaction, the sender reactions, the sender can evaluate how well the receiver has comprehended his message and if there is any illumination to be made.

From the above discussion, we can say that feedback assumes an essential part in two-way business communication. It is vital for the finishing of entire communication framework. In genuine sense, it is the substance of two-way communication. Things being what they are, what is Feedback? Feedback is unavoidable for fruitful communication. Its significance can never be disregarded or undermined.

6.22 BARRIERS TO COMMUNICATION

There are numerous reasons why interpersonal communications may come up short. In numerous communications, the message (what is said) may not be received precisely the way the sender proposed. It is, along these lines, imperative that the communicator looks for feedback to watch that their message is unmistakably caught on.

The abilities of Active Listening, Clarification and Reflection may help however the gifted communicator additionally should know about the hindrances to successful communication and how to stay away from or overcome them.

There are numerous hindrances to communication and these may happen at any stage in the communication process. Hindrances may prompt your message getting to be contorted and you along these lines danger squandering both time and/or cash by bringing on perplexity and misconception. Powerful communication includes defeating these hindrances and passing on a reasonable and concise message.

6.22.1 Communication Barriers Between People

When you communicate something specific, you expect to impart meaning, however the message itself doesn't contain meaning. The importance exists in your brain and in the psyche of your receiver. To comprehend each other, you and your receiver must have comparative implications for words, motions, manner of speaking, and different images.

Differences in Perception

The world always shells us with information: sights, sounds, fragrances, etc. Our psyches sort out this surge of sensation into a mental guide that speaks to our observation or reality. For no situation is the impression of someone in particular the same as the world itself, and no two maps are indistinguishable. As you view the world, your brain retains your encounters in one of a kind and individual way. Since your discernments are special, the thoughts you need to express contrast from other individuals' Even when two individuals have encountered the same occasion, their mental pictures of that occasion won't be indistinguishable. As senders, we pick the points of interest that appear to be vital and center our consideration on the most pertinent and general, a procedure known as particular observation. As receivers, we attempt to fit new points of interest into our current example. On the off chance that a point of interest doesn't exactly fit, we are slanted to misshape the information as opposed to revamp the example.

Incorrect filtering

Sifting is screening through before a message is gone on to another person. In business, the channels in the middle of you and your receiver are numerous; secretaries, aides, receptionists, voice-mail, and so on. Those same guards might likewise "interpret" your receiver's thoughts and reactions before passing them on to you. To overcome separating boundaries, attempt to set up more than one communication channel, wipe out whatever number middle people as could reasonably be expected, and diminish twisting by gathering message information to the minimum necessities.

Language problems

When you pick the words for your message, you flag that you are an individual from a specific society or subculture and that you know the code. The way of your code forces its own boundaries on your message. Boundaries likewise exist in light of the fact that words can be translated in more than restricted. Dialect is a subjective code that relies on upon shared definitions, yet there's a cutoff to how totally any of us have the same significance for a given word. To overcome dialect boundaries, utilize the most particular and precise words conceivable. Continuously attempt to utilize words your crowd will get it. Build the precision of your messages by utilizing dialect that depicts as opposed to assesses and by exhibiting detectable certainties, occasions, and circumstances.

Poor listening

May be the most widely recognized boundary to gathering is essentially an absence of consideration on the receiver's part. We all let our brains meander from time to time; paying little respect to how hard we attempt to focus. Individuals are basically prone to float off when they are compelled to listen to information that is hard to comprehend or that has minimal direct bearing all alone lives. Excessively few of us basically don't listen well! To overcome hindrances, rework what you have comprehended, attempt to see the circumstance through the eyes of different speakers and oppose forming a hasty opinion. Elucidate importance by asking non-debilitating inquiries, and listen without interfering.

Differing emotional states

Each message contains both a substance importance, which manages the subject of the message, and a relationship significance, which recommends the way of the connection in the middle of sender and receiver. Communication can separate when the receiver responds contrarily to both of these implications. You may need to manage individuals when they are steamed or when you are. An annoyed individual has a tendency to disregard or contort what the other individual is stating and is regularly not able to present sentiments and thoughts adequately. This is not to say that you should keep away from all communication when you are sincerely included, yet you should be aware of the more noteworthy potential for misconception that goes with stirred feelings. To overcome enthusiastic obstructions, know about the emotions that emerge in yourself and in others as you impart, and endeavor to control them. Most imperative, be aware of the more noteworthy potential for misconception that goes with passionate messages.

Differing backgrounds

Contrasts in foundation can be one of the hardest communication boundaries to succeed. Age, instruction, societal position, monetary position, social foundation, disposition, well being, magnificence, fame, religion, political conviction, even a passing inclination can all different one individual from another and make understanding troublesome. To conquer the boundaries connected with contrasting foundations, abstain from anticipating your own particular foundation or society onto others. Clear up your own particular and comprehend the foundation of others, circles of information, identities and recognitions and don't expect that sure practices mean the same thing to everybody.

6.22.2 Communication Barriers within Organizations

During the time spent communication there can be generous contrast between the information that is really planned to be passed on by the originator of communication and its beneficiary. Some piece of the information may get not achieve the beneficiary by any means, and whatever compasses may be misshaped, and may be translated by the receiver in a way not planned by the sender of information. Communication boundary is the aggregate name given to the reasons for this misfortune and bending of information amid the procedure of communication.

There are numerous sorts of communication obstructions in an organization. Significant ones of these are depicted beneath.

a. **Lack of Planning:** What should be conveyed, how, and when is not legitimately thoroughly considered and arranged.
b. **Un-clarified Assumptions:** Leaving out applicable points of interest in the communication expecting that receiver is as of now mindful of it.
c. **Semantic Distortion:** Same word or expression deciphered in distinctive way.

Poor Expression of Messages

a. **Communication Barriers in International Environment:** The obstructions as a consequence of distinctive dialects, society, and so on. Such boundaries can exist inside of a nation moreover.
b. **Poor Listening and Premature Evaluation:** The receiver may not ingest or rationally get the all information sent. One of the real explanations behind poor listening is propensity of individuals to begin assessing the information received even as the other individual is talking.
c. **Too Much Impersonal Communication:** Frequently communications come up short in light of the fact that the speaker can't set up individual security with the audience.
d. **Distrust, Threat and Fear:** Communication is a two-way prepare, one gives information and additionally gets information. On the off chance that a man is questioned or dreaded, individuals will abstain from giving him an excess of or right information. Likewise they will have less validity in information given by him.
e. **Information Overload:** Too quite a bit of information additionally brings about poor communication. Helpful information blended with extra information requires extra push to discrete the two. Likewise, right information can get stirred up with comparative wrong information and reason disarray and blunders.
f. **Other Communication Barriers:** These incorporate discernment, which makes people rationally shift through and twist information received. The recognition itself is influenced by any variables, for example, states of mind and feelings.

Contrasts in status and power likewise influence readiness of the people to impart and the way of information conveyed.

Channel Selection

To decide the fitting communication channel, distinguish the general population you need to correspond with, exploration how they get information, consider the multifaceted nature of the message you need to convey, figure the expense of imparting and choose whether you need the communication to be intelligent. The decision of channel is not straightforward; for a mind-boggling communication program, you may need to work with experts, for example, advertising or promoting communication specialists has described in following steps:

Step 1

Recognize your intended interest group. Figure out the occupation titles of the general population who settle on or impact choices about acquiring the sort of items you supply. Survey the media information packs of magazines and daily papers that claim to achieve your intended interest group. Draw up a shortlist of productions you could use for publicizing or article scope. Inquire as to whether they meet the key leaders up close and personal. In the event that they do, you can utilize the business power to impart information. Consider how you could utilize your site to correspond with the crowd. Organizations utilize the Internet to assemble preparatory information when they are considering a buy.

Step 2

Break down the message you need to impart. Use channels, for example, ads, e-mail or short messages on online networking, for example, twitter to convey a basic message, for example, a value change or new item declaration. Select a channel that permits you to treat a theme in more profundity on the off chance that you need to clarify the advantages of another item or a key change in your organization. Consider component articles in magazines read by your intended interest group, itemized specialized papers accessible from your site or talking opportunities at industry gatherings went to by your intended interest group.

Step 3

Figure the expense of imparting through the channels you have recognized. Acquire promoting rates from media distributors, approach creators and printers for quotes on delivering printed records, for example, specialized papers and compute the expense of direct deals approaches key chiefs.

Step 4

Pick intuitive channels on the off chance that you need to get feedback or screen assessments of your organization and your items. Set up a gathering or item survey page on your site to urge guests to share their perspectives. Screen online networking for material that identifies with your organization. React to remarks to construct dialog and ensure your notoriety.

Step 5

Work with communications experts to create and execute your communication system. Delegate an advertising expert to handle relations with the media – guaranteeing that official statements show up in the right productions and increasing article scope in powerful media. Select a showcasing firm or publicizing organization to make suggestions on communication channels and strategy.

Physical Barriers

There are a large group of physical variables that can keep people from having a powerful communication. Physical boundaries identify with aggravation in the quick milieu, which can meddle over the span of a viable communication.

a. Environment

A few obstructions are because of the current environment. On the off chance that you are remaining in antagonistic climate conditions, your discussion would be hampered, in light of the fact that you would not have the capacity to give careful consideration to what the other individual is stating.

The feeling in which you are having a discussion additionally has vital impact in the nature of a discussion. On the off chance that the spot is excessively boisterous, or two swarmed, you will most likely be unable to plainly listen to the speaker.

For instance, in the event that you are having a discussion with somebody along the roadside, the commotion of the passing vehicles can make it troublesome for you to focus on what you are stating, aside from meddling in powerful tuning in. Correspondingly, on the off chance that you are conversing with somebody in singing warmth, then the physical uneasiness can without much of a stretch make you unengaged in the discussion.

b. Distance

Separation likewise has vital influence in deciding the course of a discussion. For instance, if the staff in an organization is made to sit in diverse structures or distinctive floors, they may need to substitute up close and personal communication with telephone calls or messages.

This keeps the representatives to have compelling communication with one another. For instance, if a supervisor and his subordinate are situated at diverse structures of an organization, then the chief may need to give out guidelines via telephone or over the e-mail, which can in some cases lead to an absence of compelling communication.

c. Ignorance of Medium

Communication likewise incorporates utilizing signs and images to pass on an inclination or an idea. In any case, if there is an absence of lack of awareness about the medium in which sender is sending the message, the discussion can be hampered.

For instance, the utilization of signs to impart can be found in amusements like soccer and hockey, where players don't need the contradicting group to think about their arrangements and may banter through codes and signs. On the other hand, if an individual from a group is not familiar with these signs, it can prompt an absence of communication.

d. Physical Disability

- Physical handicap can likewise end up being a boundary for powerful communication.
- Individuals with physical handicaps for the most part are off guard with regards to picking up work.
- They have been underestimated through ages, and this can make them have a low self-regard and social uneasiness.
- It can bring about a physically tested individual to have face troubles in self-exposure and can hamper his interpersonal abilities.

Semantics

There is dependably a plausibility of misconception the sentiments of the sender of the message or misunderstanding a significance of it. The receiver in the light of his experience, which makes far-fetched circumstances, clarifies the words, signs, and figures utilized as a part of the communication. This happens in light of the fact that the information is not sent in basic dialect.

Perception of Reality

Discernment is comprehension of our general surroundings. Everyone sees the world in his own special way and deciphers what has been seen in yet another novel way and translates what has been seen in yet another one of a kind way. When we firmly dissent, we basically say "I am sad, our observations seem, by all accounts, to appear as something else".

Information Overload

Information over-burden happens when the measure of data to a framework surpasses its preparing limit. Leaders have genuinely restricted intellectual handling limit. Hence, when information over-burden happens, it is likely that a diminishment in choice quality will happen.

In the event that you get a message with a lot of information, you may tend to set up an obstruction on the grounds that the measure of information is coming so quick that you may experience issues easily interpreting that information. On the off chance that you are offering a thing with a quarter century elements, pick a few imperative elements to accentuate as opposed to overpowering your receiver (ho-murmur) with an information torrential slide.

6.23 IMPROVING YOUR WRITING SKILLS

Writing is a form of communication which allows people to put their feelings and ideas on paper, to organize their knowledge and beliefs into convincing arguments, and to convey meaning through well-constructed text.

Writing skills are an important part of communication, as good writing skills allow you to communicate your message with clarity and ease to a far larger audience than through face-to-face or telephone conversations. You might be called upon to write a report, plan or strategy at work; write a grant application or press release within a volunteering role. A well written CV or résumé with no spelling or grammatical mistakes is essential if you want a new job.

Poor writing skills create poor first impressions and many readers will have an immediate negative reaction if they spot a spelling or grammatical mistake. This section will teach you about writing - from grammar, spelling and punctuation, how to plan your writing, and the various processes and checks to go through before finalizing you writing.

6.24 RESUME

Resume sets out your skills and experience, it should demonstrate potential employer that why they should hire you above any of the other skilled candidates who have presented themselves for employment.

Resume is a detailed document which outline all of the life achievements, qualifications, associations, awards and skills. It's a concise document; an and focuses on specific skills and achievements, usually in relation and relevant to an employment opportunity.

Things to Do while Writing a Resume

- Start with your name, address, phone number and email address.
- If your Resume runs to more than one page, then make sure you include an identifier on every page, probably as a header or footer, and page numbers.
- Include sections on Key Skills, Knowledge and Achievements, Work Experience, and Education.

- Include everything relevant in "Work Experience" and "Education".
- Make sure that your spelling and grammar are all correct.
- Use a standard and professional-looking font such as Arial or Calibri, which is easy to read, and generally no smaller than 10 point for body text, larger for headings.

Mistakes and Pitfalls to Avoid

- Do not give any false information about yourself.
- Avoid leaving gaps in your career history
- Do not start your CV with the dull bits
- Do not include your hobbies and interests
- Don't make your CV too long
- Do not use an unprofessional email address

6.25 LETTERS

A business letter is typically a letter starting with one organization then onto the next, or between such organizations and their clients, customers and other outside gatherings. The general style of a letter relies on the relationship between the groups concerned. Business letters can have numerous sorts of contents, for example, to ask for direct information or activity from another party, to request supplies from a supplier, to point out a mistake by the letter's recipient, to answer straightforwardly to a request, to apologize for a wrong, or to pass on goodwill. A business letter is now and then helpful because it delivers a changeless composed record, and may be considered more important by the recipient than different types of communication.

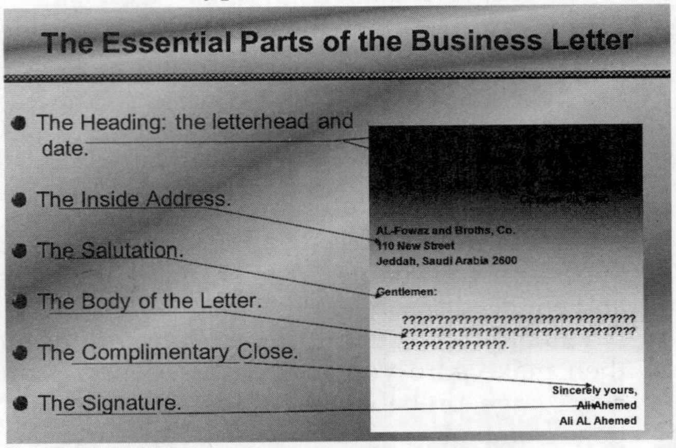

Figure 6.4 Letters

Conventional Parts of Business Letters

- **Letterhead**–Organizations usually use printed-paper where heading or letterhead is primarily designed at the top of the sheet. It bears all the necessary information about the organization's identity.
- **The date of the letter**–Date of composing. The month ought to be completely delineated and the year composed with every one of the four digits October 20, 2006 (20 October 2006 – UK style). The date is adjusted to the arrival address. The quantity of the date is proclaimed as an ordinal figure, however, the endings st, nd, rd, th, are regularly excluded in composing. The article before the quantity of the day is proclaimed however not composed. In the body of the letter, in any case, the article is written when the name of the month is not specified with the day.
- **The Inside Address**–In a business or formal letter, you should give the address of the recipient after your address. Include the recipient's name, company, address, and postal code. Add job title if appropriate. Separate the recipient's name and title with a comma. Double check that you have the correct spelling of the recipient's name. The Inside Address is always on the left margin. If an 8 1/2" x 11" paper is folded in thirds to fit in a standard 9" business envelope, the internal address can appear through the window in the envelope.
- **The Greeting/Salutation**–Also called the salutation. The type of greeting depends on your relationship with the recipient. It starts with "Dear" and dependably incorporates the individual's last name. Utilize each asset conceivable to deliver your letter to a genuine person. On the off chance that you don't have a clue about the name of your collector address it to Dear Madam/Sir (or Dear Sales Manager or Dear Human Resources Director). When in doubt, the welcome in a business letter closures in a colon (US style). It is likewise satisfactory to utilize a comma (UK style).
- **The Subject Line (optional)**–Its inclusion can help the recipient in dealing successfully with the aims of your letter. The subject sentence is preceded by the word Subject: or Re: Subject line may be emphasized by underlining, using bold font, or all capital letters. It is placed one

line below the greeting but alternatively can be located directly after the "internal address," before the "greeting".

- **The Body Paragraphs**–The body is the place you clarify why you are composing. It is the focal piece of the business letter. Ensure the beneficiary knows who you are and why you are writing yet attempt to abstain from beginning with "I." Use another section when you wish to present another thought or component into your letter. Contingent upon the letter style you pick, sections may be indented. Notwithstanding arrange, avoid a line between sections.
- **The Complimentary Close**–This short, well-mannered shutting dependably closes with a comma. It is either at the left edge, or its left side is on the inside, contingent upon the Business Letter Style that you utilize. It starts at the same section the heading does. The standard guideline of manners in Britain is that a formal letter is beginning "Dear Sir or Madam" must end "Yours dependably" while a letter is starting "Dear " must end "Yours truly". (Note: the second expression of the purpose is NOT promoted).
- **Signature and Writer's identification**–The signature is the last some portion of the letter. You should be signing your first and last names. The signature line might incorporate a second line for a title if fitting. The signature ought to begin precisely over the first letter of the signature line in the space between the nearby and the signature line. Use blue or dark ink.
- Initials, Enclosures, Copies–Initials are to be incorporated on the off chance that somebody other than the author sorts the letter. On the off chance that you include other material in the letter, put 'Fenced in an area', 'Enc.', or " Encs. ', as fitting, two lines underneath the last passage. cc implies a duplicate or duplicates are sent to another person.

Types of Business Letters

The most critical component you have to guarantee in any business letter is exactness. One of the parts of composing a business letter that requires the most precision knows which kind of business letter you are writing. Some options are available for those looking to trade in business correspondence, and you will significantly increase your odds of getting a reply if you know the form you need to send.

a. Letter of Complaint
b. Resume Cover Letter
c. Letter of Recommendation
d. Letter of Resignation
e. Job Applicant Not Hired
f. Declining Dinner Invitation
g. Reception of Gift
h. Notification of Error
i. Thanks for Job Recommendation
j. Information Request

6.26 REPORT

A report, by definition, is a "statement describing what has happened" or "describing a state of affairs". In business, there are many occasions when some form of "report" is required. It is supposed to be a detailed examination of a situation or problem, of action taken, or of the findings of an investigation. It is written in a clear, informative way, often drawing conclusions, making recommendations and suggesting courses of action. The purpose of such reports is usually to bring information to the attention of senior management authorities so that they can take any decision regarding the matters under review with full knowledge of the background, facts and circumstances. Reports can also be requested for action, or they can make suggestions to initiate action.

Business reports convey information from one person, group or company to another. According to West Virginia University, informal business reports are commonly sent through email, memos, letters or orally. Formal business reports are usually printed and might consist of one document submitted in a project or a series of reports.

Business Report Parts

The contents of business reports differ dependent on the report's purpose. However, reports typically include four parts: introduction, summary, discussion and conclusions.

- The introduction is a short outline of the report's content. This might include a "Table of Contents" or merely state an overview.
- The summary illustrates the opportunity or problem or summarizes the situation the report covers.
- The discussion includes descriptive details, such as methods used, results found and existing choices.
- The conclusion differs dependent on the reports, such as implications of each option for recommendation or analytical reports, evaluations for analytical reports, and explanations of why you think one options is best in recommendation reports.

Analytical Reports

These types of business reports include information along with analysis or interpretation from the report's writer or in response to the person who requested the report.

- A business uses analytical reports to make a decision or to work out a problem.
- Examples of analytical reports include a progress report detailing what has occurred and the writer's analysis of it, or a sales report requested by the business owner as to why sales are falling in one location and not another.

Informational Reports

- Informational reports contain information only and no commentary from the writer.
- This type of report includes data, facts and results about a specific subject in detail without any explanation or suggestions.
- This might be an informal report, such as a "minutes of meetings" report that contains actions and dialog of a meeting.
- It might be a report on applicants for a new position requested by a company president, which might include names, experience, work record and other details pertinent to the job.

Recommendation and Research Reports

- A recommendation and research report includes information, the writer's examination of the information and the suitable action or actions the writer advises.
- These reports are based on research performed by a person or group in regard to a specific problem or subject.
- A common recommendation report is policy directives.
- These reports detail the topic or problem using figures and significant facts, suggest various options and include detailed explanations of why one option is better than another option.

Preparation before Writing Reports

Everything reports need to be clear, succinct and all around organized. The way to composing a viable report is to dispense time for arranging and readiness. With careful arranging, the written work of a report will be made much less demanding. The critical phases of effective report writing are depicted beneath. Consider to what extent every stage is prone to set aside and isolate the time before the due date between the distinct phases. Make sure to leave time for precise editing and checking.

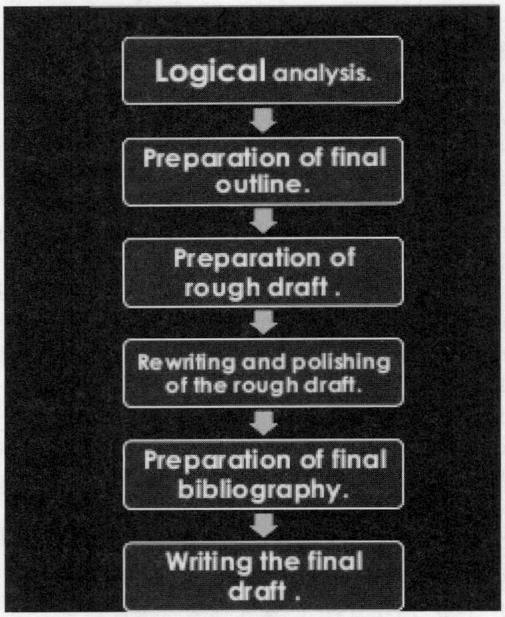

Figure 6.5 Writing Reports

Stage One: Understanding the report brief

This first stage is the most essential. You should be sure that you comprehend the motivation behind your report as portrayed in your report brief or directions. Consider whom the report is for and why it is being composed. Watch that you see everyone of the directions or necessities, and inquire as to whether anything is misty.

Stage Two: Gathering and selecting information

When you are clear about the reason for your report, you have to start to accumulate pertinent information. Your information might originate from an assortment of sources, yet the amount of information you will need will rely on upon the quantity of point of interest is required in the report. You might need to start by perusing pertinent writing to enlarge your comprehension of the point or issue before you go ahead to take a gander at different types of information, for example, polls, studies and so on. As you read and assemble information, you have to survey its importance to your report and select in like manner. Continue alluding to your report brief to offer you some assistance with deciding what is significant information.

Stage Three: Organizing your material

When you have assembled information you have to choose what will be incorporated and in what grouping it ought to be introduced. Start by gathering together focuses that are connected. These may frame segments or sections. Keep in mind to continue alluding to the report brief and be arranged to cut any information that is not specifically pertinent to the report. Pick a request for your material that is consistent and simple to take after.

Stage Four: Analyzing your material

Before you start to compose your first draft of the report, set aside time to consider and make notes on the focuses you will make utilizing the actualities and proof you have assembled. What conclusions can be drawn from the material? What are the constraints or imperfections in the confirmation? Do individual bits of confirmation struggle with each other? It is insufficient just to present the information you have accumulated; you should relate it to the issue or issue portrayed in the report brief.

Stage Five: Writing the Report

Having sorted out your material into respective areas and headings, you can start to compose the first draft of your report. You might discover it less demanding to write the rundown and substance page toward the end when you know precisely what will be incorporated. Go for a composition style that is immediate and exact. Stay away from waffle and make your focuses obviously and succinctly. Parts, areas, and even individual passages ought to be composed with an unmistakable structure. The structure portrayed beneath can be adjusted and connected to parts, segments, and even passages.

- Present the initial thought of the part/area/section.
- Clarify and extend the thought, characterizing any key terms.
- Present pertinent confirmation to bolster your point(s).
- Remark on every bit of confirmation demonstrating how it identifies with your point(s).
- Finish up your part/segment/section by either demonstrating its essentialness to the report overall or making a connection to the following part/segment/passage.

Stage Six: Reviewing and redrafting

In a perfect world, you ought to leave time to enjoy a reprieve before you audit your first draft. Be arranged to revise or modify areas in the light of your audit. Attempt to peruse the draft from the per user. Is it simple to take after with a logical structure that bodies well? Are the focuses succinctly yet unmistakably clarified and upheld by applicable proof? Composing on a word processor makes it less demanding to rework and improve areas or sections in your first draft. If you write your first draft by hand, have a go at writing every area on a different bit of paper to make redrafting less demanding.

Stage Seven: Presentation

When you are fulfilled by the substance and structure of your redrafted report, you can turn your thoughtfulness regarding the presentation. Watch that the wording of every part/area/subheading is clear and precise. Watch that you have held fast to the directions in your report brief on design and presentation. Check for consistency in the numbering of parts, areas and informative supplements. Ensure that everyone of your sources is recognized and accurately referenced. You should edit your report for blunders of spelling or language structure. In the event that time permits, write more than once. Blunders in presentation or expression make a poor impression and can make the report hard to peruse.

Main Parts of the Report

Whether you are writing a short report in memorandum format, preparing your report for a verbal presentation at a meeting or constructing a formal printed report, it is likely to contain three main parts:

- Summary
- Body
- Conclusion

A formal report may also include a table of contents, index, appendices and bibliography. There are no absolute rules about the parts and their order in a report, but there are conventions.

- Front cover
- Title page
- Foreword or covering letter
- Contents
- Summary
- Body of the report: introduction, discussion, conclusion
- Appendices
- Bibliography
- Index

Summary

The summary may vary in content, depending on the nature of the report, but is usually no longer than one or two pages and contains:

- A statement on the background to the report – purpose, scope and the name of the person or organization requesting the report.
- A summary of the main findings of the report, usually in point forms.

Body

The body of the report contains a complete discussion of all relevant issues.

- It may be structured chronologically (in order of date or time), logically (using patterns, such as cause and effect) or topically (divided according to key points or tasks).
- If the body of the report refers to the detailed supporting material, such as a survey used to collect information, this material is usually included as an appendix to the report.
- Otherwise, all relevant graphs, tables and diagrams should be included in the body of the report.

Conclusion

Depending on the type of report, the conclusion is generally where the author interprets the research, reports on the findings or makes recommendations. No new information is included at this point, apart from opinion or interpretation.

Text of the Report

Report text is a text that describes something in general. Every text has a communicative purpose. Communicative purpose of report text is to present information about something in general.

- Report text has two generic structures.
- The first is general classification it is usually in the first paragraph of the text.
- It can be a short description of the subject or it can be definitions from the subject that is described.
- The second is, description. In this part, we usually will describe the details of the topic or subject such as physical appearance, parts, qualities, habits or behavior.
- Every paragraph in the part of description usually gives us information about one feature of the subject.

6.27 WHAT IS PRESENTATION?

A presentation is the process of presenting a topic to an audience. It is typically a demonstration, introduction, lecture, or speech meant to inform, persuade, or build good will. A presentation requires you to get a message across to the listeners and contain a 'persuasive' element.

Presenting information clearly and effectively is a key skill to get your message or opinion. Whether you are a student, administrator or executive, if you wish to start up your own business, apply for a grant or stand for an elected position, you may very well be asked to make a presentation. This can be a very daunting prospect. Our guide is designed to help.

6.28 HOW IMPORTANT IS PRESENTATION SKILLS?

Presentation skills are very important for you if you want to succeed professionally. In today's business environment, as the competition in the workplace is getting more competitive. It is no longer enough for you to have the necessary capability to do the job, you should also be able to talk - write well, and present yourself attractively to your superiors. You should be capable of presenting a great idea or a plan during a meeting.

The most important element during a presentation is you, because you are the one that the audience is concentrating on. You convey who you are on the basis of your body language, your speech, and your overall mannerism. Every gesture, movement, facial expression you use reflects your personality. So it is important for you to know which gestures or movements you usually do and what should be avoided. You need to be comfortable during a presentation because it is then that you can perform at your best.

You should concentrate on is how you can communicate effectively with the listeners, because the key to have good presentation skills is not only though the transmission of the message but through the reception of the message as well.

The whole content of your presentation should be centered on catching the attention of the audience and keeping it; they should be persuaded of the merits and the benefits of what you had presented.

Content of your presentation is also essential. It does not matter if you are the most attractive person in the room with the personality to match it if the content of your presentation itself means nothing.

You should have an objective for the presentation. This will determine the content and the structure of the entire presentation. It is also important to look at the audience so that the mode of presentation would be appropriate to the knowledge and interest.

Developing presentation skills and giving an effective presentation is not an easy matter. It is said that some people are born with presentation skills but you should also remember that presentation skills can be learned. And take note that presentation skills can be developed further when it is being practiced regularly so develop your presentation skills and become an expert.

6.29 BASIC PRINCIPLES OF PRESENTATION SKILLS

When we watch celebrities, politicians, or business leaders speak on television or in public, they seem so at ease that we may wonder: are great speakers made, or are they just born that way? While it is true that some individuals are definitely born with this gift, the overwhelming majority of effective speakers have trained themselves to be so.

Either they have received formal media training or they have delivered so many speeches that over time they have learned what works for them. So what is the true secret to effective public speaking?

Here are seven principles of public speaking which help you to presenting before a group.

a. Stand erect distributing your weight on both the legs. Do not hold onto the mike or to the podium for support.
b. Have a good posture and appearance. Do not lean on the podium.
c. Be confident, relaxed and energetic. Do not play with your clothes or fingers.
d. Wear clothes that befit the occasion.
e. Convey sincerity, conviction and enthusiasm for the subject.
f. Begin the speech, after passing for a few seconds, looking over the audience.
g. Open the speech with a striking, catchy introduction looking into the eyes of the audience.
h. Have a conversational tone.
i. Establish eye contact with the audience.
j. Use gestures to emphasize and clarify your points.
k. Allow your hands, to fall naturally to your sides, when not gesturing.

l. Have enough voice projection.
m. Modulate your voice.
n. Speak at moderate speed. Do not rush through.
o. Pause before and after important ideas.
p. Have pleasant mannerisms.
q. Do not read your speech.
r. Manage time.
s. Close the speech with a striking, impressive, concluding remark.
t. Stop, while the audience is still eager to hear more.

6.29.1 Guidelines for an Effective Delivery of Speech

Even the greatest content/message will be ruined by a poor delivery. So often speakers work diligently on what they are going to say but they fail to connect because of how they are saying it. The following 10 Delivery Guidelines will help you use your delivery to deepen, rather than damage, your connection.

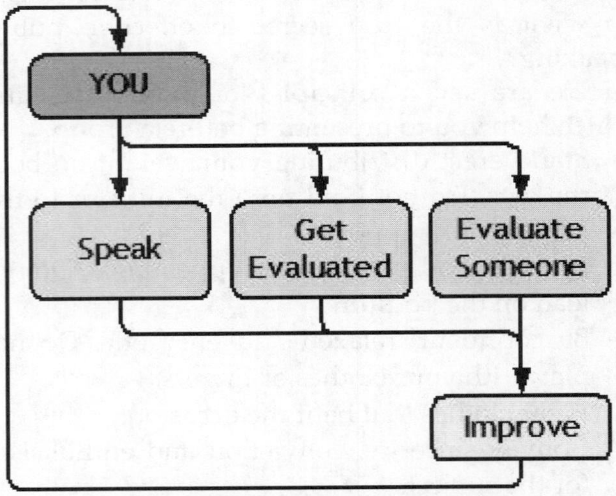

Figure 6.6 Delivery of Speech

a. **Do not move all the time**
If you are continually moving then, no development will be necessary. Your audience will never realize what's imperative. Move with a reason. At the point when there is no motivation to move, don't.
What's the primary reason for moving amid your speech?
It is the activity in your story. Let the action in your story provoke your development in front of an audience. On the off chance that you have a story in which you move from the front room to the kitchen, demonstrate that development in front of an audience. That implies you more likely than not assigned spots for the kitchen and the family room on your stage. What's more, those places must stay there for the length of that specific story. Listen to what may happen on the off chance that they don't.

b. **Do not forget about your face**
Your outward appearances are more critical than all your arm and hand developments consolidated. The eyes are undoubtedly the windows to the spirit. What you do with them can represent the moment of truth your whole speech.

c. **Use your character's gestures**
Remember that talking includes using enrapturing stories to make your exceptional focuses. Every story has its particular characters and every character likely has his or her specific manner of signaling. When you tackle the part and persona of that character, you should utilize his or her Gestures. While practicing your speech, reliably ask yourself, "How might this character say this?" at the end of the day, each character should not to look and act like you. Every character should work in an unexpected way, in light of the fact that will offer us some assistance with seeing those characters with more prominent clarity. So once more, continue inquiring: How might this character say this?

d. **Let the emotions drive**
The feelings in your story and your point will turn your developments. On the off chance that you are inebriated with your feelings while telling your story or making your point, the fitting motions will come. It will be easy. Consider it. When you are truly furious at

somebody or something, do you need to consider what Gestures to utilize? No, they come consequently. If you assemble the feeling, the Gestures will come.

e. **Use Surround-Sense Gestures (360 Degrees)**
Numerous speakers Gesture before them and possibly as an afterthought. The best speakers acknowledge there is a whole zone around them, and they use it. Don't hesitate to motion down for the lower measurement. For instance, when I talk about a blog visit my wife, and I took, I discuss the crocodiles that encompassed the vessel. By then I motion downwards with the open hand while taking a gander at where the water is assigned in front of an audience. At that point, I portray the trees that were hanging down as though they were attempting to take hold of us. By then I Gestures upwards to the upper measurement utilizing my hands to copy how the trees hung and influenced. On occasion, I indicate behind me the back of the stage or before me out into the audience. I may show my entitlement to mean the past and point to one side to connote the future as I utilize the stage as a timetable. The key is to go up, down, back, forward, and side to side with a particular end goal to paint an entire (encompass sense) scene for your audience keeping in mind the end goal to welcome them into it.

f. **Do not use the same gesture over and over again**
This is confirmation of a propensity and in all likelihood occupies from your presentation. Ask me how I know this?

g. **Watch out for Your Resting Position**
This is the position your hands tumble to when you are not utilizing a Gesture. For instance, my hands used to fall together before me with my fingers interlocking. In the time, it got to be diverting. Unquestionably film your speeches once in a while to check whether you are falling into this propensity. It kills the sound and after that quick forward the video because, in case you're utilizing a resting point, it will turn out to be exceptionally clear.

h. **Use an open hand**
It is ideal to indicate your audience with an open hand instead of a pointer. It is not so much undermining but rather more welcoming. The free hand is additionally fortunate when getting back to back to spots on the floor as you return to the focused, characters, and stories you already utilized. A non-verbal communication master as of late let me know that palms up are a great deal more inviting than palms down as you convey your message and particularly when you indicate somebody in your audience. Clearly palms down can have a stopping impact.

i. **Use bigger gestures for bigger audiences**
Try not to cross the span of your audience with the measure of your Gestures. In case, you are talking at a Commencement Ceremony to 4,000 individuals, and you give the same estimated motions that you do before a Toastmasters Club, odds are your audience won't see them. At the point when the audience gets greater, you should get greater.

Additionally, ensure you coordinate their vitality at first. For instance, if you have a laid back audience, you can not turn out shouting and energized, because they'll be searching for the closest exit. Rather, meet them on their vitality level and afterward, once you join with them there, they will tell you to your common vitality level. It is called Pacing and Leading. You should initially meet them where they are, not where you are.

j. **Smile**
Regularly the first thing to go when a speaker gets in front of an audience is his or her smile. That is grievous because the smile can unite you with your audience before you even say the single word. So smile when appropriate.

6.30 INTERVIEW SKILLS

The term "interview" has been derived from the French word "entree voir" that means "to glimpse" or "to see each other". By definition, it means a meeting for obtaining information by questioning a person or persons. In this way, an interview is a classic example of communication that takes place through the process by which meanings are exchanged between people through the use of a standard set of symbols.

An interview is a conversation between two or more people where questions are asked by the interviewer to elicit facts or statements from the interviewee. Interviews are a standard part of qualitative research. They are also used in journalism and media reporting and in various employment-related contexts. General guidelines for effective employment interview.

- **Be prepared for the interview:** Just as the interviewer has to plan out the event in advance, so has the interviewee to be prepared for it. As he/she has no control over the event, he/she has to be more careful at every step. He/she has to face an interviewer or a board of interviewers. He/she must, therefore, be very clear about the purpose of the event. If it is going to be a job interview he/she has to be well prepared for questions on his/her area of interest, his/her present position, the position he/she has applied for, the nature of the organization, its history, its current activities etc. His/her knowledge on all such questions will impress the interviewers. However he/she must be prepared for the unexpected.
- **Has a presentable appearance:** Everybody appreciates a pleasant personality. As in the case of a presentation, so in an interview, the concerned person's appearance is a part of the message. Since an interview is a formal occasion, the interviewee must be formally dressed. Anyone having conventional standards of neatness is likely to have a definite advantage over one casually dressed for an interview.
- **Be polite**. Politeness is indispensable in every situation.
- **Show interest by making effective use of body language:** Keeping eye-to-eye contact with the interviewer at once shows that the interviewee is genuinely interested in the event and keen to participate in it. He/she should also sit in a correct, confident posture, straight, balanced and not stiff in the chair offered. The hands should be neatly locked on the lap or comfortably placed on the arms of the chair.
- All the questions must be correctly and completely answered. Since the primary aim of an interview is to exchange information it should be done effectively.
- If the interviewee is not clear about a suitable answer to a question, there is no harm in admitting it. One must **never try to bluff**. Be honest.
- Avoid talking too much or making boastful statements. The interviewer is intelligent enough to find out the interview's intelligence and suitability for the job.
- Avoid criticism of the previous employer or anybody else. Negative statements are looked down upon.
- Do not forget to thank the interviewers for having spared time for you. Granting an interview is indeed a favour.
- Do not hesitate to ask any questions to seek clarification regarding the company profile, service conditions etc. It will not only satisfy your curiosity but also give the interviewer an idea of your confidence and interest in the organization. But such questions should come only towards the end of the interview and when you feel you are likely to get the job.

A successful interview is one in which both the parties – the interviewer and the interviewee – actively participate. The interviewer asks certain vitally important questions arranged according to his plan. The interviewee, on his part, gives satisfactory answers to all of them. The interviewer seeks information, the interviewee gives information. At some stage in the process, most probably towards the end, the interviewer may also seek some information that the interviewee will gladly give. In this way the purpose of the interview, mutually understood, is fulfilled.

Moreover, both the parties must be unbiased, impartial and scientific in their approach to the entire event.

6.31 TIPS FOR SUCCESSFUL COMMUNICATION

There is a great deal of communication hindrances confronted nowadays by all. The receiver does not comprehend the message proposed by the sender in the same terms and sense and in this way communication breakdown happens. It is key to arrangement and adapt up to these communication hindrances to guarantee smooth and viable communication.

a. **Eliminating Contrasts in Observation:** The organization should guarantee that it is enrolling right people at work. It's the obligation of the questioner to guarantee that the interviewee has summoned over the composed and talked dialect. There should be appropriate Induction program so that the arrangements of the organization are clear to every one of the workers. There should be legitimate trainings led for required representatives (for example, Voice and Accent preparing).

b. **Use of Simple Language:** Use of basic and clear words should be underlined. Utilization of questionable words and languages should be maintained a strategic distance from.

c. **Reduction and End of Commotion Levels:** Noise is the fundamental communication boundary which must be overcome on need premise. It is vital to recognize the wellspring of commotion and after that dispense with that source.

d. **Active Listening:** Listen mindfully and painstakingly. There is a contrast in the middle of "tuning in" and "hearing". Dynamic listening means hearing with legitimate comprehension of the message that is listened. By making inquiries the speaker can guarantee whether his/her message is comprehended or not by the receiver in the same terms as proposed by the speaker.

e. **Emotional State:** During communication one should make successful utilization of non-verbal communication. He/she ought not demonstrate his/her feelings while communication as the receiver may misconstrue the message being conveyed. For instance, if the transport of the message is in an awful disposition then the receiver may feel that the information being conveyed is bad.

f. **Simple Organizational Structure:** The organizational structure ought not be unpredictable. The quantity of progressive levels should be ideal. There should be a perfect compass of control inside of the organization. Less complex the organizational structure, more successful will be the communication.

g. **Avoid Information Overload:** The supervisors should know how to organize their work. They ought not over-burden themselves with the work. They should invest quality energy with their subordinates and should listen to their issues and feedbacks effectively.

h. **Give Constructive Feedback:** Avoid giving negative feedback. The substance of the feedback may be negative, however it should be conveyed valuably. Productive feedback will prompt successful communication between the predominant and subordinate.

i. **Proper Media Selection:** The chiefs should legitimately select the medium of communication. Straightforward messages should be passed on orally, similar to eye-to-eye collaboration or gatherings. Utilization of composed method for communication should be empowered for conveying complex messages. For critical messages updates can be given by utilizing composed method for communication, for example, Memos, Notices and so forth.

j. **Flexibility in Meeting the Objectives:** For powerful communication in an organization the chiefs should guarantee that the people are meeting their objectives convenient without skirting the formal channels of communication. There ought not be much weight on workers to meet their objectives.

6.32 BODY LANGUAGE

Body language is a vital form of communication, which can make or break your presentation. It is an essential part of emotional intelligence, which can help you bond with another person. When your body language is deliberate, it shows that you are in control and that you are happy to be where you are, doing what you are doing.

By following the body language guidelines below, you will be able to strengthen the effectiveness of your oral presentation:

Posture

Posture conveys a lot about our level of confidence. Good posture gives the impression of authority and confidence. A natural, straight open-body position is best. Let your arms rest in a relaxed way at your sides, so you do not appear stiff or rigid. Remember, the audience members want you to behave normally; they do not want to see you uncomfortable or suffering, as it makes them uncomfortable too.

Things to avoid:

- arms folded across your chest, which may make you slouch, and makes you appear closed, disconnected from the audience.
- arms clasped behind the back military style, which makes you appear too aloof.
- hands on hips, which makes you appear too matronly, like you are about to scold someone;

Gestures

From an open body position, your arms will be free to gesture as they would in normal conversation in order to support your words and emphasize certain points. In most professional presentations, you can add movement by simply pointing to the important features of your presentation.

Walking

Controlled walking can add to the effectiveness of your message. If you stay glued to one spot, you might appear rigid, inexperienced or terrified. Your movement forces the audience to refocus its attention on you and creates interest. However, make sure you move about in a relaxed, natural way.

REVIEW QUESTIONS WITH ANSWERS

1. Multiple Choice Questions

1. ________ is a relatively enduring pattern of thoughts, feelings, and behaviour which differentiate person from each other.
   a. Personality b. Personality development
   c. Social interaction d. Persona
2. Personality is derived from Latin word - "persona", meaning:
   a. Mask b. Mark
   c. Mesk d. Maek
3. According to Davis, personality is a psychic phenomenon which is:
   a. Organic b. Social
   c. A mask d. Combination of organic and social
4. ________ considers personality as a certain style which is peculiar to the individual and is determined by the characteristic organization of mental trends, complexes, emotions and sentiments.
   a. Psychological b. Sociology
   c. Attitude d. Value of person
5. ________ considers personality in terms of the status of the person in the group, like how he/she consider his/her conception about his role in the group of which he/she is a member.
   a. Psychological b. Sociology
   c. Attitude d. Value of person
6. Personality is:
   a. Not related only to body structure, but it includes both the structure and dynamics.
   b. An indivisible unit.
   c. Unique for every individual.
   d. All of the above
7. Personality is the combination of ________ factors.
   a. One b. Two

c. Three d. Four

8. Environment in which we live also effect on culture and the geographical environment sometimes determines cultural variability is ________.
   a. Ecological environment b. Social environment
   c. Physical environment d. Cultural environment
9. Personality is an individual aspect of culture, whereas ________ is a collective aspect of personality.
   a. Heredity b. Culture
   c. Particular Experiences d. None of the above
10. Personality is not just one or more aspects of behaviour, but it is one's total integrated behaviour, this characteristic of personality is known as:
    a. Organization b. Consistency or stability
    c. Dynamic d. Self-consciousness
11. Self-esteem reflects a person's subjective _______evaluation of his or her own worth.
    a. Mental b. Emotional
    c. Physical d. Social
12. ________ is the self-concept is what we think about the self.
    a. Self-Evaluation b. Self-Esteem
    c. Self-Efficiency d. Self-Analysis
13. Self Esteem is:
    a. A degree to which you value yourself.
    b. Thoughts and feelings about yourself and your place in the world.
    c. Both a and b
    d. None of the above
14. Elements of Self Esteem are:
    a. Self-confidence b. Self-respect
    c. Self-acceptance d. All of the above
15. ________ of an individual is the source of mental health.
    a. Self-confidence b. Self-respect
    c. Self-value d. Self-acceptance
16. ___________is the result of one's own evaluation based on many factor.
    a. Self-Esteem
    b. Self-Evaluation
    c. Self-Efficiency
    d. Self-Analysis
17. Self Esteem is important because:
    a. You believe, that you are worthy of happiness and of respect.
    b. It is the last step in believing in you and it builds self-confidence.
    c. It does not have a profound effect on your thinking, emotions, happiness, desires, values, and goals.
    d. You cannot feel respect and be proud even if you make a mistake.
18. Self-Esteem come from:
    a. Talk, support and spending time with your family.
    b. Your friends support and respect.
    c. Teachers who encourages you and are proud of your work.
    d. All of the above
19. To convert low self Esteem to Healthy one, you need to:
    a. Not to be kind to yourself and respect yourself
    b. Never compare yourself with others
    c. No need to Stay away from the negative self-talk
    d. Criticizing yourself
20. __________ is the extent of one's belief in its own ability to complete the task and reach towards its goals.
    a. Self-Esteem b. Self-Evaluation
    c. Self-Efficiency d. Self-Analysis
21. The following is (are) non-verbal communication:
    a. Facial expression b. Appearance
    c. Posture d. All of the above
22. The handshake that conveys confidence is:
    a. Limp b. Firm
    c. Loose d. None of these
23. Communication is the task of imparting:

a. Training b. Information
c. Knowledge d. Message

24. The whole concept of achieving success begins with how you:
a. Behave b. Think
c. Work d. All of the above

25. Which law restricts corporate communications for publicly traded companies before and during the period that new securities are being registered?
a. Securities Act of 1933 b. Sarbanes-Oxley Act of 2002
c. Investment Advisers Act of 1940 d. Investment Company Act of 1934

26. Which of the following entities cannot used for libel?
a. A politician
b. A private citizen
c. A house of worship
d. A government institution

27. What public relations pioneer is credited with being the first practitioner to insist on "a place at the management table":
a. Carl Byoir b. Edward Bernays
c. Doris Fleischman d. Arthur Page

28. What World War I-era organization introduced decentralized publicity "drives" as a strategy to mobilize U.S. public opinion to support the war?
a. The Creel Committee b. The Red Cross
c. The Council on Public Relations d. The Office of War Information

29. _____________means being specific, definite and vivid.
a. Consideration b. Completeness
c. Concreteness d. Conciseness

30. When speaking to business associates or customers, always open the conversation to questions and __________.
a. Clarify b. Clarifications
c. Confidence d. Correctness

2. State True or False for the following:

1. Self-esteem reflects a person's overall subjective emotional evaluation of his or her own worth.
2. Motivation is a theoretical construct which is used to explain the appearance of the person.
3. Body language or Posture, is a verbal form of communication.
4. Hygiene is a set of practices which are performed for the preservation of health.
5. Every person has a unique personality which characterizes an individual.
6. Time management starts with the choices and decisions you make based on the values you hold.
7. Time is precious, some respond to this fact of life with focus and purpose whereas others freak out.
8. Your daily plan should not revolve around working on tasks and activities.
9. Stress is an emotional/bodily reaction to physical, psychological or emotional demands.
10 Attitudes is defined as response to people, place, things or events in life.
11. It is not necessary for a speaker to solicity a warm response from an audience, thus a speaker should never smile.
12. If it is necessary to read a speech from a manuscript, you should first apologize for having to read the speech.
13. A human-interest story is considered to be an effective opening for a speech.
14. Eye contact with the entire audience is very important for any good speaker.
15. When using a visual aid in public speaking, it is not necessary to maintain eye contact with your audience as you describe the visual aid.

3. Match the following:

1. Communication	a. Level of confidence
2. Feedback	b. To share
3. Message	c. Reaction or response

4. Conference	d. Fundamental thought
5. Posture conveys	e. Forms of formal communication
6. Poor Self Esteem	f. Feel good
7. Healthy Self Esteem	g. Negative feelings
8. Etiquettes	h. Non-verbal
9. Attitude	i. Code of behaviour
10. Gestures	j. Mental and emotional entity

4. Fill in the blanks:

1. Personality has existence only in relation to the ________.
2. ________ is the capacity that a person has to introspect, it includes gaining an understanding of and insight into one's strengths.
3. To understand our personality, we need to understand the ________.
4. In social psychology, ________ is the process of looking at oneself to assess aspects which are important to one's identity.
5. ________ is a process of communication by which one person reveals information about himself or herself to another.
6. ________ is a person's belief in his or her ability to complete a future task or solve a future problem.
7. ________ is an ability to do what needs to be done, without the influence from other people or situations
8. There are a number of ______ involved in self-motivation.
9. ________ is a kind of planning and exercising conscious control over the amount of time spent on the specific activities.
10. Time management include creating an environment conducive to ______.
11. The general style of a ______ relies upon the relationship between the groups concerned.
12. The most critical component has to guarantee in any business letter is ______.
13. A letter of ________ for a gathering that offered you some assistance with getting an occupation ought to be proficient and respectful.
14. A ________ letter that requests information should make the request specific and entirely understandable.
15. Business reports are ________ that present data and information to diverse per users.

Answers

1. 1. b 2. a 3. d 4. a 5. b 6. d
7. d 8. c 9. b 10. a 11 c 12 b
13. c 14. d 15. c 16. a 17. a 18. d
19. b 20. c 21. d 22. b 23. b 24. d
25. a 26. d 27. d 28. a 29. c 30. b

2. 1. T 2. F 3. F 4. T 5. T 6. T
7. T 8. F 9. T 10. T 11 F 12 F
13. T 14. T 15. F

3. 1. b 2. c 3. d 4. e 5. a 6. g
7. f 8. i 9. j 10. h

4. 1. External World 2. Self-Awareness
3. Nature of our mind 4. Self-Analysis
5. Self-Disclosure 6. Self-Efficacy
7. Self-Motivation 8. Skills
9. Time management 10. Effectiveness
11. Letter 12. Exactness
13. Thankfulness 14. Business
15. Documents

Short Answers Questions

1. Write short notes on the following:
(a) Stress
(b) Attitude
(c) Time management

Ans a. Stress is an emotional/bodily reaction to physical, psychological or emotional demands.

b. It is defined as response to people, place, things or events in life. Basically, a person's viewpoint, mind set and belief makes an attitude.

c. Time management is a kind of planning and exercising conscious control over the amount of time spent on the specific activities, to increase effectiveness, efficiency or productivity.

2. What is Personality?

Ans Personality is the constant pattern of thinking, feeling and acting. It may be considered as a combination of individual thought, characteristics, behaviours, attitude or it is the product of social interaction in group life as every person living in society has different traits such as skin, color, weight, etc.

3. What do you mean by an Attitude?

Ans Attitude is a psychological construct, or its a mental and emotional entity which inheres in, or characterizes a person. It is an acquired state through experiences. It is an individual's predisposed state of mind regarding a value and it is precipitated through a responsive expression toward a person, place, thing, or event which influences individual's thought and action. An attitude is a persistent tendency which is to feel and then behave in a particular way toward some object.

4. Define Gestures.

Ans It is a form of non-verbal communication in which body actions communicates a particular message, either with or without speech. Gestures includes the movement of the hands, face, or other parts of the body.

5. How will you develop a positive personality?

Ans To develop a positive personality:

- Have a Positive Outlook in Life.
- Entertain Positive Thoughts.
- Maintain a Positive Attitude.

6. What are causes of Stress?

Ans Causes of Stress are:

- Expectations of others or which we place on yourself.
- Physical environment, which include noise, movement etc.
- Internal environment such as academic pressure, frustration, social life, etc.

7. What are different ways to manage stress?

Ans Ways to manage stress are:

- Add balance to life.
- Know your strength and weakness.
- Exercise regularly.

8. How stress effects our Health?

Ans When we are in a stressful situation, we may notice that our heartbeat speeds up, our breathing gets faster, our muscles tense, and we start sweating. This kind of stress is short-term and temporary or acute stress, and our body usually recovers quickly from it.

9. What are different elements of Communication?

Ans Different elements of Communication are Connection, Sender/Encoder, Message, Medium, Recipient/Decoder and Feedback.

10. Write any two main objectives of communication.

Ans The main objectives of communication are:

- **Conveying the right message:** The main objective of communication is to pass on the right message to one side individual, i.e., to the individual for whom it is implied.
- **Effectiveness of policies:** The organization defines policies and projects to manage the workforce. These should be conveyed appropriately to the individuals who are truly responsible for the execution of work to accomplish the organizational objectives.

11. Explain different types of attitude.

Ans There are three types of attitude:

- **Positive attitude:** Individual will pay attention to the good in people. Situation, event, etc. They will not consider a mistake or failure as a hurdle but as an opportunity. They learn from mistakes and move forward in life.
- **Negative attitude:** Individual will ignore the good and pay attention to the bad in people, situation, events, etc. They also complain about changes, rather than adapting to the changing environment. They blame their failure on others.

- **Neutral attitude:** individual do not give enough importance to situations or events. They ignore the problem, leaving it for someone else to solve. They do not feel the need to change.

12. Define Etiquettes. What are good Etiquettes?

Ans Etiquettes is a code of behaviour which delineates expectations for social behaviour according to contemporary conventional norms within a society, social class, or group. Good etiquettes are:

- Hold doors open for other people
- Speak polity
- Listen to another person
- Don't speak loud on your cell phone.

13. What are two main approaches to the study of personality?

Ans The two main approaches to the study of personality are:

(a) Psychological: It considers personality as a certain style which is peculiar to the individual and is determined by the characteristic organization of mental trends, complexes, emotions and sentiments. The psychological approach enables a person to understand the phenomena of personality disorganization and the role of wishes, of mental conflict.

(b) Sociological: It considers personality in terms of the status of the person in the group, like how he/she consider his/her conception about his role in the group of which he/she is a member. Basically, what others think of us also plays a very important role in the formation of our personality.

14. What are the characteristics of personality?

Ans The characteristics of personality are:

(a) It is not related only to body structure, but it includes both the structure and dynamics.

(b) It is unique for every individual.

(c) It expresses consistency and regularity.

(d) It is defined in terms of behaviour.

15. What are the factors of Personality?

Ans Personality is the combination of four factors:

(a) Physical Environment: Environment in which we live also effect on culture and the geographical environment sometimes determines cultural variability. Also, physical environment determines the cultural development and the culture in turn determines personality, so the relationship between personality and environment becomes clear.

(b) Heredity: Similarities in man's personality is due to his common heredity. Every human group inherits the same general set of biological needs and capacities which explain some of our similarities in personality. Man, originates from the union of male and female germ cells into a single cell which is formed at the moment of conception.

(c) Culture: Personality is the subjective aspect of culture and regarded as two sides of the same coin. Personality is an individual aspect of culture, whereas culture is a collective aspect of personality."

(d) Particular Experiences: Personality can also be determined by the particular and unique experiences. There are two types of experiences one which is from continuous association with one's group, and the other arise suddenly. The people who meet daily has a major influence on personality. The personality of parents affect more a child's personality.

16. Explain any two determinants which affects personality.

Ans The determinants which affects personality are:

(a) Self-Awareness: Self-awareness is the capacity that a person has to introspect, it includes gaining an understanding of and insight into one's strengths, qualities, weakness, defects, ideas, thoughts, beliefs, ideals, responses, reactions, attitude, emotions and motivations.

(b) Self-Discipline: It is the suppression of base desires, which is understood as a form of self-control restraint and control. Discipline is when one uses reason to determine the best course of action regardless of one's desires, which may be the opposite of excited.

17. Why Self Esteem is important?

Ans Self Esteem is important because it impact on life and choices of an individual. Self-value of an individual is the source of mental health. Self Esteem is the idea which you have about yourself like how valuable and important you think you are. It is the result of one's own evaluation based on many factors. It involves self-beliefs, emotions such as accomplishment, depression, pride and humiliation as gathered or accumulated in our own mind.

18. What is self-motivation?

Ans It is an ability to do what needs to be done, without the influence from other people or situations. People with self-motivation can find a reason and strength to complete a task without giving up.

It is the force which drives you to do things. Self-motivation is a key life skill of personal development and an emotional intelligence.

19. Explain different types of Vertical Communication.

Ans Vertical communication is of the following two types:

(a) Downward Communication: The communication by top hierarchy with their subordinates is called downward communication. This communication includes orders, rules, information, policies, instructions, etc. The chief advantage of the downward communication is that the subordinates get useful timely information, which helps them in their work performance.

(b) Upward Communication: This is quite the reverse of the downward communication. This flows from the subordinates to the superiors. The subject matter of this communication includes suggestions, reactions, reports, complaints, etc. This sort of communication helps the superiors in taking decisions.

20. "Writing skills are an important part of communication" Comment.

Ans Writing is a form of communication which allows people to put their feelings and ideas on paper, to organize their knowledge and beliefs into convincing arguments, and to convey meaning through well-constructed text.

Writing skills are an important part of communication, as good writing skills allow you to communicate your message with clarity and ease to a far larger audience than through face-to-face or telephone conversations. You might be called upon to write a report, plan or strategy at work; write a grant application or press release within a volunteering role. A well written CV or resume with no spelling or grammatical mistakes is essential if you want a new job.

21. What are the general guidelines for effective employment interview?

Ans General guidelines for effective employment interview are:

- Be prepared for the interview: Just as the interviewer has to plan out the event in advance, so has the interviewee to be prepared for it. As he/she has no control over the event, he/she has to be more careful at every step. He/she has to face an interviewer or a board of interviewers. He/she must, therefore, be very clear about the purpose of the event.
- Has a presentable appearance: Everybody appreciates a pleasant personality. As in the case of a presentation, so in an interview, the concerned person's appearance is a part of the message. Since an interview is a formal occasion, the interviewee must be formally dressed. Anyone having conventional standards of neatness is likely to have a definite advantage over one casually dressed for an interview.
- Show interest by making effective use of body language: Keeping eye-to-eye contact with the interviewer at once shows that the interviewee is genuinely interested in the event and keen to participate in it. He/she should also sit in a correct, confident posture, straight, balanced and not stiff in the chair offered. The hands should be neatly locked on the lap or comfortably placed on the arms of the chair.

EXERCISE

1. Write short notes on the following:
   (a) Positive attitude
   (b) Self-motivation
   (c) Stress management
   (d) Etiquettes & Manner
   (e) Formal communication
   (f) Resume
   (g) Report
2. What are the Determinants of personality?
3. How a person can build a Positive Personality?
4. Define Self Esteem.
5. From where does Self-Esteem come from?
6. Differentiate between Healthy Self-Esteem and Poor Self-Esteem.
7. What do you mean by Self-Efficacy?
8. Define communication process.
9. What are the objectives of Communication?
10. Briefly explain the categories of Communication.
11. What are the barriers to Communication?
12. What is Presentation?
13. Differentiate between Internal communication and External Communication.
14. Discuss different attribute of communication.
15. What do you mean by Formal and Informal Communication?
16. How will you improve your writing skills?
17. Explain different types of Vertical Communication.

Important Definitions and Terminologies

8-bit, 16-bit, 32-bit

The 8-bit, 16-bit and 32-bit specifications are the computer's internal word size, which is the amount of data the processor can hold in its registers and work on at the same time. Large-scale supercomputers hold 64 bits. All things being equal, a 16-bit computer works twice as fast as an 8-bit computer; however, this specification measures only one aspect of a computer performance.

5G

It is the fifth generation of wireless, popularly known as 5G.

6LoWpan

6LoWPAN is an acronym of IPv6 over Low Power Wireless Personal Area Networks.

Access Bus

Access bus is a new standard intended to connect relatively low-speed devices such as keyboards, mice, modems, and printers.

Access time

The time interval between the instant at which data is called from a storage device and the instant delivery begins.

Acoustic sensors

Acoustic sensors measure sound levels and convert that information into digital or analog data signals.

Active Transducers

In *Active Transducers,* the energy from the input is used as a control signal in the process of transferring energy from power supply to proportional output.

Actuators

Actuators are devices which is a contrast to sensors. It transforms electrical signals into physical movements.

Alphanumeric

A combination of letters, digits, and special characters used to form an expression, such as a part number. An example of an alphanumeric expression follows:

PN A-10036-001

Notice that alphabetical, numeric, spaces, and punctuation characters may exist in an alphanumeric expression.

ALU (Arithmetic Logic Unit)

It is one of the components of the Central Processing Unit (CPU) of the computer which performs all mathematical and logical operations.

AMQP

Advanced Message Queuing Protocol (AMQP) is an open source published standard for asynchronous messaging by wire.

Analog sensors

Analog sensors produce an analog output i.e. a continuous output signal with respect to the quantity being measured and typically require analog-to-digital conversion.

Analog transmission

A continuously varying electromagnetic wave that may be propagated over a variety of media.

Analytical Reports

These types of business reports include information along with analysis or interpretation from the report's writer or in response to the person who requested the report.

Architecture

The overall design, construction, organization and interconnecting of the various components of a computer system. It refers particularly to the processor hardware and the size and ordering sequence of its bytes.

Arduino

Arduino first and foremost is an open-source computer hardware and software company.

Arduino Uno

The Arduino Uno is one kind of microcontroller board based on ATmega328.

ARM Microcontroller

The ARM microcontroller stands for Advance Risk Machine; it is one of the extensive and most licensed processor cores in the world.

Artificial intelligence (AI)

A branch of computer science that deals with computers that possess reasoning, learning, and thinking capabilities that resemble those of human beings.

ASCII (American Standard Code for Information Interchange)

A standard coding system for computers. ASCII-7 is a 7-bit code and its extended version ASCII-8 is an 8-bit code.

Attitude

Attitude is a psychological construct, or its a mental and emotional entity which inheres in, or characterizes a person.

Authorization

The process of determining what types of activities are permitted. Usually, authorization is in the context of authentication: once you have authenticated a user, they may be authorized different types of access or activity.

AVR microcontroller

AVR microcontroller was developed in the year of 1996 by Atmel Corporation. The AVR microcontrollers are modified harvard RISC architecture with separate memories for data and program and speed of AVR is high when compare to 8051 and PIC.

Bandwidth

The range of frequencies available for data transmission. The wider the bandwidth of a communications system, the more data it can transmit in a given period of time. It is expressed in Kilobits per seconds. The bandwidth determines the rate at which information can be sent through a communication channel.

Bar Code

A coding structure in which characters are represented by means of a series of parallel bars.

Baud

A unit for measuring data transmission speed. It is used to describe the capacity of a carrier. In general usage, baud is identical to bits per second.

Baud rate

The speed of data transmission, usually in bits per second.

BCD (Binary Coded Decimal)

One of the early coding systems used by computers which is based on the idea of converting each digit of a decimal number into its binary equivalent rather than converting the entire decimal value into a pure binary form.

Binary operators

Operators that act upon two operands are referred to as binary operators.

BIOS (Basic Input Output System)

BIOS is responsible for handling the details of input/output operations including the task of relating a program's logical records to a peripheral device physical records.

Biosensor

A Biosensor is an analytical device that detects changes in Biological processes and converts them into an electrical signal.

Bit

Stands for binary digit. The values are 1 or 0 (zero).

BLE

BLE stands for Bluetooth Low Energy. Bluetooth Low Energy uses the same 2.4 GHz radio frequencies as classic Bluetooth but uses less power to transmit distance over a short distance.

Blockchain

Blockchain is the technology of Digital Crypto-Currency Bitcoin.

Bluetooth

An open specification for short-range wireless transmission of voice and data that is currently under development. Bluetooth provides a simple, low-cost method of linking Personal Digital Assistants (PDAs), cellular phones, laptops, and other information appliances.

Boolean

Variables of this type can take only one of the two values, True or False.

Boolean Data Type

Comparisons in Python can generate only one of two possible responses: True or False. These data types are called booleans.

Bootloader

Bootloader, is basically the initial piece of code which runs whenever any micro-controller is powered up or resets.

Bots

A bot short for "robot" and also called an Internet bot is an automated program that runs over the Internet.

Breadboard

A breadboard is a circuit board that is used to make temporary circuits and prototyping.

Brute force

A brute force attack (also known as brute force cracking) is an attempt to crack a password or username or find a hidden web page, or find the key used to encrypt a message, using a trial and error approach.

Bug

An error in a computer program that causes it to produce an incorrect or unexpected result.

Campus network

A set of LAN segments and building networks in a geographical area that is a few miles in diameter.

Capacitor

A capacitor is a device that stores electrical energy in an electric field.

CISC

CISC stands for complex instruction set computer. It allows the user to insert a single instruction as an alternative to many simple instructions.

Clock Pulse

A clock pulse is a signal that is used to synchronize the operations of an electronic system. Clock Pulses are continuous, precisely spaced changes in voltage.

Clock rate

Inverse of clock cycle time, usually measured in Mhz.

Closed loop control system

Control system in which the output has an effect on the input quantity in such a manner that the input quantity will adjust itself based on the output generated is called *closed loop control system*

Cloud computing

Cloud computing or on-demand computing is an Internet-based computing service which involves the use of the network of remote servers rather than local server.

CoAP

CoAP is an internet-utility protocol created specifically for connecting devices with limited (constrained) resources such as a small memory or short battery life.

COM1, COM2, COM3, COM4 or comm port

Serial ports used for connecting peripherals, such as, mouse, joystick etc.

Comment

Any text to the right of # symbol.

Compiler

A system software package that converts a high-level language program to machine language codes.

Compound statement

Group of statements.

Concatenation

Adds values on either side of the operator.

Conditional Branching

It is the ability of a program to decide whether or not to execute code based on the value of an expression.

Conditional Transfer

An instruction that may change the sequence of instructions being followed, depending upon the result of an operation.

Configuration

An initial set of system values, such as the number of buffers DOS will use, the number of simultaneously open files it will allow, and specific devices that will be supported.

Connector

A symbol used to transfer flow between different pages of a lengthy flowchart.

Constants

Fixed values in a program.

Control Registers

CPU registers employed to control CPU operation. Most of these registers are not user-visible.

Counter

A variable used to count something, usually initialized to zero and then incremented.

Cryptography

A system of secret communications to improve the security of confidential computerized files.

Cycle time

The time interval between the instant at which a read/write command is given to a memory and the instant when the next such instruction can be issued to the memory (also known as memory cycle time).

Dashboard

Dashboard displays information about the IoT ecosystem to users and enables them to control their IoT ecosystem.

Data-link layer

Layer 2 of the OSI reference model. This layer provides reliable transit of data across a physical link. The data-link layer is concerned with physical addressing, network topology, line discipline, error notification, ordered delivery of frames, and flow control.

Data type

The kind of data that a variable may hold in a programming language is called the *data type*.

DDS

DDS (Data Distribution Service) is an IoT standard for real-time, scalable and high-performance machine-to-machine communication.

Debugging

A process of finding and removing the bugs from a computer program.

Definite Loops

The simplest kind of loop is called a definite loop. This is a loop that will execute a definite number of times.

Delimiter

A character or string used to indicate where a string should be split.

Denial of service attacks

Denial of service attacks prevents the legal users of System from accessing or using the resources, information or capabilities of the system.

Digital sensors

Digital sensors work with discrete or digital data that can be directly interfaced with the digital controller.

Digital signal

A discrete or discontinuous signal, such as voltage pulses.

Dumb terminal

A terminal that has no local processing capability.

Duplex

A data communication facility on which data can be transmitted in two directions. A facility where information travels both ways.

Eavesdropping

It refers to unauthorised access to another person's or organization's data while the data is on its way on the network.

Electronic mail

A general term to describe the transmission of messages by the use of computing systems and telecommunications facilities.

Embedded system

An Embedded system is a system that has computer hardware and software embedded to perform specific tasks.

Encryption

Converting stored or transmitted data to a coded form in order to prevent it from being read by unauthorized persons. Also application of a specific algorithm to alter the appearance of data, making it incomprehensible to those who are not authorized to see the information.

EPROM (Erasable Programmable Read Only Memory)

A semiconductor memory which allows the eraser of the information stored in it by exposure to ultraviolet light. Later new information can be stored in it.

Ergonomics

The science that focuses on how machines and other things should be designed and arranged so that people can interact with them in a comfortable and efficient way.

Error

A procedure that leads to an incorrect result.

Error Message

A statement that appears on your screen when your computer is unable to continue processing. The message tells you what the problem is and how to solve it.

Exceptions

An exception is an error that occurs when a program is executed.

Executable file

Any "runnable" application program with a file extension of . COM, .EXE, or .BAT. The term is sometimes extended to include files that don't run by themselves but do contain program code, such as .OVL and .PIF files.

Execution time

The total time required to execute a program on a particular system is called its execution time for that computer system.

Expression

Any valid combination of operators, literals and variables.

Extended ASCII

Extended ASCII provides added capability by allowing for 128 additional characters, such as accented letters, graphics characters, and special symbols.

Fiber-optic cable

Physical medium capable of conducting modulated light transmission. Fiber-optic cable is not susceptible to electromagnetic interference, and is capable of high data rates. Also a data transmission medium made of tiny threads of glass or plastic that can transmit huge amount of information at the speed of light.

File Transfer Protocol

Permits files to be transferred from one computer to another using a TCP connection. A related but less common file transfer protocol. Trivial File Transfer Protocol (TFTP), uses UDP rather than TCP to transfer file data.

Firewall

Router or remote-access server (or several routers or access servers) designated as a buffer between connected networks. A firewall uses access lists and other methods to ensure the security of a network. Also a system or combination of systems that enforces a boundary between two or more networks.

float

Numbers with fractions or decimal points.

Fog Computing

Fog computing is a type of network architecture that links cloud computing to the Internet of Things (IoT).

Function

A named sequence of statements.

Gestures

It is a form of non-verbal communication in which body actions communicates a particular message, either with or without speech.

Global scope

A global scope refers to the objects available through the code execution since their inception.

Half duplex

Capability for data transmission in only one direction at a time between a sending station and a receiving station.

HTTP

Hypertext transport protocol, the Internet protocol that defines how a Web server responds to requests for files, made via anchors and URLs.

Hydraulic actuators

Hydraulic actuators consist of a cylinder or fluid motor that utilizes hydraulic power to facilitate mechanical process.

I/O (Input/Output)

Pertaining to the techniques, media, and devices used for man-machine interaction

Identifiers

Names given to program elements, such as variables, functions, and arrays.

IDLE

An Integrated Development Environment. It is a basic editor and interpreter environment.

IIoT

The Industrial Internet of Things (IIoT) is the use of Internet of Things (IoT) technologies in manufacturing.

Incrementation

A process wherein numerical value added to the variable each time one goes round the loop.

Infinite loop

A loop that never ends.

Infrared sensors (IR)

An infrared sensor is a sensor which is used to sense certain characteristics of its surroundings by either emitting or detecting infrared radiation.

int

Basic integer data type.

Interface

The point at which independent systems or diverse groups interact. It consists of the devices, rules or conventions by which one component of a system communicates with another. It is also the point of communication between a person and a computer.

Internet Protocol (IP)

A low-level protocol that routes packets of data across separate networks tied together by routers to form the Internet or an intranet. Data travels in packets called IP datagrams.

Interoperability

Interoperability is the ability of two or more systems or components to exchange data and use information.

Interpreter

An interpreter is a program that translates one statement of a high-level language program in to machine codes and executes it and then translates and executes the next statement of the program and so forth.

IoT

Internet of Things (IoT) is a system of interconnected objects, usually called smart devices, through the Internet.

IoT ecosystem

The IoT ecosystem is a connection of various kind of devices that sense and analyze the data and communicates with each other over the networks.

IP Spoofing

An attack whereby a system attempts to illicitly impersonate another system by using its IP network address.

IPv6

IPv6 is the latest revision of the Internet Protocol (IP), the communications protocol that provides an identification and location system for computers on networks.

ISO

International Organization for Standardization. International organization that is responsible for a wide range of standards, including those relevant to networking. ISO developed the OSI reference model, a popular networking reference model.

ISO protocol

A communication protocol to interconnect geographically dispersed heterogeneous computers. This protocol has been standardized by the International Standards Organization (ISO).

Iteration

A process of executing a statement or a set of statements repeatedly.

Jumper wires

Jumper wires are simply wires that have connector pins at each end, allowing them to be used to connect two points to each other without soldering.

K (Kilo)

Used to represent $2^{10} = 1024$ in computers only.

Latency

Delay between the time a device requests access to a network and the time it is granted permission to transmit.

LCD

(Liquid Crystal Display) is the technology used for displays in notebook and other smaller computers.

LED

Light Emitting Diode or simply LED is one of the most commonly used sources of light now-a-days.

Letterhead

Organizations usually use printed-paper where heading or letterhead is primarily designed at the top of the sheet. It bears all the necessary information about the organization's identity.

LiFi(Light Fidelity)

It is a new wireless technology that offers high speed data transmission based on Visible Light Communication (VLC) principle.

Lilypad Arduino USB

The LilyPad Arduino USB is the perfect board for e-textiles and wearables projects.

Local Area Network (LAN)

Network that connects computers that are in the same building or campus, usually with cables.

Local scope

A local scope refers to the local objects available in the current function.

Logical operators

Symbols used to show a logical relationship between two data items.

Loop

A sequence of instructions that is executed repeatedly until a terminal condition occurs.

Looping

A process of repeating a series of steps a certain number of times.

LoRaWAN

LoRaWAN is a newly developed long-range wide-area network wireless technology designed for IoT applications.

LTE-A

LTE-A, or LTE Advanced, delivers an important upgrade to LTE technology by increasing not only its coverage, but also reducing its latency and raising its throughput.

Microcontroller

Microcontroller is like a mini computer with a CPU along with RAM, ROM, serial ports, timers, and IO peripherals all embedded on a single chip.

Microcontroller 8051

8051 microcontroller is an 8-bit family of microcontroller is developed by the Intel in the year 1981. This is one of the popular families of microcontroller.

Microprocessor

A LSI chip which contains the entire CPU of a computer, except main memory.

Millisecond

One-thousandth of a second.

Module

A file containing definitions, i.e., functions and statements.

Modulo operator(%)

The % operator finds the modulus of its first operand relative to the second.

MQTT

Message Queue Telemetry Transport (MQTT) is an open light-weight easy-to-implement messaging protocol for M2M communications.

Network

An inter-connection of computer systems and/or peripheral devices with carriers and data communications devices for the purpose of exchanging data and information.

NFC

NFC is a set of the communication-based protocol used for communication between two devices in the range of approximately 10 cm.

Open-loop control system

Open-loop control system is a control system where its control action only depends on input signal and does not depend on its output response.

OSI reference model

Open System Interconnection reference model. Network architectural model that consists of seven layers, each of which specifies particular network functions such as addressing, flow control, error control encapsulation, and reliable message transfer. The OSI reference model is used universally as a method for teaching and understanding network functionality.

Passive Transducers

In Passive Transducers, the energy from the input is directly converted into the output. For example, a Thermocouple is a passive transducer.

Password

A code by which a user gains access to a computer system. It is used for security purposes.

Personality

Personality is the constant pattern of thinking, feeling and acting.

Phishing

It is an attempt of acquiring sensitive information such as usernames, passwords, and credit card details, by hacker in an electronic communication.

PIC Microcontroller

Peripheral Interface Controller (PIC) is microcontroller developed by a Microchip, PIC microcontroller is fast and simple to implement program when you contrast other microcontrollers like 8051.

Potentiometer

A potentiometer is used to detect the position. It generally has various ranges of resistors connected to different poles of the switch.

Proximity sensor

A device that detects the presence or absence of a nearby object, or properties of that object, and converts it into signal which can be easily read by user or a simple electronic instrument without getting in contact with them.

Pseudocode

A program analysis tool that is used for planning program logic. It is an imitation of actual computer instructions written in ordinary English language.

Ransomware

Ransomware is a type of malicious software that blocks access to a computer system or data, usually by encrypting it.

Relational operators

It compares the values of its operands.

Renesas Microcontroller

Renesas is latest automotive microcontroller family that offers high performance feature with exceptionally low power consumption over a wide and versatile extend of items.

Report

A report, by definition, is a "statement describing what has happened" or "describing a state of affairs".

Resistor

A resistor is an electrical component that limits or regulates the flow of electrical current in an electronic circuit.

Resume

Resume sets out your skills and experience, it should demonstrate potential employer that why they should hire you above any of the other skilled candidates who have presented themselves for employment.

RFID

RFID stands for Radio Frequency Identification. The acronym refers to small electronic devices that consist of a small chip and an antenna.

RISC

RISC stands for Reduced Instruction Set Computers. It reduces the operational time by shortening the clock cycle per instruction.

Scope

The scope of a variable determines the portion of the program where you can access a particular identifier.

Security

The issues of protecting data from unauthorized use, tampering, or destruction are collectively referred to as security issues.

Self-motivation

It is an ability to do what needs to be done, without the influence from other people or situations.

Self esteem

Self esteem is crucial and is a cornerstone of a positive attitude towards living.

Sensors

Sensors are a key component that helps you to collect live data from the surrounding environment.

Serial port

Connector on your computer that is used for connecting Modem for serial communication. You can also connect joystick, mouse and serial printers to a serial port.

Server

Node or software program that provides services to clients. Also the main high-capacity computer where all the information is stored. Also a system that shares resources with one or more workstations on a network.

Session layer

Layer 5 of the OSI reference model. This layer establishes, manages, and terminates sessions between applications and manages data exchange between presentation-layer entities.

Sigfox

Sigfox is a cellular style system that enables remote devices to connect using ultra-narrow band, to provide low power low data rate, and low cost communications for remote connected devices.

Snooping

Snooping refers to unauthorized access to someone else's data, email or computer activity.

Statement

A unit of code.

Stepper Motors

Stepper motors (DC motor) are electromechanical, converting a digital pulse into rotational movement or displacement.

Strain Gauge

A strain gauge is used to detect pressure when a load is applied. It works on the principle of resistance.

Stress

Stress is an emotional/bodily reaction to physical, psychological or emotional demands.

String

A string is an ordered sequence of characters.

Substring

A part or a subset of another string.

TCP/IP

A protocol stack, designed to connect different network on which the Internet is based. The suite includes protocols for remote login (Telnet), file transfer (FTP), E-mail (SMTP), etc. TCP/IP can work with any hardware or operating system.

Thermistor

It is a temperature sensitive resistor that changes its physical resistance with the change in temperature.

Thermocouple

These are voltage devices that indicate temperature measuring with a change in voltage.

Thread

A very new IP-based IPv6 networking protocol aimed at the home automation environment.

Transducer

A transducer is a device that converts one form of energy into another form of energy.

Unicode Strings

Unicode strings give us a consistent way to process character data from a variety of character encodings.

Variable

A variable is a programming construct that uses a certain part of memory to represent a specific item of data that we wish to keep track of in a program.

Verify/Compile

It checks the errors present in your sketch and informs you about the memory space occupied by the variables in the console area.

Virus

A replicating code segment that attaches itself to a program or data file.

void loop()

This function is the next important function in the Sketch. It consists of that part of the code that needs to be continuously executed in a loop over and over again.

void setup()

This is the first routine that begins when the Arduino starts functioning.

while Loop

It evaluates a test expression before allowing entry into the loop.

Worm

Worm is a program made to replicate automatically. A worm replicates continuously until the entire hard disk space and memory are used up.

WoT

Web of Things (WoT) is a computing concept that describes a future where everyday objects are fully integrated with the Web.

X-10

X-10 is a protocol for communication among IoT devices, mainly in the home automation sector.

XMPP

The Extensible Messaging and Presence Protocol (XMPP) is an open technology for real-time communication originally designed for chats and messages exchange applications.

Z-Wave

Z-Wave is a wireless network standard that consumes very low power and it is widely used for connecting smart devices in the Internet of Things (IoT).

Zigbee

Zigbee is a low powered, low cost standard on a wireless mesh network designed for battery-powered devices and cheaper alternative to Bluetooth.

Solved Sample Paper–1

Total Time : 3 Hours

Total Marks 100
(Part One - 40 Part Two - 60)

PART – ONE

1. Multiple Choice Questions

1.1 Microcontroller used in Arduino UNO prototyping board is:
a. ATmega328m b. ATmega328p
c. ATmega2560 d. ATmega356p

1.2 Which of the following is not a main element of IoT?
a. People b. Process
c. Security d. Things

1.3 To easily interface add-on modules with Arduino we can use:
a. General PCB b. Connectivity circuit boards
c. Arduino shields d. Other high-end Arduino boards

1.4 Which symbol is used in Arduino to calculate Modulo?
a. #
b. $
c. %
d. !

1.5 With respect to the body language, the handshake conveys the confidence is:
a. Firm
b. Limp
c. Loose
d. Incomplete

1.6 A program written with the IDE for Arduino is called ________.
a. IDE source b. Source code
c. Sketch d. All of the above

1.7 How many digital pins are there on the UNO board?
a. 14
b. 12
c. 16
d. 20

1.8 What is the use of Thermostat in Nest Thermostat E?
a. Save energy
b. Show the use of energy
c. Supports in some devices only
d. Won't work at some conditions

1.9 Which devices measures gases or liquid?
a. Proximity sensor
b. Pressure sensor
c. Temperature sensor
d. Touch sensor

1.10 All code in an Arduino sketch is processed from:
a. Top to bottom b. Bottom to top
c. Any order d. None of these

2. State True or False:

2.1 Arduino program statement for generating one second delay is delay(100);.

2.2 In ATmega328p, p stands for pico power.

2.3 Mirai botnet attack was originated from IoT cameras.

2.4 M135 is one of the commonly used gas sensors in MQ sensor series.

2.5 trim() removes all whitespace characters from a String.

2.6 Arduino provides IDE Environment

2.7 MQTT is created by Andy Stanford-Clark.

2.8 IoT devices are naturally vulnerable to security threats.

2.9 Arduino boards are a Microcontroller which is capable of reading input from sensors to controlling motors and etc.

2.10 Arduino IDE consists of two functions setup() and build().

3. Match the following:

3.1	Default bootloader for Arduino	a.	sketch
3.2	PWM pins in Arduino UNO	b.	0-255
3.3	Informal Communication	c.	Optiboot
3.4	Analog Read method in Arduino UNO returns value range	d.	1999
3.5	Open source Operating System	e.	6
3.6	Program written in Arduino IDE	f.	setup()
3.7	The term "IoT" was coined in	g.	Grapevine
3.8	Single line comment	h.	0-1023
3.9	Analog Write method in Arduino UNO accepts value range	i.	//
3.10	Function called once in Arduino program	j.	Windows
		k.	Linux

4. Fill in the blanks:

a. Thermocouple	b. Massimo Banzi
c. Square	d. Self-Analysis
e. Exhaustive	f. Security
g. Sheilds	h. M2M communication
i. Embedded Controller	j. Self-Disclosure

4.1 __________ are pre built circuit boards that fit on top of Android.

4.2 MQTT is mainly used for __________.

4.3 ________ is a process of communication by which one person reveals information about himself or herself to another.

4.4 __________ is the process of looking at oneself to assess aspects which are important to one's identity.

4.5 PWM is basically, a _______ wave with a varying high and low time.

4.6 The founder of Arduino project is ___________.

4.7 Another name for a microcontroller is ________.

4.8 A ________ converts thermal energy into electrical energy.

4.9 The brute force attacks are known as an ________ key search.

4.10 Passwords are used to improve the ________ of a network.

PART – TWO

(Answer any four questions)

5. a. What is Brute Force Attack?

b. What is the role of setup method in an Arduino program?

6. a. Discuss role of IoT in Home Automation.

b. What is Z-Wave? What are its advantages.

c. What is Internet of Things (IoT)? What is meant by Things in IoT?

7. a. Write important characteristics for IOT Protocols.

b. Why MQTT is considered better than HTTP in IoT?

8. a. Write a program to interface LCD with Arduino board and display "Hello World" on it.

b. Write a program for Sequential LED ON-OFF.

9. Briefly explain the following:

a. Ransomware

b. Control system

c. Microcontrollers

d. Presentation

Answers to Objective Type Questions

1.	1.1	b	1.2	c	1.3	c	1.4	c	1.5	a
	1.6	c	1.7	a	1.8	a	1.9	b	1.10	a
2.	2.1	T	2.2	T	2.3	T	2.4	T	2.5	T
	2.6	T	2.7	T	2.8	T	2.9	T	2.10	F
3.	3.1	c	3.2	f	3.3	g	3.4	h	3.5	k
	3.6	a	3.7	d	3.8	i	3.9	b	3.10	e
4.	4.1	g	4.2	h	4.3	j	4.4	d	4.5	c
	4.6	b	4.7	i	4.8	a	4.9	e	4.10	f

Answers to Descriptive Type Questions

5.a A Brute Force Attack is the simplest method to gain access to a site or server (or anything that is password protected). It tries various combinations of usernames and passwords again and again until it gets in. The longer the password, the more combinations that will need to be tested. However, if the password is weak it could merely take seconds with hardly any effort.

5.b In the setup() function, you set initial conditions of variables when necessary, and run any preliminary code that you only want to run once.

6.a In smart homes, various sensors are deployed, which provide intelligent and automated services to the user. They help in automating daily tasks and help in maintaining a routine for individuals. They help in energy conservation by turning off lights and electronic gadgets automatically. For example, an application can automatically turn on the AC when the humidity rises. Or, when there is a gas leak, it can turn all the lights off. Smart home applications are really beneficial for ill people. Their health is monitored and relatives are informed immediately in case of emergencies.

6.b Z-Wave is a wireless network standard that consumes very low power and it is widely used for connecting smart devices in the Internet of Things (IoT) like home automation, lighting controls, security systems, Energy saving etc.

Advantages of Z-wave are:

(a) Easy to install the system.
(b) Uses low-energy radio waves to communicate.
(c) Uses a simpler protocol than some others, which can enable faster and simpler development.

6.c. Internet of Things (IoT) means when things or objects are more connected to the Internet rather than people. The *Things* in IoT is defined as objects that can be the person or machine with a built-in sensor having IP addresses with the ability to collect and transfer the data over the Internet.

7.a The important characteristics for IOT Protocols are:

(a) Speed: Amount of data that can be transferred / second.
(b) Latency: amount of time a message takes to be transferred.
(c) Power consumption.
(d) Security
(e) Availability of software stacks.

7.b HTTP is the best known protocol that powers the Web (WWW). However because of the high protocol overhead HTTP is not likely to be a major IOT protocol. MQTT (Message Queuing Telemetry Transport) has emerged as the main IOT messaging protocol because it is lightweight and easy to use.

8.a

```
// Arduino Code to print "Hello World!" message on the LCD.
// include the library code:
#include <LiquidCrystal.h>

// Creates an LCD object. Parameters: (rs, enable, d4, d5, d6, d7)
LiquidCrystal lcd(12, 11, 5, 4, 3, 2);
void setup()
{
  // set up the LCD's number of columns and rows:
  lcd.begin(16, 2);
  // Clears the LCD screen and moves the cursor to the upper left corner.
```

(cont...)

```
  lcd.clear();
}
void loop()
{
  // Print a message to the LCD.
  lcd.print(" Hello world!");
  // set the cursor to column 0, line 1
  // (note: line 1 is the second row, since counting begins with 0):
  lcd.setCursor(0, 1);
  // Print a message to the LCD
  lcd.print(" Message printed");
}
```

Figure 1 Program for Q8(a)

8 b

```
//Sketch for Sequential LED ON-OFF
void setup() {
  //set gpio pin {0,1,2,3} as output
  pinMode(0, OUTPUT);
  pinMode(1, OUTPUT);
  pinMode(2, OUTPUT);
  pinMode(3, OUTPUT);
}
void loop() {
  //turn LED ON one by one
  for (int i = 0; i < 4; i++) {
    digitalWrite(i, HIGH);
    delay(1000);
  }
  //turn LED OFF one by one
  for (int i = 3; i >= 0; i--) {
    digitalWrite(i, LOW);
    delay(1000);
  }
}
```

Figure 2 Program for Q8(b)

9.a Ransomware is a form of malware that encrypts a victim's files. The attacker then demands a ransom from the victim to restore access to the data upon payment.

b A control system as a system responds to input signals from the plant (a system to be controlled) and/or an operator and causes the plant or equipment to operate in the desired manner. Control systems usually involve one or more input devices, a controller, one or more output devices, power supplies, and any associated information connections.

c. Microcontrollers (embedded processors) are processors (or specialized microprocessors) that have many peripherals to interact with real-world sensors and actuators. Microcontrollers are typically employed in scenarios that must have low power consumption, operate fan-less, thus must have low power dissipation. Also, often micro-controllers run relatively simpler set of instructions.

d. A presentation is the process of presenting a topic to an audience. It is typically a demonstration, introduction, lecture, or speech meant to inform, persuade, or build good will. A presentation requires you to get a message across to the listeners and contain a 'persuasive' element.

Solved Sample Paper–2

Total Time : 3 Hours

Total Marks 100
(Part One - 40 Part Two - 60)

PART – ONE

1. Multiple Choice Questions

1.1 Botnet is often used to launch __________ attack

a. DoS
b. DDoS
c. Brute force
d. Passive

1.2 The IIoT stands for

a. Indepth Internet of T
b. Innovative Internet of Things
c. Industrial Internet of Things
d. Information Internet of Things

1.3 The default method(s) in Arduino program is/are:

a. Only loop()
b. Only setup()
c. setup() and loop()
d. Can be either loop() or setup()

1.4 Which of the following communication medium supports highest data rate?

a. Optical fiber
b. Wifi
c. Ethernet
d. Bluetooth

1.5 __________ are pre built circuit boards that fit on top of Android.

a. Sensor
b. Data types
c. Breadboard
d. Sheilds

1.6 Arduino shields are also called as __________.

a. Extra peripherals
b. Add on modules
c. Connectivity modules
d. Another Arduinos

1.7 What is the default bootloader of the Arduino UNO?

a. Optiboot bootloader
b. AIR-boot
c. Bare box
d. GAG

1.8 Which is the software or a programming language used for controlling of Arduino?

a. Assembly Language
b. C Languages
c. JAVA
d. Any Language

1.9 Which sensor is LM35?

a. Pressure sensor
b. Humidity sensor
c. Temperature sensor
d. Touch sensor

1.10 Communication is the task of imparting:

a. Training
b. Information
c. Knowledge
d. Message

2. State True or False:

2.1 The thermostat controls half of our energy bills.

2.2 ATmega328p is a microcontroller which is 32KB of flash ROM and 8-bit microcontroller.

2.3 IPv6 over Low power wireless personal area network.

2.4 Motivation is a theoretical construct which is used to explain the appearance of the person.

2.5 Hygiene is a set of practices which are performed for the preservation of health.

2.6 *Associativity* means that in the same expression if you have two operators of the same precedence, they are evaluated from left to right.

2.7 The / operation for integers gives the quotient after division.

2.8 The percentage sign (%) is used as the modulo operator.

2.9 Integrity is a set of rules that limits access to information.

2.10 Injection Injects application code which can execute operating system commands as the user running the web application.

3. Match the following:

3.1	IPv4	a.	Scan content on webpages
3.2	MQTT	b.	32 bit address
3.3	DHT11 sensor	c.	Light weight
3.4	Arduino shields	d.	Temperature & Humidity
3.5	Default bootloader	e.	Add on modules
3.6	Sketch	f.	Optiboot
3.7	Personality	g.	A program written with the IDE for Arduino
3.8	Etiquettes	h.	MACIONIS
3.9	Web crawlers	i.	Scrape content
3.10	Malicious bots	j.	code of behaviour

4. Fill in the blanks:

a. Microcontroller	b. Massimo Banzi
c. Fog Computing	d. Lilypad
e. Kevin Ashton	f. Microprocessor
g. mask	h. Analog
i. Report	j. PWM
k. mirai	l. Nano

4.1 __________ IC contains memory, input-output peripherals along with processing capability.

4.2 Analog Write method is used for __________ pins in Arduino.

4.3 The term Internet of Things was first coined by __________.

4.4 Modern PC has __________ as main component in CPU.

4.5 __________is medium weighted extension of cloud computing in IoT domain.

4.6 __________ is designed to launch botnet attacks rom IoT.

4.7 The founder of Arduino project is __________.

4.8 Personality is derived from Latin word - persona meaning __________.

4.9 The statement describing what has happened is called __________.

4.10 __________ board of Arduino family can be used to sewn into clothing.

PART – TWO

(Answer any four questions)

5. a. What do you mean by determinants of personality? Explain motivation and self-esteem in detail.

b. Write Pros and Cons of Symmetric cryptography algorithms.

6. a. What is Blockchain? How does blockchain works?

b. Differentiate between Microprocessor and Microcontroller.

7. a. Explain Sensors and Actuators with example.

b. How setup() is different from loop()?

8. a. Write a program to interface LED on pin no. 8 and blink with the delay of 1 sec.

b. Write a program that automatically turn lights on when an LDR sensor detects darkness.

9. Briefly explain the following:

a. Stress

b. Botnet

c. Fog Computing

d. 6LoWpan

Answers to Objective Type Questions

1.	1.1	b	1.2	c	1.3	c	1.4	a	1.5	d
	1.6	b	1.7	a	1.8	d	1.9	c	1.10	b
2.	2.1	T	2.2	T	2.3	T	2.4	F	2.5	T
	2.6	T	2.7	T	2.8	T	2.9	F	2.10	T
3.	3.1	b	3.2	c	3.3	d	3.4	e	3.5	f
	3.6	g	3.7	h	3.8	j	3.9	a	3.10	i
4.	4.1	a	4.2	j	4.3	e	4.4	f	4.5	c
	4.6	k	4.7	b	4.8	g	4.9	i	4.10	d

Answers to Descriptive Type Questions

5.a Determinants are some very important traits which affects personality. Firstly, knowing self is must, as it helps in monitoring our self continually and works as a very effective tool to improve our self consistently.

Motivation is a theoretical construct which is used to explain the behaviour. It gives the reasons for people's actions, desires, and needs. Motivation can also be defined as one's direction to behaviour, or what causes a person to want to repeat a behaviour. A motive is what prompts the person to act in a certain way, or at least develop an inclination for specific behaviour.

Self-Esteem reflects a person's overall subjective emotional evaluation of his or her own worth. It is a kind of judgment of oneself and an attitude toward the self. It encompasses of beliefs about oneself, and emotional states.

5.b Pros: Faster than asymmetric cryptography.

Cons: Difficult to distribute and protect the shared secret key securely.

6.a Blockchain is an incorruptible digital ledger of economic transactions that can be programmed to record not only financial transactions but virtually everything of value. In simple terms, it is a decentralized distributed database of immutable records that are managed by a group of computers but not owned by any single entity. It is stored as a database or a flat-file. It is consists of immutable records of data called blocks with are linked using cryptography. It is nothing but a process to encrypt and secure data communication from third parties in reading private messages. Once the data has been recorded, it will not be changed. It works like a digital notary with timestamps to avoid tampering of information.

6.b Difference between Microprocessor and Microcontroller are:

- Microprocessor widely used in the computer system. And microcontroller is used in embedded system.
- Microprocessor is used in Personal Computers whereas Micro Controller is used in an embedded system.
- The microprocessor uses Von Neumann architecture where data and program present in the same memory module. The microcontroller uses Harvard architecture. In this module, data and program get stored in separate memory.
- Microprocessor requires external components to operate. So, the Cost of the microprocessor is higher than the microcontroller.
- Microprocessor consists of only a Central Processing Unit, whereas Micro Controller contains a CPU, Memory, I/O all integrated into one chip.
- Microprocessor uses an external bus to interface to RAM, ROM, and other peripherals, on the other hand, Microcontroller uses an internal controlling bus.

7.a Sensors are devices that responds to a physical quantity with a signal and Actuators are devices that respond to signals with physical movement (or similar action) can be considered as Transducers.

For example, a Microphone is a Sensor, which converts sound waves into electrical signals and a Loudspeaker is an Actuator, which converts electrical signals into audio signals.

7.b setup() is called once in the program when a sketch starts after power-up. It is used to initialize variables, input and output pin modes, and other libraries needed in the sketch.

loop() is used after setup() been called, function loop() is executed repeatedly in the main program. It controls the board until the board is powered off or is reset.

8.a

```
void setup() {
pinMode(8,OUTPUT);
}
void loop() {

digitalWrite(8,HIGH);
delay(1000);
digitalWrite(8,LOW);
delay(1000);
}
```

Figure 1 Program for Q8a

b

```
//Program that automatically turn lights on when an LDR sensor detects
darkness.
int sensorPin = A0; // select the input pin for LDR
int sensorValue = 0; // variable to store the value coming from the sensor
void setup() {
  Serial.begin(9600); //sets serial port for communication
}
void loop() {
  sensorValue = analogRead(sensorPin); // read the value from the sensor
  Serial.println(sensorValue); //prints the values coming from the sensor
on the screen
  delay(100);
}
```

Figure 2 Program for Q8b

9.a Stress is an emotional/bodily reaction to physical, psychological or emotional demands. Stress is your body's way of responding to demand or threat. Consider an example, when you sense danger - whether real or imagined your body's defences kick into high gear in a rapid, automatic process known as the "fight-or-flight" reaction, or the stress response.

b Botnets consist of many bots working together, may be used to gain unauthorized access to computer systems and infect computers . For example , The attack used the Mirai IoT Botnet, taking control of over 600,000 IoT devices to flood Dyn with traffic in a massive DDoS attack. The devices seemed to be mostly routers and IP cameras. IP cameras are frequently targeted IoT devices.

c Fog computing also known as Edge Computing is a term created by Cisco and it extends the concept of cloud computing to the network edge, making it ideal for Internet of Things (IoT) and other applications that require real-time interactions. It refers to a decentralized computing structure, where resources, including the data and applications, get placed in logical locations between the data source and the cloud. The fog computing platform lies between the cloud servers and the users. In a fog-enabled environment, the devices at the fog layer usually perform operations related to networking such as routers, gateways, bridges, and hubs.

d 6LoWPAN is an acronym of IPv6 over Low Power Wireless Personal Area Networks. It is a protocol that is primarily intended for long-range wireless battery-operated IoT devices in regional, national, or global networks. It is specifically known for its ability to communicate in long-range with the least power consumption and detects the signals below the noise level. This protocol is mainly used in smart cities, where there is a large network with millions and millions of devices connected to each other that function with less power, memory, low-cost mobile secure communication in IoT devices, and a wide range of industrial applications.

Unsolved Sample Paper–1

Total Time : 3 Hours

Total Marks 100
(Part One - 40 Part Two - 60)

PART – ONE

1. Multiple Choice Questions

1.1 DHT11 is __________ sensor.
a. Proximity sensor b. Humidity sensor
c. Touch sensor d. Pressure sensor

1.2 Resolution is expressed in __________
a. Bytes b. Bits
c. Word d. Nibble

1.3 Which of the following needs a clock?
a. Only Asynchronous b. Only synchronous
c. Both synchronous and Asynchronous d. Sometimes Synchronous

1.4 QoS stands for ____________.
a. Quality of storage
b. Quality of service
c. Quality of security
d. Quality of swarms

1.5 Which of the following is not a standard protocol used in IoT domain?
a. Wifi
b. Z-wave
c. Zigbee
d. LoMe

1.6 Which layer is CoAP?
a. Control layer b. Transport layer
c. Service layer d. All of the above

1.7 MQTT is mainly used for __________
a. M2M communication
b. Device communication
c. Internet communication
d. Wireless communication

1.8 Full form of MQTT _____
a. Message Queuing Telemetry Transport
b. Message Queuing Telegram Transport
c. Message Queue Telegram Transport
d. Message Queue Telemetry Transport

1.9 The handshake that conveys confidence is:
a. Limp
b. Loose
c. Firm
d. None of these

1.10 Elements of Self Esteem are:
a. Self-confidence b. Self-respect
c. Self-acceptance d. All of the above

2. State True or False:

2.1 The total resistance of resistor is low when connected in series.

2.2 Microprocessor has only processing capability, no serial interface or interrupts are available.

2.3 Capacitor blocks AC and allows DC to pass through.

2.4 Ohms law calculates the power consumed by an electrical appliance.

2.5 IIoT targets applications related to health and fitness.

2.6 Time management is primarily creating an environment conducive to effectiveness.

2.7 Stress is an emotional reaction to physical and psychological demands.

2.8 Depression is Physical signs if you are suffering from chronic stress.

2.9 Bots that operate on social media platforms are known as Malicious bots.

2.10 Blockchain was invented by a person using the name 'Satoshi Nakamoto' in 2008 to serve as the public transaction ledger of the cryptocurrency bitcoin.

3. Match the following:

3.1	MQTT	a.	temporary circuits and prototyping
3.2	Attitude	b.	Message oriented
3.3	Bitcoin	c.	Wearable e-textile technology
3.4	Internet of Things	d.	Satoshi Nakamoto
3.5	Breadboard	e.	Kevin Ashton
3.6	The Founder of Arduino project	f.	Mental and emotional entity
3.7	Resistor	g.	Massimo Banzi
3.8	Serial Plotter	h.	Text editing program
3.9	Arduino IDE	i.	Real-time graph
3.10	Lilypad Arduino	j.	An electrical component

4. Fill in the blanks:

a. Crystal oscillator	b. GND
c. Automation	d. Self-esteem
e. LEDs	f. Smart meters
g. Posture	h. Machine-to-Human
i. Network	j. Application Layer

4.1 __________ reflects a person's overall subjective emotional evaluation of his or her own worth.

4.2 __________ is a non-verbal form of communication which is showed through facial expressions, gestures, posture, and body movements.

4.3 The __________ helps Arduino in dealing with time issues.

4.4 There are several ________ pins on the Arduino, any of which can be used to ground your circuit.

4.5 ________ are small, powerful lights that are used in many different applications.

4.6 ________ refers to a set of technologies that enable machines to interact with human beings.

4.7 _________ means to manage everyday tasks without human intervention.

4.8 _________ read and analyze consumption patterns of power at regular and peak load times.

4.9 The ________ layer is responsible for connecting to other smart things, network devices, and servers.

4.10 _________ This layer is responsible for delivering application specific services to the user.

PART – TWO

(Answer any four questions)

5. a. What is a sensor? Explain its working with example.

b. What are the different communication modes available to connect things n an IoT domain?

c. What is the role of setup() method in an Arduino program?

6. a. Explain Five-layer-IoT Architecture with diagram.

b. What is RFID? What are its advantages and disadvantags.

c. How IPv6 is different from IPv4.

7. a. What is an IOT? What is the difference between IOT devices and embedded devices?

b. What impacts will the Internet of Things (IoT) have on Agriculture Sector?

8. a. Write a program to interface LEDs at pins 10, 11, 12, 13 and button 7. The press of button changes the pattern of LED glow. (Considering four pattern of LED glow.

b. Write a program to interface LED and Buzzer with Arduino board, so that buzzer is put on whenever LED is on and Buzzer is put off when LED is off.

9. Briefly explain the following:

a. Microcontroller

b. OSI Model

c. Stress management

d. Etiquettes & manners

Unsolved Sample Paper–2

Total Time : 3 Hours

Total Marks 100
(Part One - 40 Part Two - 60)

PART – ONE

1. Multiple Choice Questions

1.1 IoT devices are naturally vulnerable to ________ threats.

a. Sensors b. Heterogeneity
c. Security d. Connectivity

1.2 In asymmetric key cryptography, the private key is kept by:

a. Receiver b. Sender and receiver
c. Sender d. All the connected devices to the network

1.3 The most common form of authentication:

a. Password b. Smart cards
c. PIN d. Digital certificates

1.4 What kind of electronic document contains a!public!key?

a. PIN
b. Digital certificate
c. PAN
d. Biometrics

1.5 What type of attack tries to guess password by trying common words:

a. Dictionary attack
b. Brute force attack
c. Man in the middle attack
d. Smurf attack

1.6 Which of the following terms indicates that information is to be read only by those people for whom it is intended?

a. Availability b. Accounting
c. Integrity d. Confidentiality

1.7 The setup() defines

a. Pin functionality using the pinMode function
b. Initial state of pins
c. Initialize classes and variables
d. All of the above

1.8 Some of the compile errors are:

a. Missing semicolons or parentheses
b. Missing variable initializations
c. Misspellings & wrong capitalizations
d. All of the above

1.9 What is Artificial Intelligence?

a. Putting your intelligence into Computer
b. Programming with your own intelligence
c. Making a machine intelligent
d. Putting more memory into computer

1.10 Dictionary attacks is a kind of:

a. Injection attacks b. Brute force attack
c. Session Hijacking d. None of the above

2. State True or False:

2.1 Motivation is a theoretical construct which is used to explain the appearance of the person.

2.2 If it is necessary to read a speech from a manuscript, you should first apologize for having to read the speech.

2.3 In blockchain, each blocks is linked backward to the previous block.

2.4 Firewalls cannot protect against viruses.

2.5 Signature algorithms!are used to create digital signatures.

2.6 Media in which the signals are not guided through a solid medium are known as unguided media.

2.7 Unshielded Twisted Pair (UTP) is a very flexible, low cost media, and can be used for either voice or data communications.

2.8 Routers and gateways operate in the network layer.

2.9 Physical layer is the lowest layer of the OSI reference model.

2.10 When the feedback signal is positive then system called positive feedback system.

3. Match the following:

3.1	A manual control system	a.	Connectionless protocol
3.2	Feed forward control	b.	Predictive control
3.3	An undesired input signal	c.	Open loop control system
3.4	Body Area Networks	d.	Noise
3.5	Bluetooth	e.	Base station
3.6	A cellular network	f.	Wearables
3.7	X-10	g.	Wireless Personal Area Network
3.8	Sigfox	h.	Home automation sector
3.9	MQTT	i.	Ultra Narrow Band
3.10	UDP	j.	Bandwidth efficient

4. Fill in the blanks:

a. TCP	b. IPv6
c. Sensor	d. Skills
e. Self-Efficacy	f. IaaS
g. Embedded system	h. Request-Response
i. Publish-Subscribe	j. Fog computing

4.1 ________ is a person's belief in his or her ability to complete a future task or solve a future problem.

4.2 There are a number of ______ involved in self-motivation.

4.3 _______ is a connection-oriented protocol.

4.4 _______ uses a 128-bit address.

4.5 A _______ is a device that is used to sense a physical condition or event.

4.6 ________ provides a cloud-based platform for servers, storage, memory, bandwidth and computing power on demand.

4.7 An _______ is a system that has computer hardware and software embedded to perform specific tasks.

4.8 ________ is the physical location of the devices, which are much closer to the users than the cloud servers.

4.9 ________ is a communication model in which the client sends requests to the server and the server responds to the requests.

4.10 ________ is a communication model that involves publishers, brokers and consumers.

PART – TWO

(Answer any four questions)

5. a. What are Things in IoT domain? What is meant by connected things.

b. Write a C program to depict an IoT uses where LED is switched ON once the button is pressed and released and next time button is pressed and released, the LED is switched OFF.

6. a. Explain the different functional blocks in a IoT ecosystem.

b. Discuss the role of digital, analog and PWM pin in Arduino UNO.

7. a. What are the determinants of personality? Explain motivation and self-esteem in detail.

b. Write a C program to interface DHT sensor and LED. The program will switch ON LED once the temperature rises above 25 degrees?

8. a. What is the use of BLE in IOT?

b. What are the challenges in IOT?

9. Briefly explain the following:

a. Arduino shields

b. PWM

c. ZigBee protocol

d. Positive attitude

MCQ & Practical Assignment – 1

Multiple Choice Questions

1. Which of the following cannot be considered an IoT device?
   a. Smartwatch b. Andriod phone
   c. Laptop d. Tubelight
2. IoT is based on __________ technology.
   a. Hardware b. Software
   c. None d. Both of these
3. What is the standard form of RFID?
   a. Radio frequency identification
   b. Radio waves frequency identification
   c. Radio frequency interdependent
   d. Radio wave frequency independent
4. What is an IoT network?
   a. A collection of networked devices
   b. A collection of interconnected devices
   c. A collection of signaled devices
   d. None of the above
5. What type of interface is used by fingerprint sensors to collect data?
   a. IPI interface
   b. UART interface
   c. I2P interface
   d. None
6. ________ is a security mechanism used in WIFI.
   a. WPA b. HTTP
   c. MLA d. None of these
7. ______ allows us to control electronic components.
   a. RETful API b. RESTful API
   c. HTTP d. MQTT
8. MQTT stands for ________
   a. MQ telemetry things
   b. MQ transport telemetry
   c. MQ transport things
   d. MQ telemetry transport
9. MQTT is __________ protocol.
   a. Machine to Machine
   b. Internet of Things
   c. Machine to Machine and Internet of Things
   d. Machine Things
10. The huge number of devices connected to the Internet of Things has to communicate automatically, not via humans. What is this called?
    a. Skynet b. Bot 2 Bot
    c. Machine 2 Machine d. intercloud
11. What is the sensor/protocol used in GSN?
    a. HTTP b. CoAP protocol
    c. MQTT protocol d. XMPP protocol
12. Which one of these is the most important factor to be considered in an IoT implementation:
    a. Scalability
    b. Power efficiency
    c. Efficient and scalable addressing schemes
    d. All of these
13. Which of these statements regarding sensors is TRUE?
    a. Sensors are input devices
    b. Sensors can be analog as well as digital
    c. Sensors respond to some external stimuli
    d. All of these
14. MQTT stands for:
    a. Message Queue Telemetry transport
    b. Multiple queue telemetry transport
    c. Multiple query transport technique
    d. Multiple query transport technique
15. Which topology is supported by Z wave:
    a. Star b. Mesh
    c. Tree d. All of these
16. The WSN nodes are prone to:
    a. Malicious attacks b. Eavesdropping
    c. Interference d. All of these
17. Which of the following is not a sensor?
    a. Barometer
    b. Light dependent Resistor
    c. DHT
    d. Relay
18. Arduino IDE consists of 2 functions. What are they?
    a. Build() and loop()
    b. Setup() and build()
    c. Setup() and loop()
    d. Loop() and build() and setup()

19. How many digital pins are there in the UNO board?
    a. 14 b. 12
    c. 16 d. 20
20. How many analog pins are used in Arduino Mega board?
    a. 16 b. 14
    c. 12 d. 8
21. ________ are pre built circuit boards that fit on top of Android.
    a. Sensor b. Data types
    c. Breadboard d. Sheilds
22. A program written with the IDE for Arduino is called ________.
    a. IDE source b. Sketch
    c. Cryptography d. Source code
23. Relay is a kind of:
    a. Sensor b. Actuator
    c. Hub d. Router
24. IoT promotes the creation of IoT terminal industry ________.
    a. Devices b. Network
    c. Clusters d. Things
25. A________ is the component that executes a program in an IoT system.
    a. Micro converter b. Microcontroller
    c. Microsensor d. None
26. Which of the following is not LPWAN technologies?
    a. LORA b. SIGFOX
    c. NB-IoT d. Bluetooth
27. The frequency rate of the z-wave is?
    a. 708.49 GHz b. 888.42 GHz
    c. 908.42 GHz d. 928.49 GHz
28. Arduino UNO is?
    a. Protocol b. Network
    c. Software d. Hardware device
29. What is the advantage of MQTT over HTTP?
    a. More secure b. Lightweight
    c. Both (a) and (b) d. None of the above
30. Remotes enables entities that utilize IoT devices to connect and control them using a dashboard.
    a. Smartphones
    b. Tablets & PCs
    c. Smartwatches
    d. All of the above
31. The RFID is a useful IoT architecture layer of the perception layer for ________.
    a. Object identifying
    b. Tracking
    c. Exchanging useful information
    d. All of the above
32. The entity in IoT is ________.
    a. Businesses b. Consumers
    c. Governments d. All of the above
33. ZigBee is based on which of the following standard?
    a. IEEE 802.5
    b. IEEE 802.15.4
    c. IEEE 802.4.13
    d. None of the above
34. Mostly used protocols in IoT is?
    a. ZigBee b. MQTT
    c. XMPP d. All of the above
35. WiFi-ah (HaLow) is designed specifically for?
    a. Low data rate b. Long-range sensors
    c. Controllers d. All of the above
36. Acronym of 6LoWPAN is ________
    a. IPV6 over low power wireless personal area network
    b. IPv6 over low energy wire personal area network
    c. IPv4 over low power wireless private area network
    d. IPv4 over longrange wireless private area network
37. What is LoRa stands for?
    a. Level Range Radio b. Low Radio Range
    c. Long Range Radio d. None
38. Which of the following is not the concern of IoT?
    a. Privacy b. Data storage
    c. Security d. Throughput
39. Which is the lowest layer of IoT architecture?
    a. Firmware b. Cloud
    c. Smart Devices d. Gateway
40. Which of the following are IoT platforms?
    a. AWS IOT
    b. Microsoft Azure IOT
    c. PTC ThingWorx
    d. All of the above

41. The analog signal in _______ is _________.
    a. Continuous, frequency
    b. Continuous, time
    c. Discrete, frequency
    d. Discrete, time
42. What is the full form of?
    a. Higher Data Level Communication
    b. Higher Data Link Communication
    c. High-level Data Link Control
    d. High Data Level Control
43. What is another name for I2C?
    a. Signal wire interface
    b. UART
    c. Two wire interfaces
    d. USART
44. Which of the following is a way to connect IoT devices with data?
    a. Internet b. Network
    c. Cloud d. Automata
45. Which layer is used for wireless connection in IoT devices?
    a. Transport layer b. Data link layer
    c. Network layer d. Application layer
46. What is the role of big data in the smart grid architecture of IoT?
    a. Locked the data b. Store data
    c. Filter the data d. None of the these
47. The main function of______ is to route the processed data and send it to the database or network for its appropriate use.
    a. Gateway b. Microcontrollers
    c. Sensors d. Processor
48. Actuators can be:
    a. Displays b. Motors
    c. Sound d. All of the above
49. Examples of sensors are:
    a. Gas sensor
    b. Water quality sensor
    c. Moisture sensor
    d. All of these
50. Different kinds of signals are:
    a. Mechanical, thermal
    b. Magnetic, Electric
    c. Chemical, Radiation
    d. All of the above
51. In AVR, which registers are there for the I/O programming of ports?
    a. Port b. Pin
    c. DDR d. All of the mentioned
52. On reset DDR registers of all ports are set to:
    a. 0 b. 1
    c. Both 0 and 1 d. None of the mentioned
53. Which of the following statements are correct?
    a. PIN register of a port is used to bring data into CPU from pins
    b. PORT register is used to send data out to pins
    c. DDR register is used to control the direction of a port
    d. All of the mentioned
54. Which of the following is not a single bit instruction in AVR?
    a. SBI b. PORT
    c. CBI d. All of the mentioned
55. ADC stand for?
    a. Digital to Analog converter
    b. Analog to digital converter
    c. Analog converter
    d. None of these
56. Which data type is not suitable for storing a number 65000 in a 32-bit system?
    a. Signed short b. Unsigned short
    c. Long d. int
57. Which of the following is a User-defined data type?
    a. Typedef int Boolean
    b. Typed enum {Moon, Tue, Wed, Thu, Fri} Workdays;
    c. Struct {char name[10], int age};
    d. All of the mentioned
58. Which of the datatypes have size that is variable?
    a. Int b. Struct A
    c. Float d. Double
59. Which of the following is not a correct variable type?
    a. Float b. Real c. Int d. double
60. In mathematics and computer programing, which is the correct order of mathematical operators?
    a. Addition, subtraction, multiplication, division
    b. Division, multiplication, addition, subtraction
    c. Multiplication, addition, division, subtraction
    d. Addition, division, modulus, subtraction

61. Which of the following data type will throw an error on modulus operation(%)?
    a. Char b. Short
    c. Int d. Float
62. Which among the following are the fundamental arithmetic operators, i.e. performing the desired operation can be done using that operator only?
    a. +, - b. +, -. %
    c. +, -, *, / d. +, -, *, /, %
63. A pointer is:
    a. A keyword used to create variables
    b. A variable that stores address of an instruction
    c. A variable that stores address of other variable
    d. All of the above
64. The operator used to get value at address stored in a pointer variable is:
    a. * b. &
    c. && d. ||
65. Which of the following is not a valid variable name declaration in C?
    a. Int Mark_1; b. Int mark1;
    c. Int_mark1; d. Int 1mark;
66. The format identifier "%d" is used for ________ datatype.
    a. Int b. Char
    c. Long d. float
67. Which is the correct order of data types with respect to their size?
    a. Int > char > float
    b. Char > int > float
    c. Char < double < int
    d. Char < int < double
68. Which among the following operator has the highest priority?
    a. Comma operator
    b. Conditional operator
    c. Relational operator
    d. Unary plus operator
69. Which of the following is not an arithmetic operation?
    a. a*=5; b. a/=5; c. a!=5; d. a%=5;
70. Which one out of these is in a format which is not readable by the user?
    a. Encryption b. Passwords
    c. Text d. None of these
71. With two-factor Authentication, which attack can be users vulnerable to?
    a. Ransome ware attack
    b. Man-in-the middle attack
    c. Cross Attack
    d. Radiant attack
72. Which of the following is not LPWAN technologies?
    a. LORA b. SIGFOX
    c. NB-IoT d. Bluetooth
73. Behavior that we repeat regularly and automatically.
    a. Habit b. Behaviour
    c. Heredity d. None of the above
74. The power within ourselves that inspires us to do something.
    a. Psychological awareness
    b. Self-awareness
    c. Emotional self-awareness
    d. Self-motivation
75. Personality is derived from latin word – "persona", meaning:
    a. Mask b. Mark
    c. Mesk d. Maek
76. Which of the following devices is used to measure the gases or liquid?
    a. Optical sensor b. Gas sensor
    c. Smoke sensor d. Pressure sensor
77. Which of the following bit defines the address bit in the control register?
    a. ML b. MM
    c. RXWake d. None of these
78. Which of the following topology is used to ZigBee Smart Energy?
    a. Bus topology b. Ring topology
    c. Star topology d. Any topology
79. Which of the following touch sensors is used in a cell phone?
    a. Resistive touch sensors
    b. Human sensor
    c. Capacitive touch sensors
    d. Follow sensor
80. What are the challenges in IoT?
    a. Energy consumption
    b. Security
    c. Network congestion
    d. All of the above

81. _____ involves delivering different types of services over the Internet.
   a. Physical computing
   b. Chemical computing
   c. Mechanism
   d. Cloud computing

82. A ________ is an established set of rules that determines how data is transmitted between different devices in the same network.
   a. Network connection
   b. TCP IP protocol
   c. Network protocol
   d. TCP protocol

83. ________ is an open source electronic platform base on easy to use hardware and software.
   a. Servo motor b. Arduino
   c. CPU d. GPU

84. Which protocol is lightweight?
   a. MQTT b. HTTP c. CoAP d. SPI

85. The core element is operated by ________.
   a. PaaS b. IoT service provider
   c. SaaS d. IaaS

86. IRS P3 satellite uses which of the following sensors?
   a. PAN b. LISS-III
   c. MOS d. LISS-II

87. Bluetooth allows the station to define a quality of
   a. Time level b. Service level
   c. Data level d. Segment level

88. A Bluetooth network is called
   a. Wireless Network b. WAN
   c. Piconet d. LAN

89. In the IPv4 layer, the datagram is of
   a. Fixed length
   b. Variable length
   c. Global length
   d. 0 length

90. IPv6 does not use ____________ type of address.
   a. Broadcast b. Multicast
   c. anycast d. unicast

91. IANA stands for:
   a. Internal assessment numerical access
   b. Internet association numbers authority
   c. International aid for network automation
   d. Internet assigned numbers authority

92. Machine learning is
   a. The selective acquisition of knowledge through the use of manual programs
   b. The autonomous acquisition of knowledge through the use of manual programs
   c. The selective acquisition of knowledge through the use of computer programs
   d. The autonomous acquisition of knowledge through the use of computer programs

93. What is the TCP name for a transport service access point
   a. Node b. Pipe
   c. Port d. None of the mentioned

94. How many time loop function runs in Arduino IDE:
   a. Four b. Forever
   c. One d. Five

95. MQTT is:
   a. Based on client-server architecture
   b. Based on publish-subscribe architecture
   c. Based on both of the above
   d. Based on none of the above

96. Which is the correct operator for power (x^y)?
   a. x^y b. x^^y
   c. x**y d. None of the mentioned

97. What is WPA?
   a. Wi-fi protected access
   b. Wired process access
   c. Wired protected access
   d. Wi-fi process access

98. Standard port number for secure MQTT is:
   a. 1883 b. 8000
   c. 8883 d. 8888

99. Bluetooth 5.0 promises:
   a. 4x speed, 2x range, 2x data
   b. 6x speed, 3x range, 3x data
   c. 2x speed 4x range 8x data
   d. 3x speed 4x range 8x data

100. Term SSL and TLS stand for:
   a. Secure Socket layers and transport layer session
   b. Secure socket layers and transport layer security
   c. Secure socket layout and transport level session
   d. Session socket layers and transport layer session

Answers to Multiple Choice Questions

1.	d	2.	d	3.	a	4.	b	5.	b
6.	a	7.	a	8.	d	9.	c	10.	c
11.	b	12.	d	13.	d	14.	a	15.	d
16.	d	17.	d	18.	c	19.	a	20.	a
21.	d	22.	b	23.	b	24.	c	25.	b
26.	d	27.	c	28.	d	29.	c	30.	d
31.	d	32.	d	33.	b	34.	d	35.	d
36.	a	37.	c	38.	d	39.	c	40.	d
41.	b	42.	c	43.	c	44.	c	45.	b
46.	b	47.	a	48.	d	49.	d	50.	d
51.	d	52.	a	53.	d	54.	b	55.	b
56.	b	57.	d	58.	b	59.	b	60.	b
61.	d	62.	a	63.	c	64.	a	65.	d
66.	a	67.	d	68.	d	69.	c	70.	a
71.	b	72.	d	73.	a	74.	d	75.	a
76.	d	77.	b	78.	c	79.	c	80.	b
81.	d	82.	c	83.	b	84.	a	85.	b
86.	c	87.	d	88.	c	89.	b	90.	a
91.	d	92.	d	93.	c	94.	b	95.	b
96.	c	97.	a	98.	c	99.	c	100.	b

Sample Practical Questions with Answers

1. Write a program to interface LCD with Arduino board and display "This is Covid-19 Pandemic always wear the mask" on it

Answer

```
// Printing message on LCD
#include<LiquidCrystal.h>
LiquidCrystal lcd (5, 4, 3, 2, 1, 0); // sets the interfacing pins
void setup()
{
lcd.begin(16,2); // initializes the 16x2 LCD
}
void loop()
{
lcd.setCursor (0,0); //sets the cursor at row 0 column 0
lcd.print ("This is Covid-19 Pandemic always wear the mask"); // prints message
lcd.setCursor (0,1); //sets the cursor at row 0 column 1
lcd.print (millis()/1000); // prints no. of seconds since reset
}
```

2. To interface LED with Arduino and write a program to turn ON LED for 2 sec after every 3 seconds.

Answer

```
// A program to turn ON LED for 2 sec after every 3 seconds.
void setup() {
  // initialize digital pin LED_BUILTIN as an output.
  pinMode(LED_BUILTIN, OUTPUT);
}

// the loop function runs over and over again forever
void loop() {
  digitalWrite(LED_BUILTIN, HIGH); // turn the LED on (HIGH is the voltage level)
  delay(2000);                     // wait for a second (2 sec = 2000ms)
  digitalWrite(LED_BUILTIN, LOW);  // turn the LED off by making the voltage LOW
  delay(3000);                     // wait for a second (3 sec = 3000ms)
}
```

3. Using LDR to activate a buzzer and an LED. When light shines on LDR; the buzzer will give alarm and the LED will flash.

Answer

```
//Using LDR to activate a buzzer and an LED.
const int ledPin = 13;
const int buzzerPin = 12;
const int ldrPin = A0;
void setup () {
Serial.begin(9600);
pinMode(ledPin, OUTPUT);
pinMode(buzzerPin, OUTPUT);
pinMode(ldrPin, INPUT);
}
void loop() {
int ldrStatus = analogRead(ldrPin);
```

```
if (ldrStatus >= 400) {
tone(buzzerPin, 100);
digitalWrite(ledPin, HIGH);
delay(100);
noTone(buzzerPin);

digitalWrite(ledPin, LOW);
delay(100);
Serial.println("ALARM ACTIVATED");
}
else {
noTone(buzzerPin);
digitalWrite(ledPin, LOW);
Serial.println("ALARM DEACTIVATED");
}
}
```

4. **Turn an LED on for one second, off for one second, and repeat forever.**

Answer

```
// Turn an LED on for one second, off for one second,
and repeat forever.

void setup()
{
  pinMode(13, OUTPUT);
}
void loop()
{
 digitalWrite(13, HIGH);   // Turn on the LED
 delay(1000);       // Wait for one second
 digitalWrite(13, LOW);   // Turn off the LED
 delay(1000);       // Wait for one second
}
```

5. **Write a program to Blink default Light Emitting Diode(LED) on Arduino board with the delay of 2 sec.**

Answer

```
// A program to turn ON LED with the delay of 2 sec.
void setup() {
 // initialize digital pin LED_BUILTIN as an output.
 pinMode(LED_BUILTIN, OUTPUT);
}

// the loop function runs over and over again forever
void loop() {
 digitalWrite(LED_BUILTIN, HIGH);  // turn the LED
 on (HIGH is the voltage level)
 delay(2000);                 // wait for a second (2 sec =
 2000ms)
 digitalWrite(LED_BUILTIN, LOW);  // turn the LED
 off by making the voltage LOW
 delay(2000);                 // wait for a second (2 sec =
 2000ms)
}
```

MCQ & Practical Assignment – 2

Multiple Choice Questions

1. The standard form of CGI is:
   a. Common gateway of interest
   b. Common gate interface
   c. Common gateway interdependent
   d. None
2. The standard form of ICT is:
   a. Inter connected technology
   b. International connection technology
   c. Inter communication technology
   d. Information and communication Technology
3. Which transport layer protocols is used by DHCP?
   a. RSVP b. TCP
   c. DCCP d. UDP
4. Which layer is called a port layer in OSI model?
   a. Session b. Application
   c. Presentation d. Transport
5. Router operate at _______ layer of OSI reference model?
   a. Layer 2 (data link)
   b. Layer 3 (Network)
   c. Layer 1 (Physical)
   d. Layer 4 (Transport)
6. Each IP Packet must contain:
   a. Only destination IP address
   b. Only source IP address
   c. Source and Destination IP addresses
   d. None of the above
7. What is the standard length of MAC address:
   a. 16 bits b. 32 bits
   c. 48 bits d. 64 bits
8. What is secure shell (SSH)?
   a. A router b. A firewall
   c. A network protocol d. Python shell
9. Which one of the following protocols is lightweight?
   a. IP b. HTTP
   c. MQTT d. CoAP
10. Raspbian is:
    a. Assembler b. Language
    c. Compiler d. Operating system
11. The storage is _________ in IoT.
    a. Limited b. Unlimited
    c. Not available d. All of these
12. Which of the following languages does GSN work on?
    a. Python b. Java
    c. C++ d. Android
13. Which of the following topology is used for ZigBee smart energy?
    a. Bus topology b. Ring topology
    c. Star topology d. None of the above
14. Which of the following layers provides end-to-end communication in iot?
    a. Logical layer b. Data link layer
    c. Transport layer d. Session layer
15. Which devices measures gases or liquid?
    a. Proximity sensor b. Pressure sensor
    c. Temperature sensor d. Touch sensor
16. DHT11 is _____________ sensor.
    a. Proximity sensor b. Humidity sensor
    c. Touch sensor d. Pressure sensor
17. IoT devices can easily lead to catastrophe without _________.
    a. Software b. Devices
    c. Cloud d. Management system
18. Which is the future application of IoT?
    a. QoS in communication
    b. Role of green IoT system
    c. Secure communication
    d. Multimedia communication
19. Which of the given wireless technologies used in IoT, consumes the least amount of power?
    a. Zigbee b. Bluetooth
    c. Wi-fi d. GSM/CDMA
20. Which of the following is not types of voice service in the IoT?
    a. Mono-directional voice
    b. Hybrid-directional voice
    c. Voice-recognition
    d. Bi-directional voice

21. Which is the at the lowest layer in the IoT architecture?
    a. Smart devices b. Gateway
    c. Cloud d. Service management
22. Which is/are key characterisitcs of IoT?
    a. Safety b. Connectivity
    c. Heterogeneity d. All of the above
23. The role of sensor in smart grid architecture of IoT is to ________.
    a. Provide security b. Filter data
    c. Store data d. Transfer data
24. An IoT network is a collection of ________ devices.
    a. Signal b. Machine to Machine
    c. Interconnected d. Network to network
25. Which one of the following is not an IoT device?
    a. Amazon echo voice controller
    b. Google home
    c. Nest smoke alarm
    d. None of these
26. Among the following layers, identify the one which is used for wireless connection in IoT devices.
    a. Datalink layer
    b. Transport layer
    c. Network layer
    d. Application layer
27. Identify the protocol used to link all devices in IoT.
    a. UDP b. TCP/IP
    c. HTTP d. Network
28. Arduino IDE is written in which programming language
    a. Java b. C/C++
    c. JavaScript d. Python
29. PubNub publishes and subscribes ________ in order to send and receive messages.
    a. Network b. Account
    c. Portal d. Keys
30. Which of the following is false about IoT devices?
    a. IoT devices use the internet for collecting and sharing data
    b. IoT devices need microcontrollers
    c. IoT devices use wireless technology
    d. IoT devices are completely safe
31. Which of the following is not a fundamental component of an IoT system?
    a. Sensors
    b. Connectivity and data processing
    c. User interface
    d. Transformer
32. What is the full form of IIOT?
    a. Index Internet of Things
    b. Incorporate Internet of Things
    c. Industrial Internet of Things
    d. Intense Internet of Things
33. Which of the following is not related to Arduino IDE IoT software?
    a. Serial monitor b. Verify
    c. Upload d. Terminate
34. IoT gateway must provide ________
    a. Protocol abstraction
    b. Data storage
    c. Security with hardware
    d. Simple and fast installation
35. What IoT collects?
    a. Device data
    b. Machine generated data
    c. Sensor data
    d. Human generated data
36. What is the full form of IDE in Arduino IDE IoT software?
    a. Intra Defence Environment
    b. Intra Development Environment
    c. Integrated Development Environment
    d. Integrated Deployed Environment
37. Which of these is a part of the Sensing Layer of the IoT Service Oriented Architecture?
    a. Service integration
    b. Service repository
    c. Business logic
    d. Data sensing and actuation protocols
38. REST API follows ________ communication model.
    a. Exclusive pair b. Push pull
    c. Publish subscribe d. Request response
39. The term IoT was coined in?
    a. 1998 b. 2000 c. 1999 d. 2001
40. Which of the following IoT gateway must provide?
    a. Security with hardware
    b. Protocol abstraction
    c. Simple and fast installation
    d. Data storage

41. Through which network does Open IoT manage registration, deployment of sensors?
a. X-GSN b. LSM c. GSN d. HTTP
42. Identify the java extension file in IoT.
a. .exe b. .jar c. .py d. .c
43. Identify the protocol used to link all devices in IoT
a. TCP/IP b. UDP
c. Network d. HTTP
44. Identify the service which permits the changes to IoT services.
a. Update
b. Enable from suspension
c. Registered service status
d. Enable
45. ITS stands for ________
a. Intelligent transportation security
b. Internet travel services
c. Internet transport security
d. Intelligent transportation services
46. Which of the following allows to monitor the application?
a. Endpoints b. Hypermedia
c. Boot d. Actuators
47. In which of the following terms in resolution expressed?
a. Nibble b. bytes c. Bits d. Word
48. SLA stands for ________
a. System-level argument
b. Service local area
c. System local area
d. Service level argument
49. The standard length of the MAC address is________
a. 8 bits b. 16 bits
c. 48 bits d. 32 bits
50. Through API, _____ service portability is enabled
a. Network b. Services
c. Device d. Systems
51. Identify the challenge coming under securing the information.
a. Presence detection b. Power consumption
c. Security d. Signaling
52. Total types in which IoT platform is divided
a. 2 b. 4 c. 3 d. 5
53. What is stands for SBC is?
a. Standard business center
b. Standard building center
c. Smart business center
d. Smart building center
54. Service is termed as ________ in SOA
a. Developer service b. Business service
c. Network service d. Software service
55. Identify the incorrect advantage of IoT
a. Security
b. Improve customer engagement
c. Enhanced data collection
d. Reduce waste
56. Who operates the core element?
a. SaaS b. PaaS
c. IaaS d. IoT service provider
57. VNC stands for ________.
a. Virtual network computing
b. Virtual network communication
c. Virtual network computers
d. None
58. ________ are the inter connectors.
a. Web b. Internet
c. Network d. APIs
59. Most IoT problems are addressed at ________ layer
a. TCP b. IP c. API d. UDP
60. Global sensor network is built for:
a. Reducing cost and time for development
b. Reducing cost and increasing time for development
c. Increasing cost and increasing time for development
d. Increasing cost and decreasing time for development
61. ____________ is uniquely identifiable embedded computing devices.
a. Internet b. IoT A
c. BigData d. Cloud
62. ____________ is most visible component of RFID?
a. Tag b. Antenna
c. Reader d. Middleware
63. RFID works on what principle?
a. Thumb rule
b. Modulation

c. Electromagnetic induction
d. None of above

64. What is full form of RFID?
a. Radio frequency identifier
b. Rapid frequency identifier
c. Radio frequency implied
d. Rapid frequency identifier

65. Which of the following cannot be considered an IoT device?
a. Smartwatch b. Andriod phone
c. Laptop d. Tubelight

66. Which is not an IoT platform?
a. Xiaomi Cloud
b. Google Cloud
c. Myntra
d. AWS (Amazon Web services)

67. What is the standard form of RFID?
a. Radio Frequency Identification
b. Radio Waves Frequency Identification
c. Radio Frequency InterDependent
d. Radio Wave Frequency Independent

68. At which level does the router operate in the OSI reference model?
a. Data link b. Network
c. Physical d. None of these

69. What is an IoT network?
a. a collection of networked devices
b. a collection of Interconnected devices
c. a collection of signaled devices
d. None of the above

70. Full-Form of VNC
a. Virtual network of computers
b. Very network of computers
c. Virtual network for communication
d. Virtual network computing

71. Which one out of these is not a Data Link Layer Technology?
a. Bluetooth b. Wifi
c. HTTP d. Mobile Hotspot

72. What is the standard form of LLN?
a. Lower Lossy Network
b. Low Power Lossy Network
c. Lossy Low Power Network
d. Low Lossy Powered Network

73. What type of interface is used by fingerprint sensors to collect data?
a. IPI interface b. UART interface
c. I2P interface d. None

74. Which of the following things is mandatory for the IoT gateway to provide?
a. Simple and secure installation
b. Data network and storage
c. Software security
d. Protocol abstraction

75. Full form of HART:
a. Highway address Remote transmitter
b. Highway addressable remote transducer
c. Highway addressable router transmitter
d. Highway address remote transmitter

76. What do API systems enable?
a. Network service portability is allowed by API
b. Systems service portability is allowed by API
c. Device service portability is allowed by API
d. All of these

77. What do RETful API systems allow the user?
a. To enhance security
b. To modify communication capability
c. To control electronic components
d. All of these

78. LTE stands for:
a. Long Terminal evolution
b. Lower Terminal evolution
c. Long term evolution
d. None of these

79. What is blockchain?
a. A distributed ledger on a peer-to-peer network
b. A type cryptocurrency
c. An exchange
d. A centralized ledger

80. The poor security practices could include(s):
a. No system hardening
b. No mechanism for updating software
c. An exchange
d. A centralized ledger

81. Which statement(s) are true about a brute force attack?
a. Crack a password or username
b. Find a hidden web page

c. Find the key used to encrypt a message
d. All of the above

82. Dictionary attacks is a kind of:
a. Injection attacks b. Brute force attack
c. Session Hijacking d. None of the above

83. Bonet is often used to launch ________ attack.
a. DoS b. DDoS
c. Brute force d. Passive

84. To secure your data on IoT devices:
a. Keep changing your passwords
b. Update your every device
c. Avoid using devices that are risky
d. All of the above

85. Microprocessor are mainly used in devices like:
a. Calculators
b. Games machine
c. Military applications
d. All of the above

86. What are the applications areas of microcontroller?
a. Security alarms b. Mp3 players
c. Microwave oven d. All of the above

87. Name application areas of AVR microcontroller are:
a. Robotics and Embedded system
b. Automobile and security systems
c. Industrial automation devices
d. All of the above

88. Fog computing is utilized to ________ all debris into a single platform.
a. Integrate b. Store
c. Task d. Flexible

89. Fog node is ________
a. Floor b. Wing
c. Individual room d. Floor and wing

90. The header size is variable in ________.
a. IPv4 b. IPv6
c. Both a and b d. None of the above

91. What is the standard form of RREPs?
a. Route Requests b. Route Reply Requests
c. Route Replies d. None of the above

92. Blockchain networks are much _____ and deal with no real single point of failure.
a. Simpler b. Easier to scale
c. Convenient d. Faster

93. What does a block in a Blockchain have?
a. Header & Digital ledger
b. Bitcoins & Input
c. Transactions & bitcoins
d. Header & Transaction

94. ________ receive verify, gather and execute transactions.
a. Miner nodes b. Smart contracts
c. Light wallets d. Ethereum full node

95. The function of a sensor is to ________.
a. Detect events within specified environment
b. Track and transfer data to computer processor
c. Both a and b
d. Separate physical parameters

96. These machines can use stored data for a limited time period only.
a. Reactive Machine b. Self-Awareness
c. Limited Machine d. Theory of mind

97. KBS in AI stands for?
a. Knowledge based scenario
b. Knowledge based system
c. Knowledge based segments
d. Knowing Best system

98. ________ consists of two different metals connected at two points.
a. Thermistor
b. Resistance Thermometer
c. Thermocouple
d. Semiconductor based sensor

99. Which of the following is not a configuration of a smart sensor?
a. Transducer b. Network interface
c. Processor d. None of the mentioned

100. The Bluetooth technology operates in the ISM band at ________.
a. 2.4 to 2.485 GHz b. 1.4 to 2.485 GHz
c. 2.4 to 2.485 MHz d. None of the above

Answers to Multiple Choice Questions

1.	d	2.	d	3.	d	4.	a	5.	b
6.	c	7.	c	8.	c	9.	c	10.	d
11.	a	12.	b	13.	c	14.	c	15.	b
16.	b	17.	d	18.	b	19.	c	20.	b
21.	a	22.	d	23.	c	24.	c	25.	d

26.	a	27.	b	28.	b	29.	d	30.	d
31.	d	32.	c	33.	d	34.	a	35.	b
36.	c	37.	d	38.	d	39.	c	40.	b
41.	a	42.	b	43.	a	44.	a	45.	d
46.	a	47.	c	48.	d	49.	c	50.	d
51.	a	52.	b	53.	c	54.	b	55.	a
56.	d	57.	a	58.	d	59.	c	60.	a
61.	b	62.	b	63.	c	64.	a	65.	d
66.	c	67.	a	68.	b	69.	b	70.	d
71.	c	72.	b	73.	b	74.	d	75.	b
76.	b	77.	c	78.	c	79.	a	80.	d
81.	d	82.	b	83.	b	84.	d	85.	d
86.	d	87.	d	88.	a	89.	d	90.	a
91.	c	92.	b	93.	d	94.	a	95.	a
96.	c	97.	b	98.	c	99.	d	100.	b

Sample Practical Questions with Answers

1. **To interface Push button with Arduino/Raspberry Pi and write a program to turn ON or OFF LED when push button is pressed.**

Answer

```
// A program to turn ON or OFF LED when push button is pressed.
// Initialize pin numbers for pushbutton and LED:

const int buttonPin = 2;
const int ledPin =  13;

int buttonState = 0;      // variable for reading the pushbutton status

void setup() {
  // initialize the LED pin as an output:
  pinMode(ledPin, OUTPUT);
  // initialize the pushbutton pin as an input:
  pinMode(buttonPin, INPUT);
}

void loop() {
  // read the state of the pushbutton value:
  buttonState = digitalRead(buttonPin);

  // check if the pushbutton is pressed i.e., buttonState is HIGH

  if (buttonState == HIGH) {
    // turn LED on:
    digitalWrite(ledPin, HIGH);
  } else {
    // turn LED off:
    digitalWrite(ledPin, LOW);
  }
}
```

2. **Write Arduino program for LED fade-in and fade-out. The programmer can decide the points when the LED should fade.**

Answer

```
// Program for LED fade-in and fade-out
int led = 9;          // PWM pin the LED is attached
int brightness = 0;   // brightness of LED
int fadeAmount = 5;   // point when LED should fade

// the setup routine runs once when reset is pressed:
void setup() {
  // declare pin 9 to be an output:
  pinMode(led, OUTPUT);
}

// the loop routine runs forever:
void loop() {
  // set the brightness of pin 9:
  analogWrite(led, brightness);

  // change the brightness for next time:
  brightness = brightness + fadeAmount;

  // reverse the direction of the fading at the ends of the fade:
  if (brightness <= 0 || brightness >= 255) {
    fadeAmount = -fadeAmount;
  }
```

```
// wait for 30 milliseconds to see the dimming effect
delay(30);
}
```

3. Write a program to interface security password with Arduino board to show green light for correct password and red light for incorrect password.

Answer

```
//a program to interface security password with Arduino board to show green
//light for correct password and red light for incorrect password.

#include <LiquidCrystal.h> //include LCD library (standard library)
#include <Keypad.h> //include keypad library - first you must install library

#define redLED 10 //define the LED pins
#define greenLED 11

char* password ="1234"; //create a password
int pozisyon = 0; //keypad position

const byte rows = 4; //number of rows on the keypad
const byte cols = 4; // //number of columns on the keypad
// keymap defines the key pressed according to the row and column
char keyMap [rows] [cols] = { //define the symbols on the buttons of the keypad

  {'1', '2', '3', 'A'},
  {'4', '5', '6', 'B'},
  {'7', '8', '9', 'C'},
  {'*', '0', '#', 'D'}
};

// Code that shows the keypad connections to the arduino terminals
// where the pins are connected to on the arduino
byte rowPins [rows] = {1, 2, 3, 4};
byte colPins [cols] = {5, 6, 7, 8};

//initialize an instance of the keypad class
Keypad myKeypad = Keypad( makeKeymap(keyMap), rowPins, colPins, rows, cols);

LiquidCrystal lcd (A0, A1, A2, A3, A4, A5); // pins of the LCD. (RS, E, D4, D5, D6, D7)

void setup(){

 lcd.begin(16, 2);
 pinMode(redLED, OUTPUT); //set the LED as an output
 pinMode(greenLED, OUTPUT);
 setLocked (true); //state of the password
}

void loop(){

 char whichKey = myKeypad.getKey(); //define which key is pressed with getKey

 lcd.setCursor(0, 0);
 lcd.print("  Welcome");
 lcd.setCursor(0, 1);
 lcd.print(" Enter Password");

 if(whichKey == '*' || whichKey == '#' || whichKey == 'A' ||    //define invalid keys
 whichKey == 'B' || whichKey == 'C' || whichKey == 'D'){

  pozisyon=0;
  setLocked (true);
  lcd.clear();
  lcd.setCursor(0, 0);
  lcd.print(" Invalid Key!");
  delay(1000);
  lcd.clear();
 }
 if(whichKey == password [pozisyon]){

  pozisyon ++;
```

```
 }
 if(pozisyon == 4){
  setLocked (false);
  lcd.clear();
  lcd.setCursor(0, 0);
  lcd.print("*** Verified ***");
  delay(3000);
  lcd.clear();
  lcd.setCursor(0, 0);
  lcd.print("Your lock");
  lcd.setCursor(0, 1);
  lcd.print("is now open");
  delay(3000);
  lcd.clear();
 }
 delay(100);
}

void setLocked(int locked){
 if(locked){
  digitalWrite(redLED, HIGH);
  digitalWrite(greenLED, LOW);
  }
  else{
   digitalWrite(redLED, LOW);
   digitalWrite(greenLED, HIGH);
  }
 }
```

4. Write a program to interface Button, buzzer and LED, whenever the button is pressed the buzzer gives beeps and LED blinks.

Answer

```
// A program to interface Button, buzzer and LED
const int buzpin=A0;
const int buttonpin1=8;
const int ledpin1=2;
int buttonstate1;

void setup() {
 // put your setup code here, to run once:
Serial.begin(9600);
pinMode(buzpin, OUTPUT);
pinMode(buttonpin1, INPUT);
pinMode(ledpin1, OUTPUT);
}

void loop() {
 // put your main code here, to run repeatedly:
buttonstate1=digitalRead(buttonpin1);
if (buttonstate1==HIGH){
 tone(buzpin,1);
 digitalWrite(ledpin1,HIGH);
}
else{
digitalWrite(ledpin1,LOW);
noTone(buzpin);
}
}
```

5. Write a program to make the buzzer buzz and LED blink.

Answer

```
int led = 13;  // LED connected to pin 13
int sound = 8; // piezo buzzer connected to pin 8

void setup()
{
 pinMode(led, OUTPUT);  // sets the LED as output
 pinMode(sound, OUTPUT); // sets the buzzer alarm
 as output
}

void loop() // run the program continuously
{
 digitalWrite(led, HIGH); // turn the LED on
 tone(sound, 1000, 250); // play a tone with 1000 Hz
 for 250 ms
 delay(2000);        // wait for 2 seconds
 digitalWrite(led, LOW); // turn the LED off
 tone(sound, 6000, 250); // play a tone with 6000 Hz
 for 250 ms
 delay(2000);        // wait for 2 seconds
}
```

MCQ & Practical Assignment – 3

Multiple Choice Questions

1. NFC is an example of ________ wireless networks.
   a. Long-range b. Medium-range
   c. Short-range d. Wide-area
2. With two-factor Authentication, which attack can be users vulnerable to?
   a. Ransome ware attack
   b. Man-in-the-middle attack
   c. Cross attack
   d. Radiant attack
3. Cloud computing must work ______ with fog computing to provide a seamless end to end customer experiences.
   a. Seamlessly b. Scalable
   c. Control d. Multiple services
4. Lack of broadband _______ and connectivity is a major issue in establishing smart cities
   a. Storage b. Bandwidth
   c. Address d. Services
5. A commercial building may contain mainly ______ component
   a. Memory b. Fog node
   c. Cloud nodes d. Sensors
6. IoT devices use _______ for security.
   a. Cloud b. Software
   c. Immutable d. Fognode
7. ____________ practice of using a network of remote servers hosted on the Internet of store.
   a. Mist computing
   b. Fog computing
   c. Cloud computing
   d. Mobile cloud computing
8. BATM stands for ____________.
   a. Bounded access transaction machine
   b. Broadcast ATM
   c. Bitcoin ATM
   d. Blockchain ATM
9. What is a DApp?
   a. A type of crytocurrenty
   b. A condiment
   c. A type of blockchain
   d. A dencentralized application
10. Arduino shields are also called as__________
    a. Extra peripherals
    b. Add-on modules
    c. Connectivity modules
    d. Another Arduinos
11. Which is the software or a programming language used for controlling of Arduino?
    a. Assembly language b. C languages
    c. Java d. Any language
12. What are the uses of Arduino?
    a. Inexpensive
    b. Cross-platform
    c. Open source and extensible software
    d. All of the above
13. What are the types of Arduino?
    a. Arduino UNO
    b. Arduino Mega
    c. Arduino Deumilanove
    d. All of these
14. What are Arduino UNO Salient features?
    a. PWM (Plus width modulation) outputs
    b. Input pins (analog)
    c. DC current (max)
    d. All of the above
15. What is PWM?
    a. A built-in-library to control CD motor
    b. A type of oscilloscope used with microcontrollers as Arduino
    c. Is a technique for getting analog results with digital means
    d. Is a technique for getting digital results with analog means
16. What are the steps to program an Arduino?
    a. Declaration of Variables
    b. Initialization
    c. Control Code
    d. All of the above
17. What are the basic Arduino Functions?
    a. AnalogRead(pin)

b. AnalogWrite(pin, value)
c. Serial.begin(baud rate)
d. All of the above

18. What is the role of gateway is smart grid architecture of IoT?
a. Store data b. Manage data
c. Collect data d. Security

19. IoT data scalability includes ___________.
a. Protocol abstraction
b. Simple and fast installation
c. Security with hardware
d. Data storage

20. What is the example for smart grid edge device for utility?
a. Smart Meters b. Smart Home
c. Smart Car d. Smart Collage

21. In ___________ layer, various application platforms are built as required by the services needs of smart grid.
a. Perception layer
b. Smart network layer
c. Smart Application layer
d. Data layer

22. ___________ enables seamless integration of LoWPAN devices with internet leveraging.
a. IETF 6LoWPAN
b. IEFT CoAP
c. RFID/NFC
d. IEEE 802.15.4. LoWPAN

23. ___________ resources are identified by Uniform Resource Identifiers
a. CoAP b. HMTP
c. MQTT d. TCP/IP

24. Which protocol interacts asynchronously over UDP?
a. HMTP b. CoAP
c. MQTT d. TCP/IP

25. WSN stands for ________
a. Wired Sensor Network
b. Wireless Sensor Network
c. Wired Service Network
d. Wireless Service Network

26. Without ______ computers embedded in house keys are worthless.
a. Data
b. Services
c. Both Data and Services
d. Neither data nor services

27. Barometer is which type of sensor _______.
a. Pressure sensor
b. Touch sensor
c. Temperature sensor
d. Humidity sensor

28. _________ is a community that is working together to establish an IoT architecture
a. Eclipse IoT b. Red Hat
c. Intercloud d. Bot 2 Bot

29. _________ is a modular and cloud based platform.
a. Eclipse Kura
b. Red Hat
c. Intercloud
d. Eclipse Kapua

30. What is the use of Ping command
a. To know network speed
b. None of the above
c. To test a host on the network is reachable
d. To test storage device

31. Which of the following statement is true?
a. All arithmetic operators have the same level of precedence.
b. The modulus operator % can be used only with integers
c. A unary expression consists of only one operand with no operators
d. The operators <=, >=, and != all enjoy the same level of priority.

32. What is the use of sizeof() operator?
a. To get the size of data types or variable in bytes
b. To get the size of variables only
c. To get the size of the structure only
d. None of the above

33. Which of the following comments about the ++ operator are correct?
a. It is a unary operator
b. The operand can come before or after the operator
c. It cannot be applied to an expression
d. All of the above

34. If a=5 and b=2 then printf("%d", a+++b); will?
a. Results in a syntax error

b. Print 8
c. Print 10
d. None of the above

35. What is/are the consequences of driving the LED in the form of an output function?
a. Pin sources the current when made low without glowing LED
b. Pin sinks the current when made high without glowing LED
c. Pin sources the current when made high by glowing LED
d. Pin sinks the current when made low by glowing LED

36. Which control lines/s acts/s as an initiator by apprising LCD about the inception of data transmission by the microcontroller?
a. Enable (EN)
b. Register Select (RS)
c. Read/write (RW)
d. All of the above

37. When can a LCD display the text form of data?
a. Only when RS line is high
b. Only when RW lines is high
c. Only when RS line is low
d. Only when RW line is low

38. What type of signal does the analogWrite() function output?
a. Pulse width modulated signal
b. Pulse code modulated signal
c. Pulse amplitude modulated signal
d. Frequency modulated signal

39. Can the anlogRead() function be used from any digital pin?
a. No, it cannot
b. Yes, it can, but only on certain Arduino boards
c. Yes, it can
d. Yes, it can, but only through certain pins

40. Which Arduino board is famous for integration with fabric-based projects?
a. The Lilypad b. The UNO
c. The Mega d. The Nano

41. What is the use of the IR Sensor?
a. Object Detection b. Humidity detection
c. Image processing d. GPS

42. How many pins are present in the IR sensor?
a. 1 b. 3 c. 2 d. 4

43. What mode should we put the Arduino pin to, for object detection to work with the IR sensor?
a. Analog b. Digital
c. PCM d. TDM

44. What is the full form of the LDR sensor?
a. Lithium Diode Resistor
b. Light Diaphragm resistor
c. Lithium Disk resistor
d. Light dependent Resistor

45. __________ is referred to as identification of authentic user and origin of information.
a. Availability
b. Confidentiality
c. Authenticity
d. Integrity

46. In the following, what is used to maintain and ensure the confidentiality of data or information/
a. Decryption of data
b. Locking of data
c. Encryption of data
d. Backup of data

47. What defines cyber security?
a. It act as a protector against cyber-attacks
b. It provides security from cyber-terrorist
c. It act as a protective shield against malware
d. All of the above

48. Which one monitors all the user's activity on the internet and transmits all the information to someone else in the background?
a. Adware b. Malware
c. Spyware d. None of the above

49. Which statement(s) are true about a brute force attack
a. Crack a password or username
b. Find a hidden web page
c. Find the key used to encrypt a message
d. All of the above

50. To secure your data on IoT devices
a. Keep changing your password
b. Update your every device
c. Avoid using devices that are risky
d. All of the above

51. Which of the following is threat to IoT device?
a. Virus b. Natural disaster
c. Spoofing d. All of the above

52. This output signal is feedback so that it subtract from the input signal
    a. Negative feedback
    b. Positive feedback
    c. Both a and b
    d. None of the above
53. A system the utilize a device to control the process without using feedback
    a. Open-loop control system
    b. Closed-loop feedback control system
    c. Regulator
    d. All of above
54. A system that uses a measurement of the output and compares it with the desired output:
    a. Open-Loop control system
    b. Closed-Loop feedback control system
    c. Both a and b
    d. All of the above
55. It is control system that has only one input and one output
    a. SISO b. MIMO
    c. Both a and b d. None of the above
56. Which of the following is not a guided medium?
    a. Twisted-pair b. Fiber optic cable
    c. Coaxial cable d. Atmosphere
57. The inner core of an optical fiber is __________ in composition.
    a. Glass or plastic b. Biometallic
    c. Copper d. Liquid
58. The OSI layer that arranges signals into logical units of information called frames:
    a. Transport b. Physical
    c. Data-link d. Application
59. Transmission media are usually categorized as
    a. Fixed and unfixed
    b. Guided and unguided
    c. Determinate or indeterminate
    d. None of the above
60. Which type of cable has glass center core
    a. UTP b. Fibre-Optic
    c. STP d. Coaxial
61. A wireless network uses _______ waves to transmit signals.
    a. Radio b. Microwave
    c. Sound d. Mechanical
62. Which layer of the osi model does data compression
    a. Network b. Data link
    c. Physical d. Presentation
63. End to end connection is established by __________ protocol of the TCP/IP suite.
    a. IP b. UDP
    c. TCP d. All of these
64. Bits from physical layer are converted into frames by the
    a. Data link layer b. Network layer
    c. Transport layer d. None of these
65. The main function of transport layer is:
    a. Node-to-Node delivery
    b. Process-to-process delivery
    c. Synchronization
    d. Updating and maintenance of routine tables
66. Smart phones can be used in IoT setup with __________ application categories.
    a. 2 b. 3 c. 4 d. 5
67. Which symbol is used in Ardino to calculate module
    a. # b. $ c. % d. !
68. To easily interface add-on modules with Arduino we can use
    a. General PCB
    b. Connectivity circuit boards
    c. Arduino shields
    d. Other high-end Arduino boards
69. All code in an Arduino sketch is processed from
    a. Top to bottom b. Bottom to top
    c. Any order d. None of these
70. Almost all statement written in arduino language must end with a
    a. Comma (,) b. Colon (☺
    c. Semicolon (;) d. Fullstop (.)
71. Which of the following statement true about a sketch?
    a. It is a name that Arduino uses for a program
    b. It's the unit of code that is uploaded to run on an Arduino board
    c. Both a and b
    d. None of these
72. Advantage(s) of Arduino
    a. Easy to learn
    b. Huge community

c. Many third-party libraries
d. All of the above

73. Full Form of GPIO is:
a. Ground pin input/output
b. General pin input/output
c. General purpose input/output
d. None of these

74. The setup() defines
a. Pin functionality using the pinMode function
b. Initial state of pins
c. Initialize classes and variables
d. All of the above

75. The SPI pins are:
a. Pins 10 (SS), 11 (MOSI)
b. 12 (MISO), 13 (SCK)
c. Both a and b
d. None of these

76. Some of the compile errors are
a. Missing semicolons or parentheses
b. Missing variable initialization
c. Misspellings & Wrong capitalizations
d. All of the above

77. Communication helps officials to ________ the employees.
a. Eliminate b. Motivate
c. Threaten d. Apprise

78. The document that is used to communicate within the organization is called:
a. Letter b. Memo
c. E-mail d. Telex

79. ____________ is a relatively enduring pattern of thoughts, feelings, and behaviour which differentiate person from each other.
a. Personality
b. Personality development
c. Social interaction
d. Persona

80. Personality is derived from Latin word "persona", meaning:
a. Mask b. Mark
c. Mesk d. Maek

81. According to Davis, personality is a psychic phenomenon which is:
a. Organic
b. Social
c. A mask
d. Combination or organic and social

82. ___________ considers personality as a certain style which is peculiar to the individual and is dertermined by the characteristic organization of mental trends, complexes, emotions and sentiments.
a. Psychological b. Sociology
c. Attitude d. Value of person

83. What is a private key?
a. A key on your key chain
b. A key given to the public
c. A key NOT to be given to the public
d. A key that opens a secret door

84. The term bot comes from robot. An internet bot may also known as
a. Web robot b. WWW robot
c. Both a and b d. None of these

85. Which statements are true about a brute force attack.
a. Crack a password or username
b. Find a hidden web page
c. Find the key used to encrypt a message
d. All of the above

86. 6LoWPAN Adaption layer contains?
a. Header compression
b. Fragmentation
c. Layer 2 forwarding
d. Header compression, Fragmentation, and Layer 2 forwarding

87. In which cases gateway will appear?
a. Industrial Automation
b. Building automation
c. Transportation
d. Industrial & Building Automation

88. Who will use their own IoT business models?
a. Pass b. Saas
c. Iaas d. Service provider

89. ______________ tags, devices, smart phones useful in identification.
a. IETF 6LoWPAN
b. IEFT CoAP
c. RFID/NFC
d. IEEE 802.15.4.LoWPAN

90. How many types of Arduinos do we have?
 a. 5 b. 6 c. 8 d. 6
91. With respect to the body language, the handshake conveys the confidence is:
 a. Limp
 b. Firm
 c. Loose
 d. Incomplete knowledge
92. Botnet is often used to launch attack.
 a. Dos b. DDOS
 c. Brute force d. Passive
93. What do you mean by micro in microcontroller?
 a. Distance between 2 IC's
 b. Distance between 2 transistors
 c. Size of a controller
 d. Distance between 2 pins
94. Which among the following is more powerful?
 a. Rasberry Pi 2 model
 b. Rasberry Pi 3 model
 c. Galieo Gen 2 Board
 d. Galieo Gen 1 Board
95. How many digital I/O pins are there in Board?
 a. 29 b. 15 c. 25 d. 20
96. What is pin connect block?
 a. All pins are having a function without reserved
 b. Some pins are reserved
 c. Pins have more than one function
 d. Multiplexing of some pins
97. What is the size of ADC and DAC?
 a. 16 bit b. 10 bit c. 8 bit d. 32 bit
98. Number of I/O ports in the 8051 microcontroller?
 a. 3 ports
 b. 4 ports
 c. 5 ports
 d. 4 ports with last port having 5 pins
99. FCP stands for __________.
 a. Fiber channel protocol
 b. Field channel protocol
 c. Fast channel protocol
 d. Fiber carrying protocol
100. UDP packets are called as:
 a. Segments b. Checksum
 c. Frames d. Datagrams

Answers to Multiple Choice Questions

1.	c	2.	b	3.	a	4.	b	5.	d
6.	c	7.	c	8.	c	9.	d	10.	b
11.	d	12.	d	13.	d	14.	d	15.	c
16.	d	17.	d	18.	c	19.	c	20.	a
21.	c	22.	a	23.	a	24.	b	25.	b
26.	c	27.	a	28.	a	29.	d	30.	c
31.	b	32.	a	33.	d	34.	b	35.	d
36.	a	37.	a	38.	a	39.	d	40.	a
41.	a	42.	b	43.	b	44.	d	45.	c
46.	c	47.	d	48.	c	49.	d	50.	d
51.	c	52.	a	53.	a	54.	b	55.	a
56.	d	57.	a	58.	c	59.	b	60.	b
61.	a	62.	c	63.	c	64.	a	65.	a
66.	c	67.	c	68.	c	69.	a	70.	c
71.	d	72.	d	73.	c	74.	d	75.	c
76.	d	77.	b	78.	b	79.	b	80.	a
81.	d	82.	a	83.	c	84.	c	85.	d
86.	d	87.	d	88.	d	89.	c	90.	c
91.	b	92.	b	93.	b	94.	b	95.	d
96.	c	97.	b	98.	b	99.	a	100.	d

Sample Practical Questions with Answers

1. Write a program to interface LEDs on pin number 11, 12, and 13 and blink alternatively at delay of 1 second.

Answer

```
int led = 13;
int led2 = 12;
int led3 = 11;
// the setup routine runs once when you press reset:
void setup() {
// initialize the digital pin as an output.
pinMode(led, OUTPUT);
pinMode(led2, OUTPUT);
pinMode(led3, OUTPUT);
}
// the loop routine runs over and over again forever:
void loop() {
```

```
digitalWrite(led, HIGH); // turn the LED on (HIGH is the voltage level)
delay(1000); // wait for a second
digitalWrite(led, LOW); // turn the LED off by making the voltage LOW
delay(1000);
{ digitalWrite(led2, HIGH);
delay(1000);
digitalWrite(led2, LOW);
delay(1000);
}
{ digitalWrite(led3, HIGH);
delay(1000);
digitalWrite(led3, LOW);
delay(1000);
}// wait for a second
}
```

2. Write a program that automatically turn lights on when an LDR sensor detects darkness.

Answer

```
//Program that automatically turn lights on when an LDR sensor detects darkness.
int sensorPin = A0; // select the input pin for LDR
int sensorValue = 0; // variable to store the value coming from the sensor
void setup() {
Serial.begin(9600); //sets serial port for communication
}
void loop() {
sensorValue = analogRead(sensorPin); // read the value from the sensor
Serial.println(sensorValue); //prints the values coming from the sensor on the screen
delay(100);
}
```

3. (a) Write a program to blink default Light Emitting Diode (LED) on Arduino board with delay of 2 seconds.

Answer

```
// Program for default LED blinking with dely of 2 sec.
int led = 13;
// the setup routine runs once when you press reset
void setup() {
// initialize the digital pin as an output.
pinMode(led, OUTPUT);
}
// the loop routine runs over and over again forever:
void loop() {
digitalWrite(led, HIGH); // turn the LED on (HIGH)
delay(2000); // wait for 2 second
digitalWrite(led, LOW); // turn the LED off (LOW)
delay(2000);
}// wait for 2 second
```

(b) Write a program/sketch for controlling LED using switch.

Answer

```
//Sketch for controlling LED using switch
int pushButton = 2;
int LED = 13;
void setup() {
// make the pushbutton's pin as input:
pinMode(pushButton, INPUT_PULLUP);
//configure pin as input with pullup enabled
pinMode(LED, OUTPUT);
//configure pin as output
}
void loop() {
// read the input pin:
int buttonState = digitalRead(pushButton);
digitalWrite(LED, (!(buttonState)));
//turn led on when switch pressed
delay(10); // delay in between reads for stability
}
```

4. (a) Write a program to interface LCD with Arduino board and display "Hello World" on it.

Answer

```
// Arduino Code to print "Hello World!" message on the LCD.
// include the library code:
#include <LiquidCrystal.h>
```

```
// Creates an LCD object. Parameters: (rs, enable, d4, d5, d6, d7)
LiquidCrystal lcd(12, 11, 5, 4, 3, 2);
void setup()
{
// set up the LCD's number of columns and rows:
lcd.begin(16, 2);
// Clears the LCD screen and moves the cursor to the upper left corner.
lcd.clear();
}
void loop()
{
// Print a message to the LCD.
lcd.print(" Hello world!");
// set the cursor to column 0, line 1
// (note: line 1 is the second row, since counting begins with 0):
lcd.setCursor(0, 1);
// Print a message to the LCD
lcd.print(" Message printed");
}
```

(b) Write a program for Sequential LED ON-OFF.

Answer

```
//Sketch for Sequential LED ON-OFF
void setup() {
//set gpio pin {0,1,2,3} as output
pinMode(0, OUTPUT);
pinMode(1, OUTPUT);
pinMode(2, OUTPUT);
pinMode(3, OUTPUT);
}
void loop() {
//turn LED ON one by one
for (int i = 0; i < 4; i++) {
digitalWrite(i, HIGH);
delay(1000);
}
}
```

5. **(a) Write a program that Lights multiple LEDs in sequence, then in reverse.**

Answer

```
// Lights multiple LEDs in sequence, then in reverse.
int timer = 100; // The higher the number, the slower the timing.
int ledPins[] = {
2, 7, 4, 6, 5, 3
}; // an array of pin numbers to which LEDs are attached
int pinCount = 6; // the no. of pins (i.e. the length of the array)
void setup() {
// the array elements are numbered from 0 to (pinCount - 1).
// use a for loop to initialize each pin as an output:
for (int thisPin = 0; thisPin < pinCount; thisPin++) {
pinMode(ledPins[thisPin], OUTPUT);
}
}
void loop() {
// loop from the lowest pin to the highest:
for (int thisPin = 0; thisPin < pinCount; thisPin++) {
// turn the pin on:
digitalWrite(ledPins[thisPin], HIGH);
delay(timer);
// turn the pin off:
digitalWrite(ledPins[thisPin], LOW);
}
// loop from the highest pin to the lowest:
for (int thisPin = pinCount - 1; thisPin >= 0; thisPin--) {
// turn the pin on:
digitalWrite(ledPins[thisPin], HIGH);
delay(timer);
// turn the pin off:
digitalWrite(ledPins[thisPin], LOW);
}
}
```

(b) Write a program to run pattern(s) on LEDs connected at pin 3, 4, 5.

Answer

Pattern example:

on, on, on

on, off, off

off, on, off

off, off, on

off, off, off

```
// Program to run pattern(s) on LEDs connected at pins 3, 4. 5
// Defining LEDs
int redLED = 3;
int greenLED = 4;
int blueLED = 5;
int del = 1000; // Milliseconds of delay
void setup() {
 // Making the LEDs outputs
pinMode(redLED,OUTPUT);
pinMode(greenLED, OUTPUT);
pinMode(blueLED, OUTPUT);
}
void loop() {
// blink in pattern on, on, on
Serial.print("Blink in pattern");
digitalWrite(redLED,HIGH);
digitalWrite(greenLED,HIGH);
digitalWrite(blueLED,HIGH);
delay(del);
// blink in pattern on, off, off
digitalWrite(redLED,HIGH);
digitalWrite(greenLED,LOW);
digitalWrite(blueLED,LOW);
delay(del);
// blink in pattern off, on, off
digitalWrite(redLED,LOW);
digitalWrite(greenLED,HIGH);
digitalWrite(blueLED,LOW);
delay(del);
// blink in pattern off, off, on
digitalWrite(redLED,LOW);
digitalWrite(greenLED,LOW);
digitalWrite(blueLED,HIGH);
delay(del);
// blink in pattern off, off, off
digitalWrite(redLED,LOW);
digitalWrite(greenLED,LOW);
digitalWrite(blueLED,LOW);
delay(del);
}
```

6. **(a) Write a program to run pattern for Multiple LEDs Pattern Generation using Arduino Uno. Note that 12 LEDs are connected on digital pins of Arduino from pin no 2 - 13. All LEDs ground are shorted with Arduino ground.**

Pattern example:

Patten 1 : Turning on all LEDs in increasing order and turning off in decreasing order.

Pattern 2: Turning on one led at a time in increasing and decreasing order.

Pattern 3: Turning on all even number LEDs and then odd number LEDs.

Answer

```
const int led1 = 2;
const int led2 = 3;
const int led3 = 4;
const int led4 = 5;
const int led5 = 6;
const int led6 = 7;
const int led7 = 8;
const int led8 = 9;
const int led9 = 10;
const int led10 = 11;
const int led11 = 12;
const int led12 = 13;
int a = 2;
```

```
void setup()
{
pinMode(led1, OUTPUT);
pinMode(led2, OUTPUT);
pinMode(led3, OUTPUT);
pinMode(led4, OUTPUT);
pinMode(led5, OUTPUT);
pinMode(led6, OUTPUT);
pinMode(led7, OUTPUT);
pinMode(led8, OUTPUT);
pinMode(led9, OUTPUT);
pinMode(led10, OUTPUT);
pinMode(led11, OUTPUT);
pinMode(led12, OUTPUT);
}
void loop()
{
//pattern 1
// Turning on all LEDs in increasing order and turning off in decreasing order
for (a = 2; a <= 13; a++)
{
digitalWrite(a, HIGH);
delay(50);
}
for (a = 13; a >= 2; a--)
{
digitalWrite(a, LOW);
delay(50);
}
//pattern 2
//Turning on one led at a time in increasing and decreasing order
for (a = 2; a <= 13; a++)
{
digitalWrite(a, HIGH);
delay(50);
digitalWrite(a, LOW);
}
for (a = 13; a >= 2; a--)
{
digitalWrite(a, HIGH);
delay(50);
digitalWrite(a, LOW);
}
//pattern 3
//Turning on all even number LEDs and then odd number LEDs.
for (a = 2; a <= 13; a++) {
if ((a % 2) == 0) {
digitalWrite(a, HIGH);
delay(50);
}
}
for (a = 13; a <= 2; a--) {
if ((a % 2) == 1) {
digitalWrite(a, HIGH);
delay(50);
}
}
//turning OFF ALL LEDs
for (a = 13; a >= 2; a--)
{
digitalWrite(a, LOW);
delay(50);
}
}
```

(b) Write a program to interface DHT sensor and LED. Put your hand on the LM35 (a temperature sensor) and that should push the temperature higher than 25 degrees and the LED will light.

Answer

```
// Program to switch on LED once the temperature rises above 25 degrees
#define lm35Pin A2
#define ledPin 12
```

```
//this sets the ground pin to LOW and the input voltage pin to high
void setup()
{
Serial.begin(9600);
pinMode(ledPin, INPUT);
digitalWrite(ledPin,0);
}
//main loop
void loop()
{
int rawvoltage= analogRead(lm35Pin);//Read Temperature
float millivolts= (rawvoltage/1024.0) * 5000;
float celsius= millivolts/10;
Serial.print(celsius);
Serial.print(" degrees Celsius, ");
if(celsius >25)
{
digitalWrite(ledPin,1);
}
else
{
digitalWrite(ledPin,0);
}
delay(1000);
}
```

Specimen Answersheet for Writing Answers to Objective Questions

PAPER CODE ______ DATE ______

1. Multiple choice

(shade the box corresponding to your answer)

	a	b	c	d
1.1.				
1.2.				
1.3.				
1.4.				
1.5.				
1.6.				
1.7.				
1.8.				
1.9.				
1.10.				

2. Selecting TRUE or FALSE statements

(shade the box corresponding to your answer)

	True	False
2.1.		
2.2.		
2.3.		
2.4.		
2.5.		
2.6.		
2.7.		
2.8.		
2.9.		
2.10.		

3. Matching words/phrases in two columns

(write the alphabet corresponding to your answer in the box)

3.1.
3.2.
3.3.
3.4.
3.5.
3.6.
3.7.
3.8.
3.9.
3.10.

4. Fill in the blanks

(write the alphabet corresponding to your answer)

4.1.
4.2.
4.3.
4.4.
4.5.
4.6.
4.7.
4.8.
4.9.
4.10.